Course	Accounting Principles I
Course Number	**ACC 2010**
	Wright State University

D0886331

http://create.mheducation.com

ISBN-10: 0077827554   ISBN-13: 9780077827557

Contents

Credits

CHAPTER

Accounting Information and Decision Making

Learning Objectives

AFTER STUDYING THIS CHAPTER, YOU SHOULD BE ABLE TO:

■ **LO1** Describe the two primary functions of financial accounting.

■ **LO2** Identify the three fundamental business activities that financial accounting measures.

■ **LO3** Discuss how financial accounting information is communicated through financial statements.

■ **LO4** Describe the role that financial accounting plays in the efficient distribution of society's resources.

■ **LO5** Explain the term generally accepted accounting principles (GAAP) and describe the role of GAAP in financial accounting.

■ **LO6** Identify career opportunities in accounting.

Appendix

■ **LO7** Explain the nature of the conceptual framework used to develop generally accepted accounting principles.

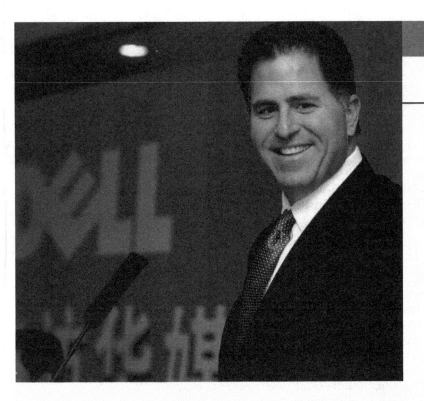

DELL INCORPORATED: COMPUTING THE SUCCESS OF AN ENTREPRENEUR

Michael was not your average college student. Since age 12, when he started his first business venture selling stamps, he realized that if you have a good idea, work hard, and treat customers with special care, you can make money—and sometimes, a lot of money. After a series of small, successful business ventures through high school, at age 19 Michael came up with his next business idea. In 1984, with an initial investment of only $1,000, he started a company that custom-built personal computers for sale directly to customers. The company enjoyed immediate success. In 1988, the company offered for sale to the public 3,500,000 shares of stock for $8.50 per share and changed its name to **Dell Incorporated**.

By the age of 26, Michael Dell had become the youngest CEO of a company ever included on the prestigious **Fortune** 500 list. Better yet, Dell's stock enjoyed greater growth than any other stock during the 1990s. By December 31, 1999, each share had increased in value nearly 60,000%. If you had invested just $1,000 in Dell at its initial public offering in 1988, your investment would have increased to nearly $600,000 by the end of 1999!

What if instead of investing $1,000 in Dell in 1988, you had invested $1,000 in **Polaroid Corporation**, most famous for its instant-film cameras? You would have watched your $1,000 shrink to $0 by 2001, when the company declared bankruptcy.

How do investors decide where to invest their money? Thousands of stocks are available in the United States, and thousands more on stock exchanges around the world. How do investors separate the successful companies from the unsuccessful companies?

The key source of information investors use to identify successful and unsuccessful companies is financial accounting—the subject of this book. As you read through the chapters, you'll begin to understand the information that financial accounting provides to investors making business decisions. And as the contrast between Dell and Polaroid demonstrates, the payoffs for understanding (or failing to understand) the financial position of a company can be quite large.

Feature Story

PART A

ACCOUNTING AS A MEASUREMENT/ COMMUNICATION PROCESS

Welcome to accounting. A common misconception about this course is that it is a math class, much like college algebra, calculus, or business statistics. You will soon see that this is *not* a math class. Don't say to yourself, "I'm not good at math so I probably won't be good at accounting." Though it's true that we use numbers heavily throughout each chapter, accounting is far more than adding, subtracting, and solving for unknown variables. So, what exactly is accounting? We'll take a close look at this next.

Defining Accounting

■ **LO1**

Describe the two primary functions of financial accounting.

Accounting is "the language of business." More precisely, accounting is a system of maintaining records of a company's operations and communicating that information to decision makers. Perhaps the earliest use of such systematic recordkeeping dates back thousands of years to ancient Mesopotamia (present-day Iraq), where records were kept of delivered agricultural products. Using accounting to maintain a record of multiple transactions allowed for better exchange among individuals and aided in the development of more complex societies.[1] In this class, you'll learn how to read, interpret, and communicate using the language of business.

Today, many millions of people every day must make informed decisions about companies. While investors and creditors (lenders) are the primary users of financial accounting information, there are many others. Illustration 1–1 identifies some of those people and examples of decisions they make about the companies.

ILLUSTRATION 1–1

Decisions People Make About Companies

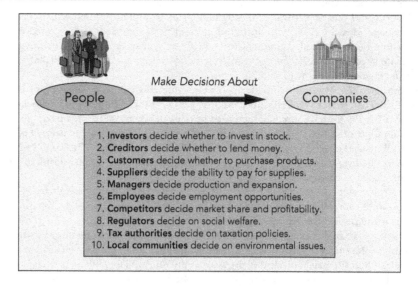

Make Decisions About

People → Companies

1. **Investors** decide whether to invest in stock.
2. **Creditors** decide whether to lend money.
3. **Customers** decide whether to purchase products.
4. **Suppliers** decide the ability to pay for supplies.
5. **Managers** decide production and expansion.
6. **Employees** decide employment opportunities.
7. **Competitors** decide market share and profitability.
8. **Regulators** decide on social welfare.
9. **Tax authorities** decide on taxation policies.
10. **Local communities** decide on environmental issues.

People and organizations need useful information in order to make good decisions. This is where accounting plays a key role. As Illustration 1–2 shows, **the functions of accounting are to *measure* the activities of the company and *communicate* those measurements to people.**

We classify accounting into two broad categories: managerial accounting and financial accounting. **Managerial accounting** deals with the methods accountants use to provide information to an organization's *internal* users—that is, its own managers. These are the subjects of another course.

[1]S. Basu and G. Waymire. 2006. Recordkeeping and Human Evolution. *Accounting Horizons* 20(3): 201–229.

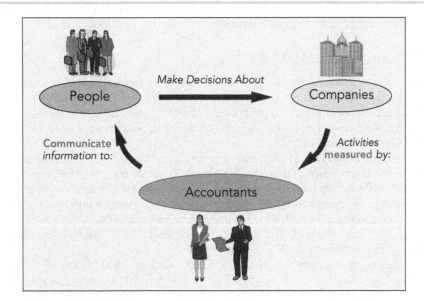

ILLUSTRATION 1–2
Functions of
Accounting

In this class, we focus on financial accounting. The two primary functions of financial accounting are to measure business activities of a company and to communicate those measurements to *external* parties for decision-making purposes. The two primary external users of financial accounting information (users outside the firm) are investors and creditors. **Investors** make decisions related to buying and selling the company's stock (shares of ownership): Is the company profitable? Will the company's stock increase in value? **Creditors** make decisions related to lending money to the company: Will the company be able to repay its debt when it comes due? Will it be able to pay interest in the meantime?

 KEY POINT

The functions of financial accounting are to measure business activities of a company and to communicate information about those activities to investors and creditors and other outside users for decision-making purposes.

User's Guide For learning objectives throughout the book, you will see boxed sections, like this one, titled *Key Point*. These boxed items will highlight the central focus of the learning objectives.

Business Activities to Measure

The first of financial accounting's functions is to measure business activities. A business engages in three fundamental activities—financing, investing, and operating.

■ **LO2**
Identify the three fundamental business activities that financial accounting measures.

- Financing activities are transactions involving external sources of funding. There are two basic sources of this external funding—the owners of the company who invest their own funds in the business, and creditors who lend money to the company. With this financing, the company engages in investing activities.
- Investing activities include the purchase and sale of (1) long-term resources such as land, buildings, equipment, and machinery and (2) any resources not directly related to a company's normal operations. Once these investments are in place, the company has the resources needed to run the business and can perform operating activities.
- Operating activities include transactions that relate to the primary operations of the company, such as providing products and services to customers and the associated costs of doing so, like utilities, taxes, advertising, wages, rent, and maintenance.

The first role of financial accounting is to measure (or keep a record of) a company's financing, investing, and operating activities. Let's look at an example.

EXAMPLE OF BUSINESS ACTIVITIES

Suppose you want to start a computer-repair business. You estimate that it will cost approximately $10,000 to get the business up and going. However, you have only $1,000 available, so you need to get funding of $9,000 elsewhere. You begin by borrowing $2,000 from a local bank, which you agree to repay a year later. Thus, the bank is your creditor.

To raise the remaining $7,000, you organize your business as a corporation. A corporation is an entity that is legally separate from its owners. The corporation raises external funding by selling shares of ownership (typically referred to as common stock) in the corporation. Each share of stock represents a unit of ownership. Many of the corporations with which you are familiar, such as Coca-Cola, American Eagle, Apple Inc., Ford Motor Co., Microsoft, and Starbucks have millions of stockholders and therefore millions of owners.

For your computer-repair business, let's say you issue 800 shares of common stock for $10 each. With your original $1,000, you buy 100 shares of stock, giving you one-eighth ownership in the corporation (your 100 shares ÷ 800 shares total). Other investors purchase the remaining 700 shares, giving them seven-eighths ownership in the company.

In this example, the *financing* activities of the company are cash inflows of $2,000 from creditors and $8,000 from investors.

Creditors (local bank)	$ 2,000	} Financing
Investors (you and others)	8,000	
	$10,000	

With this financing of $10,000, your company purchases a truck costing $6,000 and equipment costing $3,000. With these resources in place, you are ready to begin operations. You start by purchasing advertising in the local newspaper for $200 and paying for the first month's office rent of $800.

You've now engaged in the second and third types of business activities: Your *investing* activities include the purchase of the truck and equipment; they involve the purchase of long-term resources. Advertising and office rent are examples of *operating* activities; they are more directly related to normal operations.

Truck	$ 6,000	} Investing
Equipment	3,000	
Advertising	200	} Operating
Office rent	800	
	$10,000	

HOW TO MEASURE BUSINESS ACTIVITIES

How should accountants measure these business activities? In other words, what information would a company's investors and creditors be interested in knowing to make informed decisions about your computer-repair business? **Ultimately, investors and creditors want to know about the company's resources and their claims to those resources.** Accounting uses some conventional categories to describe such resources and claims.

Assets, liabilities, and stockholders' equity.   We measure resources owned by a company as assets. Recall that with the start-up funds of $10,000, your computer-repair business bought a truck ($6,000) and equipment ($3,000). You will measure the $9,000 as assets. Other assets typical of most businesses include such items as cash, inventories, supplies, and buildings. Cash is a resource used to make purchases; inventories represent resources used to make product sales to customers; supplies include resources used to perform basic business functions; and buildings are resources used by employees as a location from which to operate a company.

As discussed earlier, two parties claim the resources of the company—creditors and investors. Amounts owed to creditors are liabilities. The computer-repair business has a liability of $2,000 to a local bank. Other examples of liabilities are amounts owed to suppliers, workers, utility companies, and governments (in the form of taxes). Liabilities must be paid by a specified date.

Investors, or owners, claim any resources of the company not owed to creditors. You can see this relationship in home ownership: Your house (an asset) is worth $300,000. The bank that helped finance its purchase holds a $200,000 mortgage (a liability). Your *equity* in the house is $100,000. For a corporation, we refer to owners' claims to resources as stockholders' equity, since stockholders are the owners of the corporation.

We express the relationship among the three measurement categories in what is called the basic accounting equation, depicted in Illustration 1–3. It shows that a company's resources equal creditors' and owners' claims to those resources.

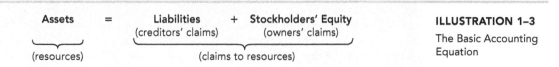

Assets	=	**Liabilities** (creditors' claims)	+	**Stockholders' Equity** (owners' claims)
(resources)		(claims to resources)		

ILLUSTRATION 1–3
The Basic Accounting Equation

Another way to think about this relationship is to replace the parenthetical descriptions under each of the three parts of the equation:

Assets	=	**Liabilities**	+	**Stockholders' Equity**
(company owns)		(company owes)		(difference)

Also, as with any equation, we can move the components (by following mathematical rules you learned in high school). For example, to isolate stockholders' equity, we can subtract liabilities from both sides of the equal sign.

Assets	−	**Liabilities**	=	**Stockholders' Equity**
(company owns)		(company owes)		(difference)

Thus, the computer-repair business has assets of $9,000 but liabilities of $2,000. How much equity do stockholders have? They have $9,000 − $2,000, or $7,000.

The accounting equation illustrates a fundamental model of business valuation. The value of a company to its owners equals total resources of the company minus amounts owed to creditors. Creditors expect to receive only resources equal to the amount owed them. Stockholders, on the other hand, can claim all resources in excess of the amount owed to creditors.

User's Guide Pay close attention to the accounting categories we define here. These may be new terms for you. We promise that very soon they will be second nature to you.

Revenues, expenses, and dividends.   Of course, all businesses intend to increase the amount of their resources through their operations and eventually to own more than they owe. We broadly define such increases as profits. (Later, we'll define profits a bit more narrowly.) Because stockholders claim all resources in excess of amounts owed to creditors, profits of the company, which add to total resources, are claimed solely by stockholders, the owners of the company.

We calculate a company's profits by comparing its revenues and expenses. Revenues are the amounts earned from selling products or services to customers. For example, when your computer-repair business provides services to a customer, it earns revenues. When McDonald's sells you a burger, fries, and drink, McDonald's earns revenue.

However, as you've probably heard, "It takes money to make money." To operate your computer-repair business, for example, you purchased advertising ($200) and paid the first month's rent ($800). We record these amounts as expenses. Expenses are the costs of providing products and services. You'll record expenses of $1,000 for your computer-repair business.

When McDonald's sells you a Big Mac, it incurs expenses for two all-beef patties, special sauce, lettuce, cheese, pickles, onions, and a sesame-seed bun. McDonald's also pays the person who took your order, the cook behind the partition, and the person who cleans up after you're gone. Then there's the cost of having and maintaining the building, TV ads, expenses of the corporate headquarters, utilities, equipment maintenance, income taxes, interest on debt, and many, many more.

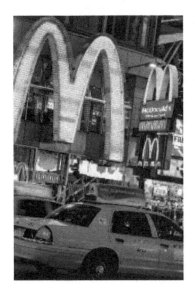

We measure the difference between revenues and expenses as net income. All businesses want revenues to be greater than expenses, producing a positive net income. However, if expenses exceed revenues, as happens from time to time, the difference between them is a negative amount—a **net loss**. You'll notice the use of the term *net* to describe a company's profitability. In business, the term *net* is used often to describe the difference between two amounts. Here, we measure revenues *net* of (or minus) expenses to calculate the net income or net loss.

Common Terms Other common names for net income include *earnings* and *profit*.

Illustration 1–4 reports McDonald's revenues, expenses, and net income from its operations around the world.

ILLUSTRATION 1–4	($ in millions)	Revenues	–	Expenses	=	Net Income
Revenue and Expenses for McDonald's Corporation, as of 2009	United States	$7,943.8	–	$4,712.1	=	$3,231.7
	Europe	9,273.8	–	6,685.7	=	2,588.1
	Asia/Pacific, Middle East, Africa	4,337.0	–	3,347.5	=	989.5

Notice that McDonald's generates only about one-third of its revenues in the United States, but almost half its net income comes from the United States. This means that McDonald's is able to make more profit per dollar of revenue in the United States than anywhere else in the world.

If the corporation has positive net income, it typically will distribute to its owners, the stockholders, some of those profits. It does so by making cash payments to its stockholders (usually every three months), in payments called dividends. McDonald's, for example, has paid a dividend to stockholders every three months for over 30 years. In 2009, McDonald's paid dividends of $2.05 per share. If you owned 100 shares of McDonald's stock, you would have received $205.00 from McDonald's in cash. Unlike creditors, who lend money to the company in expectation of being repaid, stockholders are not guaranteed regular cash payments from the firm.

Match the term with the appropriate definition.

1. _____ Assets
2. _____ Liabilities
3. _____ Stockholders' equity
4. _____ Dividends
5. _____ Revenues
6. _____ Expenses

A. Costs of selling products or services.
B. Amounts earned from sales of products or services.
C. Amounts owed.
D. Distributions to stockholders.
E. Owners' claims to resources.
F. Resources owned.

Solution:

1. F; 2. C; 3. E; 4. D; 5. B; 6. A

In summary, the measurement role of accounting is to create a record of the financing, investing, and operating activities of the company. To make this possible, the firm must maintain an accurate record of its assets, liabilities, stockholders' equity, revenues, expenses, and dividends. Be sure you understand the meaning of these items. We will refer to them throughout this book. Illustration 1–5 summarizes the business activities and the categories that measure them.

	Activities Related to:	Measurement Category
Financing Activities	• Borrowing • Stockholders' investment • Distributions to stockholders	• Liabilities • Stockholders' equity • Dividends
Investing Activities	• Resources owned by the company	• Assets
Operating Activities	• Sales to customers • Costs of selling to customers	• Revenues • Expenses

ILLUSTRATION 1–5

Business Activities and Their Measurement

KEY POINT

Financing activities include transactions with creditors and owners. Investing activities generally include the purchase or disposal of productive assets. Operating activities relate to earning revenues and incurring expenses.

As you learn to measure business activities, you will often find it helpful to consider both sides of the transaction: When someone pays cash, someone else receives cash; when someone borrows money, another lends money. Likewise, an expense for one company can be a revenue for another company; one company's asset can be another company's liability. Throughout this book, you will find discussions of the "flip side" of certain transactions, indicated by the icon you see here in the margin. In addition, certain homework problems, also marked by the icon, will ask you specifically to address the "flip side" in your computations. (See page 39 for the first such example.)

Flip Side

FORMS OF BUSINESS ORGANIZATION

The computer-repair business introduced earlier was organized as a corporation. Other common business forms include sole proprietorships and partnerships. A sole proprietorship is a business owned by one person, whereas a partnership is a business owned by two or more persons. If you had decided to start the computer-repair business without outside investors, you could have formed a sole proprietorship. Or, you and a friend could have formed a partnership.

To decide on a form of business organization, you need to understand their advantages and disadvantages. The major *advantage* of the corporate form of business is the limited liability of the corporation's stockholders. **Limited liability** means the stockholders are not held personally responsible for the financial obligations of the corporation. If the business fails, stockholders can lose no more than the investment they already made by purchasing stock. In other words, stockholders are not obligated to pay the corporation's remaining debts out of their own pockets. In contrast, if a sole proprietorship or partnership is unable to pay its legal obligations to creditors, the owner(s) may be forced to surrender personal assets, such as homes, cars, computers, and furniture to satisfy those debts.

The *disadvantage* of the corporate form of business is the higher tax burden on the owners. Generally, the corporate income tax rate is greater than the individual income tax rate. Moreover, a corporation's income is taxed twice—first when the company earns it and pays corporate income taxes on it, and then again when stockholders pay personal income taxes on amounts the firm distributes to them as dividends. This is called *double taxation*. Any income of a sole proprietorship or a partnership is taxed only once, and at the personal income tax rate.

Because most of the largest companies in the United States are corporations, in this book we will primarily focus on accounting from a corporation's perspective. Focusing on corporations also highlights the importance of financial accounting—to measure and communicate activities of a company when owners (shareholders) are typically separated from management of the company. (A more detailed discussion of the advantages and disadvantages of a corporation can be found in Chapter 10.)

Communicating through Financial Statements

■ LO3
Discuss how financial accounting information is communicated through financial statements.

We've discussed that different business activities produce assets, liabilities, stockholders' equity, dividends, revenues, and expenses, and that the first important role of financial accounting is to record the relevant transactions of a company. Its second vital role is to communicate these business activities to those outside the company. The primary means of communicating business activities is through financial statements. Financial statements are periodic reports published by the company for the purpose of providing information to external users. We have four primary financial statements:

1. Income statement
2. Statement of stockholders' equity
3. Balance sheet
4. Statement of cash flows

These financial statements give investors and creditors the key information they need when making decisions about a company: Should I buy the company's stock? Should I lend money to the company? Is management efficiently operating the company? Without these financial statements, it would be difficult for those outside the company to see what's going on inside.

Let's go through a simple set of financial statements to see what they look like. We'll start with the income statement of a simple, fictitious company. Actual companies' financial statements often report items you haven't yet encountered. However, because actual companies' financial information will be useful in helping you understand certain accounting topics, we'll sample them often throughout the book.

THE INCOME STATEMENT

The income statement is a financial statement that reports the company's revenues and expenses over an interval of time. It shows whether the company was able to generate enough revenue to cover the expenses of running the business. If revenues exceed expenses, then the company reports *net income:*

Revenues − Expenses = Net income

If expenses exceed revenues, then the company reports a *net loss.*

Now, let's look at our fictitious company. On January 1 Eagle Golf Academy begins operations by offering lessons to junior golfers. The lessons include a variety of skills intended to develop players for a top university golf program and perhaps even one day playing on the PGA Tour. For the first month of operations, Eagle Golf Academy reports its income statement as shown in Illustration 1–6.

Common Terms Other common names for the income statement include *statement of operations* and *statement of income.*

ILLUSTRATION 1–6

Income Statement for Eagle Golf Academy

EAGLE GOLF ACADEMY Income Statement For the month ended January 31	
Revenues:	
Service revenue	$6,360
Expenses:	
Salaries expense	3,100
Rent expense	500
Supplies expense	800
Interest expense	100
Utilities expense	960
Other expenses	400
Total expenses	5,860
Net income	$ 500

Notice the heading of the income statement: It includes the company's name, the title of the financial statement, and the time period covered by the financial statement. The three major captions in the income statement include **revenues** and **expenses,** discussed earlier, and the difference between them—**net income.**

We can determine from the income statement that for the month of January Eagle Golf Academy earns revenues of $6,360. This means that Eagle provides golf training and bills customers for a total of $6,360. Total expenses associated with generating those revenues, including salaries, rent, supplies, and other items listed here, are $5,860. These are typical costs that we might expect of any company. The income statement shows that revenues *exceed* expenses ($6,360 is greater than $5,860), and thus the academy is able to report net income of $500.

The fact that Eagle reports a positive net income is, in some sense, a signal of the company's success. The company is able to charge its customers a price higher than the costs of running the business. Do you assume most companies sell their products and services for a profit? It's not as easy as you might think. In recent years, **American Airlines, OfficeMax, Eastman Kodak, Ford Motor Co., Goodyear Tire and Rubber, ConocoPhillips, CBS, U.S. Cellular, Gateway, Sirius Satellite Radio, Sprint PCS, Blockbuster,** and hundreds of others have reported net losses.

KEY POINT

The income statement compares revenues and expenses for the current period to assess the company's ability to earn a profit from running its operations.

Decision Point

User's Guide Decision Points in each chapter highlight specific decisions related to chapter topics that can be made using financial accounting information.

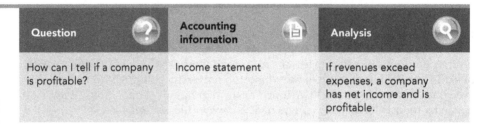

Question	Accounting information	Analysis
How can I tell if a company is profitable?	Income statement	If revenues exceed expenses, a company has net income and is profitable.

THE STATEMENT OF STOCKHOLDERS' EQUITY

The statement of stockholders' equity is a financial statement that summarizes the changes in stockholders' equity over an interval of time. The reporting period coincides with the time period covered by the income statement.

Stockholders' equity has two primary components—common stock and retained earnings. Recall that common stock represents amounts invested by stockholders (the owners of the corporation) when they purchase shares of stock. Common stock is an *external* source of stockholders' equity.

Common Terms
Another common name for retained earnings is *profits reinvested in the business.*

Retained earnings, on the other hand, is an *internal* source of stockholders' equity. Retained earnings represents the cumulative amount of net income, earned over the life of the company, that has *not* been distributed to stockholders as dividends. Since all profits of the company are owned by stockholders, any net income in excess of dividends paid to stockholders represents stockholders' equity retained in the business. Thus, both common stock and retained earnings make up total stockholders' equity. This concept is shown in Illustration 1–7.

ILLUSTRATION 1–7
Components of Stockholders' Equity

You will notice that some financial statements have parentheses around some amounts. As you will learn as you study this book, accounting convention uses parentheses to highlight negative amounts (such as the subtraction of dividends here) or to show cash outflows (which we will point out later).

Suppose Eagle obtains financing in January by issuing common stock for $25,000. This transaction will distribute shares of common stock to investors in return for the company's receiving cash of $25,000. Let's say that at the end of January, Eagle pays dividends of $200 to stockholders. Illustration 1–8 (next page) shows the statement of stockholders' equity for Eagle Golf Academy.

When the company begins operations on January 1, the balances of common stock and retained earnings are $0. Once the company issues common stock, its balance increases to **$25,000**. The balance of retained earnings always increases by the amount of net income less any dividends paid to stockholders—here, $500 − $200 = $300. **The name *retained earnings* is descriptive. The balance of retained earnings represents the amount of "earnings retained" (not paid out in the form of dividends) over the life of the company.**

EAGLE GOLF ACADEMY Statement of Stockholders' Equity For the month ended January 31			
	Common Stock	Retained Earnings	Total Stockholders' Equity
Beginning balance (Jan. 1)	$ -0-	$ -0-	$ -0-
Issuance of common stock	25,000		25,000
Add: Net income for January		500	500
Less: Dividends		(200)	(200)
Ending balance (Jan. 31)	$25,000	$ 300	$25,300

ILLUSTRATION 1–8

Statement of Stockholders' Equity for Eagle Golf Academy

Retained earnings includes net income less dividends. Note that the items shown here in blue come from the income statement.

COMMON MISTAKE

Dividends represent the payment of cash but are not considered an expense in running the business. Students sometimes mistakenly include the amount of dividends as an expense in the income statement, rather than as a distribution of net income in the statement of stockholders' equity.

User's Guide Throughout each chapter, you will see sections titled *Common Mistake*. Information in these boxes will help you avoid common mistakes on exams, quizzes, and homework.

By adding common stock and the retained earnings of $300, we calculate the balance of total stockholders' equity at January 31 to be **$25,300**. In accounting terms, this amount represents the value of the firm to its owners, the stockholders. The company creates value *externally* through investment by owners (common stock) and *internally* by generating and retaining profits (retained earnings).

KEY POINT

The statement of stockholders' equity reports information related to changes in common stock and retained earnings each period. The change in retained earnings equals net income less dividends for the period.

Decision Point

Question ?	Accounting information	Analysis
Was the change in company value (stockholders' equity) the result of external or internal sources?	Statement of stockholders' equity	When a company sells common stock, company value increases due to external sources (stockholders). When a company has profits during the year in excess of dividends paid, company value increases due to internal sources (company operations).

THE BALANCE SHEET

The balance sheet is a financial statement that presents the financial position of the company on a particular date. The financial position of a company is summarized by the basic accounting equation (see Illustration 1–3): **Assets = Liabilities + Stockholders' Equity.** As discussed earlier, this equation provides a fundamental model of business valuation. Assets are the resources owned by the company, and liabilities are amounts owed to creditors. Stockholders have equity in the company to the extent that assets exceed liabilities. Creditors also need to understand the balance sheet; it's the company's assets that will be used to pay liabilities (the amounts due creditors) as they become due.

The income statement is like a video (shows events over time), whereas a balance sheet is like a photograph (shows events at a point in time).

Illustration 1–9 shows the balance sheet of Eagle Golf Academy. The first thing to notice is the time period included in the heading. Recall that the income statement and statement of stockholders' equity both show activity over an *interval of time*. The balance sheet, in contrast, reports assets, liabilities, and stockholders' equity at a *point in time*. For example, Eagle's income statement shows revenue and expense activity occurring *from* January 1 to January 31; its balance sheet shows assets, liabilities, and stockholders' equity of the company *on* January 31.

ILLUSTRATION 1–9

Balance Sheet for Eagle Golf Academy

Total assets must equal total liabilities and stockholders' equity.

We show the stockholders' equity items in purple here, to indicate they came from the statement of stockholders' equity (Illustration 1–8).

EAGLE GOLF ACADEMY				
Balance Sheet				
January 31				
Assets			**Liabilities**	
Cash	$ 6,200		Accounts payable	$ 2,300
Accounts receivable	2,700		Salaries payable	300
Supplies	1,500		Interest payable	100
Equipment, net	23,600		Utilities payable	960
Other assets	5,500		Notes payable	10,000
			Other liabilities	540
			Total liabilities	14,200
			Stockholders' Equity	
			Common stock	25,000
			Retained earnings	300
			Total stockholders' equity	25,300
			Total liabilities and	
Total assets	$39,500		stockholders' equity	$39,500

Common Terms
Another common name for the balance sheet is *statement of financial position*.

For Eagle Golf Academy on January 31, total assets equal $39,500 and include some of the typical resources owned by most businesses, such as cash, supplies, and equipment. You'll learn about many other assets as you go through this book. Total liabilities equal $14,200 and include amounts owed to regular vendors (accounts payable), as well as amounts owed for other items such as employee salaries, interest, and utilities. As you'll begin to learn, many liabilities are referred to as "payables" to signify amounts that must be paid.

The difference between assets and liabilities of **$25,300** represents stockholders' equity. Total stockholders' equity includes the amount of common stock plus the amount of retained earnings from the statement of stockholders' equity. Notice that the amounts listed in the balance sheet show that the accounting equation balances:

Assets	=	Liabilities	+	Stockholders' Equity
(resources)		(creditors' claims)		(owners' claims)
$39,500	=	$14,200	+	$25,300

KEY POINT

The balance sheet demonstrates that the company's resources (assets) equal creditors' claims (liabilities) plus owners' claims (stockholders' equity) to those resources.

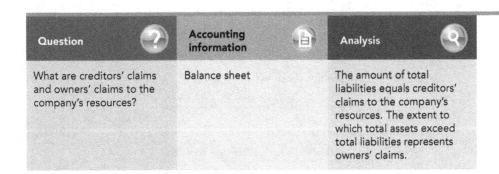

Decision Point

Question	Accounting information	Analysis
What are creditors' claims and owners' claims to the company's resources?	Balance sheet	The amount of total liabilities equals creditors' claims to the company's resources. The extent to which total assets exceed total liabilities represents owners' claims.

THE STATEMENT OF CASH FLOWS

The statement of cash flows is a financial statement that measures activities involving cash receipts and cash payments over an interval of time. We can classify all cash transactions into three categories that correspond to the three fundamental business activities—operating, investing, and financing—we discussed earlier in the chapter:

- **Operating cash flows** include cash receipts and cash payments for transactions involving revenues and expenses.
- **Investing cash flows** generally include cash transactions for the purchase and sale of investments and productive long-term assets. Long-term assets are resources owned by a company that are thought to provide benefits for more than one year.
- **Financing cash flows** include cash transactions with lenders, such as borrowing money and repaying debt, and with stockholders, such as issuing stock and paying dividends.

The statement of cash flows can be an important source of information to investors and creditors. For example, investors use the relationship between net income (revenues minus expenses) and operating cash flows (cash flows from revenue and expense activities) to forecast a company's future profitability. Creditors compare operating cash flows and investing cash flows to assess a company's ability to repay debt. Financing activities provide information to investors and creditors about the mix of external financing of the company. ●

Illustration 1–10 (next page) provides the statement of cash flows for Eagle Golf Academy. Notice that the three sections in the statement of cash flows show the types of inflows and outflows of cash during the period. Inflows are shown as positive amounts; outflows are shown in parentheses to indicate negative cash flows. The final line in each section shows, in the right-most column, the difference between inflows and outflows as *net cash flow* for that type of activity.

Decision Maker's Perspective

User's Guide *Decision Maker's Perspective* sections discuss the usefulness of accounting information to decision makers such as investors, creditors, and company managers.

 KEY POINT

The statement of cash flows reports cash transactions from operating, investing, and financing activities.

ILLUSTRATION 1–10

Statement of Cash Flows for Eagle Golf Academy

Remember, amounts in parentheses indicate outflows of cash, consistent with accounting convention.

EAGLE GOLF ACADEMY Statement of Cash Flows For the month ended January 31		
Cash Flows from Operating Activities		
Cash inflows:		
From customers	$ 4,200	
Cash outflows:		
For salaries	(2,800)	
For rent	(6,000)	
Net cash flows from operating activities		($4,600)
Cash Flows from Investing Activities		
Purchase equipment	(24,000)	
Net cash flows from investing activities		(24,000)
Cash Flows from Financing Activities		
Issue common stock	25,000	
Borrow from bank	10,000	
Pay dividends	(200)	
Net cash flows from financing activities		34,800
Net increase in cash		6,200
Cash at the beginning of the month		-0-
Cash at the end of the month		$6,200

The total of the net cash flows from operating, investing, and financing activities equals the *net change in cash* during the period. For Eagle, that net change in cash for January was an increase of **$6,200.** To this change, we add the beginning balance of cash. Because this is the first month of operations for Eagle, cash at the beginning of the month is zero. Thus, the ending balance of cash is the same as that reported in the balance sheet in Illustration 1–9. This reconciliation of the beginning and ending cash balances emphasizes that the statement of cash flows explains *why* the cash reported in the balance sheet changed.

THE LINKS AMONG FINANCIAL STATEMENTS

The four financial statements are linked, because events that are reported in one financial statement often affect amounts reported in another. Many times, a single business transaction, such as receiving cash from a customer when providing services, will affect more than one of the financial statements. Providing services to a customer, for example, results in revenues recorded in the income statement, which are used to calculate net income. Net income, in turn, is reported in the calculation of retained earnings in the statement of stockholders' equity. Then, the ending balance of retained earnings is reported in the balance sheet. **Thus, any transaction that affects the income statement ultimately affects the balance sheet through the balance of retained earnings.** The cash received from customers will be reported as part of the ending cash balance in the balance sheet and as part of operating cash flows in the statement of cash flows.

Illustration 1–11 shows the links among the financial statements of Eagle Golf Academy in Illustrations 1–6, 1–8, 1–9, and 1–10. Link (1) shows that net income from the income statement is reported in the statement of stockholders' equity as part of the calculation of retained earnings. Link (2) shows that after we calculate the balance of retained earnings, the amount of total stockholders' equity can be reported in the balance sheet. Finally, link (3) demonstrates that the balance of cash in the balance sheet equals the amount of cash reported in the statement of cash flows.

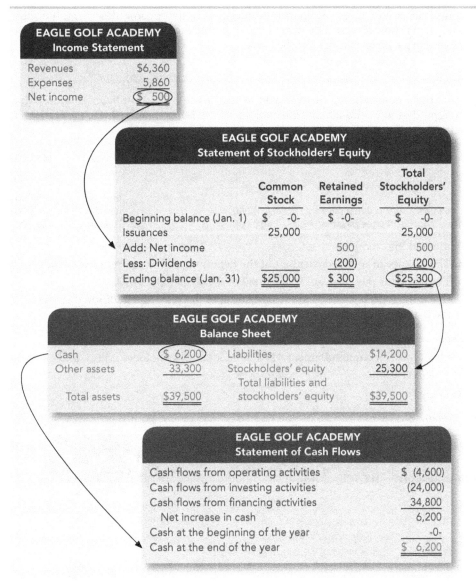

ILLUSTRATION 1–11

Relationship between
Financial Statements

[1] Notice that
the amount of net
income on the income
statement reappears
in the statement of
stockholders' equity.

[2] Notice that the ending
balance in the statement
of stockholders' equity
reappears in the balance
sheet.

[3] Notice that the
amount of cash in the
balance sheet reappears
as the ending cash
balance in the statement
of cash flows.

KEY POINT

All transactions that affect revenues or expenses reported in the income statement ultimately affect the balance sheet through the balance in retained earnings.

OTHER INFORMATION REPORTED TO OUTSIDERS

Financial statements provide a summary of the most important financial accounting information. Two other sources of information provide important detail: (1) management's discussion and analysis and (2) note disclosures to the financial statements. Publicly traded firms are required to report both of these items in their annual reports, along with the financial statements we've discussed.

The **management discussion and analysis** (MD&A) section typically includes management's views on significant events, trends, and uncertainties pertaining to the company's operations and resources. **Note disclosures** offer additional information either to explain the information presented in the financial statements or to provide information not included in the financial statements. For example, companies are required to report total revenues in the income statement, but they also often report revenues itemized by geographic region in a note disclosure. We'll discuss these items throughout the book.

Let's Review

Test your understanding of what you've read so far. The Computer Shop repairs laptops, desktops, and mainframe computers. On December 31, 2012, the company reports the following year-end amounts:

Assets:	Cash	$10,000	**Revenues:**	Service	$65,000
	Supplies	8,000			
	Equipment, net	26,000			
			Expenses:	Rent	6,000
Liabilities:	Accounts payable	4,000		Supplies	14,000
	Notes payable	10,000		Salaries	40,000

Additional information:

a. The balance of retained earnings at the beginning of the year is $7,000.

b. The company pays dividends of $1,000 on December 31, 2012.

c. Common stock is $15,000 at the beginning of the year, and additional shares are issued for $4,000 during 2012.

Suggested Homework:
BE1-5, BE1-6;
E1-6, E1-7, E1-8;
P1-3A&B, P1-5A&B

Required:

Prepare the (1) income statement, (2) statement of stockholders' equity, and (3) balance sheet.

Solution:

1. Income statement:

THE COMPUTER SHOP
Income Statement
For the year ended Dec. 31, 2012

Revenues:	
Service revenue	$65,000
Expenses:	
Rent expense	6,000
Supplies expense	14,000
Salaries expense	40,000
Net income	$ 5,000

2. Statement of stockholders' equity:

THE COMPUTER SHOP
Statement of Stockholders' Equity
For the year ended Dec. 31, 2012

	Common Stock	Retained Earnings	Total Stockholders' Equity
Beginning balance (Jan. 1)	$15,000	$ 7,000	$22,000
Issuance of common stock	4,000		4,000
Add: Net income		5,000	5,000
Less: Dividends		(1,000)	(1,000)
Ending balance (Dec. 31)	$19,000	$11,000	$30,000

3. Balance sheet:

THE COMPUTER SHOP
Balance Sheet
December 31, 2012

Assets		Liabilities	
Cash	$10,000	Accounts payable	$ 4,000
Supplies	8,000	Notes payable	10,000
Equipment	26,000	**Stockholders' Equity**	
		Common stock	19,000
		Retained earnings	11,000
		Total liabilities and	
Total assets	$44,000	stockholders' equity	$44,000

FINANCIAL ACCOUNTING INFORMATION

To this point, you've had a simple, first look at how companies measure and communicate financial information to external users. Subsequent chapters will provide an even more detailed view of this measurement/communication process. However, before proceeding, it's important to first consider why we are studying financial accounting. Does it matter? In other words, does the use of financial accounting information result in better business decisions?

Is Financial Accounting Important?

One of the rewarding things about studying financial accounting is that it does matter! The concepts in this course have an impact on everyday business decisions as well as wide-ranging economic consequences. We'll see an example of this next and then more examples throughout the rest of this book.

■ LO4
Describe the role that financial accounting plays in the efficient distribution of society's resources.

Most prospering economies in the world today are structured around free markets. In free markets, firms are allowed to compete and customers are free to choose from a variety of products and services. From which company do you prefer to buy a notebook computer—**Dell**, **Hewlett-Packard**, or **Apple**? Competition among these companies helps determine the prices they charge customers and the amounts they spend on computer components, salaries, manufacturing and distribution facilities, warranties, research and development, and other business-related activities. Can these companies offer you the notebook computer you want for a price above their costs? If they can, they'll earn a profit and stay in business. If they cannot, they'll eventually go out of business. Because companies know they are directly competing with each other, they work harder and more efficiently to please you, the customer.

Successful companies use their resources efficiently to sell products and services for a profit. When a company is able to make a profit, investors and creditors are willing to transfer their resources to it, and the company will expand its profitable operations even further.

Unsuccessful companies either offer lower-quality products and services or do not efficiently keep their costs low. In either case, they are not profitable. When a company is unprofitable, investors will neither invest in nor lend to the firm. Without these sources of financing, eventually the company will fail. Clearly, you don't want to invest in an unsuccessful company and then watch your investment shrink as the company loses your money. But how do investors and creditors know the successful companies from the unsuccessful companies? Here's where financial accounting enters the picture. Investors and creditors rely heavily on financial accounting information in making investment and lending decisions.

As Illustration 1–12 demonstrates, investors and creditors have cash they are willing to invest. How do they decide which investment option provides the better opportunity? Most often, they analyze companies' financial accounting information in making their decision. In fact, **financial accounting information is essential to making good business decisions.**

ILLUSTRATION 1–12

Use of Financial Accounting Information in Investing and Lending Decisions

KEY POINT

Financial accounting serves an important role by providing information useful in investment and lending decisions.

To demonstrate the importance of financial accounting information to investment decisions, we can look at the relationship between changes in stock prices and changes in net income over 20 years. As an investor, you will make money from an increase in the stock price of a company in which you invest (you can sell the stock for more than you bought it). So as an investor, you are looking for companies whose stock price is likely to increase. Is there a way to find such companies? Interestingly, there is: **No other single piece of company information better explains companies' stock price performance than does financial accounting net income,** the bottom line in the income statement.

What if you were able to accurately predict the direction of companies' changes in net income over the next year—that is, whether it would increase or decrease—and then you invested $1,000 in companies that were going to have an *increase?* In contrast, what if instead you invested in companies that would have a *decrease* in net income? Illustration 1–13 shows what would happen to your $1,000 investment over 20 years for each scenario.

ILLUSTRATION 1–13

Relationship between Changes in Stock Prices and Changes in Net Income over a 20-Year Period

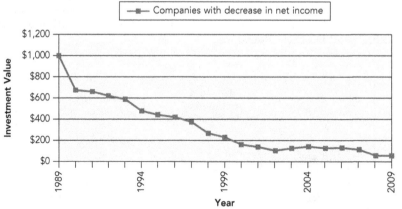

*Amounts in this chart represent the investment growth based on the median stock return of each group each year. Companies included in this analysis are all U.S. companies with listed stocks, which averages about 6,000 companies per year.

You can see that if you had invested $1,000 in companies with an increase in net income, your investment would have increased to $18,225 over the 20-year period. (The amount would have been much higher without the extraordinary events surrounding the financial crisis in 2008.) If instead you had invested $1,000 in companies with a decrease in net income, your $1,000 investment would have shrunk to $49 over this same period. This dramatic difference in the value of the investment demonstrates the importance of financial accounting information to investors. This book will provide you a thorough understanding of how net income is calculated and presented in financial statements. As you can see from the charts above, if you are able to predict the change in financial accounting's measure of profitability—net income—then you can predict the change in stock prices as well.

Investors and creditors also use information reported in the balance sheet. Consider a company's total liabilities, often referred to as *total debt*. Expanding debt levels limit management's ability to respond quickly and effectively to business situations. The "overhanging" debt, which involves legal obligation of repayment, restricts management's ability to engage in new profit-generating activities. Increased debt levels also increase interest payment burdens on the company. Failure to pay interest or to repay debt can result in creditors forcing the company to declare bankruptcy and go out of business. Understandably, then, investors and creditors keep a close eye on the company's debt level and its ability to repay.

 KEY POINT

No single piece of company information better explains companies' stock price performance than does financial accounting net income. A company's debt level is an important indicator of management's ability to respond to business situations and the possibility of bankruptcy.

Rules of Financial Accounting

Recall that accounting serves two main functions in our society: It (1) measures business activities and (2) communicates those measurements to investors and creditors. Although this process might seem straightforward, it's not always. How do we measure assets? When do we record revenues? What do we classify as an expense? How should we present financial statements? These are all important issues, and the answers are not always simple.

Because financial accounting information is so vital to investors and creditors, formal reporting standards have been established. All companies that sell their stock to the public must follow these rules and must publish financial statements in accordance with those rules. The rules of financial accounting are called generally accepted accounting principles, often abbreviated as GAAP (pronounced *gap*). The fact that all companies use these same rules is critical to financial statement users. It allows them to accurately *compare* financial information among companies when they are making decisions about where to lend or invest their resources.

■ **LO5**
Explain the term generally accepted accounting principles (GAAP) and describe the role of GAAP in financial accounting.

CURRENT STANDARD SETTING

Today, financial accounting and reporting standards in the United States are established primarily by the Financial Accounting Standards Board (FASB) (pronounced either by the letters themselves or as *faz-be*). The FASB is an independent, private-sector body with full-time voting members and a very large support staff. Members include representatives from the accounting profession, large corporations, financial analysts, accounting educators, and government agencies.

Not all countries follow the same accounting and reporting standards. For example, accounting practices in the United Kingdom differ from those in the United States, and those in the United States differ from those in Japan. In recent years,

For information about the activities of the Financial Accounting Standards Board, see its website, *www.fasb.org*.

the accounting profession has undertaken a project whose goal is to eliminate differences in accounting standards around the world. The standard-setting body responsible for this convergence effort is the International Accounting Standards Board (IASB), as detailed in the following box.

User's Guide Boxed sections on *International Financial Reporting Standards* (IFRS) are included throughout the text to emphasize the growing importance of international accounting standards throughout the world. They discuss specific instances in which U.S. GAAP and international standards differ. Appendix E at the back of the book provides more detail about differences between IFRS and U.S. GAAP.

For information about the activities of the International Accounting Standards Board, see its website, *www.iasb.org*.

INTERNATIONAL FINANCIAL REPORTING STANDARDS (IFRS)

The global counterpart to the FASB is the International Accounting Standards Board (IASB). In many ways, this organization functions like the FASB. The IASB's objectives are (1) to develop a single set of high-quality, understandable global accounting standards, (2) to promote the use of those standards, and (3) to bring about the convergence of national accounting standards and international accounting standards around the world. In 2002, the FASB and IASB signed the Norwalk Agreement, formalizing their commitment to convergence of U.S. and international accounting standards. The standards being developed and promoted by the IASB are called International Financial Reporting Standards (IFRS) (pronounced either by the letters or as *eye-furs*).

For more discussion, see Appendix E.

More than 100 countries have chosen to forgo their own country-specific standards and either require or allow International Financial Reporting Standards as their national standards. That movement, coupled with the convergence of U.S. GAAP and IFRS, has caused many to predict that soon both sets of rules, or perhaps only IFRS, will be acceptable for financial reporting in the United States.

KEY POINT

The rules of financial accounting are called generally accepted accounting principles (GAAP). The Financial Accounting Standards Board (FASB) is an independent, private body that has primary responsibility for the establishment of GAAP in the United States.

HISTORICAL PERSPECTIVE ON STANDARD SETTING

Pressures on the accounting profession to establish uniform accounting standards began to surface after the stock market crash of 1929. The Dow Jones Industrial Average, a major stock market index in the United States, fell 40% over the period September 3 to October 29 that year. The Dow bottomed out in July 1932, after losing 89% of its value.

Many blamed financial accounting for the stock market crash and the ensuing Great Depression of the 1930s. At the time of the crash, accounting practices and reporting procedures were not well established, providing the opportunity for companies to engage in inaccurate financial reporting to enhance their reported performance. This led to many stocks being valued too highly. As investors began to recognize this, their confidence in the stock market fell. They panicked and sold stocks in a frenzy. The Dow did not reach precrash levels again until 1954.

The 1933 Securities Act and the 1934 Securities Exchange Act were designed to restore investor confidence in financial accounting. The 1933 act sets forth accounting and disclosure requirements for initial offerings of securities (stocks and bonds). The 1934 act created a government agency, the **Securities and Exchange Commission (SEC).** The 1934 act gives the SEC the power to require companies that publicly trade their stock to prepare periodic financial statements for distribution to investors and creditors.

While Congress has given the SEC both the power and the responsibility for setting accounting and reporting standards for publicly traded companies, the SEC has delegated the primary responsibility for setting accounting standards to the private sector, currently the FASB. Note that the SEC delegated only the responsibility, not the authority, to set these standards. The power still lies with the SEC. If the SEC does not agree with a particular standard issued by the FASB, it can force a change in the standard. In fact, it has done so in the past.

THE ROLE OF THE AUDITOR

It is the responsibility of management to apply GAAP when communicating with investors and creditors through financial statements. Unfortunately, however, sometimes those in charge of preparing financial statements do not always follow the rules. Instead, some purposely provide misleading financial accounting information, commonly referred to as "cooking the books." The phrase implies that the accounting records ("books") have been presented in an altered form ("cooked"). Managers may cook the books for several reasons, such as to hide the poor operating performance of the company or to increase their personal wealth at stockholders' expense.

To help ensure that management has in fact appropriately applied GAAP, the SEC requires independent outside verification of the financial statements of publicly traded companies. Such independent examination is done by auditors, who are hired by a company as an independent party to express a professional opinion of the accuracy of that company's financial statements. They are not employees of the company they are auditing. Auditors provide an independent opinion of the extent to which financial statements are prepared in compliance with GAAP. If they find mistakes or fraudulent reporting behavior, auditors require the company to correct all significant information before issuing financial statements.

Illustration 1–14 presents an excerpt from the report of the independent auditors for **Dell**'s financial statements. The auditor's report indicates that Dell's financial statements for the period mentioned have been prepared in conformity with GAAP.

ILLUSTRATION 1–14

Excerpts from the 2009 Independent Auditor's Report of Dell Incorporated

User's Guide In this book, information from actual companies is illustrated using a flipped page in the lower-right corner.

DELL INCORPORATED
Report of Independent Registered Public Accounting Firm

To the Board of Directors and
Shareholders of Dell Inc.:

In our opinion, the consolidated financial statements listed in the accompanying index present fairly, in all material respects, the financial position of Dell Inc. and its subsidiaries at January 29, 2010, and January 30, 2009, and the results of their operations and their cash flows for each of the three years in the period ended January 29, 2010, in conformity with accounting principles generally accepted in the United States of America.

   Our audits of financial statements included examining, on a test basis, evidence supporting the amounts and disclosures in the financial statements, assessing the accounting principles used and significant estimates made by management, and evaluating the overall financial statement presentation. We believe that our audits provide a reasonable basis for our opinion.

Auditors play a major role in investors' and creditors' decisions by adding credibility to a company's financial statements.

OBJECTIVES OF FINANCIAL ACCOUNTING

After measuring business activities and communicating those measurements to investors and creditors, what do financial accountants hope to have achieved? What benefit will their services have brought to users of financial statements? The FASB has explicitly stated the specific objectives of financial accounting. These objectives are presented in Illustration 1–15.

ILLUSTRATION 1–15

Objectives of Financial Accounting

Financial accounting should provide information that:

1. Is useful to investors and creditors in making decisions.
2. Helps to predict cash flows.
3. Tells about economic resources, claims to resources, and changes in resources and claims.

The first objective is specific to investors and creditors. In addition to those users, though, financial accounting information is likely to have general usefulness to other groups of external users, who are interested in essentially the same financial aspects of a business as are investors and creditors. Some of these other groups were discussed in Illustration 1–1.

The second objective refers to the specific cash flow information needs of investors and creditors. The third objective emphasizes the need for information about economic resources (assets) and claims to those resources (liabilities and stockholders' equity) and their changes over time.

KEY POINT

The primary objective of financial accounting is to provide useful information to investors and creditors in making decisions.

Underlying these three key objectives is a conceptual framework that is the foundation upon which financial accounting is built. We discuss the FASB's conceptual framework in detail in the appendix to this chapter.

An Ethical Foundation

Like all structures, accounting requires a strong foundation. For accounting, part of that foundation is the ethical behavior of those who practice its rules. You have probably encountered the topic of ethics in other business courses. Ethics refers to a code or moral system that provides criteria for evaluating right and wrong behavior. Investors, creditors, government, and the general public rely on general ethical behavior among those who record and report the financial activities of businesses. A lack of public trust in financial reporting can undermine business and the economy. Indeed, the dramatic collapse of Enron in 2001 and the dismantling of the international public accounting firm of Arthur Andersen in 2002 severely shook investors' confidence in the stock market. Some questioned the credibility of corporate America as well as the accounting profession itself.

Public outrage over accounting scandals at high-profile companies increased the pressure on lawmakers to pass measures that would restore credibility and investor confidence in the financial reporting process. These pressures resulted in the issuance of the Public Company Accounting Reform and Investor Protection Act of 2002, commonly referred to as the Sarbanes-Oxley Act (SOX), named for the two congressmen who sponsored the bill. The Sarbanes-Oxley Act provides for the regulation of auditors and the types of services they furnish to clients, increases accountability of corporate executives, addresses conflicts of interest for securities analysts, and provides for stiff criminal penalties for violators. These increased requirements have dramatically increased the need for good accounting and, at the same time, highlighted the value of accounting information to investors and creditors. We discuss the specific provisions of SOX in more detail in Chapter 4.

Important as such legislation is in supporting the ethical foundation of accounting, it is equally important that accountants themselves have their own personal standards for ethical conduct. You cannot, though, just go out and suddenly obtain ethics when you need them. ("I'd like a pound of ethics, please.") Rather, accountants need to *develop* their ability to identify ethical situations and know the difference between right and wrong in the context of the accounting topics you will learn in this course. One of the keys to ethical decision making is having an appreciation for how your actions affect others.

When you face ethical dilemmas in your professional life (and indeed in your personal life), you can apply the following simple framework as you think through what to do:

1. Identify the ethical situation and the people who will be affected (the stakeholders).
2. Specify the options for alternative courses of action.
3. Understand the impact of each option on the stakeholders.
4. Make a decision.

Throughout the book, we will discuss some ethical decisions relating to accounting and will make clear their financial impact. These discussions will give you opportunities to practice some ethical decision making in a classroom setting.

 ETHICAL DILEMMA

 You have been the manager of a local restaurant for the past five years. Because of increased competition, you notice you're getting fewer customers. Despite all your attempts to attract new customers and cut costs, the restaurant's profitability continues to decline. The restaurant owner tells you that if this year's profit is lower than last year's, you'll lose your job.

When preparing financial statements at the end of the year, you notice that this year's profit *is* lower. You know that by purposely understating certain expenses, you can falsely report higher profits to the owner for this year. That will allow you to keep your job for at least one more year and look for a new job in the meantime.

What should you do? What if you really believe the lower profitability is caused by factors outside your control? Would this make the false reporting acceptable?

User's Guide
Throughout the book, you will see boxed discussions of *Ethical Dilemmas*. These dilemmas are designed to raise your awareness of accounting issues that have ethical ramifications.

CAREERS IN ACCOUNTING

PART C

At this point in your college career, you may be uncertain of your major. Here are three important questions to consider when you make your choice: (1) Will you enjoy your major as a career? (2) Will you be good at your chosen field? (3) Will you be well paid?

After completing the first course in accounting, you will have some idea of the answers to the first two questions. You will find out whether you might enjoy accounting. You will also find out through exams, quizzes, and homework whether you have the aptitude to be good at it. Realize, however, that besides being good at

CAREER CORNER

Over 20,000 employees join public accounting firms in entry-level jobs each year, and thousands more go into other areas of accounting. While financial accountants learn how to measure business transactions and prepare financial reports, they also learn a great deal about the business itself. Because of this widespread business knowledge, accountants often play a key role on the management team. In fact, it should come as no surprise to learn that most chief financial officers (CFOs) started their careers as accountants.

Accounting, because of its dynamic and professional nature, offers an attractive career option. You can learn more about a career in accounting by visiting the website of the American Institute of Certified Public Accountants (*www.aicpa.org*). There, you can look under the *Career Development and Workplace Issues* link to find current information about job opportunities, salaries, work life for women, how to write a resume, how to interview, and other general career advice. For salary and other job-related information, consult the website of the U.S. Bureau of Labor Statistics (*www.bls.gov/oco/ocos001.htm*) or go to *careers-in-accounting.com*. In 2009, entry-level jobs ranged between $50,000 and $70,000, with $55,000 as the norm for Big-4 firms.

Is an accounting degree right for you?

the technical side of accounting, you will need interpersonal skills such as working well in teams, making presentations to clients, and leading co-workers in complex projects. As for the third question, someone definitely will pay you to be an accountant, as we discuss in the following section.

Demand for Accounting

One of the greatest benefits of an accounting degree is the wide variety of job opportunities it opens to you. With an accounting degree you can apply for almost any position available to finance majors. However, it doesn't work the other way: Finance majors often lack the accounting background necessary to apply for accounting positions.

For the past several years, accounting has ranked as one of the top majors on university campuses. Accounting firms are anticipating a 20% increase in new hires over the next several years. Because of their importance in our society, accountants are in high demand. And because of this high demand, accounting salaries are on the rise. Starting salaries are among the highest of all majors across the university.

Career Options in Accounting

User's Guide
Throughout the book, you will see sections titled *Career Corner.* These sections highlight a link between a particular topic and a career.

■ **LO6**
Identify career opportunities in accounting.

The first big decision a student makes as an accounting graduate is the choice between a career in public accounting and a career in private accounting.

PUBLIC ACCOUNTING

Public accounting firms are professional service firms that traditionally have focused on three areas: auditing, tax preparation/planning, and business consulting. We already have discussed the role of *auditors* in attesting to the accuracy of companies' financial statements. *Tax preparation/planning* is an increasingly important activity in the United States, as the complexity of tax laws related to personal and corporate taxes continues to increase. *Business consulting* is perhaps the most lucrative activity of accountants. Managers who want to better understand their companies' financial strengths and weaknesses often turn to public accountants for guidance. Who knows the business activities better than the one measuring and communicating them?

If you choose a career in public accounting, the next big decision is whether to work for one of the "Big 4" public accounting firms (**Deloitte**, **Ernst & Young**, **PricewaterhouseCoopers**, and **KPMG**) or one of the thousands of medium or smaller-sized firms. The Big 4 firms are huge, each having annual revenues in the billions. They audit almost all the Fortune 500 companies in the United States and most of the largest companies around the world, and they hire thousands of accounting majors each year. The thousands of smaller international, regional, and local accounting firms also hire thousands of accounting majors right out of college.

Most public accountants become *Certified Public Accountants (CPAs)*. You become a CPA by passing the four parts of the CPA exam and meeting minimum work experience requirements (in some states). Most states require that you have 150 semester hours (225 quarter hours) of college credit to take the exam. Becoming a CPA can provide a big boost in salary and long-term job opportunities.

PRIVATE ACCOUNTING

A career in **private accounting** means providing accounting services to the company that employs you. Every major company in the world hires accountants. Just think of all the accounting issues at Dell, for example. Dell, and all other large companies, need accountants with training and experience in financial accounting, management accounting, taxation, internal auditing, and accounting information systems. Whereas working as a public accountant provides the advantage of experience working with a number of different clients, private accountants sometimes earn higher starting salaries. In fact, many accounting students begin their careers in public accounting, gaining experience across a wide array of companies and industries, and then eventually switch over to one of their favorite clients as private accountants. Other students take positions directly in private accounting right out of college.

Because of their special training and valuable knowledge base, both public and private accountants are expanding their roles to include the following: financial planning, information technology development, financial analysis, forensic accounting, information risk management, investment banking, environmental accounting, tax law, FBI work, management consulting, and much, much more. Illustration 1–16 outlines just a few of the many career options in accounting.

	Public Accounting (Big 4 and Non-Big 4)	Private Accounting	
Clients	Corporations Governments Nonprofit organizations Individuals	Your particular employer	**ILLUSTRATION 1–16** Some of the Career Options in Accounting
Traditional roles	Auditors Tax preparers/planners Business consultants	Financial accountants Managerial accountants Budget analysts Internal auditors Tax preparers Payroll managers	
Expanding roles	Financial planners Information technology developers Financial analysts Forensic accountants Information risk managers Investment bankers Environmental accountants Financial advisors Tax lawyers	Information managers Management advisors Tax planners Acquisition specialists FBI agents Sports agents	
Other career options	Governmental accounting, sole proprietorships, and education.		

A recent survey by *BusinessWeek* on ideal employers for undergraduate business majors listed the Big 4 public accounting firms in the top 12 of all companies in the United States. Three of the Big 4 were in the top five. All of the firms in the list hire accountants. This is a great time to be an accounting major.

KEY POINT

Because of the high demand for accounting graduates, wide range of job opportunities, and increasing salaries, this is a great time to obtain a degree in accounting.

APPENDIX

CONCEPTUAL FRAMEWORK

■ **LO7**
Explain the nature of the conceptual framework used to develop generally accepted accounting principles.

The FASB establishes financial accounting standards based on a **conceptual framework,** which you can think of as the "theory" of accounting. In much the same way that our nation's Constitution provides the underlying principles that guide the "correctness" of all laws, the FASB's conceptual framework prescribes the correctness of financial accounting rules. Having a conceptual framework provides standard setters with a benchmark for creating a consistent set of financial reporting rules now and in the future. It also provides others with a *written* framework so that everyone understands the underlying concepts that accountants are to consider in preparing and interpreting financial accounting information.

KEY POINT

The conceptual framework provides an underlying foundation for the development of accounting standards and interpretation of accounting information.

In the chapter, we discussed the three objectives of financial accounting as outlined in the FASB's conceptual framework. To satisfy these stated objectives, accounting information should possess certain characteristics. What are the desired characteristics? Illustration 1–17 provides a graphical depiction of the qualitative characteristics of accounting information.

ILLUSTRATION 1–17   Qualitative Characteristics of Accounting Information

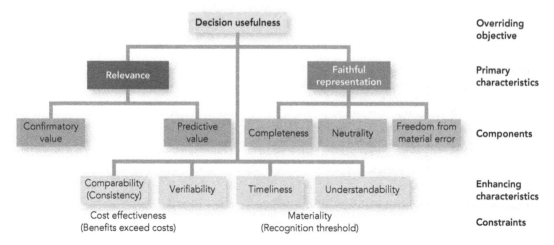

Notice that at the top of the figure is decision usefulness—the ability of the information to be useful in decision making. Accounting information should help investors, lenders, and other creditors make important decisions about providing funds to a company.

PRIMARY QUALITATIVE CHARACTERISTICS

The two primary decision-specific qualitative characteristics that make accounting information useful are *relevance* and *faithful representation.* Both are critical. No matter how representative, if information is not relevant to the decision at hand, it is useless. Conversely, relevant information is of little value if it does not accurately represent the underlying activity.

Relevance. To have relevance, accounting information should possess *confirmatory value* and/or *predictive value.* Generally, useful information will possess both of these components. For example, the ability of **Dell** to report a positive net income confirms that its management is effectively and efficiently using the company's resources to sell quality products. In this case, net income has *confirmatory value.* At the same time, reporting a positive and growing net income for several consecutive years should provide information that has *predictive value* for the company's future cash-generating ability.

Faithful representation. To be a faithful representation of business activities, accounting information should be complete, neutral, and free from material error. *Completeness* means including all information necessary for faithful representation of the business activity the firm is reporting. For example, when Dell reports inventory in its balance sheet, investors understand it to represent *all* items (and only those items) that are intended for sale to customers in the ordinary course of business. If the amount reported for inventory includes only some of the items to be sold, then it lacks completeness. Adequate note disclosure is another important component of completeness. Dell must disclose in the notes to the financial statements the method it used to calculate inventory reported on its balance sheet. (We discuss alternative inventory methods in Chapter 6.)

Neutrality means to be unbiased, and this characteristic is highly related to the establishment of accounting standards. Sometimes a new accounting standard may favor one group of companies over others. In such cases, the FASB must convince the financial community that this was a *consequence* of the standard, and not an *objective* used to set the standard. For example, the FASB requires that all research and development (R&D) costs be reported as an expense in the income statement, reducing the current year's net income. The FASB's objective in adopting this approach was not to weaken the financial appearance of those companies in R&D-intensive industries, such as telecommunications, pharmaceuticals, and software, even though that may have been the effect.

Freedom from material error indicates that reported amounts reflect the best available information. As you'll come to find out in this course, some amounts reported in the financial statements are based on estimates, and the accuracy of those estimates is subject to uncertainty. Because of this, financial statements are not expected to be completely free of error, but they are expected to reflect management's unbiased judgments.

 KEY POINT

To be useful for decision making, accounting information should have relevance and faithful representation.

ENHANCING QUALITATIVE CHARACTERISTICS

Four enhancing qualitative characteristics are comparability, verifiability, timeliness, and understandability. Comparability refers to the ability of users to see similarities and differences between two different business activities. For example, how does Dell's net income compare with net income for other computer manufacturers such as Hewlett-Packard or Gateway? Comparability also refers to the ability of users to see similarities and differences in the same company over time. How does Dell's net income this year compare to last year's? Closely related to the notion of comparability is consistency. Consistency refers to the use of similar accounting procedures either over time for the same company, or across companies at the same point in time. Comparability of financial information is the overriding goal, while consistency of accounting procedures is a means of achieving that goal.

Verifiability implies a consensus among different measurers. For instance, different graders will arrive at the same exam score for multiple-choice tests, but they are more likely to differ in scoring essay exams. Multiple-choice tests are highly verifiable. The same idea holds in the business world. For example, the price Dell paid to purchase a patent from another company is usually highly verifiable because there is an exchange at a certain point in time. In contrast, the fair value of a patent for a product Dell developed internally over an extended period is more subjective and less verifiable.

Firms must also disclose information related to net income that is *timely*. Timeliness refers to information being available to users early enough to allow them to use it in the decision process. Large companies like Dell are required to report information related to net income within 40 days after the end of the quarter and within 60 days after the end of the year.

Understandability means that users must be able to understand the information within the context of the decision they are making. This is a user-specific quality because users will differ in their ability to comprehend any set of information.

PRACTICAL CONSTRAINTS ON ACHIEVING DESIRED QUALITATIVE CHARACTERISTICS

Sometimes, certain information involves more time and effort than the information is worth. For example, if a friend asks what you did today, she probably wants to know the general outline of your day, but does not want to hear a recital of every move you made. Similarly, there may be practical constraints (limits) on each of the qualitative characteristics of accounting information.

One such constraint is cost effectiveness, which suggests that financial accounting information is provided only when the benefits of doing so exceed the costs. For example, knowing the profit margin earned by Dell in each country provides decision-useful information to investors and creditors. However, this information is also helpful to the company's current and potential competitors such as Hewlett-Packard and Apple as they make their own expansion plans. The competitive costs of providing this information may outweigh the benefits.

A related constraint on the type of information we provide is the concept of materiality. Materiality reflects the impact of financial accounting information on investors' and creditors' decisions. Unless an item is *material* in amount or nature—that is, sufficient in amount or nature to affect a decision—it need not be reported in accordance with GAAP. Based on the concept of materiality, Dell probably does not record all its assets as assets. Most companies record assets such as wastebaskets and staplers as *expenses*, even though these items will benefit the company for a long period. Recording a $6 wastebasket as a current expense instead of a long-term asset for a multi-billion dollar company like Dell has no impact on investors' decisions.

UNDERLYING ASSUMPTIONS

Four basic assumptions underlie GAAP. As pictured in Illustration 1–18, they are (1) the economic entity assumption, (2) the monetary unit assumption, (3) the periodicity assumption, and (4) the going concern assumption.

GAAP

UNDERLYING ASSUMPTIONS			
Economic Entity	Monetary Unit	Periodicity	Going Concern

ILLUSTRATION 1-18

Assumptions That Underlie GAAP

Economic Entity Assumption. The economic entity assumption states that we can identify all economic events with a particular economic entity. In other words, only business transactions involving Dell should be reported as part of Dell's financial accounting information. Another key aspect of this assumption is the distinction between the economic activities of owners and those of the company. For example, Michael Dell's personal residence is not an asset of Dell Incorporated.

Monetary Unit Assumption. Information would be difficult to use if, for example, we listed assets as "three machines, two trucks, and a building." According to the monetary unit assumption, in order to *measure* financial statement elements, we need a unit or scale of measurement. The dollar in the United States is the most appropriate common denominator to express information about financial statement elements and changes in those elements. In Europe, the common denominator is the euro. Dell has operations throughout the world, so it must translate all its financial information to U.S. dollars under the monetary unit assumption.

Periodicity Assumption. The periodicity assumption relates to the qualitative characteristic of *timeliness*. External users need *periodic* information to make decisions. The periodicity assumption divides the economic life of an enterprise (presumed to be indefinite) into artificial time periods for periodic financial reporting. Corporations, like Dell, whose securities are publicly traded are required to provide financial information to the SEC on a quarterly *and* an annual basis.

Going Concern Assumption. The going concern assumption states that in the absence of information to the contrary, a business entity will continue to operate indefinitely. This assumption is critical to many broad and specific accounting principles. It provides justification for measuring many assets based on their original costs (a practice known as the *historical cost principle*). If we knew an enterprise was going to cease operations in the near future, we would measure assets and liabilities not at their original costs but at their current liquidation values.

In addition to the four basic assumptions that underlie GAAP are four principles (historical cost, full disclosure, realization, and matching) that guide the application of GAAP. We will explain each of these in an appropriate context in later chapters.

KEY POINTS BY LEARNING OBJECTIVE

LO1 Describe the two primary functions of financial accounting.

The functions of financial accounting are to measure business activities of a company and to communicate information about those activities to investors and creditors and other outside users for decision-making purposes.

LO2 Identify the three fundamental business activities that financial accounting measures.

Financing activities include transactions with lenders and owners. Investing activities generally include the purchase or disposal of productive assets. Operating activities relate to earning revenues and incurring expenses.

LO3 Discuss how financial accounting information is communicated through financial statements.

The income statement compares revenues and expenses for the current period to assess the company's ability to earn a profit from running its operations.

The statement of stockholders' equity reports information related to changes in common stock and retained earnings each period. The change in retained earnings equals net income less dividends for the period.

The balance sheet demonstrates that the company's resources (assets) equal creditors' claims (liabilities) plus owners' claims (stockholders' equity) to those resources.

The statement of cash flows reports cash transactions from operating, investing, and financing activities.

All transactions that affect revenues or expenses reported in the income statement ultimately affect the balance sheet through the balance in retained earnings.

LO4 Describe the role that financial accounting plays in the efficient distribution of society's resources.

Financial accounting serves an important role by providing information useful in investment and lending decisions.

No single piece of company information better explains companies' stock price performance than does financial accounting net income. A company's debt level is an important indicator of management's ability to respond to business situations and the possibility of bankruptcy.

LO5 Explain the term generally accepted accounting principles (GAAP) and describe the role of GAAP in financial accounting.

The rules of financial accounting are called generally accepted accounting principles (GAAP). The Financial Accounting Standards Board (FASB) is an independent, private body that has primary responsibility for the establishment of GAAP in the United States.

The primary objective of financial accounting is to provide useful information to investors and creditors in making decisions.

LO6 Identify career opportunities in accounting.

Because of the high demand for accounting graduates, the wide range of job opportunities, and increasing salaries, this is a great time to obtain a degree in accounting.

Appendix

LO7 Explain the nature of the conceptual framework used to develop generally accepted accounting principles.

The conceptual framework provides an underlying foundation for the development of accounting standards and interpretation of accounting information.

To be useful for decision making, accounting information should have relevance and faithful representation.

GLOSSARY

Accounting: A system of maintaining records of a company's operations and communicating that information to decision makers. **p. 4**

Accounting equation: Equation that shows a company's resources (assets) equal creditors' and owners' claims to those resources (liabilities and stockholders' equity). **p. 7**

Assets: Resources owned by a company. **p. 7**

Auditors: Trained individuals hired by a company as an independent party to express a professional opinion of the accuracy of that company's financial statements. **p. 23**

Balance sheet: A financial statement that presents the financial position of the company on a particular date. **p. 13**

Comparability: The ability of users to see similarities and differences between two different business activities. **p. 30**

Consistency: The use of similar accounting procedures either over time for the same company, or across companies at the same point in time. **p. 30**

Corporation: An entity that is legally separate from its owners. **p. 6**

Cost effectiveness: Financial accounting information is provided only when the benefits of doing so exceed the costs. **p. 30**

Decision usefulness: The ability of the information to be useful in decision making. **p. 29**

Dividends: Cash payments to stockholders. **p. 8**

Economic entity assumption: All economic events with a particular economic entity can be identified. **p. 31**

Ethics: A code or moral system that provides criteria for evaluating right and wrong behavior. **p. 24**

Expenses: Costs of providing products and services. **p. 8**

Faithful representation: Accounting information that is complete, neutral, and free from material error. **p. 29**

Financial accounting: Measurement of business activities of a company and communication of those measurements to external parties for decision-making purposes. **p. 5**

Financial Accounting Standards Board (FASB): An independent, private body that has primary responsibility for the establishment of GAAP in the United States. **p. 21**

Financial statements: Periodic reports published by the company for the purpose of providing information to external users. **p. 10**

Financing activities: Transactions involving external sources of funding. **p. 5**

Generally accepted accounting principles (GAAP): The rules of financial accounting. **p. 21**

Going concern assumption: In the absence of information to the contrary, a business entity will continue to operate indefinitely. **p. 31**

Income statement: A financial statement that reports the company's revenues and expenses over an interval of time. **p. 11**

International Accounting Standards Board (IASB): An international accounting standard-setting body responsible for the convergence of accounting standards worldwide. **p. 22**

International Financial Reporting Standards (IFRS): The standards being developed and promoted by the International Accounting Standards Board. **p. 22**

Investing activities: Transactions involving the purchase and sale of (1) long-term resources such as land, buildings, equipment, and machinery and (2) any resources not directly related to a company's normal operations. **p. 5**

Liabilities: Amounts owed to creditors. **p. 7**

Materiality: The impact of financial accounting information on investors' and creditors' decisions. **p. 30**

Monetary unit assumption: A unit or scale of measurement can be used to measure financial statement elements. **p. 31**

Net income: Difference between revenues and expenses. **p. 8**

Operating activities: Transactions involving the primary operations of the company, such as providing products and services to customers and the associated costs of doing so, like utilities, taxes, advertising, wages, rent, and maintenance. **p. 5**

Partnership: Business owned by two or more persons. **p. 9**

Periodicity assumption: The economic life of an enterprise (presumed to be indefinite) can be divided into artificial time periods for financial reporting. **p. 31**

Relevance: Accounting information that possesses confirmatory value and/or predictive value. **p. 29**

Retained earnings: Cumulative amount of net income earned over the life of the company that has not been distributed to stockholders as dividends. **p. 12**

Revenues: Amounts earned from selling products or services to customers. **p. 8**

Sarbanes-Oxley Act (SOX): Formally titled the Public Company Accounting Reform and Investor Protection Act of 2002, this act provides regulation of auditors and the types of services they furnish to clients, increases accountability of corporate executives, addresses conflicts of interest for securities analysts, and provides for stiff criminal penalties for violators. **p. 24**

Sole proprietorship: A business owned by one person. **p. 9**

Statement of cash flows: A financial statement that measures activities involving cash receipts and cash payments over an interval of time. **p. 15**

Statement of stockholders' equity: A financial statement that summarizes the changes in stockholders' equity over an interval of time. **p. 12**

Stockholder's equity: Stockholders', or owners', claims to resources, which equal the difference between total assets and total liabilities. **p. 7**

Timeliness: Information being available to users early enough to allow them to use it in the decision process. **p. 30**

Understandability: Users must understand the information within the context of the decision they are making. **p. 30**

Verifiability: A consensus among different measurers. **p. 30**

SELF-STUDY QUESTIONS

■ LO1
1. Based on the introductory section of this chapter, which course is most like financial accounting?
   a. College algebra.
   b. Foreign language.
   c. Molecular biology.
   d. Physical education.

■ LO2
2. Financial accounting serves which primary function(s)?
   a. Measures business activities.
   b. Communicates business activities to interested parties.
   c. Makes business decisions on behalf of interested parties.
   d. Both a. and b. are functions of financial accounting.

■ LO2
3. Financing activities of a company include which of the following?
   a. Selling products or services to customers.
   b. Using cash to purchase long-term assets such as machinery.
   c. Borrowing money from the bank.
   d. Paying salaries to employees.

■ LO2
4. Investing activities of a company include which of the following?
   a. Paying salaries to workers.
   b. Using cash to purchase long-term assets such as equipment.
   c. Issuing common stock to investors.
   d. Borrowing money from the bank.

■ LO3
5. Which financial statement conveys a company's ability to generate profits in the current period?
   a. Income statement.
   b. Statement of cash flows.
   c. Balance sheet.
   d. Statement of stockholders' equity.

■ LO3
6. Which financial statement shows that a company's resources equal claims to those resources?
   a. Income statement.
   b. Statement of stockholders' equity.
   c. Balance sheet.
   d. Statement of cash flows.

■ LO4
7. Why does financial accounting have a positive impact on our society?
   a. It entails a detailed transaction record necessary for filing taxes with the Internal Revenue Service (IRS).
   b. It allows investors and creditors to redirect their resources to successful companies and away from unsuccessful companies.
   c. It prevents competitors from being able to steal the company's customers.
   d. It provides a system of useful internal reports for management decision making.

■ LO5
8. The body of rules and procedures that guide the measurement and communication of financial accounting information is known as:
   a. Standards of Professional Compliance (SPC).
   b. Code of Ethical Decisions (COED).
   c. Rules of Financial Reporting (RFP).
   d. Generally Accepted Accounting Principles (GAAP).

9. What is a benefit to a career in accounting?   ■ LO6
   a. High salaries.
   b. Wide range of job opportunities.
   c. High demand for accounting graduates.
   d. All of the above.

10. What are the two primary qualitative characteristics identified by the Financial   ■ LO7
    Accounting Standards Board's (FASB) conceptual framework?
    a. Relevance and faithful representation.
    b. Materiality and efficiency.
    c. Comparability and consistency.
    d. Costs and benefits.

Check out
www.mhhe.com/succeed
for more multiple-choice
questions.

Note: For answers, see the last page of the chapter.

REVIEW QUESTIONS

1. Explain what it means to say that an accounting class is not the same as a math class.   ■ LO1

2. Identify some of the people interested in making decisions about a company.   ■ LO1

3. What is the basic difference between financial accounting and managerial accounting?   ■ LO1

4. What are the two primary functions of financial accounting?   ■ LO1

5. What are the three basic business activities that financial accounting seeks to   ■ LO2
   measure and communicate to external parties? Define each.

6. What are a few of the typical financing activities for a company like **United Parcel**   ■ LO2
   Service, Inc. (UPS), the world's largest package delivery company and a leading
   global provider of specialized transportation and logistics services?

7. What are a few of the typical investing activities for a company like **Trump**   ■ LO2
   Entertainment Resorts, Inc., a leading gaming company that owns and operates
   casinos, resorts, and hotels?

8. What are a few of the typical operating activities for a company like **Oracle**   ■ LO2
   Corporation, one of the world's leading suppliers of software for information
   management?

9. What are the three major legal forms of business organizations? Which one is   ■ LO2
   chosen by most of the largest companies in the United States?

10. Provide the basic definition for each of the account types: assets, liabilities,   ■ LO2
    stockholders' equity, dividends, revenues, and expenses.

11. What are the major advantages and disadvantages of each of the legal forms of   ■ LO2
    business organizations?

12. What are the four primary financial statements? What basic information is shown   ■ LO3
    on each?

13. What does it mean to say that the income statement, statement of stockholders'   ■ LO3
    equity, and statement of cash flows measure activity over an *interval of time*, but
    the balance sheet measures activity at a *point in time?*

14. Give some examples of the basic revenues and expenses for a company like   ■ LO3
    The Walt Disney Company.

15. What is the accounting equation? Which financial statement reports the accounting   ■ LO3
    equation?

■ LO3 16. Give some examples of the basic assets and liabilities of a company like **Walmart Stores, Inc.**

■ LO3 17. "The retained earnings account is a link between the income statement and the balance sheet." Explain what this means.

■ LO3 18. What are the three types of cash flows reported in the statement of cash flows? Give an example of each type of activity for a company like **Oakley, Inc.,** a designer, manufacturer, and distributor of high-performance eyewear, footwear, watches, and athletic equipment.

■ LO3 19. In addition to financial statements, what are some other ways to disclose financial information to external users?

■ LO4 20. How does financial accounting have an impact on society?

■ LO5 21. What is meant by GAAP? Why should companies follow GAAP in reporting to external users?

■ LO5 22. Which body is primarily responsible for the establishment of GAAP in the United States? What body serves this function on an international basis?

■ LO5 23. In general terms, explain the terms U.S. GAAP and IFRS.

■ LO5 24. What was the primary reason for the establishment of the 1933 Securities Act and the 1934 Securities Exchange Act? What power does the Securities and Exchange Commission (SEC) have?

■ LO5 25. What is the role of the auditor in the financial reporting process?

■ LO5 26. What are the three primary objectives of financial reporting?

■ LO6 27. What are some of the benefits to obtaining a degree in accounting? What is the difference between a career in public accounting and private accounting? What are some of the traditional careers of accounting graduates? What new areas are accountants expanding into?

■ LO7 28. Discuss the terms *relevance* and *faithful representation* as they relate to financial accounting information.

■ LO7 29. What are the two components of relevance? What are the three components of faithful representation?

■ LO7 30. What is meant by the terms *cost effectiveness* and *materiality* in financial reporting?

■ LO7 31. Define the four basic assumptions underlying GAAP.

BRIEF EXERCISES

connect |ACCOUNTING

Define accounting **(LO1)**

BE1–1 Indicate whether the definition provided is true or false.

(True/False)   Accounting can be defined as:

1. _____ The language of business.
2. _____ A measurement/communication process.
3. _____ A mathematics course.

Identify the different types of business activities **(LO2)**

BE1–2 Match each business activity with its description.

Business Activities	Descriptions
1. _____ Financing	a. Transactions related to revenues and expenses.
2. _____ Investing	b. Transactions with lenders and owners.
3. _____ Operating	c. Transactions involving the purchase and sale of productive assets.

BE1–3 Match each form of business organization with its description.

Identify the different forms of business organizations (**LO2**)

Business Organizations	Descriptions
1. _____ Sole proprietorship	a. Business owned by two or more persons.
2. _____ Partnership	b. Entity legally separate from its owners.
3. _____ Corporation	c. Business owned by a single person.

BE1–4 Match each account type with its description.

Recognize the different account classifications (**LO2**)

Account Classifications	Descriptions
1. _____ Assets	a. Amounts earned from sales of products or services.
2. _____ Liabilities	b. Owners' claims to resources.
3. _____ Stockholders' equity	c. Distributions to stockholders.
4. _____ Dividends	d. Costs of selling products or services.
5. _____ Revenues	e. Resources owned.
6. _____ Expenses	f. Amounts owed.

BE1–5 Match each financial statement with its description.

Describe each financial statement (**LO3**)

Financial Statements	Descriptions
1. _____ Income statement	a. Change in owners' claims to resources.
2. _____ Statement of stockholders' equity	b. Profitability of the company.
3. _____ Balance sheet	c. Change in cash as a result of operating, investing, and financing activities.
4. _____ Statement of cash flows	d. Resources equal creditors' and owners' claims to those resources.

BE1–6 Determine on which financial statement you find the following items.

Determine the location of items in financial statements (**LO3**)

Financial Statements	Items
1. _____ Income statement	a. The change in retained earnings due to net income and dividends.
2. _____ Statement of stockholders' equity	b. Amount of cash received from borrowing money from a local bank.
3. _____ Balance sheet	c. Revenue earned from sales to customers during the year.
4. _____ Statement of cash flows	d. Total amounts owed to workers at the end of the year.

BE1–7 Each of these parties plays a role in the quality of financial reporting. Match each group with its function.

Identify different groups engaged in providing high-quality financial reporting (**LO5**)

Groups	Functions
1. _____ Financial Accounting Standards Board	a. Group that has been given power by Congress to enforce the proper application of financial reporting rules for companies whose securities are publicly traded.
2. _____ International Accounting Standards Board	b. Independent, private-sector group that is primarily responsible for setting financial reporting standards in the United States.
3. _____ Securities and Exchange Commission	c. Independent intermediaries that help to ensure that management appropriately applies financial reporting rules in preparing the company's financial statements.
4. _____ Auditors	d. Body that is attempting to develop a single set of high-quality, understandable global accounting standards.

Identify the objectives of financial accounting (**LO5**)

BE1–8 Indicate which of the following are objectives of financial accounting.

(Yes/No)	Objectives
1. _____	Provide information that is useful to investors and creditors.
2. _____	Guarantee that businesses will not go bankrupt.
3. _____	Provide information about resources and claims to resources.
4. _____	Prevent competitors from offering lower-priced products.
5. _____	Provide information to help users in predicting future cash flows.
6. _____	Maximize tax revenue to the federal government.

Identify careers for accounting majors (**LO6**)

BE1–9 Below are possible career opportunities for those earning a degree in accounting. Indicate whether the statement related to each career is true or false.

(True/False) Someone earning a degree in accounting could pursue the following career:

1. _____   Auditor
2. _____   Tax preparer
3. _____   Business consultant
4. _____   Financial planner
5. _____   Forensic investigator
6. _____   Tax planner
7. _____   Financial analyst
8. _____   Information technology developer
9. _____   Investment banker
10. _____   Tax lawyer
11. _____   FBI agent
12. _____   Information risk manager

Identify the components of relevance (**LO7**)

BE1–10 Match each of the components of relevance with its definition.

Relevance	Definitions
1. _____ Confirmatory value	a. Information is useful in helping to forecast future outcomes.
2. _____ Predictive value	b. Information provides feedback on past activities.

Identify the components of faithful representation (**LO7**)

BE1–11 Match each of the components of faithful representation with its definition.

Faithful Representation	Definition
1. _____ Freedom from material error	a. All information necessary to describe an item is reported.
2. _____ Neutrality	b. Information that does not bias the decision maker.
3. _____ Completeness	c. Reported amounts reflect the best available information.

EXERCISES

Identify the different types of business activities (**LO2**)

E1–1 The following provides a list of transactions and a list of business activities.

Transactions	Business Activities
1. _____ Borrow from the bank.	a. Financing
2. _____ Provide services to customers.	b. Investing
3. _____ Issue common stock to investors.	c. Operating
4. _____ Purchase land.	
5. _____ Pay rent for the current period.	
6. _____ Pay dividends to stockholders.	
7. _____ Purchase building.	

Required:

Match the transaction with the business activity by indicating the letter that corresponds to the appropriate business activity.

E1–2 Falcon Incorporated has the following transactions with Wildcat Corporation.

Identify account classifications and business activities (LO2)

Flip Side of E1–3

Transactions	Falcon's Related Account
1. Falcon purchases common stock of Wildcat.	Investment
2. Falcon borrows from Wildcat by signing a note.	Notes payable
3. Wildcat pays dividends to Falcon.	Dividend revenue
4. Falcon provides services to Wildcat.	Service revenue
5. Falcon pays interest to Wildcat on borrowing.	Interest expense

Required:
1. For each transaction, indicate whether Falcon would classify the related account as an (a) asset, (b) liability, or (c) stockholders' equity to be reported in the balance sheet; a (d) revenue or (e) expense to be reported in the income statement; or an (f) dividend to be reported in the statement of stockholders' equity.
2. Classify the type of activity as financing, investing, or operating.

E1–3 The transactions in this problem are identical to those in E1–2, but now with a focus on Wildcat.

Identify account classifications and business activities (LO2)

Flip Side of E1–2

Transactions	Wildcat's Related Account
1. Falcon purchases common stock of Wildcat.	Common stock
2. Falcon borrows from Wildcat by signing a note.	Notes receivable
3. Wildcat pays dividends to Falcon.	Dividend
4. Falcon provides services to Wildcat.	Service fee expense
5. Falcon pays interest to Wildcat on borrowing.	Interest revenue

Required:
1. For each transaction, indicate whether Wildcat would classify the related account as an (a) asset, (b) liability, or (c) stockholders' equity to be reported in the balance sheet; a (d) revenue or (e) expense to be reported in the income statement; or an (f) dividend to be reported in the statement of stockholders' equity.
2. Classify the type of activity as financing, investing, or operating.

E1–4 Eagle Corp. operates Magnetic Resonance Imaging (MRI) clinics throughout the Northeast. At the end of the current period, the company reports the following amounts: Assets = $40,000; Liabilities = $22,000; Dividends = $2,000; Revenues = $12,000; Expenses = $8,000.

Calculate net income and stockholders' equity (LO2)

Required:
1. Calculate net income.
2. Calculate stockholders' equity at the end of the period.

E1–5 Cougar's Accounting Services provides low-cost tax advice and preparation to those with financial need. At the end of the current period, the company reports the following amounts: Assets = $17,000; Liabilities = $14,000; Revenues = $26,000; Expenses = $32,000.

Calculate net loss and stockholders' equity (LO2)

Required:
1. Calculate net loss.
2. Calculate stockholders' equity at the end of the period.

E1–6 Below are the account balances for Cowboy Law Firm at the end of December.

Prepare an income statement (LO3)

Accounts	Balances
Cash	$ 4,400
Salaries expense	1,700
Accounts payable	2,400
Retained earnings	4,300
Utilities expense	1,100
Supplies	12,800
Service revenue	8,300
Common stock	5,000

Required:

Use only the appropriate accounts to prepare an income statement.

Prepare a statement of stockholders' equity (LO3)

E1–7 At the beginning of the year (January 1), Buffalo Drilling has $10,000 of common stock outstanding and retained earnings of $7,200. During the year, Buffalo reports net income of $7,500 and pays dividends of $2,200. In addition, Buffalo issues additional common stock for $7,000.

Required:

Prepare the statement of stockholders' equity at the end of the year (December 31).

Prepare a balance sheet (LO3)

E1–8 Wolfpack Construction has the following account balances at the end of the year.

Accounts	Balances
Equipment	$21,000
Accounts payable	2,000
Salaries expense	28,000
Common stock	10,000
Land	13,000
Notes payable	15,000
Service revenue	34,000
Cash	5,000
Retained earnings	?

Required:

Use only the appropriate accounts to prepare a balance sheet.

Prepare a statement of cash flows (LO3)

E1–9 Tiger Trade has the following cash transactions for the period.

Accounts	Amounts
Cash received from sale of products to customers	$ 35,000
Cash received from the bank for long-term loan	40,000
Cash paid to purchase factory equipment	(45,000)
Cash paid to merchandise suppliers	(11,000)
Cash received from the sale of an unused warehouse	12,000
Cash paid to workers	(23,000)
Cash paid for advertisement	(3,000)
Cash received for sale of services to customers	25,000
Cash paid for dividends to stockholders	(5,000)

Required:

1. Calculate the ending balance of cash, assuming the balance of cash at the beginning of the period is $4,000.
2. Prepare a statement of cash flows.

Compute missing amounts from financial statements (LO3)

E1–10 Each of the following independent situations represents amounts shown on the four basic financial statements.

1. Revenues = $25,000; Expenses = $17,000; Net income = _____.
2. Increase in stockholders' equity = $16,000; Issuance of common stock = $10,000; Net income = $11,000; Dividends = _____.
3. Assets = $23,000; Stockholders' equity = $17,000; Liabilities = _____.
4. Total change in cash = $24,000; Net operating cash flows = $32,000; Net investing cash flows = ($15,000); Net financing cash flows = _____.

Required:

Fill in the missing blanks using your knowledge of amounts that appear on the financial statements.

E1–11 During its first five years of operations, Red Raider Consulting reports net income and pays dividends as follows.

Calculate the balance of retained earnings (LO3)

Year	Net Income	Dividends	Retained Earnings
1	$1,200	$ 500	_____
2	1,700	500	_____
3	2,100	1,000	_____
4	3,200	1,000	_____
5	4,400	1,000	_____

Required:

Calculate the balance of retained earnings at the end of each year. Note that retained earnings will always equal $0 at the beginning of year 1.

E1–12 Below is information related to retained earnings for five companies.

Calculate amounts related to the balance of retained earnings (LO3)

1. **Coca-Cola** reports an increase in retained earnings of $2.2 billion and net income of $4.9 billion. What is the amount of dividends?
2. **Pepsico** reports an increase in retained earnings of $2.4 billion and dividends of $1.6 billion. What is the amount of net income?
3. **Google** reports an increase in retained earnings of $1.5 billion and net income of $1.5 billion. What is the amount of dividends?
4. **Sirius Satellite Radio** reports beginning retained earnings of −$1.8 billion, net loss of $0.9 billion, and $0 dividends. What is the amount of ending retained earnings?
5. **Abercrombie & Fitch** reports ending retained earnings of $1.36 billion, net income of $0.33 billion, and dividends of $0.05 billion. What is the amount of beginning retained earnings?

Required:

Calculate the answer to each.

E1–13 Below is balance sheet information for five companies.

Use the accounting equation to calculate amounts related to the balance sheet (LO3)

1. **ExxonMobil** reports total assets of $208 billion and total liabilities of $97 billion. What is the amount of stockholders' equity?
2. **Citigroup** reports total liabilities of $1,400 billion and stockholders' equity of $100 billion. What is the amount of total assets?
3. **Amazon.com** reports total assets of $3.7 billion and total stockholders' equity of $0.2 billion. What is the amount of total liabilities?
4. **Nike** reports an increase in assets of $1.1 billion and an increase in liabilities of $0.4 billion. What is the amount of the change in stockholders' equity?
5. **Kellogg** reports a decrease in liabilities of $0.24 billion and an increase in stockholders' equity of $0.03 billion. What is the amount of the change in total assets?

Required:

Calculate the answer to each.

E1–14 Below is cash flow information for five companies.

Calculate missing amounts related to the statement of cash flows (LO3)

1. **Kraft Foods** reports operating cash flows of $3.5 billion, investing cash flows of $0.5 billion, and financing cash flows of −$4.0 billion. What is the amount of the change in total cash?
2. **Sara Lee** reports operating cash flows of $1.3 billion, investing cash flows of −$0.2 billion, and financing cash flows of −$1.2 billion. If the beginning cash amount is $0.6 billion, what is the ending cash amount?
3. **Performance Food Group** reports operating cash flows of $0.08 billion, investing cash flows of $0.53 billion, and a change in total cash of $0.05 billion. What is the amount of cash flows from financing activities?
4. **Smithfield Foods** reports operating cash flows of $0.50 billion, financing cash flows of $0.32 billion, and a change in total cash of $0.01 billion. What is the amount of cash flows from investing activities?

5. **Tyson Foods** reports investing cash flows of –$1.22 billion, financing cash flows of $0.93 billion, and a change in total cash of $0.01 billion. What is the amount of cash flows from operating activities?

Required:
Calculate the answer to each.

Identify the purpose of qualitative characteristics (LO7)

E1–15 The qualitative characteristics outlined in the FASB's conceptual framework include:

Primary Characteristics		Enhancing Characteristics
Relevance	**Faithful Representation**	f. Comparability
a. Confirmatory value	c. Completeness	g. Verifiability
b. Predictive value	d. Neutrality	h. Timeliness
	e. Freedom from material error	i. Understandability

Consider the following independent situations.
1. In deciding whether to invest in **Southwest Airlines** or **American Airlines**, investors evaluate the companies' income statements. _____
2. To provide the most reliable information about future sales, **Walmart**'s management provides unbiased estimates of the decline in inventory value each year. _____
3. In deciding whether to loan money, **Wells Fargo** uses balance sheet information to forecast the probability of bankruptcy. _____
4. **IBM** is required to issue public financial statements within 60 days of its year-end. _____
5. Employees of **Starbucks** can use the company's financial statements to understand the efficiency with which management has conducted operations over the past year. _____
6. When first requiring firms to prepare a statement of cash flows, the FASB's intent was not to discourage or promote investment in the automobile industry. _____
7. When **Harley-Davidson** reports revenue for the year, the amount includes sales not only in the United States but also those outside the United States. _____
8. The amount of total assets reported by **General Mills** can be substantiated by its auditors. _____
9. The **Cheesecake Factory** prepares its balance sheet in a clear format using basic accounting terminology to allow users to easily comprehend the company's assets, liabilities, and stockholders' equity. _____

Required:
Determine which qualitative characteristic best applies to each situation. Note: Each of the nine characteristics is used once and only once.

Identify business assumptions underlying GAAP (LO7)

E1–16 Below are the four underlying assumptions of generally accepted accounting principles.

Assumptions	Descriptions
1. _____ Economic entity	a. A common denominator is needed to measure all business activities.
2. _____ Going concern	b. Economic events can be identified with a particular economic body.
3. _____ Periodicity	c. In the absence of information to the contrary, it is anticipated that a business entity will continue to operate indefinitely.
4. _____ Monetary unit	d. The economic life of a company can be divided into artificial time intervals for financial reporting.

Required:
Match each business assumption with its description.

*For additional exercises, visit **www.mhhe.com/succeed** for Exercises: Set B.*

PROBLEMS: SET A

P1–1A Below are typical transactions for **Hewlett-Packard**.

Classify business
activities (LO2)

Type of Business Activity	Transactions
1. _____	Pay amount owed to the bank for previous borrowing.
2. _____	Pay utility costs.
3. _____	Purchase equipment to be used in operations.
4. _____	Provide services to customers.
5. _____	Purchase office supplies.
6. _____	Purchase a building.
7. _____	Pay workers' salaries.
8. _____	Pay for research and development costs.
9. _____	Pay taxes to the IRS.
10. _____	Sell common stock to investors.

Required:

Indicate whether each transaction is classified as a financing, investing, or operating activity.

P1–2A Account classifications include assets, liabilities, stockholders' equity, dividends, revenues, and expenses.

Assign account
classifications (LO2)

Account Classifications	Accounts	Related Transactions
1. _____	Common stock	Sale of common stock to investors.
2. _____	Equipment	Equipment used for operations.
3. _____	Salaries payable	Amounts owed to employees.
4. _____	Service revenue	Sales of services to customers.
5. _____	Utilities expense	Cost of utilities.
6. _____	Supplies	Purchase of office supplies.
7. _____	Research and development expense	Cost of research and development.
8. _____	Land	Property used for operations.
9. _____	Income tax payable	Amounts owed to the IRS for federal income taxes.
10. _____	Interest payable	Amount of interest owed on borrowing.

Required:

For each transaction, indicate whether the related account would be classified as an (a) asset, (b) liability, or (c) stockholders' equity to be reported in the balance sheet; a (d) revenue or (e) expense to be reported in the income statement; or an (f) dividend to be reported in the statement of stockholders' equity.

P1–3A Longhorn Corporation provides low-cost food delivery services to senior citizens. At the end of the year, the company reports the following amounts:

Prepare financial
statements (LO3)

Cash	$ 1,300	Service revenue	$ 62,700
Equipment	24,000	Cost of goods sold (food expense)	52,400
Accounts payable	3,400		
Delivery expense	1,600	Buildings	30,000
Salaries expense	4,500	Supplies	2,400
		Salaries payable	900

User's Guide Problems marked with this icon can be solved using Microsoft Excel templates.

In addition, the company had common stock of $30,000 at the beginning of the year and issued an additional $3,000 during the year. The company also had retained earnings of $16,200 at the beginning of the year.

Required:

Prepare the income statement, statement of stockholders' equity, and balance sheet for Longhorn Corporation.

P1–4A Below are incomplete financial statements for Bulldog, Inc.

Understand the format of financial statements and the links among them **(LO3)**

BULLDOG, INC. Income Statement	
Revenues	$34,000
Expenses:	
Salaries	(a)
Advertising	5,000
Utilities	3,000
Net income	(b)

BULLDOG, INC. Statement of Stockholders' Equity	Common Stock	Retained Earnings	Total S. Equity
Beginning balance	$ 9,000	$6,000	$15,000
Issuances	1,000		1,000
Add: Net income		(c)	(c)
Less: Dividends		(2,000)	(2,000)
Ending balance	$10,000	$9,000	$19,000

BULLDOG, INC. Balance Sheet			
Assets		**Liabilities**	
Cash	$ 3,000	Accounts payable	(d)
Accounts receivable	2,000	**Stockholders' Equity**	
Supplies	8,000	Common stock	(e)
Equipment	9,000	Retained earnings	(f)
Total assets	$22,000	Total liabilities and stockholders' equity	(g)

Required:

Calculate the missing amounts.

Prepare financial statements **(LO3)**

P1–5A Cornhusker Company provides the following information at the end of 2012.

Cash remaining	$ 3,800
Rent expense for the year	6,000
Land that has been purchased	20,000
Retained earnings	?
Utility expense for the year	3,900
Accounts receivable from customers	6,200
Service revenue earned during the year	32,000
Salary expense for the year	12,300
Accounts payable to suppliers	1,700
Dividends paid to shareholders during the year	2,200
Common stock that has been issued prior to 2012	15,000
Salaries owed at the end of the year	1,900
Insurance expense for the year	2,500

Required:

Prepare the income statement, statement of stockholders' equity, and balance sheet for Cornhusker Company on December 31, 2012. No common stock is issued during 2012, and the balance of retained earnings at the beginning of 2012 equals $6,300.

Identify underlying assumptions of GAAP **(LO7)**

P1–6A The four underlying assumptions of generally accepted accounting principles are economic entity, monetary unit, periodicity, and going concern. Consider the four independent situations below.

1. McAdam's is a local restaurant. Due to a bad shipment of potatoes, several of the company's customers become ill, and the company receives considerable bad publicity. Revenues are way down, several of its bills are past due, and the company

is making plans to close the restaurant at the end of the month. The company continues to report its assets in the balance sheet at historical (original) cost.

2. Uncle Sam's Tax Services is owned and operated by Sam Martin. The company has the usual business assets: land, building, cash, equipment, and supplies. In addition, Sam decides to buy a boat for him and his family to enjoy on the weekends. Sam includes the boat as an asset on the balance sheet of Uncle Sam's Tax Services.

3. Tison International, a U.S.-based company, has operations in the United States and in Europe. For the current year, the company purchased two trucks in the United States for $10,000 and three trucks in Europe for €20,000 (euros). Because of the differences in currencies, the company reported "Five Trucks" with no corresponding amount in the balance sheet.

4. Trumpets Etc. sells specialty music equipment ranging from African bongo drums to grand pianos. Because of the fluctuating nature of the business, management decides to publish financial statements only when a substantial amount of activity has taken place. Its last set of financial statements covered a period of 14 months, and the set of financial statements before that covered a period of 18 months.

Required:
For each situation, indicate which of the underlying assumptions of GAAP is violated.

P1–7A Listed below are nine terms and definitions associated with the FASB's conceptual framework.

Understand the components of the FASB's conceptual framework (**LO7**)

Terms	Definitions
1. _____ Completeness	a. Requires the consideration of the costs and value of information.
2. _____ Comparability	b. Ability to make comparisons between firms.
3. _____ Neutrality	c. Comprehending the meaning of accounting information.
4. _____ Understandability	d. Including all information necessary to report the business activity.
5. _____ Cost effectiveness	e. The business will last indefinitely unless there is evidence otherwise.
6. _____ Verifiability	f. Recording transactions only for the company.
7. _____ Decision usefulness	g. Implies consensus among different measures.
8. _____ Economic entity assumption	h. Accounting should be useful in making decisions.
9. _____ Going concern assumption	i. Accounting information should not favor a particular group.

Required:
Pair each term with its related definition.

PROBLEMS: SET B

P1–1B Below are typical transactions for **Caterpillar Inc.**

Classify accounts (**LO2**)

Type of Business Activity	Transactions
1. _____	Pay for advertising.
2. _____	Pay dividends to stockholders.
3. _____	Collect cash from customer for previous sale.
4. _____	Purchase a building to be used for operations.
5. _____	Purchase equipment.
6. _____	Sell land.
7. _____	Receive a loan from the bank by signing a note.
8. _____	Pay suppliers for purchase of supplies.
9. _____	Provide services to customers.
10. _____	Invest in securities of another company.

Required:

Indicate whether each transaction is classified as a financing, investing, or operating activity.

Assign business transactions to account classifications (LO2)

P1–2B Account classifications include assets, liabilities, stockholders' equity, dividends, revenues, and expenses.

Account Classifications	Accounts	Related Transactions
1. _____	Cash	Receive cash from customers.
2. _____	Service revenue	Provide services to customers.
3. _____	Supplies	Purchase supplies.
4. _____	Buildings	Purchase factory for
5. _____	Advertising expense	operations.
6. _____	Equipment	Pay for cost of advertising.
7. _____	Interest expense	Purchase equipment for
8. _____	Accounts payable	operations.
9. _____	Dividends	Pay for cost of interest.
10. _____	Notes payable	Purchase supplies on credit.
		Distribute cash to stockholders.
		Borrow from the bank.

Required:

For each transaction, indicate whether the related account would be classified as an (a) asset, (b) liability, or (c) stockholders' equity to be reported in the balance sheet; a (d) revenue or (e) expense to be reported in the income statement; or an (f) dividend to be reported in the statement of stockholders' equity.

Prepare financial statements (LO3)

P1–3B Gator Investments provides financial services related to investment selections, retirement planning, and general insurance needs. For the current year, the company reports the following amounts:

Advertising expense	$ 32,500	Service revenue	$122,600
Buildings	140,000	Interest expense	2,500
Salaries expense	64,100	Utilities expense	14,500
Accounts payable	5,400	Equipment	22,000
Cash	4,500	Notes payable	25,000

In addition, the company had common stock of $100,000 at the beginning of the year and issued an additional $10,000 during the year. The company also had retained earnings of $21,300 at the beginning of the year and paid dividends of $4,200.

Required:

Prepare the income statement, statement of stockholders' equity, and balance sheet for Gator Investments.

Understand the format of financial statements and the link among them (LO3)

P1–4B Below are incomplete financial statements for Cyclone, Inc.

CYCLONE, INC.
Income Statement

Revenues	(a)
Expenses:	
Salaries	$12,000
Rent	6,000
Advertising	4,000
Net income	(b)

CYCLONE, INC.
Statement of Stockholders' Equity

	Common Stock	Retained Earnings	Total S. Equity
Beginning balance	$13,000	$6,000	$19,000
Issuances of stock	(c)		(c)
Add: Net income		4,000	4,000
Less: Dividends		(d)	(d)
Ending balance	$15,000	$7,000	$22,000

CYCLONE, INC. Balance Sheet			
Assets		**Liabilities**	
Cash	$ 1,000	Accounts payable	$3,000
Supplies	(e)	**Stockholders' Equity**	
Land	5,000	Common stock	(g)
Building	15,000	Retained earnings	(h)
		Total liabilities and	
Total assets	(f)	stockholders' equity	(i)

Required:

Calculate the missing amounts.

P1–5B Tar Heel Corporation provides the following information at the end of 2012.

Prepare financial statements **(LO3)**

Salaries payable to workers at the end of the year	$ 2,300
Advertising expense for the year	9,400
Building that has been purchased	70,000
Supplies at the end of the year	3,600
Retained earnings	36,000
Utility expense for the year	5,000
Note payable to the bank	20,000
Service revenue earned during the year	64,400
Salary expense for the year	25,700
Accounts payable to suppliers	6,700
Dividends paid to shareholders during the year	(?)
Common stock that has been issued, including $5,000 that was issued this year	25,000
Cash remaining	4,200
Interest expense for the year	1,600
Accounts receivable from customers	12,200

Required:

Prepare the income statement, statement of stockholders' equity, and balance sheet for Tar Heel Corporation on December 31, 2012. The balance of retained earnings at the beginning of the year equals $23,300.

P1–6B The four underlying assumptions of generally accepted accounting principles are economic entity, monetary unit, periodicity, and going concern. Consider the following four independent situations.

Identify underlying assumptions of GAAP **(LO7)**

1. Fine Groceries has over 1,000 grocery stores throughout the Northwest. Approximately 200,000 customers visit its stores each day. Because of the continual nature of grocery sales, the company does not publish an income statement. The company feels that it has an indefinite life and a periodic report would mislead investors.
2. Pacific Shipping provides delivery of packages between the United States and Japan. During the current year, the company delivered 3,000 packages for its U.S. customers totaling $25,000 in revenue. For its Japanese customers, the company delivered 1,000 packages totaling ¥1,000,000 (yen). The company's income statement indicates that total revenue equals 4,000 packages delivered with no corresponding amount in the income statement.
3. Schuster Typewriter has provided some of the finest typewriters in town for the past 50 years. Because of the advance of electronic word processors and computers, customer demand has dwindled over the years to almost nothing in the current year and the company can no longer pay its debts. For the most recent year, the company reports its assets in the balance sheet at historical (original) cost.

4. John Brewer Carpet specializes in the installation of carpet and wood flooring. The company has the usual business expenses: salaries, supplies, utilities, advertising, and taxes. John took his wife and two daughters to Disney World. John reported the airfare and hotel expenses in the income statement of John Brewer Carpet.

Required:

For each situation, indicate which of the underlying assumptions of GAAP is violated.

Understand the components of the FASB's conceptual framework (LO7)

P1–7B Listed below are several terms and definitions associated with the FASB's conceptual framework.

Terms	Definitions
1. _____ Predictive value	a. Decreases in equity resulting from transfers to owners.
2. _____ Relevance	b. Business transactions are measured using a common denominator.
3. _____ Timeliness	c. The indefinite life of a company can be broken into definite periods.
4. _____ Dividends	d. Information helps in understanding prior activities.
5. _____ Confirmatory value	e. Agreement between a measure and the phenomenon it represents.
6. _____ Faithful representation	f. Information arrives prior to the decision.
7. _____ Materiality	g. Information is related to the decision at hand.
8. _____ Monetary unit assumption	h. Information is useful in predicting the future.
9. _____ Periodicity assumption	i. Concerns the relative size of an item and its effect on decisions.

Required:

Pair each term with its related definition.

For additional problems, visit www.mhhe.com/succeed for Problems: Set C.

ADDITIONAL PERSPECTIVES

Continuing Problem

Great Adventures

(The Great Adventures problem continues in each chapter.)

AP1–1 Tony Matheson plans to graduate from college in May 2012 after spending four years earning a degree in sports and recreation management. Since beginning T-ball at age five, he's been actively involved in sports and enjoys the outdoors. Each summer growing up, he and his father would spend two weeks at a father/son outdoor camp. These fond memories are part of the reason he chose his major. He wants to remain involved in these outdoor activities and provide others with the same adventures he was able to share with his dad. He decides to start an outdoor adventure company. However, he's not sure he has the business background necessary to do this.

This is where Suzie Ramos can help. Suzie also plans to graduate in May 2012 with a major in business. Suzie and Tony first met their sophomore year and have been friends ever since as they share a strong interest in sports and outdoor activities.

They decide to name their company Great Adventures. They will provide clinics for a variety of outdoor activities such as kayaking, mountain biking, rock climbing, wilderness survival techniques, orienteering, backpacking, and other adventure sports.

Required:

1. What are the three primary forms of business organizations Tony and Suzie might choose for Great Adventures? Explain the advantages and disadvantages of each. Which form do you recommend for Great Adventures?

2. Discuss some of the typical financing, investing, and operating activities that a company like Great Adventures is likely to have.
3. What specific account names for assets, liabilities, stockholders' equity, revenues, and expenses would the company likely use to record its business transactions?
4. To report company performance, Suzie plans to prepare the four primary financial statements. Explain the type of information provided by each statement.

American Eagle Outfitters, Inc.

Financial Analysis

AP1–2 Financial information for American Eagle is presented in Appendix A at the end of the book.

Required:

1. Determine the amounts American Eagle reports for total assets, total liabilities, and total stockholders' equity in the balance sheet for the most recent year. Verify that the basic accounting equation balances.
2. American Eagle refers to its income statement using another name. What is it?
3. Determine the amounts American Eagle reports for net sales and net income in its income statement for the most recent year.
4. For investing activities, what are the largest inflows and largest outflows for the most recent year reported in the statement of cash flows? For financing activities, what are the largest inflows and largest outflows?
5. Who is the company's auditor? (See the Report of Independent Registered Public Accounting Firm.) What does the report indicate about the amounts reported in the company's financial statements?

The Buckle, Inc.

Financial Analysis

Buckle

AP1–3 Financial information for The Buckle is presented in Appendix B at the end of the book.

Required:

1. Determine the amounts The Buckle reports for total assets, total liabilities, and total stockholders' equity in the balance sheet for the most recent year. Verify that the basic accounting equation balances.
2. The Buckle refers to its income statement using another name. What is it?
3. Determine the amounts The Buckle reports for net sales and net income in its income statement for the most recent year.
4. For investing activities, what are the largest inflows and largest outflows for the most recent year reported in the statement of cash flows? For financing activities, what are the largest inflows and largest outflows?
5. Who is the company's auditor? (See the Report of Independent Registered Public Accounting Firm.) What does the report indicate about the amounts reported in the company's financial statements?

American Eagle Outfitters, Inc. vs. The Buckle, Inc.

Comparative Analysis

AP1–4 Financial information for American Eagle is presented in Appendix A at the end of the book, and financial information for The Buckle is presented in Appendix B at the end of the book.

Required:

1. Which company reports higher total assets?
2. Which company reports higher total liabilities? Does this always mean this company has a higher chance of not being able to repay its debt and declare bankruptcy? Explain.
3. What relevant information do total assets and total liabilities provide to creditors deciding whether to lend money to American Eagle versus The Buckle?

Buckle

4. Which company reports higher net income? Does this always mean this company's operations are more profitable? Explain.
5. What relevant information does net income provide to investors who are deciding whether to invest in American Eagle versus The Buckle?

Ethics

AP1–5 Management has the responsibility of accurately preparing financial statements when communicating with investors and creditors. Another group, auditors, serves an independent role by helping to ensure that management has in fact appropriately applied GAAP in preparing the company's financial statements. Auditors examine (audit) financial statements to express a professional, independent opinion. The opinion reflects the auditors' assessment of the statements' fairness, which is determined by the extent to which they are prepared in compliance with GAAP.

Suppose an auditor is being paid $1,000,000 by the company to perform the audit. In addition, the company plans to pay the auditor $500,000 over the next year for business consulting advice and another $200,000 for preparing its tax returns. The auditor and management of the company have always shared a friendly relationship, which partly explains the company's willingness to give the auditor additional work for $700,000.

Required:
How might an auditor's ethics be challenged while performing an audit?

Internet Research

AP1–6 The purpose of this research case is to introduce you to the Internet home pages of the Securities and Exchange Commission (SEC) and the Financial Accounting Standards Board (FASB).

Required:
1. Access the SEC home page on the Internet (*www.sec.gov*). Under "About the SEC," choose "What We Do." What is the mission of the SEC? Why was the SEC created? What are the two objectives of the 1933 Securities Act? The 1934 Securities Exchange Act established the SEC. What does the 1934 Act empower the SEC to require?
2. Access *www.sec.gov/investor/pubs/begfinstmtguide.htm*. What are the four main financial statements discussed by the SEC? What does each report? What information is disclosed in the notes and management discussion and analysis (MD&A)?
3. Access the FASB home page on the Internet (*www.fasb.org*). Select "Facts About FASB." Describe the mission of the FASB. What is the relation between the SEC and the FASB?
4. Obtain a copy of the annual report of **ConocoPhillips** for the most recent year. You can find the annual report at the company's website (*www.conocophillips.com*) in the investor information section or at the SEC's website (*www.sec.gov*) using EDGAR (Electronic Data Gathering, Analysis, and Retrieval). The SEC requires that Form 10-K, which includes the annual report, be filed on EDGAR. Answer the following questions:
   (a) Did ConocoPhillips prepare the four financial statements discussed by the SEC?
   (b) In the MD&A section, how does the company describe its business environment?
   (c) Find the note disclosures to the financial statements. What does the disclosure on segment information discuss?

Written Communication

AP1–7 Maria comes to you for investment advice. She asks, "Which company's stock should I buy? There are so many companies to choose from and I don't know anything about any of them."

Required:

Respond to Maria by explaining the two functions of financial accounting. Specifically address the four financial statements reported by companies and the information contained in each. Also explain the role of the auditor in the preparation of financial statements. What advice can you give her about finding a company's stock to buy?

Answers to the Self-Study Questions
1. b   2. d   3. c   4. b   5. a   6. c   7. b   8. d   9. d   10. a

CHAPTER

The Accounting Information System

Learning
Objectives

AFTER STUDYING THIS CHAPTER, YOU SHOULD BE ABLE TO:

- **LO1** Identify the basic steps in measuring external transactions.
- **LO2** Analyze the impact of external transactions on the accounting equation.
- **LO3** Assess whether the impact of external transactions results in a debit or credit to an account balance.
- **LO4** Record transactions using debits and credits.
- **LO5** Post transactions to T-accounts in the general ledger.
- **LO6** Prepare a trial balance.

WALMART: **SHELVES OF BUSINESS TRANSACTIONS**

Walmart opened its first store in Rogers, Arkansas, in 1962. By 1967, the company had increased to 24 stores totaling $12,600,000 in sales, and the following year it expanded operations to Missouri and Oklahoma. Today, Wal-Mart Stores, Inc. (the parent company) is the world's largest retailer with over $400,000,000,000 in sales. (That's $400 billion!) With nearly 2 million employees worldwide, it's the largest private employer in the United States and Mexico and one of the largest in Canada. Each year Walmart purchases from over 60,000 vendors merchandise totaling $300 billion. More than 175 million customers visit Walmart stores each week.

With its huge numbers of financial transactions and relationships with customers, suppliers, employees, and government agencies, Walmart poses a challenge to potential investors and lenders who need to understand its financial position today. Obviously, its past performance represents a success story. Sam Walton, Walmart's founder, started his career at J. C. Penney in 1940, earning just $75 per month. In 2009, the Walton family's net worth totaled nearly $90 billion (*www.forbes.com*). If you had invested $1,000 in Walmart in 1970 when it first issued stock, your investment would have grown to more than $1 million by the end of 2009.

But is Walmart still a good investment? Would you want to invest $1,000 today? While the past provides useful information, what is the current financial position of Walmart? What is its potential for the future? For investors to fully understand the financial position and profitability of any company, a system must be in place that can summarize and communicate thousands (or even billions) of economic events.

As you may realize by now, summarizing and communicating economic events is the role of financial accounting. In this chapter, we review the process accountants use to identify, analyze, record, and summarize economic events affecting a company's financial position. Having a firm grasp of this process is key to your understanding of financial accounting.

54   CHAPTER 2   The Accounting Information System

MEASURING BUSINESS ACTIVITIES

In this chapter, we examine the accounting information process using a manual accounting system. Most business enterprises use a computerized accounting system due to the sheer volume of data they must process. Computerized data processing is fast, accurate, and affordable. Our focus on a manual accounting information system, though, will provide you an essential understanding of the basic model that underlies the computerized programs.

This chapter provides a foundation for the remaining chapters. We'll consider the *measurement role* of financial accounting and examine the process firms use to identify, analyze, record, and summarize the external economic events affecting their financial position.

Measurement of External Transactions

■ LO1
Identify the basic steps in measuring external transactions.

Recall from Chapter 1 that the two roles of financial accounting are to (1) measure business activities of the company and (2) communicate those measurements to external parties for decision-making purposes. The business activities, or transactions, we want to measure and communicate are classified as either external or internal. External transactions are transactions the firm conducts with a separate economic entity. Examples are selling products to a customer, purchasing supplies from a vendor, paying salaries to an employee, and borrowing money from a bank. Internal transactions are events that affect the financial position of the company but do not include an exchange with a separate economic entity. Examples are using supplies on hand and earning revenues after having received cash in advance from a customer. In this chapter, we focus on the measurement of external transactions. We save internal transactions for Chapter 3.

KEY POINT

External transactions are transactions between the company and separate economic entities. Internal transactions do not include an exchange with a separate economic entity.

Measuring external transactions is a six-step process, as outlined in Illustration 2–1. These steps are the foundation for the remaining chapters in this book. Make sure you understand them before you proceed.

The first step in the measurement process involves gathering information about a transaction. Source documents such as sales invoices, bills from suppliers, and signed contracts provide information related to external transactions. These source documents usually identify the date and nature of each transaction, the participating parties, and the monetary terms. For example, a sales invoice might identify the date of sale, the customer, the specific items sold, the dollar amount of the sale, and the payment terms.

Companies record the effects of transactions in accounts. An account provides a summary of the effects of all transactions related to a particular item over a period of time. For instance, *asset accounts* include Cash, Supplies, and Equipment. All transactions affecting cash are summarized in the Cash account; all transactions affecting supplies are summarized in the Supplies account; and so on. Examples of *liability accounts* include Accounts Payable, Salaries Payable, Utilities Payable, and Taxes Payable. *Stockholders' equity accounts* include Common Stock and Retained Earnings. A list of all account names used to record transactions of a company is referred to as the chart of accounts. (Later in the chapter, we'll see a preliminary chart of accounts. A comprehensive chart of accounts provided at the back of the

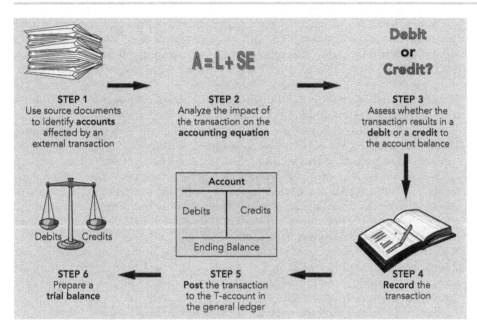

ILLUSTRATION 2–1
Six Steps in Measuring External Transactions

book includes all accounts used in the book. Keep this handy for reference throughout the course.)

In this chapter and throughout the remainder of the book, you'll learn how to compute the balance of each account and eventually use these account balances to prepare the financial statements introduced in Chapter 1. But first, let's work through steps 2–6 of the measurement process to see how external business transactions are summarized in account balances.

 KEY POINT

The six-step measurement process (Illustration 2–1) is the foundation of financial accounting.

Effects of Transactions on the Basic Accounting Equation

The activities we want to record are those that affect the financial position of the company. That means they affect the accounting equation you learned about in Chapter 1. Remember, the basic accounting equation shows that resources of the company (asset accounts) are equal to claims to those resources by creditors (liability accounts) and owners (stockholders' equity accounts).

■ **LO2**
Analyze the impact of external transactions on the accounting equation.

$$\underbrace{\textbf{Assets}}_{\text{(resources)}} = \underbrace{\textbf{Liabilities} + \textbf{Stockholders' Equity}}_{\text{(claims to resources)}}$$

The basic accounting equation

When **Walmart** borrows cash from a bank, its financial position is affected because assets (cash) increase and liabilities (the loan payable to the bank) increase. So, Walmart records that event in its accounting records. On the other hand, when

Walmart hires Ralph as a front-door greeter, that action doesn't change the company's assets, liabilities, or stockholders' equity; Walmart's financial position is unaffected the day Ralph is hired, and until he begins work. Yes, Walmart hopes that hiring Ralph will favorably affect its financial position in the future, but the hiring itself does not.

Recall that the basic accounting equation must always remain in balance: The left side (assets) equals the right side (liabilities plus stockholders' equity). **Each transaction will have a dual effect.** If an economic event increases one side of the equation, then it also increases the other side of the equation by the same amount. That's what happens, for example, when Walmart borrows cash.

Sometimes, though, a transaction will not affect the *total* of either side. Let's say **Wendy's** buys new cash registers for its stores, paying cash. One asset (equipment) goes up; another asset (cash) goes down by the same amount. There's no change to assets *as a whole*. The accounting equation remains in balance. You can tell whether a transaction affects the accounting equation by considering its impact on the company's total resources—its total assets.

As the balance in an account changes, we record the increase or decrease in that specific account. Let's say we have $50,000 in cash. That's the *balance* in the Cash account. Now say a transaction causes cash to increase by $1,000. The balance in the Cash account is now $51,000.

To see the effect of each transaction, ask yourself these questions:

1. **"What is one account in the accounting equation affected by the transaction? Does that account increase or decrease?"**
2. **"What is a second account in the accounting equation affected by the transaction? Does that account increase or decrease?"**

After noting the effects of the transaction on the accounting equation, ask yourself this:

3. **"Do assets equal liabilities plus stockholders' equity?"**

The answer to the third question must be "yes." **At least two accounts will be affected by every transaction or economic event.** While some economic events will affect *more* than two accounts, most events we record affect only two accounts.

The best way to understand the impact of a transaction on the accounting equation is to see it demonstrated by a few examples. Let's return to the Eagle Golf Academy from Chapter 1. Illustration 2–2 (next page) summarizes the external transactions for Eagle in January, the first month of operations. (You may also want to refer back to the financial statements in Illustrations 1–6, 1–8, and 1–9 to remind yourself how the transactions will eventually be reported.) Note that business activities usually occur in this same order for a new company—obtain external *financing*, use those funds to *invest* in long-term productive assets, and then begin normal *operations*. We discussed these business activities in Chapter 1.

On the following pages, we discuss the impact of these 10 transactions on the accounting equation.

TRANSACTION (1): ISSUE COMMON STOCK

To begin operations, Eagle Golf Academy needs cash. To generate cash from external sources, Eagle sells shares of common stock for $25,000. Let's reflect on this for a moment. Imagine being the sole owner of Eagle Golf Academy. To get your business going, you take $25,000 from your personal funds and invest it in your business. Although your personal cash decreased, the cash of your company *increased*, and so did your equity or ownership interest in the company's assets. Now, imagine instead

Transaction	Date	External Transactions in January	Type of Activity
(1)	Jan. 1	Sell shares of common stock for $25,000 to obtain the funds necessary to start the business.	Financing
(2)	Jan. 1	Borrow $10,000 from the local bank and sign a note promising to repay the full amount of the debt in three years.	Financing
(3)	Jan. 1	Purchase equipment necessary for giving golf training, $24,000 cash.	Investing
(4)	Jan. 1	Pay one year of rent in advance, $6,000 ($500 per month).	Operating
(5)	Jan. 6	Purchase supplies on account, $2,300.	Operating
(6)	Jan. 12	Provide golf training to customers for cash, $3,600.	Operating
(7)	Jan. 17	Provide golf training to customers on account, $2,500.	Operating
(8)	Jan. 23	Receive cash in advance for 10 golf training sessions to be given in the future, $600.	Operating
(9)	Jan. 28	Pay salaries to employees, $2,800.	Operating
(10)	Jan. 30	Pay cash dividends of $200 to shareholders.	Financing

ILLUSTRATION 2–2

External Transactions of Eagle Golf Academy

that the company is organized as a corporation and that by investing $25,000 in it you are becoming one of its many stockholders or owners.

Eagle Golf Academy   Investors

Stock Certificate

(1) Issue common stock

It's time to ask the three questions we asked earlier:

1. **"What is one account in the accounting equation affected by the transaction? Does that account increase or decrease?"**

   Answer: **Cash.** Cash is a resource owned by the company, which makes it an asset. The company receives cash from you, so cash and total assets **increase** by $25,000.

2. **"What is a second account in the accounting equation affected by the transaction? Does that account increase or decrease?"**

   Answer: **Common Stock.** Common Stock is a stockholders' equity account. Issuing common stock to you in exchange for your $25,000 increases the amount of common stock owned by stockholders, so common stock and total stockholders' equity both **increase.**

   Issuing common stock for cash increases both sides of the accounting equation:

Assets	=	Liabilities	+	Stockholders' Equity
Cash ↑ +$25,000	=			Common Stock ↑ +$25,000

TRANSACTION (1)

Initial investment of $25,000 by stockholders

3. "Do assets equal liabilities plus stockholders' equity?"

Answer: **Yes.**

Note that the accounting equation balances. If one side of the equation increases, so does the other side. We can use this same series of questions to understand the effect of *any* business transaction. Let's try another one.

 COMMON MISTAKE

It's sometimes tempting to *decrease* cash as a way of recording an investor's initial investment. However, we account for transactions *from the company's perspective*, and the company *received* cash from the stockholder—an increase in cash.

TRANSACTION (2): BORROW FROM THE BANK

Seeking cash from another external source, Eagle Academy borrows $10,000 from the bank and signs a note promising to repay it in the future.

(2) Borrow from bank

Eagle Golf Academy   IOU   Bank

1. "What is one account in the accounting equation affected by the transaction? Does that account increase or decrease?"

Answer: **Cash.** Cash is a resource owned by the company, which makes it an asset. The company receives cash, so cash and total assets **increase.**

2. "What is a second account in the accounting equation affected by the transaction? Does that account increase or decrease?"

Answer: **Notes Payable.** Notes payable represent amounts owed to creditors (the bank in this case), which makes them a liability. The company incurs debt when signing the note, so notes payable and total liabilities **increase.**

Borrowing by signing a note causes both assets and liabilities to increase:

TRANSACTION (2)

Borrow $10,000 from the bank and sign a long-term note

Assets	=	Liabilities	+	Stockholders' Equity
Cash ↑ +$10,000	=	Notes Payable ↑ +$10,000		

3. "Do assets equal liabilities plus stockholders' equity?"

Answer: **Yes.**

After these two transactions, the accounting equation remains in balance. The total resources of the company equal $35,000. Creditors' claims to those resources total $10,000, and the remaining resources of $25,000 were provided by stockholders. Illustration 2–3 summarizes the effects of the two financing activities we've analyzed so far.

Assets	=	Liabilities	+	Stockholders' Equity
Financing Activities:				
(1) Cash ↑ +$ 25,000				Common Stock ↑ +$ 25,000
(2) Cash ↑ +$ 10,000		Notes Payable ↑ +$ 10,000		
Total **$35,000** =		**$10,000** +		**$25,000**

ILLUSTRATION 2–3

Summary of Initial Financing Transactions of Eagle Golf Academy

Regardless of the number of transactions occurring during the period, the accounting equation always must remain in balance. For brevity, we do not address the three-question process for Eagle's remaining eight transactions, but you should ask yourself those questions until you feel comfortable with the process.

KEY POINT

After each transaction, the accounting equation must always remain in balance. In other words, assets must always equal liabilities plus stockholders' equity.

TRANSACTION (3): PURCHASE EQUIPMENT

Once Eagle obtains financing by issuing common stock and borrowing from the bank, the company can invest in long-term assets necessary to operate the business.

Eagle Golf Academy   Supplier

(3) Purchase equipment

Buying equipment from a supplier causes one asset to increase and another asset to decrease:

Assets	=	Liabilities	+	Stockholders' Equity
Equipment ↑ +$24,000				
Cash ↓ −$24,000				

TRANSACTION (3)

Purchase equipment with cash, $24,000

Notice that purchasing one asset (equipment) with another asset (cash) has no effect on the category totals in the accounting equation. One asset increases, while another asset decreases. Once we add transaction (3) to the accounting equation, we see in Illustration 2–4 (next page) that the accounting equation remains in balance.

TRANSACTIONS (4) AND (5): INCUR COSTS FOR RENT AND SUPPLIES

Eagle Academy now engages in some operating transactions: It pays one year of rent in advance, $6,000, and purchases supplies on account, $2,300. Because the rent paid is for occupying space in the future, we don't want to record it as an expense immediately. Instead, we record it as an asset representing the right to occupy the space in the future. We call the asset *prepaid rent* and, as we discuss later in the course, we'll report this amount as expense over the next 12 months, as the time we've prepaid

ILLUSTRATION 2–4

Summary of Initial Financing and Investing Transactions of Eagle Golf Academy

Assets		=	Liabilities		+	Stockholders' Equity	
Financing Activities:							
(1) Cash ↑	+$25,000					Common Stock ↑	+$25,000
(2) Cash ↑	+$10,000		Notes Payable ↑	+$10,000			
Subtotal	$35,000	=		$10,000	+		$25,000
Investing Activities:							
(3) Equipment ↑	+$24,000						
Cash ↓	−$24,000						
Total	$35,000	=		$10,000	+		$25,000

expires. Other common examples of prepaid assets include prepaid insurance and prepaid advertising. These items often are purchased prior to their use.

(4) Incur costs for rent

Purchasing rent in advance causes one asset to increase and one asset to decrease:

TRANSACTION (4)

Pay one year of rent in advance, $6,000

Assets		=	Liabilities	+	Stockholders' Equity
Prepaid Rent ↑	+$6,000				
Cash ↓	−$6,000				

Next, Eagle purchases supplies with the promise to pay cash in the future. This promise creates a liability. We refer to a liability of this type, in which we purchase something on account, as an *account payable*.

(5) Incur costs for supplies

Purchasing supplies with the promise to pay cash in the future causes an asset (supplies) to increase and also causes a liability (accounts payable) to increase:

TRANSACTION (5)

Purchase supplies on account, $2,300

Assets		=	Liabilities		+	Stockholders' Equity
Supplies ↑	+$2,300	=	Accounts Payable ↑	+$2,300		

Effects of Transactions on the Expanded Accounting Equation

To better understand how revenues increase stockholders' equity, let's expand the accounting equation. As discussed in Chapter 1, we can divide stockholders' equity into its two components—common stock and retained earnings. Common stock represents investments by stockholders. Retained earnings represents net income earned over the life of the company that has *not* been distributed to stockholders as dividends. Both of these amounts represent stockholders' claims to the company's resources. Next, we can split retained earnings into its three components—revenues, expenses, and dividends. Illustration 2–5 presents the expanded accounting equation, which shows these components.

ILLUSTRATION 2–5

Expanded Accounting Equation

Be sure to notice the effects of revenues, expenses, and dividends on retained earnings (and therefore on total stockholders' equity) in the expanded accounting equation:

1. We *add* revenues to calculate retained earnings. That's because revenues increase net income, and net income increases stockholders' claims to resources. **Therefore, an *increase* in revenues has the effect of *increasing* stockholders' equity in the basic accounting equation.**

2. We *subtract* expenses and dividends to calculate retained earnings. Expenses reduce net income, and dividends represent a distribution of net income to stockholders. Both expenses and dividends reduce stockholders' claims to the company's resources. **Therefore, an *increase* in expenses or dividends has the effect of *decreasing* stockholders' equity in the basic accounting equation.**

 KEY POINT

The expanded accounting equation demonstrates that revenues increase retained earnings while expenses and dividends decrease retained earnings. Retained earnings is a component of stockholders' equity.

TRANSACTIONS (6) AND (7): PROVIDE SERVICES TO CUSTOMERS

To see an example of how revenue affects the expanded accounting equation, let's look at the two revenue transactions for Eagle Golf Academy. In transaction (6), Eagle provides golf training to customers who pay cash at the time of the service, $3,600.

(6) Provide golf training
for cash

Eagle Golf Academy   Training   Customers

Providing training to customers for cash causes both assets and stockholders' equity to increase:

TRANSACTION (6)	Assets	=	Liabilities	+	Stockholders' Equity	
					Common Stock	+	Retained Earnings

TRANSACTION (6)

Provide golf training
to customers for cash,
$3,600

Cash ↑ +$3,600 =   Common Stock +   Retained Earnings
                                                              +$3,600 ◄

Revenues − Expenses − Dividends
Service
Revenue ↑

Notice that an increase in Service Revenue (↑) increases stockholders' equity by increasing the Retained Earnings account (+$3,600). Therefore, the basic accounting equation remains in balance (Assets = Liabilities + Stockholders' Equity).

As shown in Illustration 2–5, revenues are a component of retained earnings. When a company earns revenue, the amount of retained earnings (or net income) in the business increases. We can increase retained earnings by increasing its revenue component. Stated another way, an increase in revenues increases net income, which increases retained earnings, which increases total stockholders' equity:

In transaction (7), other customers receive golf training but promise to pay $2,500 cash at some time in the future. The fact that some customers do not pay cash at the time of the service doesn't prevent Eagle from recording revenue. Eagle has *earned* the revenue by providing services. In addition, the *right* to receive cash from a customer is something of value the company owns, and therefore is an asset. When a customer does not immediately pay for services with cash, we traditionally say the services are performed "on account," and we record an *account receivable*.

(7) Provide golf training
on account

Eagle Golf Academy   Training   Customers

Providing services to customers on account causes both assets and stockholders' equity to increase:

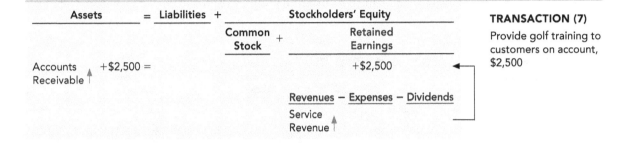

TRANSACTION (7)

Provide golf training to customers on account, $2,500

TRANSACTION (8): RECEIVE CASH IN ADVANCE FROM CUSTOMERS

Companies sometimes receive cash in advance from customers. Let's assume that Eagle receives $600 from customers for golf training to be provided later. In this case, Eagle cannot now report revenue from training because it has yet to provide the training to *earn* those revenues. Instead, the advance payment from customers creates an obligation for the company to perform services in the future. This future obligation is a liability (or debt), most commonly referred to as *unearned revenue*.

Eagle Golf Academy

Training

Customers

(8) Receive cash in advance

Receiving cash in advance causes both assets and liabilities to increase:

TRANSACTION (8)

Receive cash in advance from customers, $600

COMMON MISTAKE

Don't let the account name fool you. Even though the term *revenue* appears in the account title for *unearned revenue*, this is not a revenue account. *Unearned* indicates that the company has yet to earn this revenue and therefore is still obligated to provide the service in the future. This current obligation creates a liability.

TRANSACTION (9): INCUR COSTS FOR SALARIES

Companies incur a variety of expenses in generating revenues. Eagle Academy incurs salaries expense of $2,800.

Labor

Eagle Golf Academy

Employee

(9) Incur salary costs

Paying salaries for the current period causes assets and stockholders' equity to decrease:

TRANSACTION (9)

Pay salaries to workers, $2,800

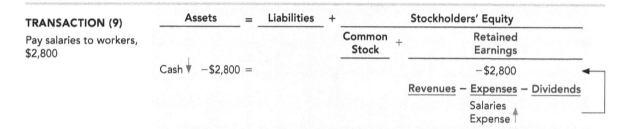

Notice that an *increase* in Salaries Expense (↑) results in a *decrease* in Retained Earnings (−$2,800). As a result, the accounting equation remains in balance, with both sides decreasing by $2,800. The concept of expenses flowing into retained earnings is the same concept that we see in transactions (6) and (7) where revenues also flow into retained earnings, but in the opposite direction. **Expenses *reduce* net income and therefore *reduce* the amount of retained earnings,** a stockholders' equity account. Stated another way, an increase in expenses decreases net income, which decreases retained earnings, which decreases total stockholders' equity:

Beyond salaries expense, companies have a number of other expenses. Most expense accounts are labeled with the *expense* title. For instance, common expense accounts include Supplies Expense, Utilities Expense, Rent Expense, Advertising Expense, Interest Expense, and Insurance Expense.

TRANSACTION (10): PAY DIVIDENDS

The final financing transaction of Eagle Golf Academy for the month is the payment of a $200 cash dividend to stockholders. Recall from the previous chapter that a dividend represents a payment of cash to the owners (stockholders) of the company. Normally a company wouldn't pay dividends after only a month in business, but we make this assumption here for purposes of illustration.

(10) Pay dividends

Reduced Claims to Company's Resources

Eagle Golf Academy   Investors

Paying dividends causes assets and stockholders' equity to decrease:

TRANSACTION (10)

Pay dividends to stockholders, $200

Assets	=	Liabilities	+	Stockholders' Equity	
				Common Stock +	Retained Earnings
Cash▼ −$200 =					−$200
					Revenues − Expenses − Dividends
					Dividends↑

Like expenses, dividends *reduce* **retained earnings, but dividends are** *not* **expenses.** Instead, dividends are distributions of part of the company's net income to the owners, reducing the amount of earnings that have been retained in the business. Therefore, an *increase* in Dividends (⬆) results in a *decrease* in Retained Earnings (−$200). The accounting equation remains in balance, with both sides decreasing by $200. Because retained earnings is a stockholders' equity account, when retained earnings decreases, so does stockholders' equity.

 COMMON MISTAKE

Students often believe a payment of dividends to owners increases stockholders' equity. Remember, you are accounting for the resources *of the company.* While stockholders have more personal cash after dividends have been paid, the company in which they own stock has *fewer* resources (less cash).

Illustration 2–6 summarizes all 10 of the month's transactions we just analyzed for Eagle Golf Academy.

Assets		=	Liabilities		+	Stockholders' Equity	
Financing Activities:							
(1) Cash ⬆	+$ 25,000					Common Stock ⬆	+$ 25,000
(2) Cash ⬆	+$ 10,000		Notes Payable ⬆	+$ 10,000			
Subtotal	**$35,000** =			**$10,000** +			**$25,000**
Investing Activities:							
(3) Equipment ⬆	+$ 24,000						
Cash ⬇	−$ 24,000						
Subtotal	**$35,000** =			**$10,000** +			**$25,000**
Operating Activities:							
(4) Prepaid Rent ⬆	+$ 6,000						
Cash ⬇	−$ 6,000						
(5) Supplies ⬆	+$ 2,300		Accounts Payable ⬆	+$ 2,300			
(6) Cash ⬆	+$ 3,600					Service Revenue ⬆	+$ 3,600
(7) Accounts Receivable ⬆	+$ 2,500					Service Revenue ⬆	+$ 2,500
(8) Cash ⬆	+$ 600		Unearned Revenue ⬆	+$ 600			
(9) Cash ⬇	−$ 2,800					Salaries Expense ⬆	−$ 2,800
Subtotal	**$41,200** =			**$12,900** +			**$28,300**
Financing Activity:							
(10) Cash ⬇	−$ 200					Dividends ⬆	−$ 200
Total	**$41,000** =			**$12,900** +			**$28,100**

ILLUSTRATION 2–6

Summary of All 10 External Transactions of Eagle Golf Academy

Let's Review

Bogey Incorporated has the following transactions during May:

May   1 Purchase a storage building by obtaining a loan of $5,000.
May   6 Provide services on account to customers, $1,800.
May 12 Pay $1,200 cash for advertising in May.
May 17 Repay $1,000 of the amount borrowed on May 1.
May 25 Purchase office supplies for $800 cash.

Required:

Indicate how each transaction affects the accounting equation.

Solution:

	Assets	=	Liabilities	+	Stockholders' Equity
May 1	+$5,000		+$5,000		
May 6	+$1,800				+$1,800
May 12	−$1,200				−$1,200
May 17	−$1,000		−$1,000		
May 25	+$ 800				
	−$ 800				
	+$4,600	=	+$4,000	+	+$ 600

Suggested Homework:
**BE2-2, BE2-3;
E2-2, E2-3, E2-4;
P2-1A&B, P2-2A&B**

PART B   DEBITS AND CREDITS

As we saw in the previous section, external transactions have the effect of increasing or decreasing account balances. While the terms *increase* and *decrease* are well understood, accountants more often use the terms *debit* and *credit* to indicate whether an account balance has increased or decreased. Here, we introduce those terms, discuss their effect on account balances, and show how we record transactions using debits and credits.

Effects on Account Balances in the Basic Accounting Equation

■ **LO3**
Assess whether the impact of external transactions results in a debit or credit to an account balance.

You will need to learn how to increase and decrease account balances using the terms debit and credit because that's the language of accounting. Although debit and credit are derived from Latin terms, today *debit* simply means "left" and *credit* means "right." Their use dates back to 1494 and a Franciscan monk by the name of Luca Pacioli. It is easy to visualize the use of these directional signals by means of an accounting convention called a "T-account."

A T-account is a simplified presentation of an account, in the shape of the letter T. Across the top, we show the account title. On the two sides created by the vertical rule, we record debits and credits, as Illustration 2–7 shows. The left side of the T-account is the debit column. The right side is the credit column.

ILLUSTRATION 2–7
T-Account Format

Account Title	
Debit	Credit

The effect that debits and credits have on various accounts depends on the nature of the specific account. Illustration 2–8 summarizes the effects that debits and credits have on the accounts in the basic accounting equation.

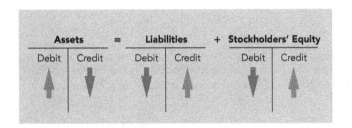

ILLUSTRATION 2–8

Debit and Credit Effects on Accounts in the Basic Accounting Equation

We refer to *increases* in accounts on the left side of the accounting equation— assets—as debits. Just the opposite is true for accounts on the right-hand side of the accounting equation: **We refer to *increases* in liabilities and stockholders' equity as credits.**

The rules reverse for *decreases* in accounts: Assets decrease with a credit. Liabilities and stockholders' equity decrease with a debit.

COMMON MISTAKE

Students sometimes hear the phrase "assets are the debit accounts" and believe it indicates that assets can only be debited. This is incorrect! Assets, or any account, can be *either* debited or credited. Rather, this phrase indicates that debiting the asset account will increase the balance, and that an asset account normally will have a debit balance. Similarly, the phrase "liabilities and stockholders' equity are the credit accounts" does *not* mean that these accounts cannot be debited. They will be debited when their balances decrease. Rather, the phrase means that crediting the liabilities and stockholders' equity accounts increases their balances, and they normally will have a credit balance.

KEY POINT

For the basic accounting equation (Assets = Liabilities + Stockholders' Equity), accounts on the left side are increased with *debits*. Accounts on the right side are increased with *credits*. The opposite is true to decrease any of these accounts.

Now, let's look again at the transactions of Eagle Golf Academy, but this time using debits and credits rather than increases and decreases to record the account changes. As we do, ask yourself these three questions for each transaction:

1. **"Is there an increase or decrease in the *first* account involved in the transaction? Should I record that increase or decrease with a debit or a credit?"**
2. **"Is there an increase or decrease in the *second* account involved in the transaction? Should I record that increase or decrease with a debit or a credit?"**
3. **"Do total debits equal total credits?"**

The answer to this last question must be "yes."

Recall our first example: Eagle issues common stock for cash of $25,000 in transaction (1).

TRANSACTION (1)

Initial investment of $25,000 by stockholders

Assets		=	Liabilities	+	Stockholders' Equity	
Cash ↑	+$25,000	=			Common Stock ↑	+$25,000

Cash	
Debit	Credit
25,000	

Common Stock	
Debit	Credit
	25,000

1. **"Is there an increase or decrease in the *first* account involved in the transaction? Should I record that increase or decrease with a debit or a credit?"**

   Answer: **Cash increases.** Cash is an asset, and assets have a debit balance. We record an increase in cash with a **debit** to the Cash account.

2. **"Is there an increase or decrease in the *second* account involved in the transaction? Is that increase or decrease recorded with a debit or a credit?"**

   Answer: **Common Stock increases.** Common Stock is a stockholders' equity account, and stockholders' equity has a credit balance. We record an increase in common stock with a **credit** to the Common Stock account.

3. **Do total debits equal total credits?**

   Answer: **Yes.**

   The bank borrowing of $10,000 in transaction (2) has the following effects:

TRANSACTION (2)

Borrow $10,000 from the bank and sign a long-term note

Assets		=	Liabilities		+	Stockholders' Equity
Cash ↑	+$10,000	=	Notes Payable ↑	+$10,000		

Cash	
Debit	Credit
10,000	

Notes Payable	
Debit	Credit
	10,000

1. **"Is there an increase or decrease in the *first* account involved in the transaction? Should I record that increase or decrease with a debit or a credit?"**

   Answer: **Cash increases.** Cash is an asset, and assets have a debit balance. We record an increase in cash with a **debit** to the Cash account.

2. **"Is there an increase or decrease in the *second* account involved in the transaction? Should I record that increase or decrease with a debit or a credit?"**

   Answer: **Notes Payable increases.** Notes payable are liabilities, and liabilities have a credit balance. We record an increase to notes payable with a **credit** to the Notes Payable account.

3. **Do total debits equal total credits?**

   Answer: **Yes.**

   To record a decrease in an account, see transaction (3), in which Eagle pays cash to purchase equipment. Recall that this transaction results in an increase in equipment and a decrease in cash, both asset accounts.

Assets	=	Liabilities	+	Stockholders' Equity
Equipment ↑ +$24,000				
Cash ↓ −$24,000				

TRANSACTION (3)

Purchase equipment with cash, $24,000

Equipment

Debit	Credit
24,000	

Cash

Debit	Credit
	24,000

1. **"Is there an increase or decrease in the *first* account involved in the transaction? Should I record that increase or decrease with a debit or a credit?"**

   Answer: **Equipment increases.** Equipment is an asset, and assets have a debit balance. We record an increase in equipment with a **debit** to the Equipment account.

2. **"Is there an increase or decrease in the *second* account involved in the transaction? Should I record that increase or decrease with a debit or a credit?"**

   Answer: **Cash decreases.** Cash is an asset, and assets have a debit balance. We record a decrease in cash with a **credit** to the Cash account.

3. **Do total debits equal total credits?**

   Answer: **Yes.**

Effects on Account Balances in the Expanded Accounting Equation

Remember that accounts on the *left* side of the accounting equation (assets) increase with debits or the *left* side of an account. Accounts on the *right* side of the accounting equation (liabilities and stockholders' equity) increase with credits or the *right* side of an account. This was demonstrated in Illustration 2–8.

As we discussed previously in Illustration 2–5, we can expand the basic accounting equation to include the components of stockholders' equity (common stock and retained earnings) and the components of retained earnings (revenues, expenses, and dividends). Because common stock and retained earnings are part of stockholders' equity, it follows directly that we increase both with a credit. We saw this demonstrated for transaction (1) in the section above: Common stock increased, so we credited that account.

Revenues *increase* retained earnings ("there's more to keep"). Retained Earnings is a credit account, so we increase revenues with a credit. Expenses, on the other hand, *decrease* retained earnings ("there's less to keep"). Thus, we do the opposite of what we do with revenues: We increase expenses with a debit. **A debit to an expense is essentially a debit to Retained Earnings, decreasing the account.** Similarly, dividends *decrease* retained earnings, so we also record an increase in dividends with a debit. In Illustration 2–9 (next page) we show the effects of debits and credits on the components of stockholders' equity in the expanded accounting equation.

ILLUSTRATION 2–9   Debit and Credit Effects on Accounts in the Expanded Accounting Equation

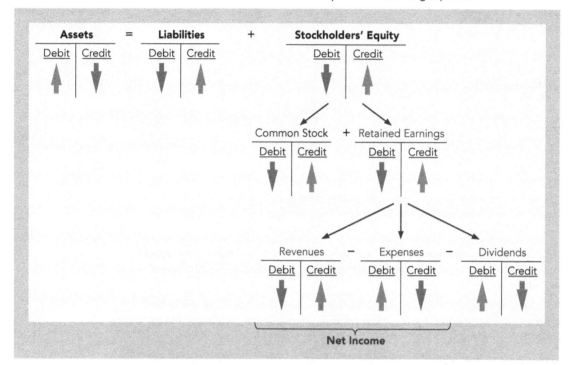

KEY POINT

The Retained Earnings account is a stockholders' equity account that normally has a credit balance. The Retained Earnings account has three components—revenues, expenses, and dividends. Revenues increase the balance of retained earnings. Expenses and dividends decrease the balance of retained earnings. Therefore, we increase revenues with a credit (similar to retained earnings) and increase expenses and dividends with a debit (opposite of retained earnings).

To see an example of the revenue, expense, and dividend components of retained earnings, let's refer back to transactions (6), (9), and (10) for Eagle Golf Academy: When providing services to customers for cash, in transaction (6), the company earns revenue. The impact of this revenue transaction on the related accounts is shown below.

TRANSACTION (6)

Provide training to customers for cash, $3,600

Paying workers' salaries for the current period in transaction (9) represents an expense and looks like this:

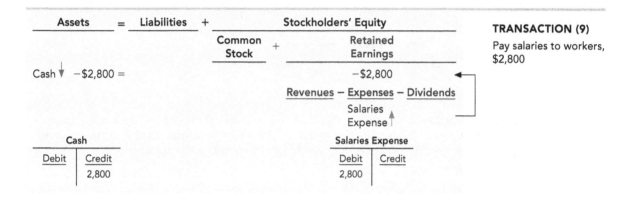

TRANSACTION (9)

Pay salaries to workers, $2,800

Eagle will record the payment of dividends in transaction (10) as:

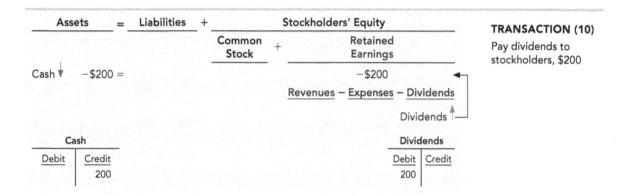

TRANSACTION (10)

Pay dividends to stockholders, $200

In the last two transactions, both expenses and dividends are increasing. These accounts have debit balances, so we increase their account balances with *debits*. However, retained earnings (a component of stockholders' equity) has a *credit* balance. A debit to an expense or a debit to Dividends is the same as a debit to Retained Earnings, reducing the balance of stockholders' equity.

Decision Point

Question	Accounting information	Analysis
How much profit has a company earned over its lifetime for its owners and retained for use in the business?	Retained earnings	The balance of retained earnings provides a record of all revenues and expenses (which combine to make net income) less dividends over the life of the company.

Illustration 2–10 (next page) provides a simple memory aid that can help you remember debits and credits. Remember the acronym **DEALOR** and you'll be able to recall the effect that debits and credits have on account balances.

ILLUSTRATION 2–10
Effects of Debit and Credit on Each Account Type

	DEALOR	
	Dividends Expenses Assets	Liabilities Owners' equity Revenues
Debit and Credit Rules:	Debit ↑ Credit ↓	Debit ↓ Credit ↑

Common Terms Another common name for stockholders' equity is *owners' equity,* since stockholders are the owners of a corporation.

The three accounts on the left, or debit, side of **DEALOR**—**D**ividends, **E**xpenses, and **A**ssets—increase with a debit. The three accounts on the right, or credit, side—**L**iabilities, **O**wners' (stockholders') equity, and **R**evenues—increase with a credit.

Let's Review

Bogey Incorporated has the following transactions during May:

May 1 Purchase a storage building by obtaining a loan of $5,000.
May 6 Provide services on account to customers, $1,800.
May 12 Pay $1,200 cash for advertising in May.
May 17 Repay $1,000 of the amount borrowed on May 1.
May 25 Purchase office supplies for $800 cash.

Required:

For each transaction, (1) identify the two accounts involved, (2) the type of account, (3) whether the transaction increases or decreases the account balance, and (4) whether the increase or decrease would be recorded with a debit or credit.

Solution:

Date	(1) Accounts Involved	(2) Account Type	(3) Increase or Decrease	(4) Debit or Credit
May 1	Buildings	Asset	Increase	Debit
	Notes Payable	Liability	Increase	Credit
May 6	Accounts Receivable	Asset	Increase	Debit
	Service Revenue	Revenue	Increase	Credit
May 12	Advertising Expense	Expense	Increase	Debit
	Cash	Asset	Decrease	Credit
May 17	Notes Payable	Liability	Decrease	Debit
	Cash	Asset	Decrease	Credit
May 25	Supplies	Asset	Increase	Debit
	Cash	Asset	Decrease	Credit

Suggested Homework:
BE2-5, BE2-6;
E2-6, E2-7;
P2-3A&B

Recording Transactions

■ **LO4**
Record transactions using debits and credits.

We have just seen how to assess whether the impact of an external transaction results in a debit or credit to an account balance. Next, we'll learn how to formally record transactions using those same debits and credits in a journal. A **journal** provides a chronological record of all transactions affecting a firm. Prior to the widespread use of computers, companies recorded their transactions in paper-based journals. Thus, the term *journal entry* was used to describe the format for recording a transaction. Today, nearly all companies have easy access to computers, and paper-based journals have become obsolete, but the term *journal entry* continues to be commonly used. Illustration 2–11 shows the format we'll use throughout the book to record a company's transactions.

Date	Debit	Credit	**ILLUSTRATION 2–11**
Account Name	Amount		Format for a Recorded Transaction, or Journal Entry
Account Name		Amount	
(Description of transaction)			

The entry that records a transaction has a place for the date of the transaction, the relevant account names, debit amounts, credit amounts, and a description of the transaction. We first list the account to be debited; below that, and indented to the right, we list the account to be credited. The entry has two amount columns—one for debits, one for credits. Because the amounts always represent dollar amounts (not number of units, for example), the dollar sign ($) is not used. As you might expect, the left-hand column is for debits, the right-hand column is for credits. **The amount of the debit must always equal the amount of the credit.** It is acceptable to include a description of the transaction at the bottom. (For learning purposes, we include descriptions.)

 COMMON MISTAKE

Many students forget to indent the credit account names. For the account credited, be sure to indent both the account name and the amount.

Think of recording a transaction as if you're writing a sentence form of the "accounting language." For example, "On January 1, Eagle Golf Academy issues shares of common stock for cash of $25,000." Here is this same sentence about transaction (1) written in the language of accounting:

January 1	Debit	Credit	**TRANSACTION (1)**
Cash (+A)	25,000		Initial investment of $25,000 by stockholders
Common Stock (+SE)		25,000	
(Issue common stock for cash)			

Just as every English sentence uses at least one noun and one verb, every accounting sentence includes at least one debit and one credit. While not a formal part of recording transactions, we'll use a notation in parentheses beside the account name in the first few chapters of this book to help you get more familiar with the effect of debits and credits on the account balance. Thus, the entry shows that transaction (1) causes total assets to increase (+A) and total stockholders' equity to increase (+SE). You will need to learn to read and write in the language of accounting as this is the language used throughout the business world.

Accounting is the language of business.

Let's try a few more transactions. In transaction (2), Eagle Academy borrows $10,000 from the bank. Eagle records the transaction as:

TRANSACTION (2)

Borrow $10,000 from the bank and sign a long-term note

January 1	Debit	Credit
Cash *(+A)*	**10,000**	
Notes Payable *(+L)*		**10,000**
(Borrow by signing long-term note)		

Both total assets and total liabilities increase by $10,000.

In transaction (3), Eagle Academy purchases equipment for $24,000 cash. Eagle records the transaction as:

TRANSACTION (3)

Purchase equipment with cash, $24,000

January 1	Debit	Credit
Equipment *(+A)*	**24,000**	
Cash *(−A)*		**24,000**
(Purchase equipment for cash)		

Here, one asset increases, while another asset decreases. We record the remaining transactions of Eagle Academy later in the chapter.

 KEY POINT

For each transaction, total debits must equal total credits.

Let's Review

Bogey Incorporated has the following transactions during May:

> May 1 Purchase a storage building by obtaining a loan of $5,000.
> May 6 Provide services on account to customers, $1,800.
> May 12 Pay $1,200 cash for advertising in May.
> May 17 Repay $1,000 of the amount borrowed on May 1.
> May 25 Purchase office supplies for $800 cash.

Required:

Record each transaction.

Solution:

May 1	Debit	Credit
Buildings *(+A)*	**5,000**	
Notes Payable *(+L)*		**5,000**
(Purchase building with note payable)		

May 6	Debit	Credit
Accounts Receivable *(+A)*	**1,800**	
Service Revenue *(+R, +SE)*		**1,800**
(Provide services on account)		

May 12	Debit	Credit
Advertising Expense (+E, −SE)	1,200	
Cash (−A)...		1,200
(Pay advertising)		

May 17	Debit	Credit
Notes Payable (−L)	1,000	
Cash (−A)...		1,000
(Repay portion of note)		

May 25	Debit	Credit
Supplies (+A)	800	
Cash (−A)...		800
(Purchase supplies for cash)		

Suggested Homework:
BE2-7, BE2-8;
E2-8, E2-10, E2-11;
P2-5A&B, P2-6A&B

Posting

The journal provides in a single location a chronological listing of every transaction affecting a company. As such, it serves as a handy way to review specific transactions and to locate any accounting errors at their original source. But it's not a convenient format for calculating account balances to use in preparing financial statements. You don't need to stretch your imagination too far to see that even for a very small company with few transactions, calculating account balances from a journal would very soon become unmanageable. Just imagine how lengthy the journal would be for **Walmart**. If each sales transaction with a customer took about one inch of space, the journal would be over 150,000 miles long by the end of the year.

■ **LO5**
Post transactions to T-accounts in the general ledger.

To make the process more efficient, we transfer information about transactions recorded in the journal to the specific accounts in the general ledger. The *general ledger* includes all accounts used to record the company's transactions. The names of these accounts are listed in the *chart of accounts*. Illustration 2–12 provides the chart of accounts for Eagle Golf Academy based on the 10 transactions we've covered to this point. Later, we'll introduce other transactions and accounts for Eagle. In addition, at the back of the book, you'll see a comprehensive chart of accounts that includes *all accounts* used throughout the book.

ILLUSTRATION 2–12

Preliminary Chart of Accounts for Eagle Golf Academy

EAGLE GOLF ACADEMY Chart of Accounts (preliminary)		
Assets	**Liabilities**	**Stockholders' Equity**
Cash	Accounts Payable	Common Stock
Accounts Receivable	Unearned Revenue	
Supplies	Notes Payable	Dividends:
Prepaid Rent		Dividends
Equipment		
		Revenues:
		Service Revenue
		Expenses:
		Salaries Expense

The process of transferring the debit and credit information from the journal to individual accounts in the general ledger is called posting. **Since we post all transactions to the general ledger, each account provides in one location a collection of all transactions that affect that account.** Computerized systems automatically and instantly post information from the journal to the general ledger accounts.

A formal general ledger account includes an account title, account number, date, and columns for increases, decreases, and the cumulative balance. As described earlier, accounts are easier to visualize if we use the T-account format. With the additional information learned since we first discussed T-accounts, we can now more formally define a T-account as a simplified form of a general ledger account with space at the top for the account title and two sides for recording debits and credits. Consistent with our previous discussion of debits and credits, the left side of the T-account is the debit column. The right side is the credit column.

Let's see how debits and credits are posted to a T-account by looking at Illustration 2–13, where we have posted the cash transactions of Eagle Golf Academy. (The corresponding transaction numbers are included in parentheses, simply for teaching purposes.) For each transaction that involves cash, we post the debit in the journal as a debit to the T-account. Similarly, we post every credit in the journal as a credit to the T-account. Note that we do not have to put "+" signs or "−" signs beside the numbers in the T-account. With all transactions collected in one place, we can now easily calculate the *ending balance* of cash. We calculate the ending balance of $6,200 by totaling all debits and subtracting the total of all credits.

ILLUSTRATION 2–13

Cash T-Account for Transactions of Eagle Golf Academy

	Cash		
	Debits	**Credits**	
	(1) 25,000		
Total	(2) 10,000		
Debits		(3) 24,000	Total
(Increases)		(4) 6,000	Credits
=	(6) 3,600		(Decreases)
$39,200	(8) 600		=
		(9) 2,800	$33,000
		(10) 200	
Ending Balance	→ Bal. 6,200		

To review:

- For assets (such as cash), an amount in the debit or left column *always* means an increase in the balance. An amount in the credit or right column *always* means a decrease in the balance.
- Just the opposite is true for liabilities and stockholders' equity: A debit to a liability or stockholders' equity T-account *always* means a decrease, and a credit *always* means an increase.

Also, notice that transactions (5) and (7) are not posted to Eagle's Cash T-account. These transactions did not include the receipt or payment of cash, and therefore they do not affect the balance of cash. Only transactions that involve cash affect the balance of cash and are posted to the Cash T-account.

 COMMON MISTAKE

Some students think the term "debit" *always* means increase and "credit" *always* means decrease. While this is true for assets, it is *not* true for liabilities and stockholders' equity. Liabilities and stockholders' equity are increased by credits and decreased by debits.

KEY POINT

Posting is the process of transferring the debit and credit information from transactions recorded in the journal to the T-accounts in the general ledger.

Summary of the Measurement Process

To better understand the measurement of external transactions, let's apply the first five steps outlined in Illustration 2–1 to each of the 10 transactions of Eagle Golf Academy. These steps are detailed in Illustrations 2–14 through 2–23.

Step 1: Use source documents to analyze **accounts** affected.	**Cash** (asset) and **common stock** (stockholders' equity) both increase by $25,000.

Step 2: Determine impact on **accounting equation.**

Assets	=	Liabilities	+	Stockholders' Equity
+$25,000	=			+$25,000
(Cash ↑)				(Common Stock ↑)

Step 3: Determine **debits** and **credits** for accounts.

1. Assets increase with a debit, so **debit** Cash, $25,000.
2. Stockholders' equity increases with a credit, so **credit** Common Stock, $25,000.

Step 4: **Record** transaction.

January 1	Debit	Credit
Cash	25,000	
Common Stock		25,000

Step 5: **Post** to T-accounts.

Cash		Common Stock	
(1) **25,000**			(1) **25,000**
Bal. 25,000			Bal. 25,000

ILLUSTRATION 2–14

Transaction (1): Issue Shares of Common Stock for $25,000

Step 1: Use source documents to analyze **accounts.**	**Cash** (asset) and **notes payable** (liability) increase by $10,000.

Step 2: Determine impact on **accounting equation.**

Assets	=	Liabilities	+	Stockholders' Equity
+$10,000	=	+$10,000		
(Cash ↑)		(Notes Payable ↑)		

Step 3: Determine **debits** and **credits** for accounts.

1. Assets increase with a debit, so **debit** Cash for $10,000.
2. Liabilities increase with a credit, so **credit** Notes Payable for $10,000.

Step 4: **Record** transaction.

January 1	Debit	Credit
Cash	10,000	
Notes Payable		10,000

Step 5: **Post** to T-accounts.

Cash		Notes Payable	
(1) 25,000			(2) **10,000**
(2) **10,000**			
Bal. 35,000			Bal. 10,000

ILLUSTRATION 2–15

Transaction (2): Borrow $10,000 from the Bank and Sign a Long-Term Note

ILLUSTRATION 2–16

Transaction (3): Purchase Equipment with Cash, $24,000

Step 1: Use source documents to analyze **accounts**.	**Equipment** (asset) increases and **cash** (asset) decreases by $24,000.
Step 2: Determine impact on **accounting equation**.	Assets = Liabilities + Stockholders' Equity +$24,000 −$24,000 = (Equipment ↑) (Cash ↓)
Step 3: Determine **debits** and **credits** for accounts.	1. Assets increase with a debit, so **debit** Equipment, $24,000. 2. Assets decrease with a credit, so **credit** Cash, $24,000.
Step 4: **Record** transaction.	January 1 Debit Credit Equipment 24,000 Cash 24,000
Step 5: **Post** to T-accounts.	Equipment Cash (3) **24,000** (1) 25,000 (3) **24,000** (2) 10,000 Bal. 24,000 Bal. 11,000

ILLUSTRATION 2–17

Transaction (4): Pay One Year of Rent in Advance, $6,000

Step 1: Use source documents to analyze **accounts**.	**Prepaid rent** (asset) increases and **cash** (asset) decreases by $6,000.
Step 2: Determine impact on **accounting equation**.	Assets = Liabilities + Stockholders' Equity +$6,000 −$6,000 = (Prepaid Rent ↑) (Cash ↓)
Step 3: Determine **debits** and **credits** for accounts.	1. Assets increase with a debit, so **debit** Prepaid Rent for $6,000. 2. Assets decrease with a credit, so **credit** Cash for $6,000.
Step 4: **Record** transaction.	January 1 Debit Credit Prepaid Rent 6,000 Cash 6,000
Step 5: **Post** to T-accounts.	Prepaid Rent Cash (4) **6,000** (1) 25,000 (3) 24,000 (2) 10,000 (4) **6,000** Bal. 6,000 Bal. 5,000

ILLUSTRATION 2–18

Transaction (5): Purchase Supplies on Account, $2,300

Step 1: Use source documents to analyze **accounts**.	**Supplies** (asset) increases and **accounts payable** (liability) increases by $2,300.
Step 2: Determine impact on **accounting equation**.	Assets = Liabilities + Stockholders' Equity +$2,300 = +$2,300 (Supplies ↑) (Accounts Payable ↑)
Step 3: Determine **debits** and **credits** for accounts.	1. Assets increase with a debit, so **debit** Supplies for $2,300. 2. Liabilities increase with a credit, so **credit** Accounts Payable for $2,300.

(continued)

Step 4: Record transaction.	January 6		Debit	Credit
	Supplies		2,300	
		Accounts Payable		2,300

Step 5: Post to T-accounts.	Supplies			Accounts Payable	
	(5) **2,300**				(5) **2,300**
	Bal. 2,300				Bal. 2,300

ILLUSTRATION 2–18 *(concluded)*

Step 1: Use source documents to analyze **accounts**.	**Cash** (asset) and **service revenue** (revenue) increase by $3,600.

ILLUSTRATION 2–19

Transaction (6): Provide Golf Training to Customers for Cash, $3,600

Step 2: Determine impact on **accounting equation**.	Assets	=	Liabilities	+	Stockholders' Equity
	+$3,600	=			+$3,600
	(Cash ↑)				(Service Revenue ↑)

Step 3: Determine **debits** and **credits** for accounts.	1. Assets increase with a debit, so **debit** Cash for $3,600. 2. Revenues increase with a credit, so **credit** Service Revenue for $3,600. The increase in revenues increases stockholders' equity.

Step 4: Record transaction.	January 12		Debit	Credit
	Cash		3,600	
		Service Revenue		3,600

Step 5: Post to T-accounts.	Cash			Service Revenue	
	(1) 25,000	(3) 24,000			(6) **3,600**
	(2) 10,000	(4) 6,000			
	(6) **3,600**				
	Bal. 8,600				Bal. 3,600

Step 1: Use source documents to analyze **accounts**.	**Accounts receivable** (asset) and **service revenue** (revenue) increase by $2,500.

ILLUSTRATION 2–20

Transaction (7): Provide Golf Training to Customers on Account, $2,500

Step 2: Determine impact on **accounting equation**.	Assets	=	Liabilities	+	Stockholders' Equity
	+$2,500	=			+$2,500
	(Accounts Receivable ↑)				(Service Revenue ↑)

Step 3: Determine **debits** and **credits** for accounts.	1. Assets increase with a debit, so **debit** Accounts Receivable for $2,500. 2. Revenues increase with a credit, so **credit** Service Revenue for $2,500. The increase in revenues increases stockholders' equity.

Step 4: Record transaction.	January 17		Debit	Credit
	Accounts Receivable		2,500	
	Service Revenue			2,500

Step 5: Post to T-accounts.	Accounts Receivable			Service Revenue	
	(7) **2,500**				(6) 3,600
					(7) **2,500**
	Bal. 2,500				Bal. 6,100

ILLUSTRATION 2–21

Transaction (8): Receive Cash in Advance for Golf Training to Be Given Next Month, $600

| Step 1:
Use source documents to analyze **accounts.** | **Cash** (asset) and **unearned revenue** (liability) increase by $600. |

| Step 2:
Determine impact on **accounting equation.** | |

Assets	=	Liabilities	+	Stockholders' Equity
+$600	=	+$600		
(Cash ↑)		(Unearned Revenue ↑)		

| Step 3:
Determine **debits** and **credits** for accounts. | 1. Assets increase with a debit, so **debit** Cash for $600.
2. Liabilities increase with a credit, so **credit** Unearned Revenue for $600. |

| Step 4:
Record transaction. | |

January 23	Debit	Credit
Cash	600	
Unearned Revenue		600

Step 5: Post to T-accounts.

Cash		Unearned Revenue
(1) 25,000 | (3) 24,000		(8) **600**
(2) 10,000 | (4) 6,000		
(6) 3,600 |		
(8) **600** |		
Bal. 9,200 |		Bal. 600

ILLUSTRATION 2–22

Transaction (9): Pay Salaries to Employees for Work during the Month, $2,800

| Step 1:
Use source documents to analyze **accounts.** | **Cash** (asset) decreases and **salaries expense** (expense) increases by $2,800. |

| Step 2:
Determine impact on **accounting equation.** | |

Assets	=	Liabilities	+	Stockholders' Equity
− $2,800	=			− $2,800
(Cash ▼)				(Salaries Expense ↑)

| Step 3:
Determine **debits** and **credits** for accounts. | 1. Assets decrease with a credit, so **credit** Cash for $2,800.
2. Expenses increase with a debit, so **debit** Salaries Expense for $2,800. The increase in expenses decreases stockholders' equity. |

| Step 4:
Record transaction. | |

January 28	Debit	Credit
Salaries Expense	2,800	
Cash		2,800

Step 5: Post to T-accounts.

Cash		Salaries Expense
(1) 25,000 | (3) 24,000		(9) **2,800**
(2) 10,000 | (4) 6,000		
(6) 3,600 | (9) **2,800**		
(8) 600 |		
Bal. 6,400 |		Bal. 2,800

ILLUSTRATION 2–23

Transaction (10): Pay Cash Dividends of $200 to Shareholders

| Step 1:
Use source documents to analyze **accounts.** | **Cash** (asset) decreases and **dividends** (dividends) increase by $200. |

| Step 2:
Determine impact on **accounting equation.** | |

Assets	=	Liabilities	+	Stockholders' Equity
−$200	=			−$200
(Cash ▼)				(Dividends ↑)

| Step 3:
Determine **debits** and **credits** for accounts. | 1. Assets decrease with a credit, so **credit** Cash for $200.
2. Dividends increase with a debit, so **debit** Dividends for $200. The increase in dividends decreases stockholders' equity. |

(continued)

Step 4: **Record** transaction.	January 30		Debit	Credit	**ILLUSTRATION 2-23** *(concluded)*
	Dividends		200		
	Cash			200	

Step 5: **Post** to T-accounts.	Dividends			Cash		
	(10) **200**		(1) 25,000	(3) 24,000		
			(2) 10,000	(4) 6,000		
			(6) 3,600	(9) 2,800		
			(8) 600	(10) **200**		
	Bal. 200		Bal. 6,200			

A summary of the external transactions recorded for Eagle Golf Academy is provided in Illustration 2–24.

January 1	Debit	Credit	**ILLUSTRATION 2-24**
Cash (+A)	25,000		Summary of External
Common Stock (+SE)		25,000	Transactions Recorded
(*Issue common stock for cash*)			for Eagle Golf
January 1			Academy
Cash (+A)	10,000		
Notes Payable (+L)		10,000	
(*Borrow by signing long-term note*)			
January 1			
Equipment (+A)	24,000		
Cash (−A)		24,000	
(*Purchase equipment for cash*)			
January 1			
Prepaid Rent (+A)	6,000		
Cash (−A)		6,000	
(*Prepay rent with cash*)			
January 6			
Supplies (+A)	2,300		
Accounts Payable (+L)		2,300	
(*Purchase supplies on account*)			
January 12			
Cash (+A)	3,600		
Service Revenue (+R, +SE)		3,600	
(*Provide training to customers for cash*)			
January 17			
Accounts Receivable (+A)	2,500		
Service Revenue (+R, +SE)		2,500	
(*Provide training to customers on account*)			
January 23			
Cash (+A)	600		
Unearned Revenue (+L)		600	
(*Receive cash in advance from customers*)			
January 28			
Salaries Expense (+E, −SE)	2,800		
Cash (−A)		2,800	
(*Pay workers' salaries*)			
January 30			
Dividends (+D, −SE)	200		
Cash (−A)		200	
(*Pay cash dividends*)			

Illustration 2–25 provides the general ledger accounts after posting the external transactions summarized in Illustration 2–24. Account balances are in bold, and transaction numbers are shown in parentheses.

ILLUSTRATION 2–25   Posting of External Transactions of Eagle Golf Academy to General Ledger Accounts

| Assets | = | Liabilities | + | Stockholders' Equity |

Cash

(1)	25,000	(3)	24,000
(2)	10,000	(4)	6,000
(6)	3,600	(9)	2,800
(8)	600	(10)	200
Bal. 6,200			

Accounts Receivable

| (7) | 2,500 | |
| **Bal. 2,500** | | |

Accounts Payable

| | (5) | 2,300 |
| | **Bal. 2,300** | |

Common Stock

| | (1) | 25,000 |
| | **Bal. 25,000** | |

Retained Earnings

| | | 0 |
| | | 0 |

Supplies

| (5) | 2,300 | |
| **Bal. 2,300** | | |

Prepaid Rent

| (4) | 6,000 | |
| **Bal. 6,000** | | |

Unearned Revenue

| | (8) | 600 |
| | **Bal. 600** | |

Service Revenue

	(6)	3,600
	(7)	2,500
	Bal. 6,100	

Salaries Expense

| (9) | 2,800 | |
| **Bal. 2,800** | | |

Equipment

| (3) | 24,000 | |
| **Bal. 24,000** | | |

Notes Payable

| | (2) | 10,000 |
| | **Bal. 10,000** | |

Dividends

| (10) 200 | |
| **Bal. 200** | |

Transaction numbers are shown in parentheses. Account balances are in bold.

■ LO6
Prepare a trial balance.

Trial Balance

After we've posted transactions to the general ledger accounts, **the sum of the accounts with debit balances should equal the sum of the accounts with credit balances.** This is expected because debits were equal to credits for every transaction posted to those ledger accounts. To prove this to be the case and to check for completeness, we prepare a trial balance. A trial balance is a list of all accounts and their balances at a particular date, showing that total debits equal total credits. Another purpose of the trial balance is to assist us in preparing adjusting entries (for *internal* transactions). We discuss adjusting entries in Chapter 3.

Using the account balances calculated in Illustration 2–25, we can now prepare the trial balance of Eagle Golf Academy. The trial balance appears in Illustration 2–26 (next page). Notice that accounts are listed with the debit balances in one column and the credit balances in another column. Asset, expense, and dividend accounts normally have debit balances. Liability, stockholders' equity, and revenue accounts normally have credit balances.

 COMMON MISTAKE

Be careful. Just because the debits and credits are equal in a trial balance does not necessarily mean that all balances are correct. A trial balance could contain offsetting errors. For example, if we overstate cash and revenue each by $1,000, both accounts will be in error, but the trial balance will still balance, since the overstatement to cash increases debits by $1,000 and the overstatement to revenue increases credits by $1,000.

EAGLE GOLF ACADEMY Trial Balance January 31		
Accounts	Debit	Credit
Cash	$ 6,200	
Accounts Receivable	2,500	
Supplies	2,300	
Prepaid Rent	6,000	
Equipment	24,000	
Accounts Payable		$ 2,300
Unearned Revenue		600
Notes Payable		10,000
Common Stock		25,000
Retained Earnings		0
Dividends	200	
Service Revenue		6,100
Salaries Expense	2,800	
Totals	$44,000	$44,000

ILLUSTRATION 2–26

Trial Balance of Eagle Golf Academy

Total debits equal total credits.

It may seem unusual that the Retained Earnings account has a balance of $0. As we explained earlier, retained earnings is a composite of three other types of accounts—revenues, expenses, and dividends. Those three accounts have balances at this point, but those balances haven't yet been transferred to retained earnings. This transfer is known as the *closing process,* and we will discuss it in Chapter 3. Since this is the first period of the company's operations, retained earnings will start at $0. As time goes by, the retained earnings balance will be the accumulated net amount of revenues minus expenses and dividends.

Decision Point

Question	Accounting information	Analysis
How does the accounting system capture the effects of a company's external transactions?	Account balances	The effects of external transactions are summarized by recording increases and decreases to account balances during the year.

ORDER OF ACCOUNTS

The trial balance is used *for internal purposes only* and provides a check on the equality of the debits and credits. Since the trial balance is not a published financial statement to be used by external parties, there is no required order for listing accounts in the trial balance. However, most companies list accounts in the following order: assets, liabilities, stockholders' equity, dividends, revenues, and expenses. As we'll see in Chapter 3, the trial balance simplifies preparation of the published financial statements. Asset, liability, and stockholders' equity accounts are reported in the balance sheet. Dividends are reported in the statement of stockholders'

CAREER CORNER

The accuracy of account balances is essential for providing useful information to decision makers, such as investors and creditors. That's why the Securities and Exchange Commission (SEC) requires all companies with publicly traded stock to have their reported account balances verified by an independent auditor. Independent auditors use their understanding of accounting principles and business practices to provide reasonable assurance that account balances are free from material misstatements resulting from errors and fraud. Tens of thousands of audits are conducted each year. Because of the huge demand for auditors, many accounting majors choose auditing, also referred to as public accounting, as their first career. For an auditor to legally certify a company's account balances, the auditor must be designated as a Certified Public Accountant (CPA).

equity. Revenue and expense accounts are reported in the income statement. Having the accounts listed in order of those classifications in the trial balance makes it easier to prepare the financial statements.

KEY POINT

A trial balance is a list of all accounts and their balances at a particular date. Debits must equal credits, but that doesn't necessarily mean that all account balances are correct.

KEY POINTS BY LEARNING OBJECTIVE

LO1 Identify the basic steps in measuring external transactions.

External transactions are transactions between the company and separate economic entities. Internal transactions do not include an exchange with a separate economic entity.

The six-step measurement process (Illustration 2–1) is the foundation of financial accounting.

LO2 Analyze the impact of external transactions on the accounting equation.

After each transaction, the accounting equation must always remain in balance. In other words, assets always must equal liabilities plus stockholders' equity.

The expanded accounting equation demonstrates that revenues increase retained earnings while expenses and dividends decrease retained earnings. Retained earnings is a component of stockholders' equity.

LO3 Assess whether the impact of external transactions results in a debit or credit to an account balance.

For the basic accounting equation (Assets = Liabilities + Stockholders' Equity), accounts on the left side are increased with *debits*. Accounts on the right side are increased with *credits*. The opposite is true to decrease any of these accounts.

The Retained Earnings account is a stockholders' equity account that normally has a credit balance. The Retained Earnings account has three components—revenues, expenses, and dividends. Revenues increase the balance of Retained Earnings, while expenses and dividends decrease the balance of Retained Earnings. Therefore, we increase revenues with a credit (similar to retained earnings) and increase expenses and dividends with a debit (opposite of retained earnings).

LO4 Record transactions using debits and credits.

For each transaction, total debits must equal total credits.

LO5 Post transactions to T-accounts in the general ledger.

Posting is the process of transferring the debit and credit information from transactions recorded in the journal to the T-accounts in the general ledger.

LO6 Prepare a trial balance.

A trial balance is a list of all accounts and their balances at a particular date. Debits must equal credits, but that doesn't necessarily mean that all account balances are correct.

GLOSSARY

Account: A summary of the effects of all transactions related to a particular item over a period of time. **p. 54**

Chart of accounts: A list of all account names used to record transactions of a company. **p. 54**

External transactions: Transactions the firm conducts with a separate economic entity. **p. 54**

General ledger: All accounts used to record the company's transactions. **p. 75**

Internal transactions: Events that affect the financial position of the company but do not include an exchange with a separate economic entity. **p. 54**

Journal: A chronological record of all transactions affecting a firm. **p. 72**

Posting: The process of transferring the debit and credit information from the journal to individual accounts in the general ledger. **p. 76**

T-account: A simplified form of a general ledger account with space at the top for the account title and two sides for recording debits and credits. **pp. 66 and 76**

Trial balance: A list of all accounts and their balances at a particular date, showing that total debits equal total credits. **p. 82**

SELF-STUDY QUESTIONS

1. Which of the following represents an external transaction?   ■ LO1
   a. Lapse of insurance due to passage of time.
   b. Use of office supplies by workers over time.
   c. Payment of utility bill.
   d. Depreciation of equipment.

2. Which of the following is *not* a step in the process of measuring external   ■ LO1
   transactions?
   a. Analyze the impact of the transaction on the accounting equation.
   b. Record the transaction using debits and credits.
   c. Post the transaction to the T-account in the general ledger.
   d. All of the above are steps in the measurement process of external
      transactions.

3. Which of the following transactions causes an increase in total assets?   ■ LO2
   a. Pay workers' salaries for the current month.
   b. Receive cash payment from a customer billed in the previous period.
   c. Issue common stock in exchange for cash.
   d. Purchase office equipment for cash.

4. Which of the following transactions causes an increase in stockholders' equity? ■ LO2
   a. Pay dividends to stockholders.
   b. Obtain cash by borrowing from a local bank.
   c. Provide services to customers on account.
   d. Purchase advertising on a local radio station.

5. Which of the following causes the accounting equation *not* to balance?   ■ LO2
   a. Increase assets; increase liabilities.
   b. Decrease assets; increase expenses.
   c. Increase assets; increase dividends.
   d. Decrease liabilities; increase revenues.

6. A debit is used to increase which of the following accounts?   ■ LO3
   a. Utilities Expense.
   b. Accounts Payable.
   c. Service Revenue.
   d. Common Stock.

■ LO3

7. A credit is used to increase which of the following accounts?
   a. Dividends.   c. Cash.
   b. Insurance Expense.   d. Service Revenue.

■ LO4

8. Providing services to customers on account for $100 is recorded as:

a. Accounts Receivable	100	
Service Revenue......................................		100
b. Cash..	100	
Accounts Receivable.............................		100
c. Service Revenue	100	
Accounts Receivable.............................		100
d. Service Expense	100	
Accounts Payable..................................		100

■ LO5

9. Posting is the process of:
   a. Analyzing the impact of the transaction on the accounting equation.
   b. Obtaining information about external transactions from source documents.
   c. Transferring the debit and credit information from the journal to individual accounts in the general ledger.
   d. Listing all accounts and their balances at a particular date and showing the equality of total debits and total credits.

■ LO6

Check out
www.mhhe.com/succeed
for more multiple-choice
questions.

10. A trial balance can best be explained as a list of:
    a. The income statement accounts used to calculate net income.
    b. Revenue, expense, and dividend accounts used to show the balances of the components of retained earnings.
    c. The balance sheet accounts used to show the equality of the accounting equation.
    d. All accounts and their balances at a particular date.

Note: For answers, see the last page of the chapter.

REVIEW QUESTIONS

■ LO1

1. Explain the difference between external transactions and internal transactions. If a company purchases supplies from a local vendor, would this be classified as an external or internal transaction?

■ LO1

2. List the steps we use to measure external transactions.

■ LO2

3. Each external transaction will have a dual effect on the company's financial position. Explain what this means.

■ LO2

4. Describe the impact of each of these external transactions on the accounting equation.
   a. Receive a loan from the bank.
   b. Pay employee salaries for the current period.
   c. Receive cash from customers for services provided in the current period.
   d. Purchase equipment by paying cash.

■ LO2

5. Jerry believes that "dual effect" indicates that, for all transactions, one account will increase and one account will decrease. Is Jerry correct? Explain.

■ LO3

6. What is the normal balance (debit or credit) of assets, liabilities, stockholders' equity, revenues, and expenses?

■ LO3

7. Jenny has learned that assets have debit balances, while liabilities have credit balances. Based on this, she believes that asset accounts can only be debited and liabilities can only be credited. Is Jenny correct? When would we credit an asset and when would we debit a liability?

8. For each of the following accounts, indicate whether we use a debit or a credit to *increase* the balance of the account.   ■ LO3

   a. Cash.   c. Utilities Expense.

   b. Salaries Payable.   d. Service Revenue.

9. For each of the following accounts, indicate whether we use a debit or a credit to *decrease* the balance of the account. (Compare your answers to those for Question 8.)   ■ LO3

   a. Cash.   c. Utilities Expense.

   b. Salaries Payable.   d. Service Revenue.

10. Suzanne knows that an increase to an expense reduces retained earnings (a stockholders' equity account). However, she also knows that expense accounts have a *debit* balance, while retained earnings normally has a *credit* balance. Are these two pieces of information consistent? Explain.   ■ LO3

11. What is a journal? What is a journal entry?   ■ LO4

12. Provide the proper format for recording a transaction.   ■ LO4

13. Explain the phrase "debits equal credits."   ■ LO4

14. Record each of the following external transactions using debits and credits.   ■ LO4

   a. Receive cash of $1,200 for providing services to a customer.

   b. Pay rent of $500 for the current month.

   c. Purchase a building for $10,000 by signing a note with the bank.

15. Describe the events that correspond to the following transactions.   ■ LO4

	Debit	Credit
a. Supplies	20,000	
Cash		20,000
b. Accounts Receivable	30,000	
Service Revenue		30,000
c. Accounts Payable	10,000	
Cash		10,000

16. What does a T-account represent? What is the left side of the T-account called? What is the right side called?   ■ LO5

17. Describe what we mean by posting. Post the transactions in Question 15 to appropriate T-accounts.   ■ LO5

18. What is a general ledger? How does it relate to the chart of accounts?   ■ LO6

19. What is a trial balance? To what does the term "balance" refer?   ■ LO6

20. If total debits equal total credits in the trial balance, does this indicate that all transactions have been properly accounted for? Explain.   ■ LO6

BRIEF EXERCISES

connect
|ACCOUNTING

BE2–1 Below are the steps in the measurement process of external transactions. Arrange them from first (1) to last (6).

List steps in the measurement process (**LO1**)

   _____ a. Post the transaction to the T-accounts in the general ledger.

   _____ b. Assess whether the impact of the transaction results in a debit or credit to the account balance.

_____ c. Use source documents to identify accounts affected by external transactions.

_____ d. Analyze the impact of the transaction on the accounting equation.

_____ e. Prepare a trial balance.

_____ f. Record transactions using debits and credits.

Balance the accounting equation (LO2)

BE2–2 Using the notion that the accounting equation (Assets = Liabilities + Stockholders' Equity) must remain in balance, indicate whether each of the following transactions is possible.

a. Cash increases; Accounts Payable decreases.

b. Service Revenue increases; Salaries Payable increases.

c. Advertising Expense increases; Cash decreases.

Balance the accounting equation (LO2)

BE2–3 Suppose a local company has the following balance sheet accounts:

Accounts	Balances
Land	$ 8,000
Equipment	?
Salaries Payable	3,300
Notes Payable	?
Supplies	1,600
Cash	6,200
Stockholders' Equity	12,500
Accounts Payable	1,200
Prepaid Rent	2,200

Calculate the missing amounts assuming the business has total assets of $30,000.

Analyze the impact of transactions on the accounting equation (LO2)

BE2–4 The following transactions occur for Badger Biking Company during the month of June:

a. Provide services to customers on account for $40,000.

b. Receive cash of $32,000 from customers in (a) above.

c. Purchase bike equipment by signing a note with the bank for $25,000.

d. Pay utilities of $4,000 for the current month.

Analyze each transaction and indicate the amount of increases and decreases in the accounting equation.

	Assets	=	Liabilities	+	Stockholders' Equity
(a)					
(b)					
(c)					
(d)					

Understand the effect of debits and credits on accounts (LO3)

BE2–5 For each of the following accounts, indicate whether a debit or credit is used to increase (+) or decrease (−) the balance of the account. The solution for the first one is provided as an example.

Account	Debit	Credit
Asset	+	−
Liability		
Common Stock		
Retained Earnings		
Dividend		
Revenue		
Expense		

BE2–6 Fill in the blanks below with the word "debit" or "credit."

a. The balance of an *asset* account increases with a _____ and decreases with a _____.

b. The balance of a *liability* account increases with a _____ and decreases with a _____.

c. The balance of a *stockholders' equity* account increases with a _____ and decreases with a _____.

d. The balance of a *revenue* account increases with a _____ and decreases with a _____.

e. The balance of an *expense* account increases with a _____ and decreases with a _____.

Understand the effect of debits and credits on accounts (LO3)

BE2–7 The following transactions occur for the Panther Detective Agency during the month of July:

a. Purchase a truck and sign a note payable, $14,000.

b. Purchase office supplies for cash, $500.

c. Pay $700 in rent for the current month.

Record the transactions. The company uses the following accounts: Cash, Supplies, Equipment (for the truck), Notes Payable, and Rent Expense.

Record transactions (LO4)

BE2–8 The following transactions occur for Cardinal Music Academy during the month of October:

a. Provide music lessons to students for $12,000 cash.

b. Purchase prepaid insurance to protect musical equipment over the next year for $3,600 cash.

c. Purchase musical equipment for $15,000 cash.

d. Obtain a loan from a bank by signing a note for $20,000.

Record the transactions. The company uses the following accounts: Cash, Prepaid Insurance, Equipment, Notes Payable, and Service Revenue.

Record transactions (LO4)

BE2–9 Consider the following T-account for cash.

Analyze T-accounts (LO5)

Cash	
12,000	7,200
3,400	1,400
2,500	4,500

1. Compute the balance of the Cash account.

2. Give some examples of transactions that would have resulted in the $3,400 posting to the account.

3. Give some examples of transactions that would have resulted in the $1,400 posting to the account.

BE2–10 The following transactions occur for the Wolfpack Shoe Company during the month of June:

a. Provide services to customers for $25,000 and receive cash.

b. Purchase office supplies on account for $15,000.

c. Pay $6,000 in salaries to employees for work performed during the month.

1. Analyze each transaction. For each transaction, indicate by how much each category in the accounting equation increases or decreases.

Analyze the impact of transactions on the accounting equation, record transactions, and post (LO2, 3, 4, 5)

	Assets	=	Liabilities	+	Stockholders' Equity
(a)					
(b)					
(c)					

2. Record the transactions. The company uses the following accounts: Cash, Supplies, Accounts Payable, Salaries Expense, and Service Revenue.

3. Post the transactions to T-accounts. Assume the opening balance in each of the accounts is zero.

Prepare a trial balance (LO6)

BE2–11 Using the following information, prepare a trial balance. Assume all asset, dividend, and expense accounts have debit balances and all liability, stockholders' equity, and revenue accounts have credit balances. List the accounts in the following order: assets, liabilities, stockholders' equity, dividends, revenues, and expenses.

Cash	$5,600	Dividends	$ 400
Salaries Payable	600	Rent Expense	1,500
Prepaid Rent	800	Accounts Receivable	3,400
Accounts Payable	1,500	Common Stock	5,200
Retained Earnings	1,300	Service Revenue	6,100
Salaries Expense	2,000	Advertising Expense	1,000

Correct a trial balance (LO6)

BE2–12 Your study partner is having trouble getting total debits to equal total credits in the trial balance. Prepare a corrected trial balance by placing each account balance in the correct debit or credit column.

Trial Balance		
Accounts	**Debit**	**Credit**
Cash	$ 6,300	
Accounts Receivable		$ 1,600
Equipment	9,400	
Accounts Payable	2,900	
Unearned Revenue		1,200
Common Stock	10,000	
Retained Earnings		3,200
Dividends	700	
Service Revenue		3,500
Salaries Expense	2,200	
Utilities Expense		600
Total	$31,500	$10,100

EXERCISES

connect |ACCOUNTING

Identify terms associated with the measurement process (LO1)

E2–1 Listed below are several terms and phrases associated with the measurement process for external transactions.

List A	List B
_____ 1. Account	a. Record of all transactions affecting a firm.
_____ 2. Analyze transactions	b. Determine the dual effect of economic events on the accounting equation.
_____ 3. Journal	c. List of accounts and their balances.
_____ 4. Post	d. Summary of the effects of all transactions related to a particular item over a period of time.
_____ 5. Trial balance	e. Transfer balances from the journal to the ledger.

Required:
Pair each item from List A with the item from List B to which it is most appropriately associated.

Analyze the impact of transactions on the accounting equation (LO2)

E2–2 Below are the external transactions for Shockers Incorporated.
1. Issue common stock in exchange for cash.
2. Purchase equipment by signing a note payable.
3. Provide services to customers on account.

4. Pay rent for the current month.
5. Pay insurance for the current month.
6. Collect cash from customers on account.

	Assets	=	Liabilities	+	Stockholders' Equity
1.	Increase	=	No effect	+	Increase
2.					
3.					
4.					
5.					
6.					

Required:
Analyze each transaction. Under each category in the accounting equation, indicate whether the transaction increases, decreases, or has no effect. The first item is provided as an example.

E2–3 Green Wave Company plans to own and operate a storage rental facility. For the first month of operations, the company had the following transactions.

1. Issue 10,000 shares of common stock in exchange for $32,000 in cash.
2. Purchase land for $19,000. A note payable is signed for the full amount.
3. Purchase storage container equipment for $8,000.
4. Hire three employees for $2,000 per month.
5. Receive cash of $12,000 in rental fees for the current month.
6. Purchase office supplies for $2,000 on account.
7. Pay employees $6,000 for the first month's salaries.

Analyze the impact of transactions on the accounting equation (LO2)

Required:
For each transaction, describe the dual effect on the accounting equation. For example, in the first transaction, (1) assets increase and (2) stockholders' equity increases.

E2–4 Boilermaker House Painting Company incurs the following transactions for September.

1. Paint houses in the current month for $15,000 on account.
2. Purchase painting equipment for $16,000 cash.
3. Purchase office supplies on account for $2,500.
4. Pay workers' salaries of $3,200 for the current month.
5. Purchase advertising to appear in the current month, $1,200.
6. Pay office rent of $4,400 for the current month.
7. Receive $10,000 from customers in (1) above.
8. Receive cash of $5,000 in advance from a customer who plans to have his house painted in the following month.

Analyze the impact of transactions on the accounting equation (LO2)

Required:
For each transaction, describe the dual effect on the accounting equation. For example, for the first transaction, (1) assets increase and (2) stockholders' equity increases.

E2–5 At the beginning of April, Owl Corporation has a balance of $12,000 in the Retained Earnings account. During the month of April, Owl had the following external transactions.

1. Issue common stock for cash, $10,000.
2. Provide services to customers on account, $7,500.
3. Provide services to customers in exchange for cash, $2,200.
4. Purchase equipment and pay cash, $6,600.
5. Pay rent for April, $1,200.
6. Pay workers' salaries for April, $2,500.
7. Pay dividends to stockholders, $1,500.

Understand the components of retained earnings (LO2)

Required:

Using the external transactions above, compute the balance of Retained Earnings at April 30.

Indicate the debit or credit balance of accounts **(LO3)**

E2–6 Below is a list of common accounts.

Accounts	Debit or Credit
Cash	1. _____
Service Revenue	2. _____
Salaries Expense	3. _____
Accounts Payable	4. _____
Equipment	5. _____
Retained Earnings	6. _____
Utilities Expense	7. _____
Accounts Receivable	8. _____
Dividends	9. _____
Common Stock	10. _____

Required:

Indicate whether the normal balance of each account is a debit or a credit.

Associate debits and credits with external transactions **(LO3)**

E2–7 Below are several external transactions for Hokies Company.

	Account Debited	Account Credited
Example: Purchase equipment in exchange for cash.	*Equipment*	*Cash*
1. Pay a cash dividend.		
2. Pay rent in advance for the next three months.		
3. Provide services to customers on account.		
4. Purchase office supplies on account.		
5. Pay salaries for the current month.		
6. Issue common stock in exchange for cash.		
7. Collect cash from customers for services provided in (3) above.		
8. Borrow cash from the bank and sign a note.		
9. Pay for the current month's utilities.		
10. Pay for office supplies purchased in (4) above.		

Hokies uses the following accounts:

Accounts Payable	Equipment	Accounts Receivable
Cash	Supplies	Utilities Expense
Prepaid Rent	Rent Expense	Service Revenue
Common Stock	Notes Payable	Retained Earnings
Salaries Payable	Salaries Expense	Dividends

Required:

Indicate which accounts should be debited and which should be credited.

Record transactions **(LO4)**

E2–8 Terapin Company engages in the following external transactions for November.

1. Purchase equipment in exchange for cash of $22,400.
2. Provide services to customers and receive cash of $5,800.
3. Pay the current month's rent of $1,100.
4. Purchase office supplies on account for $900.
5. Pay employees' salaries of $1,600 for the current month.

Required:

Record the transactions. Terapin uses the following accounts: Cash, Supplies, Equipment, Accounts Payable, Service Revenue, Rent Expense, and Salaries Expense.

E2–9 Below are recorded transactions of Yellow Jacket Corporation for August.

Identify transactions **(LO4)**

	Debit	Credit
1. Equipment	8,800	
Cash		8,800
2. Accounts Receivable	3,200	
Service Revenue................................		3,200
3. Salaries Expense	1,900	
Cash		1,900
4. Cash	1,500	
Unearned Revenue		1,500
5. Dividends	900	
Cash		900

Required:

Provide an explanation for each transaction.

E2–10 Sun Devil Hair Design has the following transactions during the month of February.

Record transactions **(LO4)**

February 2	Pay $600 for radio advertising for February.
February 7	Purchase beauty supplies of $1,200 on account.
February 14	Provide beauty services of $2,400 to customers and receive cash.
February 15	Pay workers' salaries for the current month of $800.
February 25	Provide beauty services of $900 to customers on account.
February 28	Pay utility bill for the current month of $200.

Required:

Record each transaction. Sun Devil uses the following accounts: Cash, Accounts Receivable, Supplies, Accounts Payable, Service Revenue, Advertising Expense, Salaries Expense, and Utilities Expense.

E2–11 Bearcat Construction begins operations in March and has the following transactions.

Record transactions **(LO4)**

March 1	Issue common stock for $16,000.
March 5	Obtain $8,000 loan from the bank by signing a note.
March 10	Purchase construction equipment for $20,000 cash.
March 15	Purchase advertising for the current month for $1,000 cash.
March 22	Provide construction services for $17,000 on account.
March 27	Receive $12,000 cash on account from March 22 services.
March 28	Pay salaries for the current month of $5,000.

Required:

Record each transaction. Bearcat uses the following accounts: Cash, Accounts Receivable, Notes Payable, Common Stock, Service Revenue, Advertising Expense, and Salaries Expense.

E2–12 Consider the recorded transactions below.

Post transactions to T-accounts **(LO5)**

	Debit	Credit
1. Accounts Receivable	7,400	
Service Revenue		7,400
2. Supplies...	1,800	
Accounts Payable		1,800
3. Cash	9,200	
Accounts Receivable........................		9,200
4. Advertising Expense	1,200	
Cash		1,200
5. Accounts Payable	2,700	
Cash		2,700
6. Cash	1,000	
Unearned Revenue		1,000

Required:

Post each transaction to T-accounts and compute the ending balance of each account. The beginning balance of each account before the transactions is: Cash, $2,400; Accounts Receivable, $3,200; Supplies, $300; Accounts Payable, $2,500; Unearned Revenue, $200. Service Revenue and Advertising Expense each have a beginning balance of zero.

Prepare a trial balance (LO6)

E2–13 Below is the complete list of accounts of Sooner Company and the related balance at the end of April. All accounts have their normal debit or credit balance. Cash, $2,900; Prepaid Rent, $6,400; Accounts Payable $3,300; Common Stock, $30,000; Service Revenue, $24,400; Salaries Expense, $7,200; Accounts Receivable, $5,100; Land, $50,000; Unearned Revenue, $1,800; Retained Earnings, $20,500; Supplies Expense, $8,400.

Required:

Prepare a trial balance with the list of accounts in the following order: assets, liabilities, stockholders' equity, revenues, and expenses.

Prepare a trial balance (LO6)

E2–14 Below is the complete list of accounts of Fightin' Blue Hens Incorporated and the related balance at the end of March. All accounts have their normal debit or credit balance. Supplies, $1,200; Buildings, $45,000; Salaries Payable, $400; Common Stock, $25,000; Accounts Payable, $1,700; Utilities Expense, $2,700; Prepaid Insurance, $1,300; Service Revenue, $18,500; Accounts Receivable, $3,200; Cash, $2,500; Salaries Expense, $5,400; Retained Earnings, $15,700.

Required:

Prepare a trial balance with the list of accounts in the following order: assets, liabilities, stockholders' equity, revenues, and expenses.

Record transactions, post to T-accounts, and prepare a trial balance (LO4, 5, 6)

E2–15 Green Wave Company plans to own and operate a storage rental facility. For the first month of operations, the company has the following transactions.

1. Issue 10,000 shares of common stock in exchange for $32,000 in cash.
2. Purchase land for $19,000. A note payable is signed for the full amount.
3. Purchase storage container equipment for $8,000 cash.
4. Hire three employees for $2,000 per month.
5. Receive cash of $12,000 in rental fees for the current month.
6. Purchase office supplies for $2,000 on account.
7. Pay employees $6,000 for the first month's salaries.

Required:

1. Record each transaction. Green Wave uses the following accounts: Cash, Supplies, Land, Equipment, Common Stock, Accounts Payable, Notes Payable, Service Revenue, and Salaries Expense.
2. Post each transaction to T-accounts and compute the ending balance of each account. Since this is the first month of operations, all T-accounts have a beginning balance of zero.
3. After calculating the ending balance of each account, prepare a trial balance.

Record transactions, post to T-accounts, and prepare a trial balance (LO4, 5, 6)

E2–16 Boilermaker House Painting Company incurs the following transactions for September.

1. Paint houses in the current month for $15,000 on account.
2. Purchase painting equipment for $16,000 cash.
3. Purchase office supplies on account for $2,500.
4. Pay workers' salaries of $3,200 for the current month.
5. Purchase advertising to appear in the current month for $1,200 cash.
6. Pay office rent of $4,400 for the current month.
7. Receive $10,000 from customers in (1) above.
8. Receive cash of $5,000 in advance from a customer who plans to have his house painted in the following month.

Required:

1. Record each transaction. Boilermaker uses the following accounts: Cash, Accounts Receivable, Supplies, Equipment, Accounts Payable, Unearned Revenue, Common Stock, Retained Earnings, Service Revenue, Salaries Expense, Advertising Expense, and Rent Expense.
2. Post each transaction to T-accounts and compute the ending balance of each account. At the beginning of September, the company had the following account balances: Cash, $21,100; Accounts Receivable, $1,200; Supplies, $400; Equipment, $6,400; Accounts Payable, $1,100; Common Stock, $20,000; Retained Earnings, $8,000. All other accounts had a beginning balance of zero.
3. After calculating the ending balance of each account, prepare a trial balance.

For additional exercises, visit www.mhhe.com/succeed for Exercises: Set B.

PROBLEMS: SET A

P2–1A Below is a list of activities for Jayhawk Corporation.

Analyze the impact of transactions on the accounting equation (LO2)

Transaction	Assets	=	Liabilities	+	Stockholders' Equity
1. Issue common stock in exchange for cash.	Increase	=	No effect	+	Increase
2. Purchase business supplies on account.					
3. Pay for legal services for the current month.					
4. Provide services to customers on account.					
5. Pay employee salaries for the current month.					
6. Provide services to customers for cash.					
7. Pay for advertising for the current month.					
8. Repay loan from the bank.					
9. Pay dividends to stockholders.					
10. Receive cash from customers in (4) above.					
11. Pay for supplies purchased in (2) above.					

Required:

For each activity, indicate whether the transaction increases, decreases, or has no effect on assets, liabilities, and stockholders' equity.

P2–2A Below is a list of activities for Purple Cow Incorporated.

Analyze the impact of transactions on the accounting equation (LO2)

Transaction	Assets	=	Liabilities	+	Stockholders' Equity
1. Provide services to customers on account, $1,600.	+$1,600	=	$0	+	+$1,600
2. Pay $400 for current month's rent.					
3. Hire a new employee, who will be paid $500 at the end of each month.					

(continued)

(concluded)

Transaction	Assets	=	Liabilities	+	Stockholders' Equity
4. Pay $100 for advertising aired in the current period.					
5. Purchase office supplies for $400 cash.					
6. Receive cash of $1,000 from customers in (1) above.					
7. Obtain a loan from the bank for $7,000.					
8. Receive a bill of $200 for utility costs in the current period.					
9. Issue common stock for $10,000 cash.					
10. Pay $500 to employee in (3) above.					
Totals	_____	=	_____	+	_____

Required:

For each activity, indicate the impact on the accounting equation. After doing so for all transactions, ensure that the accounting equation remains in balance.

Identify the type of account and its normal debit or credit balance (LO3)

P2–3A Below is a list of typical accounts.

Accounts	Type of Account	Normal Balance (Debit or Credit)
1. Salaries Payable		
2. Common Stock		
3. Prepaid Rent		
4. Buildings		
5. Utilities Expense		
6. Equipment		
7. Rent Expense		
8. Notes Payable		
9. Salaries Expense		
10. Insurance Expense		
11. Cash		
12. Service Revenue		

Required:

For each account, indicate (1) the type of account and (2) whether the normal account balance is a debit or credit. For the type of account, choose from asset, liability, stockholders' equity, dividend, revenue, or expense.

Correct recorded transactions (LO4)

P2–4A Below are several transactions for Scarlet Knight Corporation. A junior accountant, recently employed by the company, proposes to record the following transactions.

External Transaction	Accounts	Debit	Credit
1. Owners invest $10,000 in the company and receive common stock.	Common Stock	10,000	
	Cash		10,000
2. Receive cash of $3,000 for services provided in the current period.	Cash	3,000	
	Service Revenue		3,000
3. Purchase office supplies on account, $200.	Supplies	200	
	Cash		200
4. Pay $500 for next month's rent.	Rent Expense	500	
	Cash		500
5. Purchase office equipment with cash of $1,700.	Cash	1,700	
	Equipment		1,700

Required:
Assess whether the junior accountant correctly proposes how to record each transaction. If incorrect, provide the correction.

P2–5A Jake owns a lawn maintenance company, and Luke owns a machine repair shop. For the month of July, the following transactions occurred.

Record transactions **(LO4)**

Flip Side of P2–6A

July 3	Jake provides lawn services to Luke's repair shop on account, $400.
July 6	One of Jake's mowers malfunctions. Luke provides repair services to Jake on account, $350.
July 9	Luke pays $400 to Jake for lawn services provided on July 3.
July 14	Luke borrows $500 from Jake by signing a note.
July 18	Jake purchases advertising in a local newspaper for the remainder of July and pays cash, $100.
July 20	Jake pays $350 to Luke for services provided on July 6.
July 27	Luke performs repair services for other customers for cash, $700.
July 30	Luke pays employees' salaries for the month, $200.
July 31	Luke pays $500 to Jake for money borrowed on July 14.

Required:
Record the transactions for Jake's Lawn Maintenance Company.

P2–6A Refer to the transactions described in P2–5A.

Analyze the impact of transactions on the accounting equation and record transactions **(LO2, 4)**

Flip Side of P2–5A

Jake's Lawn Maintenance Company				Luke's Repair Shop			
Assets	=	Liabilities	+	Stockholders' Equity	Assets	=	Liabilities	+	Stockholders' Equity
July 3	+$400	=	$0	+	+$400	$0	=	+$400	+	–$400
6										
9										
14										
18										
20										
27										
30										
31										

Required:
1. Record each transaction for Luke's Repair Shop.
2. Using the format shown above, indicate the impact of each transaction on the accounting equation for each company.

P2–7A Below are the account balances of Bruins Company at the end of November.

Prepare a trial balance **(LO6)**

Accounts	Balances	Accounts	Balances
Cash	$30,000	Common Stock	$40,000
Accounts Receivable	40,000	Retained Earnings	25,000
Supplies	1,000	Dividends	1,000
Prepaid Rent	2,000	Service Revenue	55,000
Equipment	?	Salaries Expense	20,000
Accounts Payable	16,000	Rent Expense	11,000
Salaries Payable	4,000	Interest Expense	2,000
Interest Payable	2,000	Supplies Expense	6,000
Unearned Revenue	8,000	Utilities Expense	5,000
Notes Payable	20,000		

Required:

Prepare a trial balance by placing amounts in the appropriate debit or credit column and determining the balance of the Equipment account.

Complete the steps in the measurement of external transactions (**LO4, 5, 6**)

P2–8A Below are the transactions for Ute Sewing Shop for March, the first month of operations.

March 1	Issue common stock in exchange for cash of $2,000.
March 3	Purchase sewing equipment by signing a note with the local bank, $1,700.
March 5	Pay rent of $500 for March.
March 7	Martha, a customer, places an order for alterations to several dresses. Ute estimates that the alterations will cost Martha $700. Martha is not required to pay for the alterations until the work is complete.
March 12	Purchase sewing supplies for $120 on account. This material will be used to provide services to customers.
March 15	Martha receives altered dresses and pays $700 to Ute.
March 19	Bob needs 100 pairs of overalls expanded as he purchased too many small and medium sizes. He pays $600 to Ute for services and expects the overalls to be completed by March 25.
March 25	Bob receives his completed overalls.
March 30	Pay utilities of $85 for the current period.
March 31	Pay dividends of $100 to stockholders.

Required:

1. Record each transaction.
2. Post each transaction to the appropriate T-accounts.
3. Calculate the balance of each account at March 31.
4. Prepare a trial balance as of March 31.

Ute uses the following accounts: Cash, Supplies, Equipment, Accounts Payable, Unearned Revenue, Notes Payable, Common Stock, Dividends, Service Revenue, Rent Expense, and Utilities Expense.

Complete the steps in the measurement of external transactions (**LO4, 5, 6**)

QB

P2–9A Pirates Incorporated had the following balances at the beginning of September.

PIRATES INCORPORATED Trial Balance		
Accounts	**Debits**	**Credits**
Cash	$ 5,500	
Accounts Receivable	1,500	
Supplies	6,600	
Land	10,200	
Accounts Payable		$6,500
Notes Payable		2,000
Common Stock		8,000
Retained Earnings		7,300

The following transactions occur in September.

September 1	Provide services to customers for cash, $3,700.
September 2	Purchase land with a long-term note for $5,400 from Crimson Company.
September 4	Receive an invoice for $400 from the local newspaper for an advertisement that appeared on September 2.
September 8	Provide services to customers on account for $5,000.
September 10	Purchase supplies on account for $1,000.
September 13	Pay $3,000 to Crimson Company for a long-term note.

September 18   Receive $4,000 from customers on account.
September 20   Pay $800 for September's rent.
September 30   Pay September's utility bill of $1,500.
September 30   Pay employees $3,000 for salaries for the month of September.
September 30   Pay a cash dividend of $1,000 to shareholders.

Required:

1. Record each transaction.
2. Post each transaction to the appropriate T-accounts.
3. Calculate the balance of each account at September 30. (*Hint:* Be sure to include the balance at the beginning of September in each T-account.)
4. Prepare a trial balance as of September 30.

PROBLEMS: SET B

P2–1B Below is a list of activities for Tigers Corporation.

Analyze the impact of transactions on the accounting equation (**LO2**)

Transaction	Assets	=	Liabilities	+	Stockholders' Equity
1. *Obtain a loan at the bank.*	*Increase*	*=*	*Increase*	*+*	*No effect*
2. Purchase a machine to use in operations for cash.					
3. Provide services to customers for cash.					
4. Pay workers' salaries for the current month.					
5. Repay loan from the bank in (1) above.					
6. Customers pay cash in advance of services.					
7. Pay for maintenance costs in the current month.					
8. Pay for advertising in the current month.					
9. Purchase office supplies on account.					
10. Provide services to customers on account.					
11. Pay dividends to stockholders.					

Required:

For each activity, indicate whether the transaction increases, decreases, or has no effect on assets, liabilities, and stockholders' equity.

P2–2B Below is a list of activities for Vikings Incorporated.

Analyze the impact of transactions on the accounting equation (**LO2**)

Transaction	Assets	=	Liabilities	+	Stockholders' Equity
1. *Issue common stock in exchange for cash, $15,000.*	*+ $15,000*	*=*	*$0*	*+*	*+$15,000*
2. Obtain a loan from the bank for $9,000.					
3. Receive cash of $1,200 in advance from customers.					
4. Purchase supplies on account, $2,400.					

(continued)

(concluded)

Transaction	Assets	=	Liabilities	+	Stockholders' Equity
5. Pay one year of rent in advance, $12,000.					
6. Provide services to customers on account, $3,000.					
7. Repay $4,000 of the loan in (2) above.					
8. Pay the full amount for supplies purchased in (4) above.					
9. Provide services to customers in (3) above.					
10. Pay cash dividends of $1,000 to stockholders.					
Totals		=		+	

Required:

For each activity, indicate the impact on the accounting equation. After doing all the transactions, ensure that the accounting equation remains in balance.

Identify the type of account and its normal debit or credit balance **(LO3)**

P2–3B Below is a list of typical accounts.

Accounts	Type of Account	Normal Balance (Debit or Credit)
1. Supplies		
2. Advertising Expense		
3. Prepaid Insurance		
4. Supplies Expense		
5. Accounts Payable		
6. Equipment		
7. Dividends		
8. Accounts Receivable		
9. Retained Earnings		
10. Unearned Revenue		
11. Service Revenue		
12. Utilities Payable		

Required:

For each account, indicate (1) the type of account and (2) whether the normal account balance is a debit or credit. For type of account, choose from asset, liability, stockholders' equity, dividend, revenue, or expense.

Correct recorded transactions **(LO4)**

P2–4B Below are several transactions for Crimson Tide Corporation. A junior accountant, recently employed by the company, proposes to record the following transactions.

External Transaction	Accounts	Debit	Credit
1. Pay cash dividends of $700 to stockholders.	Cash	700	
	Dividends		700
2. Provide services on account for customers, $2,400.	Cash	2,400	
	Service Revenue		2,400
3. Pay a $400 utilities bill for the current period.	Utilities Expense	400	
	Cash		400
4. Receive cash of $300 from previously billed customers.	Cash	300	
	Service Revenue		300
5. Pay for supplies previously purchased on account, $1,100.	Supplies Expense	1,100	
	Cash		1,100

Required:

Assess whether the junior accountant correctly proposes how to record each transaction. If incorrect, provide the correction.

P2–5B Eli owns an insurance office, while Olivia operates a maintenance service that provides basic custodial duties. For the month of May, the following transactions occurred.

Record transactions **(LO4)**

Flip Side of P2–6B

May 2	Olivia decides that she will need insurance for a one-day special event at the end of the month and pays Eli $200 in advance.
May 5	Olivia provides maintenance services to Eli's insurance offices on account, $375.
May 7	Eli borrows $400 from Olivia by signing a note.
May 14	Olivia purchases maintenance supplies from Spot Corporation, paying cash of $150.
May 19	Eli pays $375 to Olivia for maintenance services provided on May 5.
May 25	Eli pays the utility bill for the month of May, $125.
May 28	Olivia receives insurance services from Eli equaling the amount paid on May 2.
May 31	Eli pays $400 to Olivia for money borrowed on May 7.

Required:

Record each transaction for Eli's Insurance Services.

P2–6B Refer to the transactions described in P2–5B.

Analyze the impact of transactions on the accounting equation and record transactions **(LO2, 4)**

Flip Side of P2–5B

	Eli's Insurance Services				Olivia's Maintenance Services		
	Assets	= Liabilities	+ Stockholders' Equity		Assets	= Liabilities	+ Stockholders' Equity
May 2	+$200	= +$200	+ $0		+$200 −$200	= $0	+ $0
5							
7							
14							
19							
25							
28							
31							

Required:

Record transactions for Olivia's Maintenance Services. Then, using the format shown, indicate the impact of each transaction on the accounting equation for each company.

P2–7B Below are account balances of Ducks Company at the end of September.

Prepare a trial balance **(LO6)**

Accounts	Balances	Accounts	Balances
Cash	$20,000	Retained Earnings	$12,000
Accounts Receivable	13,000	Dividends	3,000
Supplies	6,000	Service Revenue	?
Prepaid Insurance	4,000	Salaries Expense	8,000
Equipment	23,000	Insurance Expense	7,000
Accounts Payable	6,000	Advertising Expense	1,000
Salaries Payable	3,000	Supplies Expense	9,000
Utilities Payable	1,000	Entertainment Expense	5,000
Unearned Revenue	8,000	Utilities Expense	1,000
Common Stock	24,000		

Required:

Prepare a trial balance by placing amounts in the appropriate debit or credit column and determining the balance of the Service Revenue account.

Complete the steps in the measurement of external transactions (LO4, 5, 6)

P2–8B Below are the transactions for Salukis Car Cleaning for June, the first month of operations.

June 1	Obtain a loan of $60,000 from the bank by signing a note.
June 2	Issue common stock in exchange for cash of $30,000.
June 7	Purchase car wash equipment for $65,000 cash.
June 10	Purchase cleaning supplies of $7,000 on account.
June 12	Wash 400 cars for $10 each. All customers pay cash.
June 16	Pay employees $800 for work performed.
June 19	Pay for advertising in a local newspaper, costing $400.
June 23	Wash 500 cars for $10 each on account.
June 29	Pay employees $850 for work performed.
June 30	A utility bill of $1,300 for the current month is paid.
June 30	Pay dividends of $500 to stockholders.

Required:

1. Record each transaction.
2. Post each transaction to the appropriate T-accounts.
3. Calculate the balance of each account.
4. Prepare a trial balance for June.

Salukis uses the following accounts: Cash, Accounts Receivable, Supplies, Equipment, Accounts Payable, Notes Payable, Common Stock, Dividends, Service Revenue, Salaries Expense, Advertising Expense, and Utilities Expense.

Complete the steps in the measurement of external transactions (LO4, 5, 6)

P2–9B Buckeye Incorporated had the following trial balance at the beginning of November.

BUCKEYE INCORPORATED Trial Balance		
Accounts	**Debits**	**Credits**
Cash	$2,200	
Accounts Receivable	500	
Supplies	600	
Equipment	8,400	
Accounts Payable		$1,500
Notes Payable		3,000
Common Stock		6,000
Retained Earnings		1,200

The following transactions occur in November.

November 1	Issue common stock in exchange for $12,000 cash.
November 2	Purchase equipment with a long-term note for $2,500 from Spartan Corporation.
November 4	Purchase supplies for $1,200 on account.
November 10	Provide services to customers on account for $8,000.
November 15	Pay creditors on account, $1,000.
November 20	Pay employees $2,000 for the first half of the month.
November 22	Provide services to customers for $10,000 cash.
November 24	Pay $1,000 on the note from Spartan Corporation.
November 26	Collect $6,000 on account from customers.
November 28	Pay $1,000 to the local utility company for November gas and electricity.
November 30	Pay $4,000 rent for November.

Required:
1. Record each transaction.
2. Post each transaction to the appropriate T-accounts.
3. Calculate the balance of each account at November 30. (*Hint:* Be sure to include the balance at the beginning of November in each T-account.)
4. Prepare a trial balance as of November 30.

*For additional problems, visit **www.mhhe.com/succeed** for Problems: Set C.*

ADDITIONAL PERSPECTIVES

Great Adventures

(This is a continuation of the Great Adventures problem from Chapter 1.)

Continuing Problem

AP2–1 Tony and Suzie graduate from college in May 2012 and begin developing their new business. They begin by offering clinics for basic outdoor activities such as mountain biking or kayaking. Upon developing a customer base, they'll hold their first adventure races. These races will involve four-person teams that race from one checkpoint to the next using a combination of kayaking, mountain biking, orienteering, and trail running. In the long run, they plan to sell outdoor gear and develop a ropes course for outdoor enthusiasts.

On July 1, 2012, Tony and Suzie organize their new company as a corporation, Great Adventures Inc. The articles of incorporation state that the corporation will sell 20,000 shares of common stock for $1 each. Each share of stock represents a unit of ownership. Tony and Suzie will act as co-presidents of the company. The following business activities occur during July.

July 1	Suzie purchases $10,000 of Great Adventures' common stock using cash she saved during college.
1	Tony purchases $10,000 of Great Adventures' common stock by borrowing from a local bank using his personal vehicle as collateral.
1	Suzie purchases a one-year insurance policy for $4,800 ($400 per month) to cover injuries to participants during outdoor clinics.
2	The company pays legal fees of $1,500 associated with incorporation.
4	Suzie purchases office supplies of $1,800 on account.
7	Suzie pays advertising of $300 to a local newspaper for an upcoming mountain biking clinic to be held on July 15. Attendees will be charged $50 the day of the clinic.
8	Tony purchases 10 mountain bikes, paying $12,000 cash.
15	On the day of the clinic, Great Adventures receives cash of $2,000 from 40 bikers. Tony conducts the mountain biking clinic.
22	Because of the success of the first mountain biking clinic, Tony holds another mountain biking clinic and the company receives $2,300.
24	Suzie pays advertising of $700 to a local radio station for a kayaking clinic to be held on August 10. Attendees can pay $100 in advance or $150 on the day of the clinic.
30	Great Adventures receives cash of $4,000 in advance from 40 kayakers for the upcoming kayak clinic.

Required:
1. Record each transaction in July.
2. Post each transaction to T-accounts.
3. Prepare a trial balance.

Financial Analysis

American Eagle Outfitters, Inc.

AP2–2 Financial information for **American Eagle** is presented in Appendix A at the end of the book.

Required:

1. Is American Eagle's company size increasing? To answer, calculate the percentage change in total assets and percentage change in net sales for the most recent year.
2. Is American Eagle's total profitability increasing? Determine your answer by calculating the percentage change in net income for the most recent year.
3. Did American Eagle issue any common stock in the most recent year?
4. Do you see the term *debit* or *credit* listed in the balance sheet? Which account types in the balance sheet increase with a debit and which ones increase with a credit?
5. Do you see the term *debit* or *credit* listed in the income statement? Which account types in the income statement increase with a debit? Which increase with a credit?

Financial Analysis

The Buckle, Inc.

AP2–3 Financial information for **The Buckle** is presented in Appendix B at the end of the book.

Required:

1. Is The Buckle's company size increasing? Determine your answer by calculating the percentage change in total assets and percentage change in net sales for the most recent year.
2. Is The Buckle's total profitability increasing? Determine your answer by calculating the percentage change in net income for the most recent year.
3. Did The Buckle issue any common stock in the most recent year?
4. Do you see the term *debit* or *credit* listed in the balance sheet? Which account types in the balance sheet increase with a debit and which ones increase with a credit?
5. Do you see the term *debit* or *credit* listed in the income statement? Which account types in the income statement increase with a debit? Which increase with a credit?

Comparative Analysis

American Eagle Outfitters, Inc., vs. The Buckle, Inc.

AP2–4 Financial information for **American Eagle** is presented in Appendix A at the end of the book, and financial information for **The Buckle** is presented in Appendix B at the end of the book.

Required:

Determine which company's growth rate in total assets, net sales, and net income is greater. Why do you think this might be the case?

Ethics

AP2–5 Larry has been the chief financial officer (CFO) of Maxima Auto Service for the past 10 years. The company has reported profits each year it's been in business. However, this year has been a tough one. Increased competition and the rising costs of labor have reduced the company's profits. On December 30, Larry informs Robert, the company's president and Larry's closest friend for the past 10 years, that it looks like the company will report a net loss (total expenses will be greater than total revenues) of about $50,000 this year.

The next day, December 31, while Larry is preparing the year-end reports, Robert stops by Larry's office to tell him that an additional $75,000 of revenues needs to be reported and that the company can now report a profit. When Larry asks about the source of the $75,000, Robert tells him, "Earlier in the month some customers paid for auto services with cash, and with this cash I bought additional assets for the company. That's why the $75,000 never showed up in the bank statement. I just forgot to tell you about this earlier." When Larry asks for more specifics about these transactions, Robert mumbles, "I can't recall where I placed the customer sales invoices or the purchase receipts for the assets, but don't worry; I know they're here.

We've been friends for a lot of years and you can trust me. Now, let's hurry and finish those reports and I'll treat you to dinner tonight at the restaurant of your choice."

Required:
Discuss the ethical dilemma Larry faces.

Internet Research

AP2–6 Obtain a copy of the annual report of **Apple Inc.** for the most recent year. You can find the annual report at the company's website (*www.apple.com*) in the investor information section or at the Securities and Exchange Commission's website (*www.sec .gov*) using **EDGAR** (Electronic Data Gathering, Analysis, and Retrieval). Form 10-K, which includes the annual report, is required to be filed on **EDGAR**. Search or scroll within the annual report to find the financial statements.

Required:
Determine the following from the company's financial statements:
1. What amount does the company report for accounts receivable? What does this amount represent?
2. What amount does the company report for accounts payable? What does this amount represent?
3. The company reports a single amount for accrued expenses in the liability section of the balance sheet. What are some possible liabilities included in this amount?
4. What amount does the company report for common stock? What does this amount represent?
5. Determine whether the company's total assets equal total liabilities plus total stockholders' (or shareholders') equity.
6. Apple refers to its income statement as the statement of operations. What amount does the company report for net sales? This amount represents sales of the company's products over what period of time?
7. What are some of the expenses listed in the income statement?
8. Do the company's total revenues exceed total expenses? By how much?

Written Communication

AP2–7 Barth Interior provides decorating advice to its clients. Three recent transactions of the company include:
a. Providing decorating services of $500 on account to one of its clients.
b. Paying $1,200 for an employee's salary in the current period.
c. Purchasing office equipment for $2,700.

Required:
Write a memo to your instructor describing each step of the six-step measurement process presented in Illustration 2–1 for each of the three transactions.

Answers to the Self-Study Questions
1. c   2. d   3. c   4. c   5. c   6. a   7. d   8. a   9. c   10. d

CHAPTER

The Financial Reporting Process

Learning
Objectives

AFTER STUDYING THIS CHAPTER, YOU SHOULD BE ABLE TO:

■ **LO1** Record revenues using the revenue recognition principle and expenses using the matching principle.

■ **LO2** Distinguish between accrual-basis and cash-basis accounting.

■ **LO3** Demonstrate the purposes and recording of adjusting entries.

■ **LO4** Post adjusting entries and prepare an adjusted trial balance.

■ **LO5** Prepare financial statements using the adjusted trial balance.

■ **LO6** Demonstrate the purposes and recording of closing entries.

■ **LO7** Post closing entries and prepare a post-closing trial balance.

FEDERAL EXPRESS: **DELIVERING PROFITS TO INVESTORS**

Wouldn't it be great to put $1,000 into the stock market and watch your investment really grow? As a student, you may not have a lot of extra money right now, but someday you will. Which stock should you buy? Where should you buy it?

The largest stock exchange in the world in terms of value traded each day is the New York Stock Exchange (NYSE), nicknamed the "Big Board." The value of shares traded on the NYSE was approximately $20 trillion in 2009. Another popular place to find stocks is the NASDAQ (an acronym for National Association of Securities Dealers Automated Quotations system). This is an electronic stock exchange in the United States that lists more companies and, on average, trades more shares per day than any other securities market in the world. Together, the NYSE and NASDAQ offer investors thousands of stocks from which to choose. Thousands more are listed on other stock exchanges throughout the world.

With so many choices, how do you tell the winning stocks from the losing stocks? The single piece of information that best distinguishes them is *net income.* Recall that net income equals revenues minus expenses for each reporting period. It measures how profitable the business is. Since stockholders are the owners of the business, any profits of the company belong solely to them (and not to creditors). Therefore, as net income increases, so does the value of the company to its stockholders.

To see the power of net income in explaining movements in stock prices, consider the following information for **Federal Express (FedEx)**. Over the 20-year period from 1990–2009, FedEx's net income increased in 14 of 20 years. For the other six years, net income decreased. What happened to FedEx's stock price in each of these years? In the years that net income increased, FedEx's stock price *rose* an average of 21.0%. In contrast, in the years that net income decreased, FedEx's stock price *fell* an average of 9.6%. The goal is clear: Predict the direction of the change in net income and you'll predict the change in stock prices.

PART A

ACCRUAL-BASIS ACCOUNTING

Net income, while certainly not the only consideration, is an essential aspect of good investment decisions. Investors know that any information they gather to help in predicting net income will lead to more profitable investments. Given the importance of net income to investors, standard setters have devoted considerable attention to the proper measurement of the two primary components of net income—revenues and expenses. In this section, we look at important principles behind reporting of revenues and expenses and at their effect on accounting.

Revenue and Expense Reporting

■ LO1
Record revenues using the revenue recognition principle and expenses using the matching principle.

If accounting information is to be useful in making decisions, accountants must measure and report revenues and expenses in a way that clearly reflects the ability of the company to create value for its owners, the stockholders. To do this, we use accrual-basis accounting, in which we record revenues when we earn them (the revenue recognition principle) and we record expenses with related revenues (the matching principle). We discuss these two principles next.

REVENUE RECOGNITION PRINCIPLE

A company records revenues when it sells its product or provides its service to a customer. For example, revenues are recorded when **Federal Express** delivers a package, **Reebok** sells a pair of shoes, **AMC Theatres** sells a movie ticket, **American Eagle** sells a shirt, or **GEICO** provides insurance coverage. The overriding concept in understanding how to properly record revenue is the revenue recognition principle. The revenue recognition principle states that we record revenue in the period in which we *earn* it. If a company sells products or provides services to a customer in 2012, the firm should report the revenue in its 2012 income statement. If the company sells products or provides services to a customer in 2013, it should report the revenue in the 2013 income statement, and so on.

Recognize revenue when it is earned.

To illustrate, suppose Calvin wants to surprise his wife Ruby with a 12-day, Hawaiian cruise to celebrate their 35th wedding anniversary. He books the cruise with **Carnival Cruise Lines**. He makes reservations and pays for the cruise in November 2012, but the cruise is not scheduled to sail until April 2013. When does Carnival report revenue from the ticket sale? Although the company receives Calvin's cash from the ticket sale in November 2012, it does not report revenue at this time because it has not substantially fulfilled its obligation to Calvin. It has not yet provided the services. Carnival will recognize the revenue in April 2013 when the cruise occurs.

It works the other way, too. Suppose that, anticipating the cruise, Calvin buys a Jimmy Buffett CD from **Best Buy**. Rather than paying cash, Calvin uses his Best Buy card to buy the CD on account. Even though Best Buy doesn't receive cash immediately from Calvin, it still records the revenue at the time it sells the CD.

 KEY POINT

The revenue recognition principle states that we should recognize revenue in the period in which we *earn* it, not necessarily in the period in which we receive cash.

MATCHING PRINCIPLE

You've heard it said, "It takes money to make money." That's true for all businesses. To make money from the sale of goods and services, companies must spend money on such essentials as advertising, workers' salaries, utilities, office rent, equipment, and business supplies. We've discussed how use of the revenue recognition principle affects when we record revenues. Now let's discuss when we record *expenses,* the costs associated with producing these revenues.

The matching principle states that we recognize expenses *in the same period as the revenues they help to generate.* Implied in this principle is a *cause-and-effect* relationship between revenue and expense recognition. In a given period, we report revenue as it is earned, according to the revenue recognition principle. It's logical, then, that in the same period we should also record all expenses incurred to generate that revenue. The result is a measure—net income—that matches current period accomplishments (revenues) and sacrifices (expenses). That's the matching principle.

To see how the matching principle is applied, let's look back at Calvin and Ruby's Hawaiian cruise. What costs does Carnival Cruise Lines incur in order to generate the revenue from providing a cruise in April 2013? Some of the costs necessary to operate a cruise ship include:

1. The purchase of supplies the month before the cruise to prepare for sailing.
2. The purchase of fuel in the month of the cruise.
3. The payment of the captain's and other crew members' salaries in the month after the cruise.

Regardless of when Carnival actually pays the cash for these costs, the company should "expense the costs"—report the costs as expenses—in April. By doing this, Carnival reports the expenses in the same period as the revenue the expenses helped to generate. Illustration 3–1 shows how these costs would be expensed using the matching principle.

> Expenses are reported with the revenues they help to generate.

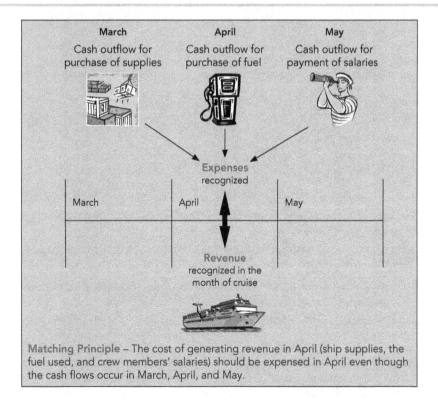

ILLUSTRATION 3–1
Matching Principle

Matching Principle – The cost of generating revenue in April (ship supplies, the fuel used, and crew members' salaries) should be expensed in April even though the cash flows occur in March, April, and May.

It's easy to see how these costs helped to generate the ticket revenue in April. Purchasing ship supplies is necessary for providing a cruise. Likewise, fuel is necessary for the ship to sail. Salaries are necessary to pay workers to operate the ship and serve the guests. All three costs are necessary to generate the ticket revenue in April, so we record them as expenses in April.

Of course, these are but a few of the costs of a cruise. Some costs are only indirectly related to producing revenue. For example, salaries paid in April 2013 to an office worker at Carnival's executive offices in Miami, Florida, are not directly related to the ticket revenue. But even such indirect costs contribute to overall operations, including cruise revenue, and so are expensed in April.

Sometimes it's impossible to determine in which period or periods, if any, revenues will occur. For example, consider the cost of advertising. Calvin may have booked the April 2013 cruise because of an advertisement (television, radio, print, Internet, cell phone) by Carnival back in November 2012. In theory, it would be ideal for Carnival to record the cost of this advertisement as an expense in April at the same time it records the revenue the advertisement helped to generate. However, it's difficult to determine when, how much, or even whether additional revenues occur as a result of a particular series of ads. Because of this obstacle, firms generally recognize advertising expenditures as expenses *in the period the ads are provided*, with no attempt made to match them with related revenues.

KEY POINT

The matching principle states that we recognize expenses in the same period as the revenues they help to generate. Expenses include those directly and indirectly related to producing revenues.

Decision Point

Question ?	Accounting information 📄	Analysis 🔍
Can the company earn revenues that exceed the cost of doing so?	Revenues and expenses reported in the income statement	Revenues measure the amount earned during the year. Expenses measure the cost of earning those revenues. Together, these two combine to measure net income, or profitability.

Accrual-Basis Compared with Cash-Basis Accounting

■ LO2
Distinguish between accrual-basis and cash-basis accounting.

In the preceding section, we discovered the following about accrual-basis accounting:

1. We record revenues when we earn them (the revenue recognition principle) and *not necessarily when we receive cash*.
2. We record expenses with related revenues (the matching principle) and *not necessarily when we pay cash*.

Under accrual-basis accounting, we record revenue and expense transactions *at the time the earnings-related activities occur.*

Cash-basis accounting is not part of generally accepted accounting principles (GAAP).

Cash-basis accounting provides an alternative way of recording revenues and expenses. Under cash-basis accounting, we record *revenues at the time we receive cash and expenses at the time we pay cash.* For example, recall in our Carnival example that Calvin purchased tickets in November 2012, for a Hawaiian cruise in April 2013. Under cash-basis accounting, the cruise line would report revenue in November 2012, at the time Calvin pays cash for the cruise, and it would record expenses as it pays cash for them over several months (rather than recording revenue in April 2013 in accord with the revenue recognition principle and related expenses in April 2013 in accord with the matching principle).

Cash-basis accounting may seem appealing because it is essentially how we think about the inflow and outflow of cash from our bank accounts. However, **because cash-basis accounting violates both the revenue recognition principle and the matching principle, it is generally not accepted in preparing financial statements.** We briefly study cash-basis accounting, though, to help provide a better understanding of the advantages and disadvantages of accrual-basis accounting.

Illustrations 3–2 and 3–3 demonstrate the timing difference between accrual-basis and cash-basis accounting by referring back to our example in Illustration 3–1 involving Ruby and Calvin's Hawaiian cruise.

		Recognize Revenue?		
		Accrual-Basis	**Cash-Basis**	
November 2012	Company receives cash from Ruby and Calvin for Hawaiian cruise next April.	No	Yes	**ILLUSTRATION 3–2** Accrual-Basis Revenue versus Cash-Basis Revenue
April 2013	Company provides cruise services to Ruby and Calvin.	Yes	No	

		Recognize Expense?		
		Accrual-Basis	**Cash-Basis**	
March 2013	Company pays cash for supplies to be used *next* month.	No	Yes	**ILLUSTRATION 3–3** Accrual-Basis Expense versus Cash-Basis Expense
April 2013	Company uses supplies purchased *last* month.	Yes	No	
	Company pays cash for fuel used during the cruise *this* month.	Yes	Yes	
	Employees earn salaries but will not be paid until *next* month.	Yes	No	
May 2013	Company pays cash to employees for salaries earned *last* month.	No	Yes	

Under both accrual-basis and cash-basis accounting, all revenues and expenses are eventually recorded for the same amount. In fact, over the life of the company, accrual-basis net income equals cash-basis net income. **The difference between the two methods is in the timing of when we record those revenues and expenses.** Under accrual-basis accounting, we record revenues when earned and expenses when we incur them. Under cash-basis accounting, we record revenues and expenses at the time we receive or pay cash.

 KEY POINT

The difference between accrual-basis accounting and cash-basis accounting is *timing.* Under accrual-basis accounting, we record revenues when we earn them (revenue recognition principle) and record expenses with the revenue they help to generate (matching principle). Under cash-basis accounting, we record revenues when we receive cash and expenses when we pay cash. Cash-basis accounting is not allowed for financial reporting purposes.

Let's Review

Cavalier Company experienced the following set of events:

May: *Receives cash* from customers for services to be provided in June.
June: *Provides services* to customers who prepaid in May.
May: *Pays cash* for supplies but does not use them.
June: *Uses the supplies* purchased in May.

Required:

1. Indicate in which month Cavalier records revenues under:
   a. Accrual-basis accounting
   b. Cash-basis accounting

2. Indicate in which month Cavalier records expenses under:
   a. Accrual-basis accounting
   b. Cash-basis accounting

Suggested Homework:
BE3-4, BE3-5;
E3-3, E3-4;
P3-1A&B; P3-2A&B

Solution:

1a. June   1b. May   2a. June   2b. May

PART B   THE MEASUREMENT PROCESS

In Chapter 2, we discussed the initial part of the accounting cycle process, measurement of external transactions. In this chapter, we will complete the accounting cycle process summarized in Illustration 3–4. First we continue the measurement process by recording adjusting entries (or internal transactions). Following adjusting entries, we will prepare financial statements and then close the books at the end of the period.

ILLUSTRATION 3–4
Steps in the
Accounting Cycle

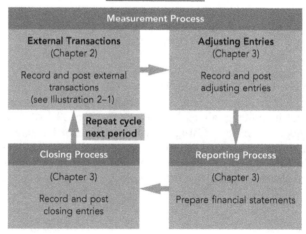

ACCOUNTING CYCLE

Adjusting Entries

■ **LO3**
Demonstrate the
purposes and
recording of
adjusting entries.

At the end of a reporting period, even if we've accurately recorded every external transaction that occurred and accurately posted those transactions to appropriate accounts, our account balances are not updated for preparing financial statements. Before we can prepare the financial statements, we need to bring several of the accounts up-to-date. That's the purpose of adjusting entries. We use adjusting entries to record events that have occurred but that we have not yet recorded.

To envision the process, think of your auto insurance. Insurance companies require you to pay for insurance in advance. On the day you purchased the insurance, you actually bought an *asset* representing insurance coverage over a future period. With each passing day, however, the length of your policy is lapsing, decreasing your insurance asset. Tomorrow you will have one day less insurance coverage than you do today.

The same holds true for a business and its insurance coverage. Although it's true that the company's asset is declining daily, it is unnecessary (and in fact impractical) to record the lapsing of the insurance coverage each day. Recording the expense is necessary, though, when it's time to prepare financial statements at the end of the reporting period. Thus, we use an end-of-period *adjusting entry*. In the case of the insurance coverage, the business adjusts downward the balance of the asset (prepaid insurance) and records insurance expense for the amount of the policy that has lapsed.

If we do not record the adjusting entry for the part of the insurance policy that has lapsed, then total assets will be overstated and expenses will be understated, causing net income to be overstated. This kind of misstatement can mislead users of financial statements. Because adjusting entries allow for proper application of the revenue recognition principle (revenues) or the matching principle (expenses), they are a *necessary part of accrual-basis accounting*. They must be recorded at the end of each period before the company prepares its financial statements.

 KEY POINT

Adjusting entries are a necessary part of accrual-basis accounting. They help to record revenues in the period earned and expenses in the period they are incurred to generate those revenues. Another benefit is that, by properly recording revenues and expenses, we correctly state assets and liabilities.

It is useful to group adjusting entries into two broad categories—prepayments and accruals—that can be further divided into four subcategories: prepaid expenses, unearned revenues, accrued expenses, and accrued revenues. These four occur as follows.

Prepayments
Prepaid expenses—We paid cash (or had an obligation to pay cash) for the purchase of an asset *before* we incurred the expense.
Unearned revenues—We received cash and recorded a liability *before* we earned the revenue.

Accruals
Accrued expenses—We paid cash *after* we incurred the expense and recorded a liability.
Accrued revenues—We received cash *after* we earned the revenue and recorded an asset.

Let's consider each of these situations. The easiest way to understand adjusting entries is to look at some examples. So, look back to the external transactions of Eagle Golf Academy from Chapter 2. For easy reference, we've restated these transactions in Illustration 3–5 (next page). We will prepare all adjusting entries on January 31, to account for revenue and expense transactions that have not been recorded by the end of the month.

PREPAID EXPENSES

Prepaid expenses are the costs of assets acquired in one period that will be expensed in a future period (like the insurance coverage mentioned previously). The cash outflow (or obligation to pay cash, in the case of assets bought on account)

	Transaction	Date	External Transactions in January	Type of Activity
ILLUSTRATION 3–5 External Transactions of Eagle Golf Academy	(1)	Jan. 1	Sell shares of common stock for $25,000 to obtain the funds necessary to start the business.	Financing
	(2)	Jan. 1	Borrow $10,000 from the local bank and sign a note promising to repay the full amount of the debt in three years.	Financing
	(3)	Jan. 1	Purchase equipment necessary for giving golf training, $24,000 cash.	Investing
	(4)	Jan. 1	Pay one year of rent in advance, $6,000 ($500 per month).	Operating
	(5)	Jan. 6	Purchase supplies on account, $2,300.	Operating
	(6)	Jan. 12	Provide golf training to customers for cash, $3,600.	Operating
	(7)	Jan. 17	Provide golf training to customers on account, $2,500.	Operating
	(8)	Jan. 23	Receive cash in advance for 10 golf training sessions to be given in the future, $600.	Operating
	(9)	Jan. 28	Pay salaries to employees, $2,800.	Operating
	(10)	Jan. 30	Pay cash dividends of $200 to shareholders.	Financing

from the purchase of an asset occurs before we record the expense. Examples are the purchase of equipment or supplies and the payment of rent or insurance in advance. These payments *create future benefits,* so we record them as assets at the time of purchase. The benefits provided by these assets *expire in future periods,* so we expense their cost in those future periods. **The adjusting entry for a prepaid expense always includes a debit to an expense account (increase an expense) and a credit to an asset account (decrease an asset).**

Eagle Golf Academy has three prepaid expenses during January: It purchases rent, supplies, and equipment. Each of these items provides future benefits and was recorded as an asset at the time of purchase. By the end of January, the company has used a portion of each asset, and that portion no longer represents a future benefit. The amount of the asset used represents an expense as well as a reduction of the asset. We'll look at each prepaid expense in turn.

Prepaid rent. Let's begin with transaction (4) in which Eagle Golf Academy purchases one year of rent in advance for $6,000 ($500 per month). The benefits from using the rented space occur evenly over time, with one month's cost attributable to January, one month to February, and so on. Therefore, we need to record one month of the asset's cost as an expense in January and include it in that month's income statement, along with the revenue it helped to produce. At the same time, the asset account has one month's less benefit with each passing month, requiring us to reduce the balance of the asset.

The end-of-period **adjusting entry** for expiration of prepaid rent is below.

January 31	Debit	Credit
Rent Expense (+E, −SE)	500	
Prepaid Rent (−A)		500
(Reduce prepaid rent due to the passage of time)		

User's Guide At this point in the book, below each journal entry we begin to include simple accounting equation analyses, to show the effects of the journal entry on the balance sheet and income statement.

Notice that the adjusting entry includes a $500 expense (+E), which reduces net income and stockholders' equity (−SE). At the same time, the balance in the asset account, Prepaid Rent, decreases (−A) by $500 and will now have a balance of $5,500 (= $6,000 − $500). We adjust any other assets that expire over time (such as prepaid insurance) in a similar manner.

Supplies.   In transaction (5), Eagle purchases supplies for $2,300 on account on January 6. Even though cash will be paid later, the cost of supplies (or obligation to pay cash for supplies) is incurred on January 6. Suppose that at the end of January a count of supplies reveals that only $1,500 of supplies remains. What happened to the other $800 of supplies? Apparently, this is the amount of supplies used during the month. Since it's not cost-efficient to record the consumption of supplies every day, we make a single adjusting entry at the end of the month for the total amount used during the period.

The end-of-period **adjusting entry** for supplies is below.

January 31	Debit	Credit
Supplies Expense (+E, −SE)	800	
Supplies (−A)		800
(Consume supplies during the current period)		

This entry simultaneously records the $800 of supplies used as an expense and reduces the balance of the Supplies account to the $1,500 amount that still remains.

Depreciable assets.   In transaction (3), Eagle purchases equipment for $24,000 cash. Let's assume that, at the time of purchase, Eagle estimates the equipment will be useful for the next five years (60 months). Because one month (January) has passed since the purchase of this asset, Eagle has used one month of the asset's estimated 60-month useful life. In addition, the company has used one month of the asset's cost to produce revenue in January. Therefore, we should *match* the cost (expense) with the revenue it helps to produce. Although this creates a situation much like that of prepaid rent or of supplies, we record the reduction in the cost of assets with longer lives using a concept called depreciation.

Depreciation is the process of allocating the cost of an asset, such as equipment, to expense. We discuss it in detail in Chapter 7; here we will cover only the basics.

The end-of-period **adjusting entry** to record one month of depreciation for equipment is below.

January 31	Debit	Credit
Depreciation Expense (+E, −SE)	400	
Accumulated Depreciation (−A)		400
(*Depreciate equipment = $24,000 ÷ 60 months = $400 per month*)		

This entry reduces the Equipment account by $400. Notice, however, that we didn't reduce Equipment directly, by crediting the asset account itself. Instead, we reduced the asset *indirectly* by crediting an account called *Accumulated Depreciation*. The Accumulated Depreciation account is called a *contra account*. A contra account is an account with a balance that is opposite, or "contra," to that of its related accounts.

The normal balance in the Accumulated Depreciation contra asset account is a *credit*, which is opposite to the normal *debit* balance in an asset account. The reason we use a contra account is to keep the original balance of the asset intact while reducing its current balance indirectly. In the balance sheet, we report equipment at its current *book value*, which equals its original cost less accumulated depreciation.

Illustration 3–6 shows how **American Airlines** records accumulated depreciation for its property and equipment. The net amount of property and equipment represents the book value, or amount of the assets' original costs less accumulated depreciation. As you will see in Chapter 7, depreciation is an *estimate* based on expected useful life and is an attempt to *allocate the cost of the asset over the useful life.* It is a calculation internal to the company and does not necessarily represent market value (what the asset could be sold for in the market).

AMERICAN AIRLINES		
Balance Sheet (partial)		
($ in millions)		
Assets		
Flight equipment, at cost	$19,601	
Less: Accumulated depreciation	(7,147)	
Book value of flight equipment		$12,454
Other equipment and property, at cost	5,132	
Less: Accumulated depreciation	(2,762)	
Book value of other equipment and property		2,370

ILLUSTRATION 3–6

Reporting Depreciation of Property and Equipment for American Airlines

 ETHICAL DILEMMA

 You have recently been employed by a large retail chain that sells sporting goods. One of your tasks is to help prepare financial statements for external distribution. The chain's largest creditor, National Savings & Loan, requires that financial statements be prepared according to generally accepted accounting principles (GAAP). During the months of November and December 2012, the company spent $1 million on a major TV advertising campaign. The $1 million included the costs of producing the commercials as well as the broadcast time purchased to run them. Because the advertising will be aired in 2012 only, you decide to charge all the costs to advertising expense in 2012, in accordance with requirements of GAAP.

The company's chief financial officer (CFO), who hired you, asks you for a favor. Instead of charging the costs to advertising expense, he asks you to set up an asset called prepaid advertising and to wait until 2013 to record any expense. The CFO explains, "This ad campaign has produced significant sales in 2012; but I think it will continue to bring in customers throughout 2013. By recording the ad costs as an asset, we can match the cost of the advertising with the additional sales in 2013. Besides, if we expense the advertising in 2012, we will show an operating loss in our income statement. The bank requires that we continue to show profits in order to maintain our loan in good standing. Failure to remain in good standing could mean we'd have to fire some of our recent hires." What should you do?

UNEARNED REVENUES

We record unearned revenues when a company receives cash in advance from a customer for products or services to be provided in the future. When customers pay cash in advance, we debit cash and credit a liability. This liability reflects the company's obligation to provide goods or services to the customer in the future. Once it has provided these products or services, the company can record revenue earned and reduce its obligation to the customer. **The adjusting entry for an unearned revenue always includes a debit to a liability account (decrease a liability) and a credit to a revenue account (increase a revenue).**

In transaction (8), Eagle receives $600 in advance from customers who will be given 10 golf lessons ($60 per lesson) in the future. Later, as Eagle provides that training to customers, it reduces the liability to customers and can record the service revenue because it now has earned it. Assume that by the end of January Eagle has provided one of the 10 training sessions paid for in advance.

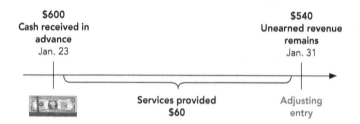

The end-of-period **adjusting entry** to account for the revenue earned is below.

January 31	Debit	Credit
Unearned Revenue (−L)	60	
Service Revenue (+R, +SE)		60
(Provide services to customers who paid in advance)		

Balance Sheet					Income Statement			
			Stockholders' Equity					
			Common	Retained				Net
Assets	=	Liabilities +	Stock +	Earnings	Revenues −	Expenses	=	Income
	=	−60		+60	+60		=	+60

Illustration 3–7 shows an example of unearned revenue for **Apple Inc.**

ILLUSTRATION 3–7

Reporting Unearned Revenues and Other Current Liabilities for Apple Inc.

Common Terms
Another common name for unearned revenue is *deferred revenue.*

APPLE INC. Balance Sheet (partial) ($ in thousands)	
Current liabilities:	
Accounts payable	$ 5,601
Unearned revenue	10,305
Other current liabilities*	3,376
Total current liabilities	$19,282

*Includes amounts owed for taxes, salaries, advertising, and other operating costs.

Most of Apple's unearned revenue comes from sales of the popular iPhone. When you purchase an iPhone, Apple does not immediately record revenue from the sale. Instead, the company spreads this revenue over the next 24 months (the life of a typical iPhone contract). In other words, if you purchase an iPhone today, Apple initially records the entire sale as unearned revenue and then begins to recognize revenue (and decrease unearned revenue) as the company earns this revenue each month for the next 24 months.

Now that we've discussed prepaid expenses and unearned revenues (prepayments), let's look at the two other categories of adjusting entries—accrued expenses and accrued revenues. Accruals are the opposite of prepayments. **Accruals occur when the cash flow occurs *after* either the expense is incurred or the revenue is earned.** Walking through some examples using our Eagle Golf Academy illustration will demonstrate both types of accruals.

ACCRUED EXPENSES

When a company has incurred an expense but hasn't yet paid cash or recorded an obligation to pay, it still should record the expense. This is referred to as an accrued expense. **The adjusting entry for an accrued expense always includes a debit to an expense account (increase an expense) and a credit to a liability account (increase a liability).**

Accrued salaries.   Eagle pays total salaries to its employees of $100 per day. For the first four weeks (28 days), Eagle pays $2,800 cash to employees. For simplicity, we combined each of these four weeks in transaction (9) in Illustration 3–5. For the remaining three days in January, employees earn additional salaries of $300, but Eagle doesn't plan to pay the employees until the end of the week, February 4. However, Eagle must record the $300 salaries expense in the month employees worked (January). Stated differently, the salaries expense *accrues* during January even though the company won't pay the expense until February.

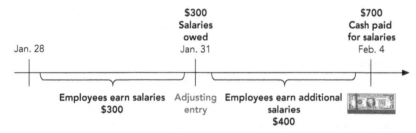

The end-of-period adjusting entry for accrued salaries is below.

January 31	Debit	Credit
Salaries Expense (+E, −SE)	300	
Salaries Payable (+L)		300
(Owe for salaries earned by employees in the current period)		

Accrued utility costs.   At the end of January, Eagle receives a utility bill for $960 associated with operations in January. Eagle plans to pay the bill on February 6. Even though it won't pay the cash until February, Eagle must record the utility costs for January as an expense in January. The firm records the corresponding obligation to the utility company at the same time.

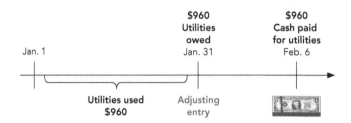

The end-of-period **adjusting entry** is below.

January 31	Debit	Credit
Utilities Expense (+E, −SE)	960	
Utilities Payable (+L)		960
(Owe for utilities costs in the current period)		

Accrued interest. In transaction (2), Eagle borrows $10,000 from the bank to begin operations. Assume the bank charges Eagle annual interest of 12% (or 1% per month) on the borrowed amount. Interest is due by the end of the year, but repayment of the $10,000 borrowed is not due for three years. By the end of the first month, the loan has accrued interest of $100, calculated as follows:

Amount of note payable	×	Annual interest rate	×	Fraction of the year	=	Interest
$10,000	×	12%	×	1/12	=	$100

Notice that we multiplied by 1/12 to calculate the interest for one month (out of 12). If we had calculated interest for a two-month period, we would have multiplied by 2/12; for three months we would have multiplied by 3/12; and so on.

Although Eagle won't pay the $100 until the end of the year, it is a cost of using the borrowed funds during January and therefore is an expense for January.

The end-of-period **adjusting entry** for interest payable is below.

January 31	Debit	Credit
Interest Expense (+E, −SE)	100	
Interest Payable (+L)		100
(Owe for interest charges in the current period)		

Balance Sheet					Income Statement			
			Stockholders' Equity					
Assets	=	Liabilities	+	**Common Stock**	**Retained Earnings**	Revenues	− Expenses	= **Net Income**
	=	+100			−100		+100	= −100

COMMON MISTAKE

When recording the interest payable on a borrowed amount, students sometimes mistakenly credit the liability associated with the principal amount (Notes Payable). We record interest payable in a *separate account* (Interest Payable), to keep the balance owed for principal separate from the balance owed for interest.

ACCRUED REVENUES

When a company has earned revenue but hasn't yet received cash or recorded an amount receivable, it still should record the revenue. This is referred to as an accrued revenue. **The adjusting entry for an accrued revenue always includes a debit to an asset account (increase an asset) and a credit to a revenue account (increase a revenue).**

Interest receivable. We can see an example of accrued revenues if we review the flip side of transaction (2), which we discussed in the previous section. The bank lends Eagle Golf Academy $10,000 and charges Eagle annual interest of 12% (or 1% per month) on the borrowed amount. By the end of the month, interest has been earned each day, but the bank has not yet recorded the interest because it is impractical to record interest on a daily basis. At the end of January, the bank records interest revenue earned of $100 (= $10,000 × 12% × 1/12). The bank's adjusting entry for January will include a debit to Interest Receivable and a credit to Interest Revenue for $100. Note that this is the same amount that Eagle Golf Academy, the borrower, records as Interest Expense.

Flip Side

Accounts receivable. Revenue also accrues when a firm performs services but has not yet collected cash or billed the customer. Suppose, for instance, that Eagle provides $200 of golf training to customers from January 28 to January 31. However, it usually takes Eagle one week to mail bills to customers and another week for customers to pay. Therefore, Eagle expects to receive cash from these customers during February 8–14. Because Eagle earned the revenue in January (regardless of when cash receipt takes place), Eagle should recognize in January the service revenue and the amount receivable from those customers.

The end-of-period **adjusting entry** is below.

January 31	Debit	Credit
Accounts Receivable (+A)	200	
Service Revenue (+R, +SE)		200
(Bill customers for services provided during the current period)		

 KEY POINT

Adjusting entries are needed when cash flows or obligations occur *before* the earnings-related activity (prepayment) or when cash flows occur *after* the earnings-related activity (accrual).

NO ADJUSTMENT NECESSARY

Notice that we did not make any adjusting entries associated with transaction (1) or (10) for Eagle Golf Academy. Transaction (1) is the sale of common stock, and transaction (10) is the payment of dividends to common stockholders. **Neither of these transactions involves the recognition of revenues or expenses and therefore will not require month-end adjusting entries.**

Similarly, **transactions in which we (1) receive cash at the same time we earn revenue or (2) pay cash at the same time we incur an expense will not require adjusting entries.** For example, when Eagle provides golf training to customers for cash [transaction (6)], the company records revenue at the same time it records the cash received, and no corresponding month-end adjusting entry is needed.

 KEY POINT

Adjusting entries are *unnecessary* in two cases: (1) for transactions that do not involve revenue or expense activities and (2) for transactions that result in revenues or expenses being recorded at the same time as the cash flow.

Below are four scenarios for a local **Midas Muffler** shop for the month of September.

Scenario 1: On September 1, the balance of maintenance supplies totals $400. On September 15, the shop purchases an additional $200 of maintenance supplies. By the end of September, only $100 of maintenance supplies remains.

Scenario 2: On September 4, Midas receives $6,000 cash from a local moving company in an agreement to provide truck maintenance of $1,000 each month for the next six months, beginning in September.

Scenario 3: Mechanics have worked the final four days in September, earning $600, but have not yet been paid. Midas plans to pay its mechanics on October 2.

Scenario 4: Customers receiving $250 of maintenance services from Midas on September 29 have not been billed as of the end of the month. These customers will be billed on October 3 and are expected to pay the full amount owed on October 6.

Required:

For each of the scenarios:

1. Indicate the type of adjusting entry needed.
2. Record the transaction described and the month-end adjusting entry.

Solution:

Scenario 1: Adjusting entry type: Prepaid expense.

September 15 (external transaction)	Debit	Credit
Supplies (+A)	200	
Cash (−A)		200
(*Purchase maintenance supplies for cash*)		

September 30 (month-end adjusting entry)	Debit	Credit
Supplies Expense (+E, −SE)	500	
Supplies (−A)		500
(*Consume supplies*)		
(*$400 + $200 − $100 = $500*)		

Scenario 2: Adjusting entry type: Unearned revenue.

September 4 (external transaction)	Debit	Credit
Cash (+A)	6,000	
Unearned Revenue (+L)		6,000
(*Receive cash in advance from customers*)		

September 30 (month-end adjusting entry)	Debit	Credit
Unearned Revenue (−L)	1,000	
Service Revenue (+R, +SE)		1,000
(*Provide first of six months of services*)		

Scenario 3: Adjusting entry type: Accrued expense.

September 30 (month-end adjusting entry)	Debit	Credit
Salaries Expense (+E, −SE)	600	
Salaries Payable (+L)		600
(*Owe for salaries earned by employees in the current period*)		
October 2 (external transaction)	Debit	Credit
Salaries Payable (−L)	600	
Cash (−A)		600
(*Pay salaries owed*)		

Scenario 4: Adjusting entry type: Accrued revenue.

September 30 (month-end adjusting entry)	Debit	Credit
Accounts Receivable (+A)	250	
Service Revenue (+R, +SE)		250
(*Provide maintenance service on account*)		
October 6 (external transaction)	Debit	Credit
Cash (+A)	250	
Accounts Receivable (−A)		250
(*Collect cash from customers previously billed*)		

Suggested Homework:
BE3-6, BE3-10;
E3-7, E3-8;
P3-3A&B, P3-4A&B

Post Adjusting Entries

■ **LO4**
Post adjusting entries and prepare an adjusted trial balance.

To complete the measurement process, we need to update balances of assets, liabilities, revenues, and expenses for adjusting entries. In Illustration 3–8, we summarize the eight adjusting entries of Eagle Golf Academy recorded earlier. To update balances, we post the adjustments to the appropriate accounts in the general ledger, as demonstrated in Illustration 3–9.

ILLUSTRATION 3–8

Summary of Adjusting Entries for Eagle Golf Academy

January 31	Debit	Credit
(a) Rent Expense (+E, −SE)	500	
Prepaid Rent (−A)		500
(*Reduce prepaid rent due to the passage of time*)		
(b) Supplies Expense (+E, −SE)	800	
Supplies (−A)		800
(*Consume supplies during the current period*)		
(c) Depreciation Expense (+E, −SE)	400	
Accumulated Depreciation (−A)		400
(*Depreciate equipment*)		
($24,000 ÷ 60 months = $400 per month)		
(d) Unearned Revenue (−L)	60	
Service Revenue (+R, +SE)		60
(*Provide services to customers who paid in advance*)		
(e) Salaries Expense (+E, −SE)	300	
Salaries Payable (+L)		300
(*Owe for salaries earned by employees in the current period*)		

ILLUSTRATION 3–8

Summary of Adjusting Entries for Eagle Golf Academy *(continued)*

(f) **Utilities Expense** (+*E*, −*SE*)	960	
Utilities Payable (+*L*)		960
(Owe for utilities costs in the current period)		
(g) **Interest Expense** (+*E*, −*SE*)	100	
Interest Payable (+*L*)		100
(Owe for interest charges in the current period)		
(h) **Accounts Receivable** (+*A*)	200	
Service Revenue (+*R*, +*SE*)		200
(Bill customers for services provided during the month)		

ILLUSTRATION 3–9   Posting Adjusting Entries (in red) of Eagle Golf Academy to General Ledger Accounts

Assets	=	Liabilities	+	Stockholders' Equity

Cash

(1)	25,000	(3)	24,000
(2)	10,000	(4)	6,000
(6)	3,600	(9)	2,800
(8)	600	(10)	200
Bal.	**6,200**		

Accounts Receivable

(7)	2,500	
(h)	200	
Bal.	**2,700**	

Supplies

(5)	2,300		
		(b)	800
Bal.	**1,500**		

Prepaid Rent

(4)	6,000		
		(a)	500
Bal.	**5,500**		

Equipment

(3)	24,000	
Bal.	**24,000**	

Accumulated Depreciation

		(c)	400
		Bal.	**400**

Accounts Payable

		(5)	2,300
		Bal.	**2,300**

Unearned Revenue

		(8)	600
(d)	60		
		Bal.	**540**

Salaries Payable

		(e)	300
		Bal.	**300**

Utilities Payable

		(f)	960
		Bal.	**960**

Interest Payable

		(g)	100
		Bal.	**100**

Notes Payable

		(2)	10,000
		Bal.	**10,000**

Common Stock

		(1)	25,000
		Bal.	**25,000**

Dividends

(10)	200	
Bal.	**200**	

Supplies Expense

(b)	800	
Bal.	**800**	

Depreciation Expense

(c)	400	
Bal.	**400**	

Utilities Expense

(f)	960	
Bal.	**960**	

Retained Earnings

			0
		Bal.	**0**

Service Revenue

		(6)	3,600
		(7)	2,500
		(d)	60
		(h)	200
		Bal.	**6,360**

Rent Expense

(a)	500	
Bal.	**500**	

Salaries Expense

(9)	2,800	
(e)	300	
Bal.	**3,100**	

Interest Expense

(g)	100	
Bal.	**100**	

- Amounts in black represent external transactions in January. Numbers in parentheses refer to transaction numbers in Illustration 3–5.
- Amounts in red represent month-end adjusting entries. Letters in parentheses refer to adjusting entries in Illustration 3–8.
- Amounts in **bold** represent ending balances.

COMMON MISTAKE

Students sometimes mistakenly include the Cash account in an adjusting entry. An adjusting entry will never include the Cash account. Note that no adjusting entries are posted to the Cash account in Illustration 3–9.

KEY POINT

We post adjusting entries to the T-accounts in the general ledger to update the account balances.

ADJUSTED TRIAL BALANCE

After we have posted the adjusting entries to the general ledger accounts, we're ready to prepare an *adjusted* trial balance. An adjusted trial balance is a list of all accounts and their balances *after we have updated account balances for adjusting entries*. Illustration 3–10 shows the relationship between an unadjusted trial

ILLUSTRATION 3–10

Unadjusted Trial Balance and Adjusted Trial Balance for Eagle Golf Academy

	EAGLE GOLF ACADEMY Unadjusted Trial Balance and Adjusted Trial Balance January 31					
Accounts	**Unadjusted Trial Balance**		**Adjustments**		**Adjusted Trial Balance**	
	Debit	**Credit**	**Debit**	**Credit**	**Debit**	**Credit**
Cash	$ 6,200				$ 6,200	
Accounts Receivable	2,500		(h) 200		2,700	
Supplies	2,300			(b) 800	1,500	
Prepaid Rent	6,000			(a) 500	5,500	
Equipment	24,000				24,000	
Accumulated Depreciation				(c) 400		$ 400
Accounts Payable		$ 2,300				2,300
Unearned Revenue		600	(d) 60			540
Salaries Payable				(e) 300		300
Utilities Payable				(f) 960		960
Interest Payable				(g) 100		100
Notes Payable		10,000				10,000
Common Stock		25,000				25,000
Retained Earnings		0				0
Dividends	200				200	
Service Revenue		6,100		(d and h) 260		6,360
Supplies Expense			(b) 800		800	
Rent Expense			(a) 500		500	
Depreciation Expense			(c) 400		400	
Salaries Expense	2,800		(e) 300		3,100	
Utilities Expense			(f) 960		960	
Interest Expense			(g) 100		100	
Totals	**$44,000**	**$44,000**			**$45,960**	**$45,960**

Total debits equal total credits.

balance (before adjustments) and an adjusted trial balance (after adjustments). The unadjusted trial balance is the one shown in Chapter 2 in Illustration 2–26. The adjusted trial balance includes the adjusted balances of all general ledger accounts shown in Illustration 3–9.

 KEY POINT

An adjusted trial balance is a list of all accounts and their balances at a particular date, after we have updated account balances for adjusting entries.

THE REPORTING PROCESS: FINANCIAL STATEMENTS

PART C

Once the adjusted trial balance is complete, we prepare financial statements. Illustration 3–11 describes the relationship between the adjusted trial balance and the financial statements. Notice the color coding of the accounts, to indicate their relationships to the financial statements.

■ **LO5**
Prepare financial statements using the adjusted trial balance.

ILLUSTRATION 3–11

Relationship between Adjusted Trial Balance and Financial Statements

EAGLE GOLF ACADEMY Adjusted Trial Balance January 31		
Accounts	**Debit**	**Credit**
Cash	$ 6,200	
Accounts Receivable	2,700	
Supplies	1,500	
Prepaid Rent	5,500	
Equipment	24,000	
Accumulated Depreciation		$ 400
Accounts Payable		2,300
Unearned Revenue		540
Salaries Payable		300
Interest Payable		100
Utilities Payable		960
Notes Payable		10,000
Common Stock		25,000
Retained Earnings		0
Dividends	200	
Service Revenue		6,360
Supplies Expense	800	
Rent Expense	500	
Depreciation Expense	400	
Salaries Expense	3,100	
Utilities Expense	960	
Interest Expense	100	
Totals	$45,960	$45,960

BALANCE SHEET
Assets
=
Liabilities
+
Stockholders'
Equity

INCOME STATEMENT
Revenues
−
Expenses
=
Net Income

STATEMENT OF STOCKHOLDERS' EQUITY

Common Stock
+
Retained Earnings
(= RE, Jan. 1 + NI − Divs)
=
Stockholders' Equity

Revenue and expense accounts are reported in the income statement. The difference between total revenues and total expenses equals net income. All asset, liability, and stockholders' equity accounts are reported in the balance sheet. The balance sheet confirms the equality of the basic accounting equation.

Income Statement

Illustration 3–12 shows the income statement of Eagle Golf Academy for the month of January. Note that, unlike the income statements shown in Chapter 1, this income statement has a *multicolumn* format: Amounts for individual items are placed in the left column, and subtotals are placed in the right column. Presenting the income statement in this manner makes it easier to see that net income equals the difference between total revenues and total expenses.

The income statement demonstrates that Eagle Golf Academy earned a profit of $500 in the month of January. The revenues earned from providing training to customers exceed the costs of providing that training.

ILLUSTRATION 3–12

Income Statement for Eagle Golf Academy

Revenues minus expenses equal net income.

EAGLE GOLF ACADEMY Income Statement For the month ended January 31		
Revenues:		
Service revenue		$6,360
Expenses:		
Salaries expense	$3,100	
Rent expense	500	
Supplies expense	800	
Depreciation expense	400	
Interest expense	100	
Utilities expense	960	
Total expenses		5,860
Net income		$ 500

Statement of Stockholders' Equity

The statement of stockholders' equity summarizes the changes in each stockholders' equity account as well as in total stockholders' equity and the accounting value of the company to stockholders (owners). Illustration 3–13 shows the statement of stockholders' equity for Eagle Golf Academy.

ILLUSTRATION 3–13

Statement of Stockholders' Equity for Eagle Golf Academy

Retained earnings includes net income from the income statement.

EAGLE GOLF ACADEMY Statement of Stockholders' Equity For the month ended January 31	Common Stock	Retained Earnings	Total Stockholders' Equity
Balance at January 1	$ -0-	$ -0-	$ -0-
Issuance of common stock	25,000		25,000
Add: Net income for January		500	500
Less: Dividends		(200)	(200)
Balance at January 31	$25,000	$300	$25,300

Total stockholders' equity increases from **$0** at the beginning of January to **$25,300** by the end of January. The increase occurs as a result of a **$25,000** investment by the owners (stockholders) when they bought common stock plus an increase of **$300** when the company earned a profit of $500 on behalf of its stockholders and distributed $200 of dividends.

You've seen that retained earnings has three components: revenues, expenses, and dividends. In the adjusted trial balance, the balance of the Retained Earnings account is its balance at the beginning of the accounting period—the balance *before* all revenue, expense, and dividend transactions. For Eagle Golf Academy, the beginning balance of Retained Earnings equals $0 since this is the first month of operations. Ending Retained Earnings equals its beginning balance of $0 plus the effects of all revenue and expense transactions (net income of $500) less dividends of **$200** paid to stockholders. Since dividends represent the payment of company resources (cash), they will have a negative effect on the stockholders' equity (retained earnings) of the company.

Classified Balance Sheet

The balance sheet you saw in Chapter 1 contained the key asset, liability, and stockholders' equity accounts, presented as a rather simple list. Here, we introduce a slightly more complex form of the balance sheet, with many more accounts. To put those accounts in an order that enables ease of understanding, we use a format called the classified balance sheet.

Common Terms
Another common name for current assets and liabilities is *short-term assets and liabilities.*

A classified balance sheet groups a company's assets, liabilities, and stockholders' equity accounts into several standard categories: We can separate assets into those that provide a benefit over the next year (*current assets*) and those that provide a benefit for more than one year (*long-term assets*). More precisely, the distinction between current and long-term assets is whether the asset will benefit the firm for more than one year or an *operating cycle,* whichever is longer. The operating cycle is the average time between purchasing or acquiring inventory and receiving cash proceeds from its sale. For nearly all firms, the operating cycle is shorter than one year. Similarly, we can divide liabilities into those due during the next year (*current liabilities*) and those due in more than one year (*long-term liabilities*).

Illustration 3–14 (next page) presents a classified balance sheet for Eagle Golf Academy. As we discuss later in the book, long-term assets are further classified into groups. Long-term asset categories include investments; property, plant, and equipment; and intangible assets:

- *Long-term investments* involve a company paying cash to invest in another company's debt or stock. We discuss long-term investments in debt and equity securities in Appendix D.
- *Property, plant, and equipment* items include long-term productive assets used in the normal course of business, such as land, buildings, equipment, and machinery. Eagle's purchase of training equipment is an example of a purchase of property, plant, and equipment. We discuss property, plant, and equipment in Chapter 7.
- *Intangible assets* are assets that lack physical substance but have long-term value to a company, such as patents, copyrights, franchises, and trademarks. We discuss intangible assets in Chapter 7.

ILLUSTRATION 3–14

Classified Balance Sheet for Eagle Golf Academy

Total assets equal current plus long-term assets.

Total liabilities equal current plus long-term liabilities.

Total stockholders' equity includes common stock and retained earnings from the statement of stockholders' equity.

Total assets must equal total liabilities plus stockholders' equity.

EAGLE GOLF ACADEMY				
Classified Balance Sheet				
January 31				
Assets			**Liabilities**	
Current assets:			Current liabilities:	
Cash	$ 6,200		Accounts payable	$ 2,300
Accounts receivable	2,700		Unearned revenue	540
Supplies	1,500		Salaries payable	300
Prepaid rent	5,500		Utilities payable	960
Total current assets	15,900		Interest payable	100
			Total current liabilities	4,200
Long-term assets:				
Equipment	24,000		Long-term liabilities:	
Less: Accum. depr.	(400)		Notes payable	10,000
			Total liabilities	14,200
Total long-term assets	23,600			
			Stockholders' Equity	
			Common stock	25,000
			Retained earnings	300
			Total stockholders' equity	25,300
Total assets	$39,500		Total liabilities and stockholders' equity	$39,500

In Illustration 3–14, notice that total assets of $39,500 equal total liabilities and stockholders' equity of $39,500. We achieve this equality only by including the correct balance of **$300** for retained earnings from the statement of stockholders' equity, *not* the balance of $0 from the adjusted trial balance.

 KEY POINT

We prepare the income statement, statement of stockholders' equity, and balance sheet from the adjusted trial balance. The income statement provides a measure of net income (profitability), calculated as revenues minus expenses. The balance sheet demonstrates that assets equal liabilities plus stockholders' equity (the basic accounting equation).

Statement of Cash Flows

The final financial statement we need to prepare is the statement of cash flows. As discussed in Chapter 1, the statement of cash flows measures activities involving cash receipts and cash payments, reflecting a company's operating, investing, and financing activities. We'll take another brief look at the statement of cash flows in the next chapter and then discuss it in detail in Chapter 11.

THE CLOSING PROCESS

Recall that revenues, expenses, and dividends are components of retained earnings. Notice that Eagle's balance sheet reports retained earnings of $300, as if all net income transactions (revenues and expenses) and dividend transactions had been recorded directly in Retained Earnings. However, instead of recording revenue, expense, and dividend transactions directly to the Retained Earnings account during the period, we recorded them to the three component accounts. This allows us to maintain individual measures of revenues, expenses, and dividends for preparing financial statements at the end of the period.

■ **LO6**
Demonstrate the purposes and recording of closing entries.

After we have reported revenues and expenses in the income statement and dividends in the statement of stockholders' equity, it's time to transfer these amounts to the Retained Earnings account itself. These three accounts—revenues, expenses, and dividends—are termed temporary accounts: We keep them for each period and then transfer the balances of revenues, expenses, and dividends to the Retained Earnings account. All accounts that appear in the balance sheet, including Retained Earnings, are permanent accounts, and we carry forward their balances from period to period. We treat only revenues, expenses, and dividends as temporary, *so it will appear as if we had recorded all these types of transactions directly in Retained Earnings* during the year. We accomplish this with closing entries.

Closing Entries

Closing entries **transfer the balances of all temporary accounts (revenues, expenses, and dividends) to the balance of the Retained Earnings account.** Here's how:

- All revenue accounts have credit balances. To transfer these balances to the Retained Earnings account, we debit each of these revenue accounts for its balance and credit Retained Earnings for the total.
- Similarly, all expense and dividend accounts have debit balances. So, we credit each of these accounts for its balance and debit Retained Earnings for the total.

By doing this, we accomplish two necessary tasks: First, we *update the balance in the Retained Earnings account to reflect transactions related to revenues, expenses, and dividends in the current period.* Second, we *reduce the balances of all revenue, expense, and dividend accounts to zero* so we can start from scratch in measuring those amounts in the next accounting period. After all, revenues, expenses, and dividends are temporary accounts, which means their balances each period must start at zero.

Closing entries serve two purposes.

KEY POINT

Closing entries serve two purposes: (1) to transfer the balances of temporary accounts (revenues, expenses, and dividends) to the Retained Earnings account, and (2) to reduce the balances of these temporary accounts to zero to prepare them for measuring activity in the next period.

For demonstration, refer back to Eagle Golf Academy. We can transfer the balances of all revenue, expense, and dividend accounts to the balance of the Retained Earnings account with the closing entries shown in Illustration 3–15.

ILLUSTRATION 3–15

Closing Entries for
Eagle Golf Academy

January 31	Debit	Credit
(a) Service Revenue..	**6,360**	
Retained Earnings..		**6,360**
(Close revenues to retained earnings)		
(b) Retained Earnings...	**5,860**	
Supplies Expense		**800**
Rent Expense...		**500**
Depreciation Expense...		**400**
Salaries Expense		**3,100**
Utilities Expense		**960**
Interest Expense		**100**
(Close expenses to retained earnings)		
(c) Retained Earnings	**200**	
Dividends...		**200**
(Close dividends to retained earnings)		

Note that closing entries transfer the balances of the components of retained earnings (revenues, expenses, and dividends) to the balance of Retained Earnings itself. Retained Earnings is credited (increased) in the first entry and then debited (decreased) in the second and third entries. Posting these amounts to the Retained Earnings account will result in the following ending balance:

Retained Earnings

		0	Beginning balance
		6,360	Total revenues
Total expenses	5,860		
Total dividends	200		
		300	Ending balance

The ending balance of Retained Earnings now includes all transactions affecting the components of the account. The ending balance of **$300** represents all revenues and expenses over the life of the company (just the first month of operations in this example) less dividends. Another way to think about the balance of Retained Earnings is that it's the amount of net income earned by the company for its owners but that has not been paid to owners in the form of dividends.

The ending balance of Retained Earnings in January will be its beginning balance in February. Then we'll close February's revenues, expenses, and dividends to Retained Earnings, and this cycle will continue each period.

 COMMON MISTAKE

Students sometimes believe that closing entries are meant to reduce the balance of Retained Eearnings to zero. Retained Earnings is a *permanent account*, representing the accumulation of all revenues, expenses, and dividends over the life of the company.

In summary, the key points about closing entries are as follows.

- We *transfer the balance of all revenue, expense, and dividend accounts to the balance of Retained Earnings.* Dollar-for-dollar, every credit to revenues is now a credit to Retained Earnings, and every debit to expenses or dividends is now a debit to Retained Earnings.
- Closing entries *increase the Retained Earnings account by the amount of revenues and decrease Retained Earnings by the amount of expenses and dividends.*
- The balance of *each revenue, expense, and dividend account equals zero after closing entries.* These accounts have temporary balances and must be closed, or "zeroed out," to prepare them for measuring activity in the next period.
- Closing entries *do not affect the balances of permanent accounts* (assets, liabilities, and permanent stockholders' equity accounts) *other than retained earnings.* Permanent accounts carry a cumulative balance throughout the life of the company.

Illustration 3–16 shows retained earnings, net income, and dividends for **Coca-Cola** over a three-year period. Notice that the balance of retained earnings increases each year by the amount of net income less dividends. Retained earnings is a permanent account and represents the cumulative total of net income less dividends over the life of the company.

CAREER CORNER

In practice, accountants do not prepare closing entries. Virtually all companies have accounting software packages that automatically update the Retained Earnings account and close the temporary accounts at the end of the year. Of course, accounting information systems go far beyond automatic closing entries. In today's competitive global environment, businesses demand information systems that can eliminate redundant tasks and quickly gather, process, and disseminate information to decision makers. Ordinary business processes—such as selling goods to customers, purchasing supplies, managing employees, and managing inventory—can be handled more efficiently with customized information systems. Employers recognize that individuals with strong information technology skills mixed with accounting knowledge add value to the company.

ILLUSTRATION 3–16

Relation between Retained Earnings, Net Income, and Dividends for Coca-Cola

	THE COCA-COLA COMPANY ($ in millions)						
Year	Beginning Retained Earnings*	+	Net Income**	−	Dividends	=	Ending Retained Earnings
2005							$31,299
2006	$31,299	+	$5,080	−	$2,911	=	33,468
2007	33,468	+	5,981	−	3,149	=	36,300
2008	36,300	+	5,807	−	3,521	=	38,586

*Beginning retained earnings is the ending retained earnings from the previous year.
**Net income equals total revenues minus total expenses.

KEY POINT

Closing entries increase retained earnings by the amount of revenues for the period and decrease retained earnings by the amount of expenses and dividends for the period.

Post Closing Entries

■ **LO7**
Post closing entries and prepare a post-closing trial balance.

After we have prepared closing entries, we post amounts to the accounts in the general ledger. Illustration 3–17 demonstrates the process of posting the closing entries. The current balance of each account reflects transactions during the period (in black), adjusting entries (in red), and closing entries (in blue).

ILLUSTRATION 3–17   Posting Closing Entries to Adjusted Balances of Ledger Accounts

| Assets | | | = | Liabilities | | + | Stockholders' Equity | | | | |

Cash

(1)	25,000	(3)	24,000
(2)	10,000	(4)	6,000
(6)	3,600	(9)	2,800
(8)	600	(10)	200
Bal.	**6,200**		

Accounts Payable

| | | (5) | 2,300 |
| | | **Bal.** | **2,300** |

Common Stock

| | | (1) | 25,000 |
| | | **Bal.** | **25,000** |

Retained Earnings

			0
		(a)	6,360
(b)	5,860		
(c)	200		
		Bal.	**300**

Accounts Receivable

(7)	2,500	
(h)	200	
Bal.	**2,700**	

Unearned Revenue

		(8)	600
(d)	60		
		Bal.	**540**

Dividends

(10)	200	
		(c)	200
Bal.	**0**	

Service Revenue

		(6)	3,600
		(7)	2,500
		(d)	60
		(h)	200
(a)	6,360		
		Bal.	**0**

Supplies

(5)	2,300	
		(b)	800
Bal.	**1,500**	

Salaries Payable

| | | (e) | 300 |
| | | **Bal.** | **300** |

Supplies Expense

(b)	800	
		(b)	800
Bal.	**0**	

Rent Expense

(a)	500	
		(b)	500
Bal.	**0**	

Prepaid Rent

(4)	6,000	
		(a)	500
Bal.	**5,500**	

Utilities Payable

| | | (f) | 960 |
| | | **Bal.** | **960** |

Depreciation Expense

(c)	400	
		(b)	400
Bal.	**0**	

Salaries Expense

(9)	2,800	
(e)	300	
		(b)	3,100
Bal.	**0**	

Equipment

| (3) | 24,000 | |
| **Bal.** | **24,000** | |

Interest Payable

| | | (g) | 100 |
| | | **Bal.** | **100** |

Utilities Expense

(f)	960	
		(b)	960
Bal.	**0**	

Interest Expense

(g)	100	
		(b)	100
Bal.	**0**	

Accumulated Depreciation

| | | (c) | 400 |
| | | **Bal.** | **400** |

Notes Payable

| | | (2) | 10,000 |
| | | **Bal.** | **10,000** |

- Amounts in black represent external transactions during January. Numbers in parentheses refer to transaction numbers in Illustration 3–5.
- Amounts in red represent month-end adjusting entries. Letters in parentheses refer to adjusting entries in Illustration 3–8.
- Amounts in blue represent month-end closing entries. Letters in parentheses refer to closing entries in Illustration 3–15.

After we post the closing entries, the **$300** balance of Retained Earnings now equals the amount shown in the balance sheet. In addition, the ending balances of all revenue, expense, and dividend accounts are now zero and ready to begin the next period.

After we post the closing entries to the ledger accounts, we can prepare a post-closing trial balance. The post-closing trial balance is a list of all accounts and their balances at a particular date *after we have updated account balances for closing entries*. The post-closing trial balance helps to verify that we prepared and posted closing entries correctly and that the accounts are now ready for the next period's transactions.

Amounts in bold represent ending balances.

Illustration 3–18 shows the post-closing trial balance for Eagle Golf Academy as of January 31.

EAGLE GOLF ACADEMY Post-Closing Trial Balance January 31		
Accounts	**Debit**	**Credit**
Cash	$ 6,200	
Accounts Receivable	2,700	
Supplies	1,500	
Prepaid Rent	5,500	
Equipment	24,000	
Accumulated Depreciation		$ 400
Accounts Payable		2,300
Unearned Revenue		540
Salaries Payable		300
Interest Payable		100
Utilities Payable		960
Notes Payable		10,000
Common Stock		25,000
Retained Earnings		300
Totals	$39,900	$39,900

ILLUSTRATION 3–18

Post-Closing Trial Balance for Eagle Golf Academy

Notice that the post-closing trial balance does not include any revenues, expenses, or dividends, because these accounts all have zero balances after closing entries. The balance of Retained Earnings has been updated from the adjusted trial balance to include all revenues, expenses, and dividends for the period.

Decision Point

Question	Accounting information	Analysis
The amounts reported for revenues and expenses represent activity over what period of time?	Income statement	Revenue and expense accounts measure activity only for the current reporting period (usually a month, quarter, or year). At the end of each period, they are closed and begin the next period at zero.

Let's Review   Below is the adjusted trial balance of Beckham Soccer Academy for October 31.

BECKHAM SOCCER ACADEMY Adjusted Trial Balance October 31		
Accounts	Debit	Credit
Cash	$ 2,600	
Supplies	3,900	
Accounts Payable		$ 1,000
Salaries Payable		300
Common Stock		3,000
Retained Earnings		1,700
Dividends	200	
Service Revenue		4,300
Salaries Expense	2,400	
Supplies Expense	700	
Rent Expense	500	
Totals	$10,300	$10,300

Required:

1. Prepare closing entries.
2. Prepare a post-closing trial balance.
3. Compare the balances of Retained Earnings in the adjusted trial balance and the post-closing trial balance.

Solution:

1. Closing entries.

October 31	Debit	Credit
Service Revenue	4,300	
Retained Earnings		4,300
(Close revenues to retained earnings)		
Retained Earnings	3,600	
Salaries Expense		2,400
Supplies Expense		700
Rent Expense		500
(Close expenses to retained earnings)		
Retained Earnings	200	
Dividends		200
(Close dividends to retained earnings)		

2. Post-closing trial balance.

BECKHAM SOCCER ACADEMY Post-Closing Trial Balance October 31		
Accounts	Debit	Credit
Cash	$2,600	
Supplies	3,900	
Accounts Payable		$1,000
Salaries Payable		300
Common Stock		3,000
Retained Earnings		2,200
Totals	$6,500	$6,500

3. The balance of Retained Earnings increases by $500 from the adjusted trial balance to the post-closing trial balance. The balance increases by the amount of net income ($700) and decreases by the amount of dividends ($200).

Suggested Homework:
BE3-19, BE3-20;
E3-17, E3-18;
P3-7A&B; P3-8A&B

KEY POINT

After we post the closing entries to the T-accounts in the general ledger, the balance of Retained Earnings equals the amount shown in the balance sheet. The balances of all revenue, expense, and dividend accounts are zero at that point.

KEY POINTS BY LEARNING OBJECTIVE

LO1 Record revenues using the revenue recognition principle and expenses using the matching principle.

The revenue recognition principle states that we should recognize revenue in the period in which we *earn* it, not necessarily in the period in which we receive cash.

The matching principle states that we recognize expenses in the same period as the revenues they help to generate. Expenses include those directly and indirectly related to producing revenues.

LO2 Distinguish between accrual-basis and cash-basis accounting.

The difference between accrual-basis accounting and cash-basis accounting is *timing*. Under accrual-basis accounting, we record revenues when we earn them (revenue recognition principle) and record expenses with the revenue they help to generate (matching

principle). Under cash-basis accounting, we record revenues when we receive cash and expenses when we pay cash. Cash-basis accounting is not allowed for financial reporting purposes.

LO3 Demonstrate the purposes and recording of adjusting entries.

Adjusting entries are a necessary part of accrual-basis accounting. They help to record revenues in the period earned and expenses in the period they are incurred to generate those revenues. Another benefit is that, by properly recording revenues and expenses, we correctly state assets and liabilities.

Adjusting entries are needed when cash flows or obligations occur *before* the earnings-related activity (prepayment) or when cash flows occur *after* the earnings-related activity (accrual).

Adjusting entries are unnecessary in two cases: (1) for transactions that do not involve revenue or expense activities and (2) for transactions that result in revenues or expenses being recorded at the same time as the cash flow.

LO4 Post adjusting entries and prepare an adjusted trial balance.

We post adjusting entries to the T-accounts in the general ledger to update the account balances.

An adjusted trial balance is a list of all accounts and their balances at a particular date after we have updated account balances for adjusting entries.

LO5 Prepare financial statements using the adjusted trial balance.

We prepare the income statement, statement of stockholders' equity, and balance sheet from the adjusted trial balance. The income statement provides a measure of net income (profitability), calculated as revenues minus expenses. The balance sheet demonstrates that assets equal

liabilities plus stockholders' equity (the basic accounting equation).

LO6 Demonstrate the purposes and recording of closing entries.

Closing entries serve two purposes: (1) to transfer the balances of temporary accounts (revenues, expenses, and dividends) to the retained earnings account and (2) to reduce the balances of these temporary accounts to zero to prepare them for measuring activity in the next period.

Closing entries increase the balance of retained earnings by the amount of revenues for the period and decrease retained earnings by the amount of expenses and dividends for the period.

LO7 Post closing entries and prepare a post-closing trial balance.

After we post the closing entries to the T-accounts in the general ledger, the balance of Retained Earnings equals the amount shown in the balance sheet. The balances of all revenue, expense, and dividend accounts are zero at that point.

GLOSSARY

Accrual-basis accounting: Record revenues when earned (the revenue recognition principle) and expenses with related revenues (the matching principle). **p. 108**

Accrued expense: When a company has incurred an expense but hasn't yet paid cash or recorded an obligation to pay. **p. 119**

Accrued revenue: When a company has earned revenue but hasn't yet received cash or recorded an amount receivable. **p. 121**

Adjusted trial balance: A list of all accounts and their balances after we have updated account balances for adjusting entries. **p. 126**

Adjusting entries: Entries used to record events that occur during the period but that have not yet been recorded by the end of the period. **p. 112**

Cash-basis accounting: Record revenues at the time cash is received and expenses at the time cash is paid. **p. 110**

Classified balance sheet: Balance sheet that groups a company's assets into current assets and long-term assets and that separates liabilities into current liabilities and long-term liabilities. **p. 129**

Closing entries: Entries that transfer the balances of all temporary accounts (revenues, expenses, and dividends) to the balance of the Retained Earnings account. **p. 131**

Contra account: An account with a balance that is opposite, or "contra," to that of its related accounts. **p. 116**

Matching principle: Recognize expenses in the same period as the revenues they help to generate. **p. 109**

Operating cycle: The average time between purchasing or acquiring inventory and receiving cash proceeds from its sale. **p. 129**

Permanent accounts: All accounts that appear in the balance sheet; account balances are carried forward from period to period. **p. 131**

Post-closing trial balance: A list of all accounts and their balances at a particular date after we have updated account balances for closing entries. **p. 135**

Prepaid expenses: The costs of assets acquired in one period that will be expensed in a future period. **p. 113**

Revenue recognition principle: Record revenue in the period in which it's earned. **p. 108**

Temporary accounts: All revenue, expense, and dividend accounts; account balances are maintained for a single period and then closed (or zeroed out) and transferred to the balance of the Retained Earnings account at the end of the period. **p. 131**

Unearned revenues: When a company receives cash in advance from a customer for products or services to be provided in the future. **p. 117**

SELF-STUDY QUESTIONS

1. On May 5, Johnson Plumbing receives a phone call from a customer needing a new   ■ **LO1**
   water heater and schedules a service visit for May 7. On May 7, Johnson installs
   the new water heater. The customer pays for services on May 10. According to
   the *revenue recognition principle*, on which date should Johnson record service
   revenue?
   a. May 5 (date of phone call).
   b. May 7 (date of service).
   c. May 10 (date of cash receipt).
   d. Evenly over the three dates.

2. On January 17, Papa's Pizza signs a contract with Bug Zappers for exterminating   ■ **LO1**
   services related to a recent sighting of cockroaches in the restaurant. Papa's pays
   for the extermination service on January 29, and Bug Zappers sprays for bugs on
   February 7. According to the *matching principle*, on which date should Papa's Pizza
   record the extermination expense?
   a. January 17 (date of the contract).
   b. January 29 (date of cash payment).
   c. February 7 (date of extermination service).
   d. Evenly over the three dates.

3. Refer to the information in self-study question 1. Using *cash-basis accounting*, on   ■ **LO2**
   which date should Johnson record service revenue?
   a. May 5 (date of phone call).
   b. May 7 (date of service).
   c. May 10 (date of cash receipt).
   d. Evenly over the three dates.

4. Refer to the information in self-study question 2. Using *cash-basis accounting*, on   ■ **LO2**
   which date should Papa's Pizza record the extermination expense?
   a. January 17 (date of the contract).
   b. January 29 (date of cash payment).
   c. February 7 (date of extermination service).
   d. Evenly over the three dates.

5. Which of the following is *not* a characteristic of adjusting entries?   ■ **LO3**
   a. Reduce the balances of revenue, expense, and dividend accounts to zero.
   b. Allow for proper application of the revenue recognition principle (revenues)
      or the matching principle (expenses).
   c. Are part of accrual-basis accounting.
   d. Are recorded at the end of the accounting period.

6. Ambassador Hotels purchases one year of fire insurance coverage on December 1   ■ **LO3**
   for $24,000 ($2,000 per month), debiting prepaid insurance. On December 31,
   Ambassador would record the following year-end adjusting entry:

	Debit	Credit
a. Insurance Expense	24,000	
Prepaid Insurance		24,000
b. Insurance Expense	2,000	
Prepaid Insurance		2,000
c. Insurance Expense	22,000	
Prepaid Insurance		22,000
d. No entry is required on December 31 because full cash payment was made on December 1 and the insurance does not expire until the following November 30.		

■ LO4

7. An adjusted trial balance:
    a. Lists all accounts and their balances at a particular date after updating account balances for adjusting entries.
    b. Is used to prepare the financial statements.
    c. Includes balances for revenues, expenses, and dividends.
    d. All the above.

■ LO5

8. Which of the following describes the information reported in the statement of stockholders' equity?
    a. Net income for the period calculated as revenues minus expenses.
    b. Equality of total assets with total liabilities plus stockholders' equity.
    c. Change in stockholders' equity through changes in common stock and retained earnings.
    d. Net cash flows from operating, investing, and financing activities.

■ LO6

9. Which of the following describes the purpose(s) of closing entries?
    a. Adjust the balances of asset and liability accounts for unrecorded activity during the period.
    b. Transfer the balances of temporary accounts (revenues, expenses, and dividends) to Retained Earnings.
    c. Reduce the balances of the temporary accounts to zero to prepare them for measuring activity in the next period.
    d. Both *b*. and *c*.

■ LO7

10. Which of the following accounts is *not* listed in a post-closing trial balance?
    a. Prepaid Rent.
    b. Accounts Payable.
    c. Salaries Expense.
    d. Retained Earnings.

Note: For answers, see the last page of the chapter.

Check out
www.mhhe.com/succeed
for more multiple-choice
questions.

REVIEW QUESTIONS

■ LO1

1. Discuss the major principle that describes recording revenues.

■ LO1

2. Discuss the major principle that describes recording expenses.

■ LO1

3. Samantha is a first-year accounting student. She doesn't think it matters that expenses are reported in the same period's income statement with the related revenues (matching principle). She feels that "as long as revenues and expenses are recorded in any period, that's good enough." Help her understand why the matching principle is important.

■ LO2

4. Describe when revenues and expenses are recognized using cash-basis accounting. How does this differ from accrual-basis accounting?

■ LO2
Flip Side of Question 7

5. Executive Lawn provides $100 of landscape maintenance to Peterson Law on April 10. Consider three scenarios:

    a. Peterson pays for the lawn service in advance on March 28.
    b. Peterson pays for the lawn service on April 10, the day of service.
    c. Peterson pays for the lawn service the following month on May 2.

    If Executive Lawn uses accrual-basis accounting, on which date would Executive Lawn record the $100 revenue for each scenario?

6. Consider the information in question 5. Using cash-basis accounting, on which date would Executive Lawn record the $100 revenue for each scenario?

■ LO2
Flip Side of Question 8

7. Peterson Law asks Executive Lawn to provide $100 of landscape maintenance. Executive Lawn provides the service on April 10. Consider three scenarios:

   a. Peterson pays for the lawn service in advance on March 28.
   b. Peterson pays for the lawn service on April 10, the day of service.
   c. Peterson pays for the lawn service the following month on May 2.

■ LO2
Flip Side of Question 5

   If Peterson Law uses accrual-basis accounting, on which date would Peterson Law record the $100 expense for each scenario?

8. Consider the information in question 7. Using cash-basis accounting, on which date would Peterson Law record the $100 expense for each scenario?

■ LO2
Flip Side of Question 6

9. Why are adjusting entries necessary under accrual-basis accounting?

10. There are two basic types of adjusting entries—prepayments and accruals. Describe each in terms of the timing of revenue and expense recognition versus the flow of cash.

■ LO3
■ LO3

11. Provide an example of a prepaid expense. The adjusting entry associated with a prepaid expense always includes a debit and credit to which account classifications?

■ LO3

12. Provide an example of an unearned revenue. The adjusting entry associated with an unearned revenue always includes a debit and credit to which account classifications?

■ LO3

13. Provide an example of an accrued expense. The adjusting entry associated with an accrued expense always includes a debit and credit to which account classifications?

■ LO3

14. Provide an example of an accrued revenue. The adjusting entry associated with an accrued revenue always includes a debit and credit to which account classifications?

■ LO3

15. Sequoya Printing purchases office supplies for $75 on October 2. The staff uses the office supplies continually on a daily basis throughout the month. By the end of the month, office supplies of $25 remain. Record the month-end adjusting entry for office supplies (assuming the balance of Office Supplies at the beginning of October was $0).

■ LO3

16. Jackson Rental receives its September utility bill of $320 on September 30 but does not pay the bill until October 10. Jackson's accountant records the utility expense of $320 on October 10 at the time of payment. Will this cause any of Jackson's accounts to be misstated at the end of September? If so, indicate which ones and the direction of the misstatement.

■ LO3

17. Global Printing publishes several types of magazines. Customers are required to pay for magazines in advance. On November 5, Global receives cash of $120,000 for prepaid subscriptions. By the end of November, Global has distributed $20,000 of magazines to customers. Record the month-end adjusting entry.

■ LO3

18. At the end of May, Robertson Corporation has provided services to customers, but it has not yet billed these customers nor have any of them paid for those services. If Robertson makes no adjusting entry associated with these unpaid services provided, will any accounts be misstated? If so, indicate which ones and the direction of the misstatement.

■ LO3

19. Fill in the blank associated with each adjusting entry:

   a. *Prepaid expense:* Debit Supplies Expense; credit _____.
   b. *Unearned revenue:* Debit _____; credit Service Revenue.
   c. *Accrued expense:* Debit _____; credit Salaries Payable.
   d. *Accrued revenue:* Debit Accounts Receivable; credit _____.

■ LO3

■ **LO4**   20. What is the purpose of the adjusted trial balance? How do the adjusted trial balance and the (unadjusted) trial balance differ?

■ **LO5**   21. Explain what is meant by the term *classified* when referring to a balance sheet.

■ **LO5**   22. At the end of the period, Sanders Company reports the following amounts: Assets = $12,000; Liabilities = $8,000; Revenues = $5,000; Expenses = $3,000. Calculate stockholders' equity.

■ **LO6**   23. What are the two purposes of preparing closing entries?

■ **LO6**   24. What does it mean to close temporary accounts? Which of the following account types are closed: assets, liabilities, dividends, revenues, and expenses?

■ **LO6**   25. Describe the debits and credits for the three closing entries required at the end of a reporting period.

■ **LO6**   26. In its first four years of operations, Chance Communications reports net income of $300, $900, $1,500, and $2,400, respectively, and pays dividends of $200 per year. What would be the balance of Retained Earnings at the end of the fourth year?

■ **LO6**   27. Matt has been told by his instructor that dividends reduce retained earnings (and therefore stockholders' equity). However, since he knows that stockholders are receiving the dividend, Matt doesn't understand how paying a dividend would *decrease* stockholders' equity. Explain this to Matt.

■ **LO7**   28. How do the adjusted trial balance and the post-closing trial balance differ? Which accounts are shown in the adjusted trial balance but not in the post-closing trial balance? Which account is shown in both trial balances but with a different balance on each?

BRIEF EXERCISES

Determine revenues to be recognized (LO1)

BE3–1 Below are transactions for Lobos, Inc., during the month of December. Calculate the amount of revenue to recognize in December. If the transaction does not require the company to recognize a revenue, indicate how it would report the transaction.
a. Receive $1,200 cash from customers for services to be provided next month.
b. Perform $900 of services during the month and bill customers. Customers are expected to pay next month.
c. Perform $2,300 of services during the month and receive full cash payment from customers at the time of service.

Determine expenses to be recognized (LO1)

BE3–2 Below are transactions for Bronco Corporation during the month of June. Calculate the amount of expense to recognize in June. If the transaction does not require an expense to be recognized, indicate how the transaction would be reported.
a. Pay $600 cash to employees for work performed during June.
b. Receive a $200 telephone bill for the month of June, but Bronco does not plan to pay the bill until early next month.
c. Pay $500 on account for supplies purchased last month. All supplies were used last month.

Calculate net income (LO1)

BE3–3 Hoya Corporation reports the following amounts: Assets = $12,000; Liabilities = $2,000; Stockholders' equity = $10,000; Dividends = $2,000; Revenues = $15,000; and Expenses = $11,000. What amount is reported for net income?

Analyze the impact of transactions on the balance of cash, cash-basis net income, and accrual-basis net income (LO1, 2)

BE3–4 Consider the following set of transactions occurring during the month of May for Bison Consulting Company. For each transaction, indicate the impact on (1) the balance of cash, (2) cash-basis net income, and (3) accrual-basis net income for May. The first answer is provided as an example.

	Cash Balance	Cash-Basis Net Income	Accrual-Basis Net Income
(a) Receive $1,500 from customers who were billed for services in April.	+$1,500	+$1,500	$0
(b) Provide $3,200 of consulting services to a local business. Payment is not expected until June.			
(c) Purchase office supplies for $400 on account. All supplies are used by the end of May.			
(d) Pay $600 to workers. $400 is for work in May and $200 is for work in April.			
(e) Pay $200 to advertise in a local newspaper in May.			
Totals			

BE3–5 Rebel Technology maintains its records using cash-basis accounting. During the year, the company received cash from customers, $40,000, and paid cash for salaries, $22,000. At the beginning of the year, customers owe Rebel $1,000. By the end of the year, customers owe $6,000. At the beginning of the year, Rebel owes salaries of $5,000. At the end of the year, Rebel owes salaries of $3,000. Determine cash-basis net income and accrual-basis net income for the year.

Determine accrual-basis and cash-basis net income (LO1, 2)

BE3–6 At the beginning of May, Golden Gopher Company reports a balance in Supplies of $400. On May 15, Golden Gopher purchases an additional $2,300 of supplies for cash. By the end of May, only $200 of supplies remains. (1) Record the purchase of supplies on May 15. (2) Record the adjusting entry on May 31. (3) Calculate the balances after adjustment on May 31 of Supplies and Supplies Expense.

Record the adjusting entry for supplies (LO3)

BE3–7 Suppose Hoosiers, a specialty clothing store, rents space at a local mall for one year, paying $19,200 ($1,600/month) in advance on October 1. (1) Record the purchase of rent in advance on October 1. (2) Record the adjusting entry on December 31. (3) Calculate the year-end adjusted balances of prepaid rent and rent expense (assuming the balance of Prepaid Rent at the beginning of the year is $0).

Record the adjusting entry for prepaid rent (LO3)

BE3–8 Mountaineer Excavation operates in a low-lying area that is subject to heavy rains and flooding. Because of this, Mountaineer purchases one year of flood insurance in advance on March 1, paying $30,000 ($2,500/month). (1) Record the purchase of insurance in advance on March 1. (2) Record the adjusting entry on December 31. (3) Calculate the year-end adjusted balances of Prepaid Insurance and Insurance Expense (assuming the balance of Prepaid Insurance at the beginning of the year is $0).

Record the adjusting entry for prepaid insurance (LO3)

BE3–9 Beaver Construction purchases new equipment for $36,000 cash on April 1, 2012. At the time of purchase, the equipment is expected to be used in operations for six years (72 months) and have no resale or scrap value at the end. Beaver depreciates equipment evenly over the 72 months ($500/month). (1) Record the purchase of equipment on April 1. (2) Record the adjusting entry for depreciation on December 31, 2012. (3) Calculate the year-end adjusted balances of Accumulated Depreciation and Depreciation Expense (assuming the balance of Accumulated Depreciation at the beginning of 2012 is $0).

Record the adjusting entry for depreciation (LO3)

BE3–10 Suppose a customer rents a vehicle for three months from Commodores Rental on November 1, paying $4,500 ($1,500/month). (1) Record the rental for Commodores on November 1. (2) Record the adjusting entry on December 31. (3) Calculate the year-end adjusted balances of the Unearned Revenue and Service Revenue accounts (assuming the balance of Unearned Revenue at the beginning of the year is $0).

Record the adjusting entry for unearned revenue (LO3)

BE3–11 Fighting Irish Incorporated pays its employees $4,200 every two weeks ($300/day). The current two-week pay period ends on December 28, 2012, and employees are paid $4,200. The next two-week pay period ends on January 11, 2013, and

Record the adjusting entry for salaries payable (LO3)

employees are paid $4,200. (1) Record the adjusting entry on December 31, 2012. (2) Record the payment of salaries on January 11, 2013. (3) Calculate the 2012 year-end adjusted balance of Salaries Payable (assuming the balance of Salaries Payable before adjustment in 2012 is $0).

Record the adjusting entry for interest payable (LO3)

Flip Side of BE3–13

BE3–12 Midshipmen Company borrows $10,000 from Falcon Company on July 1, 2012. Midshipmen repays the amount borrowed and pays interest of 12% (1%/month) on June 30, 2013. (1) Record the borrowing for Midshipmen on July 1, 2012. (2) Record the adjusting entry for Midshipmen on December 31, 2012. (3) Calculate the 2012 year-end adjusted balances of Interest Payable and Interest Expense (assuming the balance of Interest Payable at the beginning of the year is $0).

Record the adjusting entry for interest receivable (LO3)

Flip Side of BE3–12

BE3–13 Refer to the information in BE3–12. (1) Record the lending for Falcon on July 1, 2012. (2) Record the adjusting entry for Falcon on December 31, 2012. (3) Calculate the 2012 year-end adjusted balances of Interest Receivable and Interest Revenue (assuming the balance of Interest Receivable at the beginning of the year is $0).

Assign accounts to financial statements (LO5)

BE3–14 For each of the following accounts, indicate whether the account is shown in the income statement or the balance sheet:

Accounts	**Financial Statement**
1. Accounts Receivable	_____
2. Unearned Revenue	_____
3. Supplies Expense	_____
4. Salaries Payable	_____
5. Depreciation Expense	_____
6. Service Revenue	_____

Understand the purpose of financial statements (LO5)

BE3–15 Below are the four primary financial statements. Match each financial statement with its primary purpose to investors.

Financial Statements	**Purposes**
1. _____ Income statement	a. Provides measures of resources and claims to those resources at the end of the year.
2. _____ Statement of stockholders' equity	b. Provides an indication of the company's ability to make a profit during the current year.
3. _____ Balance sheet	c. Provides a measure of net increases and decreases in cash for the current year.
4. _____ Statement of cash flows	d. Shows changes in owners' claims to resources for the current year.

Prepare an income statement (LO5)

BE3–16 The following account balances appear in the 2012 adjusted trial balance of Beavers Corporation: Service Revenue, $225,000; Salaries Expense, $100,000; Supplies Expense, $15,000; Rent Expense, $21,000; Depreciation Expense, $34,000; and Delivery Expense, $13,000. Prepare an income statement for the year ended December 31, 2012.

Prepare a statement of stockholders' equity (LO5)

BE3–17 The following account balances appear in the 2012 adjusted trial balance of Bulldog Corporation: Common Stock, $20,000; Retained Earnings, $7,000; Dividends, $1,000; Service Revenue, $25,000; Salaries Expense, $15,000; and Rent Expense, $8,000. No common stock was issued during the year. Prepare the statement of stockholders' equity for the year ended December 31, 2012.

Prepare a classified balance sheet (LO5)

BE3–18 The following account balances appear in the 2012 adjusted trial balance of Blue Devils Corporation: Cash, $4,000; Accounts Receivable, $8,000; Supplies, $18,000; Equipment, $110,000; Accumulated Depreciation, $40,000; Accounts Payable, $25,000;

Salaries Payable, $15,000; Common Stock, $50,000; and Retained Earnings, _____.
Prepare the December 31, 2012, classified balance sheet including the correct balance
for retained earnings.

BE3–19 The year-end adjusted trial balance of Aggies Corporation included the
following account balances: Retained Earnings, $220,000; Service Revenue, $850,000;
Salaries Expense, $380,000; Rent Expense, $140,000; Interest Expense, $75,000; and
Dividends, $50,000. Record the necessary closing entries.

Record closing entries (LO6)

BE3–20 The year-end adjusted trial balance of Hilltoppers Corporation included the
following account balances: Cash, $4,000; Equipment, $16,000; Accounts Payable,
$2,000; Common Stock, $10,000; Retained Earnings, $7,000; Dividends, $1,000;
Service Revenue, $15,000; Salaries Expense, $10,000; and Utilities Expense, $3,000.
Prepare the post-closing trial balance.

Prepare a post-closing trial balance (LO7)

EXERCISES

E3–1 Consider the following situations:

1. **American Airlines** collects cash on June 12 from the sale of a ticket to a customer.
   The flight occurs on August 16.
2. A customer purchases sunglasses from **Eddie Bauer** on January 27 on account.
   Eddie Bauer receives payment from the customer on February 2.
3. On March 30, a customer preorders 10 supreme pizzas (without onions) from
   Pizza Hut for a birthday party. The pizzas are prepared and delivered on April 2.
   The company receives cash at the time of delivery.
4. A customer pays in advance for a three-month subscription to **Sports Illustrated**
   on July 1. Issues are scheduled for delivery each week from July 1 through
   September 30.

Determine the timing of revenue recognition (LO1)

Required:
For each situation, determine the date for which the company recognizes the revenue
under accrual-basis accounting.

E3–2 Consider the following situations:

1. **American Airlines** operates a flight from Dallas to Los Angeles on August 16. The
   pilots' salaries associated with the flight are paid on September 2.
2. **Eddie Bauer** pays cash on January 6 to purchase sunglasses from a wholesale
   distributor. The sunglasses are sold to customers on January 27.
3. On January 1, **Pizza Hut** pays for a one-year property insurance policy with
   coverage starting immediately.
4. **Sports Illustrated** signs an agreement with CBS on January 12 to provide television
   advertisements during the Super Bowl. Payment is due within 3 weeks after February 4,
   the day of the Super Bowl. Sports Illustrated makes the payment on February 23.

Determine the timing of expense recognition (LO1)

Required:
For each situation, determine the date for which the company recognizes the expense
under accrual-basis accounting.

E3–3 Refer to the situations discussed in E3–1.

Differentiate cash-basis revenues from accrual-basis revenues (LO2)

Required:
For each situation, determine the date for which the company recognizes revenue
using cash-basis accounting.

E3–4 Refer to the situation discussed in E3–2.

Differentiate cash-basis expenses from accrual-basis expenses (LO2)

Required:
For each situation, determine the date for which the company recognizes the expense
using cash-basis accounting.

146   CHAPTER 3   The Financial Reporting Process

Determine the amount of net income (LO1)

E3–5 During the course of your examination of the financial statements of Trojan Corporation for the year ended December 31, 2012, you come across several items needing further consideration. Currently, net income is $90,000.

a. An insurance policy covering 12 months was purchased on October 1, 2012, for $18,000. The entire amount was debited to Prepaid Insurance and no adjusting entry was made for this item in 2012.

b. During 2012, the company received a $3,000 cash advance from a customer for services to be performed in 2013. The $3,000 was incorrectly credited to Service Revenue.

c. There were no supplies listed in the balance sheet under assets. However, you discover that supplies costing $2,250 were on hand at December 31, 2012.

d. Trojan borrowed $60,000 from a local bank on September 1, 2012. Principal and interest at 12% will be paid on August 31, 2013. No accrual was made for interest in 2012.

Required:
Using the information in *a.* through *d.* above, determine the proper amount of net income as of December 31, 2012.

Organize the steps in the accounting cycle (LO3, 4, 5, 6, 7)

E3–6 Listed below are all the steps in the accounting cycle.

(a) Record and post adjusting entries.
(b) Post the transaction to the T-account in the general ledger.
(c) Record the transaction.
(d) Prepare financial statements (income statement, statement of stockholders' equity, balance sheet, and statement of cash flows).
(e) Record and post closing entries.
(f) Prepare a trial balance.
(g) Analyze the impact of the transaction on the accounting equation.
(h) Assess whether the transaction results in a debit or a credit to the account balance.
(i) Use source documents to identify accounts affected by external transactions.

Required:
List the steps in proper order.

Record adjusting entries (LO3)

E3–7 Golden Eagle Company prepares monthly financial statements for its bank. The November 30 and December 31 adjusted trial balances include the following account information:

| | November 30 | | December 31 | |
	Debit	Credit	Debit	Credit
Supplies	1,500		3,000	
Prepaid Insurance	6,000		4,500	
Salaries Payable		10,000		15,000
Unearned Revenue		2,000		1,000

The following information also is known:
a. Purchases of supplies in December total $3,500.
b. No insurance payments are made in December.
c. $10,000 is paid to employees during December for November salaries.
d. On November 1, a tenant pays Golden Eagle $3,000 in advance rent for the period November through January. Unearned Revenue is credited.

Required:
Show the adjusting entries that were made for supplies, prepaid insurance, salaries payable, and unearned revenue on December 31.

E3–8 Consider the following transactions for Huskies Insurance Company:

a. Equipment costing $36,000 is purchased at the beginning of the year for cash. Depreciation on the equipment is $6,000 per year.

b. On June 30, the company lends its chief financial officer $40,000; principal and interest at 6% are due in one year.

c. On October 1, the company receives $12,000 from a customer for a one-year property insurance policy. Unearned Revenue is credited.

Record year-end adjusting entries (LO3)

Required:

For each item, record the necessary adjusting entry for Huskies Insurance at its year-end of December 31. No adjusting entries were made during the year.

E3–9 Refer to the information in E3–8.

Calculate the effects of adjusting entries on net income (LO3)

Required:

For each of the adjustments in E3–8, indicate by how much net income in the income statement is higher or lower if the adjustment is not recorded.

E3–10 Consider the following situations for Shocker:

a. On November 28, 2012, Shocker receives a $3,000 payment from a customer for services to be rendered evenly over the next three months. Unearned Revenue is credited.

b. On December 1, 2012, the company pays a local radio station $2,400 for 30 radio ads that were to be aired, 10 per month, throughout December, January, and February. Prepaid Advertising is debited.

c. Employee salaries for the month of December totaling $7,000 will be paid on January 7, 2013.

d. On August 31, 2012, Shocker borrows $60,000 from a local bank. A note is signed with principal and 8% interest to be paid on August 31, 2013.

Record year-end adjusting entries (LO3)

Required:

Record the necessary adjusting entries for Shocker at December 31, 2012. No adjusting entries were made during the year.

E3–11 Refer to the information in E3–10.

Calculate the effects of adjusting entries on the accounting equation (LO3, 4)

Required:

For each of the adjustments recorded in E3–10, indicate by how much the assets, liabilities, and stockholders' equity in the December 31, 2012, balance sheet is higher or lower if the adjustment is not recorded.

E3–12 Below are transactions for Wolverine Company during 2012.

a. On December 1, 2012, Wolverine receives $3,000 cash from a company that is renting office space from Wolverine. The payment, representing rent for December and January, is credited to Unearned Revenue.

b. Wolverine purchases a one-year property insurance policy on July 1, 2012, for $12,000. The payment is debited to Prepaid Insurance for the entire amount.

c. Employee salaries of $2,000 for the month of December will be paid in early January 2013.

d. On November 1, 2012, the company borrows $10,000 from a bank. The loan requires principal and interest at 12% to be paid on October 30, 2013.

e. Office supplies at the beginning of 2012 total $900. On August 15, Wolverine purchases an additional $2,400 of office supplies, debiting the Supplies account. By the end of the year, $400 of office supplies remains.

Record year-end adjusting entries (LO3)

Required:

Record the necessary adjusting entries at December 31, 2012, for Wolverine Company. You do not need to record transactions made during the year. Assume that no financial statements were prepared during the year and no adjusting entries were recorded.

Record year-end adjusting entries (LO3)

E3–13 Below are transactions for Hurricane Company during 2012.

a. On October 1, 2012, Hurricane lends $8,000 to another company. The other company signs a note indicating principal and 8% interest will be paid to Hurricane on September 30, 2013.

b. On November 1, 2012, Hurricane pays its landlord $3,000 representing rent for the months of November through January. The payment is debited to Prepaid Rent for the entire amount.

c. On August 1, 2012, Hurricane collects $12,000 in advance from another company that is renting a portion of Hurricane's factory. The $12,000 represents one year's rent and the entire amount is credited to Unearned Revenue.

d. Depreciation on machinery is $4,500 for the year.

e. Salaries for the year earned by employees but not paid to them or recorded are $4,000.

f. Hurricane begins the year with $1,000 in supplies. During the year, the company purchases $4,500 in supplies and debits that amount to Supplies. At year-end, supplies costing $2,500 remain on hand.

Required:

Record the necessary adjusting entries at December 31, 2012, for Hurricane Company for each of the situations. Assume that no financial statements were prepared during the year and no adjusting entries were recorded.

Prepare an adjusted trial balance (LO3, 4)

E3–14 The December 31, 2012, unadjusted trial balance for Demon Deacons Corporation is presented below.

Accounts	Debit	Credit
Cash	$ 9,000	
Accounts Receivable	14,000	
Prepaid Rent	6,000	
Supplies	3,000	
Unearned Revenue		$ 2,000
Common Stock		10,000
Retained Earnings		5,000
Service Revenue		45,000
Salaries Expense	30,000	
	$62,000	$62,000

At year-end, the following additional information is available:

a. The balance of Prepaid Rent, $6,000, represents payment on October 31, 2012, for rent from November 1, 2012, to April 30, 2013.

b. The balance of Unearned Revenue, $2,000, represents payment in advance from a customer. By the end of the year, $500 of the services have been provided.

c. An additional $600 in salaries is owed to employees at the end of the year but will not be paid until January 4, 2013.

d. The balance of Supplies, $3,000, represents the amount of office supplies on hand at the beginning of the year of $1,200 plus an additional $1,800 purchased throughout 2012. By the end of 2012, only $700 of supplies remains.

Required:

1. Update account balances for the year-end information by recording any necessary adjusting entries. No prior adjustments have been made in 2012.

2. Prepare an adjusted trial balance as of December 31, 2012.

E3–15 Below are the restated amounts of net income and retained earnings for Volunteers Inc. and Raiders Inc. for the period 2003–2012. Volunteers began operations in 2004.

Calculate the balance of retained earnings **(LO5)**

	VOLUNTEERS INC. ($ in millions)		RAIDERS INC. ($ in millions)	
Year	Net Income (Loss)	Retained Earnings	Net Income (Loss)	Retained Earnings
2003	—	$0	$ 25	$10
2004	$ 20		(53)	
2005	(6)		51	
2006	31		53	
2007	125		92	
2008	20		125	
2009	(141)		(52)	
2010	567		64	
2011	349		100	
2012	350		152	

Required:
Calculate the balance of retained earnings each year for each company. Neither company paid dividends during this time.

E3–16 The December 31, 2012, adjusted trial balance for Blue Hens Corporation is presented below.

Prepare financial statements from an adjusted trial balance **(LO5)**

Accounts	Debit	Credit
Cash	$ 11,000	
Accounts Receivable	140,000	
Prepaid Rent	5,000	
Supplies	25,000	
Equipment	300,000	
Accumulated Depreciation		$125,000
Accounts Payable		11,000
Salaries Payable		10,000
Interest Payable		4,000
Notes Payable (due in two years)		30,000
Common Stock		200,000
Retained Earnings		50,000
Service Revenue		400,000
Salaries Expense	300,000	
Rent Expense	15,000	
Depreciation Expense	30,000	
Interest Expense	4,000	
Totals	$830,000	$830,000

Required:
1. Prepare an income statement for the year ended December 31, 2012.
2. Prepare a classified balance sheet as of December 31, 2012.

Record closing
entries (LO6)

E3–17 Seminoles Corporation's fiscal year-end is December 31, 2012. The following is a partial adjusted trial balance as of December 31.

Accounts	Debit	Credit
Retained Earnings		$20,000
Dividends	$ 2,000	
Service Revenue		40,000
Interest Revenue		5,000
Salaries Expense	14,000	
Rent Expense	5,000	
Advertising Expense	2,000	
Depreciation Expense	10,000	
Interest Expense	4,000	

Required:
Prepare the necessary closing entries.

Record closing
entries (LO6)

E3–18 Laker Incorporated's fiscal year-end is December 31, 2012. The following is an adjusted trial balance as of December 31.

Accounts	Debit	Credit
Cash	$ 11,000	
Supplies	34,000	
Prepaid Rent	25,000	
Accounts Payable		$ 2,000
Notes Payable		20,000
Common Stock		35,000
Retained Earnings		8,000
Dividends	3,000	
Service Revenue		55,000
Salaries Expense	19,000	
Advertising Expense	12,000	
Rent Expense	9,000	
Utilities Expense	7,000	
Totals	$120,000	$120,000

Required:
Prepare the necessary closing entries.

Record closing entries
and a post-closing trial
balance (LO6, 7)

E3–19 Refer to the adjusted trial balance in E3–16.

Required:
1. Record the necessary closing entries at December 31, 2012.
2. Prepare a post-closing trial balance.

*For additional exercises, visit **www.mhhe.com/succeed** for Exercises: Set B.*

PROBLEMS: SET A

P3–1A Consider the following transactions.

Determine accrual-basis and cash-basis revenues and expenses (LO1, 2)

Transaction	Accrual-basis		Cash-basis	
	Revenue	Expense	Revenue	Expense
1. Receive cash from customers in advance, $500.				
2. Pay utilities bill for the previous month, $100.				
3. Pay for insurance one year in advance, $1,500.				
4. Pay workers' salaries for the current month, $700.				
5. Record depreciation of building, $900.				
6. Receive cash from customers at the time of service, $1,200.				
7. Purchase office supplies on account, $230.				
8. Borrow cash from the bank, $3,000.				
9. Receive cash from customers for services performed last month, $650.				
10. Pay for advertising to appear in the current month, $350.				

Required:

For each transaction, determine the amount of revenue or expense, if any, that is recorded under accrual-basis accounting and under cash-basis accounting in the current period.

P3–2A Minutemen Law Services maintains its books using cash-basis accounting. However, the company decides to borrow $100,000 from a local bank, and the bank requires Minutemen to provide annual financial statements prepared using accrual-basis accounting as part of the creditworthiness verification. During 2012, the company records the following cash flows:

Convert cash-basis accounting to accrual-basis accounting (LO1, 2)

Cash collected from customers		$60,000
Cash paid for:		
Salaries	$35,000	
Supplies	3,000	
Rent	4,000	
Insurance	6,000	
Utilities	2,000	50,000
Net cash flows		$10,000

You are able to determine the following information:

	January 1, 2012	December 31, 2012
Accounts Receivable	$20,000	$22,000
Prepaid Insurance	-0-	3,200
Supplies	4,000	1,500
Salaries Payable	2,200	3,400

In addition, depreciation on the company's equipment is $8,000 for the year.

Required:

Prepare an accrual-basis income statement for the year ended December 31, 2012. (Ignore income taxes.)

Record adjusting entries and determine their effect on net income (LO3)

P3–3A The information necessary for preparing the 2012 year-end adjusting entries for Gamecock Advertising Agency appears below. Gamecock's fiscal year-end is December 31.

a. On July 1, 2012, Gamecock receives $5,000 from a customer for advertising services to be given evenly over the next 10 months. Gamecock credits Unearned Revenue.

b. At the beginning of the year, Gamecock's depreciable equipment has a cost of $30,000, a five-year life, and no salvage value. The equipment is depreciated evenly (straight-line depreciation method) over the five years.

c. On May 1, 2012, the company pays $3,600 for a two-year fire and liability insurance policy and debits Prepaid Insurance.

d. On September 1, 2012, the company borrows $10,000 from a local bank and signs a note. Principal and interest at 12% will be paid on August 31, 2013.

e. At year-end there is a $2,200 debit balance in the Supplies (asset) account. Only $900 of supplies remains on hand.

Required:

Record the necessary adjusting entries on December 31, 2012. No prior adjustments have been made during 2012.

Record adjusting entries (LO3)

P3–4A Crimson Tide Music Academy offers lessons in playing a wide range of musical instruments. The *unadjusted* trial balance as of December 31, 2012, appears below. December 31 is the company's fiscal year-end.

Accounts	Debits	Credits
Cash	$ 9,300	
Accounts Receivable	8,500	
Supplies	1,500	
Prepaid Rent	6,000	
Equipment	75,000	
Accumulated Depreciation		$ 10,000
Accounts Payable		6,700
Salaries Payable		-0-
Interest Payable		-0-
Utilities Payable		-0-
Notes Payable		15,000
Common Stock		35,000
Retained Earnings		14,000
Service Revenue		45,000
Salaries Expense	23,500	
Interest Expense	-0-	
Rent Expense	-0-	
Supplies Expense	-0-	
Utilities Expense	1,900	
Depreciation Expense	-0-	
Totals	$125,700	$125,700

Information necessary to prepare the year-end adjusting entries appears below.

a. Depreciation of equipment for the year is $5,000.

b. Accrued salaries at year-end should be $1,600.

c. Crimson Tide borrows $15,000 on September 1, 2012. The principal is due to be repaid in four years. Interest is payable each August 31 at an annual rate of 10%.

d. Unused supplies at year-end total $600. Crimson Tide debits Supplies at the time supplies are purchased.

e. Crimson Tide opens a second studio by purchasing one year of rent in advance on April 1, 2012, for $6,000 ($500 per month) debiting Prepaid Rent.

f. Unpaid utilities for December total $100.

Required:

Record the necessary adjusting entries on December 31, 2012.

P3–5A Boilermaker Unlimited specializes in building new homes and remodeling existing homes. Remodeling projects include adding game rooms, changing kitchen cabinets and countertops, and updating bathrooms. Below is the year-end adjusted trial balance of Boilermaker Unlimited.

Prepare financial statements from an adjusted trial balance when net income is positive **(LO5)**

BOILERMAKER UNLIMITED Adjusted Trial Balance December 31, 2012		
Accounts	**Debits**	**Credits**
Cash	$ 15,000	
Accounts Receivable	24,000	
Supplies	31,000	
Prepaid Insurance	6,000	
Equipment	500,000	
Accumulated Depreciation		$ 160,000
Accounts Payable		30,000
Salaries Payable		27,000
Utilities Payable		4,000
Notes Payable (due in 5 years)		100,000
Common Stock		150,000
Retained Earnings		79,000
Dividends	25,000	
Service Revenue—new construction		400,000
Service Revenue—remodeling		250,000
Salaries Expense	150,000	
Supplies Expense	275,000	
Depreciation Expense	40,000	
Insurance Expense	24,000	
Utilities Expense	41,000	
Interest Expense	6,000	
Service Fee Expense	63,000	
Totals	$1,200,000	$1,200,000

Required:

Prepare an income statement, statement of stockholders' equity, and classified balance sheet. In preparing the statement of stockholders' equity, note that during the year the company issued additional common stock for $20,000. This amount is included in the amount for Common Stock in the adjusted trial balance.

P3–6A The year-end financial statements of Blue Devil Tax Services are provided below.

Record closing entries and prepare a post-closing trial balance **(LO6, 7)**

BLUE DEVIL TAX SERVICES Income Statement		
Service revenue		$72,500
Expenses:		
Salaries	$45,000	
Utilities	7,200	
Insurance	4,800	
Supplies	1,600	58,600
Net income		$13,900

BLUE DEVIL TAX SERVICES Statement of Stockholders' Equity			
	Common Stock	Retained Earnings	Total S. Equity
Beg. bal., Jan. 1	$50,000	$23,500	$ 73,500
Issue stock	20,000		20,000
Net income		13,900	13,900
Dividends		(5,000)	(5,000)
Ending bal., Dec. 31	$70,000	$32,400	$102,400

BLUE DEVIL TAX SERVICES				
Balance Sheet				
Assets		**Liabilities**		
Cash	$ 3,700	Accounts payable		$ 7,500
Accounts receivable	6,200	**Stockholders' Equity:**		
Land	100,000	Common stock	$70,000	
		Retained earnings	32,400	102,400
Total assets	$109,900	Total liabs. and equities		$109,900

Required:
1. Record year-end closing entries.
2. Prepare a post-closing trial balance. (*Hint:* The balance of Retained Earnings will be the amount shown in the balance sheet.)

Complete the accounting cycle after adjusting entries (LO4, 5, 6, 7)

P3–7A Refer to P3–4A.

Required:
Complete the following steps:
1. Enter the unadjusted balances from the trial balance into T-accounts.
2. Post the adjusting entries prepared in P3–4A to the accounts.
3. Prepare an adjusted trial balance.
4. Prepare an income statement and a statement of shareholders' equity for the year ended December 31, 2012, and a classified balance sheet as of December 31, 2012. Assume that no common stock is issued during the year.
5. Record closing entries.
6. Post closing entries to the accounts.
7. Prepare a post-closing trial balance.

Complete the full accounting cycle (LO3, 4, 5, 7)

P3–8A The general ledger of Red Storm Cleaners at January 1, 2012, includes the following account balances:

Accounts	Debits	Credits
Cash	$15,000	
Accounts Receivable	7,000	
Supplies	3,000	
Equipment	10,000	
Accumulated Depreciation		$ 3,000
Salaries Payable		5,000
Common Stock		20,000
Retained Earnings		7,000
Totals	$35,000	$35,000

The following is a summary of the transactions for the year:
a. Sales of services, $50,000, of which $20,000 is on account.
b. Collect on accounts receivable, $17,000.
c. Issue shares of common stock in exchange for $5,000 cash.
d. Pay salaries, $25,000 (of which $5,000 is for salaries payable in 2011).
e. Pay repairs and maintenance expenses, $12,000.
f. Purchase equipment for $7,000 cash.
g. Pay $1,000 cash dividends to stockholders.

Required:
1. Set up the necessary T-accounts and enter the beginning balances from the trial balance. In addition to the accounts shown, the company also has accounts for Dividends, Service Revenue, Salaries Expense, Repairs and Maintenance Expense, Depreciation Expense, and Supplies Expense.

2. Record each of the summary transactions listed above.
3. Post the transaction to the accounts.
4. Prepare an unadjusted trial balance.
5. Record adjusting entries. Accrued salaries at year-end amounted to $1,000. Depreciation for the year on the equipment is $4,000. Office supplies remaining on hand at the end of the year equal $1,000.
6. Post adjusting entries.
7. Prepare an adjusted trial balance.
8. Prepare an income statement for 2012 and a classified balance sheet as of December 31, 2012.
9. Record closing entries.
10. Post closing entries.
11. Prepare a post-closing trial balance.

PROBLEMS: SET B

connect

|ACCOUNTING

P3–1B Consider the following transactions.

Determine accrual-basis and cash-basis revenues and expenses **(LO1, 2)**

	Accrual-Basis		Cash-Basis	
Transaction	Revenue	Expense	Revenue	Expense
1. Receive cash from customers at the time of service, $2,700.				
2. Issue common stock for cash, $5,000.				
3. Receive cash from customers who were previously billed, $1,200.				
4. Record depreciation of equipment, $500.				
5. Pay workers' salaries for the current month, $600.				
6. Pay for rent one year in advance, $2,400.				
7. Repay a long-term note to the bank, $2,000.				
8. Pay workers' salaries for the previous month, $750.				
9. Pay dividends to stockholders, $400.				
10. Purchase office supplies for cash, $440.				

Required:

For each transaction, determine the amount of revenue or expense, if any, that is recorded under accrual-basis accounting and under cash-basis accounting.

P3–2B Horned Frogs Fine Cooking maintains its books using cash-basis accounting. However, the company recently borrowed $50,000 from a local bank, and the bank requires the company to provide annual financial statements prepared using accrual-basis accounting as part of the creditworthiness verification. During 2012, the company records the following cash flows:

Convert cash-basis accounting to accrual-basis accounting **(LO1, 2)**

Cash collected from customers		$55,000
Cash paid for:		
Salaries	$22,000	
Supplies	8,000	
Repairs and maintenance	7,000	
Insurance	3,000	
Advertising	5,000	45,000
Net cash flows		$10,000

You are able to determine the following information:

	January 1, 2012	December 31, 2012
Accounts Receivable	$16,000	$12,000
Prepaid Insurance	1,200	3,200
Supplies	-0-	1,500
Salaries Payable	3,200	2,300

In addition, depreciation on the company's building is $6,000 for the year.

Required:

Prepare an accrual-basis income statement for 2012. (Ignore income taxes.)

Record adjusting entries and determine their effect on net income (LO3)

P3–3B The information necessary for preparing the 2012 year-end adjusting entries for Bearcat Personal Training Academy appears below. Bearcat's fiscal year-end is December 31.

a. Depreciation on the equipment for the year is $6,000.

b. Salaries earned (but not paid) from December 16 through December 31, 2012, are $3,000.

c. On March 1, 2012, Bearcat lends an employee $15,000. The employee signs a note requiring principal and interest at 8% to be paid on February 28, 2013.

d. On April 1, 2012, Bearcat pays an insurance company $12,000 for a two-year fire insurance policy. The entire $12,000 is debited to Prepaid Insurance at the time of the purchase.

e. Bearcat uses $1,200 of supplies in 2012.

f. A customer pays Bearcat $2,400 on October 31, 2012, for three months of personal training to begin November 1, 2012. Bearcat credits Unearned Revenue at the time of cash receipt.

g. On December 1, 2012, Bearcat pays $4,500 rent to the owner of the building. The payment represents rent for December 2012 through February 2013, at $1,500 per month. Prepaid Rent is debited at the time of the payment.

Required:

Record the necessary adjusting entries at December 31, 2012. No prior adjustments have been made during 2012.

Prepare adjusting entries (LO3)

P3–4B Jaguar Auto Company provides general car maintenance to customers. The company's fiscal year-end is December 31. The December 31, 2012, trial balance (before any adjusting entries) appears below.

Accounts	Debits	Credits
Cash	$ 17,000	
Accounts Receivable	14,000	
Supplies	22,000	
Prepaid Insurance	18,000	
Equipment	85,000	
Accumulated Depreciation		$ 27,000
Accounts Payable		11,000
Salaries Payable		-0-
Utilities Payable		-0-
Interest Payable		-0-
Notes Payable		30,000
Common Stock		25,000
Retained Earnings		9,000
Dividends	2,000	
Service Revenue		220,000

(continued)

(concluded)	Accounts	Debits	Credits
	Salaries Expense	153,000	
	Depreciation Expense	-0-	
	Insurance Expense	-0-	
	Supplies Expense	-0-	
	Utilities Expense	11,000	
	Interest Expense	-0-	
	Totals	$322,000	$322,000

Information necessary to prepare the year-end adjusting entries appears below.

a. Depreciation on the machines for the year is $9,000.

b. Employee salaries are paid every two weeks. The last pay period ended on December 23. Salaries earned from December 24 through December 31, 2012, are $3,000.

c. On September 1, 2012, Jaguar borrows $30,000 from a local bank and signs a note. The note requires interest to be paid annually on August 31 at 9%. The principal is due in five years.

d. On March 1, 2012, the company purchases insurance for $18,000 for a one-year policy to cover possible injury to mechanics. The entire $18,000 is debited to Prepaid Insurance at the time of the purchase.

e. $4,000 of supplies remains on hand at December 31, 2012.

f. On December 30, Jaguar receives a utility bill of $1,700 for the month. The bill will not be paid until early January 2013, and no entry is recorded when the bill is received.

Required:
Prepare the necessary adjusting entries on December 31, 2012.

P3–5B Orange Designs provides consulting services related to home decoration. Orange Designs provides customers with recommendations for a full range of home décor, including window treatments, carpet and wood flooring, paint colors, furniture, and much more. Below is the year-end adjusted trial balance of Orange Designs.

Prepare financial statements from an adjusted trial balance (LO5)

ORANGE DESIGNS Adjusted Trial Balance December 31, 2012		
Accounts	**Debits**	**Credits**
Cash	$ 5,000	
Accounts Receivable	4,000	
Supplies	2,000	
Prepaid Rent	6,000	
Buildings	110,000	
Accumulated Depreciation		$ 21,000
Accounts Payable		3,000
Salaries Payable		4,000
Utilities Payable		1,000
Notes Payable		20,000
Common Stock		50,000
Retained Earnings		15,000
Service Revenues		115,000
Salaries Expense	42,000	
Rent Expense	18,000	
Depreciation Expense	7,000	
Supplies Expense	8,000	
Advertising Expense	13,000	
Utilities Expense	12,000	
Interest Expense	2,000	
Totals	$229,000	$229,000

Required:

Prepare an income statement, statement of stockholders' equity, and classified balance sheet. In preparing the statement of stockholders' equity, note that during the year the company issued additional common stock of $10,000. This amount is included in the amount for Common Stock in the adjusted trial balance.

Record closing entries and prepare a post-closing trial balance (LO6, 7)

P3–6B The year-end financial statements of Fighting Illini Financial Services are provided below.

FIGHTING ILLINI
Income Statement

Service revenue		$84,700
Expenses:		
Salaries	$49,000	
Supplies	9,100	
Rent	7,500	
Delivery	3,700	69,300
Net income		$15,400

FIGHTING ILLINI
Statement of Stockholders' Equity

	Common Stock	Retained Earnings	Total S. Equity
Beg. bal., Jan. 1	$60,000	$32,300	$ 92,300
Issue stock	15,000		15,000
Net income		15,400	15,400
Dividends		(6,000)	(6,000)
Ending bal., Dec. 31	$75,000	$41,700	$116,700

FIGHTING ILLINI
Balance Sheet

Assets		Liabilities	
Cash	$ 6,600	Accounts payable	$ 9,100
Accounts receivable	9,200	**Stockholders' Equity**	
Land	110,000	Common stock	$75,000
		Retained earnings	41,700	116,700
Total assets	$125,800	Total liabs. and equities	$125,800

Required:

1. Record year-end closing entries.
2. Prepare a post-closing trial balance. (*Hint:* The balance of retained earnings will be the amount shown in the balance sheet.)

Complete the accounting cycle after adjusting entries (LO4, 5, 6, 7)

P3–7B Refer to P3–4B.

Required:

Complete the following steps:

1. Enter the unadjusted balances from the trial balance into T-accounts.
2. Post the adjusting entries prepared in P3–4B to the accounts.
3. Prepare an adjusted trial balance.
4. Prepare an income statement and a statement of shareholders' equity for the year ended December 31, 2012, and a classified balance sheet as of December 31, 2012. Assume that no common stock is issued during the year.
5. Record closing entries.
6. Post closing entries to the accounts.
7. Prepare a post-closing trial balance.

Complete the full accounting cycle (LO3, 4, 5 6, 7)

P3–8B The general ledger of Pipers Plumbing at January 1, 2012, includes the following account balances:

Accounts	Debits	Credits
Cash	$ 4,000	
Accounts Receivable	9,000	
Supplies	3,000	
Equipment	26,000	
Accumulated Depreciation		$ 6,000
Accounts Payable		4,000
Utilities Payable		5,000
Unearned Revenue		-0-
Common Stock		18,000
Retained Earnings		9,000
Totals	$42,000	$42,000

The following is a summary of the transactions for the year:

a. Provide plumbing services for cash, $15,000, and on account, $60,000.
b. Collect on accounts receivable, $48,000.
c. Issue shares of common stock in exchange for $10,000 cash.
d. Pay salaries for the current year, $32,000.
e. Pay for utilities expenses, $12,000, of which $5,000 represents costs for 2011.
f. Receive cash in advance from customers, $8,000.
g. Pay $2,000 cash dividends to stockholders.

Required:
1. Set up the necessary T-accounts and enter the beginning balances from the trial balance. In addition to the accounts shown, the company has accounts for Dividends, Service Revenue, Salaries Expense, Utilities Expense, Supplies Expense, and Depreciation Expense.
2. Record each of the summary transactions listed above.
3. Post the transactions to the accounts.
4. Prepare an unadjusted trial balance.
5. Record adjusting entries. Depreciation for the year on the machinery is $6,000. Plumbing supplies remaining on hand at the end of the year equal $1,000. Of the $8,000 paid in advance by customers, $6,000 of the work has been completed by the end of the year.
6. Post adjusting entries.
7. Prepare an adjusted trial balance.
8. Prepare an income statement for 2012 and a classified balance sheet as of December 31, 2012.
9. Record closing entries.
10. Post closing entries
11. Prepare a post-closing trial balance.

*For additional problems, visit **www.mhhe.com/succeed** for Problems: Set C.*

ADDITIONAL PERSPECTIVES

Great Adventures

(This is a continuation of the Great Adventures problem from earlier chapters. To complete the requirements for this problem, be sure to account for the July transactions presented in AP2-1 on p. 103.)

Continuing Problem

AP3–1 The following transactions occur over the remainder of the year.

Aug.	1	Suzie applies for and obtains a $30,000 low-interest loan for the company from the city council, which has recently passed an initiative encouraging business development related to outdoor activities. The loan is due in three years, and 6% annual interest is due each year on July 31.
Aug.	4	The company purchases 14 kayaks, costing $28,000.
Aug.	10	Twenty additional kayakers pay $3,000 ($150 each), in addition to the $4,000 that was paid in advance on July 30, on the day of the clinic. Tony conducts the first kayak clinic.
Aug.	17	Tony conducts a second kayak clinic and receives $10,500 cash.
Aug.	24	Office supplies of $1,800 purchased on July 4 are paid in full.
Sep.	1	To provide better storage of mountain bikes and kayaks when not in use, the company rents a storage shed, purchasing a one-year rental policy for $2,400 ($200 per month).
Sep.	21	Tony conducts a rock-climbing clinic. The company receives $13,200 cash.
Oct.	17	Tony conducts an orienteering clinic. Participants practice how to understand a topographical map, read an altimeter, use a compass, and orient through heavily wooded areas. Clinic fees total $17,900.
Dec.	1	Tony decides to hold the company's first adventure race on December 15. Four-person teams will race from checkpoint to checkpoint using a combination of mountain biking, kayaking, orienteering, trail running, and rock-climbing skills. The first team in each category to complete all checkpoints in order wins. The entry fee for each team is $500.
Dec.	5	To help organize and promote the race, Tony hires his college roommate, Victor. Victor will be paid $50 in salary for each team that competes in the race. His salary will be paid after the race.
Dec.	8	The company pays $1,200 to purchase a permit from a state park where the race will be held. The amount is recorded as a miscellaneous expense.
Dec.	12	The company purchases racing supplies for $2,800 on account due in 30 days. Supplies include trophies for the top-finishing teams in each category, promotional shirts, snack foods and drinks for participants, and field markers to prepare the racecourse.
Dec.	15	Forty teams pay a total of $20,000 to race. The race is held.
Dec.	16	The company pays Victor's salary of $2,000.
Dec.	31	The company pays a dividend of $4,000 ($2,000 to Tony and $2,000 to Suzie).
Dec.	31	Using his personal money, Tony purchases a diamond ring for $4,500. Tony surprises Suzie by proposing that they get married. Suzie accepts!

The following information relates to year-end adjusting entries as of December 31, 2012.

a. Depreciation of the mountain bikes purchased on July 8 and kayaks purchased on August 4 totals $8,000.

b. Six months' worth of insurance has expired.

c. Four months' worth of rent has expired.

d. Of the $1,800 of office supplies purchased on July 4, $300 remains.

e. Interest expense on the $30,000 loan obtained from the city council on August 1 should be recorded.

f. Of the $2,800 of racing supplies purchased on December 12, $200 remains.

g. Suzie calculates that the company owes $14,000 in income taxes.

Required:

1. Record transactions from August 1 through December 31.
2. Record adjusting entries as of December 31, 2012.
3. Post transactions from August 1 through December 31 and adjusting entries on December 31 to T-accounts.
4. Prepare an adjusted trial balance as of December 31, 2012.
5. For the period July 1 to December 31, 2012, prepare an income statement and statement of stockholders' equity. Prepare a classified balance sheet as of December 31, 2012.

6. Record closing entries as of December 31, 2012.
7. Post closing entries to T-accounts.
8. Prepare a post-closing trial balance as of December 31, 2012.

American Eagle Outfitters, Inc.

AP3–2 Financial information for **American Eagle** is presented in Appendix A at the end of the book.

Required:
1. For the most recent year, what amount does American Eagle report for current assets? What assets are listed as current assets? What is the ratio of current assets to total assets?
2. For the most recent year, what amount does American Eagle report for current liabilities? What liabilities are listed as current liabilities? What is the ratio of current liabilities to total liabilities?
3. List any current assets or current liabilities that likely relate to adjusting entries.
4. What is the change in retained earnings reported in the balance sheet?
5. For the most recent year, what is the amount of net income reported in the income statement?
6. Using your answers in 4 and 5, calculate the amount of dividends paid during the year. Verify your answer by looking at the retained earnings column in the statement of stockholders' equity.

The Buckle, Inc.

AP3–3 Financial information for **The Buckle** is presented in Appendix B at the end of the book.

Required:
1. For the most recent year, what amount does The Buckle, Inc., report for current assets? What assets are listed as current assets? What is the ratio of current assets to total assets?
2. For the most recent year, what amount does The Buckle, Inc., report for current liabilities? What liabilities are listed as current liabilities? What is the ratio of current liabilities to total liabilities?
3. List any current assets or current liabilities that likely relate to adjusting entries.
4. For the most recent year, what is the change in retained earnings reported in the balance sheet?
5. For the most recent year, what is the amount of net income reported in the income statement?
6. Using your answers in parts 4 and 5 above, calculate the amount of dividends paid during the year. Verify your answer by looking at the retained earnings column in the statement of stockholders' equity.

American Eagle Outfitters, Inc. vs. The Buckle, Inc.

AP3–4 Financial information for **American Eagle** is presented in Appendix A at the end of the book, and financial information for **The Buckle** is presented in Appendix B at the end of the book.

Required:
1. Determine which company maintains a higher ratio of current assets to total assets. How might this be an advantage for the company?
2. Determine which company maintains a higher ratio of current liabilities to total liabilities. How might this be a disadvantage for the company?
3. The dividend payout ratio equals dividends paid during the year divided by net income. Determine which company has a higher dividend payout ratio. Why might this be the case?

Ethics

AP3–5 You have recently been hired as the assistant controller for Stanton Temperton Corporation, which rents building space in major metropolitan areas. Customers are required to pay six months of rent in advance. At the end of 2012, the company's president, Jim Temperton, notices that net income has fallen compared to last year. In 2011, the company reported before-tax profit of $330,000, but in 2012 the before-tax profit is only $280,000. This concerns Jim for two reasons. First, his year-end bonus is tied directly to before-tax profits. Second, shareholders may see a decline in profitability as a weakness in the company and begin to sell their stock. With the sell-off of stock, Jim's personal investment in the company's stock, as well as his company-operated retirement plan, will be in jeopardy of severe losses.

After close inspection of the financial statements, Jim notices that the balance of the Unearned Revenue account is $120,000. This amount represents payments in advance from long-term customers ($80,000) and from relatively new customers ($40,000). Jim comes to you, the company's accountant, and suggests that the firm should recognize as revenue in 2012 the $80,000 received in advance from long-term customers. He offers the following explanation: "First, we have received these customers' cash by the end of 2012, so there is no question about their ability to pay. Second, we have a long-term history of fulfilling our obligation to these customers. We have always stood by our commitments to our customers and we always will. We earned that money when we got them to sign the six-month contract."

Required:

Discuss the ethical dilemma you face.

Internet Research

AP3–6 Obtain a copy of the annual report of **McDonald's Corporation** for the most recent year. You can find the annual report at the company's website (*www.mcdonalds.com*) in the investor information section or at the Securities and Exchange Commission's website (*www.sec.gov*) using EDGAR (Electronic Data Gathering, Analysis, and Retrieval). Form 10-K, which includes the annual report, is required to be filed on EDGAR. Search or scroll within the annual report to find the financial statements.

Required:

Determine the following from the company's financial statements:

1. Do the company's revenues exceed expenses? What is the amount of net income?
2. Did net income increase in the most recent year compared to the previous year?
3. Which assets are listed as current assets? Why are other assets not listed as current assets?
4. Which liabilities are listed as current liabilities? Why are other liabilities not listed as current liabilities?
5. By how much did retained earnings increase/decrease in the most recent year compared to the previous year?
6. What is the amount of dividends paid to common stockholders? This information can be found in the statement of shareholders' equity or the statement of cash flows.
7. Explain the relationship between the change in retained earnings, net income, and dividends.

Written Communication

AP3–7 You are a tutor for introductory financial accounting. You tell the students, "Recording adjusting entries is a critical step in the accounting cycle, and the two major classifications of adjusting entries are prepayments and accruals." Chris, one of the students in the class, says, "I don't understand."

Required:

Respond to Chris.

1. When do prepayments occur? When do accruals occur?

2. Describe the appropriate adjusting entry for prepaid expenses and for unearned revenues. What is the effect on net income, assets, liabilities, and stockholders' equity of not recording a required adjusting entry for prepayments?

3. Describe the required adjusting entry for accrued expenses and for accrued revenues. What is the effect on net income, assets, liabilities, and shareholders' equity of not recording a required adjusting entry for accruals?

Answers to the Self-Study Questions

1. b   2. c   3. c   4. b   5. a   6. b   7. d   8. c   9. d   10. c

CHAPTER

Cash and Internal Controls

REGAL ENTERTAINMENT: INTERNAL CONTROLS ARE A BOX-OFFICE HIT

According to research conducted by the Association of Certified Fraud Examiners (ACFE, *www.acfe.com*), U.S. organizations lose an estimated $1 *trillion* (or 7% of their total revenue) to employee fraud each year. This occurs despite increased corporate emphasis on antifraud controls and recent legislation to combat fraud. While some employees steal office supplies, inventory, and equipment, the asset most often targeted is cash. Cash fraud includes skimming cash receipts before they are recorded, stealing cash that has already been recorded, and falsely disbursing cash through fraudulent billing, expense reimbursement, or payroll.

Companies that rely heavily on cash transactions are especially susceptible to employee fraud. For example, consider a company like **Regal Entertainment Group** (NYSE: **RGC**), one of the world's largest motion picture exhibitors. The company operates almost 7,000 screens and sells about 250 million tickets per year, generating revenues each year of nearly $3 billion. The company states, "Revenues are generated principally through admissions and concessions sales with proceeds received in cash at the point of sale." The primary way a company like RGC can minimize cash losses due to employee fraud is to establish strong systems for internal control.

Toward that end, RGC makes extensive use of its point-of-service information technology for managing its theatres. The revenue streams generated by admissions and concessions are fully supported by information systems to monitor cash flow and to detect fraud and inventory theft. Simpler approaches to internal control include *separation of duties:* For example, one person sells tickets, and another collects the tickets. This prevents the ticket seller from pocketing a moviegoer's cash and then allowing admission without a ticket being produced by the ticket machine. At the end of the day, the number of tickets produced by the machine should exactly match the cash collected.

We discuss much more about fraud and ways to prevent it in this chapter. At the end of the chapter (in Problem 4-1A), you can apply your newly learned skills in preventing and detecting fraud at a movie theatre.

PART A

INTERNAL CONTROLS

We're all familiar, more or less, with the concept of fraud. Fraud occurs when a person intentionally deceives another person for personal gain or to damage that person. More specifically related to business activities, the Association of Certified Fraud Examiners (ACFE) defines occupational fraud as the use of one's occupation for personal enrichment through the deliberate misuse or misapplication of the employing organization's resources. As discussed in the chapter-opening Feature Story, occupational fraud is big business, with companies expecting to lose on average 7% of their total revenues to fraud each year. For a company like Regal Entertainment Group, 7% of total revenues would equal nearly $200 million lost to fraud in a single year. Given the high cost of occupational fraud, it's not surprising that companies are willing to spend significant amounts to prevent it.

To minimize occupational fraud, companies implement formal procedures known as internal controls. These represent a company's plan to (1) safeguard the company's assets and (2) improve the accuracy and reliability of accounting information. To accomplish this broad goal, all companies institute a variety of specific internal controls, which we discuss in this chapter.

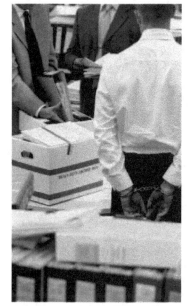

The ACFE, the world's largest antifraud organization (*www.acfe.com*), reports that theft or the misuse of the company's resources occurs in 90% of all fraud cases. Common examples include stealing cash or inventory or using the company's resources for non–work-related purposes. Because cash is the asset most commonly misappropriated, a significant portion of this chapter discusses the procedures implemented by businesses to maintain control over cash receipts and cash disbursements. We'll also work through two specific examples of cash controls: the bank reconciliation and the petty cash fund.

A second source of occupational fraud involves financial statement manipulation. Here, those in charge of communicating financial accounting information falsify reports. You may have heard the phrase "cooking the books." The phrase implies that the accounting records ("books") have been presented in an altered form ("cooked"). Managers have a variety of reasons for manipulating the numbers in financial statements, such as maximizing their compensation, increasing the company's stock price, and preserving their jobs. Strong internal controls help to minimize financial statement manipulation.

To set the stage for the importance of internal controls in general, we discuss the impact of recent accounting scandals, and the response by Congress.

Recent Accounting Scandals and Response

■ LO1
Discuss the impact of accounting scandals and the passage of the Sarbanes-Oxley Act.

Managers are entrusted with the resources of both the company's lenders (liabilities) and its owners (stockholders' equity). In this sense, managers of the company act as stewards or caretakers of the company's assets. However, in recent years some managers shirked their ethical responsibilities and misused or misreported the company's funds. In many cases, top executives misreported accounting information to cover up their company's poor operating performance. Such fraudulent activity is costly: The ACFE reports that the median loss caused by fraudulent financial statement schemes, for example, is $2,000,000 per instance. As you become more familiar with specific accounting topics throughout the remainder of this book, you'll begin to understand how amounts reported in the financial statements can be manipulated by managers.

Two of the highest-profile cases of accounting fraud in U.S. history are the collapses of Enron and WorldCom. Enron used questionable accounting practices to avoid reporting billions in debt and losses in its financial statements. WorldCom misclassified certain expenditures to overstate assets and profitability by $11 billion. Both companies hoped to fool investors into overvaluing the company's stock. Other common types of financial statement fraud include creating fictitious revenues from a fake customer, improperly valuing assets, hiding liabilities, and mismatching revenues and expenses.

As the Enron and WorldCom frauds (as well as several others) were being uncovered in 2001 and 2002, the stock prices of these companies plummeted. Investors lost nearly $200 billion as a result. Employees of these companies also suffered. Both firms declared bankruptcy, resulting in employee termination; reduced salaries and increased workloads for those who were left; and loss of employee retirement funds, stock options, and health benefits.

Recall from Chapter 1 that all public companies are required to have an independent party, an auditor, provide reasonable assurance that financial statements are free of material misstatements. So where were the auditors in the cases of Enron and WorldCom, when the external audits failed to detect billions of dollars of fraud? Both companies had the same audit firm, **Arthur Andersen**. At the time, many would have argued that Arthur Andersen was the most prestigious and most trusted audit firm in the world. How did billions of dollars of fraud go unreported?

The high-profile scandals led to an extensive investigation of Arthur Andersen by the Securities and Exchange Commission (SEC). This action, along with subsequent events, damaged the auditor's reputation so severely that most of its clients fled to other auditors to avoid being associated with the Andersen name. By the end of 2002, Arthur Andersen was no longer in business.

SARBANES-OXLEY ACT OF 2002

In response to these corporate accounting scandals and to public outrage over seemingly widespread unethical behavior of top executives, Congress passed the Sarbanes-Oxley Act, also known as the *Public Company Accounting Reform and Investor Protection Act of 2002* and commonly referred to as *SOX*. SOX applies to all companies that are required to file financial statements with the SEC and represents one of the greatest reforms in business practices in U.S. history. The act established a variety of new guidelines related to auditor-client relations and internal control procedures. Illustration 4–1 lists and discusses some of the major provisions of SOX.

Oversight board. The Public Company Accounting Oversight Board (PCAOB) has the authority to establish standards dealing with auditing, quality control, ethics, independence, and other activities relating to the preparation of audited financial reports. The board consists of five members who are appointed by the Securities and Exchange Commission.

Corporate executive accountability. Corporate executives must personally certify the company's financial statements and financial disclosures. Severe financial penalties and the possibility of imprisonment are consequences of fraudulent misstatement.

Nonaudit services. It's unlawful for the auditors of public companies to also perform certain nonaudit services, such as consulting, for their clients.

Retention of work papers. Auditors of public companies must retain all work papers for seven years or face a prison term for willful violation.

Auditor rotation. The lead auditor in charge of auditing a particular company (referred to as the *audit partner*) must rotate off that company within five years and allow a new audit partner to take the lead.

Conflicts of interest. Audit firms are not allowed to audit public companies whose chief executives worked for the audit firm and participated in that company's audit during the preceding year.

Hiring of auditor. Audit firms are hired by the audit committee of the board of directors of the company, not by company management.

Internal control. Section 404 of the act requires (a) that company management document and assess the effectiveness of all internal control processes that could affect financial reporting and (b) that company auditors express an opinion on whether management's assessment of the effectiveness of internal control is fairly stated.

ILLUSTRATION 4–1

Major Provisions of the Sarbanes-Oxley Act of 2002

The last provision listed in Illustration 4–1, internal controls under Section 404, is worth pausing over for a moment, given the topic of this chapter. Section 404 requires company management and auditors to document and assess the effectiveness of a company's internal controls—processes that could affect financial reporting. PCAOB chairman William McDonough explained the significance of this part of the law: "In the past, internal controls were merely considered by auditors; now they will have to be tested and examined in detail" (*PCAOBUS.org*, June 18, 2004). Whether you are an investor, an employee, a manager, or an auditor, understanding a company's internal controls is important.

KEY POINT

The accounting scandals in the early 2000s prompted passage of the Sarbanes-Oxley Act (SOX). Among other stipulations, SOX sets forth a variety of new guidelines related to auditor-client relations and additional internal controls. Section 404, in particular, requires company management and auditors to document and assess the effectiveness of a company's internal controls.

Framework for Internal Control

■ LO2
Identify the components, responsibilities, and limitations of internal control.

As noted above, internal control is a company's plan to (1) safeguard the company's assets and (2) improve the accuracy and reliability of accounting information. Effective internal control builds a wall to prevent misuse of company funds by employees and fraudulent or errant financial reporting. Strong internal control systems allow greater reliance by investors on reported financial statements.

COMPONENTS OF INTERNAL CONTROL

A framework for designing an internal control system was provided by the *Committee of Sponsoring Organizations (COSO)* of the Treadway Commission. Formed in 1985, COSO (*www.coso.org*) is dedicated to improving the quality of financial reporting through, among other things, effective internal controls. COSO suggests that internal control consists of five components, displayed in Illustration 4–2.

ILLUSTRATION 4–2

Components of Internal Control

Methods for collection of relevant **information and communication** in a timely manner, enabling people to carry out their responsibilities.

Continual **monitoring** of internal activities and reporting of deficiencies is required. Monitoring includes formal procedures for reporting control deficiencies.

Control activities are the policies and procedures that help ensure that management's directives are being carried out. These activities include authorizations, reconciliations, and separation of duties.

Risk assessment identifies and analyzes internal and external risk factors that could prevent a company's objectives from being achieved.

The **control environment** sets the overall ethical tone of the company with respect to internal control. It includes formal policies related to management's philosophy, assignment of responsibilities, and organizational structure.

The components of internal control are built on the foundation of the ethical tone set by top management in its control environment. From there, management assesses risks, implements specific control activities, and continuously monitors all systems. Running throughout this structure is the need for timely information and communication. Employees at all levels must understand the importance of high-quality information. Lower-level employees must report information accurately and in a timely manner to those higher in the organization. Top executives of a company then must effectively communicate this information to external parties such as investors and creditors through financial statements.

To see an example of how internal controls are linked to the information provided in financial statements, let's look at the description given by Regal Entertainment Group in its annual report (see Illustration 4–3).

REGAL ENTERTAINMENT GROUP
Notes to the Financial Statements (excerpt)

A company's internal control over financial reporting includes those policies and procedures that (1) pertain to the maintenance of records that, in reasonable detail, accurately and fairly reflect the transactions and dispositions of the assets of the company; (2) provide reasonable assurance that transactions are recorded as necessary to permit preparation of financial statements in accordance with generally accepted accounting principles, and that receipts and expenditures of the company are being made only in accordance with authorizations of management and directors of the company; and (3) provide reasonable assurance regarding prevention or timely detection of unauthorized acquisition, use, or disposition of the company's assets that could have a material effect on the financial statements.

ILLUSTRATION 4–3

Regal Entertainment's Discussion of Internal Controls and Financial Reporting

Movie theatre example.   Let's look at how the five components of internal control apply in actual practice. Here, we apply them to operating a movie theatre.

The overall attitudes and actions of management greatly affect the *control environment*. If employees notice unethical behavior or comments by management, they are more likely to behave in a similar manner, wasting the company's resources. Wouldn't you be more comfortable investing in or lending to a movie theatre if it were run by a highly ethical person, rather than someone of questionable character?

Risk assessment includes careful consideration of internal and external risk factors. Internal risks include issues such as unsafe lighting, faulty video projectors, unsanitary bathrooms, and employee incompetence with regard to food preparation. Common examples of external risks include a vendor supplying lower-grade or unsafe popcorn, moviegoers' security in the parking lot, or perhaps the decline in customer demand from DVD rentals or On Demand at home. These internal and external risk factors put the company's objectives in jeopardy.

Control activities include a variety of policies and procedures used to protect a company's assets. There are two general types of control activities: preventive and detective. *Preventive controls* are designed to keep errors or fraud from occurring in the first place. *Detective controls* are designed to detect errors or fraud that already have occurred.

Common examples of preventive controls include:

1. Separation of duties. Authorizing transactions, recording transactions, and maintaining control of the related assets should be separated among employees. The employee selling the movie ticket should not also be the employee in charge of collecting the tickets. The accountant at the movie theatre should not also have direct access to company cash by filling in as a ticket cashier or being

responsible for the daily cash deposits. Employees who have physical control of theatre inventory (candy bars, T-shirts, and so on) should not also be in charge of accounting for that inventory.

2. **Physical controls** over assets and accounting records. Each night, money from ticket sales should be placed in the theatre's safe or deposited at the bank. Important documents should be kept in fireproof files, and electronic records should be backed up daily and require user-ID and password for access. Concession supplies should be kept in a locked room with access allowed only to authorized personnel.

3. **Proper authorization** to prevent improper use of the company's resources. The theatre should establish formal guidelines on how to handle cash receipts and make purchases. For example, only management should be authorized to make purchases over a certain amount.

4. **Employee management.** The company should provide employees with appropriate guidance to ensure they have the knowledge necessary to carry out their job duties. Employees should be made fully aware of the company's internal control procedures, ethical responsibilities, and channels for reporting irregular activities.

Some examples of detective controls include:

1. **Reconciliations.** Management should periodically determine whether the amount of physical assets of the company (cash, supplies, inventory, and other property) match—reconcile with—the accounting records. For example, accounting personnel should routinely reconcile the company's cash records with those of its bank, and any discrepancy should be investigated. Later in this chapter we'll see an example of how to prepare a bank reconciliation for Starlight Drive-In.

2. **Performance reviews.** The actual performance of individuals or processes should be checked against their expected performance. For example, the amount of food sold should be compared to the number of tickets sold over a period of time. If food sales are lower than expected for a given number of tickets, employees could be wasting food, stealing food, or giving it to their friends for free. Alternatively, vendors may be supplying lower-quality food, driving down sales. Management may also wish to evaluate the overall performance of the theatre by comparing ticket sales for the current year with ticket sales for the previous year.

Monitoring of internal controls needs to occur on an ongoing basis. The theatre manager needs to actively review daily operations to ensure that control procedures work effectively. For instance, the manager should compare daily cash from ticket sales with the number of tickets issued, compare concession sales with units purchased, and make sure employees are paid only for actual hours worked.

Information and communication depend on the reliability of the accounting information system itself. If the accountant's office has papers scattered everywhere, and you learn the company still does all its accounting by hand without a computer, wouldn't you, as an investor or lender, be a bit worried? A system should be in place to ensure that current transactions of the company are reflected in current reports. Employees also should be aware of procedures in place to deal with any perceived internal control failures. For example, an anonymous tip hotline should be in place to encourage communication about unethical activities, such as an employee giving concession items for free to her friends. Employee tips historically have been the most common means of detecting employee fraud.

RESPONSIBILITIES FOR INTERNAL CONTROL

Everyone in a company has an impact on the operation and effectiveness of internal controls, but **the top executives are the ones who must take final responsibility for their establishment and success.** The CEO and CFO sign a report each year assessing whether the internal controls are adequate. Section 404 of SOX requires not only that companies document their internal controls and assess their adequacy, but that the company's auditors provide an opinion on management's assessment. A recent survey by the Financial Executives Institute of 247 executives reports that the total cost to a company of complying with Section 404 averages nearly $4 million.

The Public Company Accounting Oversight Board (PCAOB) further requires the auditor to express its own opinion on whether the company has maintained effective internal control over financial reporting. To see how this information gets reported, look at Illustration 4–4, which provides an excerpt from Regal Entertainment's auditor's report.

REGAL ENTERTAINMENT GROUP
Auditor's Report (excerpt)

In our opinion, management's assessment that Regal Entertainment Group maintained effective internal control over financial reporting is fairly stated, in all material respects, based on criteria established in *Internal Control—Integrated Framework* issued by the Committee of Sponsoring Organizations of the Treadway Commission (COSO). Also, in our opinion, Regal Entertainment Group maintained, in all material respects, effective internal control over financial reporting, based on criteria established in *Internal Control—Integrated Framework* issued by the Committee of Sponsoring Organizations of the Treadway Commission (COSO).

ILLUSTRATION 4–4

Excerpt from Regal Entertainment's Auditor's Report Related to Effectiveness of Internal Controls

LIMITATIONS OF INTERNAL CONTROL

Unfortunately, even with the best internal control systems, financial misstatements can occur. While better internal control systems will more likely detect operating and reporting errors, no internal control system can turn a bad employee into a good one.

Internal control systems are especially susceptible to collusion. Collusion occurs when two or more people act in coordination to circumvent internal controls. Going back to our movie theatre example, if the ticket cashier and the ticket taker, or the ticket cashier and the accountant, decide to work together to steal cash, theft will be much more difficult to detect. Fraud cases that involve collusion are typically several times more severe than are fraud cases involving a single perpetrator. This suggests that collusion is effective in circumventing control procedures.

Top-level employees who have the ability to override internal control features also have opportunity to commit fraud. For example, managers may be required to obtain approval from the chief financial officer (CFO) for all large purchases. However, if the CFO uses the company's funds to purchase a boat for personal use at a lake home, fewer controls are in place to detect this misappropriation. Even if lower-level employees suspect wrongdoing, they may feel intimidated to confront the issue.

Finally, because there are natural risks to running any business, **effective internal controls and ethical employees alone cannot ensure a company's success, or even survival.** Regal Entertainment recognizes the limitations of internal controls and provides an explicit discussion of this issue in its annual report, as shown in Illustration 4–5 (next page).

ILLUSTRATION 4–5

Regal Entertainment's Discussion of Limitations of Internal Controls

> **REGAL ENTERTAINMENT GROUP**
> **Management Discussion and Analysis (excerpt)**
>
> Management recognizes that there are inherent limitations in the effectiveness of any internal control over financial reporting, including the possibility of human error and the circumvention or overriding of internal control. Accordingly, even effective internal control over financial reporting can provide only reasonable assurance with respect to financial statement preparation. Further, because of changes in conditions, the effectiveness of internal control over financial reporting may vary over time.

 KEY POINT

Internal control refers to a company's plan to improve the accuracy and reliability of accounting information and safeguard the company's assets. Five key components to an internal control system are (1) control environment, (2) risk assessment, (3) control activities, (4) monitoring, and (5) information and communication.

Decision Point

Question ❓	Accounting information 📄	Analysis 🔍
Does the company maintain adequate internal controls?	Management's discussion, auditor's opinion	If management or the auditor notes any deficiencies in internal controls, financial accounting information may be unreliable.

PART B

CASH

Among all of the company's assets, cash is the one most susceptible to employee fraud. The obvious way that employees steal cash is by physically removing it from the company, such as pulling it out of the cash register and walking out the door. However, there are other, less obvious ways to commit fraud with a company's cash. An employee could falsify documents, causing the company to overreimburse the employee for certain expenses, to issue an inflated paycheck, or to make payment to a fictitious company. Because of these possibilities, companies develop strict procedures to maintain control of cash. Before discussing some of these controls, let's first get a good understanding of what "cash" includes.

Cash and Cash Equivalents

■ **LO3**

Define cash and cash equivalents.

The amount of cash recorded in a company's balance sheet includes currency, coins, and balances in savings and checking accounts, as well as items acceptable for deposit in these accounts, such as checks received from customers. *Checks* are written instruments instructing a bank to pay a specific amount from the check maker's account.

The balance of cash also includes cash equivalents, which are defined as short-term investments that have a maturity date no longer than three months *from the date of purchase*. Common examples of such investments are money market funds, Treasury bills, and certificates of deposit. The important point to understand is that cash and cash equivalents usually are combined and reported as a single asset in the balance sheet of most companies.

KEY POINT

Cash includes not only currency, coins, balances in checking accounts, and checks and money orders received from customers, but also cash equivalents, defined as investments that mature within three months (such as money market funds, Treasury bills, and certificates of deposit).

User's Guide Below is a shorthand way of showing the effects of transactions on assets, liabilities, and stockholders' equity. We use these throughout the book.

Whether a customer uses cash or a check to make a purchase, the company records the transaction as a cash sale. Let's assume a local theatre sells tickets for the entire day totaling $3,000. Some customers pay cash for those tickets, while others use a check. (Others will use credit cards or debit cards, which we discuss later.) Regardless of which method of payment customers use, the theatre records all of those ticket sales as cash sales.

	Debit	Credit	A	=	L	+	SE
Cash	3,000		+3,000				
Service Revenue		3,000					+3,000 Rev↑
(Sell tickets with cash or check)							

How Much Cash Is Enough?

Decision Maker's Perspective

Investors and creditors closely monitor the amount of cash a company holds. The company needs enough cash, or enough other assets that can quickly be converted to cash, to pay obligations as they become due. Available cash also helps a company respond quickly to new, profitable opportunities before competitors do. On the other hand, having too much cash leads to inefficient use of funds and could be a signal that a company's management does not see additional opportunities for profitable expansion. Investors usually view excess cash as a negative. ●

Cash Controls

Management must safeguard all assets against possible misuse. Again, because cash is especially susceptible to theft, internal control of cash is a key issue.

CONTROLS OVER CASH RECEIPTS

Most businesses receive payment from the sale of products and services either in the form of cash or as a check received immediately or through the mail. Internal control over cash receipts could include the following steps:

■ **LO4**
Understand controls over cash receipts and cash disbursements.

1. Record all cash receipts as soon as possible. Theft is more difficult once a record of the cash receipt has been made.
2. Open mail each day, and make a list of checks received, including the amount and payer's name.
3. Designate an employee to deposit cash and checks into the company's bank account each day, different from the person who receives cash and checks.
4. Have another employee record cash receipts in the accounting records. Verify cash receipts by comparing the bank deposit slip with the accounting records.
5. Accept credit cards or debit cards, to limit the amount of cash employees handle.

Because acceptance of credit cards and debit cards is so widespread, let's look at those controls in a bit more detail.

Acceptance of credit cards. The acceptance of credit cards provides an additional control by reducing employees' need to directly handle cash. The term *credit card* is derived from the fact that the issuer, such as **Visa** or **MasterCard**, extends credit (lends money) to the cardholder each time the cardholder uses the card. Cash in the amount of the sale automatically is deposited in the company's bank.

Credit card companies earn revenues primarily in two ways. First, the cardholder has a specified grace period before he or she has to pay the credit card balance in full. If the balance is not paid by the end of the grace period, the issuing company will charge a fee (interest). Second, credit card companies charge the *retailer*, not the customer, for the use of the credit card. This charge generally ranges from 2% to 4% of the amount of the sale.

For example, suppose a movie theatre accepts MasterCard as payment for $2,000 worth of movie tickets, and MasterCard charges the movie theatre a service fee of 3% (or $60 on sales of $2,000). Moviegoers don't pay cash to the theatre at the time of sale, but MasterCard deposits cash, less the service fee expense, into the theatre's account usually within 24 hours. Therefore, the theatre records the $2,000 credit card transaction as $1,940 cash received and $60 service fee expense.

A = L + SE		Debit	Credit
+1,940	Cash	1,940	
−60 Exp↑	Service Fee Expense..	60	
+2,000 Rev↑	Service Revenue		2,000
	(Sell tickets with credit card and 3% service fee)		

From the seller's perspective, the only difference between a cash sale and a credit card sale is that the seller must pay a fee to the credit card company for allowing the customer to use a credit card.

Decision Point

Question	Accounting information	Analysis
Should the company allow its customers to pay by using credit cards?	Credit sales, service fee expense, internal controls	When the benefits of credit card use (increased sales, reduced handling of cash by employees) exceed the costs (service fee expense and credit card fraud), the company benefits.

Acceptance of debit cards. *Debit cards* also provide an additional control for cash receipts. Like credit cards, debit cards offer customers a way to purchase goods and services without a physical exchange of cash. They differ, however, in that most debit cards (sometimes referred to as *check cards*) work just like a check and withdraw funds directly from the cardholder's bank account at the time of use. (Recall that credit cards don't remove cash from the cardholder's account after each transaction.)

Similar to credit cards, the use of debit cards by customers results in a fee being charged to the retailer. However, the fees charged for debit cards are typically much lower than those charged for credit cards. Debit card transactions are recorded similar to credit card transactions.

COMMON MISTAKE

The term *debit card* can cause some confusion for someone in the first accounting course. Throughout this course, we refer to an increase in cash as a *debit* to cash. However, using your *debit card* will result in a decrease in your cash account. It's the *merchant's* cash account, not yours, that increases and is debited. Don't let this confuse you.

ETHICAL DILEMMA

Jill is starting her sophomore year of college. The only way she can pay for tuition and school supplies is to take out a student loan. To make living costs more affordable, she shares an apartment with two other students. One week after Jill starts classes, her car breaks down. She pays a $120 towing bill to get the car to the service station, and the mechanic tells her the car has suffered major engine failure. The cost to fix the car will be $1,600, which is a fair price for such damage. Jill has enough money from her student loan to pay the bill, but she knows this will put her behind for the next several months' rent. The mechanic tells her that if she pays cash, instead of writing a check or paying with a debit card or credit card, he will charge her only $1,300. When she asks the reason for the $300 discount, he tells her, "If you pay cash, there's no record of our transaction, and I won't have to pay taxes. This will save money for both of us." What should Jill do? Another mechanic is likely to charge her full price, and she would have to pay an additional towing charge to get the car to a different mechanic.

CONTROLS OVER CASH DISBURSEMENTS

Managers should design proper controls for cash disbursements to prevent any unauthorized payments and ensure proper recording. Consistent with our discussion of cash receipts, cash disbursements include not only disbursing physical cash, but also writing checks and using credit cards and debit cards to make payments. All these forms of payment constitute cash disbursement and require formal internal control procedures. Important elements of a cash disbursement control system include the following steps:

1. Make all disbursements, other than very small ones, by check, debit card, or credit card. This provides a permanent record of all disbursements.
2. Authorize all expenditures before purchase and verify the accuracy of the purchase itself. The employee who authorizes payment should not also be the employee who prepares the check.

176   CHAPTER 4   Cash and Internal Controls

3. Make sure checks are serially numbered and signed only by authorized employees. Require two signatures for larger checks.

4. Periodically check amounts shown in the debit card and credit card statements against purchase receipts. The employee verifying the accuracy of the debit card and credit card statements should not also be the employee responsible for actual purchases.

5. Set maximum purchase limits on debit cards and credit cards. Give approval to purchase above these amounts only to upper-level employees.

6. Employees responsible for making cash disbursements should not also be in charge of cash receipts.

When the movie theatre pays $1,000 to advertise its show times, it records the following transaction, regardless of whether it pays with cash, a check, or a debit card.

A = L + SE		Debit	Credit
−1,000 Exp↑	**Advertising Expense**	**1,000**	
−1,000	**Cash**		**1,000**
	(Purchase advertising with cash, check, or debit card)		

Because credit cards allow the purchaser to delay payment for several weeks or even months, if the theatre uses a credit card to pay for the $1,000 worth of advertising, it would record the purchase as follows.

A = L + SE		Debit	Credit
−1,000 Exp↑	**Advertising Expense**	**1,000**	
+1,000	**Accounts Payable**		**1,000**
	(Purchase advertising with credit card)		

KEY POINT

Because cash is the asset of a company most susceptible to employee fraud, controls over cash receipts and cash disbursements are an important part of a company's overall internal control system. Important controls over cash receipts include separation of duties for those who handle cash and independent verification of cash receipts. Important controls over cash disbursements include payment by check, credit card, or debit card, separation of duties, and various authorization and documentation procedures.

Bank Reconciliation

■ **LO5**
Reconcile a bank statement.

Another important control used by nearly all companies to help maintain control of cash is a bank reconciliation. A **bank reconciliation** matches the balance of cash in the bank account with the balance of cash in the company's own records. If you have your own checking account, you know that the balance of cash in your checkbook often does not equal the balance of cash in your bank account. Why is that? One possibility is that you (or your bank) made a recording error. More likely, though, you've written a check or have cash receipts that haven't yet reached the bank, or maybe the bank has made an adjustment you haven't yet recorded.

It's the same for a business. A company's cash balance as recorded in its books rarely equals the cash balance reported in the bank statement. The reasons for the differences are the same as those for your personal checking account: Differences in these balances most often occur because of either timing differences or errors. It is the *possibility* of these errors, or even outright fraudulent activities, that makes the bank reconciliation a useful cash control tool.

Timing differences in cash occur when the company records transactions either before or after the bank records the same transaction. For example, when a movie theatre pays its popcorn supplier $200 by check, the company records a decrease in cash immediately, but the bank doesn't record a decrease in cash until the popcorn supplier later deposits the check. If the supplier waits a week before depositing the check, the balance of cash in the company's records will be reduced one week earlier than will the bank's.

Other times, the bank is the first to record a transaction. The bank could charge a $50 service fee for processing the company's transaction, immediately reducing the bank's record of the company's balance for cash. However, the company may not be immediately aware of this fee. Only when the monthly bank statement is sent will the company become aware of the cash reduction. In this case, the bank's balance for cash reflects a cash transaction before the company's balance can reflect the same transaction.

Errors can be made either by the company or its bank and may be accidental or intentional. An *accidental* error might occur if the company mistakenly were to record a check being written for $117 as $171 in its records, or if the bank improperly processed a deposit of $1,100 as a $1,010 deposit. An *intentional* error is the result of theft. If the company records a daily deposit of $5,000 but an employee deposits only $500 into the bank account and pockets the rest, the bank reconciliation will reveal the missing $4,500.

A bank reconciliation connects the company's cash balance to the bank's cash balance by identifying differences due to timing and errors. This concept is shown in Illustration 4–6.

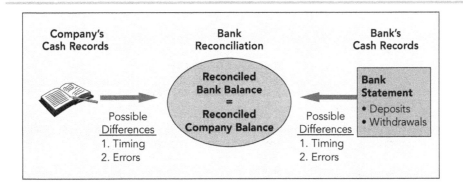

ILLUSTRATION 4–6

Bank Reconciliation

To see how a bank reconciliation is prepared, let's start by examining the bank statement of Starlight Drive-In. At the end of March, First Bank sends the bank statement in Illustration 4–7 (next page) to Starlight. Compare the bank statement with Starlight's own records of cash activity over the same period, as shown in Illustration 4–8 (next page).

First Bank's ending balance of cash ($4,100) differs from Starlight's ending balance of cash ($2,880). To understand why these two cash balances differ, we need to identify (1) timing differences created by cash activity reported by either First Bank or Starlight but not recorded by the other and (2) any errors.

ILLUSTRATION 4–7

Bank Statement

P.O. Box 26788	*First Bank*	Member FDIC
Odessa, TX 79760	*A Name You Can Trust*	
(432) 799-BANK		

Account Holder:	Starlight Drive-In	Account Number:	4061009619
	221B Baker Street		
	Odessa, TX 79760	Statement Date:	March 31, 2012

Account Summary

Beginning Balance	Deposits and Credits		Withdrawals and Debits		Ending Balance
March 1, 2012	No.	Total	No.	Total	March 31, 2012
$3,800	4	$8,600	7	$8,300	$4,100

Account Details

Deposits and Credits			Withdrawals and Debits				Daily Balance	
Date	Amount	Desc.	Date	No.	Amount	Desc.	Date	Amount
3/5	$3,600	DEP	3/8	293	$2,100	CHK	3/5	$7,400
3/9	3,000	NOTE	3/12	294	2,900	CHK	3/8	5,300
3/22	1,980	DEP	3/15		400	EFT	3/9	8,300
3/31	20	INT	3/22		750	NSF	3/12	5,400
			3/26	296	1,900	CHK	3/15	5,000
			3/28		200	DC	3/22	6,230
			3/31		50	SF	3/26	4,330
							3/28	4,130
	$8,600				$8,300		3/31	$4,100

Desc.	**DEP** Customer deposit	**INT** Interest earned	**SF** Service fees
	NOTE Note collected	**CHK** Customer check	**NSF** Nonsufficient funds
	EFT Electronic funds transfer	**DC** Debit card	

ILLUSTRATION 4–8

Company Records of
Cash Activities

STARLIGHT DRIVE-IN
Cash Account Records
March 1, 2012, to March 31, 2012

Deposits			Checks			
Date	Desc.	Amount	Date	No.	Desc.	Amount
3/5	Sales receipts	$3,600	3/6	293	Salaries	$2,100
3/22	Sales receipts	1,980	3/11	294	Rent	2,600
3/31	Sales receipts	2,200	3/21	295	Utilities	1,200
			3/24	296	Insurance	1,900
			3/30	297	Supplies	900
		$7,780				$8,700

SUMMARY OF TRANSACTIONS

Beginning Cash Balance March 1, 2012	+	Deposits	−	Checks	=	Ending Cash Balance March 31, 2012
$3,800		$7,780		$8,700		$2,880

COMMON MISTAKE

Notice that bank statements refer to an increase (or deposit) in the cash balance as a *credit* and a decrease (or withdrawal) as a *debit*. This terminology is the opposite of that used in financial accounting, where *debit* refers to an increase in cash and *credit* refers to a decrease in cash. The reason for the difference in terminology is a difference in perspective: The financial accounting records are prepared *from a company's perspective*, while the bank statement is prepared *from a bank's perspective*. When a company makes a deposit, the bank's liability to the company (a credit account) increases. When a company withdraws cash from its bank account, the bank's liability to the company decreases.

Reconciling the bank account involves three steps: (1) reconciling the bank's cash balance, (2) reconciling the company's cash balance, and (3) adjusting the company's cash balance. In the first two steps, we should catch timing differences (such as for deposits outstanding, checks outstanding, and bank memoranda) as well as errors made by either the company or the bank. In the third step, we update the company's accounting records for cash transactions that have occurred but have not yet been recorded.

STEP 1: RECONCILING THE BANK'S CASH BALANCE

First, we will reconcile the bank's cash balance. Cash transactions recorded by a company, but not yet recorded by its bank, include deposits outstanding and checks outstanding. Deposits outstanding are cash receipts of the company that have not been added to the bank's record of the company's balance. Checks outstanding are checks the company has written that have not been subtracted from the bank's record of the company's balance.

Timing differences

For example, comparing cash receipts recorded by Starlight (Illustration 4–8) to those reported as deposits in the bank statement (Illustration 4–7) reveals that cash sales receipts of $2,200 on March 31 are not yet reflected in the bank's balance by the end of March. This is a deposit outstanding.

Comparing the checks written by Starlight to those reported in the bank statement shows that the bank received checks #293, #294, and #296 by the end of March. This means checks #295 (for $1,200) and #297 (for $900) remain outstanding and are not yet reflected in the bank's balance.

Once the bank receives the deposits outstanding, the bank's cash balance will increase. Similarly, once the bank receives the checks outstanding, the bank's cash balance will decrease. We also need to check for and correct any bank errors.

The reconciled bank balance is calculated on the left side of Illustration 4–9 (next page).

STEP 2: RECONCILING THE COMPANY'S CASH BALANCE

Next, we need to reconcile the company's cash balance. What are some examples of cash transactions recorded by the bank but not yet recorded by the company? These would include items such as interest earned by the company, collections made by the bank on the company's behalf, service fees, and charges for NSF checks—customers' checks written on "nonsufficient funds," otherwise known as "bad" checks. In addition, we adjust the company's balance for any recording errors made by the company.

Six cash transactions recorded by First Bank (Illustration 4–7) are not reported in Starlight's cash records (Illustration 4–8) by the end of March:

1. Note received by First Bank on Starlight's behalf ($3,000 consisting of $2,800 plus related interest received of $200).

2. Interest earned by Starlight on its bank account ($20).

180   CHAPTER 4   Cash and Internal Controls

Timing differences

3. NSF check ($750).

4. Debit card purchase of office equipment by an employee ($200).

5. Electronic funds transfer (EFT) related to the payment of advertising ($400).

6. Service fee ($50).

 COMMON MISTAKE

Students sometimes mistake an NSF check as a bad check written *by* the company instead of one written *to* the company. When an NSF check occurs, the company must adjust its balance of cash downward to reverse the increase in cash it recorded at the time it received the check from the customer, because the customer did not have enough funds to cover the check. This bounced check will create an account receivable for the company until the customer pays the funds it owes.

Company error

In addition to the amounts related to timing differences, we need to address one other reconciling item. Comparing Starlight's record of checks written to those in the bank statement reveals an error by Starlight. Check #294 for rent was written for $2,900, but Starlight's accountant recorded it incorrectly as $2,600. First Bank processed the check for the correct amount of $2,900. This means Starlight needs to reduce its cash balance by an additional $300 for rent expense. The reconciled company balance is calculated on the right side of Illustration 4–9. (Note that the illustration shows additions to the company's account in green and subtractions from the account in red.)

ILLUSTRATION 4–9

Reconciling the Bank Statement

STARLIGHT DRIVE-IN
Bank Reconciliation
March 31, 2012

Bank's Cash Balance		*Company's* Cash Balance	
Before reconciliation	$4,100	Before reconciliation	$2,880
Deposits outstanding:	+2,200	Note received	+2,800
3/31 = $2,200		Interest earned from note	+200
		Interest earned on bank account	+20
Checks outstanding:	−2,100	NSF check	−750
#295 = $1,200		Debit card for office equipment	−200
#297 = $ 900		EFT for advertising	−400
		Service fee	−50
		Corrected rent expense error	−300
After reconciliation	$4,200	After reconciliation	$4,200

Reconciled

If the bank were aware of all deposits made and all checks written by the company, the bank's cash balance would be $4,200. Similarly, once the company adjusts its balance for information revealed in the bank statement, its cash balance is $4,200. The fact that the two balances match provides some indication that cash is not being mishandled by employees.

STEP 3: ADJUSTING THE COMPANY'S CASH BALANCE

As a final step in the reconciliation process, a company must update the balance in its Cash account, to adjust for the items used to reconcile the *company's* cash balance. We record these adjustments once the bank reconciliation is complete. Remember, these are amounts the company didn't know until it received the bank statement.

We record items that increase the company's cash by a debit to Cash. Similarly, we record items that decrease the company's cash by a credit to Cash. The entries needed to adjust Starlight's cash balance for reconciliation items are as follows.

March 31, 2012	Debit	Credit	A	=	L	+	SE
Cash	3,020		+3,020				
Notes Receivable		2,800	−2,800				
Interest Revenue		220					+220 Rev↑
(Reconcile cash increases)			A	=	L	+	SE
Accounts Receivable	750		+750				
Equipment	200		+200				
Advertising Expense	400						−400 Exp↑
Service Fee Expense	50						−50 Exp↑
Rent Expense	300						−300 Exp↑
Cash		1,700	−1,700				
(Reconcile cash decreases)							

Most of the accounts are easy to understand. We credit Notes Receivable because the note has been received, decreasing that asset account (−$2,800). We recognize interest revenue (+$220) as earned. We need to record cash outflows related to expenses (advertising, service fee, and rent) and asset purchases need to be recorded. Finally, we debit Accounts Receivable, increasing that asset account (+$750) to show that the customer who paid with an NSF check still owes the company money.

COMMON MISTAKE

Some students try to prepare adjusting entries for deposits outstanding, checks outstanding, or a bank error. The company does *not* need to adjust for these items related to reconciling the bank's balance because they are already properly recorded in the company's accounting records.

In the uncommon event that the two reconciled balances do not equal, management investigates the discrepancy to check for wrongdoing or errors by company employees or the bank. If the company cannot resolve the discrepancy, it records the difference to either Miscellaneous Expense or Miscellaneous Revenue, depending on whether it has a debit or credit balance. For example, suppose a company is unable to account for $100 of missing cash. In this event, the company records the following transaction, increasing Miscellaneous Expense and decreasing Cash.

	Debit	Credit	A	=	L	+	SE
Miscellaneous Expense	100						−100 Exp↑
Cash		100	−100				
(Record loss of $100 cash)							

KEY POINT

In a bank reconciliation we adjust the *bank's* balance for (1) cash transactions already recorded by the company but not yet recorded by the bank and (2) bank errors. Similarly, we adjust the *company's* balance for (1) cash transactions already recorded by the bank but not yet recorded by the company and (2) company errors. After we adjust both the bank balance and the company balance, the two should equal.

Let's Review

At the end of April 2012, Showtime Theatre's accounting records show a cash balance of $4,800. The April bank statement reports a cash balance of $3,700. The following information is gathered from the bank statement and company records:

Checks outstanding	$1,900	Customer's NSF check	$1,300
Deposits outstanding	1,600	Service fee	200
Interest earned	70		

In addition, Showtime discovered it correctly paid for advertising with a check for $220 but incorrectly recorded the check in the company's records for $250. The bank correctly processed the check for $220.

Required:

1. Prepare a bank reconciliation for the month of April 2012.
2. Prepare entries to adjust the balance of cash in the company's records.

Solution:

1. Bank reconciliation:

SHOWTIME THEATRE
Bank Reconciliation
April 30, 2012

Bank's Cash Balance		*Company's Cash Balance*	
Before reconciliation	$3,700	Before reconciliation	$4,800
Deposits outstanding	+1,600	Interest earned	+70
		Company error	+30
Checks outstanding	−1,900	Service fee	−200
		NSF check	−1,300
After reconciliation	$3,400	After reconciliation	$3,400

2. Entries to adjust cash balance:

April 30, 2012	Debit	Credit
Cash	100	
Interest Revenue		70
Advertising Expense		30
(Reconcile cash increases)		
Service Fee Expense	200	
Accounts Receivable	1,300	
Cash		1,500
(Reconcile cash decreases)		

Suggested Homework:
BE4-8, BE4-9;
E4-12, E4-13;
P4-2A&B, P4-3A&B

Petty Cash

■ **LO6**
Account for petty cash.

You probably pay for most of your purchases with a debit card, credit card, or check. However, it's nice to have a little cash in your wallet for emergency or impulse expenditures. For example, you might decide to buy a box of Girl Scout cookies from your neighbor or soda from a machine. In the same way, most companies like to keep a small amount of cash on hand at the company's location for minor purchases such as postage, office supplies, delivery charges, and entertainment expenses. If the office manager orders a $10 pizza for a staff meeting, it would be inconvenient and costly to write and process a check for such a small amount. Furthermore, it would be time-consuming to run to the bank for a $10 cash withdrawal. To pay for these minor purchases, companies keep some minor amount of cash on hand in a petty cash fund.

Accounting for the petty cash fund involves recording transactions to (1) establish the fund, (2) recognize expenditures from the fund, and (3) replenish the fund as the cash balance becomes sufficiently low. Management establishes a petty cash fund by writing a check for cash against the company's checking account and putting that amount of withdrawn cash in the hands of an employee who becomes responsible for it. This employee is often referred to as the *petty-cash custodian*. The fund should have just enough cash to make minor expenditures over a reasonable period (such as a week or a month). Given appropriate documentation, such as a receipt for the purchase of the $10 pizza for the staff meeting or of office supplies, the petty-cash custodian will disburse cash to reimburse the purchaser. At any given time, the cash remaining in the fund plus all receipts should equal the amount of the fund. The receipts are important to ensure proper use of the funds and for recording expenditures each time the fund is replenished.

Suppose that at the beginning of May, Starlight Drive-In establishes a petty cash fund of $500 to pay for minor purchases. Starlight establishes the fund by recording:

May 1	Debit	Credit	A	=	L	+	SE
Petty Cash (on hand)	500		+500				
Cash (checking account)		500	−500				
(Establish the petty cash fund)							

Assume Starlight has the following expenditures from the petty cash fund during May:

Date	Expenditure	Amount
May 7	Postage	$ 75
May 16	Delivery charges	85
May 20	Office group lunch	50
May 26	Office supplies	120
		$330

By the end of May, the petty cash fund has distributed $330, leaving $170 in the fund, along with receipts for $330. However, the company did not record these transactions at the time these expenditures were made. By the end of the period, the expenditures from the petty cash fund must be recorded.

May 31	Debit	Credit	A	=	L	+	SE
Postage Expense	75						−75 Exp↑
Delivery Expense	85						−85 Exp↑
Entertainment Expense	50						−50 Exp↑
Supplies	120		+120				
Petty Cash (on hand)		330	−330				
(Recognize expenditures from the petty cash fund)							

Also at the end of the period, the petty cash fund may need to be replenished. Management can withdraw cash of $330 from the checking account and give it to the petty-cash custodian so the fund's balance will once again be $500.

	Debit	Credit
May 31		
Petty Cash (on hand)	330	
Cash (checking account)		330
(*Replenish the petty cash fund at the end of the period*)		

A   =   L   +   SE
+330
−330

To maintain the control objective of separation of duties, the petty-cash custodian should not be involved in accounting for, nor in the process of writing or approving, replenishment checks.

What if only $150 is left in the petty cash fund, when there should be $170? It could be that $20 was stolen from the fund, or the fund could be missing a receipt for $20. If the question is not resolved, the firm will likely charge the $20 to Miscellaneous Expense.

 KEY POINT

To pay for minor purchases, companies keep some cash on hand in a petty cash fund. At the end of the period, expenditures from the petty cash fund are recorded, and the fund is replenished.

Reporting Cash

To this point, we've considered several internal controls related to cash. Here, we discuss how companies report cash activities. Cash activities of a business enterprise are the most fundamental events upon which investors and lenders base their decisions: Where does a company get its cash? Where does a company usually spend its cash? These are important issues in determining management's efficient use of a company's resources and in predicting future performance. Companies report cash in two ways—in the balance sheet and in the statement of cash flows.

BALANCE SHEET

As we discussed in Chapter 3, companies report cash as an asset in the balance sheet. The amount is typically reported as a current asset and represents cash available for spending at the end of the reporting period. The balance sheet provides only the final balance for cash. It does not provide any details regarding cash receipts and payments during the period.

STATEMENT OF CASH FLOWS

■ LO7
Identify the major inflows and outflows of cash.

Companies report information about cash receipts and payments during the period in a statement of cash flows. **From the statement of cash flows, investors know a company's cash inflows and cash outflows related to (1) operating activities, (2) investing activities, and (3) financing activities.** We'll provide a complete discussion of the statement of cash flows in Chapter 11. Here, we briefly introduce the basics of the statement to help you understand that its purpose is to report activity related to the key topic of this chapter—cash.

Recall from Chapter 1 the three fundamental types of business activities relating to cash:

- *Operating activities* include cash transactions involving revenue and expense events during the period. In other words, operating activities include the cash effect of the same activities that are reported in the income statement.
- *Investing activities,* as the name implies, include cash investments in long-term assets and investment securities. When the firm later sells those assets, we consider those transactions investing activities also. So, investing activities tend to involve long-term assets.

- *Financing activities* include transactions designed to raise cash or finance the business. There are two ways to do this: borrow cash from lenders or raise cash from stockholders. We also consider cash outflows to repay debt and cash dividends to stockholders to be financing activities. So, financing activities involve liabilities and stockholders' equity.

It's easiest to understand cash flow information by looking at the underlying transactions. To do this, we'll refer back to the external transactions of Eagle Golf Academy introduced in Chapters 1 through 3. For convenience, Illustration 4–10 lists those transactions and analyzes their effects on the company's cash.

Transaction	External Transactions in January	Type of Activity	Is Cash Involved?	Inflow or Outflow?
(1)	Sell shares of common stock for $25,000 to obtain the funds necessary to start the business.	Financing	Yes	Inflow
(2)	Borrow $10,000 from the local bank and sign a note promising to repay the full amount of the debt in three years.	Financing	Yes	Inflow
(3)	Purchase equipment necessary for giving golf training, $24,000 cash.	Investing	Yes	Outflow
(4)	Pay one year of rent in advance, $6,000 ($500 per month).	Operating	Yes	Outflow
(5)	Purchase supplies on account, $2,300.	Operating	No	—
(6)	Provide golf training to customers for cash, $3,600.	Operating	Yes	Inflow
(7)	Provide golf training to customers on account, $2,500.	Operating	No	—
(8)	Receive cash in advance for 10 golf training sessions to be given in the future, $600.	Operating	Yes	Inflow
(9)	Pay salaries to employees, $2,800.	Operating	Yes	Outflow
(10)	Pay cash dividends of $200 to shareholders.	Financing	Yes	Outflow

ILLUSTRATION 4–10

External Transactions of Eagle Golf Academy

Which transactions involve the exchange of cash?

Which transactions involve the exchange of cash? All transactions except (5) and (7) involve either the receipt (inflow) or payment (outflow) of cash. **Only transactions involving *cash* affect a company's *cash* flows.**

Illustration 4–11 (next page) presents the statement of cash flows for Eagle Golf Academy using what's called the *direct method* of reporting operating activities. Corresponding transaction numbers are in brackets. (In Chapter 11 we'll discuss the *indirect method*.)

From the statement of cash flows, investors and creditors can see that the major source of cash inflow for Eagle is the issuance of common stock, a financing activity. Eagle has also received cash from bank borrowing, which must be repaid. The company is also investing heavily in its future by purchasing equipment. Eagle reports this amount as an investing outflow.

With regard to the three types of business activities, the cash flow that's related most directly to the company's profitability is net cash flows from operating activities. For Eagle Golf Academy, net cash flows from operating activities are –$4,600. This means that cash *outflows* related to operating activities exceed inflows. Stated another way, cash outflows related to expense activities exceed cash inflows related to revenue activities. While Eagle reports net income of $500 in its income statement (see Illustration 3–12 in Chapter 3), these same activities are not able to generate positive cash flows for the company. Ultimately, companies must be able to generate positive operating cash flows to maintain long-term success.

ILLUSTRATION 4–11

Statement of Cash Flows for Eagle Golf Academy

Numbers in brackets correspond to the external transaction numbers of Eagle Golf Academy in Illustration 4–10.

Only transactions that involve the exchange of cash are included in the statement of cash flows.

EAGLE GOLF ACADEMY
Statement of Cash Flows
For the month ended January 31, 2012

Cash Flows from Operating Activities

Cash inflows:		
From customers [6 and 8]	$ 4,200	
Cash outflows:		
For salaries [9]	(2,800)	
For rent [4]	(6,000)	
Net cash flows from operating activities		$ (4,600)

Cash Flows from Investing Activities

Purchase equipment [3]	(24,000)	
Net cash flows from investing activities		(24,000)

Cash Flows from Financing Activities

Issue common stock [1]	25,000	
Borrow from bank [2]	10,000	
Pay dividends [10]	(200)	
Net cash flows from financing activities		34,800
Net increase in cash		6,200
Cash at the beginning of the month		-0-
Cash at the end of the month		$ 6,200

The final amount reported in the statement of cash flows, **$6,200**, is the same amount of cash reported in the balance sheet. You can verify this is the case for Eagle Golf Academy by referring back to the balance sheet reported in Illustration 3–14 in Chapter 3.

 KEY POINT

The statement of cash flows reports all cash activities for the period. *Operating activities* include those transactions involving revenue and expense activities. *Investing activities* include cash investments in long-term assets and investment securities. *Financing activities* include transactions designed to finance the business through borrowing and owner investment.

Decision Point

Question	Accounting information	Analysis
Is the company able to generate enough cash from internal sources to sustain daily operations?	Statement of cash flows	Cash flows generated from internal sources include operating and investing activities. For established companies, the sum of these amounts should be positive. Otherwise, the company will need to rely on external funding (lenders and stockholders), which is not sustainable in the long term.

A company reports in its current year each of the transactions listed below.

Let's Review

Required:

Indicate whether each transaction should be reported as an operating, investing, or financing cash flow in the company's statement of cash flows, and whether each is a cash inflow or outflow.

Transaction	Type of Cash Flow	Inflow or Outflow
1. Pay employees' salaries.		
2. Obtain a loan at the bank.		
3. Purchase a building with cash.		
4. Purchase equipment with a note payable.		

Solution:

1. Operating—outflow.   2. Financing—inflow.   3. Investing—outflow.
4. Not reported as a cash flow because no cash is involved in the transaction.

Suggested Homework:
BE4-11, BE4-12;
E4-16, E4-17;
P4-4A&B, P4-5A&B

CASH ANALYSIS
Krispy Kreme vs. Starbucks

ANALYSIS

We now look at how decision makers analyze and use information about cash. Krispy Kreme and Starbucks provide some interesting comparisons.

The difference between revenues and expenses—net income—provides an accrual-basis measure of the company's ability to create wealth for its stockholders. In general, the greater a company's net income, the greater will be the value of the company to stockholders. However, the *timing* of revenues and expenses recorded under accrual-basis accounting may differ from the timing of operating cash flows.

Earlier, we discussed an example of such a timing difference, by comparing the net income of Eagle Golf Academy ($500) to its net cash flows from operations (−$4,600). If you were considering an investment in Eagle Golf Academy, would you consider net income of $500 to be a reliable indicator of the profit-generating potential of the company, given that it has net cash flows from operating activities of −$4,600? Which number is more useful in helping us to predict the long-term profitability of the company? We refer to the ability of current net income to help us predict the future performance of a company as earnings quality. When net income does not provide a good indicator of future performance, its earnings quality is said to be low.

COMPARING NET INCOME TO CASH FLOW

One of the more common techniques used by investors for measuring earnings quality relies on comparing the trend in a company's reported net income to its trend in free cash flow. A simple way to calculate a company's free cash flow is to consider its operating cash flows plus investing cash flows during the period. This measure represents the cash that is *free* to repay debt and distribute to stockholders. Companies whose free cash flow is declining relative to the trend in net income are likely to have lower-quality earnings.

Let's look at an example: In 1937, Vernon Rudolph bought a secret doughnut recipe from a French chef in New Orleans, rented a building in Winston-Salem, North Carolina, and began selling doughnuts. Since then, Mr. Rudolph's company,

■ **LO8**
Assess earnings quality by comparing net income and cash flows.

CAREER CORNER

Financial analysts offer investment advice to their clients—banks, insurance companies, mutual funds, securities firms, and individual investors. This advice usually comes in the form of a formal recommendation (buy, hold, or sell). Before giving an opinion, analysts develop a detailed understanding of a company's operations through discussions with management, analysis of competitors, and projections of industry trends. They also develop a detailed understanding of a company's financial statements, including its earnings quality. Analysts typically do not recommend companies with lower-quality earnings.

Understanding a company's earnings quality comes from having a good grasp of accrual-basis accounting. This is why many finance majors and MBA students, pursuing careers as financial analysts, take additional accounting-related courses when earning their degrees and even after graduation.

Comparing free cash flow with net income can help in measuring the quality of earnings.

Krispy Kreme, grew into a leading branded specialty retailer across the country, producing over a billion doughnuts a year. To illustrate the preference of not relying on a single measure like net income in isolation, we compare Krispy Kreme with **Starbucks Corporation**.

As Illustrations 4–12 and 4–13 show, both Krispy Kreme and Starbucks enjoyed explosive increases in net income over the 1999–2004 period. However, their free cash flows (or strict cash-basis net incomes) tell a very different story. Notice that Krispy Kreme's free cash was falling through 2004, while Starbucks' was increasing. The pattern should have raised concerns about the long-term profit-generating ability of Krispy Kreme. Indeed, in 2005, Krispy Kreme's growth in net income could no longer be sustained and decreased dramatically because the company did not have sufficient cash to maintain profitable operations.

In comparison, Starbucks' upward trend in net income through 2004 showed no signs of slowing. However, that trend would last for only a few more years. Notice that Starbucks' free cash flow began falling in 2006, while net income continued to rise. Again, the difference in trends between net income and free cash flow should have been a warning to investors.

ILLUSTRATION 4–12

Net Income and Free Cash Flow for Krispy Kreme, 1999–2009

ILLUSTRATION 4–13

Net Income and Free Cash Flow for Starbucks Corporation, 1999–2009

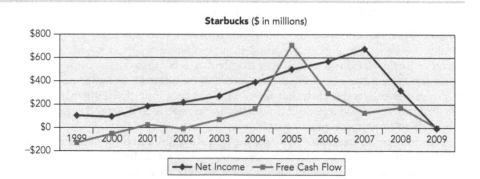

An upward trend in net income cannot be sustained indefinitely without a sufficient supply of cash. As predicted by the falling trend in free cash flow in 2006 and 2007, Starbucks' net income experienced a sharp decline beginning in 2008. These examples demonstrate the predictive ability of comparing a company's trend in net income and free cash flow. **When the trend in net income is upward while the trend in free cash flow is downward, a company is more likely to experience falling profits in the coming years.**

 KEY POINT

Companies whose free cash flow is decreasing relative to net income are likely to have lower earnings quality than are other companies, all else being equal.

Decision Point

Question	Accounting information	Analysis
How does free cash flow predict a company's net income?	Net income from the income statement and free cash flow (operating and investing) from the statement of cash flows	When free cash flow and net income have similar trends, net income is more likely to continue that trend in the future.

 KEY POINTS BY LEARNING OBJECTIVE

LO1 Discuss the impact of accounting scandals and the passage of the Sarbanes-Oxley Act.

The accounting scandals in the early 2000s prompted passage of the Sarbanes-Oxley Act (SOX). Among other stipulations, SOX sets forth a variety of new guidelines related to auditor-client relations and additional internal controls. Section 404, in particular, requires company management and auditors to document and assess the effectiveness of a company's internal controls.

LO2 Identify the components, responsibilities, and limitations of internal control.

Internal control refers to a company's plan to improve the accuracy and reliability of accounting information and safeguard the company's assets. Five key components to an internal control system are (1) control environment, (2) risk assessment, (3) control activities, (4) monitoring, and (5) information and communication.

LO3 Define cash and cash equivalents.

Cash includes not only currency, coins, balances in checking accounts, and checks and money orders received from customers, but also cash equivalents, defined as investments that mature within three months (such as money

market funds, Treasury bills, and certificates of deposit).

LO4 Understand controls over cash receipts and cash disbursements.

Because cash is the asset of a company most susceptible to employee fraud, controls over cash receipts and cash disbursements are an important part of a company's overall internal control system. Important controls over cash receipts include segregation of duties for those who handle cash and independent verification of cash receipts. Important controls over cash disbursements include payment by check, credit card, or debit card, segregation of duties, and various authorization and documentation procedures.

LO5 Reconcile a bank statement.

In a bank reconciliation we adjust the *bank's* balance for (1) cash transactions already recorded by the company but not yet recorded by the bank and (2) bank errors. Similarly, we adjust the *company's* balance for (1) cash transactions already recorded by the bank but not yet recorded by the company and (2) company errors. After we adjust both the bank balance and the company balance, the two should equal.

LO6 Account for petty cash.

To pay for minor purchases, companies keep some cash on hand in a petty cash fund. At the end of the period, expenditures from the petty cash fund are recorded, and the fund is replenished.

LO7 Identify the major inflows and outflows of cash.

The statement of cash flows reports all cash activities for the period. *Operating activities* include those transactions and events involving revenues and expenses. *Investing activities* include cash investments in long-term assets and investment securities. *Financing activities* include transactions designed to finance the business through borrowing and owner investment.

Analysis

LO8 Assess earnings quality by comparing net income and cash flows.

Companies whose free cash flow is decreasing relative to net income are likely to have lower earnings quality than are other companies, all else being equal.

GLOSSARY

Bank reconciliation: Matching the balance of cash in the bank account with the balance of cash in the company's own records. **p. 176**

Cash: Currency, coins, balances in savings and checking accounts, items acceptable for deposit in these accounts (such as checks received from customers), and cash equivalents. **p. 172**

Cash equivalents: Short-term investments that have a maturity date no longer than three months from the date of purchase. **p. 172**

Checks outstanding: Checks the company has written that have not been subtracted from the bank's record of the company's balance. **p. 179**

Collusion: Two or more people acting in coordination to circumvent internal controls. **p. 171**

Deposits outstanding: Cash receipts of the company that have not been added to the bank's record of the company's balance. **p. 179**

Earnings quality: The ability of net income to help predict future performance of the company. **p. 187**

Free cash flow: Operating cash flows plus investing cash flows during the period. **p. 187**

Internal controls: A company's plans to (1) safeguard the company's assets and (2) improve the accuracy and reliability of accounting information. **p. 166**

NSF checks: Checks drawn on nonsufficient funds, or "bad" checks from customers. **p. 179**

Occupational fraud: The use of one's occupation for personal enrichment through the deliberate misuse or misapplication of the employing organization's resources. **p. 166**

Petty cash fund: Small amount of cash kept on hand to pay for minor purchases. **p. 183**

Sarbanes-Oxley Act: Known as the *Public Company Accounting Reform and Investor Protection Act of 2002* and commonly referred to as *SOX*; the act established a variety of new guidelines related to auditor-client relations and internal control procedures. **p. 167**

Separation of duties: Authorizing transactions, recording transactions, and maintaining control of the related assets should be separated among employees. **p. 169**

SELF-STUDY QUESTIONS

■ **LO1**

1. Fraudulent reporting by management could include:
   a. Fictitious revenues from a fake customer.
   b. Improper asset valuation.
   c. Mismatching revenues and expenses.
   d. All of the above.

■ **LO1**

2. The Sarbanes-Oxley Act (SOX) mandates which of the following?
   a. Increased regulations related to auditor-client relations.
   b. Increased regulations related to internal control.
   c. Increased regulations related to corporate executive accountability.
   d. All of the above.

3. What is the concept behind *separation of duties* in establishing internal control? ■ LO2
   a. Employee fraud is less likely to occur when access to assets and access to accounting records are separated.
   b. The company's financial accountant should not share information with the company's tax accountant.
   c. Duties of middle-level managers of the company should be clearly separated from those of top executives.
   d. The external auditors of the company should have no contact with managers while the audit is taking place.

4. Which of the following is considered cash for financial reporting purposes? ■ LO3
   a. Accounts receivable.
   b. Investments with maturity dates greater than three months.
   c. Checks received from customers.
   d. Accounts payable.

5. Which of the following generally would *not* be considered good internal control of cash receipts? ■ LO4
   a. Allowing customers to pay with a debit card.
   b. Requiring the employee receiving the cash from the customer to also deposit the cash into the company's bank account.
   c. Recording cash receipts as soon as they are received.
   d. Allowing customers to pay with a credit card.

6. Which of the following adjusts the bank's balance of cash in a bank reconciliation? ■ LO5
   a. NSF checks.
   b. Service fees.
   c. An error by the company.
   d. Checks outstanding.

7. Which of the following adjusts the company's balance of cash in a bank reconciliation? ■ LO5
   a. Interest earned.
   b. Checks outstanding.
   c. Deposits outstanding.
   d. An error by the bank.

8. The purpose of a petty cash fund is to: ■ LO6
   a. Provide a convenient form of payment for the company's customers.
   b. Pay employee salaries at the end of each period.
   c. Provide cash on hand for minor expenditures.
   d. Allow the company to save cash for major future purchases.

9. Operating cash flows would include which of the following? ■ LO7
   a. Repayment of borrowed money.
   b. Payment for employee salaries.
   c. Services provided to customers on account.
   d. Payment for a new operating center.

10. A company's free cash flow is calculated as: ■ LO8
    a. The amount of cash reporting in the balance sheet.
    b. Net income less investing cash flows.
    c. Operating cash flows plus investing cash flows.
    d. Net income plus operating cash flows.

Note: For answers, see the last page of the chapter.

Check out
www.mhhe.com/succeed
for more multiple-choice
questions.

REVIEW QUESTIONS

■ LO1　1. Define occupational fraud. Describe two common means of occupational fraud.

■ LO1　2. What is internal control? Why should a company establish an internal control system?

■ LO1　3. "Managers are stewards of the company's assets." Discuss what this means.

■ LO1　4. Why are some managers motivated to manipulate amounts reported in the financial statements?

■ LO1　5. What are some of the consequences to employees when managers engage in fraudulent financial reporting?

■ LO1　6. What are some of the major provisions of the Sarbanes-Oxley Act?

■ LO2　7. Briefly describe the five components of internal control outlined by the Committee of Sponsoring Organizations (COSO).

■ LO2　8. Describe the difference between preventive controls and detective controls. What are examples of each?

■ LO2　9. What is meant by separation of duties?

■ LO2　10. Who has responsibility for internal control in an organization? According to guidelines set forth in Section 404 of the Sarbanes-Oxley Act, what role does the auditor play in internal control?

■ LO2　11. What are some limitations of internal control?

■ LO2　12. To what does collusion refer?

■ LO2　13. Is fraud more likely to occur when it is being committed by top-level employees? Explain.

■ LO3　14. Define cash and cash equivalents.

■ LO3　15. Describe how the purchase of items with a check is recorded.

■ LO4　16. Discuss basic controls for cash receipts.

■ LO4　17. What is a credit card? How are credit card sales reported?

■ LO4　18. What is a debit card? How are debit card sales reported?

■ LO4　19. Discuss basic controls for cash disbursements.

■ LO4　20. How are credit card purchases reported?

■ LO5　21. What is a bank reconciliation? How can it help in determining whether proper control of cash has been maintained?

■ LO5　22. What are two primary reasons that the company's balance of cash will differ between its own records and those of the bank?

■ LO5　23. Give some examples of timing differences in cash transactions that firms need to account for in a bank reconciliation.

■ LO5　24. After preparing a bank reconciliation, what adjustments does the company need to make to its records?

■ LO6　25. What is a petty cash fund?

■ LO6　26. Describe how management maintains control over the petty cash fund.

■ LO7　27. The change in cash for the year can be calculated by comparing the balance of cash reported in this year's and last year's balance sheet. Why is the statement of cash flows needed?

■ LO7　28. Describe the operating, investing, and financing sections of the statement of cash flows.

29. How does the relationship between net income and cash flows for the period provide an indication of the quality of earnings?   ■ LO8

30. We compared **Krispy Kreme** and **Starbucks** at the end of this chapter. What was the difference between the two companies, and why did that matter?   ■ LO8

BRIEF EXERCISES

BE4–1 Match each of the following provisions of the Sarbanes-Oxley Act (SOX) with its description.

Identify terms associated with the Sarbanes-Oxley Act **(LO1)**

Major Provisions of the Sarbanes-Oxley Act

_____ 1. Oversight board
_____ 2. Corporate executive accountability
_____ 3. Auditor rotation
_____ 4. Nonaudit services
_____ 5. Internal control

Descriptions

a. Executives must personally certify the company's financial statements.
b. Audit firm cannot provide a variety of other services to its client, such as consulting.
c. PCAOB establishes standards related to the preparation of audited financial reports.
d. Lead audit partners are required to change every five years.
e. Management must document the effectiveness of procedures that could affect financial reporting.

BE4–2 Match each of the following components of internal control with its description.

Identify terms associated with components of internal control **(LO2)**

Components of Internal Control

_____ 1. Control environment
_____ 2. Risk assessment
_____ 3. Control activities
_____ 4. Information and communication
_____ 5. Monitoring

Descriptions

a. Procedures for maintaining separation of duties.
b. Routine activities that are meant to continually observe internal control activities.
c. Transfer of data from lower managers to top executives for accurate financial reporting.
d. Formal policies to evaluate internal and external threats to achieving company objectives.
e. Overall attitude of the company with respect to internal controls.

BE4–3 Match each of the following control activities with its definition.

Define control activities associated with internal control **(LO2)**

Control Activities

_____ 1. Separation of duties
_____ 2. Physical controls
_____ 3. Proper authorization
_____ 4. Employee management
_____ 5. Reconciliations
_____ 6. Performance reviews

Definitions

a. The company should maintain security over assets and accounting records.
b. Management should periodically determine whether the amounts of physical assets of the company match the accounting records.
c. The company should provide employees with appropriate guidance to ensure they have the knowledge necessary to carry out their job duties.
d. The actual performance of individuals or processes should be checked against their expected performance.

194   CHAPTER 4   Cash and Internal Controls

e. Authorizing transactions, recording transactions, and maintaining control of the related assets should be separated among employees.

f. To prevent improper use of the company's resources, only certain employees are allowed to carry out certain business activities.

Identify cash and cash equivalents (LO3)

BE4–4 Determine whether the firm reports each of the following items as part of cash and cash equivalents in the balance sheet.

Item	Cash or Cash Equivalent? (yes/no)
1. Currency	_____
2. Inventory for sale to customers	_____
3. Balance in savings account	_____
4. Checks	_____
5. Accounts receivable	_____
6. Investments with maturities of less than three months	_____

Determine cash sales (LO4)

BE4–5 During the year, the following sales transactions occur. There is a charge of 3% on all credit card transactions. Calculate total cash sales recorded for the year.
1. Total cash sales = $400,000
2. Total check sales = $250,000
3. Total credit card sales = $500,000

Record cash expenditures (LO4)

BE4–6 Record the following transactions.
1. Pay employee salaries of $500 by issuing checks.
2. Purchase computer equipment of $900 using a credit card.
3. Pay for maintenance of $300 for a company vehicle using a debit card.

Identify terms associated with a bank reconciliation (LO5)

BE4–7 Match each term associated with a bank reconciliation with its description.

Terms	Descriptions
_____ 1. Checks outstanding	a. Cash receipts received by the company but not yet recorded by the bank.
_____ 2. NSF checks	b. Fees imposed by the bank to the company for providing routine services.
_____ 3. Company error	c. Checks written to the company that are returned by the bank as not having adequate funds.
_____ 4. Interest earned	
_____ 5. Deposits outstanding	d. Checks written by the company but not yet recorded by the bank.
_____ 6. Bank service fees	e. Money earned on the average daily balance of the checking account.
	f. The company recorded a deposit twice.

Prepare a bank reconciliation (LO5)

BE4–8 Indicate whether the firm should add or subtract each item below from its balance of cash or the bank's balance of cash in preparing a bank reconciliation. The first answer is provided as an example.

Reconciliation Items	Bank Balance	Company Balance
1. *Checks outstanding*	*Subtract*	
2. NSF checks		
3. Deposit recorded twice by company		
4. Interest earned		
5. Deposits outstanding		
6. Bank service fees		

BE4–9 Brangelina Adoption Agency's general ledger shows a cash balance of $4,583. The balance of cash in the March-end bank statement is $7,325. The bank statement reveals the following information: checks outstanding of $2,793, bank service fees of $75, and interest earned of $24. Calculate the correct balance of cash at the end of March.

Calculate the correct balance of cash (LO5)

BE4–10 Clooney Corp. establishes a petty cash fund for $200. By the end of the month, employees made the following expenditures from the fund: postage, $50; delivery, $75; supplies expense, $40; entertainment, $20. Record the expenditures from the petty cash fund, and record the entry to replenish the petty cash fund.

Record petty cash expenditures (LO6)

BE4–11 Match each type of cash flow to its definition.

Match types of cash flows with their definitions (LO7)

Types of Cash Flows	Definitions
_____ 1. Operating cash flows	a. Cash flows related to long-term assets and short-term investments.
_____ 2. Investing cash flows	b. Cash flows related to long-term liabilities and stockholders' equity.
_____ 3. Financing cash flows	c. Cash flows related to revenues and expenses.

BE4–12 Eastwood Enterprises offers horseback riding lessons. During the month of June, the company provides lessons on account totaling $4,100. By the end of the month, the company received on account $3,500 of this amount. In addition, Eastwood received $400 on account from customers who were provided lessons in May. Determine the amount of operating cash flows Eastwood will report as received from customers in June.

Determine operating cash flows (LO7)

BE4–13 On January 12, Ferrell Incorporated obtains a permit to start a comedy club, which will operate only on Saturday nights. To prepare the club for the grand opening, Ferrell purchases tables, chairs, ovens, and other related equipment for $55,000 on January 16. Ferrell pays 20% of this amount (= $11,000) in cash at the time of purchase and signs a note with Live Bank for the remaining amount. Determine the amount of investing cash flows Ferrell would report in January.

Determine investing cash flows (LO7)

BE4–14 Smith Law Firm specializes in the preparation of wills for estate planning. On October 1, 2012, the company begins operations by issuing stock for $10,000 and obtaining a loan from a local bank for $25,000. By the end of 2012, the company provides will preparation services of $32,000 cash and pays employee salaries of $23,000. In addition, Smith pays $2,000 in cash dividends to stockholders on December 31, 2012. Determine the amount of financing cash flows Smith would report in 2012.

Determine financing cash flows (LO7)

BE4–15 For each company, calculate free cash flow. Amounts in parentheses represent negative cash flows.

Calculate free cash flow (LO8)

	Operating Cash Flows	Investing Cash Flows	Financing Cash Flows
Tuohy Incorporated	$17,200	$(5,800)	$2,300
Oher Corporation	12,500	6,400	(7,100)

EXERCISES

E4–1 Below are several statements about occupational fraud.
1. For most large companies, occupational fraud is minimal and internal control procedures are unnecessary.
2. Managers have a variety of reasons for manipulating the numbers in financial statements, such as maximizing their compensation, increasing the company's stock price, and preserving their jobs.

Answer true-or-false questions about occupational fraud (LO1)

3. Internal control procedures include formal policies and procedures related to (1) safeguarding the company's assets and (2) improving the accuracy and reliability of accounting information.
4. "Cooking the books" is a phrase used by accountants to indicate the preparation of financial statements that are free of manipulation.
5. Most occupational fraud cases involve misuse of the company's resources.
6. Common types of financial statement fraud include creating fictitious revenues from a fake customer, improperly valuing assets, hiding liabilities, and mismatching revenues and expenses.

Required:
State whether the answer to each of the statements is true or false.

E4–2 Below are several statements about the Sarbanes-Oxley Act (SOX).

Answer true-or-false questions about the Sarbanes-Oxley Act (LO1)

1. SOX represents legislation passed in response to several accounting scandals in the early 2000s.
2. The requirements outlined in SOX apply only to those companies expected to have weak internal controls or to have manipulated financial statements in the past.
3. Section 404 of SOX requires both company management and auditors to document and assess the effectiveness of a company's internal control processes that could affect financial reporting.
4. Severe financial penalties and the possibility of imprisonment are consequences of fraudulent misstatement.
5. With the establishment of SOX, management now has primary responsibility for hiring an external audit firm.
6. The lead auditor in charge of auditing a particular company must rotate off that company only when occupational fraud is suspected.

Required:
State whether the answer to each of the statements is true or false.

E4–3 Below are several statements about internal controls.

Answer true-or-false questions about internal controls (LO2)

1. The components of internal control are built on the foundation of the ethical tone set by top management.
2. Once every three months, managers need to review operations to ensure that control procedures work effectively.
3. Collusion refers to the act of a single individual circumventing internal control procedures.
4. Detective control procedures are designed to detect errors or fraud that have already occurred, while preventive control procedures are designed to keep errors or fraud from occurring in the first place.
5. Fraud committed by top-level employees is more difficult to detect because those employees more often have the ability to override internal control features.
6. A good example of separation of duties would be having one person collect cash from customers and account for it, while having another person order inventory and maintain control over it.
7. Employee tips historically have been the most common means of detecting employee fraud.
8. Detective controls include reconciling the physical assets of the company with the accounting records and comparing actual performance of individuals or processes against their expected performance.
9. Effective internal controls and ethical employees ensure a company's success.

Required:
State whether the answer to each of the statements is true or false.

E4–4 Below are several scenarios related to control activities of a company.

Determine control activity violations (LO2)

1. A manufacturing company compares total sales in the current year to those in the previous year but does not compare the cost of production.

2. So that employees can have easy access to office supplies, a company keeps supplies in unlocked cabinets in multiple locations.
3. At the end of each day, a single employee collects all cash received from customers, records the total, and makes the deposit at the bank.
4. At the end of the year only, the company compares its cash records to the bank's records of cash deposited and withdrawn during the year.
5. A company encourages employees to call an anonymous hotline if they believe other employees are circumventing internal control features.
6. All employees have the authority to refund a customer's money.

Required:
For each scenario, determine which control activity is violated. Control activities include separation of duties, physical controls, proper authorization, employee management, reconciliations, and performance reviews. If no control activity is violated, state "none."

E4–5 Below are several amounts reported at the end of the year.

Currency located at the company	$ 800
Supplies	2,200
Short-term investments that mature within three months	1,700
Accounts receivable	2,500
Balance in savings account	7,500
Checks received from customers but not yet deposited	400
Prepaid rent	1,200
Coins located at the company	100
Equipment	8,400
Balance in checking account	5,200

Calculate the amount of cash to report (LO3)

Required:
Calculate the amount of cash to report in the balance sheet.

E4–6 Douglas and Son, Inc., uses the following process for its cash receipts: The company typically receives cash and check sales each day and places them in a single drawer. Each Friday, the cash clerk records the amount of cash received and deposits the money in the bank account. Each quarter, the controller requests information from the bank necessary to prepare a bank reconciliation.

Discuss internal control procedures related to cash receipts (LO4)

Required:
Discuss Douglas and Son's internal control procedures related to cash receipts, noting both weaknesses and strengths.

E4–7 Goldie and Kate operate a small clothing store that has annual revenues of about $100,000. The company has established the following procedures related to cash disbursements: The petty cash fund consists of $10,000. Employees place a receipt in the fund when making expenditures from it and obtain the necessary cash. For any expenditure not made with the petty cash fund, the employee writes a check. Employees are not required to obtain permission to write a check but are asked to use good judgment. Any check written for more than $5,000 can be signed only by Goldie or Kate.

Discuss internal control procedures related to cash disbursements (LO4)

Required:
Discuss Goldie and Kate's internal control procedures related to cash disbursements, noting both weaknesses and strengths.

E4–8 Janice Dodds opens the mail for Ajax Plumbing Company. She lists all customer checks on a spreadsheet that includes the name of the customer and the check amount. The checks, along with the spreadsheet, are then sent to Jim Seymour in the accounting department, who records the checks and deposits them daily in the company's checking account.

Discuss internal control procedures related to cash receipts (LO4)

Required:

Describe how the company could improve its internal control procedure for the handling of its cash receipts.

Reconcile timing differences in the bank's balance (LO5)

E4–9 Damon Company receives its monthly bank statement, which reports a balance of $1,750. After comparing this to the company's cash records, Damon's accountants determine that deposits outstanding total $3,200 and checks outstanding total $3,450.

Required:

Calculate the reconciled bank balance for cash.

Reconcile timing differences in the company's balance (LO5)

E4–10 Bourne Incorporated reports a cash balance at the end of the month of $2,370. A comparison of the company's cash records with the monthly bank statement reveals several additional cash transactions: bank service fees ($75), an NSF check from a customer ($250), a customer's note receivable collected by the bank ($1,100), and interest earned ($25).

Required:

Calculate the reconciled company balance for cash.

Record adjustments to the company's cash balance (LO5)

E4–11 Refer to the information in E4–10.

Required:

Prepare the necessary entries to adjust the balance of cash.

Calculate the balance of cash using a bank reconciliation (LO5)

E4–12 Spielberg Company's general ledger shows a checking account balance of $22,870 on July 31, 2012. The July cash receipts of $1,785, included in the general ledger balance, are placed in the night depository at the bank on July 31 and processed by the bank on August 1. The bank statement dated July 31 shows bank service fees of $45. The bank processes all checks written by the company by July 31 and lists them on the bank statement, except for one check totaling $1,360. The bank statement shows a balance of $22,400 on July 31.

Required:

Prepare a bank reconciliation to calculate the correct ending balance of cash on July 31, 2012.

Calculate the balance of cash using a bank reconciliation (LO5)

E4–13 On August 31, 2012, the general ledger of The Dean Acting Academy shows a balance for cash of $7,844. Cash receipts yet to be deposited into the checking account total $3,238, and checks written by the academy but not yet processed by the bank total $1,325. The company's balance of cash does not reflect a bank service fee of $25 and interest earned on the checking account of $36. These amounts are included in the balance of cash of $5,942 reported by the bank as of the end of August.

Required:

Prepare a bank reconciliation to calculate the correct ending balance of cash on August 31, 2012.

Record transactions for the petty cash fund (LO6)

E4–14 Halle's Berry Farm establishes a $400 petty cash fund on September 4 to pay for minor cash expenditures. The fund is replenished at the end of each month. At the end of September, the fund contains $70 in cash and the following receipts:

Office party decorations	$ 80
Lawn maintenance	110
Postage	65
Fuel for delivery	75

Required:

Record the establishment of the petty cash fund on September 4, the expenditures made during the month, and the replenishment of the fund on September 30.

E4–15 T. L. Jones Trucking Services establishes a petty cash fund on April 3 for $500. By the end of April, the fund has a cash balance of $72 and has receipts for the following items:

Utilities	$125
Pizza delivery (entertainment)	34
Stamps	49
Plumbing repair services	220

Required:

Record the establishment of the petty cash fund on April 3, the expenditures made during the month, and the replenishment of the fund on April 30.

E4–16 Below are several transactions for Witherspoon Incorporated, a small manufacturer of decorative glass designs.

Transaction	Cash Involved? (yes or no)	Operating, Investing, or Financing? (if cash involved)	Inflow or Outflow?
a. Borrow cash from the bank.			
b. Purchase supplies on account.			
c. Purchase equipment with cash.			
d. Provide services on account.			
e. Pay cash on account for *b.* above.			
f. Sell for cash a warehouse no longer in use.			
g. Receive cash on account for *d.* above.			
h. Pay cash to workers for salaries.			

Required:

For each transaction, indicate (1) whether cash is involved (yes or no), and, if cash is involved, (2) whether Witherspoon should classify it as operating, investing, or financing in a statement of cash flows, and (3) whether the cash is an inflow or outflow.

E4–17 Below are several transactions for Meyers Corporation for 2012.

Transaction	Inflow or Outflow of Cash?	Operating, Investing, or Financing?
a. Issue common stock for cash, $50,000.		
b. Purchase building and land with cash, $35,000.		
c. Provide services to customers on account, $7,000.		
d. Pay utilities on building, $1,000.		
e. Collect $5,000 on account from customers.		
f. Pay employee salaries, $9,000.		
g. Pay dividends to stockholders, $4,000.	_____	
Net cash flows for the year	_____	

Required:

1. For each transaction, determine the amount of the inflow or outflow of cash (indicate inflows with a "+" and outflows with a "−"). If cash is involved in the transaction, indicate whether Meyers should classify it as operating, investing, or financing in a statement of cash flows.
2. Calculate net cash flows for the year.

200   CHAPTER 4   Cash and Internal Controls

3. Assuming the balance of cash on January 1, 2012, equals $4,400, calculate the balance of cash on December 31, 2012.

Calculate operating cash flows (LO7)

E4–18 Below are cash transactions for Goldman Incorporated, which provides consulting services related to mining of precious metals.

a. Cash used for purchase of office supplies, $1,900.
b. Cash provided from consulting to customers, $45,600.
c. Cash used for purchase of mining equipment, $73,000.
d. Cash provided from long-term borrowing, $60,000.
e. Cash used for payment of employee salaries, $24,000.
f. Cash used for payment of office rent, $12,000.
g. Cash provided from sale of equipment purchased in *c.* above, $22,500.
h. Cash used to repay a portion of the long-term borrowing in *d.* above, $40,000.
i. Cash used to pay office utilities, $4,300.
j. Purchase of company vehicle, paying $10,000 cash and borrowing $15,000.

Required:
Calculate cash flows from operating activities.

Calculate investing cash flows (LO7)

E4–19 Refer to the information in E4–18.

Required:
Calculate cash flows from investing activities.

Calculate financing cash flows (LO7)

E4–20 Refer to the information in E4–18.

Required:
Calculate cash flows from financing activities.

Determine earnings quality (LO8)

E4–21 Below are amounts (in millions) for Glasco Company and Sullivan Company.

	GLASCO COMPANY		SULLIVAN COMPANY	
Year	Net Income	Free Cash Flow	Net Income	Free Cash Flow
1	$350	$420	$250	$300
4	470	630	330	210

Required:
Referring to the relation between net income and free cash flow, discuss each company's quality of earnings. Make a prediction as to which firm will have the larger increase in net income in year 5.

For additional exercises, visit www.mhhe.com/succeed for Exercises: Set B.

PROBLEMS: SET A

Discuss control procedures for cash receipts (LO4)

P4–1A The Carmike 8 Cinema is a modern theatre located close to a college campus. The cashier, located in a box office at the entrance to the theatre, receives cash from customers and operates a machine that ejects serially numbered tickets for each film. Customers then enter the theatre lobby where they can purchase refreshments at the concession stand. To gain admission to the movie, a customer hands the ticket to a ticket taker stationed some 50 feet from the box office at the entrance to the theatre lobby. The ticket taker tears the ticket in half, returns the stub to the customer, and allows the customer to enter the theatre hallway through a turnstile. The ticket taker drops the other half of the ticket stub into a locked box.

Required:
1. What internal controls are present in the handling of cash receipts?
2. What steps should the theatre manager take regularly to give maximum effectiveness to these controls?
3. Assume the cashier and the ticket taker decide to work together in an effort to steal from the movie theatre. What action(s) might they take?
4. For each idea proposed in number 3 above, what additional control features could Carmike 8 Cinema add to catch the thieves and reduce the risk of future thefts?

P4–2A Oscar's Red Carpet Store maintains a checking account with Academy Bank. Oscar's sells carpet each day but makes bank deposits only once per week. The following provides information from the company's cash ledger for the month ending February 28, 2012.

Prepare the bank reconciliation and record cash adjustments **(LO5)**

	Date	Amount		No.	Date	Amount
Deposits:	2/4	$ 2,200	Checks:	321	2/2	$ 4,200
	2/11	1,800		322	2/8	500
	2/18	2,700		323	2/12	2,000
	2/25	3,600		324	2/19	1,700
Cash receipts:	2/26–2/28	1,100		325	2/27	300
		$11,400		326	2/28	800
				327	2/28	1,400
						$10,900
Balance on February 1		$ 6,300				
Receipts		11,400				
Disbursements		(10,900)				
Balance on February 28		$ 6,800				

Information from February's bank statement and company records reveals the following additional information:

a. The ending cash balance recorded in the bank statement is $10,350.
b. Cash receipts of $1,100 from 2/26–2/28 are outstanding.
c. Checks 325 and 327 are outstanding.
d. The deposit on 2/11 includes a customer's check for $300 that did not clear the bank (NSF check).
e. Check 323 was written for $2,800 for advertising in February. The bank properly recorded the check for this amount.
f. An automatic withdrawal for Oscar's February rent was made on February 4 for $1,200.
g. Oscar's checking account earns interest based on the average daily balance. The amount of interest earned for February is $150.
h. In January, one of Oscar's suppliers, Titanic Fabrics, borrowed $5,000 from Oscar. On February 24, Titanic paid $5,200 ($5,000 borrowed amount plus $200 interest) directly to Academy Bank in payment for January's borrowing.
i. Academy Bank charged the following service fees to Oscar's: $50 for NSF check, $10 for automatic withdrawal for rent payment, and $40 for collection of the loan amount from Titanic.

Required:
1. Prepare a bank reconciliation for Oscar's checking account on February 28, 2012.
2. Record the necessary cash adjustments.

202

CHAPTER 4   Cash and Internal Controls

Prepare the bank
reconciliation and record
cash adjustments (LO5)

P4–3A The cash records and bank statement for the month of May for Diaz
Entertainment are shown below.

DIAZ ENTERTAINMENT
Cash Account Records
May 1, 2012, to May 31, 2012

Cash Balance May 1, 2012	+	Deposits	−	Checks	=	Cash Balance May 31, 2012
$5,380		$11,540		$11,620		$5,300

Deposits				Checks			
Date	Desc.	Amount	Date	No.	Desc.		Amount
5/3	Sales	$ 1,360	5/7	471	Legal fees		$ 1,200
5/10	Sales	1,790	5/12	472	Property tax		1,570
5/17	Sales	2,420	5/15	473	Salaries		3,500
5/24	Sales	2,890	5/22	474	Advertising		1,400
5/31	Sales	3,080	5/30	475	Supplies		450
			5/31	476	Salaries		3,500
		$11,540					$11,620

P.O. Box 162647
Bowlegs, OK 74830
(405) 369-CASH

Midwest Bank
Looking Out For You

Member FDIC

Account Holder:	Diaz Entertainment 124 Saddle Blvd. Bowlegs, OK 74830	Account Number:	7772854360
		Statement Date:	May 31, 2012

Beginning Balance May 1, 2012	Deposits and Credits		Withdrawals and Debits		Ending Balance May 31, 2012
	No.	Total	No.	Total	
$6,160	7	$9,530	9	$9,290	$6,400

Deposits and Credits			Withdrawals and Debits				Daily Balance	
Date	Amount	Desc.	Date	No.	Amount	Desc.	Date	Amount
5/4	$1,360	DEP	5/1	469	$ 450	CHK	5/1	$5,710
5/11	1,790	DEP	5/2	470	330	CHK	5/2	5,380
5/18	2,420	DEP	5/9	471	1,200	CHK	5/4	6,740
5/20	1,000	NOTE	5/11		300	NSF	5/9	5,540
5/20	50	INT	5/12	472	1,570	CHK	5/11	7,030
5/25	2,890	DEP	5/18	473	3,500	CHK	5/12	5,460
5/31	20	INT	5/20		500	EFT	5/18	4,380
			5/25	474	1,400	CHK	5/20	4,930
			5/31		40	SF	5/25	6,420
	$9,530				$9,290		5/31	$6,400

Desc.	**DEP** Customer deposit	**INT** Interest earned	**SF** Service fees
	NOTE Note collected	**CHK** Customer check	**NSF** Nonsufficient funds
	EFT Electronic funds transfer		

Additional information:

a. The difference in the beginning balances in the company's records and the bank
statement relates to checks #469 and #470, which are outstanding as of April 30, 2012.

b. The bank made the EFT on May 20 in error. The bank accidentally charged Diaz for
payment that should have been made on another account.

Required:
1. Prepare a bank reconciliation for Diaz's checking account on May 31, 2012.
2. Record the necessary cash adjustments.

P4–4A Below is a summary of all transactions of Pixar Toy Manufacturing for the month of August 2012.

Prepare the statement of cash flows **(LO7)**

Cash Transactions

Cash collections from:	
Customers	$ 92,500
Sale of unused warehouse	35,000
Bank borrowing	25,000
Cash payments for:	
Employee salaries	(64,300)
Office rent	(18,000)
Manufacturing equipment	(44,000)
Office utilities	(10,800)
Dividends to stockholders	(4,700)
Materials to make toys	(26,700)

Noncash Transactions

Sales to customers on account	15,400
Purchase of materials on account	12,900
Purchase equipment with promissory note to pay later	17,500

Required:
Prepare a statement of cash flows for the month of August 2012, properly classifying each of the transactions into operating, investing, and financing activities. The cash balance at the beginning of August is $24,500.

P4–5A Rocky owns and operates Balboa's Gym located in Philadelphia. The following transactions occur for the month of October:

Record transactions, post to the Cash T-account, and prepare the statement of cash flows **(LO7)**

October 2	Receive membership dues for the month of October totaling $7,500.
October 5	Issue common stock in exchange for cash, $10,000.
October 9	Purchase additional boxing equipment for $8,600, paying one-half of the amount in cash and the other one-half due by the end of the year.
October 12	Pay $1,000 for advertising regarding a special membership rate available during the month of October.
October 19	Pay dividends to stockholders, $3,400.
October 22	Pay liability insurance to cover accidents to members for the next six months, starting November 1, $6,000.
October 25	Receive cash in advance for November memberships, $4,600.
October 30	Receive, but do not pay, utilities bill for the month, $4,200.
October 31	Pay employees' salaries for the month, $6,300.

Required:
1. Record each transaction.
2. Identify the transactions involving cash.
3. Assuming the balance of cash at the beginning of October is $15,600, post each cash transaction to the Cash T-account and compute the ending cash balance.
4. Prepare a statement of cash flows for the month of October, properly classifying each of the cash transactions into operating, investing, and financing activities.
5. Verify that the net cash flows reported in the statement of cash flows equal the change in the cash balance for the month.

PROBLEMS: SET B

≡connect
|ACCOUNTING

Prepare a bank reconciliation and discuss cash procedures (LO4, 5)

P4–1B At the end of February, Howard Productions' accounting records reveal a balance for cash equal to $19,175. However, the balance of cash in the bank at the end of February is only $2,235. Howard is concerned and asks the company's accountant to reconcile the two balances. Examination of the bank statement and company records at the end of February reveals the following information:

NSF checks	$5,228	Service fees	$149
Deposits outstanding	7,642	Checks outstanding	479

In addition, during February the company's accountant wrote a check to one of its suppliers for $100. The check was recorded correctly in the company's records for $100 but processed incorrectly by the bank for $1,000. Howard has contacted the bank, which has agreed to fix the error. Finally, a petty cash fund of $3,500 was established during February. This amount was withdrawn from the checking account but not recorded.

Required:
1. Calculate the correct ending balance of cash at the end of February.
2. Discuss any problems you see with the company's cash procedures.

Prepare the bank reconciliation and record cash adjustments (LO5)

P4–2B On October 31, 2012, the bank statement for the checking account of Blockwood Video shows a balance of $12,630, while the company's records show a balance of $12,331. Information that might be useful in preparing a bank reconciliation is as follows:

a. Outstanding checks are $1,230.

b. The October 31 cash receipts of $785 are not deposited in the bank until November 2.

c. One check written in payment of utilities for $137 is correctly recorded by the bank but is recorded by Blockwood as a disbursement of $173.

d. In accordance with prior authorization, the bank withdraws $650 directly from the checking account as payment on a note payable. The interest portion of that payment is $50 and the principal portion is $600. Blockwood has not recorded the direct withdrawal.

e. Bank service fees of $24 are listed on the bank statement.

f. A deposit of $567 is recorded by the bank on October 13, but it did not belong to Blockwood. The deposit should have been made to the checking account of Hollybuster Video, a separate company.

g. The bank statement includes a charge of $75 for an NSF check. The check is returned with the bank statement, and the company will seek payment from the customer.

Required:
1. Prepare a bank reconciliation for the Blockwood checking account on October 31, 2012.
2. Record the necessary cash adjustments.

Prepare the bank reconciliation and record cash adjustments (LO5)

P4–3B The cash records and bank statement for the month of July for Glover Incorporated are shown below.

GLOVER INCORPORATED
Cash Account Records
July 1, 2012, to July 31, 2012

Cash Balance July 1, 2012	+	Deposits	−	Checks	=	Cash Balance July 31, 2012
$7,110		$8,420		$9,160		$6,370

Deposits			Checks			
Date	Desc.	Amount	Date	No.	Desc.	Amount
7/9	Sales	$2,560	7/7	531	Rent	$1,500
7/21	Sales	3,140	7/12	532	Salaries	1,960
7/31	Sales	2,720	7/19	533	Equipment	3,500
			7/22	534	Utilities	900
			7/30	535	Advertising	1,300
		$8,420				$9,160

P.O. Box 123878
Gotebo, OK 73041
(580) 377-OKIE

Fidelity Union
You Can Bank On Us

Member FDIC

Account Holder:	Glover Incorporated 519 Main Street Gotebo, OK 73041	Account Number:	2252790471
		Statement Date:	July 31, 2012

Beginning Balance July 1, 2012	Deposits and Credits		Withdrawals and Debits		Ending Balance July 31, 2012
	No.	Total	No.	Total	
$7,700	3	$5,750	7	$8,800	$4,650

Deposits and Credits			Withdrawals and Debits				Daily Balance	
Date	Amount	Desc.	Date	No.	Amount	Desc.	Date	Amount
7/10	$2,560	DEP	7/2	530	$ 590	CHK	7/2	$7,110
7/22	3,140	DEP	7/10	531	1,500	CHK	7/10	8,170
7/31	50	INT	7/14	532	1,960	CHK	7/14	6,210
			7/18		400	NSF	7/18	5,810
			7/22	533	3,800	CHK	7/22	5,150
			7/26		500	EFT	7/26	4,650
			7/30		50	SF	7/30	4,600
	$5,750				$8,800		7/31	$4,650

Desc.	**DEP** Customer deposit	**INT** Interest earned	**SF** Service fees
	NOTE Note collected	**CHK** Customer check	**NSF** Nonsufficient funds
	EFT Electronic funds transfer		

Additional information:

a. The difference in the beginning balances in the company's records and the bank statement relates to check #530, which is outstanding as of June 30, 2012.

b. Check #533 is correctly processed by the bank.

c. The EFT on July 26 relates to the purchase of office supplies.

Required:

1. Prepare a bank reconciliation for Glover's checking account on July 31, 2012.
2. Record the necessary cash adjustments.

P4–4B Below is a summary of all transactions of Dreamworks Bedding Supplies for the month of August 2012.

Prepare the statement of cash flows (LO7)

Cash Transactions

Cash collections from:	
Customers	$ 85,400
Sale of unused land	14,700
Issuance of common stock	20,000
Interest earned on savings account	200
Cash payments for:	
Employee salaries	(46,100)
Delivery truck	(32,500)
Advertising expense	(4,900)
Office supplies	(2,800)
Repayment of borrowing	(8,000)
Bedding material	(16,200)

Noncash Transactions

Sales to customers on account	11,300
Purchase of materials on account	7,400
Exchange common stock for building	82,000

206   CHAPTER 4   Cash and Internal Controls

Required:

Prepare a statement of cash flows for the month of August, properly classifying each of the transactions into operating, investing, and financing activities. The cash balance at the beginning of August is $7,300.

Record transactions, post to the Cash T-account, and prepare the statement of cash flows **(LO 7)**

P4–5B Peter loves dogs and cats. For the past several years, he has owned and operated Homeward Bound, which temporarily houses pets while their owners go on vacation. For the month of June, the company has the following transactions:

June	2	Obtain cash by borrowing $20,000 from the bank by signing a note.
June	3	Pay rent for the current month, $1,000.
June	7	Provide services to customers, $4,200 for cash and $2,500 on account.
June	11	Purchase cages and equipment necessary to maintain the animals, $7,400 cash.
June	17	Pay employees' salaries for the first half of the month, $5,500.
June	22	Pay dividends to stockholders, $1,300.
June	25	Receive cash in advance from a customer who wants to house his two dogs (Chance and Shadow) and cat (Sassy) while he goes on vacation the month of July, $1,600.
June	28	Pay utilities for the month, $2,300.
June	30	Record salaries earned by employees for the second half of the month, $5,500. Payment will be made on July 2.

Required:

1. Record each transaction.
2. Identify the transactions involving cash.
3. Assuming the balance of cash at the beginning of June is $13,700, post each cash transaction to the Cash T-account and compute the ending cash balance.
4. Prepare a statement of cash flows for the month of June, properly classifying each of the cash transactions into operating, investing, and financing activities.
5. Verify that the net cash flows reported in the statement of cash flows equal the change in the cash balance for the month.

*For additional problems, visit **www.mhhe.com/succeed** for Problems: Set C.*

ADDITIONAL PERSPECTIVES

Continuing Problem

Great Adventures

(This is a continuation of the Great Adventures problem from earlier chapters.)

AP4–1 An examination of the cash activities during the year shows the following.

GREAT ADVENTURES
Cash Account Records
July 1, 2012, to December 31, 2012

Deposits			Checks/Debit Cards			
Date	Desc.	Amount	Date	No.	Desc.	Amount
7/1	Stock sale	$ 20,000	7/1	101	Insurance	$ 4,800
7/15	Clinic receipts	2,000	7/2	102	Legal fees	1,500
7/22	Clinic receipts	2,300	7/7	DC	Advertising	300
7/30	Clinic receipts	4,000	7/8	103	Bikes	12,000
8/1	Borrowing	30,000	7/24	DC	Advertising	700
8/10	Clinic receipts	3,000	8/4	104	Kayaks	28,000

(continued)

(concluded)

Deposits			Checks/Debit Cards			
Date	Desc.	Amount	Date	No.	Desc.	Amount
8/17	Clinic receipts	10,500	8/24	DC	Office supplies	1,800
9/21	Clinic receipts	13,200	9/1	105	Rent	2,400
10/17	Clinic receipts	17,900	12/8	106	Race permit	1,200
12/15	Race receipts	20,000	12/16	107	Salary	2,000
			12/31	108	Dividend	2,000
			12/31	109	Dividend	2,000
		$122,900				$58,700

SUMMARY OF TRANSACTIONS

Beginning Cash Balance July 1, 2012	+	Deposits	−	Checks	=	Ending Cash Balance December 31, 2012
$0		$122,900		$58,700		$64,200

Suzie has not reconciled the company's cash balance with that of the bank since the company was started. She asks Summit Bank to provide her with a six-month bank statement. To save time, Suzie makes deposits at the bank only on the first day of each month.

Summit Bank
Leading You to the Top

Member FDIC

Account Holder: Great Adventures, Inc.

Account Number: 1124537774

Statement Date: Dec. 31, 2012

Account Summary

Beginning Balance July 1, 2012	Deposits and Credits		Withdrawals and Debits		Ending Balance December 31, 2012
	No.	Total	No.	Total	
$0	8	$103,400	11	$52,900	$50,500

Account Details

Deposits and Credits			Withdrawals and Debits				Daily Balance	
Date	Amount	Desc.	Date	No.	Amount	Desc.	Date	Amount
7/1	$ 20,000	DEP	7/1	101	$ 4,800	CHK	7/1	$15,200
8/1	8,300	DEP	7/7	102	1,500	CHK	7/7	13,400
8/1	30,000	DEP	7/7		300	DC	7/14	1,400
9/1	13,500	DEP	7/14	103	12,000	CHK	7/24	700
9/30	200	INT	7/24		700	DC	8/1	39,000
10/1	13,200	DEP	8/9	104	28,000	CHK	8/9	11,000
11/1	17,900	DEP	8/24		1,800	DC	8/24	9,200
12/31	300	INT	9/2	105	2,400	CHK	9/1	22,700
			9/30		100	SF	9/2	20,300
			12/10	106	1,200	CHK	9/30	20,400
			12/31		100	SF	10/1	33,600
							11/1	51,500
							12/10	50,300
	$103,400				$52,900		12/31	$50,500

Desc.	**DEP** Customer deposit	**INT** Interest earned	**SF** Service fees
	CHK Customer check	**DC** Debit card	

208   CHAPTER 4   Cash and Internal Controls

After comparing the two balances, Suzie has some concern because the bank's balance of $50,500 is substantially less than the company's balance of $64,200.

Required:

1. Discuss any problems you see with Great Adventures' internal control procedures related to cash.
2. Prepare Great Adventures' bank reconciliation for the six-month period ended December 31, 2012, and any necessary entries to adjust cash.
3. How did failure to reconcile the bank statement affect the reported amounts for assets, liabilities, stockholders' equity, revenues, and expenses?

Financial Analysis

American Eagle Outfitters, Inc.

AP4–2 Financial information for **American Eagle** is presented in Appendix A at the end of the book.

Required:

1. What does the Report of Independent Registered Public Accounting Firm indicate about American Eagle's internal controls?
2. In the summary of significant accounting policies, how does American Eagle define cash equivalents?
3. What is the amount of cash reported in the two most recent years? By how much has cash increased/decreased?
4. Determine the amounts American Eagle reports for net cash flows from operating activities, investing activities, and financing activities in its statement of cash flows for the most recent year. What are total cash flows for the year?
5. Compare your answers in question 4 to the increase/decrease you calculated in question 3. (Note: Include any effect of exchange rates on cash as an additional cash flow in question 4.)
6. What does American Eagle's trend in net income versus free cash flows over the three most recent years suggest about the company's earnings quality?

Financial Analysis

The Buckle, Inc.

AP4–3 Financial information for **The Buckle** is presented in Appendix B at the end of the book.

Required:

1. What does the Report of Independent Registered Public Accounting Firm indicate about The Buckle's internal controls?
2. In the summary of significant accounting policies, how does The Buckle define cash equivalents?
3. What is the amount of cash reported in the two most recent years? By how much has cash increased/decreased?
4. Determine the amounts The Buckle reports for net cash flows from operating activities, investing activities, and financing activities in its statement of cash flows for the most recent year. What are total cash flows for the year?
5. Compare your answers in question 4 to the increase/decrease you calculated in question 3. (Note: Include any effect of exchange rates on cash as an additional cash flow in question 4.)
6. What does The Buckle's trend in net income versus free cash flows over the three most recent years suggest about the company's earnings quality?

American Eagle Outfitters, Inc., vs. The Buckle, Inc.

AP4–4 Financial information for **American Eagle** is presented in Appendix A at the end of the book, and financial information for **The Buckle** is presented in Appendix B at the end of the book.

Comparative Analysis

Required:

1. Which company has a greater amount of cash relative to total assets? What might this mean about the two companies' potential growth opportunities?
2. Based on the trend in net income versus free cash flows over the three most recent years, which company would you predict to have a greater percentage increase in net income in the following year? Why?

Ethics

AP4–5 Between his freshman and sophomore years of college, Jack takes a job as ticket collector at a local movie theatre. Moviegoers purchase a ticket from a separate employee outside the theatre and then enter through a single set of doors. Jack takes half their ticket, and they proceed to the movie of their choice.

Besides trying to earn enough money for college the next year, Jack loves to watch movies. One of the perks of working for the movie theatre is that all employees are allowed to watch one free movie per day. However, in the employee handbook it states that friends and family of employees are not allowed to watch free movies. In addition, employees must pay full price for all concession items.

Soon after starting work at the theatre, Jack notices that most other employees regularly bring their friends and family to the movie without purchasing a ticket. When Jack stops them at the door to ask for their ticket, they say, "Jack, no one really follows that policy. Just be cool and let us in. You can do the same." Jack even notices that upper management does not follow the policy of no family and friends watching free movies. Furthermore, employees commonly bring their own cups to get free soft drinks and their own containers to eat free popcorn.

Jack considers whether he should also start bringing friends and family and enjoying the free popcorn and beverages. He reasons, "Why should I be the only one following the rules? If everyone else is doing it, including upper management, what harm would it be for me to do it too? After all, when you watch a movie you aren't really stealing anything, and popcorn and drinks cost hardly anything. Plus, I really need to save for college."

Required:

Discuss the ethical dilemma Jack faces.

Internet Research

AP4–6 Financial accounting information can often be found at financial websites. These websites are useful for collecting information about a company's stock price, analysts' forecasts, dividend history, historical financial accounting information, and much more. One such site is Yahoo! Finance (*finance.yahoo.com*).

Required:

1. Visit Yahoo! Finance and get a stock quote for **Google**. To do this, type "GOOG" in the "Get Quotes" box. Under "Financials" click on the "Cash Flow" link. Calculate Google's free cash flows for the three most recent years.
2. Calculate **IBM**'s free cash flows in the same way by typing "IBM" in the "Get Quotes" box.

3. Compare the trends in free cash flows between the companies. What would explain differences between these two companies' free cash flows?
4. Click on "Historical Prices" and compare the trend in these companies' stock prices over the same three-year period used to calculate free cash flows.

Written Communication

AP4–7 Consider the following independent situations:

1. John Smith is the petty-cash custodian. John approves all requests for payment out of the $200 fund, which is replenished at the end of each month. At the end of each month, John submits a list of all accounts and amounts to be charged, and a check is written to him for the total amount. John is the only person ever to tally the fund.
2. All of the company's cash disbursements are made by check. Each check must be supported by an approved voucher, which is in turn supported by the appropriate invoice and, for purchases, a receiving document. The vouchers are approved by Dean Leiser, the chief accountant, after reviewing the supporting documentation. Betty Hanson prepares the checks for Leiser's signature. Leiser also maintains the company's check register (the cash disbursements journal) and reconciles the bank account at the end of each month.
3. Fran Jones opens the company's mail and lists all checks and cash received from customers. A copy of the list is sent to Jerry McDonald who maintains the general ledger accounts. Fran prepares and makes the daily deposit at the bank. Fran also maintains the subsidiary ledger for accounts receivable, which is used to generate monthly statements to customers.

Required:

Write a memo to your instructor indicating the apparent internal control weaknesses and suggest alternative procedures to eliminate the weaknesses.

Answers to the Self-Study Questions
1. d   2. d   3. a   4. c   5. b   6. d   7. a   8. c   9. b   10. c

CHAPTER

5

Receivables and Sales

AFTER STUDYING THIS CHAPTER, YOU SHOULD BE ABLE TO:

- **LO1** Recognize accounts receivable.
- **LO2** Calculate net revenues using discounts, returns, and allowances.
- **LO3** Record an allowance for future uncollectible accounts.
- **LO4** Apply the procedure to write off accounts receivable as uncollectible.
- **LO5** Use the aging method to estimate future uncollectible accounts.
- **LO6** Contrast the allowance method and direct write-off method when accounting for uncollectible accounts.
- **LO7** Apply the procedure to account for notes receivable, including interest calculation.

Analysis

- **LO8** Calculate key ratios investors use to monitor a company's effectiveness in managing receivables.

Appendix

- **LO9** Estimate uncollectible accounts using the percentage-of-credit-sales method.

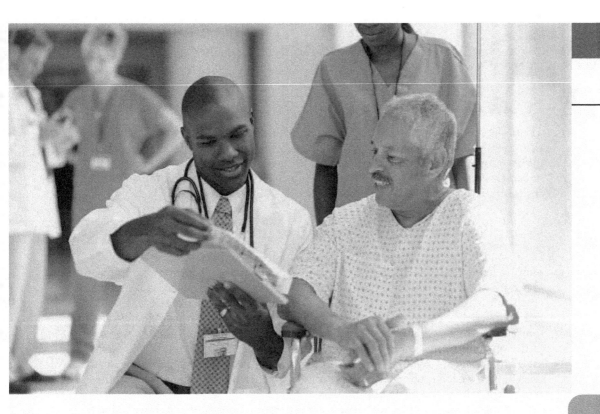

TENET HEALTHCARE: BAD DEBTS CAUSE PAIN TO INVESTORS

Feature
Story

Tenet Healthcare Corporation is one of the largest hospital chains in the United States. The company operates 50 hospitals in 12 states, employs over 57,000 people, admits more than 500,000 patients, and has nearly 4,000,000 outpatient visits each year. For the period 2007–2009, the company reported net operating revenues of $26 billion. Everything seems fine, right?

Wrong. Over this same period, Tenet reported profits of only $145 million. That's a profit of only one-half of a penny for every dollar of revenue. One of the reasons for Tenet's poor operating performance was the cost of "uncompensated care." Uncompensated care occurs when patients receive services but are either unwilling or unable to pay. Though hospitals try to minimize these costs, federal law requires that patients not be denied emergency treatment due to inability to pay. Uncompensated care is a problem for the entire health-care industry.

Tenet reports uncompensated care in three ways: (1) as charity care, (2) as discounted services, and (3) as provisions for bad debts. For patients who are financially unable to pay for their health-care services, Tenet does not pursue collection of amounts that qualify as charity care. Also, it offers discounted services to patients who have no insurance or are underinsured. The company instituted a program of discounted services to reduce the reported amounts of bad debts. Bad debts occur when customers have been billed but never pay, and the company decides to recognize that fact in its accounting records. In reality, the three types of uncompensated care are difficult to separate, and all have a negative economic impact on the company's operations.

Over the period 2007–2009, Tenet reported the following amounts (in millions) for each of these categories of uncompensated care:

Year	Charity Care	Discounted Services	Provision for Bad Debts	Total
2007	$121	$ 342	$ 555	$1,018
2008	113	359	628	1,100
2009	118	365	697	1,180
Total	$352	$1,066	$1,880	$3,298

Tenet's profits would have been dramatically higher without the cost of more than $3 billion in uncompensated care. Tenet states in its annual report, ". . . unless our business mix shifts toward a greater number of insured patients or the trend of higher co-payments and deductibles reverses, we anticipate this high level of uncollectible accounts to continue." In 2010, health-care industry troubles, such as Tenet's, sparked a heated national debate over the need for health-care reform in the United States.

PART A   RECOGNIZING ACCOUNTS RECEIVABLE

As you learned in Chapter 2, companies sometimes provide goods or services to customers, not for cash, but on account. Formally, accounts receivable represent the amount of cash owed to a company by its customers from the sale of products or services on account. To understand accounts receivable, we need to start with *credit sales*, from which accounts receivable originate.

Credit Sales and Accounts Receivable

■ **LO1**
Recognize accounts receivable.

Have you ever sold a product or service to someone and accepted that person's promise to pay you in the future? For example, did you ever sell a candy bar as part of a fund-raiser and have the person promise to pay you later? If so, you made a credit sale. Credit sales transfer products and services to a customer today while bearing the risk of collecting payment from that customer in the future. Credit sales transactions are also known as *sales on account* or *services on account*. As we saw in the opening story, Tenet Healthcare provides a considerable number of credit sales for health care–related services, but many of its credit customers never pay. In this chapter, we focus on recording credit sales and dealing with the likelihood that some customers will not pay as promised.

Credit sales are common for large business transactions in which buyers don't have sufficient cash available or in which credit cards cannot be used because the transaction amount exceeds typical credit card limits. They typically include an informal credit agreement supported by an invoice and require payment within 30 to 60 days after the sale. **Even though the seller does not receive cash at the time of the credit sale, the firm records revenue immediately, as long as future collection from the customer is reasonably certain.**

Along with the recognized revenue, at the time of sale the seller also obtains a legal right to receive cash from the buyer. **The legal right to *receive* cash is valuable and represents an asset of the company.** This asset is referred to as accounts receivable (sometimes called *trade receivables*), and the firm records it at the time of a credit sale.

To see how companies record credit sales, consider an example. Suppose Link's Dental charges $500 for teeth whitening. Dee Kay decides to have her teeth whitened on March 1 but doesn't pay cash at the time of service. She promises to pay the $500 whitening fee to Link by March 31. Link's Dental records the following at the time of the whitening.

March 1	Debit	Credit
Accounts Receivable	500	
Service Revenue		500
(*Provide services on account*)		

A = L + SE
+500
+500 Rev↑

Notice that instead of debiting Cash, as in a cash sale, Link's Dental debits another asset—Accounts Receivable—for the credit sale.

 KEY POINT

Companies record an asset (accounts receivable) and revenue when they sell products and services to their customers on account, expecting payment in the future.

As you study receivables, realize that one company's right to *collect* cash corresponds to another company's (or individual's) obligation to *pay* cash. One company's account receivable is the flip side of another company's account payable. In Chapter 6 we discuss accounts payable in the context of inventory purchases on account. In Chapter 8 we again discuss accounts payable, but in the context of current liabilities.

Flip Side

OTHER TYPES OF RECEIVABLES

Other types of receivables are less common than accounts receivable. *Nontrade receivables* are receivables that originate from sources other than customers. They include tax refund claims, interest receivable, and loans by the company to other entities, including stockholders and employees. When receivables are accompanied by formal credit arrangements made with written debt instruments (or notes), we refer to them as *notes receivable*. We'll consider notes receivable later in this chapter.

Net Revenues

From time to time, companies offer discounts to customers. These discounts offer ways to quickly sell old inventory, attract new customers, reward long-term loyal customers, and encourage customers to pay quickly on their accounts. However, while these discounts may be beneficial to the company's long-term success, they can reduce the amount of revenue reported in the current period. In addition, the company's revenues are reduced when customers return unsatisfactory products or demand allowances for inferior services. Therefore, it is important for managers to consider not only their companies' total revenues, but also net revenues. Net revenues refer to a company's total revenues less any amounts for discounts, returns, and allowances. We discuss these items next.

■ **LO2**
Calculate net revenues using discounts, returns, and allowances.

TRADE DISCOUNTS

Trade discounts represent a reduction in the listed price of a product or service. Companies typically use trade discounts to provide incentives to larger customers or consumer groups to purchase from the company. Trade discounts also can be a way to change prices without publishing a new price list or to disguise real prices from competitors.

When recording a transaction, companies don't recognize trade discounts *directly*. Instead, they recognize trade discounts *indirectly* by recording the sale at the discounted price. For example, let's go back to Link's Dental, which typically charges $500 for teeth whitening. Assume that in order to entice more customers, Dr. Link offers a 20% discount on teeth whitening to any of his regular patients. Since Dee Kay is one of Dr. Link's regular patients, she can take advantage of the special discount and have her teeth whitened for only $400.

March 1	Debit	Credit
Accounts Receivable	400	
Service Revenue		400
(Make credit sale of $500 with a 20% trade discount)		

A	=	L	+	SE
+400				
				+400 Rev↑

Notice that Link's Dental records the trade discount *indirectly* by recognizing revenue equal to the discounted price, which is $500 less the trade discount of $100 (= $500 × 20%).

SALES DISCOUNTS

Unlike a trade discount, a sales discount represents a reduction, not in the selling price of a product or service, but in the amount to be paid by a credit customer if payment is made within a specified period of time. It's a discount intended to provide incentive for quick payment.

Discount terms, such as 2/10, n/30, are a shorthand way to communicate the amount of the discount and the time period within which it's available. The term "2/10," pronounced "two ten," for example, indicates the customer will receive a 2% discount if the amount owed is paid within 10 days. The term "n/30," pronounced "net thirty," means that if the customer does *not* take the discount, full payment is due within 30 days.

Assume Link's Dental wants Dee to pay quickly on her teeth whitening bill and offers her terms of 2/10, n/30. This means that if Dee pays within 10 days, the amount due ($400 after the trade discount) will be reduced by 2% (or $8 = $400 × 2%). Let's consider two alternatives—taking or not taking the sales discount.

With the sales discount. Let's see what happens when Dee pays within 10 days: Assume that Dee pays on March 10, which is within the 10-day discount period. Link's Dental records the following transaction when it receives payment.

March 10	Debit	Credit
Cash	392	
Sales Discounts	8	
Accounts Receivable		400
(*Collect cash on account with a 2% sales discount*)		

Balance Sheet					Income Statement		
			Stockholders' Equity				
			Common	Retained			Net
Assets	=	Liabilities +	Stock	+ Earnings	Revenues	− Expenses =	Income
+392	=			−8	−8		= −8
−400							
−8							

Notice that Link receives only $392 cash, the full amount owed less the 2% sales discount. **We record the sales discount as a** contra revenue account. A contra revenue account is an account with a balance that is opposite, or "contra," to that of its related revenue account. The reason we use a contra revenue account is to be able to keep a record of the total revenue separate from the reduction in that revenue due to quick payment. In this case, Service Revenue has a credit balance of $400, and its related contra revenue account—Sales Discounts—has a debit balance of $8. The net effect is that sales discounts increase, reducing net revenues of the company to $392. It's easier to see the relationship between these two accounts by looking at the partial income statement of Link's Dental in Illustration 5–1.

ILLUSTRATION 5–1

Partial Income Statement Reporting Revenues Net of Sales Discounts

LINK'S DENTAL Income Statement (partial)		
Service revenues	$400	
Less: Sales discounts	(8)	
Net service revenues		$392

Link provides a service with a normal price of $500. However, after the trade discount of $100 and the sales discount of $8, Link's income statement reports net revenue of $392.

Also notice that Link's Dental credits Accounts Receivable for $400, even though it receives only $392 cash. The reason is that the $400 balance in Accounts Receivable is "paid in full" by the combination of the $392 cash payment and the $8 sales discount. Dee owes $0 after paying $392. The balance of Accounts Receivable now equals $0, as demonstrated in Illustration 5–2.

	Accounts Receivable			
Credit sale	Mar. 1 400		Collection of $392	**ILLUSTRATION 5–2**
		Mar. 10 400	on account	Balance of Accounts Receivable after Credit Sale and Subsequent Collection on Account
Ending balance	Bal. 0			

Without the sales discount. For our second scenario, assume that Dee waits until March 31 to pay, which is *not* within the 10-day discount period. Link's Dental records the following transaction at the time it collects cash from Dee.

March 31	Debit	Credit		A	=	L	+	SE
Cash	400			+400				
Accounts Receivable		400		−400				
(Collect cash on account)								

Notice that there is no indication in recording the transaction that the customer does not take the sales discount. This is the typical way to record a cash collection on account when no sales discounts are involved. Accounts Receivable is credited for $400 to reduce its balance to $0, representing the amount owed by the customer after payment.

SALES RETURNS AND ALLOWANCES

In some cases, customers may not be satisfied with a product or service purchased. If a customer returns a product, we call that a sales return. After a sales return, (a) we reduce the customer's account balance if the sale was on account or (b) we issue a cash refund if the sale was for cash.

Sometimes, because of a deficiency in the company's product or service, the seller reduces the customer's balance owed or provides at least a partial refund while allowing the customer to keep the product. Such a reduction or partial refund is called a sales allowance. Suppose on March 5, after she gets her teeth whitened but before she pays, Dee notices that another local dentist is offering the same procedure for $350, which is $50 less than Link's discounted price of $400. Dee brings this to Dr. Link's attention and because his policy is to match any competitor's pricing, he offers to reduce Dee's account balance by $50. Link's Dental records the following sales allowance.

March 5	Debit	Credit
Sales Allowances	50	
Accounts Receivable		50
(Make sales allowance for credit sale)		

Balance Sheet					Income Statement		
			Stockholders' Equity				
			Common	Retained			Net
Assets	=	Liabilities +	Stock	+ Earnings	Revenues	− Expenses =	Income
−50	=			−50	−50	=	−50

This reduction of accounts receivable indicates that Dee owes less after the allowance—she now owes only $350.

Firms sometimes combine their sales returns and sales allowances in a *single* Sales Returns and Allowances account. **Like sales discounts, sales returns and allowances are contra revenue accounts.** We report both sales discounts and sales returns and allowances as reductions in the related revenue account, causing a reduction in net income.

 KEY POINT

Sales discounts, returns, and allowances are contra revenue accounts. We subtract the balances in these accounts from total revenues when calculating net revenues.

Decision Point

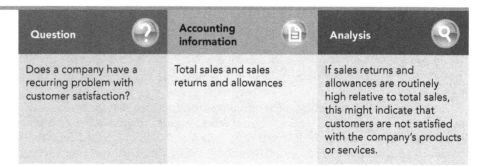

Question	Accounting information	Analysis
Does a company have a recurring problem with customer satisfaction?	Total sales and sales returns and allowances	If sales returns and allowances are routinely high relative to total sales, this might indicate that customers are not satisfied with the company's products or services.

 COMMON MISTAKE

Students sometimes misclassify contra revenue accounts—sales discounts, returns, and allowances—as expenses. Like expenses, contra revenues have normal debit balances and reduce the reported amount of net income. However, contra revenues represent *direct reductions* of revenues, whereas expenses represent the separate costs of generating revenues. Misclassifying contra revenue accounts as expenses overstates revenues and expenses but leaves bottom-line net income unaffected.

Let's Review

Snap-Crackle-Pop (SCP) Chiropractic normally charges $120 for a full spinal adjustment. Currently, the company is offering a $20 discount to senior citizens. In addition, SCP offers terms 2/10, n/30 to all customers receiving services on account. The following events occur.

June 18   David, age 72, calls to set up an appointment.
June 20   David visits SCP and receives a spinal adjustment for the discounted price.
June 29   David pays for his office visit.

Required:

1. On what date should SCP record patient revenue?
2. Record patient revenue for SCP.
3. Record the cash collection for SCP assuming SCP receives David's payment in full on June 29 (within the discount period).
4. Calculate the balance of Accounts Receivable using a T-account format, and then calculate the balance of net revenue as shown in the income statement after the cash payment is received.

Solution:

1. SCP should record patient revenue on June 20—the date the service is provided.

2. Record patient revenue:

June 20	Debit	Credit
Accounts Receivable	100	
Service Revenue		100
(Provide services on account)		
(Revenue = $120 less $20 trade discount)		

3. Record receipt of David's payment in full within the discount period:

June 29	Debit	Credit
Cash	98	
Sales Discounts	2	
Accounts Receivable		100
(Collect cash on account with a 2% sales discount)		
(Sales discount = $100 × 2%)		

4. Balance of Accounts Receivable and calculation of net revenue after receipt of cash payment:

Accounts Receivable	
Jun. 20 100	
	Jun. 29 100
Bal. 0	

Service revenue (from *Requirement 2*)	$100
Less: Sales discounts (from *Requirement 3*)	(2)
Net revenue	$ 98

Suggested Homework:
BE5-1, BE5-2;
E5-2, E5-3;
P5-2A&B

VALUING ACCOUNTS RECEIVABLE

PART B

The right to receive cash from a customer is a valuable resource for the company. **This is why accounts receivable is an asset, reported in the company's balance sheet.** If the company expects to receive the cash within one year, it classifies the receivable as a current asset; otherwise it classifies the receivable as a long-term asset.

What, though, is the *value* of being owed $100? If you are confident the person will actually pay you $100 in the near future, then you might consider the right to receive the money to be worth $100. However, if the person is unable to pay you anything, then your right to collect $100 is worth $0. Of course there are many possibilities in between. To be useful to decision makers, accounts receivable should be reported at the amount of cash the firm *expects* to collect, an amount known as net realizable value.

 KEY POINT

We recognize accounts receivable as assets in the balance sheet and report them at their *net realizable value*, that is, the amount of cash we expect to collect.

220   CHAPTER 5   Receivables and Sales

Allowance Method

■ **LO3**
Record an allowance
for future uncollectible
accounts.

We know that companies often are not able to collect all of their accounts receivable from customers. Rather than accept only cash payment at the time of sale, should companies extend credit to their customers by allowing them to purchase on account? **The upside of extending credit to customers is that it boosts sales by allowing customers the ability to purchase on account and pay cash later.** Just think of how many times you wanted to buy food, clothes, electronics, or other items that you could afford, but you didn't have cash with you. You're not alone. Many customers may not have cash readily available to make a purchase or, for other reasons, simply prefer to buy on credit.

   The downside of extending credit to customers is that not all customers will pay fully on their accounts. Even the most well-meaning customers may find themselves in difficult financial circumstances beyond their control, limiting their ability to repay debt. Customers' accounts that we no longer consider collectible are uncollectible accounts, or *bad debts*.

   We account for uncollectible accounts using what's called the allowance method. This method involves *allowing for the possibility* that some accounts will be uncollectible at some point in the future.[1] Be sure to understand this key point. Using the allowance method we account for events (customers' bad debts) that have *not yet* occurred but that are likely to occur. This is different from other transactions you've learned about to this point. Those earlier transactions involved recording events that have already occurred, such as purchasing supplies, paying employees, and providing services to customers. **Under the allowance method, companies are required to *estimate* future uncollectible accounts and record those estimates in the current year.**

The allowance method
estimates future
uncollectible accounts.

   Before seeing exactly how to record the allowance method, let's first think about the effects that uncollectible accounts should have on the financial position of the company. Uncollectible accounts have the effect of (1) reducing assets (accounts receivable) by an estimate of the amount we don't expect to collect and (2) increasing expenses (bad debt expense) to reflect the cost of offering credit to customers. Illustration 5–3 demonstrates how the effects of uncollectible accounts should therefore be reflected in the financial statements.

ILLUSTRATION 5–3

The Financial
Statement Effects of
Accounting for Future
Uncollectible Accounts

   An account we do not expect to collect has no value. Thus, we need to reduce assets because we don't expect to collect the entire accounts receivable (assets). At the same time, failure to collect a customer's cash represents a cost inherent in using credit sales. The cost of uncollectible accounts is an operating expense, decreasing net income by the uncollectible amount. Next, let's see how to record bad debts so that both of these effects are captured in the financial statements—the reduction in assets and the increase in operating expenses.

---

[1]Later in the chapter, we'll look at a second method—the direct write-off method. The direct write-off method is used for tax purposes but is generally not permitted for financial reporting.

KEY POINT

Under the allowance method, companies are required to *estimate* future uncollectible accounts and record those estimates in the current year. Estimated uncollectible accounts reduce assets and increase expenses.

ESTIMATING UNCOLLECTIBLE ACCOUNTS

Now that we have discussed the impact of uncollectible accounts in the financial statements, let's see how we record them. To use the allowance method, a company first estimates at the end of the *current* year how much in uncollectible accounts will occur in the *following* year. Consider an example of future uncollectible accounts for Kimzey Medical Clinic, which specializes in emergency outpatient care. Because it doesn't verify the patient's health insurance before administering care, Kimzey knows that a high proportion of fees for emergency care provided will not be collected.

In 2012, Kimzey bills customers $50 million for emergency care it provided. By the end of the year, $20 million remains due from customers, but how much of this amount does Kimzey expect *not* to collect in the following year? Let's suppose that in previous years approximately 30% of accounts receivable were not collected; Kimzey decides to base this year's estimate on that same percentage. Estimating uncollectible accounts based on the percentage of accounts receivable expected not to be collected is known as the percentage-of-receivables method. This method sometimes is referred to as the *balance sheet method,* because we base the estimate of bad debts on a balance sheet amount—accounts receivable.[2]

Using the 30% estimate, Kimzey expects that $6 million of its accounts receivable (or 30% of $20 million) likely will never be collected. It makes the following year-end adjustment to allow for these future uncollectible accounts.

December 31, 2012 ($ in millions)	Debit	Credit
Bad Debt Expense	6	
Allowance for Uncollectible Accounts		6
(*Estimate future bad debts*)		
($20 million × 30% = $6 million)		

Balance Sheet					Income Statement		
			Stockholders' Equity				
			Common	Retained			Net
Assets	**= Liabilities +**		**Stock +**	**Earnings**	**Revenues –**	**Expenses =**	**Income**
−6	=			−6		+6 =	−6

The effect of the adjustment in the financial statements reflects the impact of the transaction on the financial position of the company. Because the nature of the accounts in this adjusting entry differs somewhat from those in other year-end adjusting entries we covered in Chapter 3, let's look closer.

Bad debt expense. First, bad debt expense represents the cost of the estimated future bad debts. Kimzey estimates that it will not collect 30% of its accounts receivable, and so records Bad Debt Expense of $6 million. We include this expense

Common Terms Bad debt expense sometimes is referred to as *uncollectible accounts expense.*

---

[2]In the appendix to this chapter, we'll consider a second method, the *percentage-of-credit-sales method* (also referred to as the *income statement method*). In practice, companies are required to follow the percentage-of-receivables method, so that will be our focus here.

in the same income statement as the credit sales with which these bad debts are associated. By doing so, we properly "match" expenses (bad debts) with the revenues (credit sales) they help to generate. Illustration 5–4 shows the partial income statement for Kimzey Medical Clinic after estimating bad debt expense.

ILLUSTRATION 5–4

Partial Income Statement Showing Estimated Bad Debt Expense

| KIMZEY MEDICAL CLINIC |
| Income Statement (partial) |
| For the year ended 2012 |

($ in millions)	
Credit sales	$50
Bad debt expense	(6)
	$44

Match expenses with their related revenues.

In the 2012 income statement, we reduce the $50 million of revenue from credit sales by $6 million for estimated future bad debts. Even though the company reports credit sales of $50 million, the expected profits on these sales, after considering the cost of future bad debts, is only $44 million.

KEY POINT

Adjusting for estimates of future uncollectible accounts matches expenses (bad debts) in the same period as the revenues (credit sales) they help to generate.

Common Terms The allowance for uncollectible accounts is sometimes referred to as the *allowance for doubtful accounts.*

Allowance for uncollectible accounts. Second, we adjust for future bad debts by making an allowance for uncollectible accounts. The contra asset account Allowance for Uncollectible Accounts represents the amount of accounts receivable we do not expect to collect. Earlier in the chapter, we discussed *contra revenue* accounts—sales discounts, returns, and allowances. Recall that these accounts provide a way to *reduce revenue indirectly.* In the same way, the allowance account provides a way to *reduce accounts receivable indirectly* to its *net realizable value,* rather than decreasing the accounts receivable balance itself.

We report the allowance for uncollectible accounts in the asset section of the balance sheet, but it represents a reduction in the balance of accounts receivable. The difference between total accounts receivable and the allowance for uncollectible accounts is referred to as net accounts receivable, which is net realizable value. Illustration 5–5 (next page) demonstrates the concept behind accounting for future uncollectible accounts and how the accounts receivable portion of Kimzey's year-end balance sheet appears.

Report accounts receivable at net realizable value.

After we estimate uncollectible accounts to be $6 million, we reduce the $20 million balance of accounts receivable and report them at their net realizable value of $14 million. But is this estimate correct? Only time will tell. Kimzey's prediction of $6 million for uncollectible accounts might be too high, or it might be too low. In either case, it's generally more informative than making no estimate at all. (Later in the chapter, we'll find out how close the estimate is.)

KEY POINT

Recording an allowance for uncollectible accounts correctly reports accounts receivable at their net realizable value.

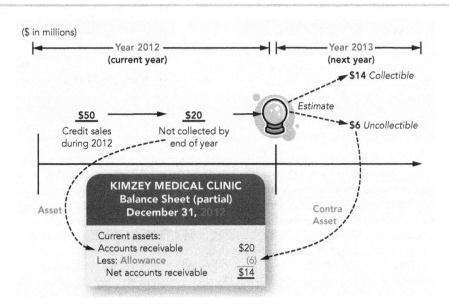

ILLUSTRATION 5-5

Accounting for Uncollectible Accounts and the Accounts Receivable Portion of the Balance Sheet

 COMMON MISTAKE

Because Allowance for Uncollectible Accounts has a normal credit balance, students sometimes misclassify this account as a liability, which also has a normal credit balance. Instead, a contra asset represents a reduction in a related asset.

Decision Point

Question	Accounting information	Analysis
Are the company's credit sales policies too lenient?	Accounts receivable and the allowance for uncollectible accounts	A high ratio of the allowance for uncollectible accounts to total accounts receivable could be an indication that the company extends too much credit to high-risk customers.

WRITING OFF ACCOUNTS RECEIVABLE

To continue with our example of Kimzey Medical Clinic, let's suppose that on February 23, 2013 (the following year), Kimzey receives notice that one of its former patients, Bruce Easley, has filed for bankruptcy protection against all creditors. Based on this information, Kimzey believes it is unlikely Bruce will pay his account of $4,000. Remember, Kimzey previously allowed for the likelihood that *some* of its customers would not pay, though it didn't know which ones. Now that it *knows* a specific customer will not pay, it can adjust the allowance and reduce the accounts receivable balance itself. Upon receiving news of this *actual* bad debt, Kimzey records the following.

■ **LO4**
Apply the procedure to write off accounts receivable as uncollectible.

February 23, 2013	Debit	Credit
Allowance for Uncollectible Accounts	4,000	
Accounts Receivable		4,000
(Write off a customer's account)		

What is the effect in Kimzey's financial statements when writing off Bruce's account receivable? **Overall, the write-off of the account receivable has no effect on total amounts reported in the balance sheet or in the income statement.** Notice that there is no decrease in total assets and no decrease in net income with the write-off. Here's why: **We have already recorded the negative effects of the bad news.** Kimzey recorded those effects when it *estimated* future bad debts at the end of 2012 and both reduced assets and recorded the bad debt expense. Now, when Bruce declares bankruptcy in the following year, 2013, we have already established the allowance for this bad debt. The write-off on February 23, 2013, reduces both an asset account (Accounts Receivable) and its contra asset account (Allowance for Uncollectible Accounts), leaving the *net* receivable unaffected. Thus, the write-off results in no change to total assets.

 COMMON MISTAKE

Students often mistakenly record bad debt expense when they write off an uncollectible account. The bad debt expense was recorded in a prior year at the time of estimating uncollectible accounts.

COLLECTION OF ACCOUNTS PREVIOUSLY WRITTEN OFF

Later in 2013, on September 8, Bruce's bankruptcy proceedings are complete. Kimzey had expected to receive none of the $4,000 Bruce owed. However, after liquidating all assets, Bruce is able to pay each of his creditors 25% of the amount due them. So, when Kimzey receives payment of $1,000 (= $4,000 × 25%), it makes the following two entries.

September 8, 2013	Debit	Credit
Accounts Receivable	1,000	
Allowance for Uncollectible Accounts		1,000
(Reestablish portion of account previously written off)		
Cash	1,000	
Accounts Receivable		1,000
(Collect cash on account)		

Balance Sheet						Income Statement		
				Stockholders' Equity				
				Common	Retained			Net
Assets	=	Liabilities	+	Stock	+ Earnings	Revenues	− Expenses	= Income
+1,000	=							
−1,000								
+1,000								
−1,000								
0								

The first entry simply reverses a portion of the previous entry that Kimzey made on February 23 to write off the account. The second entry records the collection of the account receivable. Notice that in both entries the debit entry increases total assets by the same amount that the credit entry decreases total assets. **Therefore, collecting cash on an account previously written off has no effect on total assets and no effect on net income.**

Let's assume that total accounts written off by Kimzey during 2013 equaled $5 million but that $1 million of this amount was ultimately collected by the end of the year. The time line of events related to accounts receivable of Kimzey during 2012 and 2013 is this:

1. At the end of 2012, accounts receivable total $20 million.
2. Kimzey makes an adjustment at the end of 2012 for *estimated* bad debts of $6 million.
3. In 2013, *actual* accounts Kimzey writes off as uncollectible total $5 million.
4. Of the $5 million in accounts written off earlier, $1 million later appears receivable.
5. Kimzey receives $1 million cash for the accounts reestablished in (4).

Illustration 5–6 summarizes the impact of each of these events (also numbered 1–5 there) in calculating net accounts receivable.

($ in millions)	2012		2013		
	(1) Accounts Receivable Total $20	**(2)** *Estimate* Bad Debts in 2013 to Be $6	**(3)** Write Off *Actual* Bad Debts of $5	**(4)** Reestablish Previous Write-offs of $1	**(5)** Collect Cash from Previous Write-offs of $1
Accts. receiv.	$20	$20	$15	$16	$15
Less: Allowance	(0)	(6)	(1)	(2)	(2)
Net accts. receiv.	$20	$14	$14	$14	$13

ILLUSTRATION 5–6

Balance of Kimzey's Net Accounts Receivable

Net accounts receivable decline for two of these events. First, as we *estimate* future bad debts, we recognize the likelihood that we will not collect cash for some accounts. Second, once the company receives payment from customers, their account balances are no longer receivable.

On the other hand, writing off *actual* bad debts and reestablishing those previous write-offs when it appears that customers will pay has no effect on net accounts receivable.

Notice that the balance of the allowance account is $2 million at the end of 2013. Does the fact that the allowance account has a nonzero ending balance mean that Kimzey's estimate of uncollectible accounts for 2013 was *wrong?* Perhaps. On the other hand, it may only mean that some of the $15 million in accounts receivable has not yet proven uncollectible but eventually will. In any case, when we make estimates in accounting, it's highly unlikely they will prove exactly correct.

Users of financial statements must realize that some of the amounts reported in financial statements are estimates, and estimating the future almost always results in some inaccuracy. Illustration 5–7 (next page) provides an excerpt from the annual report of **Tenet Healthcare Corporation.**

 KEY POINT

Writing off a customer's account as uncollectible reduces the balance of accounts receivable but also reduces the contra asset—allowance for uncollectible accounts. The net effect is that there is no change in the *net* receivable (accounts receivable less the allowance) or in total assets. We recorded the decrease to assets as a result of the bad debt when we established the allowance for uncollectible accounts in a prior year.

ILLUSTRATION 5–7

Excerpt from
Tenet Healthcare
Corporation's
Annual Report

> **TENET HEALTHCARE CORPORATION**
> **Notes to the Financial Statements (excerpt)**
>
> The preparation of financial statements, in conformity with accounting principles generally accepted in the United States of America, requires us to make estimates and assumptions that affect the amounts reported in the Consolidated Financial Statements and these accompanying notes. We regularly evaluate the accounting policies and estimates we use. In general, we base the estimates on historical experience and on assumptions that we believe to be reasonable given the particular circumstances in which we operate. Although we believe all adjustments considered necessary for fair presentation have been included, actual results may vary from those estimates.

ESTIMATING UNCOLLECTIBLE ACCOUNTS IN THE FOLLOWING YEAR

At the end of 2013, Kimzey must once again estimate uncollectible accounts and make a year-end adjustment. Suppose that in 2013 Kimzey bills customers for services totaling $80 million, and $30 million is still receivable at the end of the year. Of the $30 million still receivable, let's say Kimzey again uses the percentage-of-receivables method and estimates 30% (or $9 million) will not be collected. For what amount would Kimzey record the year-end adjustment for bad debts in 2013? Before answering, let's first examine the current balance of the allowance account, as shown in Illustration 5–8.

ILLUSTRATION 5–8

Balance of Kimzey's
Allowance for
Uncollectible Accounts

	Allowance for Uncollectible Accounts ($ in millions)		
Write off account	5	6	Beginning balance for 2013
		1	Collection of previous write-off
		2	Balance before adjustment
		?	Year-end adjustment
		9	Estimated ending balance for 2013

Notice that the balance before the year-end adjustment in this example is a $2 million *credit*. **A *credit* balance before adjustment indicates that last year's estimate of uncollectible accounts may have been too high.** However, it's possible that some of the estimated uncollectible accounts have not proven bad yet. **A *debit* balance before adjustment indicates that last year's estimate was too low.**

Based on all available information at the end of 2013, Kimzey estimates that the allowance for uncollectible accounts should be $9 million. This means the allowance account needs to increase from its current balance of $2 million credit to the estimated ending balance of $9 million credit. Kimzey can accomplish this by adjusting the account for $7 million as follows:

A = L + SE	December 31, 2013	Debit	Credit
−7 Exp↑	**Bad Debt Expense**	7	
−7	Allowance for Uncollectible Accounts		7
	(*Estimate future bad debts*)		

In its 2013 income statement, Kimzey will report bad debt expense of $7 million along with other operating expenses of, say, $50 million. This is shown in Illustration 5–9.

ILLUSTRATION 5–9
Bad Debt Expense in the Income Statement

KIMZEY MEDICAL CLINIC
Income Statement
For the year ended 2013

($ in millions)		
Revenue from credit sales		$80
Expenses:		
Bad debt expense	$ 7	
Other operating expenses	50	57
Net income		$23

In the 2013 balance sheet, Kimzey will report the allowance account at the best estimate of its appropriate balance, $9 million. This is shown in Illustration 5–10.

ILLUSTRATION 5–10
Accounts Receivable Portion of the Balance Sheet

KIMZEY MEDICAL CLINIC
Balance Sheet (partial)
December 31, 2013

Assets

Current assets ($ in millions):		
Accounts receivable	$30	
Less: Allowance for uncollectible accounts	(9)	
Net accounts receivable		$21

The process of estimating an allowance for uncollectible accounts, writing off bad debts in the following period, and then reestimating the allowance at the end of the period is one that occurs throughout the company's life.

AGING OF ACCOUNTS RECEIVABLE

■ **LO5**
Use the aging method to estimate future uncollectible accounts.

In our example for Kimzey Medical Clinic, we estimated future uncollectible accounts by applying a *single* estimated percentage to total accounts receivable (30%). Management can estimate this percentage using historical averages, current economic conditions, industry comparisons, or other analytical techniques. A more accurate method than assuming a single percentage uncollectible for all accounts is to consider the *age* of various accounts receivable, and use a higher percentage for "old" accounts than for "new" accounts. This is known as the aging method. For instance, accounts that are 60 days past due are older than accounts that are 30 days past due. **The older the account, the less likely it is to be collected.**

Let's return to Kimzey Medical Clinic to see how an aging of accounts receivable can be used to estimate uncollectible accounts. Recall that accounts receivable at the end of 2013 totaled $30 million. Illustration 5–11 (next page) shows Kimzey's accounts receivable aging schedule at the end of 2013.

Each age group has its own estimate of the percent uncollectible. Summing the estimated allowance for each age group results in a total estimated allowance of **$8** million. Because the allowance has a balance of $2 million before adjustment at the end of 2013 (refer back to Illustration 5–8), it needs a **$6** million adjustment. In other words, the $2 million current balance in the allowance account needs an upward adjustment of $6 million to reach the $8 million estimated ending balance for 2013. Illustration 5–12 (next page) demonstrates this calculation.

ILLUSTRATION 5–11

Kimzey's Accounts Receivable Aging Schedule

($ in millions)

Age Group (days past due)	Accounts Receivable	×	Estimated Percent Uncollectible	=	Estimated Allowance
0–60	$20		20%		$4.0
61–120	5		30%		1.5
121–180	4		40%		1.6
More than 180	1		90%		0.9
Total	$30				$8.0

ILLUSTRATION 5–12

Balance of Kimzey's Allowance for Uncollectible Accounts

Allowance for Uncollectible Accounts
($ in millions)

Write off account	5	6	Beginning balance for 2013
		1	Collection of previous write-off
		2	Balance before adjustment
		?	Year-end adjustment
		8	Estimated ending balance for 2013

To adjust the allowance from its current balance of $2 million credit to the estimated balance of $8 million credit, we record the following:

A	=	L	+	SE			
				−6 Exp↑			
−6							

December 31, 2013	Debit	Credit
Bad Debt Expense	6	
Allowance for Uncollectible Accounts		6
(*Estimate future bad debts*)		

Illustration 5–13 presents **Tenet Healthcare**'s policy of estimating uncollectible accounts.

ILLUSTRATION 5–13

Excerpt from Tenet Healthcare Corporation's Annual Report

TENET HEALTHCARE CORPORATION
Notes to the Financial Statements (excerpt)

We provide for an allowance against accounts receivable that could become uncollectible by establishing an allowance to reduce the carrying value of such receivables to their estimated net realizable value. We estimate this allowance based on the aging of our accounts receivable by hospital, our historical collection experience by hospital and for each type of payer over an 18-month look-back period, and other relevant factors. There are various factors that can impact collection trends, such as changes in the economy, which in turn have an impact on unemployment rates and the number of uninsured and underinsured patients, the volume of patients through the emergency department, the increased burden of co-payments and deductibles to be made by patients with insurance, and business practices related to collection efforts. These factors continuously change and can have an impact on collection trends and our estimation process.

The following tables present the approximate aging by payer of our continuing operations' net accounts receivable.

Age	Medicare	Medicaid	Managed Care	Indemnity, Self-pay, and Other	Total
0–60 days	94%	63%	78%	26%	69%
61–120 days	3	24	12	27	15
121–180 days	3	11	5	13	6
Over 180 days	0	2	5	34	10
Total	100%	100%	100%	100%	100%

KEY POINT

Using the aging method to estimate uncollectible accounts is more accurate than applying a single percentage to all accounts receivable. The aging method recognizes that the longer accounts are past due, the less likely they are to be collected.

Question		Accounting information		Analysis		**Decision Point**
How likely is it that the company's accounts receivable will be collected?		Notes to the financial statements detailing the age of individual accounts receivable		Older accounts are less likely to be collected.		

Let's Review

Community Medical is an outpatient health facility that provides minor surgical and other health-related services to the local community. Many of the patients do not have medical insurance. These customers are required to pay for services within 30 days of receiving treatment. At the beginning of 2012, Community Medical's allowance for uncollectible accounts was a $100,000 credit.

Required:

1. Record the write-off of $120,000 of accounts receivable during 2012.
2. Estimate the allowance for future uncollectible accounts using the following ages and estimated percentage uncollectible at the end of 2012:

Age Group	Amount Receivable	Estimated Percent Uncollectible	Estimated Amount Uncollectible
Not yet due	$600,000	10%	
1–45 days past due	200,000	20	
More than 45 days past due	50,000	60	
Total	$850,000		

3. Use a T-account to determine the year-end adjustment to the allowance account.
4. Record the year-end adjustment for bad debts expense.
5. Prepare a partial balance sheet showing accounts receivable and the allowance for uncollectible accounts.

Solution:

1. Write-off of accounts receivable during 2012:

	Debit	Credit
Allowance for Uncollectible Accounts	120,000	
Accounts Receivable		120,000

2. Estimate of the allowance for future uncollectible accounts:

Age Group	Amount Receivable	Estimated Percent Uncollectible	Estimated Amount Uncollectible
Not yet due	$600,000	10%	$ 60,000
1–45 days past due	200,000	20%	40,000
More than 45 days past due	50,000	60%	30,000
Total	$850,000		$130,000

3. Year-end adjustment to the allowance account:

Allowance for Uncollectible Accounts		
	100,000	Beginning balance
Write-offs 120,000		
Balance before adjustment 20,000		
	?	Year-end adjustment
	130,000	Estimated ending balance

4. Year-end adjustment for bad debt expense:

December 31, 2012	Debit	Credit
Bad Debt Expense	150,000	
Allowance for Uncollectible Accounts		150,000*

*Notice from the T-account in *Requirement* 3 that the balance of the allowance account before adjustment is a $20,000 *debit*. Based on the estimated allowance of a $130,000 *credit*, we need a credit adjustment of $150,000. Of this adjustment, $20,000 is needed to get the allowance account to a zero balance, and the remaining $130,000 credit adjusts the account to the estimated ending balance.

5. Balance sheet:

COMMUNITY MEDICAL
Balance Sheet (partial)
December 31, 2012

Assets		
Current assets:		
Accounts receivable	$850,000	
Less: Allowance for uncollectible accounts	(130,000)	
Net accounts receivable		$720,000

Suggested Homework:
BE5-5, BE5-8;
E5-11, E5-12;
P5-4A&B, P5-6A&B

Direct Write-Off Method

■ LO6
Contrast the allowance method and direct write-off method when accounting for uncollectible accounts.

We've just seen how the allowance method of accounting for uncollectible accounts works. However, if uncollectible accounts are not anticipated or are immaterial, or if it's not possible to reliably estimate them, we need not make an allowance for them. **In these rare situations, we do not estimate uncollectible accounts, but we write off any bad debts that do arise as bad debt expense at that time.**

For example, suppose a company provides services for $10,000 on account in 2012, but makes no allowance for uncollectible accounts at the end of the year. On September 17, 2013, an account of $2,000 is considered uncollectible. The company records the write-off as follows.

A	=	L	+	SE
				−2,000 Exp↑
−2,000				

September 17, 2013	Debit	Credit
Bad Debt Expense	2,000	
Accounts Receivable		2,000
(*Write off uncollectible account directly*)		

The direct write-off method typically is not acceptable for financial reporting.

Recording bad debt expense at the time we know the account to be uncollectible is known as the direct write-off method. **The direct write-off method is used for tax purposes but is generally not permitted for financial reporting.** Can you guess why? Accounts receivable generated from the credit sales in 2012 are recorded in 2012, but no allowance is made for the possibility that some of these accounts will not be collected. As a result, in 2012 assets are overstated and operating expenses are understated. This is why the direct write-off method of accounting for uncollectible accounts is not permitted for financial reporting purposes except in limited circumstances. Specifically, **a firm must use the allowance method if it is probable that the firm will not collect a material amount of receivables and it can reasonably estimate that amount.**

Illustration 5–14 highlights the difference between the allowance method and the direct write-off method for our example.

	2012		2013	
	(Year-end estimated bad debts = $2,000)		**(Actual bad debts = $2,000)**	
	Year-end adjustment		**Write-off**	
Allowance method (estimate)	Bad Debt Expense 2,000		Allowance 2,000	
	Allowance 2,000		Accounts Receivable 2,000	
Direct write-off method	No Adjustment		Bad Debt Expense 2,000	
			Accounts Receivable 2,000	

ILLUSTRATION 5–14

Comparing the Allowance Method and the Direct Write-off Method for Recording Uncollectible Accounts

Assume that at the end of 2012 we *estimate* $2,000 of accounts receivable won't be collected. For simplicity, also assume that our estimate of future bad debts turns out to be correct, and actual bad debts in 2013 total $2,000.

Under the allowance method, future bad debts are *estimated* and recorded as an expense and a reduction in assets in 2012. Under the direct write-off method, though, we make no attempt to estimate future bad debts. We record bad debt expense in the period the account proves uncollectible. In this case, we report the bad debt expense and reduction in assets in 2013. Notice that, either way, the ultimate effect is a $2,000 debit to Bad Debt Expense and a $2,000 credit to Accounts Receivable. **The difference is in the timing.**

 COMMON MISTAKE

Some students erroneously think firms should reduce total assets and record bad debt expense at the time the bad debt actually occurs. However, companies *anticipate* future bad debts and establish an allowance for those estimates.

 KEY POINT

The direct write-off method reduces accounts receivable and records bad debt expense at the time the account receivable proves uncollectible. If the credit sale occurs in a prior reporting period, bad debt expense is not properly matched with revenues (credit sales). Also, accounts receivable will be overstated in the prior period. The direct write-off method typically is not acceptable for financial reporting.

Managing Bad Debt Estimates

While the allowance method is conceptually superior to the direct write-off method and more accurately reports assets and matches revenues and expenses, it does have one disadvantage. This disadvantage arises from the fact that reported amounts under the allowance method represent management estimates. If so inclined, management could use these estimates to manipulate reported earnings.[3] For example, if management wants to boost earnings in the current year, it can intentionally

Decision Maker's Perspective

---

[3]M. McNichols, G. P. Wilson, and L. De Angelo. 1988. Evidence of Earnings Management from the Provision for Bad Debts. *Journal of Accounting Research* (26): 1–40.

underestimate future uncollectible accounts. Similarly, if a company is having an especially good year and management wants to "reserve" earnings for the future, it can intentionally *overestimate* future uncollectible accounts. Having a large expense in the current year means there is less of a charge to bad debt expense in a future year, increasing future earnings. Other expenses, such as rent expense, are much more difficult to manipulate because their reported amounts don't rely on management estimates. These expenses are evidenced by past transactions, and their amounts are verifiable to the penny using a receipt or an invoice.

HealthSouth Corporation appears to have used estimates of uncollectible accounts to manipulate earnings. In the early 1990s, HealthSouth reported large amounts of bad debt expense, building large reserves in the allowance account. Then in the mid-1990s, as additional earnings were needed to meet analysts' expectations, HealthSouth was able to report low amounts for bad debt expense because of the previously inflated allowance account. In 1999, when it became apparent that HealthSouth's earnings were falling dramatically, the company took a "big bath" by reporting a very large charge to bad debt expense. Some companies feel that if they are going to have a bad year, they might as well release all the bad news at once. This makes it possible to report better news in future years. ●

 ETHICAL DILEMMA

 Philip Stanton, the executive manager of Thomson Pharmaceutical, receives a bonus if the company's net income in the current year exceeds net income in the past year. By the end of 2012, it appears that net income for 2012 will easily exceed net income for 2011. Philip has asked Mary Beth Williams, the company's controller, to try to reduce this year's income and "bank" some of the profits for future years. Mary Beth suggests that the company's bad debt expense as a percentage of accounts receivable for 2012 be increased from 10% to 15%. She believes 10% is the more accurate estimate but knows that both the corporation's internal and external auditors allow some flexibility in estimates. What is the effect of increasing the estimate of bad debts from 10% to 15% of accounts receivable? Does Mary Beth's proposal present an ethical dilemma?

PART C

NOTES RECEIVABLE

Notes receivable are similar to accounts receivable but are more formal credit arrangements evidenced by a written debt instrument, or *note*. Notes receivable typically arise from loans to other entities (including affiliated companies); loans to stockholders and employees; and occasionally the sale of merchandise, other assets, or services.

Accounting for Notes Receivable

■ **LO7**
Apply the procedure to account for notes receivable, including interest calculation.

Like accounts receivable, notes receivable are assets and therefore have a normal debit balance. We classify notes receivable as either *current* or *noncurrent*, depending on the expected collection date. If the time to maturity is longer than one year, the note receivable is a long-term asset.

As an example, let's say that, on February 1, 2012, Kimzey Medical Clinic provides services of $10,000 to a patient, Justin Payne, who is not able to pay immediately. In place of payment, Justin offers Kimzey a six-month, 12% promissory note. Because of the large amount of the receivable, Kimzey agrees to accept the promissory note as a way to increase the likelihood of eventually receiving payment. In addition, because of the delay in payment, Kimzey would like to charge interest on the outstanding balance. A formal promissory note provides an explicit statement of the interest charges. Illustration 5–15 shows an example of a typical note receivable.

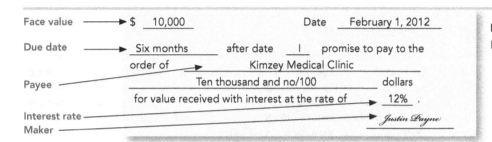

ILLUSTRATION 5–15

Note Receivable

Kimzey records the note as follows.

February 1, 2012	Debit	Credit	A	=	L	+	SE
Notes Receivable	10,000		+10,000				
Service Revenue		10,000					+10,000 Rev↑
(Accept a six-month, 12% note receivable for services provided)							

Another example of the use of notes receivable is to replace existing accounts receivable. For example, suppose that Justin received $10,000 of services on account, but Kimzey originally recorded the amount due as a typical account receivable. Over time, it became apparent that Justin would not be able to pay quickly, so Kimzey required Justin to sign a six-month, 12% promissory note on February 1, 2012. When Justin signs the note, Kimzey records the following transaction to reclassify the existing account receivable as a note receivable.

February 1, 2012	Debit	Credit	A	=	L	+	SE
Notes Receivable	10,000		+10,000				
Accounts Receivable		10,000	−10,000				
(Reclassify an existing account receivable as a six-month, 12% note receivable)							

Recognize that the transaction has no impact on the accounting equation; it is simply a matter of reclassifying assets. One asset (notes receivable) increases, while another asset (accounts receivable) decreases.

How would the patient, Justin Payne, record the previous transaction? By signing the note, Justin has an account payable that becomes reclassified as a note payable. He records the issuance of the note payable on February 1 as follows.

Flip Side

February 1, 2012	Debit	Credit	A	=	L	+	SE
Accounts Payable	10,000				−10,000		
Notes Payable		10,000			+10,000		
(Reclassify account payable as a six-month, 12% note payable)							

Flip Side

Just as one company's account payable is another company's account receivable, there is also a note payable for every note receivable. For every dollar a company earns in interest revenue, another company incurs a dollar of interest expense. We address notes payable in Chapter 8, but if you have a good understanding of notes receivable, then you have a head start with its flip side—notes payable.

KEY POINT

Notes receivable are similar to accounts receivable except that notes receivable are more formal credit arrangements made with a written debt instrument, or *note*.

INTEREST CALCULATION

Many of the same issues we discussed concerning accounts receivable, such as allowing for uncollectible accounts, apply also to notes receivable. The one issue that usually applies to notes receivable but not to accounts receivable is interest. You're probably familiar with the concept of interest. You may be earning interest on money in a savings account or checking account, and you might be paying interest on student loans, a car loan, or a credit card.

In the previous example, Kimzey issued a six-month, 12% promissory note. The "12%" indicates the *annual* interest rate charged by the payee. The terms of the six-month note mean that Kimzey will charge Justin Payne one-half year of interest, or 6%, on the face value. Interest on Kimzey's note receivable is calculated as follows.

Interest calculation

Interest	=	Face value	×	Annual interest rate	×	Fraction of the year
$600	=	$10,000	×	12%	×	6/12

KEY POINT

We calculate interest as the face value of the note multiplied by the stated annual interest rate multiplied by the appropriate fraction of the year that the note is outstanding.

COLLECTION OF NOTES RECEIVABLE

We record the collection of notes receivable the same way as collection of accounts receivable, except that we also record interest earned as interest revenue in the income statement.

Continuing the previous example, suppose that on August 1, 2012, the maturity date, Justin repays the note and interest in full as promised. Kimzey will record the following.

A = L + SE		Debit	Credit
+10,600	August 1, 2012		
−10,000	Cash	10,600	
	Notes Receivable		10,000
+600 Rev	Interest Revenue		600
	(Collect note receivable and interest)		
	(Interest revenue = $10,000 × 12% × 6/12)		

Over the six-month period, Kimzey earns interest revenue of $600. The credit to Notes Receivable reduces the balance in that account to $0, which is the amount Justin owes after payment to Kimzey.

ACCRUED INTEREST

It frequently happens that a note is issued in one year and the maturity date occurs in the following year. For example, what if Justin Payne issued the previous six-month note to Kimzey on November 1, 2012, instead of February 1, 2012? In that case, the $10,000 face value (principal) and $600 interest on the six-month note are not due until May 1, 2013. The length of the note (six months) and interest rate (12%) remain the same, and so the total interest charged to Justin remains the same. However, Kimzey will earn interest revenue in two separate accounting periods (assuming Kimzey uses a calendar year): for two months of the six-month note in 2012 (November and December), and for four months in the next year (January through April). Illustration 5–16 demonstrates the calculation of interest revenue over time. Interest receivable from Kimzey's six-month, $10,000, 12% note is $100 per month (= $10,000 × 12% × 1/12).

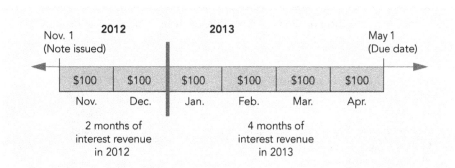

ILLUSTRATION 5–16

Calculating Interest Revenue over Time for Kimzey Medical Clinic

Because Kimzey earns two months of interest in 2012, it must accrue that interest as revenue on December 31, 2012 (even though no cash has been collected). The adjustment to accrue interest revenue follows.

December 31, 2012	Debit	Credit	A	=	L	+	SE
Interest Receivable	200		+200				
Interest Revenue		200					+200 Rev↑
(Accrue interest revenue)							
(Interest revenue = $10,000 × 12% × 2/12)							

On May 1, 2013, the maturity date, Kimzey records the collection of the note receivable and interest receivable from 2012 as well as the revenue related to the remaining four months' interest earned in 2013.

May 1, 2013	Debit	Credit	A	=	L	+	SE
Cash	10,600		+10,600				
Notes Receivable		10,000	−10,000				
Interest Receivable		200	−200				
Interest Revenue		400					+400 Rev↑
(Collect note receivable and interest)							
(Interest revenue = $10,000 × 12% × 4/12)							

On May 1, 2013, Kimzey has received the note receivable recorded on November 1, 2012, and the interest receivable recorded on December 31, 2012, and has eliminated their balances. The remaining four months' interest occurs in 2013, and Kimzey recognizes it as revenue in 2013.

KEY POINT

We record interest earned on notes receivable but not yet collected by the end of the year as interest receivable and interest revenue.

Let's Review

General Hospital has a policy of lending any employee up to $3,000 for a period of 12 months at a fixed interest rate of 9%. Chevy Chase has worked for General Hospital for more than 10 years and wishes to take his family on a summer vacation. On May 1, 2012, he borrows $3,000 from General Hospital to be repaid in 12 months.

Required:

1. Record the loan of cash and acceptance of the note receivable by General Hospital.
2. Record General Hospital's year-end adjustment to accrue interest revenue.
3. Record the collection of the note with interest from Chevy Chase on May 1, 2013.

Solution:

1. Acceptance of the note receivable:

May 1, 2012	Debit	Credit
Notes Receivable	3,000	
Cash		3,000
(*Accept note receivable*)		

2. Year-end adjustment to accrue interest revenue:

December 31, 2012	Debit	Credit
Interest Receivable	180	
Interest Revenue (8 months' interest)		180
(*Accrue interest revenue*)		
(*Interest revenue = $3,000 × 9% × 8/12*)		

3. Collection of the note with interest:

May 1, 2013	Debit	Credit
Cash	3,270	
Notes Receivable		3,000
Interest Receivable		180
Interest Revenue (4 months' interest)		90
(*Collect note receivable and interest*)		
(*Interest revenue = $3,000 × 9% × 4/12*)		

Suggested Homework:
BE5-10, BE5-11;
E5-15, E5-17;
P5-8A&B

ANALYSIS

RECEIVABLES ANALYSIS
Tenet vs. LifePoint

The amount of a company's accounts receivable is influenced by a variety of factors, including the level of sales, the nature of the product or service sold, and credit and collection policies. These factors are, of course, related. For example, a change in credit policies could affect sales. More liberal credit policies—allowing customers a longer time to pay or offering cash discounts for early payment—often are initiated with the specific objective of increasing sales volume.

Management's choice of credit and collection policies results in trade-offs. For example, when a company attempts to boost sales by allowing customers more time to pay, that policy also creates an increase in the required investment in receivables and may increase bad debts because older accounts are less likely to be collected. Offering discounts for early payment may increase sales volume, accelerate customer payment, and reduce bad debts, but at the same time it reduces the amount of cash collected from customers who take advantage of the discounts.

 CAREER CORNER

Companies that make large amounts of credit sales often employ credit analysts. These analysts are responsible for deciding whether to extend credit to potential customers. To make this decision, credit analysts focus on the customer's credit history (such as delinquency in paying bills) and information about current financial position, generally found using amounts in the financial statements. When the credit risk is too high, the analyst will advise management to reject the customer's request for goods and services, or perhaps limit the amount of credit extended. Management must then face a difficult trade-off: the potential gains from additional customer revenues versus the risk of an eventual uncollectible account. Credit analysts are most commonly employed by financial institutions ranging from banks to credit rating agencies and investment companies.

Investors, creditors, and financial analysts can gain important insights by monitoring a company's investment in receivables. Two important ratios that help in understanding the company's effectiveness in managing receivables are the *receivables turnover ratio* and the *average collection period*. We discuss those measures and then compare them for **Tenet Healthcare Corporation** and **LifePoint Hospitals**.

■ **LO8**
Calculate key ratios investors use to monitor a company's effectiveness in managing receivables.

RECEIVABLES TURNOVER RATIO

The receivables turnover ratio shows the number of times during a year that the average accounts receivable balance is collected (or "turns over"). We calculate it as follows:

$$\text{Receivables turnover ratio} = \frac{\textbf{Net credit sales}}{\textbf{Average accounts receivable}}$$

Let's say net credit sales are $400,000 for the year and the average accounts receivable balance is $40,000. In that case, we could say the turnover ratio is 10 ($400,000/$40,000), or that average receivables were collected 10 times during the year.

Note that the lower half of the receivables turnover ratio—average accounts receivable—is typically measured as the beginning accounts receivable plus the ending accounts receivable divided by two. So, our average of $40,000 might be the result of having a $35,000 balance at the beginning of the year and a $45,000 balance at the end of the year.

$$\text{Receivables turnover ratio} = \frac{\$400,000}{(\$35,000 + \$45,000)/2} = 10$$

AVERAGE COLLECTION PERIOD

The average collection period is another way to express the same efficiency measure. We calculate the average collection period as:

$$\text{Average collection period} = \frac{\textbf{365 days}}{\textbf{Receivables turnover ratio}}$$

238   CHAPTER 5   Receivables and Sales

It shows the approximate number of days the average accounts receivable balance is outstanding. If the turnover is 10 times a year (365 days), then the average balance is collected every 36.5 days.

$$\text{Average collection period} = \frac{365 \text{ days}}{10} = 36.5 \text{ days}$$

Companies typically strive for a high receivables turnover ratio and a correspondingly low average collection period. As a company's sales increase, receivables also likely will increase. If the percentage increase in receivables is greater than the percentage increase in sales, the receivables turnover ratio will decline (and the average collection period will increase). This could indicate that customers are dissatisfied with the product or that the company's payment terms for attracting new customers are too generous, which, in turn, could increase sales returns and bad debts.

Of course, what's "high" and what's "low" for these ratios depends on the situation. Companies may wish to evaluate these ratios relative to the prior year's ratios, ratios of other firms in the same industry, or specific targets set by management.

Decision Point

Question ?	Accounting information 📄	Analysis 🔍
Is the company effectively managing its receivables?	Receivables turnover ratio and average collection period	A high receivables turnover ratio (or low average collection period) generally indicates that the company's credit sales and collection policies are effective.

Now let's compare **Tenet Healthcare Corporation** to **LifePoint Hospitals**. The calculations of the receivables turnover ratio and average collection period for each company for 2008 and 2009, along with their net income for those years, are shown in Illustration 5–17.

ILLUSTRATION 5–17

Comparison of Receivables Ratios between Tenet Healthcare Corporation and LifePoint Hospitals

TENET HEALTHCARE CORPORATION					
	Net Sales (in millions)	Average Accounts Receivable (in millions)	Receivables Turnover Ratio	Average Collection Period	Net Income
2008	$8,585	$1,361	$\frac{\$8,585}{\$1,361} = 6.31$	$\frac{365}{6.31} = 57.8$	$ 32
2009	$9,014	$1,248	$\frac{\$9,014}{\$1,248} = 7.22$	$\frac{365}{7.22} = 50.6$	$197

LIFEPOINT HOSPITALS					
2008	$2,701	$ 310	$\frac{\$2,701}{\$310} = 8.71$	$\frac{365}{8.71} = 41.9$	$103
2009	$2,963	$ 321	$\frac{\$2,963}{\$321} = 9.23$	$\frac{365}{9.23} = 39.5$	$134

From Illustration 5–17, we see that LifePoint has a much higher receivables turnover, indicating that the company more efficiently collects cash from patients than does Tenet. The average collection period is much longer for Tenet. Better management of receivables by LifePoint may help explain the company's more profitable operations. Over the two-year period, LifePoint's net income is greater than that of Tenet, even though its revenue is only about one-third.

Having enough cash is important to running any business. The more quickly a company can collect its receivables, the more quickly it can use that cash to generate even more cash by reinvesting in the business and generating additional sales.

 KEY POINT

The receivables turnover ratio and average collection period can provide an indication of management's ability to collect cash from customers in a timely manner.

PERCENTAGE-OF-CREDIT-SALES METHOD

APPENDIX

In the chapter, we estimated uncollectible accounts based on a percentage of accounts receivable at the end of the period. You learned that this method is the *percentage-of-receivables method* or the *balance sheet method,* because we base the estimate of bad debts on a balance sheet amount—accounts receivable.

As an alternative, we can estimate uncollectible accounts based on the percentage of credit sales for the year, aptly referred to as the *percentage-of-credit-sales method* or the *income statement method,* because we base the estimate of bad debts on an income statement amount—credit sales. In this appendix, we consider the percentage-of-credit-sales method.

■ **LO9**
Estimate uncollectible accounts using the percentage-of-credit-sales method.

Let's rework the example in the chapter for Kimzey Medical Clinic (see Illustrations 5–8 to 5–10 and their discussion). During 2013, Kimzey bills customers $80 million for services, with $30 million in accounts receivable remaining at the end of the year. The balance of the allowance account, before adjustment, is a $2 million credit. For the percentage-of-receivables method, we'll use the estimate for uncollectible accounts used in the chapter—30% of receivables. For the percentage-of-credit-sales method, let's assume Kimzey expects 10% of credit sales to be uncollectible. Kimzey bases the 10% estimate on a number of factors, such as the average percentage of uncollectibles each year over the past several years.

Illustration 5–18 demonstrates the differences in the two methods when adjusting for estimates of uncollectible accounts.

Percentage-of-Receivables Method (repeated from chapter)	Percentage-of-Credit Sales Method
Estimate of Uncollectible Accounts	Estimate of Uncollectible Accounts
• 30% of ending accounts receivable will not be collected.	• 10% of credit sales will not be collected.
• 30% of $30 million = $9 million.	• 10% of $80 million = $8 million.
• Adjust from $2 million existing balance.	• Ignore $2 million existing balance.

Adjustment ($ in millions)		Adjustment ($ in millions)	
Bad Debt Expense	7	Bad Debt Expense	8
Allowance for Uncoll. Accts.	7	Allowance for Uncoll. Accts.	8

ILLUSTRATION 5–18

Adjusting for Estimates of Uncollectible Accounts

Notice that the two methods for estimating uncollectible accounts result in different adjustments. Because the amounts of the adjustments differ, the effects on the financial statements differ. Recall that the balance of the allowance account before adjustment is a $2 million credit. After adjustment, the balance of the allowance account will differ between the two methods, as will the amount of bad debt expense. Illustration 5–19 summarizes the differences in financial statement effects.

ILLUSTRATION 5–19

Financial Statement Effects of Estimating Uncollectible Accounts

Percentage-of-Receivables Method ($ in millions)		Percentage-of-Credit-Sales Method ($ in millions)	
Income Statement Effect		Income Statement Effect	
Revenues	$80	Revenues	$80
Bad debt expense	(7)	Bad debt expense	(8)
Net income	$73	Net income	$72
Balance Sheet Effect		Balance Sheet Effect	
Accounts receivable	$30	Accounts receivable	$30
Less: Allowance	(9)*	Less: Allowance	(10)*
Net accounts receivable	$21	Net accounts receivable	$20
* $9 = $2 + $7 (adjustment)		* $10 = $2 + $8 (adjustment)	

From an income statement perspective, some argue that the percentage-of-credit-sales method provides a better method for estimating bad debts because expenses (bad debts) are better matched with revenues (credit sales). A better matching of expenses and revenues results in a more accurate measure of net income for the period. From a balance sheet perspective, though, the percentage-of-receivables method is preferable because assets (net accounts receivable) are reported closer to their net realizable value.

The current emphasis on better measurement of assets (balance sheet focus) outweighs the emphasis on better measurement of net income (income statement focus). **This is why the percentage-of-receivables method (balance sheet method) is the preferable method, while the percentage-of-credit-sales method (income statement method) is allowed only if amounts do not differ significantly from estimates using the percentage-of-receivables method.**

KEY POINT

When applying the percentage-of-credit-sales method, we adjust the allowance for uncollectible accounts for the current year's credit sales that we don't expect to collect (rather than adjusting at the end of the year for the percentage of accounts receivable we don't expect to collect).

KEY POINTS BY LEARNING OBJECTIVE

LO1 Recognize accounts receivable.

Companies record an asset (accounts receivable) and revenue when they sell products and services to their customers on account, expecting payment in the future.

LO2 Calculate net revenues using discounts, returns, and allowances.

Sales discounts, returns, and allowances are contra revenue accounts. We subtract the balances in these accounts from total revenues when calculating net revenues.

LO3 Record an allowance for future uncollectible accounts.

We recognize accounts receivable as assets in the balance sheet and record them at their net realizable values, that is, the amount of cash we expect to collect.

Under the allowance method, companies are required to *estimate* future uncollectible accounts and record those estimates in the current year. Estimated uncollectible accounts reduce assets and increase expenses.

Adjusting for estimates of future uncollectible accounts matches expenses (bad debts) in the same period as the revenues (credit sales) they help to generate.

Recording an allowance for uncollectible accounts correctly reports accounts receivable at their net realizable value.

LO4 Apply the procedure to write off accounts receivable as uncollectible.

Writing off a customer's account as uncollectible reduces the balance of accounts receivable but also reduces the contra asset—allowance for uncollectible accounts. The net effect is that there is no change in the *net* receivable (accounts receivable less the allowance) or in total assets. We recorded the decrease to assets as a result of the bad debt when we established the allowance for uncollectible accounts in a prior year.

LO5 Use the aging method to estimate future uncollectible accounts.

Using the aging method to estimate uncollectible accounts is more accurate than applying a single percentage to all accounts receivable. The aging method recognizes that the longer accounts are past due, the less likely they are to be collected.

LO6 Contrast the allowance method and direct write-off method when accounting for uncollectible accounts.

The direct write-off method reduces accounts receivable and records bad debt expense at the time the account receivable proves uncollectible. If the credit sale occurs in a prior reporting period, bad debt expense is not properly matched with revenues (credit sales). Also, accounts receivable will be overstated in the prior period. The direct write-off method typically is not acceptable for financial reporting.

LO7 Apply the procedure to account for notes receivable, including interest calculation.

Notes receivable are similar to accounts receivable except that notes receivable are more formal credit arrangements made with a written debt instrument, or *note*.

We calculate interest as the face value of the note multiplied by the stated annual interest rate multiplied by the appropriate fraction of the year.

We record interest earned on notes receivable but not yet collected by the end of the year as interest receivable and interest revenue.

Analysis

LO8 Calculate key ratios investors use to monitor a company's effectiveness in managing receivables.

The receivables turnover ratio and average collection period can provide an indication of management's ability to collect cash from customers in a timely manner.

Appendix

LO9 Estimate uncollectible accounts using the percentage-of-credit-sales method.

When applying the percentage-of-credit-sales method, we adjust the allowance for uncollectible accounts for the current year's credit sales that we don't expect to collect (rather than adjusting at the end of the year for the percentage of accounts receivable we don't expect to collect).

GLOSSARY

Accounts receivable: The amount of cash owed to the company by its customers from the sale of products or services on account. **p. 214**

Aging method: Using a higher percentage for "old" accounts than for "new" accounts when estimating uncollectible accounts. **p. 227**

Allowance for uncollectible accounts: Contra asset account representing the amount of accounts receivable that we do not expect to collect. **p. 222**

Allowance method: Recording an adjustment at the end of each period to allow for the possibility of future uncollectible accounts. The adjustment has the effects of reducing assets and increasing expenses. **p. 220**

Average collection period: Approximate number of days the average accounts receivable balance is outstanding. It equals 365 divided by the receivables turnover ratio. **p. 237**

Bad debt expense: The amount of the adjustment to the allowance for uncollectible accounts, representing the cost of estimated future bad debts charged to the current period. **p. 221**

Contra revenue account: An account with a balance that is opposite, or "contra," to that of its related revenue account. **p. 216**

Credit sales: Transfer of products and services to a customer today while bearing the risk of collecting payment from that customer in the future. Also known as *sales on account* or *services on account*. **p. 214**

Direct write-off method: Recording bad debt expense at the time we know the account is uncollectible. **p. 230**

Net accounts receivable: The difference between total accounts receivable and the allowance for uncollectible accounts. **p. 222**

Net realizable value: The amount of cash the firm expects to collect. **p. 219**

Net revenues: A company's total revenues less any discounts, returns, and allowances. **p. 215**

Notes receivable: Formal credit arrangements evidenced by a written debt instrument, or *note*. **p. 232**

Percentage-of-receivables method: Method of estimating uncollectible accounts based on the percentage of accounts receivable expected not to be collected. **p. 221**

Receivables turnover ratio: Number of times during a year that the average accounts receivable balance is collected (or "turns over"). It equals net credit sales divided by average accounts receivable. **p. 237**

Sales allowance: Seller reduces the customer's balance owed or provides at least a partial refund because of some deficiency in the company's product or service. **p. 217**

Sales discount: Reduction in the amount to be paid by a credit customer if payment on account is made within a specified period of time. **p. 215**

Sales return: Customer returns a product. **p. 217**

Trade discount: Reduction in the listed price of a product or service. **p. 215**

Uncollectible accounts: Customers' accounts that no longer are considered collectible. **p. 220**

SELF-STUDY QUESTIONS

■ LO1

1. Accounts receivable are best described as:
   a. Liabilities of the company that represent the amount owed to suppliers.
   b. Amounts that have previously been received from customers.
   c. Assets of the company representing the amount owed by customers.
   d. Amounts that have previously been paid to suppliers.

■ LO2

2. On March 17, Fox Lumber sells materials to Whitney Construction for $12,000, terms 2/10, n/30. Whitney pays for the materials on March 23. What amount would Fox record as revenue on March 17?
   a. $12,400.
   b. $11,760.
   c. $12,000.
   d. $12,240.

■ LO2

3. Refer to the information in the previous question. What is the amount of net revenues (sales minus sales discounts) as of March 23?
   a. $0.
   b. $11,760.
   c. $12,000.
   d. $12,240.

■ LO3

4. Suppose the balance of Allowance for Uncollectible Accounts at the end of the current year is $400 (*credit*) before any adjustment. The company estimates future uncollectible accounts to be $3,200. At what amount would bad debt expense be reported in the current year's income statement?
   a. $400.
   b. $2,800.
   c. $3,200.
   d. $3,600.

■ LO3

5. Suppose the balance of Allowance for Uncollectible Accounts at the end of the current year is $400 (*debit*) before any adjustment. The company estimates future

uncollectible accounts to be $3,200. At what amount would bad debt expense be reported in the current year's income statement?
a. $400.
b. $2,800.
c. $3,200.
d. $3,600.

6. The entry to record a write-off of accounts receivable will include: ■ LO4
a. A debit to Bad Debt Expense.
b. A debit to Allowance for Uncollectible Accounts.
c. No entry because an allowance for uncollectible accounts was established in an earlier period.
d. A debit to Service Revenue.

7. Kidz Incorporated reports the following aging schedule of its accounts receivable with the estimated percent uncollectible. What is the total estimate of uncollectible accounts using the aging method?   ■ LO5

Age Group	Amount Receivable	Estimated Percent Uncollectible
0–60 days	$20,000	2%
61–90 days	6,000	15%
More than 90 days past due	2,000	50%
Total	$28,000	

a. $1,150.
b. $1,900.
c. $2,300.
d. $5,900.

8. The direct write-off method is generally not permitted for financial reporting purposes because: ■ LO6
a. Compared to the allowance method, it would allow greater flexibility to managers in manipulating reported net income.
b. This method is primarily used for tax purposes.
c. It is too difficult to accurately estimate future bad debts.
d. Expenses (bad debts) are not properly matched with the revenues (credit sales) they help to generate.

9. On January 1, 2012, Roberson Supply borrows $10,000 from Nees Manufacturing by signing a 9% note due in eight months. Calculate the amount of interest revenue Nees will record on September 1, 2012, the date that the note is due.   ■ LO7
a. $300.
b. $600.
c. $900.
d. $1,000.

10. At the beginning of 2012, Clay Ventures has total accounts receivable of $100,000. By the end of 2012, Clay reports net credit sales of $900,000 and total accounts receivable of $200,000. What is the receivables turnover ratio for Clay Ventures?   ■ LO8
a. 2.0.
b. 4.5.
c. 6.0.
d. 9.0.

Check out
www.mhhe.com/succeed
for more multiple-choice
questions.

Note: For answers, see the last page of the chapter.

REVIEW QUESTIONS

■ LO1   1. When recording a credit sale, what account do we debit? Describe where this account is reported in the financial statements.

■ LO1   2. What is the difference between a trade receivable and a nontrade receivable?

■ LO2   3. Explain the difference between a trade discount and a sales discount. Where are sales discounts reported in the income statement?

■ LO2   4. Briefly explain the accounting treatment for sales returns and allowances. Where are these accounts reported in the income statement?

■ LO2   5. Revenue can be earned at one point or over a period. Provide an example of each.

■ LO3   6. Explain the correct way companies should account for uncollectible accounts receivable (bad debts).

■ LO3   7. What two purposes do firms achieve by estimating future uncollectible accounts?

■ LO3   8. How does accounting for uncollectible accounts conform to the concept of the matching principle?

■ LO3   9. What are the financial statement effects of establishing an allowance for uncollectible accounts?

■ LO3   10. Describe the year-end adjustment to record the allowance for uncollectible accounts.

■ LO3   11. Allowance for Uncollectible Accounts is a contra asset account, which means that its normal balance is a credit. However, it is possible for the account to have a debit balance before year-end adjustments are recorded. Explain how this could happen.

■ LO3   12. We report accounts receivable in the balance sheet at their *net realizable value*. Explain what this term means.

■ LO4   13. When we have established an allowance for uncollectible accounts, how do we write off an account receivable as uncollectible? What effect does this write-off have on the reported amount of total assets and net income at the time of the write-off?

■ LO4   14. If at the end of the year Allowance for Uncollectible Accounts has a credit balance before any adjustment, what might that tell us about last year's estimate of future uncollectible accounts?

■ LO5   15. What does the *age* of accounts receivable refer to? How can we use an aging method to estimate uncollectible accounts receivable?

■ LO6   16. Discuss the differences between the allowance method and the direct write-off method for recording uncollectible accounts. Which of the two is acceptable under financial accounting rules?

■ LO7   17. Notes receivable differ from accounts receivable in that notes receivable represent *written* debt instruments. What is one other common difference between notes receivable and accounts receivable?

■ LO7   18. With respect to notes receivable, explain what each of these represent: (a) face value, (b) annual interest rate, and (c) fraction of the year.

■ LO7   19. What will be the total interest earned on a 6%, $2,000 note receivable that is due in nine months?

■ LO7   20. Interest on a note receivable typically is due along with the face value at the note's maturity date. If the end of the accounting period occurs before the maturity date, how do we record interest earned but not yet collected?

■ LO8   21. How is the receivables turnover ratio measured? What does this ratio indicate? Is a higher or lower receivables turnover preferable?

22. How is the average collection period of receivables measured? What does this ratio indicate? Is a higher or lower average collection period preferable? ■ **LO8**

23. How can effectively managing receivables benefit a company? ■ **LO8**

24. Which method, the percentage-of-receivables method or the percentage-of-credit-sales method, is typically used in practice? Why? ■ **LO9**

25. Explain why the percentage-of-receivables method is referred to as the *balance sheet method* and the percentage-of-credit-sales method is referred to as the *income statement method*. ■ **LO9**

BRIEF EXERCISES

BE5–1 The Giles Agency offers a 10% trade discount when providing advertising services of $1,000 or more to its customers. Audrey's Antiques decides to purchase advertising services of $2,500 (not including the trade discount), while Michael's Motors purchases only $600 of advertising. Both services are provided on account. Record both transactions for The Giles Agency, accounting for any trade discounts.

Record accounts receivable and trade discount (LO2)

BE5–2 Kelly's Jewelry reported the following amounts at the end of the year: total jewelry sales = $650,000; sales discounts = $15,000; sales returns = $40,000; sales allowances = $20,000. Compute net sales.

Calculate net sales (LO2)

BE5–3 At the end of the year, Mercy Cosmetics' balance of Allowance for Uncollectible Accounts is $500 (*credit*) before adjustment. The balance of Accounts Receivable is $20,000. The company estimates that 15% of accounts will not be collected over the next year. What adjustment would Mercy Cosmetics record for Allowance for Uncollectible Accounts?

Record the adjustment for uncollectible accounts (LO3)

BE5–4 At the end of the year, Dahir Incorporated's balance of Allowance for Uncollectible Accounts is $2,000 (*credit*) before adjustment. The company estimates future uncollectible accounts to be $10,000. What adjustment would Dahir record for Allowance for Uncollectible Accounts?

Record the adjustment for uncollectible accounts (LO3)

BE5–5 Refer to the information in BE5–4, but now assume that the balance of Allowance for Uncollectible Accounts before adjustment is $2,000 (*debit*). The company still estimates future uncollectible accounts to be $10,000. What is the adjustment Dahir would record for Allowance for Uncollectible Accounts?

Record the adjustment for uncollectible accounts (LO3)

BE5–6 At the beginning of the year, Mitchum Enterprises allows for estimated uncollectible accounts of $14,000. By the end of the year, actual bad debts total $15,000. Record the write–off to uncollectible accounts. Following the write-off, what is the balance of Allowance for Uncollectible Accounts?

Record the write-off of uncollectible accounts (LO4)

BE5–7 Barnes Books allows for possible bad debts. On May 7, Barnes writes off a customer account of $6,000. On September 9, the customer unexpectedly pays the $6,000 balance. Record the cash collection on September 9.

Record collection of account previously written off (LO4)

BE5–8 Williamson Distributors separates its accounts receivable into three age groups for purposes of estimating the percentage of uncollectible accounts.
1. Accounts not yet due = $30,000; estimated uncollectible = 5%.
2. Accounts 1–30 days past due = $10,000; estimated uncollectible = 20%.
3. Accounts more than 30 days past due = $4,000; estimated uncollectible = 30%.
Compute the total estimated uncollectible accounts.

Calculate uncollectible accounts using the aging method (LO5)

BE5–9 Brady is hired in 2012 to be the accountant for Anderson Manufacturing, a private company. At the end of 2012, the balance of Accounts Receivable is $24,000. In the past, Anderson has used only the direct write-off method to account for bad debts. Based on a detailed analysis of amounts owed, Brady believes the best estimate of future bad debts is $8,000. If Anderson continues to use the direct write-off method to account for uncollectible accounts, what adjustment, if any, would Brady record

Use the direct write-off method to account for uncollectible accounts (LO6)

at the end of 2012? What adjustment, if any, would Brady record if Anderson instead uses the allowance method to account for uncollectible accounts?

Calculate amounts related to interest (LO7)

BE5–10 Calculate the missing amount for each of the following notes receivable.

Face Value	Annual Interest Rate	Fraction of the Year	Interest
$10,000	6%	4 months	(a)
$20,000	4%	(b)	$800
$25,000	(c)	6 months	$500
(d)	8%	6 months	$600

Calculate interest revenue on notes receivable (LO7)

BE5–11 On October 1, 2012, Oberley Corporation loans one of its employees $30,000 and accepts a 12-month, 8% note receivable. Calculate the amount of interest revenue Oberley will recognize in 2012 and 2013.

Use the percentage-of-credit-sales method to adjust for uncollectible accounts (LO9)

BE5–12 At the end of the year, Brinkley Incorporated's balance of Allowance for Uncollectible Accounts is $3,000 (*credit*) before adjustment. The company estimates future uncollectible accounts to be 4% of credit sales for the year. Credit sales for the year total $125,000. What is the adjustment Brinkley would record for Allowance for Uncollectible Accounts using the percentage-of-credit-sales method?

Use the percentage-of-credit-sales method to adjust for uncollectible accounts (LO9)

BE5–13 Refer to the information in BE5–12, but now assume that the balance of Allowance for Uncollectible Accounts before adjustment is $3,000 (*debit*). The company still estimates future uncollectible accounts to be 4% of credit sales for the year. What adjustment would Brinkley record for Allowance for Uncollectible Accounts using the percentage-of-credit-sales method?

EXERCISES

Record credit sale (LO1)

E5–1 On May 7, Juanita Construction provides services on account to Michael Wolfe for $3,000. Michael pays for those services on May 13.

Required:
For Juanita Construction, record the service on account on May 7 and the collection of cash on May 13.

Record cash sales with a trade discount (LO2)

E5–2 Merry Maidens Cleaning generally charges $200 for a detailed cleaning of a normal-size home. However, to generate additional business, Merry Maidens is offering a new-customer discount of 10%. On May 1, Ms. E. Pearson has Merry Maidens clean her house and pays cash equal to the discounted price.

Required:
Record the revenue earned by Merry Maidens Cleaning on May 1.

Record credit sale and cash collection with a sales discount (LO1, 2)

E5–3 On March 12, Medical Waste Services provides services on account to Grace Hospital for $10,000, terms 3/10, n/30. Grace pays for those services on March 20.

Required:
For Medical Waste Services, record the service on account on March 12 and the collection of cash on March 20.

Record credit sale and cash collection (LO1, 2)

Flip Side of E5–5

E5–4 Refer to the information in E5–3, but now assume that Grace does not pay for services until March 31, missing the 3% sales discount.

Required:
For Medical Waste Services, record the service on account on March 12 and the collection of cash on March 31.

E5–5 Refer to the information in E5–4.

Required:

For Grace Hospital, record the purchase of services on account on March 12 and the payment of cash on March 31.

Record credit purchase and cash payment (**LO1, 2**)

Flip Side of E5–4

E5–6 On April 25, Foreman Electric installs wiring in a new home for $2,500 on account. However, on April 27, Foreman's electrical work does not pass inspection, and Foreman grants the customer an allowance of $500 because of the problem. The customer makes full payment of the balance owed, excluding the allowance, on April 30.

Record credit sales with a sales allowance (**LO1, 2**)

Required:
1. Record the credit sale on April 25.
2. Record the sales allowance on April 27.
3. Record the cash collection on April 30.
4. Calculate net sales associated with these transactions.

E5–7 During 2012, its first year of operations, Pave Construction provides services on account of $140,000. By the end of 2012, cash collections on these accounts total $100,000. Pave estimates that 30% of the uncollected accounts will be bad debts.

Record the adjustment for uncollectible accounts and calculate net realizable value (**LO3**)

Required:
1. Record the adjustment for uncollectible accounts on December 31, 2012.
2. Calculate the net realizable value of accounts receivable.

E5–8 Physicians' Hospital has the following balances on December 31, 2012, before any adjustment: Accounts Receivable = $50,000; Allowance for Uncollectible Accounts = $1,000 (credit). On December 31, 2012, Physicians' estimates uncollectible accounts to be 20% of accounts receivable.

Record the adjustment for uncollectible accounts and calculate net realizable value (**LO3**)

Required:
1. Record the adjustment for uncollectible accounts on December 31, 2012.
2. Determine the amount at which bad debt expense is reported in the income statement and the allowance for uncollectible accounts is reported in the balance sheet.
3. Calculate the net realizable value of accounts receivable.

E5–9 Southwest Pediatrics has the following balances on December 31, 2012, before any adjustment: Accounts Receivable = $120,000; Allowance for Uncollectible Accounts = $2,000 (*debit*). On December 31, 2012, Southwest estimates uncollectible accounts to be 10% of accounts receivable.

Record the adjustment for uncollectible accounts and calculate net realizable value (**LO3**)

Required:
1. Record the adjustment for uncollectible accounts on December 31, 2012.
2. Determine the amount at which bad debt expense is reported in the income statement and the allowance for uncollectible accounts is reported in the balance sheet.
3. Calculate the net realizable value of accounts receivable.

E5–10 Consider the following transactions associated with accounts receivable and the allowance for uncollectible accounts.

Identify the financial statement effects of transactions related to accounts receivable and allowance for uncollectible accounts (**LO3, 4**)

Credit Sales Transaction Cycle	Assets	Liabilities	Stockholders' Equity	Revenues	Expenses
1. Provide services on account					
2. Estimate uncollectible accounts					
3. Write off accounts as uncollectible					
4. Collect on account previously written off					

Required:

For each transaction, indicate whether it would increase (I), decrease (D), or have no effect (NE) on the account totals. (*Hint:* Make sure the accounting equation, Assets = Liabilities + Stockholders' Equity, remains in balance after each transaction.)

Record the adjustment for uncollectible accounts using the aging method **(LO5)**

E5–11 Mercy Hospital has the following balances on December 31, 2012, before any adjustment: Accounts Receivable = $60,000; Allowance for Uncollectible Accounts = $1,500 (credit). Mercy estimates uncollectible accounts based on an aging of accounts receivable as shown below.

Age Group	Amount Receivable	Estimated Percent Uncollectible
Not yet due	$40,000	10%
0–30 days past due	10,000	20%
31–90 days past due	7,000	50%
More than 90 days past due	3,000	90%
Total	$60,000	

Required:
1. Estimate the amount of uncollectible receivables.
2. Record the adjustment for uncollectible accounts on December 31, 2012.
3. Calculate the net realizable value of accounts receivable.

Record the adjustment for uncollectible accounts using the aging method **(LO5)**

E5–12 The Physical Therapy Center specializes in helping patients regain motor skills after serious accidents. The center has the following balances on December 31, 2012, before any adjustment: Accounts Receivable = $100,000; Allowance for Uncollectible Accounts = $3,000 (*debit*). The center estimates uncollectible accounts based on an aging of accounts receivable as shown below.

Age Group	Amount Receivable	Estimated Percent Uncollectible
Not yet due	$ 50,000	5%
0–60 days past due	25,000	10%
61–120 days past due	15,000	20%
More than 120 days past due	10,000	70%
Total	$100,000	

Required:
1. Estimate the amount of uncollectible receivables.
2. Record the adjustment for uncollectible accounts on December 31, 2012.
3. Calculate the net realizable value of accounts receivable.

Compare the allowance method and the direct write-off method **(LO6)**

E5–13 At the beginning of 2012, Brad's Heating & Air (BHA) has a balance of $25,000 in accounts receivable. Because BHA is a privately owned company, the company has used only the direct write-off method to account for uncollectible accounts. However, at the end of 2012, BHA wishes to obtain a loan at the local bank, which requires the preparation of proper financial statements. This means that BHA now will need to use the allowance method. The following transactions occur during 2012 and 2013.
a. During 2012, install air conditioning systems on account, $180,000.
b. During 2012, collect $175,000 from customers on account.
c. At the end of 2012, estimate that uncollectible accounts total 20% of ending accounts receivable.
d. In 2013, customers' accounts totaling $7,000 are written off as uncollectible.

Required:
1. Record each transaction using the allowance method.
2. Record each transaction using the direct write-off method.
3. Calculate the difference in net income (before taxes) in 2012 and 2013 between the two methods.

E5–14 During 2012, LeBron Corporation accepts the following notes receivable.
a. On April 1, LeBron provides services to a customer on account. The customer signs a four-month, 9% note for $6,000.
b. On June 1, LeBron lends cash to one of the company's executives by accepting a six-month, 10% note for $10,000.
c. On November 1, LeBron accepts payment for prior services by having a customer with a past-due account receivable sign a three-month, 8% note for $5,000.

Record notes receivable (LO7)

Required:
Record the acceptance of each of the notes receivable.

E5–15 On March 1, Terrell & Associates provides legal services to Whole Grain Bakery regarding some recent food poisoning complaints. Legal services total $10,000. In payment for the services, Whole Grain Bakery signs a 10% note requiring the payment of the face amount and interest to Terrell & Associates on September 1.

Record notes receivable and interest revenue (LO7)

Flip Side of E5–16

Required:
For Terrell & Associates, record the acceptance of the note receivable on March 1 and the cash collection on September 1.

E5–16 Refer to the information in E5–15.

Record notes payable and interest expense (LO7)

Flip Side of E5–15

Required:
For Whole Grain Bakery, record the issuance of the note payable on March 1 and the cash payment on September 1.

E5–17 On April 1, 2012, Shoemaker Corporation realizes that one of its main suppliers is having difficulty meeting delivery schedules, which is hurting Shoemaker's business. The supplier explains that it has a temporary lack of funds that is slowing its production cycle. Shoemaker agrees to lend $500,000 to its supplier using a 12-month, 12% note.

Record notes receivable and interest revenue (LO7)

Required:
Record the following transactions for Shoemaker Corporation.
1. The loan of $500,000 and acceptance of the note receivable on April 1, 2012.
2. The adjustment for accrued interest on December 31, 2012.
3. Cash collection of the note and interest on April 1, 2013.

E5–18 Below are amounts (in millions) from three companies' annual reports.

Calculate receivables ratios (LO8)

	Beginning Accounts Receivable (net)	Ending Accounts Receivable (net)	Net Sales
Walmart	$1,715	$2,662	$312,427
Target	$5,666	$6,194	$ 57,878
Costco Wholesale	$ 529	$ 565	$ 58,963

Required:
For each company, calculate the receivables turnover ratio and the average collection period (rounded to one decimal place). Which company appears most efficient in collecting cash from sales?

E5–19 Suzuki Supply reports the following amounts at the end of 2012 (before adjustment).

Compare the percentage-of-receivables method and the percentage-of-credit-sales method (LO9)

Credit Sales for 2012	$250,000
Accounts Receivable, December 31, 2012	45,000
Allowance for Uncollectible Accounts, December 31, 2012	1,000 (credit)

Required:
1. Record the adjustment for uncollectible accounts using the percentage-of-receivables method. Suzuki estimates 10% of receivables will not be collected.

250   CHAPTER 5   Receivables and Sales

2. Record the adjustment for uncollectible accounts using the percentage-of-credit-sales method. Suzuki estimates 2% of credit sales will not be collected.
3. Calculate the effect on net income (before taxes) and total assets in 2012 for each method.

Compare the percentage-of-receivables method and the percentage-of-credit-sales method (LO9)

E5–20 Refer to the information in E5–19, but now assume that the balance of the Allowance for Uncollectible Accounts on December 31, 2012, is $1,000 *(debit)* (before adjustment).

Required:
1. Record the adjustment for uncollectible accounts using the percentage-of-receivables method. Suzuki estimates 10% of receivables will not be collected.
2. Record the adjustment for uncollectible accounts using the percentage-of-credit-sales method. Suzuki estimates 2% of credit sales will not be collected.
3. Calculate the effect on net income (before taxes) and total assets in 2012 for each method.

For additional exercises, visit www.mhhe.com/succeed for Exercises: Set B.

PROBLEMS: SET A

Calculate the amount of revenue to recognize (LO1)

P5–1A Assume the following scenarios.

Scenario 1: During 2012, **IBM** provides consulting services on its mainframe computer for $10,000 on account. The customer does not pay for those services until 2013.

Scenario 2: On January 1, 2012, **Gold's Gym** sells a one-year membership for $1,200 cash. Normally, this type of membership would cost $1,500, but the company is offering a 20% "New Year's Resolution" discount.

Scenario 3: During 2012, **The Manitowoc Company** provides shipbuilding services to the U.S. Navy for $300,000. The U.S. Navy will pay $100,000 at the end of each year for the next three years, beginning in 2012.

Scenario 4: During 2012, **Goodyear** sells tires to customers on account for $24,000. By the end of the year, collections total $20,000. At the end of 2013, it becomes apparent that the remaining $4,000 will never be collected from customers.

Required:
For each scenario, calculate the amount of revenue to be recognized in 2012.

Record transactions related to credit sales and contra revenues (LO1, 2)

P5–2A Outdoor Expo provides guided fishing tours. The company charges $200 per person but offers a 10% discount to parties of four or more. Consider the following transactions during the month of May.

May 2   Charlene books a fishing tour with Outdoor Expo for herself and four friends at the group discount price ($900 = $180 × 5). The tour is scheduled for May 7.
May 7   The fishing tour occurs. Outdoor Expo asks that payment be made within 30 days of the tour and offers a 5% discount for payment within 15 days.
May 9   Charlene is upset that no one caught a single fish and asks management for a discount. Outdoor Expo has a strict policy of no discounts related to number of fish caught.
May 15   Upon deeper investigation, management of Outdoor Expo discovers that Charlene's tour was led by a new guide who did not take the group to some of the better fishing spots. In concession, management offers a sales allowance of 40% of the amount due.
May 20   Charlene pays for the tour after deducting the sales allowance.

Required:
1. Record the necessary transaction(s) for Outdoor Expo on each date.
2. Calculate net sales.
3. Show how Outdoor Expo would present net sales in its income statement.

P5–3A The following events occur for The Underwood Corporation during 2012 and 2013, its first two years of operations.

June 12, 2012	Provide services to customers on account for $35,000.
September 17, 2012	Receive $20,000 from customers on account.
December 31, 2012	Estimate that 40% of accounts receivable at the end of the year will not be received.
March 4, 2013	Provide services to customers on account for $50,000.
May 20, 2013	Receive $10,000 from customers for services provided in 2012.
July 2, 2013	Write off the remaining amounts owed from services provided in 2012.
October 19, 2013	Receive $40,000 from customers for services provided in 2013.
December 31, 2013	Estimate that 40% of accounts receivable at the end of the year will not be received.

Record transactions related to accounts receivable (**LO3, 4**)

Required:

1. Record transactions for each date.
2. Post transactions to the following accounts: Cash, Accounts Receivable, and Allowance for Uncollectible Accounts.
3. Calculate the net realizable value of accounts receivable at the end of 2012 and 2013.

P5–4A Pearl E. White Orthodontist specializes in correcting misaligned teeth. During 2012, Pearl provides services on account of $580,000. Of this amount, $70,000 remains receivable at the end of the year. An aging schedule as of December 31, 2012, is provided below.

Record transactions related to uncollectible accounts (**LO3, 4, 5**)

Age Group	Amount Receivable	Estimated Percent Uncollectible
Not yet due	$30,000	5%
0–90 days past due	15,000	10%
91–180 days past due	10,000	30%
More than 180 days past due	15,000	80%
Total	$70,000	

Required:

1. Calculate the allowance for uncollectible accounts.
2. Record the December 31, 2012, adjustment, assuming the balance of Allowance for Uncollectible Accounts before adjustment is $4,000 (*credit*).
3. On July 19, 2013, a customer's account balance of $7,000 is written off as uncollectible. Record the write-off.
4. On September 30, 2013, the customer whose account was written off in *Requirement* 3 unexpectedly pays the full amount. Record the cash collection.

P5–5A In an effort to boost sales in the current year, Roy's Gym has implemented a new program where members do not have to pay for their annual membership until the end of the year. The program seems to have substantially increased membership and revenues. Below are year-end amounts.

Compare the direct write-off method to the allowance method (**LO3, 6**)

	Membership Revenues	Accounts Receivable
Last year	$100,000	$ 5,000
Current year	300,000	160,000

Arnold, the owner, realizes that many members have not paid their annual membership fees by the end of the year. However, Arnold believes that no allowance for uncollectible accounts should be reported in the current year because none of the nonpaying members' accounts have proven uncollectible. Arnold wants to use the direct write-off method to record bad debts, waiting until the end of next year before writing off any accounts.

Required:

1. Do you agree with Arnold's reasoning for not reporting any allowance for future uncollectible accounts? Explain.
2. Suppose that similar programs in the past have resulted in uncollectible accounts of approximately 75%. If Arnold uses the allowance method, what should be the balance of Allowance for Uncollectible Accounts at the end of the current year?
3. Based on your answer in *Requirement* 2, for what amount will total assets and expenses be misstated in the current year if Arnold uses the direct write-off method? Ignore tax effects.

Using estimates of uncollectible accounts to overstate income (LO3)

P5–6A Willie Cheetum is the CEO of Happy Foods, a distributor of produce to grocery store chains throughout the Midwest. At the end of the year, the company's accounting manager provides Willie with the following information, before any adjustment.

Accounts receivable	$1,000,000
Estimated percentage uncollectible	10%
Allowance for uncollectible accounts	$30,000 (*credit*)
Operating income	$250,000

Willie's compensation contract states that if the company generates operating income of at least $200,000, he will get a salary bonus early next year.

Required:

1. Record the adjustment for uncollectible accounts using the accountant's estimate of 10% of accounts receivable.
2. After the adjustment is recorded in *Requirement* 1, what is the revised amount of operating income? Will Willie get his salary bonus?
3. Willie instructs the accountant to record the adjustment for uncollectible accounts using 7% rather than 10% of accounts receivable. Now will Willie get his salary bonus? Explain.
4. By how much would total assets and operating income be misstated using the 7% amount?

Overestimating future uncollectible accounts (LO3, 4)

P5–7A Humanity International sells medical and food supplies to those in need in underdeveloped countries. Customers in these countries are often very poor and must purchase items on account. At the end of 2012, total accounts receivable equal $1,200,000. The company understands that it's dealing with high credit risk clients. These countries are often in the middle of a financial crisis, civil war, severe drought, or some other difficult circumstance. Because of this, Humanity International typically estimates the percentage of uncollectible accounts to be 40% (= $480,000). Actual write-offs in 2013 total only $200,000, which means that the company significantly overestimated uncollectible accounts in 2012. It appears that efforts by the International Monetary Fund (IMF) and the United Nations (UN), and a mild winter mixed with adequate spring rains, have provided for more stable economic conditions than were expected, helping customers to pay on their accounts.

Required:

1. Record the adjustment for uncollectible accounts at the end of 2012, assuming there is no balance in Allowance for Uncollectible Accounts at the end of 2012 before any adjustment.
2. By the end of 2013, Humanity International has the benefit of hindsight to know that estimates of uncollectible accounts in 2012 were too high. How did this overestimation affect the reported amounts of total assets and expenses at the end of 2012? Ignore tax effects.

3. Should Humanity International prepare new financial statements for 2012 to show the correct amount of uncollectible accounts? Explain.

P5–8A On December 1, 2012, Liang Chemical provides services to a customer for $80,000. In payment for the services, the customer signs a three-year, 12% note. The face amount and all interest are due at the end of the third year.

Record long-term notes receivable and interest revenue (LO7)

Required:
1. Record the acceptance of the note on December 1, 2012.
2. Record the adjustment for interest revenue on December 31, 2012, 2013, and 2014.
3. Record the cash collection on December 1, 2015.

PROBLEMS: SET B

P5–1B Assume the following scenarios.

Calculate the amount of revenue to recognize (LO1)

Scenario 1: During 2012, The Hubbard Group provides services of $800,000 for repair of a state highway. The company receives an initial payment of $200,000 with the balance to be received the following year.

Scenario 2: Rolling Stone magazine typically charges $60 for a one-year subscription. On January 1, 2012, Herman, age 72, purchases a one-year subscription to the magazine and receives a 10% senior citizen discount.

Scenario 3: During 2012, Waste Management provides services on account for $20,000. The customer pays for those services in 2013.

Scenario 4: During 2012, Sysco Corporation sells grocery items to one of its customers for $250,000 on account. Cash collections on those sales are $170,000 in 2012 and $50,000 in 2013. The remaining $30,000 is written off as uncollectible in 2013.

Required:
For each scenario, calculate the amount of revenue to be recognized in 2012.

P5–2B Data Recovery Services (DRS) specializes in data recovery from crashed hard drives. The price charged varies based on the extent of damage and the amount of data being recovered. DRS offers a 20% discount to students and faculty at educational institutions. Consider the following transactions during the month of June.

Record transactions related to credit sales and contra revenues (LO1, 2)

June 10	Rashid's hard drive crashes and he sends it to DRS.
June 12	After initial evaluation, DRS e-mails Rashid to let him know that full data recovery will cost $2,000.
June 13	Rashid informs DRS that he would like them to recover the data and that he is a student at UCLA, qualifying him for a 20% educational discount and reducing the cost by $400 (= $2,000 × 20%).
June 16	DRS performs the work and claims to be successful in recovering all data. DRS asks Rashid to pay within 30 days of today's date, offering a 3% discount for payment within 10 days.
June 19	When Rashid receives the hard drive, he notices that DRS did not successfully recover all data. Approximately 25% of the data has not been recovered and he informs DRS.
June 20	DRS reduces the amount Rashid owes by 25%.
June 30	Rashid pays the amount owed.

Required:
1. Record the necessary transaction(s) for Data Recovery Services on each date.
2. Calculate net sales.
3. Show how net sales would be presented in the income statement.
4. Calculate net sales if Rashid had paid his bill on June 25.

Record transactions related to accounts receivable (LO3, 4)

P5–3B The following events occur for Morris Engineering during 2012 and 2013, its first two years of operations.

February 2, 2012	Provide services to customers on account for $32,000.
July 23, 2012	Receive $22,000 from customers on account.
December 31, 2012	Estimate that 30% of uncollected accounts will not be received.
April 12, 2013	Provide services to customers on account for $45,000.
June 28, 2013	Receive $6,000 from customers for services provided in 2012.
September 13, 2013	Write off the remaining amounts owed from services provided in 2012.
October 5, 2013	Receive $40,000 from customers for services provided in 2013.
December 31, 2013	Estimate that 30% of uncollected accounts will not be received.

Required:
1. Record transactions for each date.
2. Post transactions to the following accounts: Cash, Accounts Receivable, and Allowance for Uncollectible Accounts.
3. Calculate the net realizable value of accounts receivable at the end of 2012 and 2013.

Record transactions related to uncollectible accounts (LO3, 4, 5)

P5–4B Facial Cosmetics provides plastic surgery primarily to hide the appearance of unwanted scars and other blemishes. During 2012, the company provides services of $400,000 on account. Of this amount, $50,000 remains uncollected at the end of the year. An aging schedule as of December 31, 2012, is provided below.

Age Group	Amount Receivable	Estimated Percent Uncollectible
Not yet due	$30,000	2%
0–30 days past due	10,000	5%
31–60 days past due	7,000	10%
More than 60 days past due	3,000	20%
Total	$50,000	

Required:
1. Calculate the allowance for uncollectible accounts.
2. Record the December 31, 2012, adjustment, assuming the balance of Allowance for Uncollectible Accounts before adjustment is $300 (*debit*).
3. On April 3, 2013, a customer's account balance of $400 is written off as uncollectible. Record the write-off.
4. On July 17, 2013, the customer whose account was written off in *Requirement* 3 unexpectedly pays $100 of the amount but does not expect to pay any additional amounts. Record the cash collection.

Compare the direct write-off method to the allowance method (LO3, 6)

P5–5B Letni Corporation engages in the manufacture and sale of semiconductor chips for the computing and communications industries. During the past year, operating revenues remained relatively flat compared to the prior year but management notices a big increase in accounts receivable. The increase in receivables is largely due to the recent economic slowdown in the computing and telecommunications industries. Many of the company's customers are having financial difficulty, lengthening the period of time it takes to collect on account. Below are year-end amounts.

Age Group	Operating Revenue	Accounts Receivable	Average Age	Accounts Written Off
Two years ago	$1,200,000	$140,000	5 days	$ 0
Last year	1,500,000	150,000	7 days	1,000
Current year	1,600,000	320,000	40 days	0

Paul, the CEO of Letni, notices that accounts written off over the past three years have been minimal and, therefore, suggests that no allowance for uncollectible accounts be established in the current year. Any account proving uncollectible can be charged to next year's financial statements (the direct write-off method).

Required:

1. Do you agree with Paul's reasoning? Explain.
2. Suppose that other companies in these industries have had similar increasing trends in accounts receivable aging. These companies also had very successful collections in the past but now estimate uncollectible accounts to be 20% because of the significant downturn in the industries. If Letni uses the allowance method estimated at 20% of accounts receivable, what should be the balance of Allowance for Uncollectible Accounts at the end of the current year?
3. Based on your answer in *Requirement* 2, for what amount will total assets and expenses be misstated in the current year if Letni uses the direct write-off method? Ignore tax effects.

P5–6B Wanda B. Rich is the CEO of Outlet Flooring, a discount provider of carpet, tile, wood, and laminate flooring. At the end of the year, the company's accountant provides Wanda with the following information, before any adjustment.

Using estimates of uncollectible accounts to understate income (LO3)

Accounts receivable	$10,000,000
Estimated percentage uncollectible	3%
Allowance for uncollectible accounts	$100,000 (*credit*)
Operating income	$2,400,000

Wanda has significant stock ownership in the company and, therefore, would like to keep the stock price high. Analysts on Wall Street expect the company to have operating income of $1,800,000. The fact that actual operating income is well above this amount will make investors happy and help maintain a high stock price. Meeting analysts' expectations will also help Wanda keep her job.

Required:

1. Record the adjustment for uncollectible accounts using the accountant's estimate of 3% of accounts receivable.
2. After the adjustment is recorded in *Requirement* 1, what is the revised amount of operating income? Will Outlet Flooring still meet analysts' expectations?
3. Wanda instructs the accountant to instead record $600,000 as bad debt expense so that operating income will exactly meet analysts' expectations. By how much would total assets and operating income be misstated if the accountant records this amount?
4. Why would Wanda be motivated to manage operating income in this way?

P5–7B By the end of its first year of operations, Previts Corporation has credit sales of $650,000 and accounts receivable of $250,000. Given it's the first year of operations, Previts' management is unsure how much allowance for uncollectible accounts it should establish. One of the company's competitors, which has been in the same industry for an extended period, estimates uncollectible accounts to be 4% of ending accounts receivable, so Previts decides to use that same amount. However, actual write-offs in the following year were 20% of the $250,000 (= $50,000). Previts' inexperience in the industry led to making sales to high credit risk customers.

Underestimating future uncollectible accounts (LO3, 4)

Required:

1. Record the adjustment for uncollectible accounts at the end of the first year of operations using the 4% estimate of accounts receivable.
2. By the end of the second year, Previts has the benefit of hindsight to know that estimates of uncollectible accounts in the first year were too low. By how much did Previts underestimate uncollectible accounts in the first year? How did this underestimation affect the reported amounts of total assets and expenses at the end of the first year? Ignore tax effects.
3. Should Previts prepare new financial statements for the first year of operations to show the correct amount of uncollectible accounts? Explain.

Record long-term notes receivable and interest revenue (LO7)

P5–8B On April 15, 2012, Sampson Consulting provides services to a customer for $100,000. To pay for the services, the customer signs a three-year, 9% note. The face amount and all interest are due at the end of the third year. [*Hint:* Because the note is accepted during the middle of the month, Sampson plans to recognize one-half month of interest revenue in April 2012, and one-half month of interest revenue in April 2015.]

Required:
1. Record the acceptance of the note on April 15, 2012.
2. Record the adjustment for interest revenue on December 31, 2012, 2013, and 2014.
3. Record the cash collection on April 15, 2015.

*For additional problems, visit **www.mhhe.com/succeed** for Problems: Set C.*

ADDITIONAL PERSPECTIVES

Continuing Problem

Great Adventures

(This is a continuation of the Great Adventures problem from earlier chapters.)

AP5–1 Tony and Suzie are ready to expand Great Adventures even further in 2013. Tony believes that many groups in the community (for example, Boy Scouts, church groups, civic groups, and local businesses) would like to hold one-day outings for their members. Groups would engage in outdoor activities such as rock climbing, fishing, capture the flag, paintball, treasure hunts, scavenger hunts, nature hikes, and so on. The purpose of these one-day events would be for each member of the group to learn the importance of TEAM (Together Everyone Achieves More).

Tony knows that most people are not familiar with these types of activities, so to encourage business he allows groups to participate in the event before paying. He offers a 5% quick-payment discount to those that pay within 10 days after the event. He also guarantees that at least eight hours of outdoor activities will be provided or the customer will receive a 20% discount. For the first six months of the year, the following activities occur for TEAM operations.

Jan.	24	Great Adventures purchases outdoor gear such as ropes, helmets, harnesses, compasses, and other miscellaneous equipment for $5,000 cash.
Feb.	25	Mr. Kendall's Boy Scout troop participates in a one-day TEAM adventure. Normally, Tony would charge a group of this size $3,500, but he wants to encourage kids to exercise more and enjoy the outdoors so he charges the group only $3,000.
Feb.	28	The Boy Scout troop pays the full amount owed, less the 5% quick-payment discount.
Mar.	19	Reynold's Management has its employees participate in a one-day TEAM adventure. Great Adventures charges $4,000, and Reynold's agrees to pay within 30 days.
Mar.	27	Reynold's pays the full amount owed, less the 5% quick-payment discount.
Apr.	7	Several men from the Elks Lodge decide to participate in a TEAM adventure. They pay $7,500, and the event is scheduled for the following week.
Apr.	14	The TEAM adventure is held for members of the Elks Lodge.
May	9	Myers Manufacturing participates in a TEAM adventure. Great Adventures charges $6,000, and Myers agrees to pay within 30 days.
Jun. 1–30		Several MBA groups participate in TEAM adventures during June. Great Adventures charges $24,000 to these groups, with payment due in July.
Jun.	30	Myers Manufacturing fails to pay the amount owed within the specified period and agrees to sign a three-month, 8% note receivable to replace the existing account receivable.

Required:

1. Record TEAM adventure transactions occurring during the first six months of 2013.
2. As of June 30, 2013, Great Adventures finishes its first 12 months of operations. If Suzie wants to prepare financial statements, part of the process would involve allowing for uncollectible accounts receivable.
   a. Suppose Suzie estimates uncollectible accounts to be 10% of accounts receivable (which does not include the $6,000 note receivable from Myers Manufacturing). Record the adjustment for uncollectible accounts on June 30, 2013.
   b. Prepare a partial balance sheet showing the net accounts receivable section.

American Eagle Outfitters, Inc.

Financial Analysis

AP5–2 Financial information for American Eagle is presented in Appendix A at the end of the book.

Required:

1. Determine whether the trend in net sales has been increasing or decreasing for the past three years.
2. Where is accounts receivable reported? Explain why using net sales to calculate the receivables turnover ratio might not be a good indicator of a company's ability to efficiently manage receivables for a retail company like American Eagle, which typically sells clothing for cash.
3. Does American Eagle report an allowance for uncollectible accounts in the balance sheet? If so, how much is reported for the most recent year?

The Buckle, Inc.

Financial Analysis

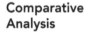

AP5–3 Financial information for The Buckle is presented in Appendix B at the end of the book.

Required:

1. Determine whether the trend in net sales has been increasing or decreasing for the past three years.
2. Where is accounts receivable reported? Explain why using net sales to calculate the receivables turnover ratio might not be a good indicator of a company's ability to efficiently manage receivables for a retail company like The Buckle, which typically sells clothing for cash.
3. Does The Buckle report an allowance for uncollectible accounts in the balance sheet? If so, how much is reported for the most recent year?

American Eagle Outfitters, Inc., vs. The Buckle, Inc.

Comparative Analysis

AP5–4 Financial information for American Eagle is presented in Appendix A at the end of the book, and financial information for The Buckle is presented in Appendix B at the end of the book.

Required:

Try to estimate each company's ratio of total current receivables to total current assets. Do you see problems with either company's management of receivables?

Ethics

AP5–5 You have recently been hired as the assistant controller for Stanton Industries. Your immediate superior is the controller who, in turn, reports to the vice president of finance.

The controller has assigned you the task of preparing the year-end adjustments. For receivables, you have prepared an aging of accounts receivable and have applied

258   CHAPTER 5   Receivables and Sales

historical percentages to the balances of each of the age categories. The analysis indicates that an appropriate balance for Allowance for Uncollectible Accounts is $180,000. The existing balance in the allowance account prior to any adjustment is a $20,000 credit balance.

After showing your analysis to the controller, he tells you to change the aging category of a large account from over 120 days to current status and to prepare a new invoice to the customer with a revised date that agrees with the new aging category. This will change the required allowance for uncollectible accounts from $180,000 to $135,000. Tactfully, you ask the controller for an explanation for the change and he tells you, "We need the extra income; the bottom line is too low."

Required:
1. What is the effect on income before taxes of the change requested by the controller?
2. Discuss the ethical dilemma you face. Consider your options and responsibilities along with the possible consequences of any action you might take.

Internet Research

AP5–6 Obtain a copy of the annual report of **Avon Products, Inc.**, for the most recent year. You can find the annual report at the company's website (*www.avon.com*) in the investor information section or at the Securities and Exchange Commission's website (*www.sec.gov*) using **EDGAR** (Electronic Data Gathering, Analysis, and Retrieval). Form 10-K, which includes the annual report, is required to be filed on EDGAR. Search or scroll within the annual report to find the financial statements.

Required:
Answer the following questions related to the company's accounts receivable and bad debts:
1. What is the amount of net accounts receivable at the end of the year? What is the amount of total accounts receivable?
2. What is the amount of bad debt expense for the year? (*Hint:* Check the statement of cash flows.)
3. Determine the amount of actual bad debt write-offs made during the year. Assume that all bad debts relate only to trade accounts receivable. Did the company underestimate or overestimate bad debts?
4. Calculate the receivables turnover ratio and average collection period for the most recent year. Assuming the industry averages for the receivables turnover ratio and average collection period are 10.5 times and 34.8 days, respectively, what do you conclude about the receivables of Avon?

Written Communication

AP5–7 You have been hired as a consultant by a parts manufacturing firm to provide advice as to the proper accounting methods the company should use in some key areas. In the area of receivables, the company president does not understand your recommendation to use the allowance method for uncollectible accounts. She stated, "Financial statements should be based on objective data rather than the guesswork required for the allowance method. Besides, since my uncollectibles are fairly constant from period to period, with significant variations occurring infrequently, the direct write-off method is just as good as the allowance method."

Required:
Draft a one-page response in the form of a memo to the president in support of your recommendation for the company to use the allowance method.

Earnings Management

AP5–8 Ernie Upshaw is the supervising manager of Sleep Tight Bedding. At the end of the year, the company's accounting manager provides Ernie with the following information, before any adjustment.

Accounts receivable	$500,000
Estimated percent uncollectible	9%
Allowance for uncollectible accounts	$20,000 (*debit*)
Operating income	$320,000

In the previous year, Sleep Tight Bedding reported operating income (after adjustment) of $275,000. Ernie knows that it's important to report an upward trend in earnings. This is important not only for Ernie's compensation and employment, but also for the company's stock price. If investors see a decline in earnings, the stock price could drop significantly, and Ernie owns a large amount of the company's stock. This has caused Ernie many sleepless nights.

Required:

1. Record the adjustment for uncollectible accounts using the accounting manager's estimate of 9% of accounts receivable.
2. After the adjustment is recorded in *Requirement* 1, what is the revised amount of operating income? Does operating income increase or decrease compared to the previous year?
3. Ernie instructs the accounting manager to record the adjustment for uncollectible accounts using 4% rather than 9% of accounts receivable. After this adjustment, does operating income increase or decrease compared to the previous year?
4. By how much would total assets and expenses be misstated using the 4% amount?

Answers to the Self-Study Questions

1. c   2. c   3. b   4. b   5. d   6. b   7. c   8. d   9. b   10. c

CHAPTER

6

Inventory and Cost of Goods Sold

BEST BUY: **TAKING INVENTORY OF ELECTRONICS SOLD**

Best Buy Co., Inc., is the largest specialty retailer of consumer goods in the United States, accounting for 17% of the specialty retail market. You are probably familiar with most of the products offered by Best Buy—computers, computer software, video games, music, DVDs, mobile phones, digital and video cameras, home appliances (washing machines, dryers, and refrigerators), and other related merchandise.

Merchandise inventory for sale to customers is the single largest asset owned by Best Buy, as it is for many retail companies. At any given time, Best Buy holds about $3 billion in inventory, or about 30% of the company's total assets. Proper management of inventory is key to the company's success.

Management of Best Buy knows there is a fine line between having too little and too much inventory. Having too little inventory reduces the selection of products available to customers, ultimately reducing sales revenue. On the other hand, in a technology-based industry where changes occur rapidly, having too much inventory can leave the store holding outdated inventory. Just think of what happens to the value of computers when the next generation becomes available. Managers don't want to get stuck with old inventory that is decreasing in value. Besides obsolescence, other costs associated with holding large inventories are storage, insurance, and shrinkage (theft). Holding less inventory provides access to money that can be invested elsewhere within the company.

For now, Best Buy seems to be taking the right steps with its inventory. Look below at the company's revenues from inventory sales compared to the cost of the inventory sold. These amounts are reported in the company's income statement. The difference between revenues and cost of goods sold (an expense) is called *gross profit*, and it has been steadily increasing over time.

	2006	2007	2008	2009
Revenues	$30,848	$35,934	$40,023	$45,015
Cost of goods sold	23,122	27,165	30,477	34,017
Gross profit	$ 7,726	$ 8,769	$ 9,546	$10,998

In this chapter, we explore how to account for the purchase and sale of inventory items. We'll see how inventory (an asset in the balance sheet) turns into cost of goods sold (an expense in the income statement) once it is sold, and how these amounts can affect business decisions.

Feature Story

PART A

UNDERSTANDING INVENTORY AND COST OF GOODS SOLD

In preceding chapters, we dealt mostly with companies that provide a service. *Service companies* such as **UPS**, **United Healthcare**, **Allstate Insurance**, and **Marriott Hotels** earn revenues by providing services to their customers. UPS delivers your packages, United Healthcare treats your medical needs, Allstate provides insurance coverage, and Marriott offers you a place to stay the night. Many companies, though, earn revenues by selling inventory rather than a service.

Part A of this chapter introduces the concept of inventory and demonstrates the different methods used to calculate the cost of inventory for external reporting. Once you understand this, then you're ready to see, in Part B and Part C, how companies actually maintain their own (internal) records of inventory transactions and the adjustments that are sometimes needed to prepare financial statements.

Inventory

■ LO1
Trace the flow of inventory costs from manufacturing companies to merchandising companies.

Companies that earn revenue by selling inventory are either *manufacturing* or *merchandising companies*. **Inventory** includes items a company intends for sale to customers. You already are familiar with several types of inventory—clothes at **The Limited**, shoes at **Payless ShoeSource**, grocery items at **Publix Super Markets**, digital equipment at **Best Buy**, building supplies at **The Home Depot**, and so on. Inventory also includes items that are not yet finished products. For instance, lumber at a cabinet manufacturer, steel at a construction firm, and rubber at a tire manufacturer are part of inventory because the firm will use them to make a finished product for sale to customers.

We report inventory as a current asset in the balance sheet—an *asset* because it represents a valuable resource the company owns, and *current* because the company expects to convert it to cash in the near term. At the end of the period, the amount the company reports for inventory is the cost of inventory *not yet sold*. What happens to the cost of the inventory sold during the period? The company reports the cost of the inventory it sold as **cost of goods sold** in the income statement.

Common Terms Cost of goods sold is also referred to as *cost of sales, cost of merchandise sold,* or *cost of products sold.*

As we'll see, determining these two amounts is a critical task in accounting for inventory. For companies that earn revenues by selling inventory, cost of goods sold often is the largest expense in the income statement. Before we explore how companies calculate cost of goods sold, we first need to consider the differences between merchandising and manufacturing companies, so that we understand the types of inventory each holds.

MERCHANDISING COMPANIES

Merchandising companies purchase inventories that are primarily in finished form for resale to customers. These companies may assemble, sort, repackage, redistribute, store, refrigerate, deliver, or install the inventory, but they do not manufacture it. They simply serve as intermediaries in the process of moving inventory from the manufacturer, the company that actually makes the inventory, to the end user.

We can broadly classify merchandising companies as wholesalers or retailers. *Wholesalers* resell inventory to retail companies or to professional users. For example, a wholesale food service company like **Sysco Corporation** supplies food to restaurants, schools, and sporting events but generally does not sell food directly to the public. Also, Sysco does not transform the food prior to sale; it just stores the food, repackages it as necessary, and delivers it.

Retailers purchase inventory from manufacturers or wholesalers and then sell this inventory to end users. You probably are more familiar with retail companies because these are the companies from which you buy products. **Best Buy**, **Target**,

Lowe's, Macy's, Gap, Sears, and McDonald's are retailers. Merchandising companies typically hold their inventories in a single category simply called *inventory*.

Common Terms
Inventory is also referred to as *merchandise inventory*.

MANUFACTURING COMPANIES

Manufacturing companies manufacture the inventories they sell, rather than buying them in finished form from suppliers. Apple Inc., Coca-Cola, Sara Lee, Harley-Davidson, ExxonMobil, Ford, Sony, and Dell are manufacturers. Manufacturing companies buy the inputs for the products they manufacture. Thus, we classify inventory for a manufacturer into three categories: (1) raw materials, (2) work in process, and (3) finished goods:

- Raw materials inventory includes the cost of components that will become part of the finished product but have not yet been used in production. (Raw materials sometimes are called *direct materials*.)
- Work-in-process inventory refers to the products that have started the production process but are not yet complete at the end of the period.
- Finished goods inventory consists of items for which the manufacturing process is complete.

Each of these inventory accounts includes its own costs. For example, Dell's raw materials inventory includes the costs of the semiconductors, circuit boards, and plastic parts that go into the production of personal computers. For its work-in-process inventory, Dell includes the cost of *raw materials* used in production, the cost of *direct labor* that we can trace directly to the goods in process, and an allocated portion of other manufacturing costs, called *overhead*. Overhead costs include costs to operate the manufacturing facility, depreciation of manufacturing equipment, and many other costs that we cannot directly link to the production of specific inventories. Once the manufacturing process is complete, Dell transfers to finished goods inventory the total cost of fully assembled but unshipped computers at the end of the reporting period. Illustration 6–1 shows inventory amounts for Dell Computers.

DELL COMPUTERS Notes to the Financial Statements (excerpt)		
($ in millions)	**2009**	**2008**
Raw materials	$454	$ 714
Work in process	150	144
Finished products	263	322
Total inventories	$867	$1,180

ILLUSTRATION 6–1

Types of Inventory for Dell Computers

At any given time, Dell holds around 70% of its inventory in a form other than finished products ready for sale to customers. Once inventory products are finished, Dell hopes to sell them as soon as possible.

 KEY POINT

Service companies earn revenues by providing services to customers. Merchandising and manufacturing companies earn revenues by selling inventory to customers.

FLOW OF INVENTORY COSTS

As you might guess, the flow of inventory costs differs depending on the type of company. Illustration 6–2 (next page) shows the flow of inventory costs for the three types of companies—service, merchandising, and manufacturing.

ILLUSTRATION 6–2

Types of Companies and Flow of Inventory Costs

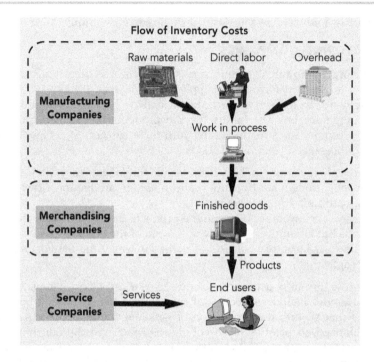

Inventory's journey begins when manufacturing companies purchase raw materials, hire workers, and incur manufacturing overhead during production. Once the products are finished, manufacturers normally pass inventories to merchandising companies, whether wholesalers or retailers. Merchandising companies then sell inventories to you, the end user. In some cases, manufacturers may sell directly to end users.

Some companies provide both services and inventories to customers. For example, **IBM** generates about half its revenues from selling its inventories of hardware and software, and the other half from providing services like consulting, systems maintenance, and financing.

In this chapter, we focus on merchandising companies, both wholesalers and retailers. Still, most of the accounting principles and procedures discussed here also apply to manufacturing companies. We do not attempt to address all the unique problems of accumulating the direct costs of raw materials and labor and allocating manufacturing overhead. We leave those details for managerial and cost accounting courses. In this course, we focus on the financial reporting implications of inventory cost flows.

Cost of Goods Sold

■ LO2

Calculate cost of goods sold.

Let's think a little more about the relationship between ending inventory in the balance sheet and cost of goods sold in the income statement. Remember that inventory represents the cost of inventory *not sold*, and cost of goods sold represents the cost of inventory *sold*. Thus, we can see that, once the inventory is sold, the amount reported for inventory becomes the amount reported for cost of goods sold. This relationship is depicted at the bottom of Illustration 6–3. Note, too, the two inventory inputs at the top of the figure: beginning inventory and purchases during the year. **The costs of *beginning inventory* plus the *additional purchases during the year* make up the cost of inventory (cost of goods) available for sale.**

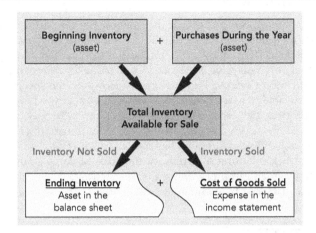

ILLUSTRATION 6–3

Relationship between Inventory and Cost of Goods Sold

To demonstrate these relationships using numbers, assume a local **Best Buy** store begins the year with $20,000 of DVD player inventory. That amount represents how much Best Buy spent to purchase the inventory of DVD players on hand at the beginning of the year. During the year, the company purchases additional DVD players for $90,000. What is the total cost of goods (DVD players) available for sale? Illustration 6–4 shows the answer: $110,000 (= $20,000 + $90,000). Now, assume that by the end of the year, the purchase cost of the remaining DVD player inventory is $30,000. What is the cost of goods sold? As Illustration 6–4 shows, the cost of the DVD players sold is $80,000 (= $110,000 − $30,000).

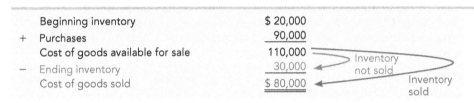

	Beginning inventory	$ 20,000
+	Purchases	90,000
	Cost of goods available for sale	110,000
−	Ending inventory	30,000
	Cost of goods sold	$ 80,000

ILLUSTRATION 6–4

Numerical Illustration of the Relationship between Inventory and Cost of Goods Sold

Of the $110,000 of goods available for sale during the year, some were not sold (ending inventory = $30,000) and some were sold (cost of goods sold = $80,000). The cost of the inventory sold (cost of goods sold) is an expense, which the company reports in the income statement (as we will see in more detail later).

 KEY POINT

Inventory is a current asset reported in the balance sheet and represents the cost of inventory *not yet sold* at the end of the period. Cost of goods sold is an expense reported in the income statement and represents the cost of inventory *sold*.

Inventory Cost Methods

To this point, we've discussed the cost of inventory without considering how we determine that cost. We do that now by considering four methods for inventory costing:

1. Specific identification
2. First-in, first-out (FIFO)
3. Last-in, first-out (LIFO)
4. Weighted-average cost

■ LO3

Determine the cost of goods sold and ending inventory using different inventory cost methods.

SPECIFIC IDENTIFICATION

The specific identification method is the method you might think of as the most logical. It matches—identifies—each unit of inventory with its actual cost. For example, an automobile has a unique serial number that we can match to an invoice identifying the actual purchase price. Fine jewelry and pieces of art are other possibilities. Specific identification works well in such cases. However, the specific identification method is practicable only for companies selling unique, expensive products. Consider the inventory at **The Home Depot** or **Sally Beauty Supply**: numerous items, many of which are relatively inexpensive. Specific identification would be very difficult for such merchandisers. Although bar codes and RFID tags now make it possible to identify and track each unit of inventory, the costs of doing so outweigh the benefits for multiple, small inventory items. For that reason, the specific identification method is used primarily by companies with unique, expensive products with low sales volume.

FIRST-IN, FIRST-OUT

For practical reasons, most companies use one of the other three inventory cost flow assumptions—FIFO, LIFO, or weighted-average cost—to determine cost of goods sold and inventory. Note the use of the word *assumptions:* Each of these three inventory cost methods *assumes* a particular pattern of inventory cost flows. However, the *actual* flow of inventory does not need to match the *assumed* cost flow in order for the company to use a particular method.

To see how the three cost flow assumptions work, let's begin with FIFO. We'll examine the inventory transactions in Illustration 6–5 for Mario's Game Shop, which sells video game cartridges. Mario has 100 units of inventory at the beginning of the year and then makes two purchases during the year—one on April 25 and one on October 19. (Note the different unit costs at the time of each purchase.) There are **1,000** game cartridges available for sale.

ILLUSTRATION 6–5

Inventory Transactions for Mario's Game Shop

Date	Transaction	Number of Units	Unit Cost	Total Cost
Jan. 1	Beginning inventory	100	$ 7	$ 700
Apr. 25	Purchase	300	9	2,700
Oct. 19	Purchase	600	11	6,600
	Total goods available for sale	**1,000**		$10,000
Jan. 1–Dec. 31	Total sales to customers	800		
Dec. 31	Ending inventory	200		

During the year, Mario sells **800** video game cartridges for $15 each. This means that **200** cartridges remain in ending inventory at the end of the year. But which 200? Do they include some of the $7 units from beginning inventory? Are they 200 of the $9 units from the April 25 purchase? Or, do they include some $11 units from the October 19 purchase? We consider these questions below.

Using the first-in, first-out (FIFO) method, we assume that the first units purchased (the first in) are the first ones sold (the first out). We assume that beginning inventory sells first, followed by the inventory from the first purchase during the year, followed by the inventory from the second purchase during the year, and so on.

In our example, which 800 units did Mario's Game Shop sell? Using the FIFO method, we *assume* they were the *first* 800 units purchased, and that all other units remain in ending inventory. These calculations are shown in Illustration 6–6.

We assume that all units from beginning inventory (100 units) and the April 25 purchase (300 units) were sold. For the final 400 units sold, we split the October 19

Inventory Transactions for Mario's Game Shop—FIFO METHOD

Purchases	Cost of Goods Available for Sale			=		Cost of Goods Sold	+	Ending Inventory
	Number of Units	× Unit Cost	= Total Cost					
Jan. 1	100	$ 7	$ 700		Sold first 800 units	$ 700		
Apr. 25	300	9	2,700			2,700		
Oct. 19	400	11	4,400			4,400		
	200	11	2,200 }		Not sold			$2,200
	1,000		$10,000	=		$7,800	+	$2,200

ILLUSTRATION 6–6

Inventory Calculation Using the FIFO Method

purchase of 600 units into two groups—400 units assumed sold and 200 units assumed not sold. We calculate cost of goods sold as the units of inventory assumed sold times their respective unit costs. [That is: $(100 \times \$7) + (300 \times \$9) + (400 \times \$11)$ in our example.] Similarly, ending inventory equals the units assumed not sold times *their* respective unit costs ($200 \times \$11$ in our example). The amount of cost of goods sold Mario reports in the income statement will be **$7,800**. The amount of ending inventory in the balance sheet will be **$2,200**.

You may have realized that we don't actually need to directly calculate both cost of goods sold and inventory. Once we calculate one, the other is apparent. Because the two amounts always add up to the cost of goods available for sale (**$10,000** in our example), knowing either amount allows us to subtract to find the other.

Realize, too, that the amounts reported for ending inventory and cost of goods sold do *not* represent the actual cost of inventory sold and not sold. That's okay. **Companies are allowed to report inventory costs by *assuming* which units of inventory are sold and not sold, even if this does not match the *actual* flow.**

LAST-IN, FIRST-OUT

Using the last-in, first-out (LIFO) method, we assume that the last units purchased (the last in) are the first ones sold (the first out). If Mario sold 800 units, we assume all the 600 units purchased on October 19 (the last purchase) were sold, along with 200 units from the April 25 purchase. That leaves 100 of the units from the April 25 purchase and all 100 units from beginning inventory assumed to remain in ending inventory (not sold). Illustration 6–7 shows calculations of cost of goods sold and ending inventory for the LIFO method.

Inventory Transactions for Mario's Game Shop—LIFO METHOD

Purchases	Cost of Goods Available for Sale			=		Cost of Goods Sold	+	Ending Inventory
	Number of Units	× Unit Cost	= Total Cost					
Jan. 1	100	$ 7	$ 700		Not sold			$ 700
Apr. 25	100	9	900					900
	200	9	1,800		Sold last 800 units	$1,800		
Oct. 19	600	11	6,600			6,600		
	1,000		$10,000			$8,400	+	$1,600

ILLUSTRATION 6–7

Inventory Calculation Using the LIFO Method

COMMON MISTAKE

Many students find it surprising that companies are allowed to report inventory costs using assumed amounts rather than actual amounts. Nearly all companies sell their actual inventory in a FIFO manner, but they are allowed to report it as if they sold it in a LIFO manner. Later, we'll see why that's advantageous.

WEIGHTED-AVERAGE COST

Using the weighted-average cost method, we assume that both cost of goods sold and ending inventory consist of a random mixture of all the goods available for sale. We assume each unit of inventory has a cost equal to the weighted-average unit cost of all inventory items. We calculate that cost at the end of the year as:

$$\text{Weighted-average unit cost} = \frac{\text{Cost of goods available for sale}}{\text{Number of units available for sale}}$$

Illustration 6–8 demonstrates the calculation of cost of goods sold and ending inventory using the weighted-average cost method. Notice that the weighted-average cost of each game cartridge is $10, even though none of the game cartridges actually cost $10. However, on average, all the game cartridges cost $10, and this is the amount we use to calculate cost of goods sold and ending inventory under the weighted-average cost method.

ILLUSTRATION 6–8

Inventory Calculation Using the Weighted-Average Cost Method

**Inventory Transactions for Mario's Game Shop—
WEIGHTED-AVERAGE COST METHOD**

		Cost of Goods Available for Sale		
Date	Transaction	Number of Units	× Unit Cost =	Total Cost
Jan. 1	Beginning inventory	100	$ 7	$ 700
Apr. 25	Purchase	300	9	2,700
Oct. 19	Purchase	600	11	6,600
		1,000		$10,000

Weighted-average unit cost $= \dfrac{\$10,000}{1,000 \text{ units}} =$ $10 per unit

Cost of goods sold	= 800 sold	×	$10 =	$ 8,000
Ending inventory	= 200 not sold	×	10 =	2,000
				$10,000

 COMMON MISTAKE

In calculating the weighted-average unit cost, be sure to use a *weighted* average of the unit cost instead of the *simple* average. In the example above, there are three unit costs: $7, $9, and $11. A simple average of these amounts is $9 [= (7 + 9 + 11) ÷ 3]. The simple average, though, fails to take into account that several more units were purchased at $11 than at $7 or $9. So we need to *weight* the unit costs by the number of units purchased. We do that by taking the total cost of goods available for sale ($10,000) divided by total number of units available for sale (1,000) for a weighted average of $10.

Illustration 6–9 depicts the concept behind the three inventory cost flow assumptions. A company begins the year with one unit of inventory and then purchases three units of inventory during the year. If the company sells two units of inventory, which two are they? Using FIFO, we assume inventory is sold in the order

ILLUSTRATION 6–9

Comparison of Cost of Goods Sold and Ending Inventory under the Three Inventory Cost Flow Assumptions

purchased: Beginning inventory is sold first, and then the first purchase during the year is sold second. Using LIFO, we assume inventory is sold in the *opposite* order that we purchased it: The last unit purchased is sold first, and the second-to-last unit purchased is sold second. Using average cost, we assume inventory is sold using an average of all inventory purchased, including the beginning inventory.

 COMMON MISTAKE

Students sometimes answer FIFO and LIFO backwards when calculating ending inventory. The reason is that these acronyms describe more directly the calculation of *cost of goods sold*, rather than ending inventory. For example, FIFO (first-in, first-out) directly suggests which inventory units are assumed sold (the first ones in) and therefore used to calculate cost of goods sold. It is implicit that the inventory units *not* sold are the last ones in and are used to calculate ending inventory.

 KEY POINT

Companies are allowed to report inventory costs by *assuming* which specific units of inventory are sold and not sold, even if this does not match the *actual* flow. The three major inventory cost flow assumptions are FIFO (first-in, first-out), LIFO (last-in, first-out), and weighted-average cost.

NASCAR Unlimited sells remote-control cars. For 2012, the company has the following beginning inventory and purchase.

Let's Review

Date	Transaction	Number of Units	Unit Cost	Total Cost
Jan. 1	Beginning inventory	120	$20	$2,400
Aug. 15	Purchase	180	15	2,700
	Total	300		$5,100

Because of technological advances, NASCAR Unlimited has seen a decrease in the unit cost of its inventory. Throughout the year, the company maintained a selling price of $30 for each remote-control car and sold a total of 280 units, which leaves 20 units in ending inventory.

Required:

1. Calculate cost of goods sold and ending inventory using the FIFO method.
2. Calculate cost of goods sold and ending inventory using the LIFO method.
3. Calculate cost of goods sold and ending inventory using the weighted-average cost method.

Solution:

1. Cost of goods sold and ending inventory using the **FIFO method:**

Purchases	Cost of Goods Available for Sale			=		Cost of Goods Sold	+	Ending Inventory
	Number of Units	× Unit Cost	= Total Cost					
Jan. 1	120	$20	$2,400		Sold first 280 units	$2,400		
Aug. 15	160	15	2,400			2,400		
	20	15	300		Not sold			$300
	300		$5,100	=		$4,800	+	$300

2. Cost of goods sold and ending inventory using the **LIFO method:**

Purchases	Cost of Goods Available for Sale			=		Cost of Goods Sold	+	Ending Inventory
	Number of Units	× Unit Cost	= Total Cost					
Jan. 1	20	$20	$ 400		Not sold			$400
	100	20	2,000		Sold last 280 units	$2,000		
Aug. 15	180	15	2,700			2,700		
	300		$5,100	=		$4,700	+	$400

3. Cost of goods sold and ending inventory using the **weighted-average cost method:**

$$\text{Weighted-average unit cost} = \frac{\$5,100}{300} = \$17$$

Cost of goods sold	=	280 sold	× $17	=	$4,760
Ending inventory	=	20 not sold	× 17	=	340
		300			$5,100

Suggested Homework:
BE6-4, BE6-5;
E6-2, E6-3;
P6-1A&B, P6-2A&B

Effects of Managers' Choice of Inventory Reporting Methods

■ **LO4**
Explain the financial statement effects and tax effects of inventory cost flow assumptions.

Companies are free to choose FIFO, LIFO, or weighted-average cost to report inventory and cost of goods sold. However, because inventory costs generally change over time, the reported amounts for ending inventory and cost of goods sold will not be the same across inventory reporting methods. These differences could cause investors and creditors to make bad decisions if they are not aware of differences in inventory assumptions.

Illustration 6–10 compares the FIFO, LIFO, and weighted-average cost methods for Mario's Game Shop (assuming rising costs). (Recall from the Feature Story at the start of the chapter, that *gross profit* is a key measure of profitability, calculated as the difference between revenues and cost of goods sold.)

	FIFO	LIFO	Weighted-Average
Balance sheet:			
Ending inventory	$ 2,200	$ 1,600	$ 2,000
Income statement:			
Sales revenue (800 × $15)	$12,000	$12,000	$12,000
Cost of goods sold	7,800	8,400	8,000
Gross profit	$ 4,200	$ 3,600	$ 4,000

ILLUSTRATION 6–10

Comparison of Inventory Cost Flow Assumptions, When Costs Are Rising

When inventory costs are rising, Mario's Game Shop will report both higher inventory in the balance sheet and higher gross profit in the income statement if it chooses FIFO. The reason is that FIFO assumes the lower costs of the earlier purchases become cost of goods sold first, leaving the higher costs of the later purchases in ending inventory. Under the same assumption (rising inventory costs), LIFO will produce the *opposite* effect: LIFO will report both the lowest inventory and the lowest gross profit. The weighted-average cost method typically produces amounts that fall between the FIFO and LIFO amounts for both cost of goods sold and ending inventory.

Accountants often call FIFO the *balance-sheet approach:* The amount it reports for ending inventory (which appears in the *balance sheet*) better approximates the current cost of inventory. The ending inventory amount reported under LIFO, in contrast, generally includes "old" inventory costs that do not realistically represent the cost of today's inventory.

> FIFO has a balance-sheet focus.

Accountants often call LIFO the *income-statement approach:* The amount it reports for cost of goods sold (which appears in the *income statement*) more realistically matches the current costs of inventory needed to produce current revenues. Recall that LIFO assumes the last purchases are sold first, reporting the most recent inventory cost in cost of goods sold. However, also note that the most recent cost is not the same as the actual cost. FIFO better approximates actual cost of goods sold for most companies, since most companies' actual physical flow follows FIFO.

> LIFO has an income-statement focus.

Decision Maker's Perspective

FIFO or LIFO?

Management must weigh the benefits of FIFO and LIFO when deciding which inventory cost flow assumption will produce a better outcome for the company. Here we review the logic behind that decision.

Why Choose FIFO?

Most companies' actual physical flow follows FIFO. Think about a supermarket, car dealership, clothing shop, electronics store, or just about any company you're familiar with. These companies generally sell their oldest inventory first (first-in, first-out). If a company wants to choose an inventory method that most closely approximates its *actual physical flow* of inventory, then for most companies FIFO makes the most sense.

> FIFO matches physical flow for most companies.

Another reason managers may want to use FIFO relates to its effect on the financial statements. **During periods of rising costs, which is the case for most companies (including our example for Mario's Game Shop), FIFO results in a (1) *higher* ending inventory, (2) *lower* cost of goods sold, and**

> FIFO generally results in higher assets and higher net income when inventory costs are rising.

CAREER CORNER

Many career opportunities are available in tax accounting. Because tax laws constantly change and are complex, tax accountants provide services to their clients not only through income tax statement preparation but also by formulating tax strategies to minimize tax payments. The choice of LIFO versus FIFO is one such example.

Tax accountants need a thorough understanding of legal matters, business transactions, and the tax code. Large corporations increasingly are looking to hire individuals with both an accounting and a legal background in tax. For example, someone who is a Certified Public Accountant (CPA) and has a law degree is especially desirable in the job market. In addition, people in nonaccounting positions also benefit greatly from an understanding of tax accounting. Whether you work in a large corporation or own a small business, virtually all business decisions have tax consequences.

LIFO generally results in tax savings.

(3) *higher* reported profit than does LIFO. Managers may want to report higher assets and profitability to increase their bonus compensation, decrease unemployment risk, satisfy shareholders, meet lending agreements, or increase stock price.

Why Choose LIFO?

If FIFO results in higher total assets and higher net income and produces amounts that most closely follow the actual flow of inventory, why would any company choose LIFO? **The primary benefit of choosing LIFO is tax savings.** LIFO results in the lowest amount of reported profits (when inventory costs are rising). While that might not look so good in the income statement, it's a welcome outcome in the tax return. When taxable income is lower, the company owes less in taxes to the Internal Revenue Service (IRS).

Can a company have its cake and eat it too by using FIFO for the income statement and LIFO for the tax return? No. The IRS established the LIFO conformity rule, which requires a company that uses LIFO for tax reporting to also use LIFO for financial reporting.

REPORTING THE LIFO DIFFERENCE

As Mario's Game Shop demonstrates, the choice between FIFO and LIFO results in different amounts for ending inventory in the balance sheet and cost of goods sold in the income statement. This complicates the way we compare financial statements: One company may be using FIFO, while a competing company may be using LIFO. To determine which of the two companies is more profitable, investors must adjust for the fact that managers' choice of inventory method has an effect on reported performance.

Because of the financial statement effects of different inventory methods, companies that choose LIFO must report the difference in the amount of inventory a company would report *if* it used FIFO instead of LIFO. (This difference is sometimes referred to as the LIFO reserve.) For some companies that have been using LIFO for a long time or for companies that have seen dramatic increases in inventory costs, the LIFO difference can be substantial. For example, Illustration 6–11 shows the effect of the LIFO difference reported by Rite Aid Corporation, which uses LIFO to account for most of its inventory.

ILLUSTRATION 6–11

Impact of the LIFO Difference on Reported Inventory of Rite Aid Corporation

RITE AID CORPORATION Notes to the Financial Statements (partial)		
($ in millions)	2009	2008
Reported inventory under LIFO	$3,509	$3,937
LIFO difference	746	563
Inventory assuming FIFO	$4,255	$4,500

If Rite Aid had used FIFO instead of LIFO, reported inventory amounts would have been $746 million greater and $563 million greater in 2009 and 2008, respectively. The magnitude of these effects can have a significant influence on investors' decisions.

Decision Point

Question	Accounting information	Analysis
When comparing inventory amounts between two companies, does the choice of inventory method matter?	The LIFO difference reported in the footnotes to the financial statements	When inventory costs are rising, FIFO results in a *higher* reported inventory. The LIFO difference can be used to compare inventory of two companies if one uses FIFO and the other uses LIFO.

CONSISTENCY IN REPORTING

Companies can choose which inventory method they prefer, even if the method does not match the actual physical flow of goods. However, once the company chooses a method, it is not allowed to frequently change to another one.[1] For example, a retail store cannot use FIFO in the current year because inventory costs are rising and then switch to LIFO in the following year because inventory costs are now falling.

However, a company need not use the same method for all its inventory. **International Paper Company**, for instance, uses LIFO for its raw materials and finished pulp and paper products, and both FIFO and weighted-average cost for other inventories. Because of the importance of inventories and the possible differential effects of different methods on the financial statements, a company informs its stockholders of the inventory method(s) being used in a note to the financial statements.

KEY POINT

Generally, FIFO more closely resembles the actual physical flow of inventory. When inventory costs are rising, FIFO results in higher reported inventory in the balance sheet and higher reported income in the income statement. Conversely, LIFO results in a lower reported inventory and net income, reducing the company's income tax obligation.

INTERNATIONAL FINANCIAL REPORTING STANDARDS (IFRS)

LIFO is not allowed under IFRS because it tends not to match the actual physical flow of inventory. FIFO and weighted-average cost are allowable inventory cost methods under IFRS. This distinction will become increasingly important as the United States moves closer to accepting IFRS for financial reporting. Will LIFO eventually disappear as a permitted inventory cost flow method? Perhaps so . . . stay tuned.

For more discussion, see Appendix E.

---

[1]When a company changes from LIFO for tax purposes, it cannot change back to LIFO until it has filed five tax returns using the non-LIFO method.

PART B

RECORDING INVENTORY TRANSACTIONS

So far, we've talked about purchases and sales of inventories and how to track their costs. We have not yet discussed how to *record* inventory transactions. We turn to that topic now.

Most companies, with the help of scanners and bar codes, keep a continual record of inventory using a perpetual inventory system. The continual—that is, perpetual—tracking of inventory helps a company to better manage its inventory levels. Just think of the losses that might occur at a video game store if the manager has no clear idea of the store's inventory and orders too many of a particular game that soon becomes obsolete when the next version or next hottest game comes out.

In contrast, a periodic inventory system does not continually modify inventory amounts, but instead *periodically* adjusts for purchases and sales of inventory at the end of the reporting period, based on a physical count of inventory on hand. Because this system does not provide a useful, continuing record of inventory, very few companies actually use the periodic inventory system in practice to maintain their own (internal) records of inventory transactions. Therefore, in this section, we will focus on how to record inventory transactions using a perpetual inventory system. Appendix A to the chapter covers the periodic system.

Perpetual Inventory System

■ **LO5**
Record inventory transactions using a perpetual inventory system.

To see how to record inventory transactions using a perpetual inventory system, we will look again at the inventory transactions for Mario's Game Shop. Recall that from January 1 through December 31, Mario sold 800 games. Now let's modify the example by giving exact dates for the sale of the 800 games—300 on July 17 and 500 on December 15. Illustration 6–12 shows the order of inventory transactions for Mario's Game Shop, including the total cost of the inventory and the total revenue from the sale of the 800 games.

ILLUSTRATION 6–12

Inventory Transactions for Mario's Game Shop

Date	Transaction	Details	Total Cost	Total Revenue
Jan. 1	Beginning inventory	100 units for $7 each	$ 700	
Apr. 25	Purchase	300 units for $9 each	2,700	
Jul. 17	Sale	300 units for $15 each		$ 4,500
Oct. 19	Purchase	600 units for $11 each	6,600	
Dec. 15	Sale	500 units for $15 each		7,500
	Totals		$10,000	$12,000

Using this information, let's see how Mario would record purchases and sales of inventory.

INVENTORY PURCHASES AND SALES

To record the purchase of new inventory, we debit Inventory (an asset) to show that the company's balance of this asset account has increased. At the same time, if the purchase was paid in cash, we credit Cash. Or more likely, if the company made the purchase on account, we credit Accounts Payable, increasing total liabilities. Thus, Mario records the first purchase of 300 units for $2,700 on April 25 as:

April 25	Debit	Credit
Inventory	2,700	
Accounts Payable		2,700
(Purchase inventory on account)		

On July 17, Mario sold 300 units of inventory on account for $15 each, resulting in total sales of $4,500. We make two entries to record the sale: (1) The first entry shows an increase to the asset account (in this case, Accounts Receivable) and an increase to Sales Revenue. (2) The second entry adjusts the Inventory and Cost of Goods Sold accounts.

Mario records as revenue the $4,500 from the July 17 sale. That amount is the price Mario charges to customers, but what did that inventory *cost* Mario? (That is, what is the cost of the goods sold?) Under the assumption that Mario uses FIFO to calculate inventory, the cost of the *first* 300 units purchased is $2,500, which is $700 of beginning inventory (100 units × $7) plus $1,800 of the April 25 purchase (200 units × $9). We record this amount as the cost of goods sold for the July 17 sale. At the same time, we maintain a continual (perpetual) record of inventory by reducing the Inventory balance by the cost of the amount sold, $2,500, as shown below.

July 17	Debit	Credit
Accounts Receivable	4,500	
Sales Revenue		4,500
(Sell inventory on account)		
($4,500 = 300 units × $15)		
Cost of Goods Sold	2,500	
Inventory		2,500
(Record cost of inventory sold)		
($2,500 = [100 units × $7] + [200 units × $9])		

By recording the sales revenue and the cost of goods sold at the same time, we can see that Mario's profit on the sale is $2,000.

On October 19, Mario purchased 600 additional units of inventory for $6,600 on account. We record that purchase as:

A = L + SE	October 19	Debit	Credit
+6,600	Inventory	6,600	
+6,600	Accounts Payable		6,600
	(Purchase inventory on account)		

On December 15, Mario sold another 500 units for $15 each on account. Again, we make two entries to record the sale. The first increases Accounts Receivable and Sales Revenue. The second adjusts the Cost of Goods Sold and Inventory accounts. What did the inventory sold on December 15 cost Mario? On the FIFO basis, the cost of goods sold is $5,300 (100 units × $9 plus 400 units × $11). Mario increases Cost of Goods Sold and decreases Inventory by that amount. Thus, we record the sale on December 15 as:

A = L + SE	December 15	Debit	Credit
+7,500	Accounts Receivable	7,500	
+7,500 Rev↑	Sales Revenue		7,500
	(Sell inventory on account)		
	($7,500 = 500 units × $15)		
A = L + SE			
−5,300 Exp↑	Cost of Goods Sold	5,300	
−5,300	Inventory		5,300
	(Record cost of inventory sold)		
	($5,300 = [100 units × $9] + [400 units × $11])		

After recording all purchases and sales of inventory for the year, we can determine the ending balance of Inventory by examining the postings to the account. Thus, Mario's ending Inventory balance is $2,200, as shown in Illustration 6–13.

ILLUSTRATION 6–13

Inventory Account for Mario's Game Shop

	Inventory		
Jan. 1 Beginning	700		
Apr. 25 Purchase	2,700	2,500	Jul. 17 Sale
Oct. 19 Purchase	6,600	5,300	Dec. 15 Sale
	10,000	7,800	
Dec. 31 Ending FIFO amount	Bal. 2,200		

KEY POINT

The perpetual inventory system maintains a continual—or *perpetual*—record of inventory purchased and sold. When companies *purchase* inventory using a perpetual inventory system, they increase the Inventory account and either decrease Cash or increase Accounts Payable. When companies *sell* inventory, they make two entries: (1) They increase an asset account (Cash or Accounts Receivable) and increase Sales Revenue, and (2) they increase Cost of Goods Sold and decrease Inventory.

Simple adjustment from FIFO to LIFO.   In the example above, we recorded inventory transactions using the FIFO assumption. Thus, Mario assumed that the 800 units sold during the year came from the first 800 units purchased. **In practice, virtually all companies maintain their own inventory records using the FIFO assumption, because that's how they typically sell their actual inventory.** However, as discussed earlier in the chapter, for preparing financial statements, many companies choose to report their inventory using the LIFO assumption. So, how does a company adjust its own inventory records maintained on a FIFO basis to a LIFO basis for preparing financial statements? The adjustment is referred to as the LIFO adjustment, and you'll see that this involves a *very simple* adjustment.

To see how easy the LIFO adjustment can be, let's refer back to our example involving Mario's Game Shop. As summarized in Illustration 6–13, Mario's ending balance of Inventory using FIFO is $2,200. Under LIFO, it is only $1,600 (see Illustration 6–7). As a result, if Mario's wants to adjust its FIFO inventory records to LIFO for preparing financial statements, it needs to adjust Inventory downward by $600 (decreasing the balance from $2,200 to $1,600). In this case, we record the LIFO adjustment at the end of the period through a decrease to Inventory and an increase to Cost of Goods Sold:

December 31	Debit	Credit
Cost of Goods Sold	600	
Inventory		600
(Record the LIFO adjustment)		

A = L + SE
           −600 Exp↑
−600

In rare situations where the LIFO Inventory balance is *greater* than the FIFO Inventory balance (such as when inventory costs are declining), the entry for the LIFO adjustment would be reversed.

Illustration 6–14 shows the Inventory account for Mario's Game Shop after the LIFO adjustment. Notice that the balance of Inventory has decreased to reflect the amount reported under the LIFO method.

	Inventory			
Jan. 1 Beginning	700			
Apr. 25 Purchase	2,700	2,500	Jul. 17 Sale	
Oct. 19 Purchase	6,600	5,300	Dec. 15 Sale	
	10,000	7,800		
FIFO amount	2,200			
		600	LIFO	
Dec. 31 Ending			adjustment	
LIFO amount	Bal. 1,600			

ILLUSTRATION 6–14

Inventory Account for Mario's Game Shop, after LIFO Adjustment

KEY POINT

Nearly all companies maintain their own inventory records on a FIFO basis, and then some prepare financial statements on a LIFO basis. To adjust their FIFO inventory records to LIFO for financial reporting, companies use a simple LIFO adjustment at the end of the period.

ADDITIONAL INVENTORY TRANSACTIONS

To this point, we've recorded inventory purchases and inventory sales transactions. So that we can discuss additional inventory topics, let's add three more inventory-related transactions to our Mario's example. Let's assume Mario also:

1. On April 25, pays freight charges of $300 for inventory purchased on April 25.
2. On April 30, pays for the units purchased on April 25, less a 2% purchase discount.
3. On October 22, returns 50 defective units from the October 19 purchase.

Next, we discuss how to record each of these three transactions.

Freight charges. A significant cost associated with inventory for most merchandising companies includes freight (also called shipping) charges. This includes the cost of shipments of inventory from suppliers, as well as the cost of shipments to customers. When goods are shipped, they are shipped with terms *FOB shipping point* or *FOB destination*. FOB stands for "free on board" and indicates *when* title (ownership) passes from the seller to the buyer. FOB *shipping point* means title passes when the seller *ships* the inventory, not when the buyer receives it. The fact that a buyer does not have actual physical possession of the inventory does not prevent transfer of title to the buyer's inventory. In contrast, if the seller ships the inventory FOB *destination*, then title does not transfer to the buyer when the inventory is shipped. The buyer would not record the purchase transaction until the shipped inventory reached its *destination*, the buyer's location.

Freight charges on incoming shipments from suppliers are commonly referred to as freight-in. **We add the cost of freight-in to the balance of Inventory.** In this case, the cost of freight is considered a cost of the purchased inventory. When Mario pays $300 for freight charges associated with the purchase of inventory on April 25, those charges would be recorded as part of the inventory cost.

A	=	L	+	SE		April 25	Debit	Credit
+300						Inventory	300	
−300						Cash		300
						(Pay freight-in charges)		

Later, when that inventory is sold, those freight charges become part of the cost of goods sold. In Mario's case, all of the units purchased on April 25 are sold by the end of the year, so the $300 freight charge would be reported as part of cost of goods sold in the income statement at the end of the year.

The cost of freight on shipments *to* customers is called freight-out. Shipping charges for outgoing inventory are reported in the income statement either as part of cost of goods sold or as an operating expense, usually among selling expenses. If a company adopts a policy of not including shipping charges in cost of goods sold, both the amounts incurred during the period as well as the income statement classification of the expense must be disclosed.[2]

To see an example of how Amazon.com accounts for freight charges, look at Illustration 6–15 (next page).

Purchase discounts. As discussed in Chapter 5, sellers often encourage prompt payment by offering *discounts* to buyers. From the seller's point of view, these are sales

---

[2]FASB ASC 605–45–50–2: Revenue Recognition–Principal Agent Considerations–Disclosure–Shipping and Handling Fees and Costs (previously "Accounting for Shipping and Handling Fees and Costs," *EITF Issue No. 00-10* [Norwalk, Conn.: FASB, 2000] par. 6).

> **AMAZON.COM, INC.**
> **Notes to the Financial Statements (excerpt)**
>
> Shipping charges to receive products from our suppliers are included in our inventory, and recognized as "Cost of sales.". . . Outbound shipping-related costs are included in "Cost of sales" and totaled $1.5 billion, $1.2 billion, and $884 million for 2008, 2007, and 2006.

ILLUSTRATION 6–15

Accounting for Shipping Costs by Amazon.com

discounts; from the buyer's point of view, they are *purchase discounts*. Purchase discounts allow buyers to trim a portion of the cost of the purchase in exchange for payment within a certain period of time. Buyers are not required to take purchase discounts, but many find it advantageous to do so.

Let's assume that Mario's supplier, Luigi Software, Inc., offers terms 2/10, n/30 for the April 25 purchase on account. This means that Mario can receive a 2% discount if payment is made within 10 days, but the total invoice is due within 30 days. Mario's policy is to take advantage of discounts offered.

For a review of credit terms, look back at page 216.

Recall that on April 25 Mario purchased 300 units on account for $9 each (or $2,700 total). When Mario makes payment on April 30, the discount would be $54 (= $2,700 × 2%). Mario has to pay only $2,646 (= $2,700 − $54) to eliminate the $2,700 amount owed. To account for the purchase discount, we subtract the discount from the balance in the Inventory account:

April 30	Debit	Credit	A	=	L	+	SE
Accounts Payable	2,700				−2,700		
Inventory		54	−54				
Cash		2,646	−2,646				
(Pay on account with a 2% purchase discount of $54)							
($54 = $2,700 × 2%)							

Just as freight charges *add* to the cost of inventory and therefore increase the cost of goods sold once those items are sold, purchase discounts *subtract* from the cost of inventory and therefore reduce cost of goods sold once those items are sold. When Mario sells the 300 units purchased on April 25, the cost of goods sold associated with those items will be the cost of the actual units ($2,700) plus freight charges ($300) less the purchase discount ($54), totaling $2,946.

Purchase returns.   Occasionally, a company will find inventory items to be unacceptable for some reason—perhaps they are damaged or are different from what was ordered. In those cases, the company returns the items to the supplier and records the purchase return as a reduction in both Inventory and Accounts Payable. For example, when Mario decides on October 22 to return 50 defective units from the 600 units purchased on October 19 for $11 each, the company would record the following transaction:

October 22	Debit	Credit	A	=	L	+	SE
Accounts Payable	550				−550		
Inventory		550	−550				
(Return inventory previously purchased on account)							
($550 = 50 defective units × $11)							

Let's Review

Camcorder Central sells high-end **Sony** camcorders and accounts for its inventory using FIFO with a perpetual system. At the beginning of March 2012, the company has camcorder inventory of $24,000 (= $240 × 100 units).

Required:

Record the following inventory transactions for Camcorder Central.
1. On March 7, Camcorder Central purchases on account 210 camcorders from Sony Corporation for $250 each, terms 2/10, n/30.
2. On March 8, Camcorder Central pays $2,000 for freight charges associated with the 210 camcorders purchased on March 7.
3. On March 10, Camcorder Central returns to Sony 10 defective camcorders from the March 7 purchase, receiving a credit of $250 for each camcorder.
4. On March 16, Camcorder Central makes full payment for inventory purchased on March 7, excluding the 10 defective camcorders returned and the 2% discount received.
5. On March 20, Camcorder Central sells 300 camcorders for $90,000 ($300 each). All sales are for cash.

Solution:

1. Camcorder Central's March 7 purchase on account of 210 camcorders from Sony Corporation for $250 each, terms 2/10, n/30:

March 7	Debit	Credit
Inventory	52,500	
Accounts Payable		52,500
(Purchase camcorders on account)		
($52,500 = $250 × 210 camcorders)		

2. Camcorder's March 8 payment for freight charges associated with the camcorders purchased on March 7:

March 8	Debit	Credit
Inventory	2,000	
Cash		2,000
(Pay for freight charges)		

3. Camcorder's March 10 return of 10 defective camcorders from the March 7 purchase, for a credit of $250 per camcorder:

March 10	Debit	Credit
Accounts Payable	2,500	
Inventory		2,500
(Return defective camcorders)		

4. Camcorder's March 16 payment for inventory purchased on March 7, excluding the returned camcorders and less the 2% discount:

March 16	Debit	Credit
Accounts Payable	50,000	
Inventory		1,000
Cash		49,000
(Make full payment for March 7 purchase)		
($1,000 = $50,000 × 2%)		

5. Camcorder's cash sale on March 20 of 300 camcorders for $300 each:

March 20	Debit	Credit
Cash	90,000	
Sales Revenue		90,000
(*Sell 300 camcorders for cash*)		
(*$90,000 = $300 × 300 camcorders*)		
Cost of Goods Sold	75,000	
Inventory		75,000
(*Record cost of camcorders sold*)		
(*Cost of 100 camcorders in beginning inventory = $24,000*)		
(*Cost of 200 camcorders purchased = $52,500 + $2,000 − $2,500 − $1,000 = $51,000*)		

Suggested Homework:
BE6-9, BE6-11;
E6-7, E6-8;
P6-3A&B, P6-6A&B

SALES TRANSACTIONS: THE OTHER SIDE OF PURCHASE TRANSACTIONS

Flip Side

For every purchase transaction, there is a sales transaction for another party. Sometimes, seeing the other side of the transaction helps us understand the economic events we are recording. In the Let's Review exercise above, Camcorder Central made a $52,500 purchase of inventory on account from Sony Corporation. Camcorder Central then returned inventory of $2,500 and received a $1,000 purchase discount for quick payment. Camcorder Central is the purchaser and Sony is the seller. We discussed returns and discounts from the seller's viewpoint in Chapter 5; here, let's briefly reexamine the transactions between Sony and Camcorder Central so we can see a side-by-side comparison of purchase and sales transactions. Illustration 6–16 shows these entries.

Purchaser			Seller		
Camcorder Central			Sony Corporation		
Purchase on Account			**Sale on Account***		
Inventory	52,500		Accounts Receivable	52,500	
Accounts Payable		52,500	Sales Revenue		52,500
Purchase Return			**Sales Return**		
Accounts Payable	2,500		Sales Return	2,500	
Inventory		2,500	Accounts Receivable		2,500
Payment on Account with Discount			**Receipt on Account with Discount**		
Accounts Payable	50,000		Cash	49,000	
Inventory		1,000	Sales Discounts	1,000	
Cash		49,000	Accounts Receivable		50,000

ILLUSTRATION 6–16

Comparison of Purchase and Sale of Inventory Transactions

*In practice, Sony also records the cost of inventory sold at the time of the sale. For simplicity, we omit this part of the transaction since Camcorder Central has no comparable transaction. We have also omitted Camcorder Central's March 20 sale of camcorders, since Sony is not party to that transaction.

KEY POINT

For most companies, freight charges are added to the cost of inventory, whereas purchase returns and purchase discounts are deducted from the cost of inventory. Some companies choose to report freight charges on outgoing shipments as part of selling expenses instead of cost of goods sold.

Multiple-Step Income Statement

■ **LO6**
Prepare a multiple-step income statement.

In Chapters 1 through 5, we presented a form of the income statement with two main categories: total revenues and total expenses. Look back at Illustration 3–12 (page 128) for an example. That format involves essentially a single calculation—total revenues minus total expenses—to get to net income. Not surprisingly, such an income statement is called a *single-step income statement*.

In this chapter, we have seen that sales and purchases of inventory typically are the most important transactions for a merchandising company. As a result, in their income statements, merchandisers report revenues and expenses from these transactions separately from other revenues and expenses. Because of this separate reporting, merchandising companies usually use a different format, called a multiple-step income statement, referring to the fact that the income statement reports *multiple* levels of income (or profitability).

Gross profit. The multiple-step income statement begins by reporting that a company's sales revenue minus cost of goods sold equals gross profit. Illustration 6–17 shows these amounts for our continuing example of Mario's Game Shop. Recall that Mario sold 800 units during the year for $15 each (or $12,000 total). This amount is reported as sales revenue.

ILLUSTRATION 6–17
Multiple-Step Income Statement

MARIO'S GAME SHOP Multiple-Step Income Statement For the year ended December 31, 2012	
Sales revenue	$12,000
Cost of goods sold	8,046
Gross profit	3,954
Selling expenses	950
General and administrative expenses	804
Operating income	2,200
Nonoperating revenues	100
Nonoperating expenses	(300)
Income before income taxes	2,000
Income tax expense	800
Net income	$ 1,200

Multiple levels of profit

From sales revenue, we subtract the cost of the 800 units sold. Again, to calculate this balance, we can look back to our transactions involving goods sold, including the cost of freight charges and the purchase discount associated with the purchase on April 25. The 800 units sold consist of the following:

	Units Sold	Unit Cost	Total Cost
Beginning inventory	100	$ 7	$ 700
Purchase on April 25	300	9	2,700
Freight charges			300
Purchase discount			(54)
Purchase on October 19	400	11	4,400
	800		$8,046

Mario would report $8,046 as the cost of goods sold.

The difference between sales of inventory and the cost of that inventory is the company's *gross profit*. Gross profit is one of the profitability measures investors use to evaluate the performance of a merchandising company. As Illustration 6–17 shows, Mario's gross profit is $3,954.

Operating income.   After gross profit, the next items reported are selling expenses and general and administrative expenses, often referred to as **operating expenses**. We discussed several types of operating expenses in earlier chapters—salaries, utilities, advertising, supplies, rent, insurance, and bad debts. These costs are normal for operating most companies. Gross profit reduced by these operating expenses is referred to as operating income (or sometimes referred to as *income from operations*). It measures profitability from *normal* operations, a key performance measure for predicting the future profit-generating ability of the company.

After operating income, a company reports **nonoperating revenues and expenses**. Nonoperating revenues and expenses arise from activities that are *not* part of the company's primary operations. Interest revenue and interest expense are examples. (In Chapter 7, we will discuss another common nonoperating item— gains and losses on the sale of long-term assets.) Investors focus less on nonoperating items than on income from operations, as these nonoperating activities often do not have long-term implications on the company's profitability.

Income before income taxes.   Combining operating income with nonoperating revenues and expenses yields income before income taxes. For Mario's Game Shop, the amount of nonoperating expenses exceeds the amount of nonoperating revenues, so income before income taxes is lower than operating income.

Net income.   Next, the company subtracts income tax expense to find its bottom-line net income. At the bottom line, net income represents the difference between all revenues and all expenses for the period. Note in Illustration 6–17 that the multiple-step income statement, unlike the single-step format, reports *multiple levels of profit*—gross profit, operating income, income before income taxes, and net income. We'll examine the multiple-step income statement again in Chapter 12, when we discuss additional income statement activities such as discontinued operations and extraordinary items.

 KEY POINT

A multiple-step income statement reports multiple levels of profitability. **Gross profit** equals sales revenue minus cost of goods sold. **Operating income** equals gross profit minus operating expenses. **Income before income taxes** equals operating income plus nonoperating revenues and minus nonoperating expenses. **Net income** equals all revenues minus all expenses.

Illustration 6–18 presents an example of a multiple-step income statement for hhgregg, Inc., a specialty retailer of consumer electronics and home appliances.

hhgregg, INC. Multiple-Step Income Statement For the year ended March 31, 2009 ($ in millions)	
Sales revenue, net	$1,397
Cost of goods sold	962
Gross profit	435
Selling, general, and administrative expenses	287
Advertising expenses	62
Other operating expenses	16
Operating income	70
Interest expense	7
Income before income taxes	63
Income tax expense	26
Net income	$ 37

Multiple levels of profit

ILLUSTRATION 6–18

Multiple-Step Income Statement for hhgregg, Inc.

The company has sales revenue of $1,397 million and cost of goods sold of $962 million, resulting in a gross profit of $435 million. After subtracting normal operating expenses, operating income is $70 million. Income before taxes equals $63 million after subtracting interest expense. The company's after-tax net income equals $37 million.

PART C

LO7
Apply the lower-of-cost-or-market method for inventories.

LOWER-OF-COST-OR-MARKET METHOD

Think about the store where you usually buy your clothes. You've probably noticed the store selling leftover inventory at deeply discounted prices after the end of each selling season to make room for the next season's clothing line. The value of the company's old clothing inventory has likely fallen below its original cost. Is it appropriate to report the reduced-value inventory at its original cost? The answer to that question has motivated accountants to use the lower-of-cost-or-market method.

When the market value of inventory falls below its original cost, companies are required to report inventory at the lower market value. Normally, the market value of inventory is considered to be the replacement cost of that inventory. In other words, what is the cost to replace the inventory item in its identical form? The cost of inventory is the amount initially recorded in the accounting records based on methods we discussed in the previous section (specific identification, FIFO, LIFO, or weighted-average cost). Once it has determined both the cost and market value of inventory, the company reports ending inventory in the balance sheet at the *lower* of the two amounts. This is known as the lower-of-cost-or-market (LCM) method to valuing inventory.

Illustration 6–19 demonstrates the concept behind the lower-of-cost-or-market method.

ILLUSTRATION 6–19

Lower-of-Cost-or-Market Method

Which is lower?

Cost	OR	Market Value
(specific identification, FIFO, LIFO, or weighted-average cost)		(replacement cost)
If:		**Then:**
Cost < Market ⟶		Report inventory at *cost*
Market < Cost ⟶		Report inventory at *market* (and report an expense)

To see how we apply the lower-of-cost-or-market method to inventory amounts, assume Mario's Game Shop sells FunStation 2 and FunStation 3. Illustration 6–20 shows information related to ending inventory at the end of 2012.

ILLUSTRATION 6–20

Calculating the Lower-of-Cost-or-Market

Inventory Items	Cost per Unit	Market per Unit	Lower-of-Cost-or-Market per Unit		Quantity		Total Lower-of-Cost-or-Market
FunStation 2	$300	$200	⟶ $200	×	15	=	$ 3,000
FunStation 3	400	450	⟶ 400	×	20	=	8,000
			Reported ending inventory			=	$11,000

Mario reports the FunStation 2 in ending inventory at market value ($200 per unit) because that's lower than its original cost ($300 per unit). The 15 FunStation 2s were originally reported in inventory at their cost of $4,500 (= 15 × $300). To reduce the inventory from that original cost of $4,500 to its lower market value of $3,000 (= 15 × $200), Mario records a $1,500 reduction in inventory with the following year-end adjustment.

December 31, 2012	Debit	Credit
Cost of Goods Sold	1,500	
Inventory		1,500
(Adjust inventory down to market value)		

Balance Sheet						Income Statement			
			Stockholders' Equity						
			Common	Retained					Net
Assets	=	Liabilities	+ Stock	+ Earnings		Revenues	− Expenses	=	Income
−1,500	=			−1,500			+1,500	=	−1,500

Notice that the write-down of inventory has the effect not only of reducing total assets, but also of reducing net income and retained earnings.

The FunStation 3 inventory, on the other hand, remains on the books at its original cost of $8,000 (= $400 × 20), since cost is less than market value. Mario does not need to make any adjustment for these inventory items.

After adjusting inventory to the lower-of-cost-or-market, the store calculates its ending Inventory balance as:

	Inventory		
Balance before LCM adjustment	12,500		
		1,500	LCM adjustment
Ending balance	Bal. 11,000		

Conservatism and the Lower-of-Cost-or-Market Method

Decision Maker's Perspective

Firms are required to report the falling value of inventory, but they are not allowed to report any increasing value of inventory. Why is this? The answer lies in the conservative nature of some accounting procedures. A *conservative* approach in accounting implies that there is more potential harm to users of financial statements if estimated *gains* turn out to be wrong than if estimated *losses* turn out to be wrong. It also guides companies, when faced with a choice, to select accounting methods that are less likely to overstate assets and net income. Therefore, companies typically do not report estimated gains. ●

286   CHAPTER 6   Inventory and Cost of Goods Sold

 KEY POINT

We report inventory at the lower-of-cost-or-market; that is, at cost (specific identification, FIFO, LIFO, or weighted-average cost) or market value (replacement cost), whichever is lower. When market value falls below cost, we adjust downward the balance of inventory from cost to market value.

Let's Review

Auto Adrenaline provides specialty car products—satellite radios, GPS navigation systems, and subwoofers. At the end of 2012, the company's records show the following amounts in ending inventory.

Inventory Items	Quantity	Cost per Unit	Market per Unit
Satellite radios	10	$100	$120
GPS navigators	20	300	350
Subwoofers	40	70	50

Required:

1. Determine ending inventory using the lower-of-cost-or-market method.
2. Record any necessary year-end adjustment entry associated with the lower-of-cost-or-market method.

Solution:

1. Ending inventory, lower-of-cost-or-market:

Inventory Items	Cost per Unit	Market per Unit	Lower-of-Cost-or-Market per Unit		Quantity		Total Lower-of-Cost-or-Market
Satellite radios	$100	$120	→ $100	×	10	=	$1,000
GPS navigators	300	350	→ 300	×	20	=	6,000
Subwoofers	70	50	→ 50	×	40	=	2,000
							$9,000

Cost is lower than market for satellite radios and GPS navigators. We get lower-of-cost-or-market by multiplying the *cost* per unit times the quantity. However, market is lower than cost for subwoofers. In that case, we get lower-of-cost-or-market by multiplying the *market* per unit times quantity.

2. Year-end adjustment associated with the lower-of-cost-or-market method:

December 31, 2012	Debit	Credit
Cost of Goods Sold	800	
Inventory		800
(Adjust inventory down to market value)		
($800 = 40 subwoofers × $20 decline in market below cost)		

Suggested Homework:
BE6-14, BE6-15;
E6-13, E6-14;
P6-4A&B

We need the $800 adjustment to reduce the reported Inventory balance of the 40 subwoofers by $20 each (from $70 to $50).

ETHICAL DILEMMA

Diamond Computers, which is owned and operated by Dale Diamond, manufactures and sells different types of computers. The company has reported profits every year since its inception in 2000 and has applied for a bank loan near the end of 2012 to upgrade manufacturing facilities. These upgrades should significantly boost future productivity and profitability.

In preparing the financial statements for the year, the chief accountant, Sandy Walters, mentions to Dale that approximately $80,000 of computer inventory has become obsolete and a write-down of inventory should be recorded in 2012.

Dale understands that the write-down would result in a net loss being reported for company operations in 2012. This could jeopardize the company's application for the bank loan, which would lead to employee layoffs. Dale is a very kind, older gentleman who cares little for his personal wealth but who is deeply devoted to his employees' well-being. He truly believes the loan is necessary for the company's sustained viability. Dale suggests Sandy wait until 2013 to write down the inventory so that profitable financial statements can be presented to the bank this year.

What should Sandy do?

INVENTORY ANALYSIS
Best Buy vs. Radio Shack

ANALYSIS

As discussed in the previous section, if managers purchase too much inventory, the company runs the risk of the inventory becoming obsolete and market value falling below cost, resulting in inventory write-downs. Outside analysts as well as managers often use the *inventory turnover ratio* to evaluate a company's effectiveness in managing its investment in inventory. In addition, investors often rely on the *gross profit ratio* to determine the core profitability of a merchandising company's operations. We discuss these ratios next.

■ **LO8**
Analyze management of inventory using the inventory turnover ratio and gross profit ratio.

INVENTORY TURNOVER RATIO

The inventory turnover ratio shows the number of times the firm sells its average inventory balance during a reporting period. It is calculated as cost of goods sold divided by average inventory.

$$\text{Inventory turnover ratio} = \frac{\textbf{Cost of goods sold}}{\textbf{Average inventory}}$$

The more frequently a business is able to sell or "turn over" its average inventory balance, the less the company needs to invest in inventory for a given level of sales. Other things equal, a higher ratio indicates greater effectiveness of a company in managing its investment in inventory.

288   CHAPTER 6   Inventory and Cost of Goods Sold

AVERAGE DAYS IN INVENTORY

Another way to measure the same activity is to calculate the average days in inventory. This ratio indicates the approximate number of days the average inventory is held. It is calculated as 365 days divided by the inventory turnover ratio.

$$\text{Average days in inventory} = \frac{365}{\text{Inventory turnover ratio}}$$

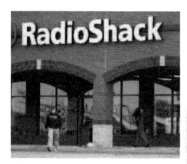

We can analyze the inventory of **Best Buy** and **Radio Shack Corporation** by calculating these ratios for both companies. Best Buy sells a large volume of commonly purchased products. In contrast, Radio Shack sells more distinct electronic items. Below are relevant amounts for each company as of February 2009 for Best Buy and December 2008 for Radio Shack.

($ in millions)	Cost of Goods Sold	Beginning Inventory	Ending Inventory
Best Buy	$34,017	$4,708	$4,753
Radio Shack	2,302	705	636

To compute the inventory turnover ratio we need the *average* inventory, which is the beginning amount of inventory plus the ending amount, divided by 2.

Best Buy   Average inventory = ($4,708 + $4,753) ÷ 2 = $4,730.5

Radio Shack   Average inventory = ($705 + $636) ÷ 2 = $670.5

We put average inventory in the denominator to compute the inventory turnover ratio, as shown in Illustration 6–21.

ILLUSTRATION 6–21

Inventory Turnover Ratios for Best Buy and Radio Shack

	Inventory Turnover Ratio	Average Days in Inventory
Best Buy	$34,017 ÷ $4,730.5 = 7.2 times	$\frac{365}{7.2}$ = 51 days
Radio Shack	$2,302 ÷ $670.5 = 3.4 times	$\frac{365}{3.4}$ = 107 days

The turnover ratio is more than twice as high for Best Buy. On average, it takes Radio Shack an additional 56 days to sell its inventory. If the two companies had the same business strategies, this would indicate that Best Buy is better at managing inventory. In this case, though, the difference in inventory turnover more likely is related to the products the two stores sell. Specialty items are not expected to sell as quickly. As we see in the next section, Radio Shack offsets its relatively low inventory turnover with a relatively high profit margin.

Decision Point

Question ?	Accounting information	Analysis
Is the company effectively managing its inventory?	Inventory turnover ratio and average days in inventory	A high inventory turnover ratio (or low average days in inventory) generally indicates that the company's inventory policies are effective.

COMMON MISTAKE

Many students use ending inventory rather than average inventory in calculating the inventory turnover ratio. Generally, when you calculate a ratio that includes an income statement item (an amount generated over a period) with a balance sheet item (an amount at a particular date), the balance sheet item needs to be converted to an amount *over the same period*. This is done by averaging the beginning and ending balances of the balance sheet item.

GROSS PROFIT RATIO

Another important indicator of the company's successful management of inventory is the gross profit ratio. It measures the amount by which the sale price of inventory exceeds its cost per dollar of sales. We calculate the gross profit ratio as gross profit divided by net sales. (Net sales equal total sales revenue less sales discounts, returns, and allowances).

$$\text{Gross profit ratio} = \frac{\text{Gross profit}}{\text{Net sales}}$$

The higher the gross profit ratio, the higher is the "markup" a company is able to achieve on its inventories. Best Buy and Radio Shack report the following information.

($ in millions)	Net Sales	−	Cost of Goods Sold	=	Gross Profit
Best Buy	$45,015		$34,017		$10,998
Radio Shack	4,225		2,302		1,923

Illustration 6–22 shows calculation of the gross profit ratio for Best Buy and Radio Shack.

	Gross Profit ÷ Net Sales	=	Gross Profit Ratio
Best Buy	$10,998 ÷ $45,015	=	24%
Radio Shack	$1,923 ÷ $4,225	=	46%

ILLUSTRATION 6–22

Gross Profit Ratios for Best Buy and Radio Shack

For Best Buy, this means that for every $1 of sales revenue, the company spends $0.76 on inventory, resulting in a gross profit of $0.24. In contrast, the gross profit ratio for Radio Shack is 46%. We saw earlier that Radio Shack's inventory turnover is about half that of Best Buy. But, we see now that Radio Shack makes up for that lower turnover with a gross profit margin about twice that of Best Buy. The products Best Buy sells are familiar goods, and competition from companies like Dell, Target, and Walmart for these high-volume items keeps sale prices low compared to costs. Because Radio Shack specializes in unique lower-volume products, there is less competition, allowing greater price markups.

As products become more highly specialized, gross profit ratios typically increase even further. For example, consider a company like Blue Coat Systems, a company that specializes in unique products and services that optimize and secure information sent over business networks or the Internet. In 2009, the company reported gross profit of $314 million on net sales of $445 million—a gross profit ratio of 71%.

 KEY POINT

The inventory turnover ratio indicates the number of times the firm sells, or turns over, its average inventory balance during a reporting period. The gross profit ratio measures the amount by which the sale price of inventory exceeds its cost per dollar of sales.

Decision Point

Question	Accounting information	Analysis
For how much is a company able to sell a product above its cost?	Gross profit and net sales	The ratio of gross profit to net sales indicates how much the sales price exceeds inventory cost for each $1 of sales.

APPENDIX A

RECORDING INVENTORY TRANSACTIONS USING A PERIODIC INVENTORY SYSTEM

■ LO9
Record inventory transactions using a periodic inventory system.

In this chapter, we discussed how to record inventory transactions using a *perpetual* inventory system. Here we discuss how to record inventory transactions using a *periodic* inventory system.

Recall that under a **perpetual inventory system** we maintain a continual—or *perpetual*—record of inventory purchased and sold. In contrast, using a **periodic inventory system** we do not continually modify inventory amounts. Instead, we *periodically* adjust for purchases and sales of inventory at the end of the reporting period, based on a physical count of inventory on hand.

To demonstrate the differences in these two systems, let's record inventory transactions under the periodic system using the same information (from Illustration 6–12) that we used to demonstrate the perpetual inventory system. We repeat those transactions in Illustration 6–23.

ILLUSTRATION 6–23

Inventory Transactions for Mario's Game Shop

Date	Transaction	Details	Total Cost	Total Revenue
Jan. 1	Beginning inventory	100 units for $7 each	$ 700	
Apr. 25	Purchase	300 units for $9 each	2,700	
Jul. 17	Sale	300 units for $15 each		$ 4,500
Oct. 19	Purchase	600 units for $11 each	6,600	
Dec. 15	Sale	500 units for $15 each		7,500
	Totals		$10,000	$12,000

To make the distinction between the perpetual system and periodic system easier, let's look at side-by-side comparisons. The perpetual entries are repeated from those in the chapter.

INVENTORY PURCHASES AND SALES

The first transaction on April 25 involves the purchase of $2,700 of inventory on account. Under the periodic system, instead of debiting the Inventory account, we debit a Purchases account. Remember, we're not continually adjusting the Inventory account under the periodic method. We use the Purchases account to temporarily track increases in inventory.

Purchase inventory on account

Perpetual System			Periodic System		
Inventory	2,700		Purchases	2,700	
Accounts Payable		2,700	Accounts Payable		2,700

The transaction on July 17 involves the sale on account of 300 units of inventory for $4,500. We record that transaction as follows.

Perpetual System			Periodic System			
Accounts Receivable	4,500		Accounts Receivable	4,500		Sell inventory on account
Sales Revenue		4,500	Sales Revenue		4,500	
Cost of Goods Sold	2,500					
Inventory		2,500	No entry for cost of goods sold			

Notice that under the periodic system, we record the revenue earned, but we don't record the reduction in inventory or the increase in cost of goods sold at the time of the sale. Instead, we will record these at the end of the period.

The final two transactions are (1) the purchase of 600 additional units of inventory for $6,600 on account on October 19 and (2) the sale of 500 units for $7,500 on account on December 15.

Perpetual System			Periodic System			
Inventory	6,600		Purchases	6,600		Purchase inventory on account
Accounts Payable		6,600	Accounts Payable		6,600	

Perpetual System			Periodic System			
Accounts Receivable	7,500		Accounts Receivable	7,500		Sell inventory on account
Sales Revenue		7,500	Sales Revenue		7,500	
Cost of Goods Sold	5,300					
Inventory		5,300	No entry for cost of goods sold			

In addition to purchases and sales of inventory, we also looked at additional inventory transactions for Mario's Game Shop that related to freight charges, purchase discounts, and purchase returns:

1. On April 25, Mario pays freight charges of $300 for inventory purchased on April 25.
2. On April 30, Mario pays for the units purchased on April 25, less a 2% purchase discount.
3. On October 22, Mario returns 50 defective units from the October 19 purchase.

Next, let's compare the perpetual system and periodic system for these transactions.

FREIGHT CHARGES

Under the perpetual system discussed in the chapter, we saw that freight charges are included as an additional cost of inventory. Here we'll see that under the periodic system, we record these charges in a separate account called Freight-in. That account will later be closed in a period-end adjustment. For freight charges of $300 associated with the April 25 purchase, we record the following transaction.

Perpetual System			Periodic System			
Inventory	300		Freight-in	300		Pay freight-in charges
Cash		300	Cash		300	

PURCHASE DISCOUNTS AND RETURNS

Under the perpetual system, purchase discounts and purchase returns are recorded as a reduction in inventory cost. Under the periodic system, these transactions are recorded in separate accounts—Purchase Discounts and Purchase Returns. In the perpetual system, we credit purchase returns and purchase discounts to Inventory. The Purchase Returns and Purchase Discounts accounts used in the periodic system are referred to as *contra purchases accounts*.

For our examples in the chapter, Mario (1) makes payment on April 30 for inventory purchased on April 25 for $2,700, receiving a $54 discount and (2) returns 50 defective units on October 22 from the 600 units purchased on account on October 19 for $11 each.

Pay on account with a 2% purchase discount of $54

Perpetual System			Periodic System		
Accounts Payable	2,700		Accounts Payable	2,700	
Inventory		54	Purchase Discounts		54
Cash		2,646	Cash		2,646

Return inventory previously purchased on account

Perpetual System			Periodic System		
Accounts Payable	550		Accounts Payable	550	
Inventory		550	Purchase Returns		550

PERIOD-END ADJUSTMENT

A period-end adjustment is needed only under the periodic system. The adjustment serves the following purposes:

1. Adjusts the balance of inventory to its proper ending balance.
2. Records the cost of goods sold for the period, to match inventory costs with the related sales revenue.
3. Closes (or zeros out) the temporary purchases accounts (Purchases, Freight-in, Purchase Discounts, and Purchase Returns).

Let's see what the period-end adjustment would look like for Mario's Game Shop using the transactions described in this appendix. In addition, recall that beginning inventory equals $700 (= 100 units × $7 unit cost) and ending inventory equals $1,650 (= 150 units × $11 unit cost).

Adjust inventory and cost of goods sold at the end of the period

Perpetual System	Periodic System		
No entry	Inventory (ending)	1,650	
	Cost of Goods Sold	8,046	
	Purchase Discounts	54	
	Purchase Returns	550	
	Purchases		9,300
	Freight-In		300
	Inventory (beginning)		700

Temporary accounts closed

Notice that (1) the balance of Inventory is updated for its ending amount of $1,650, while its beginning balance of $700 is eliminated, (2) Cost of Goods Sold is recorded for $8,046, and (3) temporary accounts related to purchases are closed to zero.

If you look carefully, you may notice that the amount of cost of goods sold above calculated under the periodic system is the same as that calculated under the perpetual system (in Illustration 6–17). To see a detailed example of this, let's reexamine the first section of the multiple-step income statement, shown again in Illustration 6–24.

The periodic system and perpetual system will always produce the same amounts for cost of goods sold and inventory when the FIFO inventory method is used.

MARIO'S GAME SHOP Multiple-Step Income Statement (partial) For the year ended December 31, 2012		
Sales revenue		$12,000
Cost of goods sold:		
Beginning inventory	$ 700	
Add: Purchases	9,300	
Freight-in	300	
Less: Purchase discounts	(54)	
Purchase returns	(550)	
Cost of goods available for sale	9,696	
Less: Ending inventory	(1,650)	
Cost of goods sold		8,046
Gross profit		$ 3,954

ILLUSTRATION 6–24

Calculation of Gross Profit in a Multiple-Step Income Statement

However, when using LIFO, the amounts for cost of goods sold and ending inventory may differ between the two systems. The reason for this difference is discussed further in more advanced accounting courses; it occurs because determining which "last" units of inventory are sold first occurs multiple times using a perpetual system but just once using a periodic system.

In practice, very few companies report inventory and cost of goods sold using the LIFO perpetual system. Instead, as discussed in Part B of the chapter, nearly all companies that report using LIFO maintain their own records on a FIFO basis and then adjust for the LIFO difference for preparing financial statements. **The inventory recording and reporting procedures discussed in Part B of the chapter reflect those used in actual practice.**

 KEY POINT

Using the periodic inventory system, we record purchases of inventory, freight-in, purchase returns, and purchase discounts to *temporary accounts* rather than directly to Inventory. These temporary accounts are closed in a period-end adjustment. In addition, at the time inventory is sold, we do not record a decrease in inventory sold; instead, we update the balance of Inventory in the period-end adjustment.

INVENTORY ERRORS

Nobody's perfect, and even accountants make mistakes. When we discover accounting errors, we always correct them. However, we don't always know when we've made an error. Errors can unknowingly occur in inventory amounts if there are mistakes in a physical count of inventory or in the pricing of inventory quantities.

APPENDIX B

■ **LO10**
Determine the financial statement effects of inventory errors.

EFFECTS IN THE CURRENT YEAR

To understand the effects of an inventory error in the financial statements, let's think again about the formula for cost of goods sold, shown in Illustration 6–25.

	Beginning Inventory		
+	Purchases		
−	Ending Inventory		Asset; Balance sheet
	Cost of Goods Sold		Expense; Income statement

ILLUSTRATION 6–25

Calculation of Cost of Goods Sold

Notice that an error in calculating ending inventory (an asset in the balance sheet) causes an error in calculating cost of goods sold (an expense in the income statement). If cost of goods sold is misstated, gross profit will be misstated as well, but in the opposite direction. This is true because gross profit equals sales *minus* cost of goods sold. The effect of the inventory error in the current year is summarized in Illustration 6–26.

ILLUSTRATION 6–26

Summary of Effects of Inventory Error in the Current Year

Inventory Error	Ending Inventory	Cost of Goods Sold	Gross Profit
Overstate ending inventory	Overstate	Understate	Overstate
Understate ending inventory	Understate	Overstate	Understate

EFFECTS IN THE FOLLOWING YEAR

To understand the effects of a current-year inventory error on financial statements in the following year, remember that the amount of ending inventory this year is the amount of beginning inventory next year. An error in ending inventory this year will create an error in beginning inventory next year. This is demonstrated in Illustration 6–27.

ILLUSTRATION 6–27

Relationship between Cost of Goods Sold in the Current Year and the Following Year

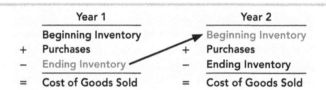

Notice that ending inventory is *subtracted* in calculating cost of goods sold in year 1 (the year of the inventory error). That same amount becomes beginning inventory in the following year and is *added* in calculating cost of goods sold. Because of this, **an error in calculating ending inventory in the current year will automatically affect cost of goods sold in the following year** *in the opposite direction.*

Consider a simple example to see how this works. Illustration 6–28 shows the correct inventory amounts for 2012 and 2013.

ILLUSTRATION 6–28

Correct Inventory Amounts

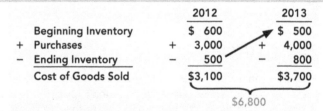

Now, assume the company mistakenly reports ending inventory in 2012 as $400, instead of $500. The effect of the mistake is shown in Illustration 6–29.

ILLUSTRATION 6–29

Incorrect Inventory Amounts

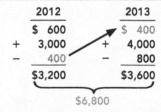

Notice three things: First, the amount reported for inventory is correct by the end of the second year, $800. This is true *even if the company had never discovered its inventory mistake* in 2012.

Second, the total amount reported for cost of goods sold over the two-year period from 2012 to 2013 is the same ($6,800) whether the error occurs or not. That's because the overstatement to cost of goods sold of $100 in 2012 is offset by an understatement of $100 in 2013. This also means that the inventory error affects gross profit in each of the two years, but the combined two-year gross profit amount is unaffected.

Third, if the combined two-year gross profit is correct, then retained earnings will also be correct by the end of 2013. Thus, the inventory error in 2012 has no effect on the accounting equation at the end of 2013. Assets (inventory) and stockholders' equity (retained earnings) are correctly stated.

KEY POINT

In the current year, inventory errors affect the amounts reported for inventory and retained earnings in the balance sheet and amounts reported for cost of goods sold and gross profit in the income statement. At the end of the following year, the error has no effect on ending inventory or retained earnings but reverses for cost of goods sold and gross profit.

KEY POINTS BY LEARNING OBJECTIVE

LO1 Trace the flow of inventory costs from manufacturing companies to merchandising companies.

Service companies earn revenues by providing services to customers. Manufacturing and merchandising companies earn revenues by selling inventory to customers.

LO2 Calculate cost of goods sold.

Inventory is a current asset reported in the balance sheet and represents the cost of inventory *not yet sold* at the end of the period. Cost of goods sold is an expense reported in the income statement and represents the cost of inventory *sold*.

LO3 Determine the cost of goods sold and ending inventory using different inventory cost methods.

Companies are allowed to report inventory costs by *assuming* which units of inventory are sold and not sold, even if this does not match the *actual* flow. The three major inventory cost flow assumptions are FIFO (first-in, first-out), LIFO (last-in, first-out), and weighted-average cost.

LO4 Explain the financial statement effects and tax effects of inventory cost flow assumptions.

Generally, FIFO more closely resembles the actual physical flow of inventory. When inventory costs are rising, FIFO results in higher reported inventory in the balance sheet

and higher reported income in the income statement. Conversely, LIFO results in a lower reported inventory and net income, reducing the company's income tax obligation.

LO5 Record inventory transactions using a perpetual inventory system.

The perpetual inventory system maintains a continual—or *perpetual*—record of inventory purchased and sold. When companies *purchase* inventory using a perpetual inventory system, they increase the Inventory account and either decrease Cash or increase Accounts Payable. When companies *sell* inventory, they make two entries: (1) They increase an asset account (Cash or Accounts Receivable) and increase Sales Revenue, and (2) they increase Cost of Goods Sold and decrease Inventory.

Nearly all companies maintain their own inventory records on a FIFO basis, and then some prepare financial statements on a LIFO basis. To adjust their FIFO inventory records to LIFO for financial reporting, companies use a simple LIFO adjustment at the end of the period.

For most companies, freight charges are added to the cost of inventory, whereas purchase returns and purchase discounts are deducted from the cost of inventory. Some companies choose to report freight charges on outgoing shipments as part of selling expenses instead of cost of goods sold.

LO6 Prepare a multiple-step income statement.

A multiple-step income statement reports multiple levels of profitability. *Gross profit* equals sales revenue minus cost of goods sold. *Operating income* equals gross profit minus operating expenses. *Income before income taxes* equals operating income plus nonoperating revenues and minus nonoperating expenses. *Net income* equals all revenues minus all expenses.

LO7 Apply the lower-of-cost-or-market method for inventories.

We report inventory at the lower-of-cost-or-market; that is, at cost (specific identification, FIFO, LIFO, or weighted-average cost) or market value (replacement cost), whichever is lower. When market value falls below cost, we adjust downward the balance of inventory from cost to market value.

Analysis

LO8 Analyze management of inventory using the inventory turnover ratio and gross profit ratio.

The inventory turnover ratio indicates the number of times the firm sells, or turns over, its average inventory balance during a reporting period. The gross profit ratio measures the

amount by which the sale price of inventory exceeds its cost per dollar of sales.

Appendixes

LO9 Record inventory transactions using a periodic inventory system.

Using the periodic inventory system, we record purchases of inventory, freight-in, purchase returns, and purchase discounts to *temporary accounts* rather than directly to Inventory. These temporary accounts are closed in a period-end adjustment. In addition, at the time inventory is sold, we do not record a decrease in inventory sold; instead, we update the balance of Inventory in the period-end adjustment.

LO10 Determine the financial statement effects of inventory errors.

In the current year, inventory errors affect the amounts reported for inventory and retained earnings in the balance sheet and amounts reported for cost of goods sold and gross profit in the income statement. At the end of the following year, the error has no effect on ending inventory or retained earnings but reverses for cost of goods sold and gross profit.

GLOSSARY

Average days in inventory: Approximate number of days the average inventory is held. It equals 365 days divided by the inventory turnover ratio. **p. 288**

Cost of goods sold: Cost of the inventory that was sold during the period. **p. 262**

Finished goods: Inventory items for which the manufacturing process is complete. **p. 263**

First-in, first-out method (FIFO): Inventory costing method that assumes the first units purchased (the first in) are the first ones sold (the first out). **p. 266**

Freight-in: Cost to transport inventory to the company, which is included as part of inventory cost. **p. 278**

Freight-out: Cost of freight on shipments to customers, which is included in the income statement either as part of cost of goods sold or as a selling expense. **p. 278**

Gross profit: The difference between sales revenue and cost of goods sold. **p. 282**

Gross profit ratio: Measure of the amount by which the sale price of inventory exceeds its cost per dollar of sales. It equals gross profit divided by net sales. **p. 289**

Income before income taxes: Operating income plus nonoperating revenues less nonoperating expenses. **p. 283**

Inventory: Items a company intends for sale to customers. **p. 262**

Inventory turnover ratio: The number of times a firm sells its average inventory balance during a reporting period. It equals cost of goods sold divided by average inventory. **p. 287**

Last-in, first-out method (LIFO): Inventory costing method that assumes the last units purchased (the last in) are the first ones sold (the first out). **p. 267**

LIFO adjustment: An adjustment used to convert a company's own inventory records maintained on a FIFO basis to LIFO basis for preparing financial statements. **p. 277**

LIFO conformity rule: IRS rule requiring a company that uses LIFO for tax reporting to also use LIFO for financial reporting. **p. 272**

Lower-of-cost-or-market (LCM) method: Method where companies report inventory in the balance sheet at the lower of cost or market value, where market value equals replacement cost. **p. 284**

Multiple-step income statement: An income statement that reports *multiple* levels of income (or profitability). **p. 282**

Net income: Difference between all revenues and all expenses for the period. **p. 283**

Operating income: Profitability from normal operations that equals gross profit less operating expenses. **p. 283**

Periodic inventory system: Inventory system that periodically adjusts for purchases and sales of inventory at the end of the reporting period based on a physical count of inventory on hand. **p. 274**

Perpetual inventory system: Inventory system that maintains a continual record of inventory purchased and sold. **p. 274**

Raw materials: Components that will become part of the finished product but have not yet been used in production. **p. 263**

Replacement cost: The cost to replace an inventory item in its identical form. **p. 284**

Specific identification method: Inventory costing method that matches or identifies each unit of inventory with its actual cost. **p. 266**

Weighted-average cost method: Inventory costing method that assumes both cost of goods sold and ending inventory consist of a random mixture of all the goods available for sale. **p. 268**

Work-in-process: Products that have started the production process but are not yet complete at the end of the period. **p. 263**

SELF-STUDY QUESTIONS

1. Which of following companies earn revenues by selling inventory? ■ LO1
   a. Service companies.
   b. Manufacturing companies.
   c. Merchandising companies.
   d. Both manufacturing and merchandising companies.

2. At the beginning of the year, Bennett Supply has inventory of $3,500. During the   ■ LO2
   year, the company purchases an additional $12,000 of inventory. An inventory count
   at the end of the year reveals remaining inventory of $4,000. What amount will
   Bennett report for cost of goods sold?
   a. $11,000.
   b. $11,500.
   c. $12,000.
   d. $12,500.

3. Madison Outlet has the following inventory transactions for the year: ■ LO3

Date	Transaction	Number of Units	Unit Cost	Total Cost
Jan. 1	Beginning inventory	10	$200	$2,000
Mar. 14	Purchase	15	300	4,500
				$6,500
Jan. 1–Dec. 31	Total sales to customers	12		

   What amount would Madison report for *cost of goods sold* using FIFO?
   a. $2,600.
   b. $2,900.
   c. $3,600.
   d. $3,900.

4. Which inventory cost flow assumption generally results in the lowest reported   ■ LO4
   amount for cost of goods sold when inventory costs are rising?
   a. Lower-of-cost-or-market.
   b. First-in, first-out (FIFO).
   c. Last-in, first-out (LIFO).
   d. Weighted-average cost.

5. Using a *perpetual* inventory system, the purchase of inventory on account would be   ■ LO5
   recorded as:
   a. Debit Cost of Goods Sold; credit Inventory.
   b. Debit Inventory; credit Sales Revenue.

298   CHAPTER 6   Inventory and Cost of Goods Sold

c. Debit Purchases; credit Accounts Payable.

d. Debit Inventory; credit Accounts Payable.

■ LO6   6. Which of the following levels of profitability in a multiple-step income statement represents revenues from the sale of inventory less the cost of that inventory?

a. Gross profit.

b. Operating income.

c. Income before income taxes.

d. Net income.

■ LO7   7. At the end of a reporting period, Maxwell Corporation determines that its ending inventory has a cost of $1,000 and a market value of $800. What would be the effect(s) of the adjustment to write down inventory to market value?

a. Decrease total assets.

b. Decrease net income.

c. Decrease retained earnings.

d. All of the above.

■ LO8   8. For the year, Simmons Incorporated reports net sales of $100,000, cost of goods sold of $80,000, and an average inventory balance of $40,000. What is Simmons' gross profit ratio?

a. 20%.

b. 25%.

c. 40%.

d. 50%.

■ LO9   9. Using a *periodic* inventory system, the purchase of inventory on account would be recorded as:

a. Debit Cost of Goods Sold; credit Inventory.

b. Debit Inventory; credit Sales Revenue.

c. Debit Purchases; credit Accounts Payable.

d. Debit Inventory; credit Accounts Payable.

■ LO10   10. Suppose Ajax Corporation overstates its ending inventory amount. What effect will this have on the reported amount of cost of goods sold in the year of the error?

a. Overstate cost of goods sold.

b. Understate cost of goods sold.

c. Have no effect on cost of goods sold.

Check out
www.mhhe.com/succeed
for more multiple-choice
questions.

d. Not possible to determine with information given.

Note: For answers, see the last page of the chapter.

REVIEW QUESTIONS

■ LO1   1. What is inventory? Where in the financial statements is inventory reported?

■ LO1   2. What is the primary distinction between a service company and a manufacturing or merchandising company?

■ LO1   3. What is the difference among raw materials inventory, work-in-process inventory, and finished goods inventory?

■ LO2   4. Define the cost of goods available for sale. How does it relate to cost of goods sold and ending inventory?

■ LO2   5. For a company like **Radio Shack**, what does the balance of Cost of Goods Sold in the income statement represent? What does the balance of Inventory in the balance sheet represent?

6. Cheryl believes that companies report cost of goods sold and ending inventory based on *actual* units sold and not sold. Her accounting instructor explains that most companies account for cost of goods sold and ending inventory based on *assumed* units sold and not sold. Help her understand why companies are allowed to do this. ■ LO3

7. What are the three primary cost flow assumptions? How does the specific identification method differ from these three primary cost flow assumptions? ■ LO3

8. Which cost flow assumption generally results in the highest reported amount for ending inventory when inventory costs are rising? Explain. ■ LO4

9. Which cost flow assumption generally results in the highest reported amount of net income when inventory costs are rising? Explain. ■ LO4

10. What does it mean that FIFO has a balance-sheet focus and LIFO has an income-statement focus? ■ LO4

11. Explain how LIFO generally results in lower income taxes payable when inventory costs are increasing. What is the LIFO conformity rule? ■ LO4

12. What is the difference between the *timing* of recording inventory transactions under the perpetual and periodic inventory systems? ■ LO5

13. Explain how freight charges, purchase returns, and purchase discounts affect the cost of inventory. ■ LO5

14. What is a multiple-step income statement? What information does it provide beyond "bottom-line" net income? ■ LO6

15. Explain the lower-of-cost-or-market method of reporting inventory. ■ LO7

16. How is cost determined under the lower-of-cost-or-market method? How is market value determined for this purpose? ■ LO7

17. Describe the entry to adjust from cost to market for inventory write-downs. What effects does this adjustment have on (a) assets, (b) liabilities, (c) stockholders' equity (or retained earnings), (d) revenues, (e) expenses, and (f) net income? ■ LO7

18. What is meant by the assertion that the lower-of-cost-or-market method is an example of conservatism in accounting? ■ LO7

19. What is the inventory turnover ratio? What is it designed to measure? ■ LO8

20. How is gross profit calculated? What is the gross profit ratio? What is it designed to measure? ■ LO8

21. Explain how the sale of inventory on account is recorded under a periodic system. How does this differ from the recording under a perpetual system? ■ LO9

22. What are the purposes of the period-end adjustment under the periodic inventory system? ■ LO9

23. Jeff is the new inventory manager for Alan Company. During the year-end inventory count, Jeff forgets that the company stores additional inventory in a back room, causing his final ending inventory count to be understated. Explain what effect this error will have on the reported amounts for (a) assets, (b) liabilities, (c) stockholders' equity (or retained earnings), (d) revenues, (e) expenses, and (f) net income in the current year. ■ LO10

24. Refer to the inventory error in *Question* 23. Explain what effect Jeff's error will have on reported amounts at the end of the following year, assuming the mistake is not corrected and no further mistakes are made. ■ LO10

BRIEF EXERCISES

Understand terms related to types of companies (LO1)

BE6–1 Match each of the following types of companies with its definition.

Types of Companies	Definitions
1. _____ Service company	a. Purchases goods that are primarily in finished form for resale to customers.
2. _____ Merchandising company	b. Earns revenues by providing services to customers.
3. _____ Manufacturing company	c. Produces the goods they sell to customers.

Understand terms related to inventory (LO1)

BE6–2 Match each of the following inventory classifications with its definition.

Inventory Classifications	Definitions
1. _____ Raw materials	a. Cost of items not yet complete by the end of the period.
2. _____ Work-in-process	b. Inventory that has been substantially completed.
3. _____ Finished goods	c. Basic components used to build a product.

Calculate cost of goods sold (LO2)

BE6–3 At the beginning of 2012, Bryers Incorporated reports inventory of $7,000. During 2012, the company purchases additional inventory for $22,000. At the end of 2012, the cost of inventory remaining is $9,000. Calculate cost of goods sold for 2012.

Calculate ending inventory and cost of goods sold using FIFO (LO3)

BE6–4 During 2012, Wright Company sells 320 remote control airplanes for $100 each. The company has the following inventory purchase transactions for 2012.

Date	Transaction	Number of Units	Unit Cost	Total Cost
Jan. 1	Beginning inventory	50	$72	$ 3,600
May. 5	Purchase	200	75	15,000
Nov. 3	Purchase	100	80	8,000
		350		$26,600

Calculate ending inventory and cost of goods sold for 2012 assuming the company uses FIFO.

Calculate ending inventory and cost of goods sold using LIFO (LO3)

BE6–5 Refer to the information in BE6–4. Calculate ending inventory and cost of goods sold for 2012, assuming the company uses LIFO.

Calculate ending inventory and cost of goods sold using weighted-average cost (LO3)

BE6–6 Refer to the information in BE6–4. Calculate ending inventory and cost of goods sold for 2012, assuming the company uses weighted-average cost.

Calculate ending inventory and cost of goods sold using specific identification (LO3)

BE6–7 Refer to the information in BE6–4. Calculate ending inventory and cost of goods sold for 2012, assuming the company uses specific identification. Actual sales by the company include its entire beginning inventory, 180 units of inventory from the May 5 purchase, and 90 units from the November 3 purchase.

Identify financial statement effects of FIFO and LIFO (LO4)

BE6–8 For each item below, indicate whether FIFO or LIFO will generally result in a higher reported amount when inventory costs are rising versus falling. The first answer is provided as an example.

Inventory Costs	Higher Total Assets	Higher Cost of Goods Sold	Higher Net Income
Rising	FIFO		
Declining			

BE6–9 Shankar Company uses a perpetual system to record inventory transactions. The company purchases inventory on account on February 2, 2012, for $30,000 and then sells this inventory on account on March 17, 2012, for $50,000. Record transactions for the purchase and sale of inventory.

Record inventory purchases and sales using a perpetual system (LO5)

BE6–10 Shankar Company uses a perpetual system to record inventory transactions. The company purchases inventory on account on February 2, 2012, for $30,000. In addition to the cost of inventory, the company also pays $500 for freight charges associated with the purchase on the same day. Record the purchase of inventory on February 2, including the freight charges.

Record freight charges for inventory using a perpetual system (LO5)

BE6–11 Shankar Company uses a perpetual system to record inventory transactions. The company purchases 1,000 units of inventory on account on February 2, 2012, for $30,000 ($30 per unit) but then returns 50 defective units on February 5, 2012. Record the inventory purchase on February 2 and the inventory return on February 5.

Record purchase returns of inventory using a perpetual system (LO5)

BE6–12 Shankar Company uses a perpetual system to record inventory transactions. The company purchases inventory on account on February 2, 2012, for $30,000, with terms 2/10, n/30. On February 10, the company pays on account for the inventory. Record the inventory purchase on February 2 and the payment on February 10.

Record purchase discounts of inventory using a perpetual system (LO5)

BE6–13 For each company, calculate the missing amount.

Calculate amounts related to the multiple-step income statement (LO6)

Company	Sales Revenue	Cost of Goods Sold	Gross Profit	Operating Expenses	Net Income
Lennon	$16,000	(a)	$7,000	$3,000	$4,000
Harrison	17,000	$10,000	(b)	5,000	2,000
McCartney	11,000	8,000	3,000	(c)	1,000
Starr	14,000	5,000	9,000	6,000	(d)

BE6–14 Powder Ski Shop reports inventory using lower-of-cost-or-market. Below is information related to its year-end inventory. Calculate the amount to be reported for ending inventory.

Calculate ending inventory using lower-of-cost-or-market (LO7)

Inventory	Quantity	Cost	Market
Ski jackets	15	$120	$100
Skis	20	350	400

BE6–15 Creative Technology reports inventory using lower-of-cost-or-market. Below is information related to its year-end inventory. Calculate the amount to be reported for ending inventory.

Calculate ending inventory using lower-of-cost-or-market (LO7)

Inventory	Quantity	Cost	Market
Optima cameras	100	$50	$80
Inspire speakers	40	60	50

BE6–16 Using the amounts below, calculate the inventory turnover ratio, average days in inventory, and gross profit ratio.

Calculate inventory ratios (LO8)

Net sales	$200,000
Cost of goods sold	140,000
Beginning inventory	45,000
Ending inventory	35,000

BE6–17 Refer to the information in BE6–9, but now assume that Shankar uses a periodic system to record inventory transactions. Record transactions for the purchase and sale of inventory.

Record inventory purchases and sales using a periodic system (LO9)

Record freight charges for inventory using a periodic system (LO9)

BE6–18 Refer to the information in BE6–10, but now assume that Shankar uses a periodic system to record inventory transactions. Record the purchase of inventory on February 2, including the freight charges.

Record purchase returns of inventory using a periodic system (LO9)

BE6–19 Refer to the information in BE6–11, but now assume that Shankar uses a periodic system to record inventory transactions. Record the inventory purchase on February 2 and the inventory return on February 5.

Record purchase discounts of inventory using a periodic system (LO9)

BE6–20 Refer to the information in BE6–12, but now assume that Shankar uses a periodic system to record inventory transactions. Record the inventory purchase on February 2 and the payment on February 10.

Find income statement effects of overstatement in ending inventory (LO10)

BE6–21 Ebbers Corporation overstated its ending inventory balance by $10,000 in 2012. What impact will this error have on cost of goods sold and gross profit in 2012 and 2013?

Find balance sheet effects of overstatement in ending inventory (LO10)

BE6–22 Refer to the information in BE6–21. What impact will this error have on ending inventory and retained earnings in 2012 and 2013? Ignore any tax effects.

EXERCISES

Calculate cost of goods sold (LO2)

E6–1 Russell Retail Group begins the year with inventory of $45,000 and ends the year with inventory of $35,000. During the year, the company has four purchases for the following amounts.

Purchase on February 17	$200,000
Purchase on May 6	120,000
Purchase on September 8	150,000
Purchase on December 4	400,000

Required:
Calculate cost of goods sold for the year.

Calculate inventory amounts when costs are rising (LO3)

E6–2 During 2012, TRC Corporation has the following inventory transactions.

Date	Transaction	Number of Units	Unit Cost	Total Cost
Jan. 1	Beginning inventory	40	$32	$ 1,280
Apr. 7	Purchase	120	34	4,080
Jul. 16	Purchase	190	37	7,030
Oct. 6	Purchase	100	38	3,800
		450		$16,190

For the entire year, the company sells 400 units of inventory for $50 each.

Required:
1. Using FIFO, calculate (a) ending inventory, (b) cost of goods sold, (c) sales revenue, and (d) gross profit.
2. Using LIFO, calculate (a) ending inventory, (b) cost of goods sold, (c) sales revenue, and (d) gross profit.
3. Using weighted-average cost, calculate (a) ending inventory, (b) cost of goods sold, (c) sales revenue, and (d) gross profit.
4. Determine which method will result in higher profitability when inventory costs are rising.

E6–3 During 2012, Trombley Incorporated has the following inventory transactions.

Calculate inventory amounts when costs are declining (**LO3**)

Date	Transaction	Number of Units	Unit Cost	Total Cost
Jan. 1	Beginning inventory	10	$12	$120
Mar. 4	Purchase	15	11	165
Jun. 9	Purchase	20	10	200
Nov. 11	Purchase	20	8	160
		65		$645

For the entire year, the company sells 50 units of inventory for $20 each.

Required:
1. Using FIFO, calculate (a) ending inventory, (b) cost of goods sold, (c) sales revenue, and (d) gross profit.
2. Using LIFO, calculate (a) ending inventory, (b) cost of goods sold, (c) sales revenue, and (d) gross profit.
3. Using weighted-average cost, calculate (a) ending inventory, (b) cost of goods sold, (c) sales revenue, and (d) gross profit.
4. Determine which method will result in higher profitability when inventory costs are declining.

E6–4 Bingerton Industries uses a perpetual inventory system. The company began the year with inventory of $75,000. Purchases of inventory on account during the year totaled $300,000. Inventory costing $325,000 was sold on account for $500,000.

Record inventory transactions using a perpetual system (**LO5**)

Required:
Record transactions for the purchase and sale of inventory.

E6–5 On June 5, Staley Electronics purchases 100 units of inventory on account for $10 each. After closer examination, Staley determines 20 units are defective and returns them to its supplier for full credit on June 9. All remaining inventory is sold on account on June 16 for $15 each.

Record inventory purchase and purchase return using a perpetual system (**LO5**)

Required:
Record transactions for the purchase, return, and sale of inventory.

E6–6 On June 5, Staley Electronics purchases 100 units of inventory on account for $10 each, with terms 2/10, n/30. Staley pays for the inventory on June 12.

Record inventory purchase and purchase discount using a perpetual system (**LO5**)

Required:
1. Record transactions for the purchase of inventory and payment on account.
2. Now assume payment is made on June 22. Record the payment on account.

E6–7 Littleton Books has the following transactions during May.

Record transactions using a perpetual system (**LO5**)

May 2	Purchases books on account from Readers Wholesale for $2,300, terms 2/10, n/30.
May 3	Pays freight costs of $100 on books purchased from Readers.
May 5	Returns books with a cost of $300 to Readers because part of the order is incorrect.
May 10	Pays the full amount due to Readers.
May 30	Sells all books purchased on May 2 (less those returned on May 5) for $3,000 on account.

Required:
1. Record the transactions of Littleton Books, assuming the company uses a perpetual inventory system.
2. Assume that payment to Readers is made on May 24 instead of May 10. Record this payment.

Record transactions using a perpetual system (LO5)

E6–8 Sundance Systems has the following transactions during July.

July 5   Purchases 20 laptop computers on account from Red River Supplies for $1,500 each, terms 3/10, n/30.
July 8   Returns to Red River two laptops that had defective hard drives.
July 13   Pays the full amount due to Red River.
July 28   Sells remaining 18 laptops purchased on July 5 for $2,000 each on account.

Required:

Record the transactions of Sundance Systems, assuming the company uses a perpetual inventory system.

Record transactions using a perpetual system (LO5)

Flip Side of E6–10

E6–9 DS Unlimited has the following transactions during August.

August 6   Purchases 50 handheld game devices on account from GameGirl, Inc., for $100 each, terms 1/10, n/60.
August 7   Pays $300 to Sure Shipping for freight charges associated with the August 6 purchase.
August 10   Returns to GameGirl five game devices that were defective.
August 14   Pays the full amount due to GameGirl.
August 23   Sells 30 game devices purchased on August 6 for $120 each to customers on account. The total cost of the 30 game devices sold is $3,170.

Required:

Record the transactions of DS Unlimited, assuming the company uses a perpetual inventory system.

Record transactions using a perpetual system (LO5)

Flip Side of E6–9

E6–10 Refer to the transactions in E6–9.

Required:

Prepare the transactions for GameGirl, Inc., assuming the company uses a perpetual inventory system. Assume the 50 game devices sold on August 6 to DS Unlimited had a cost to GameGirl of $80 each. The items returned on August 10 were considered worthless to GameGirl and were discarded.

Prepare a multiple-step income statement (LO6)

E6–11 Wayman Corporation reports the following amounts in its December 31, 2012, income statement.

Sales revenue	$320,000	Income tax expense	$ 40,000
Interest expense	10,000	Cost of goods sold	120,000
Salaries expense	30,000	Advertising expense	20,000
Utilities expense	40,000		

Required:

Prepare a multiple-step income statement.

Prepare a multiple-step income statement and analyze profitability (LO6)

E6–12 Tisdale Incorporated reports the following amount in its December 31, 2012, income statement.

Sales revenue	$250,000	Income tax expense	$ 20,000
Gain on land sale*	100,000	Cost of goods sold	180,000
Selling expenses	50,000	Administrative expenses	30,000
General expenses	40,000		

*On July 12, 2012, the company sold land for $400,000 that it had previously purchased for $300,000, resulting in a $100,000 gain. This is the only land owned by the company.

Required:

1. Prepare a multiple-step income statement.
2. Explain how analyzing the multiple levels of profitability can help in understanding the future profit-generating potential of Tisdale Incorporated.

E6–13 Home Furnishings reports inventory using the lower-of-cost-or-market method. Below is information related to its year-end inventory.

Calculate inventory using lower-of-cost-or-market (LO7)

Inventory	Quantity	Cost	Market
Furniture	100	$ 75	$ 90
Electronics	40	300	250

Required:
1. Calculate ending inventory under lower-of-cost-or-market.
2. Record any necessary adjustment to inventory.
3. Explain the impact of the adjustment in the financial statements.

E6–14 A company like Golf USA that sells golf-related inventory typically will have inventory items such as golf clothing and golf equipment. As technology advances the design and performance of the next generation of drivers, the older models become less marketable and therefore decline in value. Suppose that in 2012, Ping (a manufacturer of golf clubs) introduces the MegaDriver II, the new and improved version of the MegaDriver. Below are amounts related to Golf USA's inventory at the end of 2012.

Calculate inventory using lower-of-cost-or market (LO7)

Inventory	Quantity	Cost	Market
Shirts	25	$ 50	$ 60
MegaDriver	5	260	200
MegaDriver II	20	300	320

Required:
1. Calculate ending inventory under lower-of-cost-or-market.
2. Record any necessary adjustment to inventory.
3. Explain the impact of the adjustment in the financial statements.

E6–15 Lewis Incorporated and Clark Enterprises report the following amounts for 2012.

Calculate cost of goods sold, the inventory turnover ratio, and average days in inventory (LO2, 8)

	Lewis	Clark
Inventory (beginning)	$ 14,000	$ 40,000
Inventory (ending)	8,000	50,000
Purchases	120,000	150,000
Purchase returns	5,000	50,000

Required:
1. Calculate cost of goods sold for each company.
2. Calculate the inventory turnover ratio for each company.
3. Calculate the average days in inventory for each company.
4. Explain which company appears to be managing its inventory more efficiently.

E6–16 Below are amounts found in the income statements of three companies.

Calculate levels of profitability for a multiple-step income statement and the gross profit ratio (LO6, 8)

Company	Sales Revenue	Cost of Goods Sold	Operating Expenses	Nonoperating Expenses	Income Tax Expense
Henry	$12,000	$ 3,000	$4,000	$1,000	$1,000
Grace	15,000	10,000	6,000	3,000	0
James	20,000	12,000	2,000	0	2,000

Required:
1. For each company, calculate (a) gross profit, (b) operating income, (c) income before income taxes, and (d) net income.
2. For each company, calculate the gross profit ratio and indicate which company has the most favorable ratio.

306   CHAPTER 6   Inventory and Cost of Goods Sold

Record transactions using a periodic system (LO9)

E6–17 Refer to the transactions in E6–7.

Required:
1. Record the transactions of Littleton Books, assuming the company uses a periodic inventory system.
2. Record the period-end adjustment to cost of goods sold on May 31, assuming the company has no beginning or ending inventory.

Record transactions using a periodic system (LO9)

E6–18 Refer to the transactions in E6–8.

Required:
1. Record the transactions of Sundance Systems, assuming the company uses a periodic inventory system.
2. Record the period-end adjustment to cost of goods sold on July 31, assuming the company has no beginning inventory.

Record transactions using a periodic system (LO9)

E6–19 Refer to the transactions in E6–9.

Required:
1. Record the transactions of DS Unlimited, assuming the company uses a periodic inventory system.
2. Record the period-end adjustment to cost of goods sold on August 31, assuming the company has no beginning inventory and ending inventory has a cost of $1,585.

Find financial statement effects of understatement in ending inventory (LO10)

E6–20 Mulligan Corporation purchases inventory on account with terms FOB shipping point. The goods are shipped on December 30, 2012, but do not reach the company until January 5, 2013. Mulligan correctly records accounts payable associated with the purchase but does not include this inventory in its 2012 ending inventory count.

Required:
1. If an error has been made, explain why.
2. If an error has been made, indicate whether there is an understatement (U), overstatement (O), or no effect (N) on the reported amount of each financial statement element in the current year and following year. Ignore any tax effects.

	Balance Sheet			Income Statement		
Year	Assets	Liabilities	Stockholders' Equity	Revenues	Cost of Goods Sold	Gross Profit
Current	_____	_____	_____	_____	_____	_____
Following	_____	_____	_____	_____	_____	_____

*For additional exercises, visit **www.mhhe.com/succeed** for Exercises: Set B.*

PROBLEMS: SET A

Calculate ending inventory and cost of goods sold for four inventory methods (LO3)

P6–1A Sandra's Purse Boutique has the following transactions related to its top-selling Gucci purse for the month of October 2012.

Date	Transactions	Units	Cost per Unit	Total Cost
October 1	Beginning inventory	6	$800	$ 4,800
October 4	Sale	4		
October 10	Purchase	5	810	4,050
October 13	Sale	3		
October 20	Purchase	4	820	3,280
October 28	Sale	7		
October 30	Purchase	6	830	4,980
				$17,110

Required:

1. Calculate ending inventory and cost of goods sold at October 31, 2012, using the specific identification method. The October 4 sale consists of purses from beginning inventory, the October 13 sale consists of one purse from beginning inventory and two purses from the October 10 purchase, and the October 28 sale consists of three purses from the October 10 purchase and four purses from the October 20 purchase.
2. Using FIFO, calculate ending inventory and cost of goods sold at October 31, 2012.
3. Using LIFO, calculate ending inventory and cost of goods sold at October 31, 2012.
4. Using weighted-average cost, calculate ending inventory and cost of goods sold at October 31, 2012.

P6–2A Greg's Bicycle Shop has the following transactions related to its top-selling Mongoose mountain bike for the month of March 2012:

Calculate ending inventory, cost of goods sold, sales revenue, and gross profit for four inventory methods (LO3, 4, 5)

Date	Transactions	Units	Cost per Unit	Total Cost
March 1	Beginning inventory	20	$200	$ 4,000
March 5	Sale ($300 each)	15		
March 9	Purchase	10	220	2,200
March 17	Sale ($350 each)	8		
March 22	Purchase	10	230	2,300
March 27	Sale ($375 each)	12		
March 30	Purchase	8	250	2,000
				$10,500

Required:

1. Calculate ending inventory and cost of goods sold at March 31, 2012, using the specific identification method. The March 5 sale consists of bikes from beginning inventory, the March 17 sale consists of bikes from the March 9 purchase, and the March 27 sale consists of four bikes from beginning inventory and eight bikes from the March 22 purchase.
2. Using FIFO, calculate ending inventory and cost of goods sold at March 31, 2012.
3. Using LIFO, calculate ending inventory and cost of goods sold at March 31, 2012.
4. Using weighted-average cost, calculate ending inventory and cost of goods sold at March 31, 2012.
5. Calculate sales revenue and gross profit under each of the four methods.
6. Comparing FIFO and LIFO, which one provides the more meaningful measure of ending inventory? Explain.
7. If Greg's Bicycle Shop chooses to report inventory using LIFO instead of FIFO, record the LIFO adjustment.

P6–3A At the beginning of July, CD City has a balance in inventory of $2,900. The following transactions occur during the month of July.

Record transactions and prepare a partial income statement using a perpetual inventory system (LO5, 6)

July 3   Purchase CDs on account from Wholesale Music for $1,800, terms 2/10, n/30.
July 4   Pay freight charges related to the July 3 purchase from Wholesale Music, $100.
July 9   Return incorrectly ordered CDs to Wholesale Music and receive credit, $300.
July 11   Pay Wholesale Music in full.
July 12   Sell CDs to customers on account, $4,800, that had a cost of $2,500.
July 15   Receive full payment from customers related to the sale on July 12.
July 18   Purchase CDs on account from Music Supply for $2,600, terms 1/10, n/30.
July 22   Sell CDs to customers for cash, $3,700, that had a cost of $2,000.
July 28   Return CDs to Music Supply and receive credit of $200.
July 30   Pay Music Supply in full.

Required:

1. Assuming that CD City uses a perpetual inventory system, record the transactions.
2. Prepare the top section of the multiple-step income statement through gross profit for the month of July.

308   CHAPTER 6   Inventory and Cost of Goods Sold

Report inventory
using lower-of-cost-or-
market (LO7)

P6–4A A local Chevrolet dealership carries the following types of vehicles:

Inventory Items	Quantity	Cost per Unit	Market (replacement cost) per Unit	Lower-of-Cost-or-Market
Vans	3	$22,000	$20,000	_____
Trucks	6	17,000	16,000	_____
2-door sedans	2	12,000	14,000	_____
4-door sedans	7	16,000	19,000	_____
Sports cars	3	32,000	35,000	_____
SUVs	5	28,000	23,000	_____

Because of recent increases in gasoline prices, the car dealership has noticed a reduced demand for its SUVs, vans, and trucks.

Required:
1. Compute the total cost of the entire inventory.
2. Determine whether each inventory item would be reported at cost or market. Multiply the quantity of each inventory item by the appropriate cost or market amount and place the total in the "Lower-of-Cost-or-Market" column. Then determine the total for that column.
3. Compare your answers in *Requirement* 1 and *Requirement* 2 and then record any necessary adjustment to write down inventory from cost to market value.
4. Discuss the financial statement effects of using lower-of-cost-or-market to report inventory.

Calculate ending
inventory and cost of
goods sold using FIFO
and LIFO and adjust
inventory using the
lower-of-cost-or-market
method (LO3, 7)

P6–5A For 2012, Parker Games has the following inventory transactions related to its traditional board games.

Date	Transaction	Units	Cost	Total Cost
Jan. 1	Beginning inventory	100	$20	$2,000
Mar. 12	Purchase	80	15	1,200
Sep. 17	Purchase	50	8	400
		230		$3,600
Jan. 1–Dec. 31	Sales	160		

Because of the increasing popularity of electronic video games, Parker Games continues to see a decline in the demand for board games. Sales prices have decreased by over 50% during 2012. At the end of the year, Parker estimates the total cost to replace the 70 units of unsold inventory is only $400.

Required:
1. Using FIFO, calculate ending inventory and cost of goods sold.
2. Using LIFO, calculate ending inventory and cost of goods sold.
3. Determine the amount of ending inventory to report using lower-of-cost-or-market. Record any necessary adjustment under (a) FIFO and (b) LIFO.

Record transactions
using a perpetual system,
prepare a partial income
statement, and adjust
for the lower-of-cost-or-
market method
(LO2, 3, 4, 5, 6, 7)

P6–6A At the beginning of October, Bowser Co.'s inventory consists of 60 units with a cost per unit of $40. The following transactions occur during the month of October.

October 4   Purchase 120 units of inventory on account from Waluigi Co. for $50 per unit, terms 2/10, n/30.
October 5   Pay freight charges related to the October 4 purchase, $600.
October 9   Return 20 defective units from the October 4 purchase and receive credit.
October 12   Pay Waluigi Co. in full.
October 15   Sell 150 units of inventory to customers on account, $12,000. [*Hint:* The cost of units sold from the October 4 purchase includes $50 unit cost plus $6 per unit for freight less $1 per unit for the purchase discount, or $55 per unit.]
October 19   Receive full payment from customers related to the sale on October 15.

October 20   Purchase 100 units of inventory from Waluigi Co. for $60 per unit, terms 1/10, n/30.

October 22   Sell 90 units of inventory to customers for cash, $7,200.

Required:

1. Assuming that Bowser Co. uses a FIFO perpetual inventory system to maintain its inventory records, record the transactions.
2. Assuming for preparing financial statements that Bowser Co. reports inventory using LIFO, record the LIFO adjustment.
3. Suppose by the end of October that the remaining inventory is estimated to have a market value per unit of $35, record any necessary adjustment for the lower-of-cost-or-market method after the LIFO adjustment.
4. Prepare the top section of the multiple-step income statement through gross profit for the month of October after the lower-of-cost-or-market adjustment.

P6–7A Baskin-Robbins is one of the world's largest specialty ice cream shops. The company offers dozens of different flavors, from Very Berry Strawberry to lowfat Espresso 'n Cream. Assume that a local Baskin-Robbins in Raleigh, North Carolina, has the following amounts for the month of July 2012.

Prepare a multiple-step income statement and calculate the inventory turnover ratio and gross profit ratio **(LO6, 8)**

Salaries expense	$12,700	Sales revenue	$64,800
Inventory (July 1, 2012)	1,800	Interest income	2,300
Sales returns	1,200	Cost of goods sold	28,200
Utilities expense	3,100	Rent expense	5,700
Income tax expense	5,000	Interest expense	500
		Inventory (July 31, 2012)	1,200

Required:

1. Prepare a multiple-step income statement for the month ended July 31, 2012.
2. Calculate the inventory turnover ratio for the month of July. Would you expect this ratio to be higher or lower in December 2012? Explain.
3. Calculate the gross profit ratio for the month of July.

P6–8A Wawa Food Markets is a convenience store chain located primarily in the Northeast. The company sells gas, candy bars, drinks, and other grocery-related items. St. Jude Medical Incorporated sells medical devices related to cardiovascular needs. Suppose a local Wawa Food Market and St. Jude sales office report the following amounts in the same year (company names are disguised):

Use the inventory turnover ratio and gross profit ratio to analyze companies **(LO8)**

	Company 1	Company 2
Net sales	$300,000	$300,000
Cost of goods sold	90,000	240,000
Gross profit	$210,000	$ 60,000
Average inventory	$ 30,000	$ 20,000

Required:

1. For Company 1 and Company 2, calculate the inventory turnover ratio.
2. For Company 1 and Company 2, calculate the gross profit ratio.
3. After comparing the inventory turnover ratios and gross profit ratios, which company do you think is Wawa and which is St. Jude? Explain.

P6–9A Refer to the transactions of CD City in P6–3A.

Record transactions and prepare a partial income statement using a periodic inventory system **(LO9)**

Required:

1. Assuming that CD City uses a periodic inventory system, record the transactions.
2. Record the month-end adjustment to inventory, assuming that a final count reveals ending inventory with a cost of $2,370.
3. Prepare the top section of the multiple-step income statement through gross profit for the month of July.

310 CHAPTER 6 Inventory and Cost of Goods Sold

Correct inventory understatement and calculate gross profit ratio (LO8, 10)

P6–10A Over a four-year period, Jackie Corporation reported the following series of gross profits.

	2009	2010	2011	2012
Net sales	$50,000	$56,000	$64,000	$80,000
Cost of goods sold	25,000	39,000	21,000	41,000
Gross profit	$25,000	$17,000	$43,000	$39,000

In 2012, the company performed a comprehensive review of its inventory accounting procedures. Based on this review, company records reveal that ending inventory was understated by $10,000 in 2010. Inventory in all other years is correct.

Required:
1. Calculate the gross profit ratio for each of the four years based on amounts originally reported.
2. Calculate the gross profit ratio for each of the four years based on corrected amounts. Describe the trend in the gross profit ratios based on the original amounts versus the corrected amounts.
3. Total gross profit over the four-year period based on the amounts originally reported equals $124,000 (= $25,000 + $17,000 + $43,000 + $39,000). Compare this amount to total gross profit over the four-year period based on the corrected amounts.

PROBLEMS: SET B

Calculate ending inventory and cost of goods sold for four inventory methods (LO3)

P6–1B Jimmie's Fishing Hole has the following transactions related to its top-selling Shimano fishing reel for the month of June 2012:

Date	Transactions	Units	Cost per Unit	Total Cost
June 1	Beginning inventory	16	$250	$ 4,000
June 7	Sale	11		
June 12	Purchase	10	240	2,400
June 15	Sale	12		
June 24	Purchase	10	230	2,300
June 27	Sale	8		
June 29	Purchase	10	220	2,200
				$10,900

Required:
1. Calculate ending inventory and cost of goods sold at June 30, 2012, using the specific identification method. The June 7 sale consists of fishing reels from beginning inventory, the June 15 sale consists of three fishing reels from beginning inventory and nine fishing reels from the June 12 purchase, and the June 27 sale consists of one fishing reel from beginning inventory and seven fishing reels from the June 24 purchase.
2. Using FIFO, calculate ending inventory and cost of goods sold at June 30, 2012.
3. Using LIFO, calculate ending inventory and cost of goods sold at June 30, 2012.
4. Using weighted-average cost, calculate ending inventory and cost of goods sold at June 30, 2012.

Calculate ending inventory, cost of goods sold, sales revenue, and gross profit for four inventory methods (LO3, 4, 5)

P6–2B Pete's Tennis Shop has the following transactions related to its top-selling Wilson tennis racket for the month of August 2012:

Date	Transactions	Units	Cost per Unit	Total Cost
August 1	Beginning inventory	8	$150	$1,200
August 4	Sale ($175 each)	5		
August 11	Purchase	10	140	1,400
August 13	Sale ($190 each)	8		
August 20	Purchase	10	130	1,300
August 26	Sale ($200 each)	11		
August 29	Purchase	12	120	1,440
				$5,340

Required:

1. Calculate ending inventory and cost of goods sold at August 31, 2012, using the specific identification method. The August 4 sale consists of rackets from beginning inventory, the August 13 sale consists of rackets from the August 11 purchase, and the August 26 sale consists of one racket from beginning inventory and 10 rackets from the August 20 purchase.
2. Using FIFO, calculate ending inventory and cost of goods sold at August 31, 2012.
3. Using LIFO, calculate ending inventory and cost of goods sold at August 31, 2012.
4. Using weighted-average cost, calculate ending inventory and cost of goods sold at August 31, 2012.
5. Calculate sales revenue and gross profit under each of the four methods.
6. Comparing FIFO and LIFO, which one provides the more meaningful measure of ending inventory? Explain.
7. If Pete's chooses to report inventory using LIFO, record the LIFO adjustment.

P6–3B At the beginning of June, Circuit Country has a balance in inventory of $2,500. The following transactions occur during the month of June.

Record transactions and prepare a partial income statement using a perpetual inventory system (LO5, 6)

June 2　Purchase radios on account from Radio World for $2,200, terms 2/15, n/45.
June 4　Pay freight charges related to the June 2 purchase from Radio World, $300.
June 8　Return defective radios to Radio World and receive credit, $200.
June 10　Pay Radio World in full.
June 11　Sell radios to customers on account, $4,000, that had a cost of $2,700.
June 18　Receive payment on account from customers, $3,000.
June 20　Purchase radios on account from Sound Unlimited for $3,300, terms 3/10, n/30.
June 23　Sell radios to customers for cash, $4,800, that had a cost of $3,100.
June 26　Return damaged radios to Sound Unlimited and receive credit of $400.
June 28　Pay Sound Unlimited in full.

Required:

1. Assuming that Circuit Country uses a perpetual inventory system, record transactions using the following account titles: Cash, Accounts Receivable, Inventory, Accounts Payable, Sales, and Cost of Goods Sold.
2. Prepare the top section of the multiple-step income statement through gross profit for the month of June.

P6–4B A home improvement store, like **Lowe's**, carries the following items:

Report inventory using lower-of-cost-or-market (LO7)

Inventory Items	Quantity	Cost per Unit	Market (replacement cost) per Unit	Lower-of-Cost-or-Market
Hammers	100	$ 7.00	$ 7.50	_____
Saws	50	10.00	9.00	_____
Screwdrivers	130	2.00	2.60	_____
Drills	40	25.00	22.00	_____
1-gallon paint cans	160	5.50	5.00	_____
Paintbrushes	180	6.00	6.50	_____

Required:

1. Compute the total cost of inventory.
2. Determine whether each inventory item would be reported at cost or market. Multiply the quantity of each inventory item by the appropriate cost or market amount and place the total in the "Lower-of-Cost-or-Market" column. Then determine the total of that column.
3. Compare your answers in *Requirement* 1 and *Requirement* 2 and then record any necessary adjustment to write down inventory from cost to market value.
4. Discuss the financial statement effects of using lower-of-cost-or-market to report inventory.

Calculate ending inventory and cost of goods sold using FIFO and LIFO and adjust inventory using lower-of-cost-or-market (LO3, 7)

P6–5B Trends by Tiffany sells high-end leather purses. During 2012, the company has the following inventory transactions.

Date	Transaction	Units	Cost	Total Cost
Jan. 1	Beginning inventory	10	$400	$ 4,000
Apr. 9	Purchase	20	420	8,400
Oct. 4	Purchase	16	450	7,200
		46		$19,600
Jan. 1–Dec. 31	Sales	42		

Because trends in purses change frequently, Trends by Tiffany estimates that the remaining four purses have a current replacement cost at December 31 of only $250 each.

Required:

1. Using FIFO, calculate ending inventory and cost of goods sold.
2. Using LIFO, calculate ending inventory and cost of goods sold.
3. Determine the amount of ending inventory to report using lower-of-cost-or-market. Record any necessary adjustment under (a) FIFO and (b) LIFO.

Record transactions using a perpetual system, prepare a partial income statement, and adjust for the lower-of-cost-or-market method (LO2, 3, 4, 5, 6, 7)

P6–6B At the beginning of November, Yoshi Inc.'s inventory consists of 50 units with a cost per unit of $95. The following transactions occur during the month of November.

November 2	Purchase 80 units of inventory on account from Toad Inc. for $100 per unit, terms 2/10, n/30.
November 3	Pay freight charges related to the November 2 purchase, $210.
November 9	Return 10 defective units from the November 2 purchase and receive credit.
November 11	Pay Toad Inc. in full.
November 16	Sell 100 units of inventory to customers on account, $13,000. [*Hint:* The cost of units sold from the November 2 purchase includes $100 unit cost plus $3 per unit for freight less $2 per unit for the purchase discount, or $101 per unit.]
November 20	Receive full payment from customers related to the sale on November 16.
November 21	Purchase 60 units of inventory from Toad Inc. for $105 per unit, terms 1/10, n/30.
November 24	Sell 70 units of inventory to customers for cash, $8,100.

Required:

1. Assuming that Yoshi Inc. uses a FIFO perpetual inventory system to maintain its internal inventory records, record the transactions.
2. Assuming for preparing financial statements that Yoshi Inc. reports inventory using LIFO, record the LIFO adjustment.
3. Suppose by the end of November that the remaining inventory is estimated to have a market value per unit of $80, record any necessary adjustment for the lower-of-cost-or-market method after the LIFO adjustment.
4. Prepare the top section of the multiple-step income statement through gross profit for the month of November after the lower-of-cost-or-market adjustment.

P6–7B Toys "R" Us sells a variety of children's toys, games, books, and accessories. Assume that a local store has the following amounts for the month of March 2012.

Prepare a multiple-step income statement and calculate the inventory turnover ratio and gross profit ratio **(LO6, 8)**

Sales revenue	$72,300	Cost of goods sold	$35,300
Purchase discounts	2,200	Inventory (Mar. 31, 2012)	1,100
Advertising expense	5,400	Insurance expense	1,800
Rent expense	3,300	Sales discounts	2,500
Gain on sale of building	6,500	Salaries expense	8,400
Inventory (Mar. 1, 2012)	2,300	Income tax expense	3,200

Required:

1. Prepare a multiple-step income statement for the month ended March 31, 2012.
2. Calculate the inventory turnover ratio for the month of March. Would you expect this ratio to be higher or lower in December 2012? Explain.
3. Calculate the gross profit ratio for the month of March.

P6–8B Payless ShoeSource and Dillard's both offer men's formal footwear. Payless offers lower- to middle-priced footwear, whereas Dillard's offers more specialized, higher-end footwear. The average price for a pair of shoes in Payless may be about $50, whereas the average price in Dillard's may be about $175. The types of shoes offered by Dillard's are not sold by many other stores. Suppose a Payless store and a Dillard's store report the following amounts for men's shoes in the same year (company names are disguised):

Use the inventory turnover ratio and gross profit ratio to analyze companies **(LO8)**

	Company 1	Company 2
Net sales	$100,000	$100,000
Cost of goods sold	40,000	75,000
Gross profit	$ 60,000	$ 25,000
Average inventory	$ 25,000	$ 10,000

Required:

1. For Company 1 and Company 2, calculate the inventory turnover ratio.
2. For Company 1 and Company 2, calculate the gross profit ratio.
3. After comparing the inventory turnover ratios and gross profit ratios, which company do you think is Payless and which is Dillard's? Explain.

P6–9B Refer to the transactions of Circuit Country in P6–3B.

Record transactions and prepare a partial income statement using a periodic inventory system **(LO9)**

Required:

1. Assuming that Circuit Country uses a periodic inventory system, record the transactions.
2. Record the month-end adjustment to inventory, assuming that a final count reveals ending inventory with a cost of $1,860.
3. Prepare the top section of the multiple-step income statement through gross profit for the month of June.

P6–10B Sylvester has a bird shop that sells canaries. Sylvester maintains accurate records on the number of birds purchased from its suppliers and the number sold to customers. The records show the following purchases and sales during 2012.

Determine the effects of inventory errors using FIFO **(LO3, 10)**

Date	Transactions	Units	Cost per Unit	Total Cost
January 1	Beginning inventory	25	$30	$ 750
April 14	Purchase	70	32	2,240
August 22	Purchase	120	34	4,080
October 29	Purchase	85	36	3,060
		300		$10,130
Jan. 1–Dec. 31	Sales ($50 each)	270		

Sylvester uses a periodic inventory system and believes there are 30 birds remaining in ending inventory. However, Sylvester neglects to make a final inventory count at the end of the year. An employee accidentally left one of the cages open one night and 10 birds flew away, leaving only 20 birds in ending inventory. Sylvester is not aware of the lost canaries.

Required:

1. What amount will Sylvester calculate for ending inventory and cost of goods sold using FIFO, assuming he erroneously believes 30 canaries remain in ending inventory?
2. What amount would Sylvester calculate for ending inventory and cost of goods sold using FIFO if he knew that only 20 canaries remain in ending inventory?
3. What effect will the inventory error have on reported amounts for (a) ending inventory, (b) retained earnings, (c) cost of goods sold, and (d) net income (ignoring tax effects) in 2012?
4. Assuming that ending inventory is correctly counted at the end of 2013, what effect will the inventory error in 2012 have on reported amounts for (a) ending inventory, (b) retained earnings, (c) cost of goods sold, and (d) net income (ignoring tax effects) in 2013?

*For additional problems, visit **www.mhhe.com/succeed** for Problems: Set C.*

ADDITIONAL PERSPECTIVES

Continuing Problem

Great Adventures

(This is a continuation of the Great Adventures problem from earlier chapters.)

AP6–1 Now that operations for outdoor clinics and TEAM events are running smoothly, Suzie thinks of another area for business expansion. She notices that a few clinic participants wear multiuse (MU) watches. Beyond the normal timekeeping features of most watches, MU watches are able to report temperature, altitude, and barometric pressure. MU watches are waterproof, so moisture from kayaking, rain, fishing, or even diving up to 100 feet won't damage them. Suzie decides to have MU watches available for sale at the start of each clinic. The following transactions relate to purchases and sales of watches during the second half of 2013. All watches are sold for $300 each.

Jul. 17 Purchased 50 watches for $7,500 ($150 per watch) on account.
Jul. 31 Sold 40 watches for $12,000 cash.
Aug. 12 Purchased 40 watches for $6,400 ($160 per watch) cash.
Aug. 22 Sold 30 watches for $9,000 on account.
Sep. 19 Paid for watches ordered on July 17.
Sep. 27 Received full payment for watches sold on account on August 22.
Oct. 27 Purchased 80 watches for $13,600 ($170 per watch) cash.
Nov. 20 Sold 90 watches for $27,000 cash.
Dec.   4 Purchased 100 watches for $18,000 ($180 per watch) cash.
Dec.   8 Sold 40 watches for $12,000 on account.

Required:

1. (a) Calculate sales revenue, cost of goods sold, and ending inventory as of December 31, 2013, assuming Suzie uses FIFO to account for inventory.
   (b) Prepare the gross profit section of a partial income statement for transactions related to MU watches.
2. Late in December, the next generation of multiuse (MU II) watches is released. In addition to all of the features of the MU watch, the MU II watches are equipped with a global positioning system (GPS) and have the ability to download and play songs and videos off the Internet. The demand for the original MU watches is

greatly reduced. As of December 31, the estimated market value of MU watches is only $100 per watch.

(a) Record any necessary adjustment on December 31, 2013, related to this information.

(b) For what amount would MU inventory be reported in the December 31, 2013, balance sheet?

(c) Prepare an updated gross profit section of a partial income statement accounting for this additional information. Compare your answer to *Requirement* 1(b).

American Eagle Outfitters, Inc.

Financial Analysis

AP6–2 Financial information for **American Eagle** is presented in Appendix A at the end of the book.

Required:

1. In the summary of significant accounting policies, what is American Eagle's procedure in accounting for inventory?
2. For the most recent year, what is the amount of inventory in the balance sheet? What does this amount represent?
3. American Eagle refers to its cost of goods sold using a different name. What is it?
4. For the most recent year, what is the amount of cost of goods sold in the income statement? What does this amount represent?
5. Calculate American Eagle's inventory turnover ratio and average days in inventory for the most recent year.
6. Calculate American Eagle's gross profit ratio for each of the three years. Do you notice any trend?
7. For the most recent year, calculate American Eagle's ratio of operating expenses to net sales.

The Buckle, Inc.

Financial Analysis

AP6–3 Financial information for **The Buckle** is presented in Appendix B at the end of the book.

Required:

1. In the summary of significant accounting policies, what is The Buckle's procedure in accounting for inventory?
2. For the most recent year, what is the amount of inventory in the balance sheet? What does this amount represent?
3. The Buckle refers to its cost of goods sold using a different name. What is it?
4. For the most recent year, what is the amount of cost of goods sold in the income statement? What does this amount represent?
5. Calculate The Buckle's inventory turnover ratio and average days in inventory for the most recent year.
6. Calculate The Buckle's gross profit ratio for each of the three years. Do you notice any trend?
7. For the most recent year, calculate The Buckle's ratio of operating expenses to net sales.

American Eagle, Inc., vs. The Buckle, Inc.

Comparative Analysis

AP6–4 Financial information for **American Eagle** is presented in Appendix A at the end of the book, and financial information for **The Buckle** is presented in Appendix B at the end of the book.

Required:

1. Which company carries a greater inventory balance as a percentage of total assets?
2. Analyze each company's inventory using the inventory turnover ratio and average days in inventory.

3. Determine which company's operations are more profitable using the gross profit ratio.
4. Considering the companies' ratio of operating expenses to net sales, does your answer to *Requirement* 3 change? Explain.

Ethics

AP6–5 Horizon Corporation manufactures personal computers. The company began operations in 2003 and reported profits for the years 2003 through 2010. Due primarily to increased competition and price slashing in the industry, 2011's income statement reported a loss of $20 million. Just before the end of the 2012 fiscal year, a memo from the company's chief financial officer to Jim Fielding, the company controller, included the following comments:

> If we don't do something about the large amount of unsold computers already manufactured, our auditors will require us to record a write down. The resulting loss for 2012 will cause a violation of our debt covenants and force the company into bankruptcy. I suggest that you ship half of our inventory to J.B. Sales, Inc., in Oklahoma City. I know the company's president, and he will accept the inventory and acknowledge the shipment as a purchase. We can record the sale in 2012 which will boost our loss to a profit. Then J.B. Sales will simply return the inventory in 2013 after the financial statements have been issued.

Required:
Discuss the ethical dilemma faced by Jim Fielding.

Internet Research

AP6–6 Obtain copies of the annual reports of **The Coca-Cola Company** and **PepsiCo Corporation** for the most recent year. You can find the annual reports at the companies' websites (*www.coca-cola.com* and *www.pepsico.com*) in the investor information section or at the Securities and Exchange Commission's website (*www.sec.gov*) using EDGAR (Electronic Data Gathering, Analysis, and Retrieval). The SEC requires Form 10-K, which includes the annual report, to be filed on EDGAR. Search or scroll within the annual reports to find the financial statements.

Required:
1. For each company, calculate the gross profit ratio, inventory turnover ratio, and average days in inventory.
2. Compare the management of each company's investment in inventory.

Written Communication

AP6–7 You have just been hired as a consultant to Gilbert Industries, a newly formed company. The company president, Mindy Grayson, is seeking your advice as to the appropriate inventory method Gilbert should use to value its inventory and cost of goods sold. Ms. Grayson has narrowed the choice to LIFO and FIFO. She has heard that LIFO might be better for tax purposes, but FIFO has certain advantages for financial reporting to investors and creditors. You have been told that the company will be profitable in its first year and for the foreseeable future.

Required:
Prepare a report for the president describing the factors that should be considered by Gilbert in choosing between LIFO and FIFO.

Earnings Management

AP6–8 Eddie's Galleria sells billiard tables. The company has the following purchases and sales for 2012.

Date	Transactions	Units	Cost per Unit	Total Cost
January 1	Beginning inventory	150	$540	$ 81,000
March 8	Purchase	120	570	68,400
August 22	Purchase	100	600	60,000
October 29	Purchase	80	640	51,200
		450		$260,600
Jan. 1–Dec. 31	Sales ($700 each)	400		

Eddie is worried about the company's financial performance. He has noticed an increase in the purchase cost of billiard tables, but at the same time, competition from other billiard table stores and other entertainment choices have prevented him from increasing the sales price. Eddie is worried that if the company's profitability is too low, stockholders will demand he be replaced. Eddie does not want to lose his job. Since 60 of the 400 billiard tables sold have not yet been picked up by the customers as of December 31, 2012, Eddie decides incorrectly to include these tables in ending inventory. He appropriately includes the sale of these 60 tables as part of total revenues in 2012.

Required:

1. What amount will Eddie calculate for ending inventory and cost of goods sold using FIFO, assuming he erroneously reports that 110 tables remain in ending inventory?
2. What amount would Eddie calculate for cost of goods sold using FIFO if he correctly reports that only 50 tables remain in ending inventory?
3. What effect will the inventory error have on reported amounts for (a) ending inventory, (b) retained earnings, (c) cost of goods sold, and (d) net income (ignoring tax effects) in 2012?
4. Assuming that ending inventory is correctly counted at the end of 2013, what effect will the inventory error in 2012 have on reported amounts for (a) ending inventory, (b) retained earnings, (c) cost of goods sold, and (d) net income (ignoring tax effects) in 2013?

Answers to the Self-Study Questions
1. d   2. b   3. a   4. b   5. d   6. a   7. d   8. a   9. c   10. b

CHAPTER

Long-Term Assets

AFTER STUDYING THIS CHAPTER, YOU SHOULD BE ABLE TO:

- **LO1** Identify and record the major types of property, plant, and equipment.
- **LO2** Identify and record the major types of intangible assets.
- **LO3** Discuss the accounting treatment of expenditures after acquisition.
- **LO4** Calculate depreciation of property, plant, and equipment.
- **LO5** Calculate amortization of intangible assets.
- **LO6** Account for the disposal of long-term assets.

Analysis

- **LO7** Describe the relationship among return on assets, profit margin, and asset turnover.

Appendix

- **LO8** Identify impairment situations and describe the two-step impairment process.

WORLDCOM: **EXPENSES CALLED ASSETS**

Feature
Story

WorldCom was the parent company of **MCI** and recognized as the leading telecommunications company in North America. Then in 2002, a routine internal audit uncovered massive accounting fraud. The firm had recorded assets in the balance sheet that should have been recorded as *expenses* in the income statement. Although this kind of fraudulent reporting was not new, the sheer volume of the fraud set new records. By failing to record expenses, WorldCom overstated its income and assets by about $11 billion (not $11 million, but $11 *billion!*). Estimates of investor losses from the resulting bankruptcy exceeded $100 billion.

How was the fraud accomplished? When WorldCom used the telecommunication lines of another company, it paid a fee. This fee is part of normal operating costs, and it should have been recorded as an expense of the current period, to properly match the expense with the revenues it helped to generate. Instead, WorldCom recorded these operating expenses as long-term assets in the balance sheet. Failure to report these operating expenses caused net income to be overstated by billions; operating expenses were purposely misstated as assets.

What motivated WorldCom's management to commit this fraud? It appears the intention was to hide operating losses and maintain a strong stock price. If investors had known the true operating performance of WorldCom, the stock price would have tumbled.

For his role in the accounting scandal that led to the largest bankruptcy in U.S. history, Bernard Ebbers, the 63-year-old CEO of WorldCom, was sentenced to 25 years in a low-security federal prison.[1] Ebbers, who took the stand in his own defense, insisted that he knew nothing of WorldCom's fraudulent accounting, but had left the accounting to Scott Sullivan, the company's former chief financial officer (CFO). The jury did not buy Ebbers's hands-off defense. They concluded that the CEO, as head of the company, is ultimately responsible for the firm's accounting.

---

[1] J. Sandberg, D. Solomon, and R. Blumenstein. "Inside WorldCom's Unearthing of a Vast Accounting Scandal." *The Wall Street Journal* (June 27, 2002); K. Eichenwald and S. Romero. "Inquiry Finds Effort to Delay at WorldCom." *The New York Times* (July 4, 2002); K. Crawford. "Ex-WorldCom CEO Ebbers Guilty." *CNNMoney.com* (March 15, 2005); and "Bernard Ebbers Given 25-year Prison Sentence." CBC News (July 13, 2005).

Winnebago cannot make campers without its manufacturing facilities and the equipment in those facilities. In contrast, it's not physical assets, but copyrights on its computer software that give **Google** the ability to generate billions of dollars in revenue each year. Both of these types of revenue-producing assets are considered *long-term assets,* the topic of this chapter.

We classify long-term assets into two major categories:

Common Terms Tangible assets are also called *property, plant, and equipment; plant assets;* or *fixed assets.*

1. **Tangible assets.** Assets in this category include land, land improvements, buildings, equipment, and natural resources. Winnebago's land, buildings, and equipment fall into this category.

2. **Intangible assets.** Assets in this category include patents, trademarks, copyrights, franchises, and goodwill. We distinguish these assets from property, plant, and equipment by their lack of physical substance. The evidence of their existence often is based on a legal contract. Google's copyrights are intangible assets.

Long-term assets often represent a significant portion of the total assets of a company. Illustration 7–1 presents a breakdown of the total assets for **Darden Restaurants**, a publicly traded company that owns and operates restaurant chains such as Red Lobster, Olive Garden, and Longhorn Steakhouse. Notice that current assets represent only about 11% of total assets, and long-term assets make up the remaining 89%. Accounting for long-term assets, both tangible (property, plant, and equipment) and intangible, is important and is the primary focus in this chapter.

ILLUSTRATION 7–1

Balance Sheet for Darden Restaurants

DARDEN RESTAURANTS Balance Sheet (partial) May 31, 2009 and 2008 ($ in thousands)		
	2009	**2008**
Cash	$ 62,900	$ 43,200
Receivables	147,500	161,300
Inventory	247,000	216,700
Other current assets	97,400	46,700
Total current assets	554,800	467,900
Property, plant, and equipment	3,306,700	3,066,000
Intangible assets	1,058,200	1,040,800
Other long-term assets and investments	105,500	155,900
Total assets	**$5,025,200**	**$4,730,600**

To properly report both tangible and intangible assets, we need to address a variety of issues including (1) which amounts to include in their cost, (2) how to expense their costs while using them, and (3) how to record their sale or disposal at the end of their useful life. These three are the basis for the three major parts of the chapter.

PART A   ACQUISITIONS

The first issue to consider in accounting for long-term assets is how to identify them and measure their costs. To do this, we need to understand the major types of tangible and intangible assets. We begin with tangible assets, also referred to as property, plant, and equipment.

Property, Plant, and Equipment

The property, plant, and equipment category consists of land, land improvements, buildings, equipment, and natural resources. The general rule for recording all such long-term assets can be stated rather simply: **We record a long-term asset at its cost *plus* all expenditures necessary to get the asset ready for use.** Thus, the initial cost of a long-term asset might be more than just its purchase price; it also will include any additional amounts the firm paid to bring the asset to its desired condition and location for use. We use the term capitalize to describe recording an expenditure as an asset.

■ **LO1**
Identify and record the major types of property, plant, and equipment.

When we make an expenditure, we have the choice of recording it as an expense of the current period or recording it as an asset and then allocating that cost as an expense over future periods. The choice depends on when the company benefits from having the asset: in the current period or over future periods. Determining which costs to record as expenses and which to record as long-term assets is crucial. Several infamous accounting frauds were the result of inflating net income by improperly recording current expenses as long-term assets.

We look at the proper recording of land, land improvements, buildings, basket purchases, equipment, and natural resources next.

LAND

The Land account represents land a company is using in its operations. (In contrast, land purchased for investment purposes is recorded in a separate investment account.) We capitalize to Land all expenditures necessary to get the land ready for its intended use.

Such capitalized costs include the purchase price of the land plus closing costs such as fees for the attorney, real estate agent commissions, title, title search, and recording fees. If the property is subject to back taxes or other obligations, we include these amounts as well. In fact, any additional expenditure such as clearing, filling, and draining the land, or even removing old buildings to prepare the land for its intended use, become part of the land's capitalized cost. If we receive any cash from selling salvaged materials from old buildings torn down, we reduce the cost of land by that amount.

Assume, for instance, that Kyoto's Sushi Bar purchases a two-acre tract of land and an existing building for $500,000. The company plans to remove the old building and construct a new restaurant on the site. In addition to the purchase price, the company pays a sales commission of $30,000 to the real estate agent and title insurance of $3,000. Kyoto also pays $8,000 in property taxes, which includes $6,000 of back taxes (unpaid taxes from previous years) paid by Kyoto on behalf of the seller and $2,000 due for the current fiscal year after the purchase date. Shortly after closing, the company pays a contractor $50,000 to tear down the old building and remove it from the site. Kyoto is able to sell salvaged materials from the old building for $5,000 and pays an additional $6,000 to level the land.

Using the guideline of **cost *plus* all expenditures necessary to get the asset ready for use,** at what amount should Kyoto record as the cost of the land? Illustration 7–2 (next page) shows the computation for the cost of Kyoto's land.

You may wonder why Kyoto recorded only $6,000 for property taxes. That was the amount required to get the asset ready for use—Kyoto could not use the land until it paid the back taxes. The additional $2,000 in property taxes, though, relates only to the current period, and so Kyoto records that amount as an expense in the current period. All of the other costs, including the $6,000 in back property taxes, are necessary to acquire the land, so Kyoto capitalizes them. Note that the salvaged materials that were sold for $5,000 reduce the overall cost of the land.

ILLUSTRATION 7-2

Computation of the
Cost of Land

Purchase price of land (and building to be removed)	$500,000
Commissions	30,000
Back property taxes	6,000
Title insurance	3,000
Cost of removing old building	50,000
Less: Salvaged materials from old building	(5,000)
Cost of leveling the land	6,000
Total cost	$590,000

COMMON MISTAKE

Many students incorrectly add or ignore the cash received from the sale of salvaged materials. Cash received from the sale of salvaged materials *reduces* the total cost of land.

LAND IMPROVEMENTS

Beyond the cost of the land, Kyoto likely will spend additional amounts to improve the land by adding a parking lot, sidewalks, driveways, landscaping, lighting systems, fences, sprinklers, and similar additions. These are land improvements.

In Chapter 3, we briefly discussed *depreciation* as the process of allocating the cost of an asset over its life. We will discuss depreciation in detail later in this chapter. When we do so, you will discover that land is an asset we do not depreciate because its life is indefinite. However, we do depreciate land improvements. For example, the paved parking lot Kyoto adds to its new property will eventually deteriorate and be replaced. Because land improvements have limited lives, we record them separately from the land itself.

BUILDINGS

Buildings include administrative offices, retail stores, manufacturing facilities, and storage warehouses. The cost of acquiring a building usually includes realtor commissions and legal fees in addition to the purchase price. The new owner sometimes needs to remodel or otherwise modify the building to suit its needs. These additional costs are part of the building's acquisition cost.

Unique accounting issues arise when a firm constructs a building rather than purchasing it. Of course the cost of construction includes architect fees, material costs, and construction labor. New building construction likely also includes costs such as officer supervision, overhead (costs indirectly related to the construction), and capitalized interest.

Capitalized interest refers to interest costs we add to the asset account rather than recording them as interest expense. In keeping with the idea that the cost of an asset includes *all* costs of making the asset ready for its intended use, if a company borrows money to finance the construction of an asset, the interest paid to borrow the funds logically is part of the asset's cost. Capitalizing interest also is in keeping with the *matching principle*. The matching principle states that expenses are to be matched with (included on the same income statement as) the revenues they help to create. During construction of a building, no revenues are created. Revenues won't be created until after the asset is fully constructed and placed into service. Therefore, interest represents a cost similar to materials, labor, and overhead necessary in preparing an asset for use.

EQUIPMENT

Equipment is a broad term that includes machinery used in manufacturing, computers and other office equipment, vehicles, furniture, and fixtures. The cost of equipment is the actual purchase price plus all other costs necessary to prepare the asset for use. These can be any of a variety of other costs including sales tax, shipping, delivery insurance, assembly, installation, testing, and even legal fees incurred to establish title.

What about recurring costs related to equipment, such as annual property insurance and annual property taxes on vehicles? Rather than including recurring costs as part of the cost of the equipment, we expense them as we incur them, in order to properly match them with revenues generated during the same period. The question to ask yourself when deciding whether to add a cost to the asset account or record it as an expense of the current period is, *"Is this a cost of acquiring this asset and getting it ready for use, or is it a recurring cost that benefits the company in the current period?"*

Assume now that Kyoto's Sushi Bar purchases new restaurant equipment for $82,000 plus $6,500 in sales tax. Kyoto pays a freight company $800 to transport the equipment and $200 shipping insurance. The firm also pays $1,600 for one year of liability insurance on the equipment in advance. The equipment was also installed at an additional cost of $1,500. Illustration 7–3 shows the calculation of the amount at which Kyoto should record the cost of the equipment.

Purchase price	$82,000
Sales tax	6,500
Transportation	800
Shipping insurance	200
Installation	1,500
Total cost	$91,000

ILLUSTRATION 7–3

Computation of the Cost of Equipment

Thus, Kyoto should record the equipment at a total cost of $91,000. With the exception of the $1,600 annual insurance on the equipment, each of the expenditures described was necessary to bring the equipment to its condition and location for use. Kyoto will report the $1,600 insurance amount as insurance expense over the first year of coverage.

BASKET PURCHASES

Sometimes companies purchase more than one asset at the same time for one purchase price. This is known as a basket purchase. For example, assume Kyoto purchases land, building, and equipment together for $900,000. How much should we record in the separate accounts for the land, the building, and the equipment? The simple answer is that we allocate the total purchase price of $900,000 based on the estimated fair values of each of the individual assets.

The difficulty, though, is that the estimated fair values of the individual assets often exceed the total purchase price, in this case, $900,000. Let's say the estimated fair values of the land, buildings, and equipment are $200,000, $700,000, and $100,000, respectively, for a total estimated fair value of $1 million. In that case, Kyoto's total purchase of $900,000 will be allocated to the separate accounts for Land, Building, and Equipment based on their relative fair values as shown in Illustration 7–4.

	Estimated Fair Value	Allocation Percentage		Amount of Basket Purchase	Recorded Amount
Land	$ 200,000	$200,000/$1,000,000 = 20%	×	$900,000	$180,000
Building	700,000	$700,000/$1,000,000 = 70%	×	$900,000	630,000
Equipment	100,000	$100,000/$1,000,000 = 10%	×	$900,000	90,000
Total	$1,000,000				$900,000

ILLUSTRATION 7–4

Allocation of Cost in a Basket Purchase

NATURAL RESOURCES

In addition to land, buildings, and equipment, many companies depend heavily on natural resources, such as oil, natural gas, timber, and even salt. **ExxonMobil**, for example, maintains oil and natural gas deposits on six of the world's seven continents. **Weyerhaeuser** is one of the largest pulp and paper companies in the world with major investments in soft timber forests. Even salt is a natural resource, with the largest supply in the United States mined directly under the Great Lakes of North America.

We can distinguish natural resources from other property, plant, and equipment by the fact that we can physically use up, or *deplete,* natural resources. ExxonMobil's oil reserves are a natural resource that decreases as the firm extracts oil. Similarly, timber is used extensively to provide materials in the construction industry. Salt is used as a food additive and to melt icy roads in the winter.

A primary concern with regard to natural resources is sustainability. A common definition of sustainability is "meeting the needs of the present without compromising the ability of future generations to meet their own needs." The oil and gas industry is developing new sources of energy based on solar, wind, and hydro power. Another example is the timber industry, in which companies plant three new trees for every tree cut down. Companies need to find ways of replenishing the natural resources used so that we do not leave future generations without these valuable resources.

KEY POINT

Tangible assets include land, land improvements, buildings, equipment, and natural resources.

Intangible Assets

■ **LO2**
Identify and record the major types of intangible assets.

The other major category of long-term assets, intangible assets, have no physical substance. Assets in this category include patents, trademarks, copyrights, franchises, and goodwill.

Despite their lack of physical substance, intangible assets can be very valuable indeed. One of the most valuable intangible assets for many companies is their trademark or brand. *BusinessWeek* publishes an annual list of the 100 most valuable brands. Illustration 7–5 summarizes the top 10 most valuable brands in 2009. As you can see, the **Coca-Cola** brand has an estimated value of $68.7 billion. Despite this value, Coca-Cola reports trademarks on its balance sheet at only $2 billion. Later, we'll see why many intangible assets are *not* recorded on the balance sheet at their estimated values.

ILLUSTRATION 7–5

World's Top 10 Brands

Rank	Company	Country	Estimated Value
1	Coca-Cola	United States	$68.7 billion
2	IBM	United States	60.2 billion
3	Microsoft	United States	56.6 billion
4	GE	United States	47.8 billion
5	Nokia	Finland	34.9 billion
6	McDonald's	United States	32.3 billion
7	Google	United States	32.0 billion
8	Toyota	Japan	31.3 billion
9	Intel	United States	30.6 billion
10	Disney	United States	28.4 billion

Source: *BusinessWeek* (September 2009), *http://businessweek.com/go/brand/.*

Companies acquire intangible assets in two ways: (1) They *purchase* intangible assets like patents, copyrights, trademarks, or franchise rights from other entities, or (2) they *create* intangible assets internally, by developing a new product or process and obtaining a protective patent. The reporting rules for intangible assets vary depending on whether the company purchased or acquired the asset.

Reporting *purchased* intangibles is similar to reporting purchased property, plant, and equipment. **We record purchased intangible assets at their original cost plus all other costs, such as legal and filing fees, necessary to get the asset ready for use.** Filing fees include items such as the fee to record a copyright with the U.S. Copyright Office or the various fees to record a patent with the U.S. Patent and Trademark Office.

Reporting intangible assets that are *developed internally* is quite different. Rather than recording these on the balance sheet as intangible assets, **we expense to the income statement most of the costs for internally developed intangible assets as we incur those costs.** For example, the research and development (R&D) costs incurred in developing a patent internally are not recorded as an intangible asset in the balance sheet. Instead, they are expensed directly in the income statement. The reason we expense all R&D costs is the difficulty in determining the portion of R&D that benefits future periods. Conceptually, we should record as an intangible asset the portion that benefits future periods. Due to the difficulties in arriving at this estimate, current U.S. accounting rules require firms to expense all R&D costs as incurred.

 INTERNATIONAL FINANCIAL REPORTING STANDARDS (IFRS)

International accounting standards differ from U.S. accounting standards in the treatment of R&D costs. U.S. GAAP requires that we expense all research and development expenditures in the period incurred. IFRS makes a distinction between *research* activities and *development* activities. Under IFRS, research expenditures are expensed in the period incurred, consistent with U.S. GAAP. However, development costs that benefit future periods can be recorded as an intangible asset.

For more discussion, see Appendix E.

A similar argument about the difficulty of estimating benefits in future periods can be made for advertising expenses. Advertising at Coca-Cola clearly has made its trademark more valuable. Because we cannot tell what portion of today's advertising benefits future periods and how many periods it might benefit, advertising costs are not recorded as an intangible asset on the balance sheet. Instead, advertising costs are recorded as expenses in the income statement.

 KEY POINT

We record (capitalize) purchased intangible assets at their purchase price plus all costs necessary to get the asset ready for use. We expense internally generated intangible assets, such as R&D and advertising costs, as we incur them.

Let's look in more detail at how we report specific types of intangible assets.

PATENTS

A patent is an exclusive right to manufacture a product or to use a process. The U.S. Patent and Trademark Office grants this right for a period of 20 years. When a firm *purchases* a patent, it records the patent at its purchase price plus such other costs as legal and filing fees to secure the patent.

In contrast, when a firm *develops a patent internally,* it expenses the research and development costs as it incurs them. An exception to this rule is legal fees. The firm will record in the Patent asset account the legal and filing fees to secure the patent, even if it developed the patented item or process internally.

Holders of patents often need to defend their exclusive rights in court. For example, The **J.M. Smucker Company** obtained a patent on a round, crustless, frozen peanut butter and jelly sandwich sealed in an airtight foil wrapper, marketed under the name "Uncrustables." Smucker's later had to defend its patent by attempting to stop another company from making similar sandwiches. The costs of successfully defending a patent, including attorneys' fees, are added to the Patent account.

COPYRIGHTS

A copyright is an exclusive right of protection given by the U.S. Copyright Office to the creator of a published work such as a song, film, painting, photograph, book, or computer software. Copyrights are protected by law and give the creator (and his or her heirs) the exclusive right to reproduce and sell the artistic or published work for the life of the creator plus 70 years. A copyright also allows the copyright holder to pursue legal action against anyone who attempts to infringe the copyright. Accounting for the costs of copyrights is virtually identical to that of patents.

TRADEMARKS

A trademark, like the name **Coca-Cola**, is a word, slogan, or symbol that distinctively identifies a company, product, or service. The firm can register its trademark with the U.S. Patent and Trademark Office to protect it from use by others for a period of 10 years. The registration can be renewed for an indefinite number of 10-year periods, so a trademark is an example of an intangible asset whose useful life can be indefinite.

Firms often acquire trademarks through acquisition. As an example, **Hewlett-Packard (HP)** acquired all the outstanding stock of **Compaq Computer Corporation** for $24 billion, of which $1.4 billion was assigned to the Compaq trademark.

Advertising costs can factor into the cost of a trademark in a big way. For example, **Subway** aired a series of commercials featuring Jared Fogle, a student at Indiana University who lost 245 pounds eating Subway sandwiches. Certainly these ads benefited Subway. But what was the value to the company of the advertising? And for how many years will Subway receive that value? These are difficult questions. Thus, when a firm develops a trademark internally through advertising, it doesn't record the advertising costs as part of the cost of the intangible asset. Instead, it expenses the advertising costs in the income statement. Even though some advertising costs meet the definition of an asset by providing future benefits, due to the difficulty in estimating these amounts, financial accounting rules require advertising costs to be expensed as incurred.

Names can lose their trademarked status if their owners fail to prevent improper use by others. All of the following were once valuable trademarks in the United States: aspirin, escalator, cellophane, zipper, shredded wheat, corn flakes, and kerosene.

A firm can record attorney fees, registration fees, design costs, successful legal defense, and other costs directly related to securing the trademark as an intangible asset in the Trademark asset account. This is how Coca-Cola can have a trademark valued at $67 billion, but reported in the balance sheet at only $2 billion. The estimated value of the trademark is not recorded on the balance sheet; instead, only the legal, registration, and design fees are recorded. The advertising costs that create value for the trademark are recorded as advertising expense.

FRANCHISES

The last time you ordered a sandwich at Subway, you probably dealt with a franchise. Many popular retail businesses such as restaurants, auto dealerships, and hotels are set up as franchises. These are local outlets that pay for the exclusive right to use the franchisor company's name and to sell its products within a specified geographical area. Many franchisors provide other benefits to the franchisee, such as participating in the construction of the retail outlet, training employees, and purchasing national advertising.

To record the cost of a franchise, the franchisee records the initial fee as an intangible asset and then expenses that cost over the life of the franchise agreement. Additional periodic payments to the franchisor usually are for services the franchisor provides on a continuing basis, and the franchisee will expense them as incurred.

GOODWILL

Goodwill often is the largest, yet the most confusing, intangible asset recorded in the balance sheet. While most long-term assets, even intangible ones, can be separated from the company and sold individually, goodwill cannot. Goodwill represents the value of a company as a whole, over and above the value of its identifiable net assets. That value can emerge from a company's reputation, its trained employees and management team, its favorable business location, and any other unique features of the company that we are unable to associate with a specific asset.

We record goodwill as an intangible asset in the balance sheet *only* when we purchase it as part of the acquisition of another company. In this case, the acquiring company records goodwill equal to the purchase price less the fair value of the net assets acquired. The fair value of the net assets is equal to the value of all identifiable assets acquired, minus the value of all liabilities assumed.

To see how this works, assume that Enriched White Bread Company (EWB) acquires Whole Wheat Bread Company (WWB) by paying $36 million in cash. The fair values of all identifiable assets acquired are as follows ($ in millions):

Receivables	$10
Inventory	14
Property, plant, and equipment	18
Patent	8
Total	$50

In the purchase, EWB also assumes all of WWB's long-term debt, which has a fair value of $24 million at the date of acquisition. Illustration 7–6 shows how to calculate the amount EWB would report as goodwill ($10 million).

($ in millions)		
Purchase price		$36
Less:		
Fair value of assets acquired	$ 50	
Less: Fair value of liabilities assumed	(24)	
Fair value of identifiable net assets		(26)
Goodwill		$10

ILLUSTRATION 7–6

Business Acquisition with Goodwill

EWB records the acquisition as follows:

	Debit	Credit	A	=	L	+	SE
Receivables (at fair value)	10		+10				
Inventory (at fair value)	14		+14				
Property, Plant, and Equipment (at fair value)	18		+18				
Patent (at fair value)	8		+8				
Goodwill (remaining purchase price)	10		+10				
Long-Term Debt (at fair value)		24			+24		
Cash (at purchase price)		36	−36				
(Acquire Whole Wheat Bread Company)							

Most companies also create goodwill to some extent through advertising, training, and other efforts. However, as it does for other internally generated intangibles, a company must *expense* any costs it incurs in the internal generation of goodwill. Imagine how difficult it would be to estimate the amount and future benefits of internally generated goodwill. Due to this difficulty, we record goodwill only when it is acquired as part of the purchase of another business.

KEY POINT

Intangible assets include patents, copyrights, trademarks, franchises, and goodwill.

Expenditures after Acquisition

■ LO3
Discuss the accounting treatment of expenditures after acquisition.

Over the life of a long-term asset, the owners often incur additional expenditures for repairs and maintenance, additions, improvements, or litigation costs. We credit these costs to Cash or perhaps to Accounts Payable or Notes Payable, but what account do we debit? As with any other expenditure, the choice is to debit either an asset or an expense. Recall that an asset is a probable future benefit. **We capitalize an expenditure as an asset if it increases future benefits. We expense an expenditure if it benefits only the current period.** To see the choice more clearly, let's look at repairs and maintenance, additions, improvements, and litigation costs in more detail.

REPAIRS AND MAINTENANCE

The cost of an engine tune-up or the repair of an engine part for a delivery truck allows the truck to continue its productive activity. We expense repairs and maintenance expenditures like these because they maintain a given level of benefits in the period incurred. We capitalize as assets more extensive repairs that *increase* the future benefits of the delivery truck, such as a new transmission or an engine overhaul.

ADDITIONS

An addition occurs when we add a new major component to an existing asset. We should capitalize the cost of additions because they increase, rather than maintain, the future benefits from the expenditure. For example, adding a refrigeration unit to a delivery truck increases the capability of the truck beyond that originally anticipated, thus increasing its future benefits.

IMPROVEMENTS

An improvement is the cost of replacing a major component of an asset. The replacement can be a new component with the same characteristics as the old component, or a new component with enhanced operating capabilities. For example, we could replace an existing refrigeration unit in a delivery truck with a new but similar unit or with a new and improved refrigeration unit. In either case, the cost of the improvement usually increases future benefits, and we should capitalize it to the Equipment account.

LEGAL DEFENSE OF INTANGIBLE ASSETS

The expenditures after acquisition mentioned so far—repairs and maintenance, additions, and improvements—generally relate to property, plant, and equipment. Intangible assets, though, also can require expenditures after their acquisition, the most frequent being the cost of legally defending the right that gives the asset its value. For example, when The J.M. Smucker Company attempted to prevent another company from copying its peanut butter and jelly sandwich patent, it incurred legal costs. If a firm successfully defends an intangible right, it should capitalize the litigation costs and amortize them over the remaining useful life of the related intangible. However, if the defense of an intangible right is unsuccessful, then the firm should expense the litigation costs as incurred because they provide no future benefit.

MATERIALITY

Materiality relates to the size of an item that is likely to influence a decision. An item is said to be material if it is large enough to influence a decision. Materiality is an important consideration in the "capitalize versus expense" decision. There often are practical problems in capitalizing small expenditures. For example, a stapler may have a 20-year service life, but it would not be practical to capitalize and then allocate that small of a cost to expense over 20 years. Companies generally expense all costs under a certain dollar amount, say $1,000, regardless of whether future benefits are increased. It's important for a company to establish a policy for treating these expenditures and apply the policy consistently.

Illustration 7–7 provides a summary of expenditures after acquisition.

 CAREER CORNER

The legal defense of intangible asset rights often requires the services of a lawyer. Accounting and law actually have a lot in common. Some business professionals (such as those specializing in tax laws) have both a CPA license and a law degree. If you are considering a career in law, don't shy away from accounting and other business courses. The skills developed in accounting and related business courses can be quite valuable in analyzing many of the challenging research questions addressed in law school. While the most traditional career path to law is through a liberal arts degree such as political science, many students begin their legal careers with undergraduate degrees in business. In addition, an understanding of accounting and business in general will make you more valuable as an attorney.

Type of Expenditure	Definition	Period Benefited	Usual Accounting Treatment
Repairs and maintenance	Maintaining a given level of benefits	Current	**Expense**
Repairs and maintenance	Making major repairs that increase future benefits	Future	**Capitalize**
Additions	Adding a new major component	Future	**Capitalize**
Improvements	Replacing a major component	Future	**Capitalize**
Legal defense of intangible assets	Incurring litigation costs to defend the legal right to the asset	Future	**Capitalize** (Expense if defense is unsuccessful)

ILLUSTRATION 7–7
Expenditures after Acquisition

 KEY POINT

Capital expenditures (recorded as assets) benefit *future* periods. Expenses typically benefit only the *current* period.

COST ALLOCATION

PART B

When people talk about a car depreciating, they usually are talking about how much the value of the car has decreased. Depreciation in accounting, though, is different. The primary dictionary definition of depreciation differs from the definition of depreciation used in accounting:

Dictionary definition = Decrease in value (or selling price) of an asset.

Accounting definition = Allocation of an asset's cost to an expense over time.

COMMON MISTAKE

Students sometimes mistake accounting depreciation as recording the decrease in value of an asset. Depreciation in accounting is *not* a valuation process. Rather, depreciation in accounting is an allocation of an asset's cost to expense over time.

In this section, we discuss the allocation of an asset's cost over time. We use the term *depreciation* to describe that process when it applies to property, plant, and equipment. You will see that we use a different term, *depletion*, to describe the cost allocation process when it applies to natural resources. For intangible assets, the term we use is *amortization*.

Depreciation of Property, Plant, and Equipment

■ **LO4**

Calculate depreciation of property, plant, and equipment.

Depreciation in accounting is the process of allocating to an expense the cost of an asset over its service life. An asset provides benefits (revenues) to a company in future periods. To properly match the cost (expense) with the revenues it helps to generate, we allocate a portion of the asset's cost to an expense in each year that the asset provides a benefit. If the asset will provide benefits to the company for four years, for example, then we allocate a portion of the asset's cost to depreciation expense in each year for four years. Illustration 7–8 portrays this concept of depreciating an asset's original purchase cost over the periods benefited.

ILLUSTRATION 7–8

Depreciation of Long-Term Assets

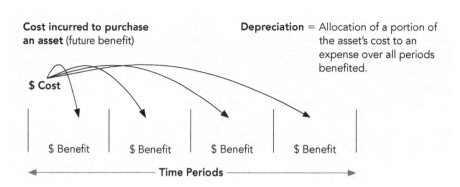

For demonstration, let's assume the local **Starbucks** pays $1,200 for equipment—say, an espresso machine. The machine is expected to have a useful life of four years. We record annual depreciation as shown below.

	Debit	Credit
Depreciation Expense	300	
Accumulated Depreciation		300
(*Depreciate equipment*)		
(*$300 = $1,200 ÷ 4 years*)		

ACCUMULATED DEPRECIATION

The credit portion of the entry requires some explanation. **Accumulated Depreciation** is a contra asset account, meaning that it reduces an asset account. Rather than credit the Equipment account directly, we instead credit its contra account, which we offset against the Equipment account in the balance sheet. The name of the account comes from the fact that the depreciation we record each period *accumulates* in the account. After one year, for instance, we have:

Equipment (cost)	$1,200
Less: Accumulated depreciation ($300 × 1 year)	(300)
= Book value	$ 900

Book value equals the original cost of the asset minus the current balance in Accumulated Depreciation. Note that by increasing accumulated depreciation each period, we are reducing the book value of equipment. The Accumulated Depreciation account allows us to reduce the book value of assets through depreciation, while maintaining the original cost of each asset in the accounting records.

Common Terms Book value sometimes is called *carrying value.*

After two years, we have:

Equipment (cost)	$1,200
Less: Accumulated depreciation ($300 × 2 years)	(600)
= Book value	$ 600

 KEY POINT

Depreciation refers to the allocation of the asset's original cost to an expense during the periods benefited. Depreciation does *not* refer to the change in value or selling price.

Depreciation requires accountants to estimate the *service life* of the asset, or its *useful life*, as well as its residual value at the end of that life. The **service life** is how long the company expects to receive benefits from the asset before disposing of it. We can measure service life in units of time or in units of activity. For example, the estimated service life of a delivery truck might be either five years or 100,000 miles. We use the terms service life and useful life interchangeably, because both terms are used in practice.

Common Terms Service life often is called *useful life.*

Depreciation also requires accountants to estimate what an asset's value will be at the end of its service life. Called **residual value**, or *salvage value*, it is the amount the company expects to receive from selling the asset at the end of its service life. A company might estimate residual value from prior experience or by researching the resale values of similar types of assets. Due to the difficulty in estimating residual value, it's not uncommon to assume a residual value of zero.

Common Terms Residual value often is called *salvage value.*

Remember: We record depreciation for land improvements, buildings, and equipment, but we *don't* record depreciation for land. Unlike other long-term assets, land is not "used up" over time.

 COMMON MISTAKE

A common mistake is to depreciate land. Land is *not* depreciated, because its service life never ends.

Generally accepted accounting principles allow us to use various methods to calculate depreciation. In the following sections, we illustrate the three most common depreciation methods used in practice: straight-line, declining-balance, and activity-based.[2] All three illustrations are based on the same business situation: Little King Sandwiches, a local submarine sandwich restaurant, purchased a new delivery truck. The specific details of that purchase are described in Illustration 7–9.

ILLUSTRATION 7–9

Data for Little King Sandwiches's Delivery Truck Purchase, to Illustrate Depreciation Methods

Cost of the new truck	$40,000
Estimated residual value	$5,000
Estimated service life	5 years or 100,000 miles

STRAIGHT-LINE DEPRECIATION

By far the most easily understood and widely used depreciation method is straight-line. With the straight-line method we allocate an *equal* amount of the depreciable cost to each year of the asset's service life. The *depreciable cost* is the asset's cost minus its estimated residual value. We simply divide the depreciable cost by the number of years in the asset's life, as shown in Illustration 7–10.

ILLUSTRATION 7–10

Formula for Straight-Line Method

$$\text{Depreciation expense} = \frac{\text{Asset's cost} - \text{Residual value}}{\text{Service life}} = \frac{\text{Depreciable cost}}{\text{Service life}}$$

$$\text{Depreciation expense} = \frac{\$40,000 - \$5,000}{5 \text{ years}} = \$7,000 \text{ per year}$$

Note that dividing the depreciable cost each year by five is the same as multiplying the depreciable cost each year by 20% ($1/5 = 0.20$).

Illustration 7–11 provides a depreciation schedule using the straight-line method.

ILLUSTRATION 7–11

Straight-Line Depreciation Schedule

LITTLE KING SANDWICHES
Depreciation Schedule—Straight-Line

| | Calculation | | | | | End-of-Year Amounts | |
| | Depreciable | | Depreciation | | Depreciation | Accumulated | Book |
Year	Cost	×	Rate	=	Expense	Depreciation	Value*
							$40,000
1	$35,000		0.20		$ 7,000	$ 7,000	33,000
2	35,000		0.20		7,000	14,000	26,000
3	35,000		0.20		7,000	21,000	19,000
4	35,000		0.20		7,000	28,000	12,000
5	35,000		0.20		7,000	35,000	5,000
Total					$35,000		

*Book value is the cost of the asset ($40,000) minus accumulated depreciation. Book value of $33,000 at the end of year 1, for example, is $40,000 minus $7,000 in accumulated depreciation.

---

[2]Some introductory financial accounting textbooks illustrate a fourth depreciation method called *sum-of-the-years'-digits*. However, use of this method has decreased dramatically over the years to the point that this method is now rarely seen in actual practice. A recent survey of depreciation methods used by large public companies is provided in Illustration 7–17.

Partial-year depreciation. We assume Little King Sandwiches bought the delivery truck at the beginning of year 1. What if it bought the truck sometime during the year instead? Then, it will record depreciation for only the portion of the first year that it owned the truck. For example, if Little King bought the truck on November 1 and its year-end is December 31, it will record depreciation for only two of the 12 months in year 1. So, depreciation expense in year 1 is $1,167 (= $7,000 × 2/12). If instead Little King bought the truck back on March 1, it will record depreciation for 10 of the 12 months in year 1. In that case, depreciation expense in year 1 is $5,833 (= $7,000 × 10/12).

In both cases, depreciation for the second, third, fourth, and fifth years still is $7,000. The partial-year depreciation for the first year does not affect the depreciation in those subsequent years. However, it does affect the depreciation treatment in the asset's final year of service life: Since the firm didn't take a full year of depreciation in year 1, it needs to record a partial year of depreciation in year 6 in order to fully depreciate the truck from its cost of $40,000 down to its residual value of $5,000. Depreciation in year 6 is $5,833 for the truck purchased on November 1 (= $7,000 − $1,167). For the truck purchased on March 1, depreciation in year 6 is $1,167 (= $7,000 − $5,833).

 COMMON MISTAKE

Many students think March 1 to the end of the year is nine months because December is the twelfth month and March is the third month. March 1 to the end of the year is actually *ten* months; it is every month except January and February.

Change in depreciation estimate. Depreciation is an *estimate*. Remember that the amount of depreciation allocated to each period is produced by two estimates—management's estimates of service life and of residual value—as well as the depreciation method chosen. Management needs to periodically review these estimates. When a change in estimate is required, the company changes depreciation in current and future years, but not in prior periods.

For example, assume that at the end of the third year Little King Sandwiches estimates the remaining service life of the delivery truck to be four more years, for a total service life of seven years rather than the original five. At this time, Little King also changes the estimated residual value to $3,000 from the original estimate of $5,000. How much should Little King record each year for depreciation in years 4 to 7? Take the book value at the end of year 3 ($19,000), subtract the new estimated residual value ($3,000), and then divide by the new remaining service life (four more years). Little King Sandwiches will record depreciation in years 4 to 7 as $4,000 per year. Illustration 7–12 shows the calculations.

Book value, end of year 3	$19,000
− New residual value	(3,000)
New depreciable cost	16,000
÷ Remaining service life	÷ 4
Annual depreciation in years 4 to 7	$ 4,000

ILLUSTRATION 7–12

Change in Depreciation Estimate

Notice that Little King Sandwiches makes all the changes in years 4 to 7. The company does not go back and change the calculations for depreciation already recorded in years 1 to 3.

ETHICAL DILEMMA

James Wright is the chief financial officer (CFO) for The Butcher Block, a major steakhouse restaurant chain. As CFO, James has the final responsibility for all aspects of financial reporting. The company is publicly traded and followed closely by the investment community. James holds regular teleconference discussions with financial analysts; in the most recent teleconference, he indicated the company is emerging nicely from the economic recession. He told the analysts that The Butcher Block should post earnings per share (net income divided by the number of shares of common stock) of at least $1.25. The analysts now expect that amount.

A couple months later, James is examining the preliminary year-end numbers. He notices that earnings per share are coming in at $1.23, two cents per share under target. He also is aware that The Butcher Block has been depreciating most of its restaurant equipment conservatively over a five-year useful life. In some cases, the equipment is used by the company for 10 years or more. He proposes to change the estimated useful life for a subset of the equipment to a more reasonable useful life of seven, rather than five, years. By depreciating over a longer useful life, depreciation expense will be lower in the current year, increasing earnings per share for the year to $1.26. It looks like The Butcher Block is going to meet analyst expectations after all.

Do you think James Wright's proposal to more accurately reflect the true depreciable life of assets is ethical? What concerns might you have?

Straight-line depreciation assumes that the benefits we derive from the use of an asset are the same each year. In some situations it might be more reasonable to assume that the asset will provide greater benefits in the earlier years of its life than in the later years. In these cases, we achieve a better matching of depreciation with revenues by using an accelerated depreciation method, with higher depreciation in the earlier years of the asset's life and lower depreciation in later years. We look at one such method next.

DECLINING-BALANCE DEPRECIATION

The declining-balance method is an accelerated depreciation method. Declining-balance depreciation will be higher than straight-line depreciation in earlier years, but lower in later years. **However, both declining-balance and straight-line will result in the same total depreciation over the asset's service life.** No matter what allocation method we use, total depreciation over the asset's service life will be equal to the depreciable cost (asset cost minus residual value).

The depreciation rate we use under the declining-balance method is a multiple of the straight-line rate, such as 125%, 150%, or 200% of the straight-line rate. The most common declining-balance rate is 200%, which we refer to as the *double-*declining-balance method since the rate is double the straight-line rate. In our illustration for Little King Sandwiches, the double-declining-balance rate would be 40% (two times the straight-line rate of 20%). Illustration 7–13 provides a depreciation schedule using the double-declining-balance method.

LITTLE KING SANDWICHES
Depreciation Schedule—Double-Declining-Balance

| Year | Calculation | | | End-of-Year Amounts | |
	Beginning Book Value	× Depreciation Rate	= Depreciation Expense	Accumulated Depreciation	Book Value*
					$40,000
1	$40,000	0.40	$16,000	$16,000	24,000
2	24,000	0.40	9,600	25,600	14,400
3	14,400	0.40	5,760	31,360	8,640
4	8,640	0.40	3,456	34,816	5,184
5	5,184		184**	35,000	**5,000**
Total			$35,000		

ILLUSTRATION 7–13
Double-Declining-Balance Depreciation Schedule

*Book value is the cost of the asset minus accumulated depreciation. Book value at the end of year 1 is $24,000, equal to the cost of $40,000 minus accumulated depreciation of $16,000. Book value at the end of **year 1** in the last column is equal to book value at the beginning of **year 2** in the second column of the schedule.
**Amount necessary to reduce book value to residual value.

A simple way to get the depreciation rate for double-declining-balance is to divide the number 2 by the estimated service life (2/5 year service life = 0.40). If the service life had been four years instead of five, what depreciation rates would we use under straight-line and under double-declining-balance? The straight-line rate is 1 divided by the four-year service life, or 1/4 = 0.25. The double-declining-balance rate is 2 divided by the four-year service life, or 2/4 = 0.50.

Notice two unusual features of declining-balance depreciation. First, we multiply the rate by *book value* (cost minus accumulated depreciation), rather than by the depreciable cost (cost minus residual value). Second, in year 5 we are not able to record depreciation expense for the entire $5,184 times 0.40, because doing so would cause the book value to fall below the expected residual value. Instead, depreciation expense in the final year is the amount that reduces book value to the expected residual value (book value beginning of year, $5,184, minus estimated residual value, $5,000, = $184).

 COMMON MISTAKE

Mistakes are commonly made in the first and last year of the calculation. In the first year, students sometimes calculate depreciation incorrectly as cost minus residual value times the depreciation rate. The correct way in the first year is to simply multiply cost times the depreciation rate. In the final year, some students incorrectly calculate depreciation expense in the same manner as in earlier years, multiplying book value by the depreciation rate. However, under the declining-balance method, depreciation expense in the final year is the amount necessary to reduce book value down to residual value.

If the estimated residual value is high enough, the asset will reach its residual value in fewer years than its expected service life. For instance, if the estimated residual value had been $10,000 rather than $5,000, the delivery truck would be fully depreciated under the double-declining-balance method in only three years, even though we used a five-year life in determining the depreciation rate.

ACTIVITY-BASED DEPRECIATION

Straight-line and declining-balance methods measure depreciation based on time. In an activity-based method, we instead allocate an asset's cost based on its *use*. For example, we could measure the service life of a machine in terms of its output

Common Terms
Activity-based depreciation is also called *units of production* or *units of output*.

(units, pounds, barrels). This method also works for vehicles such as our delivery truck, whose use we measure in miles.

We first compute the average *depreciation rate per unit* by dividing the depreciable cost (cost minus residual value) by the number of units expected to be produced. In our illustration, the depreciation rate is $0.35 per mile, calculated as shown in Illustration 7–14.

ILLUSTRATION 7–14

Formula for Depreciation Rate per Unit in Activity-Based Method

$$\text{Depreciation rate per unit} = \frac{\text{Depreciable cost}}{\text{Total units expected to be produced}}$$

$$\text{Depreciation rate} = \frac{\$40,000 - \$5,000}{100,000 \text{ expected miles}} = \$0.35 \text{ per mile}$$

To calculate the depreciation expense for the reporting period, we then multiply the per-unit rate by the number of units of activity each period. Illustration 7–15 shows a depreciation schedule using the activity-based method. The actual miles driven in years 1 to 5 were 30,000, 22,000, 15,000, 20,000, and 13,000. Notice that the activity-based method is very similar to the straight-line method, except that rather than dividing the depreciable cost by the service life in years, we divide it by the service life in expected miles.

ILLUSTRATION 7–15

Activity-Based Depreciation Schedule

LITTLE KING SANDWICHES
Depreciation Schedule—Activity-Based

		Calculation				End-of-Year Amounts	
Year	Miles Driven	×	Depreciation Rate	=	Depreciation Expense	Accumulated Depreciation	Book Value*
							$40,000
1	30,000		$0.35		$10,500	$10,500	29,500
2	22,000		0.35		7,700	18,200	21,800
3	15,000		0.35		5,250	23,450	16,550
4	20,000		0.35		7,000	30,450	9,550
5	13,000		0.35		4,550	35,000	5,000
Total	100,000				$35,000		

*Book value is the cost of the asset ($40,000) minus accumulated depreciation. Book value of $29,500 in year 1 is $40,000 minus $10,500 in accumulated depreciation.

In our illustration, the delivery truck is driven exactly 100,000 miles over the five years. What if we drive the delivery truck *less than* 100,000 miles by the end of the fifth year? Then we will continue to depreciate the truck past five years until we reach 100,000 miles. Similarly, if we drive the delivery truck more than 100,000 miles in less than five years, we will stop depreciating the truck at 100,000 miles before the five years are up. In either case, we need to depreciate the asset until the book value (cost minus accumulated depreciation) declines to the estimated residual value.

Decision Maker's Perspective

Selecting a Depreciation Method

Assume you are the chief financial officer (CFO) responsible for your company's accounting and reporting policies. Which depreciation method would you choose? Illustration 7–16 compares annual depreciation under the three alternatives we discussed.

Year	Straight-Line	Double-Declining-Balance	Activity-Based
1	$ 7,000	$16,000	$10,500
2	7,000	9,600	7,700
3	7,000	5,760	5,250
4	7,000	3,456	7,000
5	7,000	184	4,550
Total	$35,000	$35,000	$35,000

ILLUSTRATION 7–16

Comparison of Depreciation Methods

Comparing methods, we see that all three alternatives result in total depreciation of $35,000 ($40,000 cost minus $5,000 residual value). Straight-line creates an equal amount of depreciation each year. Double-declining-balance creates more depreciation in earlier years and less depreciation in later years. Activity-based depreciation varies depending on the miles driven each year.

Companies are free to choose the depreciation method they believe best reflects the pattern of an asset's use and the revenues it creates. Illustration 7–17 shows the results of a recent survey of depreciation methods used by large public companies.

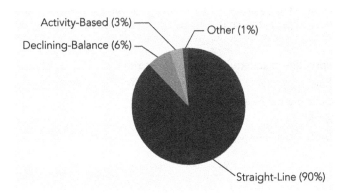

ILLUSTRATION 7–17

Use of Various Depreciation Methods

Source: *Accounting Trends and Techniques* (New York: AICPA, 2009).

Why do so many companies use the straight-line method? Many probably believe they realize benefits from their plant assets approximately evenly over these assets' service lives. Certainly another motivating factor is that straight-line is the easiest method to apply. One more important motivation is straight-line's positive effect on reported income. Straight-line produces a higher net income than accelerated methods in the earlier years of an asset's life. Higher net income can improve bonuses paid to management, increase stock prices, and reduce the likelihood of violating debt agreements with lenders. ●

DEPLETION

Earlier in the chapter we discussed natural resources like oil, natural gas, and timber. We allocate natural resources to expense through a process known as depletion. The process of recording depletion expense for natural resources is nearly identical to the activity-based method of recording depreciation. Specific details for recording depletion are covered in more advanced accounting courses.

TAX DEPRECIATION

Conflicting with the desire to report higher net income is the desire to reduce taxes by *reducing* taxable income. An accelerated method serves this objective by reducing taxable income more in the earlier years of an asset's life than does straight-line.

338   CHAPTER 7   Long-Term Assets

As a result, most companies use the straight-line method for financial reporting and the Internal Revenue Service's prescribed accelerated method (called MACRS[3]) for income tax purposes. Thus, companies record higher net income using straight-line depreciation and lower taxable income using MACRS depreciation. MACRS combines declining-balance methods in earlier years with straight-line in later years to allow for a more advantageous tax depreciation deduction. Congress, not accountants, approved MACRS rules to encourage greater investment in long-term assets by U.S. companies.

 KEY POINT

Straight-line, declining-balance, and activity-based depreciation all are acceptable depreciation methods for financial reporting. Most companies use straight-line depreciation for financial reporting and an accelerated method called MACRS for tax reporting.

Let's Review

University Hero purchases new bread ovens at a cost of $110,000. On the date of purchase, the company estimates the ovens will have a residual value of $20,000. University Hero expects to use the ovens for four years or about 9,000 total hours.

Required:

Prepare a depreciation schedule using each of the following methods:

1. Straight-line.
2. Double-declining-balance.
3. Activity-based.

   Actual oven use per year was as follows:

Year	Hours Used
1	2,200
2	2,600
3	2,300
4	2,100
Total	9,200

Solution:

1. Straight-line:

UNIVERSITY HERO
Depreciation Schedule—Straight-Line

	Calculation					End-of-Year Amounts	
Year	Depreciable Cost	×	Depreciation Rate*	=	Depreciation Expense	Accumulated Depreciation	Book Value**
1	$90,000		0.25		**$22,500**	$22,500	$87,500
2	90,000		0.25		22,500	45,000	65,000
3	90,000		0.25		22,500	67,500	42,500
4	90,000		0.25		22,500	90,000	20,000
Total					**$90,000**		

*1 ÷ 4 years = 0.25 per year
**$110,000 cost minus accumulated depreciation.

[3]Modified Accelerated Cost Recovery System.

2. Double-declining-balance:

UNIVERSITY HERO
Depreciation Schedule—Double-Declining-Balance

	Calculation				End-of-Year Amounts	
Year	Beginning Book Value	×	Depreciation Rate*	=	Depreciation Expense	Accumulated Depreciation	Book Value**
1	$110,000		0.50		**$55,000**	$55,000	$55,000
2	55,000		0.50		**27,500**	82,500	27,500
3	27,500		0.50		**7,500***	90,000	**20,000**
4					**0**	90,000	**20,000**
Total					**$90,000**		

*2 ÷ 4 years = 0.50 per year
**$110,000 cost minus accumulated depreciation.
***Amount needed to reduce book value to residual value.

3. Activity-based:

UNIVERSITY HERO
Depreciation Schedule—Activity-Based

	Calculation				End-of-Year Amounts	
Year	Hours Used	×	Depreciation Rate*	=	Depreciation Expense	Accumulated Depreciation	Book Value**
1	2,200		$10		**$22,000**	$22,000	$88,000
2	2,600		10		**26,000**	48,000	62,000
3	2,300		10		**23,000**	71,000	39,000
4	2,100				**19,000***	90,000	**20,000**
Total	9,200				**$90,000**		

*$90,000 ÷ 9,000 hours = $10/hour
**$110,000 cost minus accumulated depreciation.
***Amount needed to reduce book value to residual value.

Suggested Homework:
BE7-7, BE7-8;
E7-10, E7-11;
P7-5A&B, P7-7A&B

Amortization of Intangible Assets

Allocating the cost of property, plant, and equipment to expense is called depreciation. Allocating the cost of natural resources to expense is called depletion. Similarly, allocating the cost of *intangible* assets to expense is called amortization.

INTANGIBLE ASSETS SUBJECT TO AMORTIZATION

Most intangible assets have a finite useful life that we can estimate. For these, we allocate the asset's cost less any estimated residual value to periods in which we expect the intangible asset to contribute to the company's revenue-generating activities. This requires that we estimate the intangible asset's service life and its residual value.

The service life of an intangible asset usually is limited by legal, regulatory, or contractual provisions. For example, the legal life of a patent is 20 years. However, the estimated useful life of a patent often is less than 20 years if the benefits are not expected to continue for the patent's entire legal life. The patent for **Apple**'s iPad, for example, is amortized over fewer than 20 years, since new technology will cause the iPad to become outdated in a much shorter period.

The expected residual value of most intangible assets is zero. This might not be the case, though, if at the end of its useful life to the reporting entity the asset will

■ **LO5**
Calculate amortization of intangible assets.

benefit another entity. For example, if **Microsoft** has a commitment from another company to purchase one of its patents at the end of the patent's useful life at a determinable price, we use that price as the patent's residual value.

The method of amortization should reflect the pattern of use of the asset in generating benefits. Most companies use *straight-line amortization* for intangibles. Also, many companies credit amortization to the intangible asset account itself rather than to accumulated amortization. However, using a contra account such as Accumulated Amortization also is acceptable.

Let's look at an example: In early January, Little King Sandwiches acquires franchise rights from University Hero for $800,000. The franchise agreement is for a period of 20 years. In addition, Little King purchases a patent for a meat-slicing process for $72,000. The original legal life of the patent was 20 years, and there are 12 years remaining. However, due to expected technological obsolescence, the company estimates that the useful life of the patent is only 8 more years. Little King uses straight-line amortization for all intangible assets. The company's fiscal year-end is December 31. Little King records the amortization expense for the franchise and the patent as follows.

		Debit	Credit
A = L + SE			
−40,000 Exp↑			
−40,000	Amortization Expense	40,000	
	Franchises		40,000
	(Amortize franchise)		
	($40,000 = $800,000 ÷ 20 years)		
A = L + SE			
−9,000 Exp↑	Amortization Expense	9,000	
−9,000	Patents		9,000
	(Amortize patent)		
	($9,000 = $72,000 ÷ 8 years)		

INTANGIBLE ASSETS NOT SUBJECT TO AMORTIZATION

We don't depreciate land because it has an unlimited life. Similarly, we do *not* amortize intangible assets with indefinite useful lives. An asset's useful life is indefinite if there is no foreseeable limit on the period of time over which we expect it to contribute to the cash flows of the entity. For example, suppose Little King acquired a trademark for a line of sandwiches. Registered trademarks have a legal life of 10 years, but the trademark registration is renewable for an indefinite number of 10-year periods. We consider the life of Little King's trademark to be indefinite, so we don't amortize it.

Goodwill is the most common intangible asset with an indefinite useful life. Recall that we measure goodwill as the difference between the purchase price of a company and the fair value of all its identifiable net assets (tangible and intangible assets minus the fair value of liabilities assumed). Does this mean that goodwill and other intangible assets with indefinite useful lives will remain on a company's balance sheet at their original cost forever? Probably not. Management must review long-term assets for a potential write-down when events or changes in circumstances indicate the amount recorded for an asset in the accounting records might not be recoverable. All long-term assets are subject to these "impairment" rules, which we discuss in more detail in the appendix to this chapter.

KEY POINT

Amortization is a process, similar to depreciation, in which we allocate the cost of intangible assets over their estimated service lives. Intangible assets with an indefinite useful life (goodwill and most trademarks) are *not* amortized.

ASSET DISPOSITION: SALE, RETIREMENT, OR EXCHANGE

■ **LO6**
Account for the disposal of long-term assets.

Few things last forever. In this section we discuss what to do when we no longer use a long-term asset. A *sale* is a possibility. When a long-term asset is no longer useful but cannot be sold, we have a *retirement*. For example, Little King Sandwiches might physically remove a baking oven that no longer works and also remove it from the accounting records through a retirement entry. An *exchange* occurs when two companies trade assets. In a trade, we often use cash to make up for any difference in fair value between the assets.

Selling a long-term asset can result in either a gain or a loss. We record a *gain* if we sell the asset for *more* than its book value. Similarly, we record a *loss* if we sell the asset for *less* than its book value. A gain is a credit balance account like other revenue accounts; a loss is a debit balance account like other expense accounts. Remember, book value is the cost of the asset minus accumulated depreciation. In order to have the correct book value, it's important to record depreciation up to the date of the sale.

COMMON MISTAKE

Some students forget to update depreciation prior to recording the disposal of the asset. Depreciation must be recorded up to the date of the sale, retirement, or exchange. Otherwise, the book value will be overstated, and the resulting gain or loss on disposal will be in error as well.

To illustrate the recording of disposals, let's return to our delivery truck example for Little King Sandwiches. Assume Little King uses straight-line depreciation and records the delivery truck in the Equipment account. The specific details are summarized again in Illustration 7–18.

Original cost of the truck	$40,000
Estimated residual value	$5,000
Estimated service life	5 years

ILLUSTRATION 7–18

Data for Little King Sandwiches's Delivery Truck Purchase, to Illustrate Long-Term Asset Disposals

Sale of Long-Term Assets

If we assume that Little King sells the delivery truck at the end of year 3 for $22,000, we can calculate the gain as $3,000. Note that both the delivery truck and the related accumulated depreciation are removed. Illustration 7–19 shows the calculation.

Sale amount		$22,000
Less:		
Original cost of the truck	$40,000	
Less: Accumulated depreciation (3 years × $7,000/year)	(21,000)	
Book value at the end of year 3		19,000
Gain on sale		$ 3,000

ILLUSTRATION 7–19

Gain on Sale

We record the gain on sale as:

	Debit	Credit	A	=	L	+	SE
Cash	22,000		+22,000				
Accumulated Depreciation	21,000		+21,000				
Equipment		40,000	−40,000				
Gain		3,000					+3,000 Rev↑
(Sell equipment for a gain)							

COMMON MISTAKE

Be careful not to combine the delivery truck ($40,000) and accumulated depreciation ($21,000) and credit the $19,000 difference to the Equipment account. Instead, remove the delivery truck and accumulated depreciation from the accounting records separately. Otherwise, the Equipment and the Accumulated Depreciation accounts will incorrectly have a remaining balance after the asset has been sold.

If we assume that Little King sells the delivery truck at the end of year 3 for only $17,000 instead of $22,000, we have a $2,000 loss as calculated in Illustration 7–20.

ILLUSTRATION 7–20

Loss on Sale

Sale amount		$17,000
Less:		
Original cost of the truck	$40,000	
Less: Accumulated depreciation (3 years × $7,000/year)	(21,000)	
Book value at the end of year 3		19,000
Loss on sale		$ (2,000)

We record the loss on sale as:

A = L + SE		Debit	Credit
+17,000	Cash	17,000	
+21,000	Accumulated Depreciation	21,000	
−2,000 Exp↑	Loss	2,000	
−40,000	Equipment		40,000
	(Sell equipment for a loss)		

Decision Point

Question	Accounting information	Analysis
How different is the company's recorded book value from its actual fair value?	Gain or loss on sale	A gain on sale indicates the actual fair value is more than the recorded book value. A loss on sale indicates the opposite.

Retirement of Long-Term Assets

Now assume that Little King retires the delivery truck instead of selling it. If, for example, the truck is totaled in an accident at the end of year 3, we have a $19,000 loss on retirement as calculated in Illustration 7–21.

ILLUSTRATION 7–21

Loss on Retirement

Sale amount		$ 0
Less:		
Original cost of the truck	$40,000	
Less: Accumulated depreciation (3 years × $7,000/year)	(21,000)	
Book value at the end of year 3		19,000
Loss on retirement		$(19,000)

We record the loss on retirement as:

	Debit	Credit	A	=	L	+	SE
Accumulated Depreciation	21,000		+21,000				
Loss	19,000						−19,000 Exp↑
Equipment		40,000	−40,000				
(*Retire equipment for a loss*)							

The above entry assumes Little King did not have collision insurance coverage. If Little King had insured the truck and collected $17,000 in insurance money for the totaled vehicle, the entry would be identical to the sale for $17,000 in Illustration 7–20.

Exchange of Long-Term Assets

Now assume that Little King exchanges the delivery truck at the end of year 3 for a new truck valued at $45,000. The dealership gives Little King a trade-in allowance of $23,000 on the exchange, with the remaining $22,000 paid in cash. We have a $4,000 gain, as calculated in Illustration 7–22.

Trade-in allowance		$23,000	**ILLUSTRATION 7–22**
Less:			Gain on Exchange
Original cost of the truck	$40,000		
Less: Accumulated depreciation (3 years × $7,000/year)	(21,000)		
Book value at the end of year 3		19,000	
Gain on exchange		$ 4,000	

We record the gain on exchange as:

	Debit	Credit	A	=	L	+	SE
Equipment (new)	45,000		+45,000				
Accumulated Depreciation	21,000		+21,000				
Cash		22,000	−22,000				
Equipment (old)		40,000	−40,000				
Gain		4,000					+4,000 Rev↑
(*Exchange equipment for a gain*)							

 KEY POINT

If we dispose of an asset for *more* than book value, we record a gain. If we dispose of an asset for *less* than book value, we record a loss.

ASSET ANALYSIS
Walmart vs. Abercrombie

We have discussed the purchase, depreciation, and disposal of long-term assets. In this final section, we see how to use actual financial statement information to analyze the profitability of a company's assets. Illustration 7–23 (next page) provides selected financial data reported by **Walmart** and **Abercrombie** for use in our analysis.

ANALYSIS

■ **LO7**
Describe the relation among return on assets, profit margin, and asset turnover.

ILLUSTRATION 7–23	($ in millions)		
Selected Financial Data for Walmart and Abercrombie	**Walmart**	**2009**	**2008**
	Net sales	$405,607	$378,799
	Net income	13,400	12,731
	Total assets	163,429	163,514

	Abercrombie	**2009**	**2008**
	Net sales	$3,540	$3,750
	Net income	272	476
	Total assets	2,848	2,568

RETURN ON ASSETS

Walmart had net income of $13,400 million and Abercrombie had net income of $272 million in 2009. Since Walmart's net income is so much larger, does that mean Walmart is more profitable? Not necessarily. Walmart is also a much larger company, as indicated by total assets. Walmart's total assets were $163,429 million compared to $2,848 million for Abercrombie. A more comparable measure of profitability than income is return on assets, which equals net income divided by *average* total assets. Dividing net income by average total assets adjusts net income for differences in company size.

Common Terms Return on assets is often just called *ROA*.

 COMMON MISTAKE

Students sometimes divide by ending total assets rather than by *average* total assets. We measure net income over time, whereas we measure total assets at a *point* in time. Therefore, whenever we divide a number in the income statement by a number in the balance sheet, it's more meaningful to use an *average* balance sheet number.

The return on assets ratio is calculated for Walmart and Abercrombie in Illustration 7–24.

ILLUSTRATION 7–24	($ in millions)	Net Income	÷	Average Total Assets	=	Return on Assets
Return on Assets for Walmart and Abercrombie	**Walmart**	$13,400	÷	($163,429 + $163,514)/2	=	8.2%
	Abercrombie	$ 272	÷	($2,848 + $2,568)/2	=	10.0%

Although Walmart has a much higher net income, Abercrombie actually is more profitable, with a higher return on assets. Return on assets indicates the amount of net income generated for each dollar invested in assets.

Decision Point

Question	Accounting information	Analysis
How effectively is the company using its assets?	Return on assets ratio	A higher return on assets generally indicates a more effective use of assets.

PROFIT MARGIN AND ASSET TURNOVER

We can explore profitability further by separating return on assets into two components: profit margin and asset turnover, as shown in Illustration 7–25.

$$\text{Return on assets} = \text{Profit margin} \times \text{Asset turnover}$$

$$\frac{\text{Net income}}{\text{Average total assets}} = \frac{\text{Net income}}{\text{Net sales}} \times \frac{\text{Net sales}}{\text{Average total assets}}$$

ILLUSTRATION 7–25

Components of Return on Assets

Profit margin is net income divided by net sales. This ratio indicates the earnings per dollar of sales. Asset turnover is net sales divided by average total assets. This ratio measures the sales per dollar of assets invested.

Strategies for Increasing Return on Assets

Companies have two primary strategies for increasing their return on assets. Some companies, like Walmart, pursue a high sales volume by charging *lower prices*. Walmart is profitable as long as it can maintain or increase its asset turnover. Other companies, like Abercrombie, pursue a higher profit margin through *product differentiation* and *premium pricing*. Abercrombie is profitable as long as it can maintain or increase its high profit margins. In Illustrations 7–26 and 7–27 we calculate profit margin and asset turnover, respectively, for both companies. We then can see if our expectations regarding Walmart and Abercrombie are supported.

Decision Maker's Perspective

($ in millions)	Net Income	÷	Net Sales	=	Profit Margin
Walmart	$13,400	÷	$405,607	=	3.3%
Abercrombie	$272	÷	$ 3,540	=	7.7%

ILLUSTRATION 7–26

Profit Margin for Walmart and Abercrombie

($ in millions)	Net Sales	÷	Average Total Assets	=	Asset Turnover
Walmart	$405,607	÷	($163,429 + $163,514)/2	=	2.5 times
Abercrombie	$3,540	÷	($2,848 + $2,568)/2	=	1.3 times

ILLUSTRATION 7–27

Asset Turnover for Walmart and Abercrombie

Illustration 7–26 indicates that Abercrombie's profit margin is more than twice that for Walmart. Illustration 7–27, however, shows that Walmart has the higher asset turnover. These accounting ratios support our expectations regarding the different business strategies Walmart and Abercrombie are pursuing. To maximize profitability, a company ideally strives to increase *both* net income per dollar of sales (profit margin) and sales per dollar invested in assets (asset turnover). ●

KEY POINT

Return on assets indicates the amount of net income generated for each dollar invested in assets. Return on assets can be separated to examine two important business strategies: profit margin and asset turnover.

Decision Point

Question	Accounting information	Analysis
How much profit is being generated from sales?	Profit margin	A higher profit margin indicates a company generates a higher net income per dollar of sales.
Is the company effectively generating sales from its assets?	Asset turnover ratio	A higher asset turnover indicates a company generates a higher sales volume per dollar of assets invested.

APPENDIX

ASSET IMPAIRMENT

■ **LO8**
Identify impairment situations and describe the two-step impairment process.

Management must review long-term assets for impairment when events or changes in circumstances indicate that book value might not be recoverable. Impairment occurs when the future cash flows (future benefits) generated for a long-term asset fall below its book value (cost minus accumulated depreciation). The relationship among future cash flows, fair value, and book value can be confusing. Illustration 7–28 displays the normal relationship and the impaired relationship among these three values.

ILLUSTRATION 7–28

Relationship among Future Cash Flows, Fair Value, and Book Value

	Normal Relationship			Impaired Relationship
Largest:	Future cash flows		*Largest:*	Book value
Middle:	Fair value		*Middle:*	Future cash flows
Smallest:	Book value		*Smallest:*	Fair value

Note that future cash flows always exceed fair value. This is true since the present value of future cash flows are used in determining fair value and the present value of an amount is always less than the total of its future cash flows. If estimated future cash flows from the asset are below the book value (as in the impaired relationship column), we record an impairment loss. The *impairment loss* is equal to the difference between the asset's book value and its fair value. Thus, reporting for impairment losses is a two-step process summarized in Illustration 7–29.

ILLUSTRATION 7–29

Two-Step Impairment Process

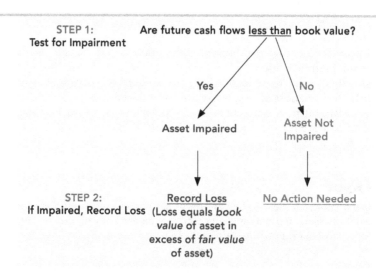

STEP 1:
Test for Impairment

Are future cash flows <u>less than</u> book value?

Yes — Asset Impaired

No — Asset Not Impaired

STEP 2:
If Impaired, Record Loss

Record Loss (Loss equals *book value* of asset in excess of *fair value* of asset)

No Action Needed

To illustrate asset impairment, suppose Little King pays $50,000 for the trademark rights to a line of specialty sandwiches. This intangible asset is not amortized because management assumes the trademark has an indefinite useful life. After several years, sales for this line of specialty sandwiches are disappointing, and management estimates the total future cash flows from sales will be only $20,000. Due to the disappointing sales, the estimated fair value of the trademark is now about $12,000. Here's how Little King determines and records the impairment loss.

STEP 1: TEST FOR IMPAIRMENT

The long-term asset is impaired since future cash flows ($20,000) are less than book value ($50,000).

STEP 2: IF IMPAIRED, RECORD THE LOSS

The loss is $38,000, calculated as the amount by which book value ($50,000) exceeds fair value ($12,000). We record the impairment loss as follows:

	Debit	Credit	A	=	L	+	SE
Loss	38,000		−38,000				
Trademarks		38,000					−38,000 Exp
(Record impairment of trademark)							

COMMON MISTAKE

Some students forget step 1 when considering impairment. Record an impairment loss only when book value exceeds *both* future cash flows and fair value.

What is the overall financial statement effect of an impairment loss? The impairment entry reduces net income in the income statement by $38,000 and reduces total assets in the balance sheet by $38,000. The new balance in the Trademarks account is $12,000, which equals its current fair value. We can write down the trademark further through impairment in future years, but we cannot write it back up under current accounting rules.

INTERNATIONAL FINANCIAL REPORTING STANDARDS (IFRS)

International accounting standards also record impairments based on a two-step impairment process. The details are covered in more advanced accounting courses. However, one important difference is this: Impairments under U.S. GAAP are permanent—the asset cannot be written back up in future periods. In contrast, impairments under IFRS rules can be reversed. Thus, under IFRS a company can record an impairment loss in one period and then write the asset back up with a corresponding gain in a later period.

For more discussion, see Appendix E.

KEY POINT

Impairment is a two-step process: **Step 1: Test for impairment:** The long-term asset is impaired if future cash flows are less than book value. **Step 2: If impaired, record impairment loss:** The impairment loss is the amount by which book value exceeds fair value.

Decision Maker's Perspective   Taking a Big Bath

In practice, determining impairment losses can be subjective. Accounting research suggests that managers sometimes use the recording of impairment losses to their advantage. Some companies time their impairment losses with other one-time losses such as losses on sales of assets, inventory write-downs, and restructuring charges, to record a big loss in one year. We refer to this practice as taking a big bath—recording all losses in one year to make a bad year even worse. Management thus cleans its slate and is able to report higher earnings in future years. Future earnings are higher because the write-down of assets in this year results in lower depreciation and amortization charges in the future. When analyzing financial statements, investors should be alert to this kind of manipulation. ●

KEY POINTS BY LEARNING OBJECTIVE

LO1 Identify and record the major types of property, plant, and equipment.

Tangible assets include land, land improvements, buildings, equipment, and natural resources.

LO2 Identify and record the major types of intangible assets.

We record (capitalize) purchased intangible assets at their purchase price plus all costs necessary to get the asset ready for use. We expense internally generated intangible assets, such as R&D and advertising costs, as we incur those costs.

Intangible assets include patents, copyrights, trademarks, franchises, and goodwill.

LO3 Discuss the accounting treatment of expenditures after acquisition.

Capital items (recorded as assets) benefit *future* periods. Expenses benefit only the *current* period.

LO4 Calculate depreciation of property, plant, and equipment.

Depreciation refers to the allocation of an asset's original cost to an expense during the periods benefited. Depreciation does *not* refer to the change in value or selling price.

Straight-line, declining-balance, and activity-based depreciation all are acceptable depreciation methods for financial reporting. Most companies use straight-line depreciation for financial reporting and an accelerated method called MACRS for tax reporting.

LO5 Calculate amortization of intangible assets.

Amortization is a process, similar to depreciation, in which we allocate the cost of intangible assets over their estimated service life. Intangible assets with an indefinite useful life (goodwill and most trademarks) are *not* amortized.

LO6 Account for the disposal of long-term assets.

If we dispose of an asset for more than book value, we record a gain. If we dispose of an asset for less than book value, we record a loss.

Analysis

LO7 Describe the relationship among return on assets, profit margin, and asset turnover.

Return on assets indicates the amount of net income generated for each dollar invested in assets. Return on assets can be separated to examine two important business strategies: profit margin and asset turnover.

Appendix

LO8 Identify impairment situations and describe the two-step impairment process.

Impairment is a two-step process. **Step 1: Test for impairment:** The long-term asset is impaired if future cash flows are less than book value. **Step 2: If impaired, record loss:** The impairment loss is the amount book value exceeds fair value.

GLOSSARY

Accelerated depreciation method: Allocates a higher depreciation in the earlier years of the asset's life and lower depreciation in later years. **p. 334**

Accumulated Depreciation: A contra asset account representing the total depreciation taken to date. **p. 330**

Activity-based method: Allocates an asset's cost based on its use. **p. 335**

Addition: Occurs when a new major component is added to an existing asset. **p. 328**

Amortization: Allocation of the cost of an intangible asset over its service life. **p. 339**

Asset turnover: Net sales divided by average total assets, which measures the sales per dollar of assets invested. **p. 345**

Basket purchase: Purchase of more than one asset at the same time for one purchase price. **p. 323**

Big bath: Recording all losses in one year to make a bad year even worse. **p. 348**

Book value: Equal to the original cost of the asset minus the current balance in Accumulated Depreciation. **p. 331**

Capitalize: Record an expenditure as an asset. **p. 321**

Capitalized interest: Interest costs recorded as assets rather than interest expense. **p. 322**

Copyright: An exclusive right of protection given to the creator of a published work such as a song, film, painting, photograph, book, or computer software. **p. 326**

Declining-balance method: An accelerated depreciation method that records more depreciation in earlier years and less depreciation in later years. **p. 334**

Depletion: Allocation of the cost of a natural resource over its service life. **p. 337**

Depreciation: Allocation of the cost of a tangible asset over its service life. **p. 330**

Franchise: Local outlets that pay for the exclusive right to use the franchisor company's name and to sell its products within a specified geographical area. **p. 326**

Goodwill: The value of a company as a whole, over and above the value of its identifiable net assets. Goodwill equals the purchase price less the fair value of the net assets acquired. **p. 327**

Impairment: Occurs when the future cash flows (future benefits) generated for a long-term asset fall below its book value (cost minus accumulated depreciation). **p. 346**

Improvement: The cost of replacing a major component of an asset. **p. 328**

Intangible assets: Long-term assets that lack physical substance, and whose existence is often based on a legal contract. **p. 324**

Land improvements: Improvements to land such as paving, lighting, and landscaping that, unlike land itself, are subject to depreciation. **p. 322**

Material: Large enough to influence a decision. **p. 329**

Natural resources: Assets like oil, natural gas, and timber that we can physically use up or deplete. **p. 324**

Patent: An exclusive right to manufacture a product or to use a process. **p. 325**

Profit margin: Net income divided by net sales; indicates the earnings per dollar of sales. **p. 345**

Repairs and maintenance: Expenses that maintain a given level of benefits in the period incurred. **p. 328**

Residual value: The amount the company expects to receive from selling the asset at the end of its service life; also referred to as *salvage value*. **p. 331**

Return on assets: Net income divided by average total assets; measures the amount of net income generated for each dollar invested in assets. **p. 344**

Service life: How long the company expects to receive benefits from the asset before disposing of it; also referred to as *useful life*. **p. 331**

Straight-line method: Allocates an equal amount of depreciation to each year of the asset's service life. **p. 332**

Trademark: A word, slogan, or symbol that distinctively identifies a company, product, or service. **p. 326**

SELF-STUDY QUESTIONS

1. We normally record a long-term asset at the: ■ LO1
   a. Cost of the asset only.
   b. Cost of the asset plus all costs necessary to get the asset ready for use.
   c. Appraised value.
   d. Cost of the asset, but subsequently adjust it up or down to appraised value.

2. Sandwich Express incurred the following costs related to its purchase of a bread machine. ■ LO1

Cost of the equipment	$20,000
Sales tax (8%)	1,600
Shipping	2,200
Installation	1,400
Total costs	$25,200

350   CHAPTER 7   Long-Term Assets

At what amount should Sandwich Express record the bread machine?
a. $20,000.
b. $21,600.
c. $23,800.
d. $25,200.

■ LO2
3. Research and development costs generated internally:
a. Are recorded as research and development assets.
b. Are capitalized and then amortized.
c. Should be included in the cost of the patent they relate to.
d. Should be expensed.

■ LO3
4. Which of the following expenditures should be recorded as an expense?
a. Repairs and maintenance that maintain current benefits.
b. Adding a major new component to an existing asset.
c. Replacing a major component of an existing asset.
d. Successful legal defense of an intangible asset.

■ LO4
5. Which of the following will maximize net income by minimizing depreciation expense in the first year of the asset's life?
a. Short service life, high residual value, and straight-line depreciation.
b. Long service life, high residual value, and straight-line depreciation.
c. Short service life, low residual value, and double-declining-balance depreciation.
d. Long service life, high residual value, and double-declining-balance depreciation.

■ LO4
6. The book value of an asset is equal to the:
a. Replacement cost.
b. Asset's cost less accumulated depreciation.
c. Asset's fair value less its historical cost.
d. Historical cost plus accumulated depreciation.

■ LO4
7. The balance in the Accumulated Depreciation account represents:
a. The amount charged to expense in the current period.
b. A contra expense account.
c. A cash fund to be used to replace plant assets.
d. The amount charged to depreciation expense since the acquisition of the plant asset.

■ LO5
8. Which of the following statements is *true* regarding the amortization of intangible assets?
a. Intangible assets with a limited useful life are not amortized.
b. The service life of an intangible asset is always equal to its legal life.
c. The expected residual value of most intangible assets is zero.
d. In recording amortization, Accumulated Amortization is always credited.

■ LO6
9. Equipment originally costing $95,000 has accumulated depreciation of $30,000. If it sells the equipment for $55,000, the company should record:
a. No gain or loss.
b. A gain of $10,000.
c. A loss of $10,000.
d. A loss of $40,000.

■ LO7

10. The return on assets is equal to the:
a. Profit margin plus asset turnover.
b. Profit margin minus asset turnover.
c. Profit margin times asset turnover.
d. Profit margin divided by asset turnover.

Check out
www.mhhe.com/succeed
for more multiple-choice
questions.

Note: For answers, see the last page of the chapter.

REVIEW QUESTIONS

1. **WorldCom** committed the largest fraud in U.S. history. What was the primary method WorldCom's management used to carry out the fraud?　　■ LO1

2. What are the two major categories of long-term assets? How do these two categories differ?　　■ LO1

3. Explain how we initially record a long-term asset.　　■ LO1

4. If University Hero initially records an expense incorrectly as an asset, how does this mistake affect the income statement and the balance sheet?　　■ LO1

5. Little King acquires land and an old building across the street from Northwestern State University. Little King intends to remove the old building and build a new sandwich shop on the land. What costs might the firm incur to make the land ready for its intended use?　　■ LO1

6. Why don't we depreciate land? What are land improvements? Why do we record land and land improvements separately?　　■ LO1

7. Equipment includes machinery used in manufacturing, computers and other office equipment, vehicles, furniture, and fixtures. What costs might we incur to get equipment ready for use?　　■ LO1

8. Where in the balance sheet do we report natural resources? Provide at least three examples of natural resource assets.　　■ LO1

9. Explain how the accounting treatment differs between purchased and internally developed intangible assets.　　■ LO2

10. What are the differences among a patent, a copyright, and a trademark?　　■ LO2

11. What is goodwill and how do we measure it? Can we sell goodwill separately from the business?　　■ LO2

12. How do we decide whether to capitalize (record as an asset) or expense a particular cost?　　■ LO3

13. Explain the usual accounting treatment for repairs and maintenance, additions, and improvements.　　■ LO3

14. Are litigation costs to defend an intangible asset capitalized or expensed? Explain your answer.　　■ LO3

15. How is the dictionary definition different from the accounting definition of depreciation?　　■ LO4

16. What factors must we estimate in allocating the cost of a long-term asset over its service life?　　■ LO4

17. What is the service life of an asset? How do we determine service life under the straight-line and the activity-based depreciation methods?　　■ LO4

18. What is residual value? How do we use residual value in calculating depreciation under the straight-line method?　　■ LO4

19. Contrast the effects of the straight-line, declining-balance, and activity-based methods on annual depreciation expense.　　■ LO4

20. Assume that Little King Sandwiches uses straight-line depreciation and University Hero uses double-declining-balance depreciation. Explain the difficulties in comparing the income statements and balance sheets of the two companies.　　■ LO4

21. Assume Little King Sandwiches depreciates a building over 40 years and University Hero depreciates a similar building over 20 years, and both companies use the straight-line depreciation method. Explain the difficulties in comparing the income statements and balance sheets of the two companies.　　■ LO4

352   CHAPTER 7   Long-Term Assets

■ LO4   22. Which depreciation method is most common for financial reporting? Which depreciation method is most common for tax reporting? Why do companies choose these methods?

■ LO5   23. Justin Time is confident that firms amortize all intangible assets. Is he right? If amortized, are intangible assets always amortized over their legal life? Explain.

■ LO6   24. What is book value? How do we compute the gain or loss on the sale of long-term assets?

■ LO7   25. Describe return on assets, profit margin, and asset turnover.

■ LO7   26. Provide an example of a company like **Abercrombie** with a high profit margin. Provide an example of a company like **Walmart** with high asset turnover.

■ LO8   27. What is an asset impairment? Describe the two-step process for recording impairments. How does recording an impairment loss affect the income statement and the balance sheet?

■ LO8   28. How do companies take a *big bath*? Explain the effect of a big bath on the current year's and future years' net income.

BRIEF EXERCISES

Determine the initial cost of land (**LO1**)

BE7–1 Fresh Veggies, Inc. (FVI), purchases land and a warehouse for $500,000. In addition to the purchase price, FVI makes the following expenditures related to the acquisition: broker's commission, $30,000; title insurance, $2,000; and miscellaneous closing costs, $5,000. The warehouse is immediately demolished at a cost of $30,000 in anticipation of building a new warehouse. Determine the amount FVI should record as the cost of the land.

Determine the initial cost of equipment (**LO1**)

BE7–2 Whole Grain Bakery purchases an industrial bread machine for $25,000. In addition to the purchase price, the company makes the following expenditures: freight, $1,500; installation, $3,000; testing, $1,000; and property tax on the machine for the first year, $500. What is the initial cost of the bread machine?

Calculate goodwill (**LO2**)

BE7–3 Kosher Pickle Company acquires all the outstanding stock of Midwest Produce for $14 million. The fair value of Midwest's assets is $11.3 million. The fair value of Midwest's liabilities is $1.5 million. Calculate the amount paid for goodwill.

Compute research and development expense (**LO2**)

BE7–4 West Coast Growers incurs the following costs during the year related to the creation of a new disease-resistant tomato plant.

Salaries for R&D	$440,000
Depreciation on R&D facilities and equipment	135,000
Utilities incurred for the R&D facilities	6,000
Patent filing and related legal costs	22,000
Payment to another company for part of the development work	110,000

What amount should West Coast Growers report as research and development (R&D) expense in its income statement?

Account for expenditures after acquisition (**LO3**)

BE7–5 Hanoi Foods incurs the following expenditures during the current fiscal year: (1) annual maintenance on its machinery, $8,900; (2) remodeling of offices, $42,000; (3) improvement of the shipping and receiving area, resulting in an increase in productivity, $25,000; and (4) addition of a security system to the manufacturing facility, $35,000. How should Hanoi account for each of these expenditures?

BE7–6 Early in the fiscal year, The Beanery purchases a delivery vehicle for $40,000. At the end of the year, the machine has a fair value of $33,000. The company controller records depreciation expense of $7,000 for the year, the decline in the vehicle's value. Explain why the controller's approach to recording depreciation expense is not correct.

Explain depreciation (LO4)

BE7–7 El Tapitio purchased restaurant furniture on September 1, 2012, for $35,000. Residual value at the end of an estimated 10-year service life is expected to be $5,000. Calculate depreciation expense for 2012 and 2013, using the straight-line method, and assuming a December 31 year-end.

Calculate partial-year depreciation (LO4)

BE7–8 Hawaiian Specialty Foods purchased equipment for $20,000. Residual value at the end of an estimated four-year service life is expected to be $2,000. The machine operated for 2,200 hours in the first year, and the company expects the machine to operate for a total of 10,000 hours. Calculate depreciation expense for the first year using each of the following depreciation methods: (1) straight-line, (2) double-declining-balance, and (3) activity-based.

Calculate depreciation (LO4)

BE7–9 In early January, Burger Mania acquired 100% of the common stock of the Crispy Taco restaurant chain. The purchase price allocation included the following items: $4 million, patent; $3 million, trademark considered to have an indefinite useful life; and $5 million, goodwill. Burger Mania's policy is to amortize intangible assets with finite useful lives using the straight-line method, no residual value, and a five-year service life. What is the total amount of amortization expense that would appear in Burger Mania's income statement for the first year ended December 31 related to these items?

Calculate amortization expense (LO5)

BE7–10 Granite Stone Creamery sold ice cream equipment for $12,000. Granite Stone originally purchased the equipment for $80,000, and depreciation through the date of sale totaled $66,000. What was the gain or loss on the sale of the equipment?

Account for the sale of long-term assets (LO6)

BE7–11 China Inn and Midwest Chicken exchanged assets. China Inn received a delivery truck and gave equipment. The fair value and book value of the equipment were $17,000 and $10,000 (original cost of $35,000 less accumulated depreciation of $25,000), respectively. To equalize market values of the exchanged assets, China Inn paid $8,000 in cash to Midwest Chicken. At what amount did China Inn record the delivery truck? How much gain or loss did China Inn recognize on the exchange?

Account for the exchange of long-term assets (LO6)

Flip Side of BE7–12

BE7–12 China Inn and Midwest Chicken exchanged assets. Midwest Chicken received equipment and gave a delivery truck. The fair value and book value of the delivery truck given were $25,000 and $28,000 (original cost of $33,000 less accumulated depreciation of $5,000), respectively. To equalize market values of the exchanged assets, Midwest Chicken received $8,000 in cash from China Inn. At what amount did Midwest Chicken record the equipment? How much gain or loss did Midwest Chicken recognize on the exchange?

Account for the exchange of long-term assets (LO6)

Flip Side of BE7–11

BE7–13 The balance sheet of Cedar Crest Resort reports total assets of $740,000 and $940,000 at the beginning and end of the year, respectively. The return on assets for the year is 20%. Calculate Cedar Crest's net income for the year.

Use the return on assets ratio (LO7)

BE7–14 Vegetarian Delights has been experiencing declining market conditions for its specialty foods division. Management decided to test the operational assets of the division for possible impairment. The test revealed the following: book value of division's assets, $28.5 million; fair value of division's assets, $20 million; sum of estimated future cash flows generated from the division's assets, $30 million. What amount of impairment loss, if any, should Vegetarian Delights record?

Determine the impairment loss (LO8)

BE7–15 Refer to the situation described in BE 7–14. Assume the sum of estimated future cash flows is $26 million instead of $30 million. What amount of impairment loss should Vegetarian Delights record?

Determine the impairment loss (LO8)

EXERCISES

Record purchase of
land **(LO1)**

E7–1 McCoy's Fish House purchases a tract of land and an existing building for
$900,000. The company plans to remove the old building and construct a new
restaurant on the site. In addition to the purchase price, McCoy pays closing costs,
including title insurance of $2,000. The company also pays $12,000 in property taxes,
which includes $8,000 of back taxes (unpaid taxes from previous years) paid by
McCoy on behalf of the seller and $4,000 due for the current fiscal year after the
purchase date. Shortly after closing, the company pays a contractor $45,000 to tear
down the old building and remove it from the site. McCoy is able to sell salvaged
materials from the old building for $3,000 and pays an additional $10,000 to level
the land.

Required:
Determine the amount McCoy's Fish House should record as the cost of the land.

Record purchase of
equipment **(LO1)**

E7–2 Orion Flour Mills purchased a new machine and made the following
expenditures:

Purchase price	$65,000
Sales tax	5,500
Shipment of machine	900
Insurance on the machine for the first year	600
Installation of machine	1,800

The machine, including sales tax, was purchased on account, with payment due in
30 days. The other expenditures listed above were paid in cash.

Required:
Record the above expenditures for the new machine.

Allocate costs in a basket
purchase **(LO1)**

E7–3 Red Rock Bakery purchases land, building, and equipment for a single purchase
price of $400,000. However, the estimated fair values of the land, building, and
equipment are $150,000, $300,000, and $50,000, respectively, for a total estimated
fair value of $500,000.

Required:
Determine the amounts Red Rock should record in the separate accounts for the land,
the building, and the equipment.

Reporting intangible
assets **(LO2)**

E7–4 Brick Oven Corporation was organized early in 2012. The following expenditures
were made during the first few months of the year:

Attorneys' fees to organize the corporation	$ 8,000
Purchase of a patent	30,000
Legal and other fees for transfer of the patent	2,000
Preopening employee salaries	70,000
Total	$110,000

Required:
Record the $110,000 in cash expenditures.

Determine acquisition
costs of land, equipment,
and patents **(LO1, 2)**

E7–5 Determine the response that best completes the following statements or
questions.

1. On December 1, 2012, Bar S purchased a $500,000 tract of land for a factory site.
   Bar S removed an old building on the property and sold the materials it salvaged

from the demolition. Bar S incurred additional costs and realized salvage proceeds during December 2012 as follows:

Demolition of old building	$40,000
Legal fees for purchase contract and recording of ownership	13,000
Title guarantee insurance	8,000
Proceeds from sale of salvaged materials	3,000

In its December 31, 2012, balance sheet, Bar S should report a balance in the Land account of

a. $558,000.

b. $561,000.

c. $564,000.

d. $521,000.

2. On October 1, 2012, Manning Corp. purchased a machine for $126,000 that was placed in service on November 30, 2012. Manning incurred additional costs for this machine, as follows:

Shipping	$3,000
Installation	4,000
Testing	5,000

In Manning's December 31, 2012, balance sheet, the machine's cost should be reported as:

a. $126,000.

b. $129,000.

c. $133,000.

d. $138,000.

3. Hanner Corp. bought Patent A for $40,000 and Patent B for $60,000. Hanner also paid acquisition costs of $5,000 for Patent A and $7,000 for Patent B. Both patents were challenged in legal actions. Hanner paid $20,000 in legal fees for a successful defense of Patent A and $30,000 in legal fees for an unsuccessful defense of Patent B. Due to the unsuccessful defense, Patent B was taken off the books. What amount should Hanner capitalize for patents?

a. $162,000.

b. $ 65,000.

c. $112,000.

d. $ 45,000.

E7–6 On March 31, 2012, Mainline Produce Corporation acquired all the outstanding common stock of Iceberg Lettuce Corporation for $34,000,000 in cash. The book values and fair values of Iceberg's assets and liabilities were as follows:

Calculate the amount of goodwill (**LO2**)

	Book Value	Fair Value
Current assets	$12,000,000	$15,000,000
Property, plant, and equipment	22,000,000	28,000,000
Other assets	2,000,000	3,000,000
Current liabilities	8,000,000	8,000,000
Long-term liabilities	12,000,000	11,000,000

Required:

Calculate the amount paid for goodwill.

356 CHAPTER 7 Long-Term Assets

Record patent and research and development expense (LO2)

E7–7 In 2012, Satellite Systems modified its model Z2 satellite to incorporate a new communication device. The company made the following expenditures:

Basic research to develop the technology	$4,000,000
Engineering design work	1,360,000
Development of a prototype device	600,000
Testing and modification of the prototype	400,000
Legal fees for patent application	80,000
Legal fees for successful defense of the new patent	40,000
Total	$6,480,000

During your year-end review of the accounts related to intangibles, you discover that the company has capitalized all the above as costs of the patent. Management contends that the device represents an improvement of the existing communication system of the satellite and, therefore, should be capitalized.

Required:

1. Which of the above costs should Satellite Systems capitalize to the Patent account in the balance sheet?
2. Which of the above costs should Satellite Systems report as research and development expense in the income statement?
3. What are the basic criteria for determining whether to capitalize or expense intangible related costs?

Match terms used in the chapter (LO2, 4)

E7–8 Listed below are several terms and phrases associated with operational assets. Pair each item from List A (by letter) with the item from List B that is most appropriately associated with it.

List A	List B
_____ 1. Depreciation	a. Exclusive right to display a word, a symbol, or an emblem.
_____ 2. Goodwill	b. Exclusive right to benefit from a creative work.
_____ 3. Amortization	c. Assets that represent contractual rights.
_____ 4. Natural resources	d. Oil and gas deposits, timber tracts, and mineral deposits.
_____ 5. Intangible assets	e. Purchase price less fair value of net identifiable assets.
_____ 6. Copyright	f. The allocation of cost for plant and equipment.
_____ 7. Trademark	g. The allocation of cost for intangible assets.

Record expenditures after acquisition (LO3)

E7–9 Sub Sandwiches of America made the following expenditures related to its restaurant:

1. Replaced the heating equipment at a cost of $250,000.
2. Covered the patio area with a clear plastic dome and enclosed it with glass for use during the winter months. The total cost of the project was $750,000.
3. Performed annual building maintenance at a cost of $24,000.
4. Paid for annual insurance for the facility at $8,800.
5. Built a new sign above the restaurant, putting the company name in bright neon lights, for $9,900.
6. Paved a gravel parking lot at a cost of $65,000.

Required:

Sub Sandwiches of America credits Cash for each of these expenditures. Indicate the account it debits for each.

Determine depreciation for the first year under three methods (LO4)

E7–10 Super Saver Groceries purchased store equipment for $21,000. Super Saver estimates that at the end of its 10-year service life, the equipment will be worth $1,000. During the 10-year period, the company expects to use the equipment for a total of 10,000 hours. Super Saver used the equipment for 1,500 hours the first year.

Required:

Calculate depreciation expense of the equipment for the first year, using each of the following methods. Round all amounts to the nearest dollar.

1. Straight-line.
2. Double-declining-balance.
3. Activity-based.

E7–11 Speedy Delivery Company purchases a delivery van for $28,000. Speedy estimates that at the end of its four-year service life, the van will be worth $4,000. During the four-year period, the company expects to drive the van 120,000 miles.

Determine depreciation under three methods (**LO4**)

Required:

Calculate annual depreciation for the four-year life of the van using each of the following methods. Round all amounts to the nearest dollar.

1. Straight-line.
2. Double-declining-balance.
3. Activity-based.

Actual miles driven each year were 33,000 miles in year 1; 36,000 miles in year 2; 28,000 miles in year 3; and 30,000 miles in year 4. Note that actual total miles of 127,000 exceed expectations by 7,000 miles.

E7–12 Togo's Sandwiches acquired equipment on April 1, 2012, for $13,000. The company estimates a residual value of $1,000 and a five-year service life.

Determine straight-line depreciation for partial periods (**LO4**)

Required:

Calculate depreciation expense using the straight-line method for 2012 and 2013, assuming a December 31 year-end.

E7–13 Tasty Subs acquired a delivery truck on October 1, 2012, for $16,500. The company estimates a residual value of $1,500 and a six-year service life.

Determine straight-line depreciation for partial periods (**LO4**)

Required:

Calculate depreciation expense using the straight-line method for 2012 and 2013, assuming a December 31 year-end.

E7–14 The Donut Stop acquired equipment for $25,000. The company uses straight-line depreciation and estimates a residual value of $5,000 and a four-year service life. At the end of the second year, the company estimates that the equipment will be useful for four additional years, for a total service life of six years rather than the original four. At the same time, the company also changed the estimated residual value to $3,000 from the original estimate of $5,000.

Determine depreciation expense for a change in depreciation estimate (**LO4**)

Required:

Calculate how much The Donut Stop should record each year for depreciation in years 3 to 6.

E7–15 Tasty Subs acquired a delivery truck on October 1, 2012, for $16,500. The company estimates a residual value of $1,500 and a six-year service life. It expects to drive the truck 100,000 miles. Actual mileage was 4,000 miles in 2012 and 17,000 miles in 2013.

Determine activity-based depreciation (**LO4**)

Required:

Calculate depreciation expense using the activity-based method for 2012 and 2013, assuming a December 31 year-end.

E7–16 On January 1, 2012, Weaver Corporation purchased a patent for $240,000. The remaining legal life is 20 years, but the company estimates the patent will be useful for only six more years. In January 2014, the company incurred legal fees of $60,000 in successfully defending a patent infringement suit. The successful defense did not change the company's estimate of useful life. Weaver Corporation's year-end is December 31.

Record amortization expense (**LO5**)

Required:

1. Record the purchase in 2012; amortization in 2012; amortization in 2013; legal fees in 2014; and amortization in 2014.
2. What is the balance in the Patent account at the end of 2014?

Record the sale of equipment (LO6)

E7–17 Abbott Landscaping purchased a tractor at a cost of $32,000 and sold it three years later for $16,000. Abbott recorded depreciation using the straight-line method, a five-year service life, and a $2,000 residual value. Tractors are included in the Equipment account.

Required:

1. Record the sale.
2. Assume the tractor was sold for $10,000 instead of $16,000. Record the sale.

Record an exchange of land (LO6)

E7–18 Salad Express exchanged land it had been holding for future plant expansion for a more suitable parcel of land along distribution routes. Salad Express reported the old land on the previously issued balance sheet at its original cost of $60,000. According to an independent appraisal, the old land currently is worth $112,000. Salad Express paid $14,000 in cash to complete the transaction.

Required:

1. What is the fair value of the new parcel of land received by Salad Express?
2. Record the exchange.

Calculate ratios (LO7)

E7–19 Under Armour, Inc., reported sales of $725,244 and net income of $38,229 in its 2008 income statement. Under Armour also reported total assets of $487,555 in its 2008 balance sheet and $390,613 in its 2007 balance sheet. All amounts are reported in thousands of dollars. (For example, "$725,244" indicates $725,244,000.)

Required:

Calculate the return on assets, the profit margin, and the asset turnover ratio for Under Armour in 2008.

Calculate impairment loss (LO8)

E7–20 Midwest Services, Inc., operates several restaurant chains throughout the Midwest. One restaurant chain has experienced sharply declining profits. The company's management has decided to test the operational assets of the restaurants for possible impairment. The relevant information for these assets is presented below.

Book value	$8.5 million
Estimated total future cash flows	7.5 million
Fair value	6.0 million

Required:

1. Determine the amount of the impairment loss, if any.
2. Repeat *Requirement* 1 assuming that the estimated total future cash flows are $9.5 million and the fair value is $8 million.

*For additional exercises, visit **www.mhhe.com/succeed** for Exercises: Set B.*

PROBLEMS: SET A

Determine the acquisition cost of land and building (LO1)

P7–1A Italian Bread Company purchased land as a factory site for $60,000. An old building on the property was demolished, and construction began on a new building. Costs incurred during the first year are listed on the next page:

Demolition of old building	$ 8,000
Sale of salvaged materials	(1,000)
Architect fees (for new building)	15,000
Legal fees (for title investigation of land)	2,000
Property taxes on the land (for the first year)	3,000
Building construction costs	500,000
Interest costs related to the construction	18,000

Required:

Determine the amounts that the company should record in the Land and the Building accounts.

P7–2A Great Harvest Bakery purchased bread ovens from New Morning Bakery. New Morning Bakery was closing its bakery business and sold its two-year-old ovens at a discount for $600,000. Great Harvest incurred and paid freight costs of $30,000, and its employees ran special electrical connections to the ovens at a cost of $4,000. Labor costs were $32,800. Unfortunately, one of the ovens was damaged during installation, and repairs cost $4,000. Great Harvest then consumed $800 of bread dough in testing the ovens. It installed safety guards on the ovens at a cost of $1,400 and placed the machines in operation.

Determine the acquisition cost of equipment **(LO1)**

Flip Side of P7–8A

Required:

1. Prepare a schedule showing the amount at which the ovens should be recorded in Great Harvest's Equipment account.
2. Indicate where any amounts not included in the Equipment account should be recorded.

P7–3A Fresh Cut Corporation purchased all the outstanding common stock of Premium Meats for $11,000,000 in cash. The book value of Premium Meats' net assets (assets minus liabilities) was $7,800,000. The book values and fair values of Premium Meats' assets and liabilities were:

Calculate and record goodwill **(LO2)**

	Book Value	Fair Value
Receivables	$1,300,000	$ 1,100,000
Property, plant, and equipment	8,000,000	9,400,000
Intangible assets	200,000	1,200,000
Liabilities	(1,700,000)	(1,700,000)
Net assets	$7,800,000	$10,000,000

Required:

1. Calculate the amount Fresh Cut paid for goodwill.
2. Record Fresh Cut's acquisition of Premium Meats.

P7–4A Several years ago, Health Services acquired a helicopter for use in emergency situations. Health Services incurred the following expenditures related to the helicopter delivery operations in 2012:

Record expenditures after acquisition **(LO3)**

1. Overhauled the engine at a cost of $7,500. Health Services estimated the work would increase the service life for an additional five years.
2. Painted the Health Services company logo on the helicopter at a cost of $6,000.
3. Added new emergency health equipment to the helicopter for $25,000.
4. Modified the helicopter to reduce cabin noise by installing new sound barrier technology at a cost of $15,000.
5. Paid insurance on the helicopter for 2012, which increased 15% over the prior year to $9,000.
6. Performed annual maintenance and repairs at a cost of $39,000.

Required:

Indicate whether Health Services should capitalize or expense each of these expenditures. How could Health Services use expenditures like these to increase reported earnings?

Determine depreciation under three methods (LO4)

P7–5A University Car Wash built a deluxe car wash across the street from campus. The new machines cost $240,000 including installation. The company estimates that the equipment will have a residual value of $30,000. University Car Wash also estimates it will use the machine for six years or about 12,000 total hours.

Required:

Prepare a depreciation schedule for six years using the following methods:

1. Straight-line.
2. Double-declining-balance.
3. Activity-based.

Actual use per year was as follows:

Year	Hours Used
1	2,600
2	2,100
3	2,200
4	1,800
5	1,600
6	1,700

Record amortization and prepare the intangible assets section (LO5)

P7–6A The following information relates to the intangible assets of University Testing Services (UTS):

a. On January 1, 2012, UTS completed the purchase of Heinrich Corporation for $3,000,000 in cash. The fair value of the net identifiable assets of Heinrich was $2,700,000.

b. Included in the assets purchased from Heinrich was a patent valued at $90,000. The original legal life of the patent was 20 years; there are 12 years remaining, but UTS believes the patent will be useful for only eight more years.

c. UTS acquired a franchise on July 1, 2012, by paying an initial franchise fee of $350,000. The contractual life of the franchise is 10 years.

Required:

1. Record amortization expense for the intangible assets at December 31, 2012.
2. Prepare the intangible asset section of the December 31, 2012, balance sheet.

Compute depreciation, amortization, and book value of long-term assets (LO4, 5)

P7–7A Solich Sandwich Shop had the following long-term asset balances as of December 31, 2012:

	Cost	Accumulated Depreciation	Book Value
Land	$ 85,000	–	$ 85,000
Building	450,000	$(85,500)	364,500
Equipment	250,000	(48,000)	202,000
Patent	200,000	(80,000)	120,000

Solich purchased all the assets at the beginning of 2010 (3 years ago). The building is depreciated over a 20-year service life using the double-declining-balance method and estimating no residual value. The equipment is depreciated over a 10-year useful life using the straight-line method with an estimated residual value of $10,000. The patent is estimated to have a five-year service life with no residual value and is amortized using the straight-line method.

Required:

1. For the year ended December 31, 2012, record depreciation expense for buildings and equipment. Land is not depreciated.
2. For the year ended December 31, 2012, record amortization expense for the patent.
3. Calculate the book value for each of the four long-term assets at December 31, 2012.

P7–8A New Morning Bakery is in the process of closing its operations. It sold its two-year-old bakery ovens to Great Harvest Bakery for $600,000. The ovens originally cost $800,000, had an estimated service life of 10 years, and an estimated residual value of $50,000. New Morning Bakery uses the straight-line depreciation method for all equipment.

Record the disposal of equipment **(LO6)**

Required:

1. Calculate the balance in the Accumulated Depreciation account at the end of the second year.
2. Calculate the book value of the ovens at the end of the second year.
3. What is the gain or loss on the sale of the ovens at the end of the second year?
4. Record the sale of the ovens at the end of the second year.

Flip Side of P7–2A

P7–9A **Dell Corporation** and **Apple Inc.** reported the following information in their 2009 annual financial statements ($ in millions):

Calculate and interpret ratios **(LO7)**

Dell Corporation	2009	2008
Net sales	$61,101	$61,133
Net income	2,478	2,947
Total assets	26,500	27,561

Apple Inc.	2009	2008
Net sales	$36,537	$32,479
Net income	5,704	4,834
Total assets	53,581	39,572

Required:

1. Calculate Dell's return on assets, profit margin, and asset turnover ratio for 2009.
2. Calculate Apple's return on assets, profit margin, and asset turnover ratio for 2009.
3. Which company has the higher profit margin and which company has the higher asset turnover? Is this consistent with the primary business strategies of these two companies?

P7–10A University Hero is considering expanding operations beyond its healthy sandwiches. Jim Axelrod, vice president of marketing, would like to add a line of smoothies with a similar health emphasis. Each smoothie would include two free health supplements such as vitamins, antioxidants, and protein. Jim believes smoothie sales should help fill the slow mid-afternoon period. Adding the line of smoothies would require purchasing additional freezer space, machinery, and equipment. Jim provides the following projections of net sales, net income, and average total assets in support of his proposal.

Calculate and interpret ratios **(LO7)**

	Sandwiches Only	Sandwiches and Smoothies
Net sales	$800,000	$1,400,000
Net income	100,000	160,000
Average total assets	400,000	800,000

Required:

1. Calculate University Hero's return on assets, profit margin, and asset turnover for sandwiches only.
2. Calculate University Hero's return on assets, profit margin, and asset turnover for sandwiches and smoothies.
3. Based on these ratios, what recommendation would you make?

PROBLEMS: SET B

Determine the acquisition cost of land and building (LO1)

P7–1B Italian Pizza Company purchased land as a factory site for $80,000. Prior to construction of the new building, the land had to be cleared of trees and brush. Construction costs incurred during the first year are listed below:

Land clearing costs	$ 4,000
Sale of firewood to a worker	(500)
Architect fees (for new building)	20,000
Title investigation of land	2,500
Property taxes on land (for the first year)	2,000
Building construction costs	300,000

Required:

Determine the amounts that the company should record in the Land and the New Building accounts.

Determine the acquisition cost of equipment (LO1)

Flip Side of P7–8B

P7–2B Sicily Pizza purchased baking ovens from New World Deli. New World Deli was closing its bakery business and sold its three-year-old ovens for $300,000. In addition to the purchase price, Sicily Pizza paid shipping costs of $15,000. Employees of Sicily Pizza installed the ovens; labor costs were $16,000. An outside contractor performed some of the electrical work for $2,800. Sicily Pizza consumed pizza dough with a cost of $1,200 in testing the ovens. It then installed new timers on the ovens at a cost of $700 and placed the machines in operation.

Required:

1. Prepare a schedule showing the amount at which Sicily Pizza should record the ovens in the Equipment account.
2. Indicate where any amounts not included in the Equipment account should be recorded.

Calculate and record goodwill (LO2)

P7–3B Northern Equipment Corporation purchased all the outstanding common stock of Pioneer Equipment Rental for $5,500,000 in cash. The book value of Pioneer's net assets (assets minus liabilities) was $3,900,000. The book values and fair values of Pioneer's assets and liabilities were:

	Book Value	Fair Value
Receivables	$ 650,000	$ 550,000
Property, plant, and equipment	4,000,000	4,700,000
Intangible assets	100,000	600,000
Liabilities	(850,000)	(850,000)
Net assets	$3,900,000	$5,000,000

Required:

1. Calculate the amount paid for goodwill.
2. Record Northern Equipment's acquisition of Pioneer Equipment Rental.

Record expenditures after acquisition (LO3)

P7–4B Stillwater Youth Programs (SYP) purchased a used school bus to use in transporting children for its after-school program. SYP incurred the following expenses related to the bus in 2012:

1. Painted the SYP logo on the bus for $3,000 to help promote the after-school program.
2. Installed new seats on the bus at a cost of $5,000.
3. Installed a DVD player and sound system to entertain the children in-transit and announce upcoming events at a cost of $1,000.
4. Paid insurance on the school bus for 2012, which increased 10% over the prior year to an annual premium of $2,800.
5. Performed annual maintenance and repairs for $1,400.
6. Overhauled the engine at a cost of $6,500, increasing the service life of the bus by an estimated three years.

Required:
Indicate whether SYP should capitalize or expense each of these expenditures. How could SYP use expenditures like these to increase reported earnings?

P7–5B Cheetah Copy purchased a new copy machine. The new machine cost $120,000 including installation. The company estimates the equipment will have a residual value of $30,000. Cheetah Copy also estimates it will use the machine for four years or about 8,000 total hours.

Determine depreciation under three methods **(LO4)**

Required:
Prepare a depreciation schedule for four years using the following methods:
1. Straight-line.
2. Double-declining-balance. (*Hint:* The asset will be depreciated in only two years.)
3. Activity-based.
Actual use per year was as follows:

Year	Hours Used
1	2,500
2	2,200
3	1,900
4	2,000

P7–6B The following information relates to the intangible assets of Lettuce Express:
a. On January 1, 2012, Lettuce Express completed the purchase of Farmers Produce, Inc., for $1,500,000 in cash. The fair value of the identifiable net assets of Farmers Produce was $1,350,000.
b. Included in the assets purchased from Farmers Produce was a patent for a method of processing lettuce valued at $45,000. The original legal life of the patent was 20 years. There are still 17 years left on the patent, but Lettuce Express estimates the patent will be useful for only 10 more years.
c. Lettuce Express acquired a franchise on July 1, 2012, by paying an initial franchise fee of $175,000. The contractual life of the franchise is seven years.

Record amortization and prepare the intangible assets section **(LO5)**

Required:
1. Record amortization expense for the intangible assets at December 31, 2012.
2. Prepare the intangible asset section of the December 31, 2012, balance sheet.

P7–7B Togo's Sandwich Shop had the following long-term asset balances as of January 1, 2012:

Compute depreciation, amortization, and book value of long-term assets **(LO4, 5)**

	Cost	Accumulated Depreciation	Book Value
Land	$ 75,000	–	$ 75,000
Building	550,000	$(104,500)	445,500
Equipment	150,000	(28,000)	122,000
Patent	100,000	(40,000)	60,000

Togo's purchased all the assets at the beginning of 2010 (3 years ago). The building is depreciated over a 20-year service life using the double-declining-balance method and estimating no residual value. The equipment is depreciated over a 10-year useful life using the straight-line method with an estimated residual value of $10,000. The patent is estimated to have a five-year service life with no residual value and is amortized using the straight-line method.

Required:
1. For the year ended December 31, 2012, record depreciation expense for buildings and equipment. Land is not depreciated.
2. For the year ended December 31, 2012, record amortization expense for the patent.
3. Calculate the book value for each of the four long-term assets at December 31, 2012.

Record the disposal of equipment (LO6)

Flip Side of P7–2B

P7–8B New Deli is in the process of closing its operations. It sold its three-year-old ovens to Sicily Pizza for $300,000. The ovens originally cost $400,000 and had an estimated service life of 10 years and an estimated residual value of $25,000. New Deli uses straight-line depreciation for all equipment.

Required:
1. Calculate the balance in the Accumulated Depreciation account at the end of the third year.
2. Calculate the book value of the ovens at the end of the third year.
3. What is the gain or loss on the sale of the ovens at the end of the third year?
4. Record the sale of the ovens at the end of the third year.

Calculate and interpret ratios (LO7)

P7–9B Nike is the market leader and **Under Armour** is an up-and-coming player in the highly competitive athletic apparel market. Reported below is selected financial information from their 2008 annual financial statements ($ in millions):

Nike Corporation	2008	2007
Net sales	$19,176.1	$18,627.0
Net income	1,486.7	1,883.4
Total assets	13,249.6	12,442.7

Under Armour	2008	2007
Net sales	$725.2	$606.6
Net income	38.2	52.6
Total assets	487.6	390.6

Required:
1. Calculate Nike's return on assets, profit margin, and asset turnover ratio for 2008.
2. Calculate Under Armour's return on assets, profit margin, and asset turnover ratio for 2008.
3. Which company has the higher profit margin and which company has the higher asset turnover?

Calculate and interpret ratios (LO7)

P7–10B Barry Sanders, likely the best running back to ever play football, has opened a successful used-car dealership. He has noted a higher than normal percentage of sales for trucks and SUVs with hauling capacity at his dealership. He is also aware that several of the best recreational lakes in the state are located nearby. Barry is considering expanding his dealership to include the sale of recreational boats. Barry provides the following projections of net sales, net income, and average total assets in support of his proposal.

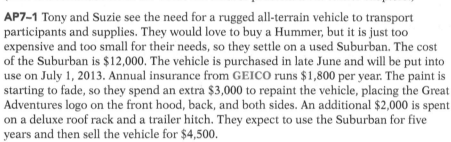

	Cars Only	Cars and Boats
Net sales	$6,400,000	$7,600,000
Net income	400,000	600,000
Average total assets	1,600,000	1,800,000

Required:

1. Calculate Barry's return on assets, profit margin, and asset turnover for cars only.
2. Calculate Barry's return on assets, profit margin, and asset turnover for cars and boats.
3. Based on these ratios, what recommendation would you make?

*For additional problems, visit **www.mhhe.com/succeed** for Problems: Set C.*

ADDITIONAL PERSPECTIVES

Great Adventures

(This is a continuation of the Great Adventures problem from earlier chapters.)

Continuing Problem

AP7–1 Tony and Suzie see the need for a rugged all-terrain vehicle to transport participants and supplies. They would love to buy a Hummer, but it is just too expensive and too small for their needs, so they settle on a used Suburban. The cost of the Suburban is $12,000. The vehicle is purchased in late June and will be put into use on July 1, 2013. Annual insurance from **GEICO** runs $1,800 per year. The paint is starting to fade, so they spend an extra $3,000 to repaint the vehicle, placing the Great Adventures logo on the front hood, back, and both sides. An additional $2,000 is spent on a deluxe roof rack and a trailer hitch. They expect to use the Suburban for five years and then sell the vehicle for $4,500.

Required:

1. Determine the amount that should be recorded for the new vehicle.
2. Indicate where any amounts not included in the Equipment account should be recorded.
3. Prepare a depreciation schedule using the straight-line method. Follow the example in Illustration 7–11, except the first and last years will have a half-year of depreciation to reflect the beginning of its service life on July 1, 2013.
4. Record the sale of the vehicle two years later on July 1, 2015, for $10,000.

American Eagle Outfitters, Inc.

Financial Analysis

AP7–2 Financial information for **American Eagle** is presented in Appendix A at the end of the book.

Required:

1. The summary of significant accounting polices is located in footnote 2 to the financial statements. Locate the section on property and equipment. What depreciation method does American Eagle use? What are the estimated useful lives for buildings, leasehold improvements, and fixtures and equipment?
2. Find footnote 7 entitled Property and Equipment. What are the cost and the book value of property and equipment? What is the trend in depreciation expense for the past three years?
3. Find footnote 9 entitled Leases. Retail stores, like American Eagle, tend to lease rather than buy their stores. What is the most common term for the store leases? What are the future minimum lease obligations under operating leases at January 30, 2010?

Financial Analysis

Buckle

The Buckle, Inc.

AP7–3 Financial information for **The Buckle** is presented in Appendix B at the end of the book.

Required:

1. The summary of significant accounting polices is located in footnote A to the financial statements. Locate the section on property and equipment. What depreciation method does The Buckle use? What are the estimated useful lives for buildings, leasehold improvements, and property and equipment?
2. Find footnote D entitled Property and Equipment. What is the cost of property and equipment? What is the trend in property and equipment for the past two years?
3. Find footnote H entitled Commitments. Retail stores, like The Buckle, tend to lease rather than buy their stores. What is the most common term for the leases? What are the future minimum rental commitments under operating leases at February 6, 2010?

Comparative Analysis

Buckle

American Eagle Outfitters, Inc., vs. The Buckle, Inc.

AP7–4 Financial information for **American Eagle** is presented in Appendix A at the end of the book, and financial information for **The Buckle** is presented in Appendix B at the end of the book.

Required:

1. Calculate American Eagle's return on assets, profit margin, and asset turnover ratio.
2. Calculate The Buckle's return on assets, profit margin, and asset turnover ratio.
3. Which company is doing better based on return on assets? Which company has the higher profit margin? Which company has the higher asset turnover?

Ethics

AP7–5 Companies often are under pressure to meet or beat Wall Street earnings projections in order to increase stock prices and also to increase the value of stock options. Some resort to earnings management practices to artificially create desired results.

Required:

1. How can a company increase earnings by changing its depreciation method?
2. How can a company increase earnings by changing the estimated service lives of depreciable assets?
3. How can a company increase earnings by changing the estimated residual value of depreciable assets?

Internet Research

AP7–6 Companies are increasingly making their accounting information, especially their annual reports, available through their websites. Select a well-known publicly traded company and go to its website. Look for the investment section, and then click on annual reports. Select the most recent annual report. If you have difficulty, try another company. Answer the following questions based on the company's most recent annual report.

Required:

1. What is the official name of the company?
2. What is its fiscal year-end?
3. At the end of the year, what is the net balance in property, plant, and equipment? (*Hint: Requirements* 3 and 4 are reported in the balance sheet.)

4. Does the company have any intangible assets? If so, how much is reported for intangible assets?
5. What is the balance in accumulated depreciation? (*Hint:* This is either in the balance sheet or in a note about property, plant, and equipment.)
6. Which method of depreciation is used? (*Hint:* It's usually disclosed in the notes under summary of accounting policies.)

Written Communication

AP7–7 At a recent luncheon, you were seated next to Mr. Fogle, the president of a local company that manufactures food processors. He heard that you were in a financial accounting class and asked:

> Why is it that I'm forced to record depreciation expense on my property when I could sell it for more than I originally paid? I thought that the purpose of the balance sheet is to reflect the value of my business and that the purpose of the income statement is to report the net change in value or wealth of a company. It just doesn't make sense to penalize my profits when the building hasn't lost any value.

At the conclusion of the luncheon, you promised to send him a short explanation of the rationale for current depreciation practices.

Required:
Prepare a memo to Mr. Fogle. Explain the accounting concept of depreciation and contrast this with the dictionary definition of depreciation.

Earnings Management

AP7–8 Edward L. Vincent is CFO of Energy Resources, Inc. The company specializes in the exploration and development of natural gas. It's near year-end, and Edward is feeling terrific. Natural gas prices have risen throughout the year, and Energy Resources is set to report record-breaking performance that will greatly exceed analysts' expectations. However, during an executive meeting this morning, management agreed to "tone down" profits due to concerns that reporting excess profits could encourage additional government regulations in the industry, hindering future profitability.

Edward decides to adjust the estimated service life of development equipment from 10 years to six years. He also plans to adjust estimated residual values on development equipment to zero as it is nearly impossible to accurately estimate residual values on equipment like this anyway.

Required:
1. Explain how the adjustment of estimated service life from 10 years to six years will affect depreciation expense and net income.
2. Explain how the adjustment of estimated residual values to zero will affect depreciation expense and net income.
3. In addition to heading off additional government regulations, why might Energy Resources have an incentive to report lower profits in the current period?

Answers to the Self-Study Questions
1. b   2. d   3. d   4. a   5. b   6. b   7. d   8. c   9. c   10. c

CHAPTER

8

Current Liabilities

Learning Objectives

AFTER STUDYING THIS CHAPTER, YOU SHOULD BE ABLE TO:

- **LO1** Distinguish between current and long-term liabilities.
- **LO2** Account for notes payable and interest expense.
- **LO3** Account for employee and employer payroll liabilities.
- **LO4** Demonstrate the accounting for other current liabilities.
- **LO5** Apply the appropriate accounting treatment for contingencies.

Analysis
- **LO6** Assess liquidity using current liability ratios.

UNITED AIRLINES: A FUTURE UP IN THE AIR

Have you ever considered buying stock in an airline? Do you think companies like **American**, **Delta**, or **United** would be a good investment? Think again. Warren Buffett, a self-made billionaire based in Omaha, Nebraska, is regarded as one of the world's top investors. In 1991 he observed that the airline industry had not made a dime for investors in a century of manned flight. Buffett acknowledged his mistake in buying stock in **US Airways**, which later filed for Chapter 11 bankruptcy along with Delta, **Northwest**, United, and others.

Companies must file for bankruptcy protection when they no longer are able to pay their liabilities as they become due. By carefully examining information in financial statements, investors and creditors can assess a company's profitability and its *liquidity*—its ability to pay currently maturing debt. Both profitability and liquidity help indicate a company's risk of filing for bankruptcy. Wise investors, like Warren Buffett, pay careful attention to these warning signs.

What are some of the current liabilities reported by companies in the airline industry? The airline industry is very labor-intensive, resulting in extensive payroll liabilities. Another substantial current liability for airlines is advance ticket sales. This liability, representing tickets sold for future flights, is in the billions of dollars for several major U.S. airlines. Airlines are well known for their frequent-flier programs. These programs have created liabilities for frequent-flier incentives exceeding $100 million. Finally, a somewhat different type of liability airlines face is contingent liabilities. A *contingent liability* is a possible liability for which payment is contingent upon another event. An example is pending litigation. All of the major airlines report contingent liabilities related to unsettled litigation.

With airlines incurring so many types of liabilities, it is no wonder many airlines have filed for bankruptcy. However, there is one shining star among companies in the airline industry—**Southwest Airlines**. Known as the airline where your "bags fly free," it is recognized in the investment community for its strong financial performance. At the end of the chapter, we compare liquidity ratios between United Airlines and Southwest Airlines, to explore whether the financial reputation of Southwest Airlines is for real.

PART A

■ LO1
Distinguish between current and long-term liabilities.

CURRENT LIABILITIES

In the four preceding chapters, we worked our way down the asset side of the balance sheet, examining cash, accounts receivable, inventory, and long-term assets. We now turn to the liabilities side of the balance sheet. In the next three chapters, we discuss how companies finance their operations through borrowing (liabilities) or additional investment by owners (stockholders' equity). Chapter 8 focuses on current liabilities and Chapter 9 on long-term liabilities. In Chapter 10, we look at stockholders' equity.

Liabilities have three essential characteristics. Liabilities are: (1) probable *future* sacrifices of economic benefits, (2) arising from *present* obligations to other entities, (3) resulting from *past* transactions or events.[1] The definition of liabilities touches on the present, the future, and the past: A liability is a present responsibility to sacrifice assets in the future due to a transaction or other event that happened in the past.

Recall that assets represent probable future *benefits*. In contrast, liabilities represent probable future *sacrifices* of benefits. What benefits are sacrificed? Most liabilities require the future sacrifice of cash. For instance, accounts payable, notes payable, and salaries payable usually are paid in cash.

Can you think of a liability that requires paying something other than cash? One such liability is unearned revenue. Remember (from Chapter 3) that this liability arises when a company receives payment in advance of providing the product or service it's selling. This obligation requires giving up inventory or services rather than cash to satisfy the debt.

Current vs. Long-Term Classification

Common Terms Current liabilities are also sometimes called *short-term liabilities.*

In a classified balance sheet, we categorize liabilities as either current or long-term. **In most cases, current liabilities are payable within one year, and long-term liabilities are payable more than one year from now.**

COMMON MISTAKE

Current liabilities are *usually*, but not always, due within one year. But for some companies (a winery, for example), it takes longer than a year to perform the activities that produce revenue. We call the time it takes to produce revenue—from "cash to cash" as the saying goes (i.e., initial investment to revenue)—the *operating cycle*. If a company has an operating cycle longer than one year, its current liabilities are defined by the operating cycle rather than by the length of a year. For now, remember that in most cases (but not all) current liabilities are due within one year.

Distinguishing between current and long-term liabilities is important in helping investors and creditors assess risk. Given a choice, most companies would prefer to report a liability as long-term rather than current, because doing so may cause the firm to appear less risky. In turn, less-risky firms may enjoy lower interest rates on borrowing and command higher stock prices for new stock listings.

The Feature Story at the beginning of this chapter pointed out that the U.S. airline industry has experienced financial difficulties in recent years, resulting in greater risk to investors. Several major airlines have been forced into bankruptcy because they were unable to pay current liabilities as they became due. In Illustration 8–1 an excerpt from the annual report of United Airlines discusses the problem.

---

[1]"Elements of Financial Statements." 1985. *Statement of Financial Accounting Concepts No. 6* (Stamford, Conn.: FASB), par. 38.

> **UNITED AIRLINES**
> **Management Discussion and Analysis (excerpt)**
>
> Over the past several years, United and indeed the entire airline industry have faced severe business challenges and fundamental industry changes which have produced material adverse impacts on earnings, financial position and liquidity. The Company had been operating under Chapter 11 bankruptcy protection since December 9, 2002, and emerged on February 1, 2006.
>
> Operating revenues for the airline industry in general, as well as for United, have been adversely impacted by several factors. The growth of low cost carriers; excess seat capacity; pricing transparency; reduced demand for high-yield business travel; global events such as the war in Iraq, the outbreak of disease as well as the fear of terrorist attacks since September 11, 2001; and the enactment of federal taxes on ticket sales to fund additional airport security measures, have caused earnings to decline.

What obligations do firms most frequently report as current liabilities? Notes payable, accounts payable, and payroll liabilities are three main categories. In addition, companies report a variety of other current liabilities, including unearned revenue, sales tax payable, and the current portion of long-term debt.

There is no prescribed order for presenting accounts within the current liabilities section of the balance sheet. However, many companies list notes payable first, followed by accounts payable, and then other current liabilities from largest to smallest. *Follow this order when preparing your homework assignments.* In keeping with this order, we discuss notes payable in the next section.

 KEY POINT

In most cases, current liabilities are payable within one year, and long-term liabilities are payable more than one year from now.

Notes Payable

In Chapter 5, we saw how companies account for notes receivable. Here, we discuss the flip side of notes receivable—notes payable. Recall that notes receivable is an asset that creates interest revenue. In contrast, notes payable is a *liability* that creates interest *expense*.

■ LO2
Account for notes
payable and interest
expense.

Very often, small firms are unable to tap into the major sources of long-term financing (such as bonds) to the extent necessary to provide for their capital needs, so they must rely heavily on short-term financing. When a company borrows cash from a bank, the bank requires the firm to sign a note promising to repay the amount borrowed plus interest. The borrower reports its liability as notes payable. About two-thirds of bank loans are short-term. Even large companies use short-term debt as a significant part of their capital structure. A major reason is that short-term funds usually offer lower interest rates than long-term debt.

Assume Southwest Airlines borrows $100,000 from Bank of America on September 1, 2012, signing a 6%, six-month note for the amount borrowed plus accrued interest due six months later on March 1, 2013. On September 1, 2012, Southwest will receive $100,000 in cash and record the following:

September 1, 2012	Debit	Credit		A	=	L	+	SE
Cash	100,000			+100,000				
Notes Payable		100,000				+100,000		
(*Issue notes payable*)								

When a company borrows money, it pays the lender **interest** in return for using the lender's money during the term of the loan. Interest is stated in terms of an annual percentage rate to be applied to the face value of the loan. Because the stated interest rate is an *annual* rate, when calculating interest for a current note payable we must adjust for the fraction of the annual period the loan spans. We calculate interest on notes as:

$$\text{Interest} = \text{Face value} \times \frac{\text{Annual}}{\text{interest rate}} \times \frac{\text{Fraction}}{\text{of the year}}$$

In the example above, how much interest cost does Southwest incur for the six-month period of the note from September 1, 2012, to March 1, 2013?

$$\$3,000 = \$100,000 \times 6\% \times 6/12$$

However, if Southwest's reporting period ends on December 31, 2012, the company can't wait until March 1, 2013, to record interest. Instead, the company records the four months' interest incurred during 2012 in an adjustment prior to preparing the 2012 financial statements. Since the firm will not pay the 2012 interest until the note becomes due (March 1, 2013), it records the $2,000 interest as **interest payable,** as follows:

	A = L + SE
−2,000 Exp↑	
+2,000	

December 31, 2012	Debit	Credit
Interest Expense (= $100,000 × 6% × 4/12)	2,000	
Interest Payable		2,000
(Record interest incurred, but not paid)		

COMMON MISTAKE

When calculating the number of months of interest, students sometimes mistakenly subtract December (month 12) from September (month 9) and get three months. However, the time from September 1 to December 31 includes both September and December, so there are four months. If you are ever in doubt, count out the months on your fingers. Your fingers never lie.

The purpose of the adjusting entry is to report four months' interest (September, October, November, and December) in 2012. Southwest will report the remaining $1,000 of interest (for January and February) in 2013. Since the firm won't actually pay the 2012 interest until March 1, 2013, its financial statements for the year ended December 31, 2012, will show interest payable of $2,000 along with notes payable of $100,000 as a current liability on the balance sheet, and the "other expenses" section of the income statement will report interest expense of $2,000.

When the note comes due on March 1, 2013, Southwest Airlines will pay the face value of the loan ($100,000) plus the entire $3,000 interest incurred ($100,000 × 6% × 6/12). The $3,000 represents six months of interest—the four months of interest ($2,000) in 2012 previously recorded as interest payable and two months of interest ($1,000) in 2013. Southwest records these transactions on March 1, 2013, as follows:

	A = L + SE
−100,000	
−1,000 Exp↑	
−2,000	
−103,000	

March 1, 2013	Debit	Credit
Notes Payable (face value)	100,000	
Interest Expense (= $100,000 × 6% × 2/12)	1,000	
Interest Payable (= $100,000 × 6% × 4/12)	2,000	
Cash		103,000
(Pay notes payable and interest)		

The entry on March 1 does the following:

- Removes the note payable ($100,000).
- Records interest expense for January and February 2013 ($1,000).
- Removes the interest payable recorded in the December 31, 2012, entry ($2,000).
- Reduces cash ($103,000).

Notice that we record interest expense incurred for four months in 2012 and two months in 2013, rather than recording all six months' interest expense in 2013 when we pay it. This is consistent with the matching principle.

 KEY POINT

We record interest expense in the period in which we *incur* it, rather than in the period in which we pay it.

How would the lender, Bank of America, record this note? For the bank it's a **note receivable** rather than a note payable, and it generates **interest revenue** rather than interest expense. (You may want to review the discussion on notes receivable in Chapter 5.) The entries for Bank of America's loan are as follows:

Flip Side

September 1, 2012	Debit	Credit	A	=	L	+	SE
Notes Receivable	100,000		+100,000				
Cash		100,000	−100,000				
(*Issue notes receivable*)							

December 31, 2012	Debit	Credit	A	=	L	+	SE
Interest Receivable	2,000		+2,000				
Interest Revenue (= $100,000 × 6% × 4/12)		2,000					+2,000 Rev↑
(*Record interest earned, but not received*)							

March 1, 2013	Debit	Credit	A	=	L	+	SE
Cash	103,000		+103,000				
Interest Revenue (= $100,000 × 6% × 2/12)		1,000					+1,000 Rev↑
Interest Receivable (= $100,000 × 6% × 4/12)		2,000	−2,000				
Notes Receivable (face value)		100,000	−100,000				
(*Collect notes receivable and interest*)							

Assume **Delta Airlines** borrows $500,000 from **Chase Bank** on November 1, 2012, signing a 9%, six-month note payable.

Let's Review

Required:

1. Record the issuance of the note payable.
2. Record the adjustment for the note payable on December 31, 2012.
3. Record the payment of the note payable at maturity.

Solution:

1. Issuance of note payable:

November 1, 2012	Debit	Credit
Cash	500,000	
Notes Payable		500,000
(Issue note payable)		

2. Adjustment for interest expense at the end of the period:

December 31, 2012	Debit	Credit
Interest Expense (= $500,000 × 9% × 2/12)	7,500	
Interest Payable		7,500
(Record interest incurred, but not paid)		

3. Payment of note at maturity:

May 1, 2013	Debit	Credit
Notes Payable	500,000	
Interest Expense (= $500,000 × 9% × 4/12)	15,000	
Interest Payable (= $500,000 × 9% × 2/12)	7,500	
Cash		522,500
(Pay note payable and interest)		

Suggested Homework:
BE8-1, BE8-2;
E8-2, E8-3;
P8-2A&B

Rather than wait until borrowing becomes necessary, many companies pre-arrange the terms of a note payable by establishing a line of credit with a bank. A line of credit is an informal agreement that permits a company to borrow up to a prearranged limit without having to follow formal loan procedures and prepare paperwork. The line of credit works like a note payable except the company is able to borrow without having to go through a formal loan approval process each time it borrows money. Banks sometimes require the company to maintain a cash balance on deposit with the bank, say, 5% of the line of credit. The recording for a line of credit is exactly the same as the recording for notes payable described earlier.

Decision Point

Question ?	Accounting information 🗎	Analysis 🔍
How can you tell the amount and interest rate of a company's line of credit?	Notes to the financial statements	Companies are required to disclose the terms of available lines of credit such as the amounts, maturity dates, and interest rates.

If a company borrows from another company rather than from a bank, the note is referred to as commercial paper. Commercial paper is sold with maturities ranging from 30 to 270 days. (Beyond 270 days, the issuing firm is required to file a registration statement with the SEC.) Since a company is borrowing directly from another company, the interest rate on commercial paper is usually lower than on a bank loan. Commercial paper has thus become an increasingly popular way for large companies to raise funds, so much so that the total dollar value of commercial paper loans outstanding has multiplied five times in the last decade.

KEY POINT

Many short-term loans are arranged under an existing line of credit with a bank, or for larger corporations in the form of commercial paper, a loan from one company to another.

Accounts Payable

Accounts payable, sometimes called *trade accounts payable,* are amounts the company owes to suppliers of merchandise or services that it has bought on credit. We discussed accounting for this very common form of current liability when we discussed inventory purchases in Chapter 6. Briefly, recall that when a company purchases items on account (if it does not pay immediately with cash), it increases a liability called Accounts Payable. Later, when the company pays the amount owed, it decreases both Cash and Accounts Payable.

Payroll Liabilities

Many companies, including those in the airline industry, are very labor-intensive. Payroll liabilities make up a significant portion of current liabilities for these companies. Here, we will look at how payroll is calculated for both the employee and the employer.

■ LO3
Account for employee and employer payroll liabilities.

Let's assume you are hired at a $60,000 annual salary with salary payments of $5,000 per month. Before you make any spending plans, though, you need to realize that your payroll check will be much *less* than $5,000 a month. Before depositing your monthly payroll check in your bank account, your employer will "withhold" amounts for (1) federal and state income taxes; (2) Social Security and Medicare; (3) health, dental, disability, and life insurance premiums; and (4) *employee* investments to retirement or savings plans. Realistically, then, your $5,000 monthly salary translates to less than $4,000 in actual take-home pay.

Now assume you are an employer. You hire an employee at a starting annual salary of $60,000. Your costs for this employee will be much *more* than $5,000 per month. Besides the $5,000 monthly salary, you will incur significant costs for (1) federal and state unemployment taxes; (2) the *employer* portion of Social Security and Medicare; (3) *employer* contributions for health, dental, disability, and life insurance; and (4) *employer* contributions to retirement or savings plans. With these additional costs, a $5,000 monthly salary could very easily create total costs in excess of $6,000 per month. Illustration 8–2 summarizes payroll costs for employees and employers. We discuss these costs below.

Employee Payroll Costs	Employer Payroll Costs
Federal and state income taxes	Federal and state unemployment taxes
Employee portion of Social Security and Medicare	Employer matching portion of Social Security and Medicare
Employee contributions for health, dental, disability, and life insurance	Employer contributions for health, dental, disability, and life insurance
Employee investments in retirement or savings plans	Employer contributions to retirement or savings plans

ILLUSTRATION 8–2

Payroll Costs for Employees and Employers

EMPLOYEE COSTS

Employers are required by law to withhold federal and state income taxes from employees' paychecks and remit these taxes to the government. The amount withheld varies according to the amount the employee earns and the number of exemptions

CAREER CORNER

When comparing compensation among different career opportunities, don't base your final decision on salary alone. Fringe benefits can sometimes make up for a lower annual salary. Various employers offer *fringe benefits*—also called "perquisites," or "perks"—that catch the attention of would-be employees: a pound of coffee every month at Starbucks, free skiing for employees at Vail Ski Resort, or scuba and kayaking in the pool at Nike's Athletic Village in Beaverton, Oregon. More common fringe benefits, and ones that many people appreciate in the long run, include employer coverage of family health insurance, educational benefits, and contributions to retirement plans.

However, remember that even more important than either salary or benefits are the training and experience the position offers. Training and experience can provide you with the skills necessary to land that big promotion or dream job in the future.

the employee claims. The IRS furnishes tax tables that assist in determining the amount withheld. If you are able to claim more exemptions, you will have less tax withheld from your paycheck. Not all states require the payment of personal income taxes: Alaska, Florida, Nevada, South Dakota, Texas, Washington, and Wyoming have no state income tax. Two others, New Hampshire and Tennessee, tax only dividend and interest income.

Employers also withhold Social Security and Medicare taxes from employees' paychecks. Collectively, Social Security and Medicare taxes are referred to as FICA taxes, named for the Federal Insurance Contribution Act (FICA). This act requires employers to withhold a 6.2% Social Security tax up to a maximum base amount plus a 1.45% Medicare tax with no maximum. Therefore, the total FICA tax is 7.65% (6.2% + 1.45%) on income up to a base amount ($106,800 in 2010) and 1.45% on all income above the base amount. For example, if you earn less than $106,800, you will have 7.65% withheld from your check all year. However, if you earn, let's say, $156,800, you would have 7.65% withheld for FICA on the first $106,800 of your annual salary and then only 1.45% withheld on the remaining $50,000 earned during the rest of the year.

Besides the required deductions for income tax and FICA taxes, employees may opt to have additional amounts withheld from their paychecks. These might include the employee portion of insurance premiums, employee investments in retirement or savings plans, and contributions to charitable organizations such as United Way. The employer records the amounts deducted from employee payroll as liabilities until it pays them to the appropriate organizations.

EMPLOYER COSTS

By law, the employer pays an additional (matching) FICA tax on behalf of the employee. The employer's limits on FICA tax are the same as the employee's. Thus, the government actually collects 15.3% (7.65% employee + 7.65% employer) on each employee's salary.

In addition to FICA, the employer also must pay federal and state unemployment taxes on behalf of its employees. The *Federal Unemployment Tax Act* (FUTA) requires a tax of 6.2% on the first $7,000 earned by each employee. This amount is reduced by a 5.4% (maximum) credit for contributions to state unemployment programs, so the net federal rate often is 0.8%. Under the *State Unemployment Tax Act* (SUTA), in many states the maximum state unemployment tax rate is 5.4%, but many companies pay a lower rate based on past employment history.

 COMMON MISTAKE

Many people think FICA taxes are paid only by the employee. The employer is required to match the amount withheld for each employee, effectively doubling the amount paid into Social Security.

Additional employee benefits paid for by the employer are referred to as fringe benefits. Employers often pay all or part of employees' insurance premiums and make contributions to retirement or savings plans. Many companies provide additional fringe benefits specific to the company or the industry, as discussed in the nearby Career Corner. For instance, an important additional fringe benefit in the airline industry is the ability for the employee and family to fly free.

To understand how employee and employer payroll costs are recorded, assume that Hawaiian Travel Agency has a total payroll for the month of January of $100,000 for its 20 employees. Its withholdings and payroll taxes are shown in Illustration 8–3.

Federal and state income tax withheld	$24,000	**ILLUSTRATION 8–3**
Health insurance premiums (Blue Cross) paid by employer	5,000	Payroll Example,
Contribution to retirement plan (Fidelity) paid by employer	10,000	Hawaiian Travel
FICA tax rate (Social Security and Medicare)	7.65%	Agency
Federal and state unemployment tax rate	6.2%	

Hawaiian Travel Agency records the *employee* salary expense, withholdings, and salaries payable on January 31 as follows:

January 31	Debit	Credit	A	=	L	+	SE
Salaries Expense	**100,000**						−100,000 Exp↑
Income Tax Payable		24,000			+24,000		
FICA Tax Payable (= 0.0765 × $100,000)		7,650			+7,650		
Salaries Payable (to balance)		68,350			+68,350		
(Record employee salary expense and withholdings)							

Hawaiian Travel Agency records its employer-provided fringe benefits as follows:

January 31	Debit	Credit	A	=	L	+	SE
Salaries Expense (fringe benefits)	**15,000**						−15,000 Exp↑
Accounts Payable (to Blue Cross)		5,000			+5,000		
Accounts Payable (to Fidelity)		10,000			+10,000		
(Record employer-provided fringe benefits)							

Hawaiian Travel Agency pays employer's FICA taxes at the same rate that the employees pay (7.65%) and also pays unemployment taxes at the rate of 6.2%. The agency records its *employer's* payroll taxes as follows:

January 31	Debit	Credit	A	=	L	+	SE
Payroll Tax Expense (total)	**13,850**						−13,850 Exp↑
FICA Tax Payable (= 0.0765 × $100,000)		7,650			+7,650		
Unemployment Tax Payable (= 0.062 × $100,000)		6,200			+6,200		
(Record employer payroll taxes)							

Hawaiian Travel Agency incurred an additional $28,850 in expenses ($15,000 for fringe benefits plus $13,850 for employer payroll taxes) beyond the $100,000 salary expense. Also notice that the FICA tax payable in the *employee* withholding is the same amount recorded for *employer* payroll tax. That's because the employee pays 7.65% and the employer matches this amount with an additional 7.65%. The amounts withheld are then transferred at regular intervals, monthly or quarterly, to their designated recipients. Income taxes, FICA taxes, and unemployment taxes are transferred to various government agencies, and fringe benefits are paid to the company's contractual suppliers.

 KEY POINT

Employee salaries are reduced by withholdings for federal and state income taxes, FICA taxes, and the employee portion of insurance and retirement contributions. The employer, too, incurs additional payroll expenses for unemployment taxes, the employer portion of FICA taxes, and employer insurance and retirement contributions.

Other Current Liabilities

■ **LO4**
Demonstrate the accounting for other current liabilities.

Additional current liabilities companies might report include unearned revenues, sales tax payable, the current portion of long-term debt, and deferred taxes. We explore each of these in more detail below.

UNEARNED REVENUES

United Airlines sells tickets and collects the cash price several days, weeks, or sometimes months before the actual flight. When does United Airlines record the revenue—when it sells the ticket, or when the flight actually takes place? Illustration 8–4 provides the answer, in United's disclosure of its revenue recognition policies.

ILLUSTRATION 8–4
Revenue Recognition Policy of United Airlines

> **UNITED AIRLINES**
> **Notes to the Financial Statements (excerpt)**
>
> **Airline Revenues**—We record passenger fares and cargo revenues as operating revenues when the transportation is provided. The value of unused passenger tickets is included in current liabilities as advance ticket sales. We periodically evaluate the balance in advance ticket sales and record any adjustments in the period the evaluation is completed.

As you can see, United waits until the actual flight occurs to record the revenues. Since the flights have not taken place, the airline has not yet earned the revenue.

United's situation is not unique. It's not uncommon for companies to require advance payments from customers that will be applied to the purchase price when they deliver goods or provide services. You've likely been one of these customers. Examples of advance payments are gift cards from clothing stores like American Eagle or restaurants like Chili's, movie tickets from Fandango, room deposits at hotels like Embassy Suites, and subscriptions for magazines like *Sports Illustrated*.

How do these companies account for the cash they receive in advance? We initially discussed unearned revenue in Chapter 3, but let's review with an example. Assume Apple Inc. sells an iTunes gift card to a customer for $100. Apple records the sale of the gift card as follows:

A	=	L	+	SE		Debit	Credit
+100					Cash	100	
		+100			Unearned Revenue		100
					(Receive cash for gift card)		

As you can see, Apple Inc. records the receipt of cash, but does not credit Sales Revenue. Rather, since the iTunes have not been downloaded yet, the company credits Unearned Revenue, a liability account. While it may seem unusual for an account called Unearned Revenue to be a liability, think of it this way: Having already collected the cash, the company now has the obligation to earn it.

When the customer purchases and downloads, say, $15 worth of music, Apple records the following:

	Debit	Credit
Unearned Revenue	15	
Sales Revenue		15
(Earn revenue from music downloaded)		

A	=	L	+	SE
		−15		
				+15 Rev↑

As the company earns revenue from music downloads, it decreases (debits) Unearned Revenue and increases (credits) Sales Revenue. The customer has a balance of $85 on his gift card, and Apple Inc. has a balance in Unearned Revenue, a liability account, of $85 for music downloads.

KEY POINT

When a company receives cash in advance, it debits Cash and credits Unearned Revenue, a current liability account. When it earns the revenue, the company debits Unearned Revenue and credits Sales Revenue.

Let's Review

The new **Dallas Cowboys** football stadium has a seating capacity of 80,000, expandable to 111,000 with standing-room-only capacity. The new stadium cost $1.15 billion, making it one of the most expensive sports stadiums ever built. The Cowboys hold eight regular season games at home; an average ticket sells for about $100 a game. Assume the Cowboys collect $48 million in season ticket sales prior to the beginning of the season. For eight home games, that's $6 million per game ($48 million ÷ 8 games).

Required:

1. Record the sale of $48 million in season tickets prior to the beginning of the season.
2. Record the $6 million in revenue recognized after the first game.

Solution:

1. Sale of $48 million in season ticket sales:

($ in millions)	Debit	Credit
Cash	48	
Unearned Revenue		48
(Sell season tickets prior to the beginning of the season)		

2. $6 million in revenue recognized after the first game:

($ in millions)	Debit	Credit
Unearned Revenue	6	
Sales Revenue		6
(Earn revenue for each home game played)		

The Cowboys would make similar entries after each home game.

Suggested Homework:
BE8-6,
E8-10;
P8-5A&B

SALES TAX PAYABLE

Most states impose a state sales tax, and many areas include a local sales tax as well. Yet, some states do not have a sales tax. Upon arriving in Oregon for the first time, Don ordered lunch at a fast-food restaurant. His meal cost $4.99. When the employee at the counter said, "You're not from Oregon, are you?", Don wondered aloud how the sales clerk could tell. The clerk politely replied, "You have five dollars and some change in your hand, but in Oregon there's no sales tax." States that currently don't impose a general state sales tax are Alaska, Delaware, Montana, New Hampshire, and Oregon. However, many cities in Alaska have *local* sales taxes. The other four states impose sales-type taxes on specific transactions such as lodging, tobacco, or gasoline sales.

Each company selling products subject to sales tax is responsible for collecting the sales tax directly from customers and periodically sending the sales taxes collected to the state and local governments. The selling company records sales revenue in one account and sales tax payable in another. **When the company collects the sales taxes, it increases (debits) Cash and increases (credits) Sales Tax Payable.**

Suppose you buy lunch in the airport for $15 plus 9% sales tax. The airport restaurant records the transaction this way:

A = L + SE		Debit	Credit
+16.35	Cash	16.35	
+15.00 Rev↑	Sales Revenue		15.00
+1.35	Sales Tax Payable (= $15 × 0.09)		1.35
	(Record sales and sales tax)		

Some companies don't separately record sales and sales tax with each sale. Instead, they choose to separate the two amounts later. Suppose you buy lunch in the airport for $21.80 that includes a 9% sales tax. How much did the restaurant charge you for the lunch, and how much does it owe the state for sales tax? If we divide the total cash paid by 1.09 (1 + 9% sales tax rate), we get $20 (= $21.80 ÷ 1.09) as the sales price, leaving $1.80 as sales tax payable. If the entire amount collected is recorded initially as sales, at some point the company will separate the sales tax portion from sales and record that amount as sales tax payable.

 KEY POINT

Sales taxes collected from customers by the seller are not an expense. Instead, they represent current liabilities payable to the government.

CURRENT PORTION OF LONG-TERM DEBT

Distinguishing between the current portion of long-term debt and long-term debt is important to management, investors, and lenders. The current portion of long-term debt is the amount that will be paid within the next year. Management needs to know this amount in order to budget the cash flow necessary to pay the current portion as it becomes due. Investors and lenders also pay attention to current debt because it provides information about a company's liquidity, a useful indicator of risk.

Long-term obligations (notes, mortgages, bonds) usually are reclassified and reported as current liabilities when they become payable within the upcoming year (or operating cycle, if longer than a year). For example, a firm reports a 10-year note payable as a long-term liability for nine years but as a current liability on the balance sheet prepared during the tenth year of its term to maturity. As another example, Southwest Airlines had total borrowings of $3,515 million at December 31, 2009, of which $190 million was payable in 2010 and the remaining $3,325 million is due after 2010. In its 2009 balance sheet, the company records the $3,515 million in current and long-term debt, as shown in Illustration 8–5.

SOUTHWEST AIRLINES
Balance Sheet (partial)
December 31, 2009
($ in millions)

Current liabilities:	
Current portion of long-term debt	$ 190
Long-term liabilities:	
Long-term debt	3,325
Total borrowings	$3,515

ILLUSTRATION 8–5
Current Portion of
Long-Term Debt

KEY POINT

We report the currently maturing portion of a long-term debt as a current liability on the balance sheet.

Current or Long-Term?

Given a choice, do you suppose management would prefer to report an obligation as a current liability or a long-term liability? Other things being equal, most managers would choose the long-term classification. The reason is that outsiders like banks, bondholders, and shareholders usually consider debt that is due currently to be riskier than debt that is not due for some time. Riskier debt means paying higher interest rates for borrowing. So, be aware that management has incentives to report current obligations as long-term. ●

Decision Maker's Perspective

DEFERRED TAXES

Net income in the income statement is *not* the same amount as taxable income reported to the Internal Revenue Service (IRS). Net income is based on financial accounting rules, while taxable income in the corporate tax return is based on tax accounting rules. There are many differences between financial accounting rules and tax accounting rules. For instance, most companies use straight-line depreciation in financial accounting, but a different depreciation method (called MACRS) for tax accounting. You will learn more about tax accounting rules in an individual or corporate income tax class.

Differences between financial accounting and tax accounting can result in a company recording financial income now, but deferring payment of some of its income tax expense to future years. In such a case, it will report a *deferred tax liability*. (Or the company may record an expense now, but deduct it for taxes in future years, in which case it will report a deferred tax asset.) As you might guess, deferred taxes can get pretty complex. For now, just remember that there are differences between net income reported on the income statement and taxable income reported on the tax return, and these differences can result in deferred tax liabilities, both current and long-term.

KEY POINT

Net income and taxable income often differ because of differences in financial accounting and tax accounting rules. These differences can result in deferred tax liabilities, in which income is reported now but the tax on the income will not be paid until future years.

PART B

■ LO5
Apply the appropriate accounting treatment for contingencies.

CONTINGENCIES

Many companies are involved in litigation disputes, in which the final outcome is uncertain. In its financial statements, does the company wait until the lawsuit is settled, or does it go ahead and report the details of the unsettled case? In this section, we discuss how to report these uncertain situations, which are broadly called contingencies. We look at both contingent liabilities and their flip side, contingent gains.

Contingent Liabilities

A contingent liability may not be a liability at all. Whether it is depends on whether an uncertain event that might result in a loss occurs or not. Examples include lawsuits, product warranties, environmental problems, and premium offers. **Philip Morris**'s tobacco litigation, **Motorola**'s cell phone warranties, **BP**'s environmental obligations, and **United**'s frequent-flier program are all contingent liabilities. To demonstrate, let's consider a litigation example.

LITIGATION AND OTHER CAUSES

Deloitte was the auditor for a client we'll call Jeeps, Inc. The client sold accessories for jeeps, such as tops, lights, cargo carriers, and hitches. One of the major issues that appeared in Deloitte's audit of Jeeps, Inc., was outstanding litigation. Several lawsuits against the company alleged that the jeep top (made of vinyl) did not hold during a major collision. The jeep manufacturer, **Chrysler**, also was named in the lawsuits. The damages claimed were quite large, about $100 million. Although the company had litigation insurance, there was some question whether the insurance company could pay because the insurance carrier was undergoing financial difficulty. The auditor discussed the situation with the outside legal counsel representing Jeeps, Inc. Legal counsel indicated that the possibility of payment was remote and that if the case went to trial, Jeeps, Inc., would almost surely win.

As the auditor, you could choose one of three options to report the situation. You could: (1) report a liability for the full $100 million or for some lesser amount, (2) provide full disclosure in a note to the financial statements but not report a liability in the balance sheet, or (3) provide no disclosure at all.

Whether we report a contingent liability (option 1) depends on two criteria: (1) the likelihood of payment and (2) the ability to estimate the amount of payment. Let's look at the options for each:

1. The likelihood of payment can be:
   a. *Probable*—likely to occur;
   b. *Reasonably possible*—more than remote but less than probable; or
   c. *Remote*—the chance is slight.

2. The ability to estimate the payment amount is either:
   a. Known or reasonably estimable; or
   b. Not reasonably estimable.

A contingent liability is recorded only if a loss is *probable* **and** the amount can be *reasonably estimated*. We record this with a debit to Loss (which acts like an expense account) and a credit to Contingent Liability.

	Debit	Credit
Loss	x,xxx	
Contingent Liability		x,xxx
(Record a contingent liability)		

INTERNATIONAL FINANCIAL REPORTING STANDARDS (IFRS)

We record a contingent liability under U.S. GAAP if it's both probable and can be reasonably estimated. IFRS rules are similar, but the threshold is "more likely than not." This is a lower threshold than "probable," and thus, contingent liabilities are more likely to be recorded under IFRS rules than under U.S. GAAP.

For more discussion, see Appendix E.

If the likelihood of payment is probable and if one amount within a range appears more likely, we record that amount. When no amount within the range appears more likely than others, we record the *minimum* amount and disclose the potential additional loss. If the likelihood of payment is *reasonably possible* rather than probable, we record no entry but make full disclosure in a note to the financial statements to describe the contingency. Finally, if the likelihood of payment is *remote,* disclosure usually is not required. Illustration 8–6 provides a summary of the accounting for contingent liabilities.

If payment is:	Known or Reasonably Estimable	Not Reasonably Estimable
Probable	Liability recorded and disclosure required	Disclosure required
Reasonably possible	Disclosure required	Disclosure required
Remote	Disclosure not required	Disclosure not required

ILLUSTRATION 8–6

Accounting Treatment of Contingent Liabilities

 KEY POINT

A contingent liability is recorded only if a loss is *probable* **and** the amount can be *reasonably estimated.*

Back to the example of Jeeps, Inc.: How do you think Deloitte, as the auditor of Jeeps, Inc., treated the litigation described earlier? Based on the response of legal counsel, the likelihood of the payment occurring was considered to be remote, so disclosure was not required. However, because the amount was so large, and because there were concerns about the firm's primary insurance carrier undergoing financial difficulty, Deloitte insisted on full disclosure of the litigation in the notes to the financial statements.

Decision Point

Question	Accounting information	Analysis
Is the company involved in any litigation?	Notes to the financial statements	Companies are required to disclose all contingencies, including litigation, with at least a reasonable possibility of payment. This information can then be used to help estimate their potential financial impact.

Illustration 8–7 provides excerpts from the disclosure of contingencies made by **United Airlines**.

ILLUSTRATION 8–7

Disclosure of Contingencies by United Airlines

UNITED AIRLINES
Notes to the Financial Statements (excerpts)

Legal and Environmental Contingencies. United Airlines has certain contingencies resulting from litigation and claims (including environmental issues) incident to the ordinary course of business. Management believes, after considering a number of factors, including (but not limited to) the views of legal counsel, the nature of contingencies to which we are subject and prior experience, that the ultimate disposition of these contingencies will not materially affect the Company's consolidated financial position or results of operations.

Contingency for Frequent-Flyer Program Awards. United's Mileage Plus frequent-flyer program awards mileage credits to passengers who fly on United, United Express, and certain other airlines that participate in the program. When a travel award level is attained by a Mileage Plus member, we record a liability for the estimated cost of such awards. The Company had recorded a liability and deferred revenue for its frequent-flyer program totaling $1.6 billion (consisting of $679 million for prepaid miles and $923 million related to award travel).

WARRANTIES

Warranties are perhaps the most common example of contingent liabilities. When you buy a new **Dell** notebook, it comes with a warranty covering the hardware from defect for either a 90-day, one-year, or two-year period depending on the product. Why does Dell offer a warranty? To increase sales, of course.

Based on the matching principle, the company needs to record the warranty expense in the same accounting period in which it sells you the product. The warranty for the computer represents an expense and a liability for Dell at the time of the sale because it meets the criteria for recording a contingent liability: Because warranties almost always entail an eventual expenditure, it's *probable* that a cost will be incurred. And even though Dell doesn't know exactly what that cost will be, it can, based on experience, *reasonably estimate* the amount. Let's look at a warranty example in more detail.

Dell introduces a new notebook computer in December that carries a one-year warranty against manufacturer's defects. Based on industry experience with similar product introductions, Dell expects warranty costs will be an amount equal to approximately 3% of sales. New notebook sales for the month of December are $1.5 million. Dell records the warranty liability on December 31 as follows:

December 31	Debit	Credit
Warranty Expense ($1.5 million × 3%)	45,000	
Warranty Liability		45,000
(Record liability for warranties)		

A = L + SE
−45,000 Exp↑
+45,000

When customers make warranty claims and Dell incurs costs to satisfy those claims, the liability is reduced. Let's say that customers make claims costing $12,000 in December. We record the warranty expenditures as follows:

December 31	Debit	Credit
Warranty Liability	12,000	
Cash		12,000
(Record actual warranty expenditures)		

A = L + SE
−12,000
−12,000

Any time you need to calculate a balance, it's often helpful to make a T-account and record the transactions. Remember, journal entries show the transaction, while T-accounts give you the balance. The balance in the Warranty Liability account at the end of December is $33,000 as follows:

	Warranty Liability		
Payment	12,000	45,000	Expense
		33,000	Balance

COMMON MISTAKE

Some students think the balance in the Warranty Liability account is equal to Warranty Expense, $45,000 in this example. Remember, the liability is increased by warranty expense but then is reduced over time by actual warranty expenditures.

Contingent Gains

A contingent gain is an existing uncertain situation that might result in a gain, which often is the flip side of contingent liabilities. In a pending lawsuit, one side—the defendant—faces a contingent liability, while the other side—the plaintiff—has a contingent gain. For example, **Polaroid** sued **Kodak** for patent infringement of its instant photography technology. Polaroid had a potential gain, while Kodak faced a potential loss.

As discussed earlier, we record contingent liabilities when the loss is probable and the amount is reasonably estimable. However, **we do not record contingent gains until the gain is certain.** The nonparallel treatment of contingent gains follows the same conservative reasoning that motivates reporting some assets (like inventory) at lower-of-cost-or-market. Specifically, it's desirable to anticipate losses, but recognizing gains should await their final settlement. Though firms do not record contingent gains in the accounts, they sometimes disclose them in notes to the financial statements.

Flip Side

KEY POINT

Unlike contingent liabilities, contingent gains are not recorded until the gain is certain and no longer a contingency.

ANALYSIS

LIQUIDITY ANALYSIS
United vs. Southwest

■ **LO6**
Assess liquidity using current liability ratios.

Liquidity refers to having sufficient cash (or other current assets convertible to cash in a relatively short time) to pay currently maturing debts. Because a lack of liquidity can result in financial difficulties or even bankruptcy, it is critical that managers as well as outside investors and lenders maintain close watch on this aspect of a company's well-being. Here we look at three liquidity measures: working capital, the current ratio, and the acid-test ratio. All three measures are calculated using current assets and current liabilities.

WORKING CAPITAL

The concept of **working capital** is straightforward. It is simply the difference between current assets and current liabilities:

$$\text{Working capital} = \text{Current assets} - \text{Current liabilities}$$

Working capital answers the question, "After paying our current obligations, how much will we have to work with?" For example, if you have $20 in your pocket and you know that you still owe $10 to your friend and $3 for parking, your working capital is $7. A large positive working capital is an indicator of liquidity—whether a company will be able to pay its current debts on time.

However, working capital is not the best measure of liquidity when comparing one company with another, since it does not control for the relative size of each company. In comparing companies, the current ratio and the acid-test ratio are better measures of a company's ability to pay its debts on time.

CURRENT RATIO

We calculate the **current ratio** by dividing current assets by current liabilities:

$$\text{Current ratio} = \frac{\text{Current assets}}{\text{Current liabilities}}$$

A current ratio greater than 1 implies more current assets than current liabilities. Recall that current assets include cash, current investments, accounts receivable, inventories, and prepaid expenses. As a rule of thumb, a current ratio of 1 or higher often reflects an acceptable level of liquidity. A current ratio of 1 indicates that for every dollar of current liabilities, the company has an equal amount of current assets. A current ratio of, say, 1.5 indicates that for every dollar of current liabilities, the company has $1.50 of current assets.

In general, the higher the current ratio, the greater the company's liquidity. But we should evaluate the current ratio, like other ratios, in the context of the industry in which the company operates and other specific circumstances. Keep in mind, though, that not all current assets are equally liquid, which leads us to another, more specific ratio for measuring liquidity.

ACID-TEST RATIO

Common Terms The acid-test ratio is also called the *quick ratio.*

The **acid-test ratio**, or *quick ratio,* is similar to the current ratio but is based on a more conservative measure of current assets available to pay current liabilities. We calculate it by dividing "quick assets" by current liabilities. **Quick assets** include only cash, current investments, and accounts receivable. By eliminating current assets, such as inventory and prepaid expenses, that are less readily convertible into cash, the acid-test ratio may provide a better indication of a company's liquidity than does the current ratio.

$$\text{Acid-test ratio} = \frac{\text{Cash} + \text{Current investments} + \text{Accounts receivable}}{\text{Current liabilities}}$$

We interpret the acid-test ratio much like the current ratio, with one difference: We know that the current assets in the top half of the ratio are only those that can be quickly converted to cash. Thus, an acid-test ratio of, say, 1.5 would indicate that for every dollar of current liabilities, the company has $1.50 of current assets that are easily convertible to cash that might be used to help pay the current liabilities as they come due. As is true for other ratios, be sure to evaluate the acid-test ratio in the context of the industry in which the company operates.

KEY POINT

Working capital is the difference between current assets and current liabilities. The current ratio is equal to current assets divided by current liabilities. The acid-test ratio is equal to quick assets (cash, current investments, and accounts receivable) divided by current liabilities. Each measures a company's liquidity, its ability to pay currently maturing debts.

Decision Point

Question	Accounting information	Analysis
Does the company have enough cash to pay current liabilities as they come due?	Working capital, current ratio, and acid-test ratio	A high working capital, current ratio, or acid-test ratio generally indicates the ability to pay current liabilities on a timely basis.

Let's compare **United Airlines**'s liquidity ratios to those of **Southwest Airlines**, considered by many to be the airline industry leader in profitability and overall financial condition.

Let's Review

Selected financial data regarding current assets and current liabilities for United and Southwest Airlines are as follows.

($ in millions)	United	Southwest
Current assets:		
Cash and cash equivalents	$3,046	$1,368
Current investments		435
Net receivables	977	574
Inventory	237	203
Other current assets	601	313
Total current assets	$4,861	$2,893
Current liabilities:		
Accounts payable	$3,231	$2,643
Short/current long-term debt	1,808	163
Other current liabilities	2,242	
Total current liabilities	$7,281	$2,806

Required:

1. Calculate working capital for United Airlines and Southwest Airlines. Is working capital adequate for each company?

2. Calculate the current ratio for United Airlines and Southwest Airlines. Which company has a better current ratio?

3. Calculate the acid-test (quick) ratio for United Airlines and Southwest Airlines. Which company has a better acid-test ratio?

Solution:

1. Working capital:

($ in millions)	Total Current Assets	−	Total Current Liabilities	=	Working Capital
United	$4,861	−	$7,281	=	$(2,420)
Southwest	$2,893	−	$2,806	=	$ 87

United Airlines actually has a negative working capital, in which its current liabilities exceed its current assets by $2.4 billion. Southwest Airlines, with positive working capital, has more liquidity.

2. Current ratio:

($ in millions)	Total Current Assets	÷	Total Current Liabilities	=	Current Ratio
United	$4,861	÷	$7,281	=	0.67
Southwest	$2,893	÷	$2,806	=	1.03

Southwest Airlines also has a higher current ratio, which would indicate better liquidity than United. Southwest has just above the "acceptable" liquidity level of 1.0.

3. Acid-test (quick) ratio:

Remember that *quick assets* equal cash + current investments + net receivables.

($ in millions)	Quick Assets	÷	Total Current Liabilities	=	Acid-Test Ratio
United	$4,023	÷	$7,281	=	0.55
Southwest	$2,377	÷	$2,806	=	0.85

Suggested Homework:
BE8-15;
E8-16;
P8-9A&B

By eliminating less-liquid current assets such as inventory, the acid-test ratio often provides a better indicator of liquidity. Once again, Southwest Airlines "wins" with an acid-test ratio of 0.85, compared to 0.55 for United Airlines.

What do the liquidity measures for United and Southwest tell us? Together, they provide an indication of a company's ability to pay its currently maturing debts. Looking at working capital, the current ratio, and the acid-test ratio, it appears that Southwest Airlines is in a better position than United to meet its current debt obligations. But remember that we should evaluate liquidity measures in the context of an industry. The airlines have faced tough times recently, between dampened demand resulting from 9/11, increasing fuel costs, and the recent recession. So, while Southwest has fared better than United, its liquidity still may not compare well with other industries.

Decision Maker's Perspective   Indicators of Liquidity

If the firm's current ratio or acid-test ratio is lower than that of the industry as a whole, does that mean liquidity is a problem? Perhaps, but perhaps not. It does, though, raise a red flag that suggests caution when assessing other aspects of the company.

It's important to remember that each ratio is but one piece of the puzzle. For example, profitability is probably the best long-run indicator of liquidity. It is difficult to maintain liquidity over a string of consecutive loss years. Another consideration is that management may be very efficient in managing current assets so that some current assets—receivables or inventory—remain at minimum amounts. This is good for the company overall, but it may result in less-impressive current and acid-test ratios. The turnover ratios we discussed in Chapters 5 and 6, such as receivables turnover and inventory turnover, help measure the efficiency of asset management in this regard. ●

COMMON MISTAKE

As a general rule, a higher current ratio is better. However, a high current ratio is not always a positive signal. Companies having difficulty collecting receivables or holding excessive inventory will also have a higher current ratio. Managers must balance the incentive for strong liquidity (yielding a high current ratio) with the need to minimize levels of receivables and inventory (yielding a lower current ratio).

Effect of Transactions on Liquidity Ratios

It also is important to understand the effect of specific transactions on the current ratio and acid-test ratio. Both ratios have the same denominator, current liabilities, so a decrease in current liabilities will increase the ratios (dividing by a smaller number makes the ratio bigger). Likewise, an increase in current liabilities will decrease the ratios (dividing by a bigger number makes the ratio smaller).

How are the ratios affected by changes in current assets? It depends on which current asset changes. Both ratios include cash, current investments, and accounts receivable. An increase in any of those will increase *both* ratios. However, only the current ratio includes inventory and other current assets. An increase to inventory or other current assets will increase the current ratio, but not the acid-test ratio.

Liquidity Management

Can management influence the ratios that measure liquidity? Yes, at least to some extent. A company can influence the timing of accounts payable recognition by asking suppliers to change their delivery schedules. For example, a large airplane manufacturer like **Boeing** or **McDonnell Douglas** might delay the shipment and billing of certain inventory parts from late December to early January, reducing accounts payable at its December year-end. Because accounts payable is included in calculating the current ratio, the timing of accounts payable recognition could mean the difference between an unacceptable ratio and an acceptable one, or between violating and complying with a debt covenant.

Suppose, for instance, a company with a current ratio of 1.25 (current assets of $5 million and current liabilities of $4 million) has entered into a *debt covenant* with its bank that requires a minimum current ratio of 1.25. A debt covenant is an agreement between a borrower and a lender that requires that certain minimum financial measures be met or the lender can recall the debt. By delaying the delivery of $1 million of inventory purchased on account, the company can increase the ratio to 1.33 (current assets of $4 million and current liabilities of $3 million). Investors and creditors should be aware of managerial activities that increase liquidity ratios, such as misclassification of current liabilities or unusual variations in accounts payable levels.

ETHICAL DILEMMA

Airport Accessories (AA) has several loans outstanding with a local bank. The loan contract contains an agreement that AA must maintain a current ratio of at least 0.90. Micah, the assistant controller, estimates that the year-end current assets and current liabilities will be $2,100,000 and $2,400,000, respectively. These estimates provide a current ratio of only 0.875. Violation of the debt agreement will increase AA's borrowing costs because the loans will be renegotiated at higher interest rates.

Micah proposes that AA purchase inventory of $600,000 on credit before year-end. This will cause both current assets and current liabilities to increase by the same amount, but the current ratio will increase to 0.90. The extra $600,000 in inventory will be used over the next year. However, the purchase will cause warehousing costs and financing costs to increase.

Micah is concerned about the ethics of his proposal. What do you think?

KEY POINTS BY LEARNING OBJECTIVE

LO1 Distinguish between current and long-term liabilities.

In most cases, current liabilities are payable within one year and long-term liabilities are payable more than one year from now.

LO2 Account for notes payable and interest expense.

We record interest expense in the period we incur it, rather than in the period in which we pay it.

Many short-term loans are arranged under an existing line of credit with a bank, or for larger corporations in the form of commercial paper, a loan from one company to another.

LO3 Account for employee and employer payroll liabilities.

Employee salaries are reduced by withholdings for federal and state income taxes, FICA taxes, and the employee portion of insurance and retirement contributions. The employer, too, incurs additional payroll expenses for unemployment taxes, the employer portion of FICA taxes, and employer insurance and retirement contributions.

LO4 Demonstrate the accounting for other current liabilities.

When a company receives cash in advance, it debits Cash and credits Unearned Revenue, a current liability account. When it earns the revenue, the company debits Unearned Revenue and credits Sales Revenue.

Sales taxes collected from customers by the seller are not an expense. Instead, they represent current liabilities payable to the government.

We report the currently maturing portion of a long-term debt as a current liability on the balance sheet.

Net income and taxable income often differ because of differences between financial accounting and tax accounting rules. These differences can result in *deferred tax liabilities*, in which income is reported now but the tax on the income will not be paid until future years.

LO5 Apply the appropriate accounting treatment for contingencies.

A contingent liability is recorded only if a loss is *probable* **and** the amount can be *reasonably estimated*.

Unlike contingent liabilities, contingent gains are not recorded until the gain is certain and no longer a contingency.

Analysis

LO6 Assess liquidity using current liability ratios.

Working capital is the difference between current assets and current liabilities. The current ratio is equal to current assets divided by current liabilities. The acid-test ratio is equal to quick assets (cash, short-term investments, and accounts receivable) divided by current liabilities. Each measures a company's liquidity, its ability to pay currently maturing debts.

GLOSSARY

Acid-test ratio: Cash, current investments, and accounts receivable divided by current liabilities; measures the availability of liquid current assets to pay current liabilities. **p. 386**

Commercial paper: Borrowing from another company rather than from a bank. **p. 374**

Contingencies: Uncertain situations that can result in a gain or a loss for a company. **p. 382**

Contingent gain: An existing uncertain situation that might result in a gain. **p. 385**

Contingent liability: An existing uncertain situation that might result in a loss. **p. 382**

Current liabilities: Debts that, in most cases, are due within one year. However, when a company has an operating cycle of longer than a year, its current liabilities are defined by the length of the operating cycle, rather than by the length of one year. **p. 370**

Current portion of long-term debt: Debt that will be paid within the next year. **p. 380**

Current ratio: Current assets divided by current liabilities; measures the availability of current assets to pay current liabilities. **p. 386**

Debt covenant: An agreement between a borrower and a lender that requires that certain minimum financial measures be met or the lender can recall the debt. **p. 389**

FICA taxes: Based on the Federal Insurance Contribution Act; tax withheld from employees' paychecks

and matched by employers for Social Security and Medicare. **p. 376**

Fringe benefits: Additional employee benefits paid for by the employer. **p. 377**

Liability: A present responsibility to sacrifice assets in the future due to a transaction or other event that happened in the past. **p. 370**

Line of credit: An informal agreement that permits a company to borrow up to a prearranged limit without having to follow formal loan procedures and prepare paperwork. **p. 374**

Liquidity: Having sufficient cash (or other assets convertible to cash in a relatively short time) to pay currently maturing debts. **p. 386**

Notes payable: Written promises to repay amounts borrowed plus interest. **p. 371**

Quick assets: Includes only cash, current investments, and accounts receivable. **p. 386**

Sales tax payable: Sales tax collected from customers by the seller, representing current liabilities payable to the government. **p. 380**

Unearned revenue: A liability account used to record cash received in advance of the sale or service. **p. 378**

Unemployment taxes: A tax to cover federal and state unemployment costs paid by the employer on behalf of its employees. **p. 376**

Working capital: The difference between current assets and current liabilities. **p. 386**

SELF-STUDY QUESTIONS

1. Which of the following statements regarding liabilities is *not* true? ■ LO1
   a. Liabilities can be for services rather than cash.
   b. Liabilities are reported in the balance sheet for almost every business.
   c. Liabilities result from future transactions.
   d. Liabilities represent probable future sacrifices of benefits.

2. Current liabilities: ■ LO1
   a. May include contingent liabilities.
   b. Include obligations payable within one year or one operating cycle, whichever is shorter.
   c. Can be satisfied only with the payment of cash.
   d. Are preferred by most companies over long-term liabilities.

3. If Express Jet borrows $100 million on October 1, 2012, for one year at 6% interest, ■ LO2
   how much interest expense does it record for the year ended December 31, 2012?
   a. $0.
   b. $1 million.
   c. $1.5 million.
   d. $6 million.

4. We record interest expense on a note payable in the period in which: ■ LO2
   a. We pay cash for interest.
   b. We incur interest.

392   CHAPTER 8   Current Liabilities

                                c. We pay cash and incur interest.
                                d. We pay cash or incur interest.

■ LO3   5. Which of the following is *not* deducted from an employee's salary?
                                a. FICA taxes.
                                b. Unemployment taxes.
                                c. Income taxes.
                                d. Employee portion of insurance and retirement payments.

■ LO4   6. The seller collects sales taxes from the customer at the time of sale and reports the
                                sales taxes as:
                                a. Sales tax expense.
                                b. Sales tax revenue.
                                c. Sales tax receivable.
                                d. Sales tax payable.

■ LO5   7. Management can estimate the amount of loss that will occur due to litigation
                                against the company. If the likelihood of loss is reasonably possible, a contingent
                                liability should be:
                                a. Disclosed but not reported as a liability.
                                b. Disclosed and reported as a liability.
                                c. Neither disclosed nor reported as a liability.
                                d. Reported as a liability but not disclosed.

■ LO5   8. Smith Co. filed suit against Western, Inc., seeking damages for patent
                                infringement. Western's legal counsel believes it is probable that Western will settle
                                the lawsuit for an estimated amount in the range of $75,000 to $175,000, with all
                                amounts in the range considered equally likely. How should Western report this
                                litigation?
                                a. As a liability for $75,000 with disclosure of the range.
                                b. As a liability for $125,000 with disclosure of the range.
                                c. As a liability for $175,000 with disclosure of the range.
                                d. As a disclosure only. No liability is reported.

■ LO6   9. The acid-test ratio is:
                                a. Current assets divided by current liabilities.
                                b. Cash and current investments divided by current liabilities.
                                c. Cash, current investments, and accounts receivable divided by current
                                   liabilities.
                                d. Cash, current investments, accounts receivable, and inventory divided by
                                   current liabilities.

■ LO6   10. Assuming a current ratio of 1.0 and an acid-test ratio of 0.75, how will the
                                purchase of inventory with cash affect each ratio?
                                a. Increase the current ratio and increase the acid-test ratio.
                                b. No change to the current ratio and decrease the acid-test ratio.
                                c. Decrease the current ratio and decrease the acid-test ratio.
Check out   d. Increase the current ratio and decrease the acid-test ratio.
www.mhhe.com/succeed
for more multiple-choice   *Note: For answers, see the last page of the chapter.*
questions.

REVIEW QUESTIONS

■ LO1   1. What are the essential characteristics of liabilities for purposes of financial reporting?

■ LO1   2. How do we define current liabilities? Long-term liabilities?

■ LO1   3. Why is it important to distinguish between current and long-term liabilities?

4. **United Airlines** served as an example throughout the chapter. Provide several examples of current liabilities in the airline industry.
■ LO1

5. Explain why we record interest in the period in which we incur it rather than in the period in which we pay it.
■ LO2

6. Bank loans often are arranged under existing lines of credit. What is a line of credit? How does a line of credit work?
■ LO2

7. How does commercial paper differ from a normal bank loan? Why is the interest rate often less for commercial paper?
■ LO2

8. Name at least four items withheld from employee payroll checks. Which deductions are required by law and which are voluntary?
■ LO3

9. Name at least four employer costs in addition to the employee's salary. Which costs are required by law and which are voluntary?
■ LO3

10. Who pays Social Security taxes: the employer, the employee, or both? How is the deduction for Social Security and Medicare (FICA) computed?
■ LO3

11. Retailers like **McDonald's, American Eagle**, and **Apple Inc.** sell quite a few gift cards. Explain how these companies account for the sale of gift cards.
■ LO4

12. *BusinessWeek* sells magazine subscriptions in advance of their distribution. (a) What journal entry would the company make at the time it sells subscriptions? (b) What journal entry would the company make each time it distributes a magazine?
■ LO4

13. Like all retailers, **Hollister** is required to collect sales tax to be remitted to state and local government authorities. Assume a local store has cash proceeds from sales of $5,325, including $325 in sales tax. What is the sales tax rate? Provide the journal entry to record the proceeds.
■ LO4

14. If $10 million of **Dell Computer Corporation**'s $130 million notes payable is due in the next year, how will the firm present this debt within the current and long-term liabilities sections of the current year's balance sheet?
■ LO4

15. Is net income reported in the income statement the same amount as taxable income in the corporate tax return? Why or why not?
■ LO4

16. Define contingent liability. Provide three common examples.
■ LO5

17. List and briefly describe the three categories of likelihood that a payment for a contingent liability will need to be made.
■ LO5

18. Under what circumstances should a firm report a contingent liability?
■ LO5

19. Suppose the firm's analysis of a contingent liability indicates that an obligation is not probable. What accounting treatment, if any, is warranted?
■ LO5

20. If a contingent liability is probable but estimable only within a range, what amount, if any, should the firm report?
■ LO5

21. Your company is the plaintiff in a lawsuit. Legal counsel advises you that your eventual victory is inevitable. "You will be awarded $2 million," your attorney confidently asserts. Describe the appropriate accounting treatment.
■ LO5

22. Current liabilities affect a company's liquidity. What is liquidity, and how do we evaluate it?
■ LO6

23. Explain the differences among working capital, the current ratio, and the acid-test ratio.
■ LO6

24. How would the following transactions affect the current ratio and the acid-test ratio? (a) Purchase of inventory with cash; and (b) sale of inventory for more than its cost. Assume that prior to these transactions the current ratio and acid-test ratio are both less than one.
■ LO6

BRIEF EXERCISES

Record notes payable (LO2)

Flip Side of BE8–2

BE8–1 On November 1, Bahama Cruise Lines borrows $3 million and issues a six-month, 6% note payable. Interest is payable at maturity. Record the issuance of the note and the appropriate adjustment for interest expense at December 31, the end of the reporting period.

Record notes receivable (LO2)

Flip Side of BE8–1

BE8–2 On November 1, Bahama National Bank lends $3 million and accepts a six-month, 6% note receivable. Interest is due at maturity. Record the acceptance of the note and the appropriate adjustment for interest revenue at December 31, the end of the reporting period.

Determine interest expense (LO2)

BE8–3 On July 1, Alaskan Adventures issues a $100,000, eight-month, 6% note. Interest is payable at maturity. What is the amount of interest expense that the company would record in a year-end adjustment on December 31?

Record commercial paper (LO2)

BE8–4 On April 1, Online Travel issues $12 million of commercial paper with a maturity on December 31 and an 8% interest rate. Record the issuance of the commercial paper and its repayment at maturity.

Calculate FICA taxes (LO3)

BE8–5 Mike Samson is a college football coach making a base salary of $640,800 a year ($53,400 per month). Employers are required to withhold a 6.2% Social Security tax up to a maximum base amount and a 1.45% Medicare tax with no maximum. Assuming the FICA base amount is $106,800, compute how much will be withheld during the year for Coach Samson's Social Security and Medicare. Through what month will Social Security be withheld? What additional amount will the employer need to contribute?

Record unearned revenues (LO4)

BE8–6 On December 18, Intel receives $250,000 from a customer toward a cash sale of $2.5 million for computer chips to be completed on January 23. The computer chips had a total production cost of $1.5 million. What journal entries should Intel record on December 18 and January 23? Assume Intel uses the perpetual inventory system.

Record sales tax (LO4)

BE8–7 During December, Far West Services makes a $1,200 credit sale. The state sales tax rate is 6% and the local sales tax rate is 2.5%. Record sales and sales tax payable.

Report current portion of long-term debt (LO4)

BE8–8 On September 1, 2012, Southwest Airlines borrows $40 million, of which $8 million is due next year. Show how Southwest Airlines would record the $40 million debt on its December 31, 2012, balance sheet.

Calculate warranty liability (LO5)

BE8–9 Sony introduces a new compact music player to compete with Apple's iPod that carries a two-year warranty against manufacturer's defects. Based on industry experience with similar product introductions, warranty costs are expected to be approximately 2% of sales. By the end of the first year of selling the product, total sales are $30 million, and actual warranty expenditures are $200,000. What amount (if any) should Sony report as a liability at the end of the year?

Determine the financial statement effect of a contingent liability (LO5)

BE8–10 Consultants notify management of Discount Pharmaceuticals that a stroke medication poses a potential health hazard. Counsel indicates that a product recall is probable and is estimated to cost the company $8 million. How will this affect the company's income statement and balance sheet this period?

Account for a contingent liability (LO5)

Flip Side of BE8–12

BE8–11 Electronic Innovators is the defendant in a $10 million lawsuit filed by one of its customers, Aviation Systems. The litigation is in final appeal, and legal counsel advises that it is probable that Electronic Innovators will lose the lawsuit. The estimated amount is somewhere between $6 and $10 million. How should Electronic Innovators account for this event?

Account for a contingent gain (LO5)

Flip Side of BE8–11

BE8–12 Aviation Systems is involved in a $10 million lawsuit filed against one of its suppliers, Electronic Innovators. The litigation is in final appeal, and legal counsel advises that it is probable that Aviation Systems will win the lawsuit and be awarded somewhere between $6 and $10 million. How should Aviation Systems account for this event?

BE8–13 The Environmental Protection Agency (EPA) is in the process of investigating a possible water contamination issue at the manufacturing facility of Northwest Forest Products. The EPA has not yet proposed a penalty assessment. Management feels an assessment is reasonably possible, and if an assessment is made, an unfavorable settlement is estimated between $20 and $30 million. How should Northwest Forest Products report this situation in its current financial statements?

Determine the financial statement effect of a contingent liability (LO5)

BE8–14 Motorola is a world leader in the development of cellular phone technology. During the year, the company becomes aware of potential costs due to (1) a product defect that is reasonably possible and can be reasonably estimated, (2) a safety hazard that is probable and cannot be reasonably estimated, and (3) a new product warranty that is probable and can be reasonably estimated. Which of these potential costs, if any, should Motorola record?

Account for contingent liabilities (LO5)

BE8–15 Under Armour has the following current assets: cash, $102 million; receivables, $94 million; inventory, $182 million; and other current assets, $18 million. Under Armour has the following liabilities: accounts payable, $98 million; current portion of long-term debt, $35 million; and long-term debt, $23 million. Based on these amounts, calculate the current ratio and the acid-test ratio for Under Armour.

Calculate current and acid-test ratios (LO6)

EXERCISES

E8–1 Match (by letter) the correct reporting method for each of the items listed below.

Determine proper classification of liabilities (LO1)

Reporting Method

C = Current liability
L = Long-term liability
D = Disclosure note only
N = Not reported

Item

_____ 1. Accounts payable.
_____ 2. Current portion of long-term debt.
_____ 3. Sales tax collected from customers.
_____ 4. Notes payable due next year.
_____ 5. Notes payable due in two years.
_____ 6. Customer advances.
_____ 7. Commercial paper.
_____ 8. Unused line of credit.
_____ 9. A contingent liability with a *probable* likelihood of occurring within the next year and can be estimated.
_____ 10. A contingent liability with a *reasonably possible* likelihood of occurring within the next year and can be estimated.

E8–2 On November 1, 2012, Aviation Training Corp. borrows $50,000 cash from Community Savings and Loan. Aviation Training signs a three-month, 6% note payable. Interest is payable at maturity. Aviation's year-end is December 31.

Record notes payable (LO2)

Required:
1. Record the note payable by Aviation Training.
2. Record the appropriate adjustment for the note by Aviation Training on December 31, 2012.
3. Record the payment of the note at maturity.

E8–3 On August 1, 2012, Trico Technologies, an aeronautic electronics company, borrows $20 million cash to expand operations. The loan is made by FirstBanc Corp. under a short-term line of credit arrangement. Trico signs a six-month, 8% promissory note. Interest is payable at maturity. Trico's year-end is December 31.

Record notes payable (LO2)
Flip Side of E8–4

396

CHAPTER 8   Current Liabilities

Required:

1. Record the issuance of the note by Trico Technologies.
2. Record the appropriate adjustment for the note by Trico on December 31, 2012.
3. Record the payment of the note by Trico at maturity.

Record notes receivable (LO2)

Flip Side of E8–3

E8–4 On August 1, 2012, Trico Technologies, an aeronautic electronics company, borrows $20 million cash to expand operations. The loan is made by FirstBanc Corp. under a short-term line of credit arrangement. Trico signs a six-month, 8% promissory note. Interest is payable at maturity. FirstBanc Corp.'s year-end is December 31.

Required:

1. Record the acceptance of the note by FirstBanc Corp.
2. Record the appropriate adjustment for the note by FirstBanc Corp., on December 31, 2012.
3. Record the receipt of cash by FirstBanc Corp. at maturity.

Determine interest expense (LO2)

E8–5 OS Environmental provides cost-effective solutions for managing regulatory requirements and environmental needs specific to the airline industry. Assume that on July 1, 2012, the company issues a one-year note for the amount of $5 million. Interest is payable at maturity.

Required:

Determine the amount of interest expense that should be recorded in a year-end adjusting entry under each of the following independent assumptions:

	Interest Rate	Fiscal Year-End
1.	12%	December 31
2.	10%	September 30
3.	9%	October 31
4.	6%	January 31

Record a line of credit (LO2)

E8–6 The following selected transactions relate to liabilities of Rocky Mountain Adventures. Rocky Mountain's fiscal year ends on December 31.

January 13	Negotiate a revolving credit agreement with First Bank that can be renewed annually upon bank approval. The amount available under the line of credit is $10 million at the bank's prime rate.
February 1	Arrange a three-month bank loan of $4 million with First Bank under the line of credit agreement. Interest at the prime rate of 7% is payable at maturity.
May 1	Pay the 7% note at maturity.

Required:

Record the appropriate entries, if any, on January 13, February 1, and May 1.

Calculate payroll withholdings and payroll taxes (LO3)

E8–7 Aspen Ski Resorts has 100 employees, each working 40 hours per week and earning $10 an hour. Although the company does not pay any health or retirement benefits, one of the perks of working at Aspen is that employees are allowed free skiing on their days off. Federal income taxes are withheld at 15% and state income taxes at 5%. FICA taxes are 7.65% of the first $106,800 earned per employee and 1.45% thereafter. Unemployment taxes are 6.2% of the first $7,000 earned per employee.

Required:

1. Compute the total salary expense, the total withholdings from employee salaries, and the actual direct deposit of payroll for the first week of January.
2. Compute the total payroll tax expense Aspen Ski Resorts will pay for the first week of January in addition to the total salary expense and employee withholdings calculated in *Requirement* 1.
3. How should Aspen Ski Resorts account for the free skiing given to employees on their days off?

E8–8 During January, Luxury Cruise Lines pays employee salaries of $2 million. Withholdings in January are $153,000 for the employee portion of FICA, $300,000 for federal income tax, $125,000 for state income tax, and $20,000 for the employee portion of health insurance (payable to **Blue Cross/Blue Shield**). The company incurs an additional $124,000 for federal and state unemployment tax and $60,000 for the employer portion of health insurance.

Record payroll (**LO3**)

Required:

1. Record the employee salary expense, withholdings, and salaries payable.
2. Record the employer-provided fringe benefits.
3. Record the employer payroll taxes.

E8–9 Airline Temporary Services (ATS) pays employees monthly. Payroll information is listed below for January, the first month of ATS's fiscal year. Assume that none of the employees exceeds the federal unemployment tax maximum salary of $7,000 in January.

Record payroll (**LO3**)

Salaries expense	$500,000
Federal and state income tax withheld	100,000
Federal unemployment tax rate	0.80%
State unemployment tax rate (after FUTA deduction)	5.40%
Social Security (FICA) tax rate	7.65%

Required:

Record salaries expense and payroll tax expense for the January pay period.

E8–10 **Apple Inc.** is the number one online music retailer through its iTunes music store. Apple sells iTunes gift cards in $15, $25, and $50 increments. Assume Apple sells $20 million in iTunes gift cards in December, and customers redeem $13 million of the gift cards.

Analyze and record unearned revenues (**LO4**)

Required:

1. Record the advance collection of $20 million for iTunes gift cards.
2. Record the revenue earned when $13 million in gift cards is redeemed.

E8–11 Two competing travel agencies provide similar services, but they record sales using different methods.

Record unearned revenue (**LO4**)

1. Eastern Travel records sales and sales tax in separate accounts. For the month of January, cash sales total $20,000, and sales tax is $1,600.
2. Western Travel records sales and sales tax together. For the month of January, cash sales total $10,800, including an 8% sales tax.

Required:

Record cash sales and the related sales tax for (1) Eastern Travel and (2) Western Travel.

E8–12 Top Sound International designs and sells high-end stereo equipment for auto and home use. Engineers notified management in December 2012 of a circuit flaw in an amplifier that poses a potential fire hazard. Further investigation indicates that a product recall is probable, estimated to cost the company $3 million. The fiscal year ends on December 31.

Analyze and record a contingent liability (**LO5**)

Required:

1. Should this contingent liability be reported, disclosed in a note only, or neither? Explain.
2. What loss, if any, should Top Sound report in its 2012 income statement?
3. What liability, if any, should Top Sound report in its 2012 balance sheet?
4. What entry, if any, should be recorded?

Determine proper treatment of a contingent liability (LO5)

E8–13 Pacific Cruise Lines is a defendant in litigation involving a swimming accident on one of its three cruise ships.

Required:

For each of the following scenarios, determine the appropriate way to report the situation. Explain your reasoning and record any necessary entry.

1. The likelihood of a payment occurring is probable, and the estimated amount is $1.2 million.
2. The likelihood of a payment occurring is probable, and the amount is estimated to be in the range of $1 to $1.5 million.
3. The likelihood of a payment occurring is reasonably possible, and the estimated amount is $1.2 million.
4. The likelihood of a payment occurring is remote, while the estimated potential amount is $1.2 million.

Record warranties (LO5)

E8–14 Computer Wholesalers restores and resells notebook computers on eBay. It originally acquires the notebook computers from corporations upgrading their computer systems, and it backs each notebook it sells with a 90-day warranty against defects. Based on previous experience, Computer Wholesalers expects warranty costs to be approximately 5% of sales. By the end of the first year, sales and actual warranty expenditures are $500,000 and $18,000, respectively.

Required:

1. Does this situation represent a contingent liability? Why or why not?
2. Record warranty expense and warranty liability for the year based on 5% of sales.
3. Record the reduction in the warranty liability and the reduction in cash of $18,000 incurred during the year.
4. What is the balance in the Warranty Liability account after the entries in *Requirements* 2 and 3?

Analyze disclosure of contingent liabilities (LO5)

E8–15 Dow Chemical Company provides chemical, plastic, and agricultural products and services to various consumer markets. The following excerpt is taken from the disclosure notes of Dow's annual report.

DOW CHEMICAL
Notes to the Financial Statements (excerpt)

Dow Chemical had accrued obligations of $381 million for environmental remediation and restoration costs, including $40 million for the remediation of Superfund sites. This is management's best estimate of the costs for remediation and restoration with respect to environmental matters for which the Company has accrued liabilities, although the ultimate cost with respect to these particular matters could range up to twice that amount. Inherent uncertainties exist in these estimates primarily due to unknown conditions, changing governmental regulations and legal standards regarding liability, and evolving technologies for handling site remediation and restoration.

Required:

1. Does the excerpt describe a contingent liability?
2. Under what conditions would Dow record such a contingency?
3. How did Dow record the $381 million?

Calculate and analyze liquidity ratios (LO6)

E8–16 Selected financial data regarding current assets and current liabilities for Royal Caribbean Cruises, Ltd., a leader in the cruise line industry, is provided:

($ in millions)	
Current assets:	
Cash and cash equivalents	$ 403
Current investments	82
Net receivables	271
Inventory	96
Other current assets	125
Total current assets	$ 977
Current liabilities:	
Accounts payable	$1,061
Short-term debt	644
Other current liabilities	969
Total current liabilities	$2,674

Required:

1. Calculate the current ratio and the acid-test ratio for Royal Caribbean.
2. Compare your calculations with those for United Airlines and Southwest Airlines reported in the chapter text. Which company appears more likely to have difficulty paying its currently maturing debts?

*For additional exercises, visit **www.mhhe.com/succeed** for Exercises: Set B.*

PROBLEMS: SET A

connect
|ACCOUNTING

P8–1A Listed below are several terms and phrases associated with current liabilities. Pair each item from List A (by letter) with the item from List B that is most appropriately associated with it.

*Review current liability terms and concepts (**LO1**)*

List A

_____ 1. An IOU promising to repay the amount borrowed plus interest.

_____ 2. Payment amount is reasonably possible and can be reasonably estimated.

_____ 3. Mixture of liabilities and equity a business uses.

_____ 4. Payment amount is probable and can be reasonably estimated.

_____ 5. A liability that requires the sacrifice of something other than cash.

_____ 6. Long-term debt maturing within one year.

_____ 7. FICA and FUTA.

_____ 8. Informal agreement that permits a company to borrow up to a prearranged limit.

_____ 9. Classifying liabilities as either current or long-term helps investors and creditors assess this.

_____ 10. Amount of note payable × annual interest rate × fraction of the year.

List B

a. Recording of a contingent liability.

b. Unearned revenues.

c. The riskiness of a business's obligations.

d. Disclosure of a contingent liability.

e. Interest on debt.

f. Payroll taxes.

g. Line of credit.

h. Capital structure.

i. Note payable.

j. Current portion of long-term debt.

400   CHAPTER 8   Current Liabilities

Record notes payable and
notes receivable (LO2)

P8–2A Precision Castparts, a manufacturer of processed engine parts in the automotive and airline industries, borrows $40 million cash on October 1, 2012, to provide working capital for anticipated expansion. Precision signs a one-year, 8% promissory note to Midwest Bank under a prearranged short-term line of credit. Interest on the note is payable at maturity. Each firm has a December 31 year-end.

Required:

1. Prepare the journal entries on October 1, 2012, to record (a) the notes payable for Precision Castparts and (b) the notes receivable for Midwest Bank.
2. Record the adjustments on December 31, 2012, for (a) Precision Castparts and (b) Midwest Bank.
3. Prepare the journal entries on September 30, 2013, to record payment of (a) the notes payable for Precision Castparts and (b) the notes receivable for Midwest Bank.

Record payroll (LO3)

P8–3A Caribbean Tours' total payroll for the month of January was $500,000. The following withholdings, fringe benefits, and payroll taxes apply:

Federal and state income tax withheld	$50,000
Health insurance premiums (Blue Cross) paid by employer	9,000
Contribution to retirement plan (Fidelity) paid by employer	20,000
FICA tax rate (Social Security and Medicare)	7.65%
Federal and state unemployment tax rate	6.20%

Assume that none of the withholdings or payroll taxes has been paid by the end of January (record them as payables), and no employee's cumulative wages exceed the relevant wage bases.

Required:

1. Record the employee salary expense, withholdings, and salaries payable.
2. Record the employer-provided fringe benefits.
3. Record the employer payroll taxes.

Record payroll (LO3)

P8–4A Vacation Destinations offers its employees the option of contributing up to 6% of their salaries to a voluntary retirement plan, with the employer matching their contribution. The company also pays 100% of medical and life insurance premiums. Assume that no employee's cumulative wages exceed the relevant wage bases. Payroll information for the first biweekly payroll period ending February 14 is listed below.

Wages and salaries	$1,000,000
Employee contribution to voluntary retirement plan	42,000
Medical insurance premiums	21,000
Life insurance premiums	4,000
Federal and state income tax withheld	250,000
Social Security tax rate	6.20%
Medicare tax rate	1.45%
Federal and state unemployment tax rate	6.20%

Required:

1. Record the employee salary expense, withholdings, and salaries payable.
2. Record the employer-provided fringe benefits.
3. Record the employer payroll taxes.

Record unearned
revenues (LO4)

P8–5A The University of Michigan football stadium, built in 1927, is the largest college stadium in America, with a seating capacity of 107,500 fans. Assume the stadium sells out all six home games before the season begins, and the athletic department collects $64.5 million in ticket sales.

Required:

1. What is the average price per season ticket and average price per individual game ticket sold?
2. Record the advance collection of $64.5 million in ticket sales.
3. Record the revenue earned after the first home game is completed.

P8–6A Texas Roadhouse opened a new restaurant in October. During its first three months of operation, the restaurant sold gift cards in various amounts totaling $2,500. The cards are redeemable for meals within one year of the purchase date. Gift cards totaling $728 were presented for redemption during the first three months of operation prior to year-end on December 31. The sales tax rate on restaurant sales is 4%, assessed at the time meals (not gift cards) are purchased. Texas Roadhouse will remit sales taxes in January.

Record unearned revenues and sales taxes (LO4)

Required:

1. Record (in summary form) the $2,500 in gift cards sold (keeping in mind that, in actuality, the firm would record each sale of a gift card individually).
2. Record the $728 in gift cards redeemed, including the 4% sales tax assessed.
3. Determine the balance in the Unearned Revenue account (remaining liability for gift cards) Texas Roadhouse will report on the December 31 balance sheet.

P8–7A The ink-jet printing division of Environmental Printing has grown tremendously in recent years. Assume the following transactions related to the ink-jet division occur during the year ended December 31, 2012.

Record contingencies (LO5)

Required:

Record any amounts as a result of each of these contingencies.

1. Environmental Printing was sued for $10 million by Addamax. Plaintiff alleges that the defendants formed an unlawful joint venture and drove it out of business. The case is expected to go to trial later this year. The likelihood of payment is reasonably possible.
2. Environmental Printing is the plaintiff in an $8 million lawsuit filed against a competitor in the high-end color-printer market. Environmental Printing expects to win the case and be awarded between $5.5 and $8 million.
3. Environmental Printing recently became aware of a design flaw in one of its ink-jet printers. A product recall appears probable. Such an action would likely cost the company between $400,000 and $800,000.

P8–8A Dinoco Petroleum faces three potential contingency situations, described below. Dinoco's fiscal year ends December 31, 2012, and it issues its 2012 financial statements on March 15, 2013.

Record contingencies (LO5)

Required:

Determine the appropriate means of reporting each situation for the year ended December 31, 2012, and record any necessary entries. Explain your reasoning.

1. In the initial trial, Dinoco lost a $120 million lawsuit resulting from a dispute with a supplier. The case is under appeal. Although Dinoco is unable to predict the outcome, it does not expect the case to have a material adverse effect on the company.
2. In November 2011, the state of Texas filed suit against Dinoco, seeking civil penalties and injunctive relief for violations of environmental laws regulating hazardous waste. On January 12, 2013, Dinoco reached a settlement with state authorities. Based upon discussions with legal counsel, it is probable that it will require $140 million to cover the cost of violations.
3. Dinoco is the plaintiff in a $200 million lawsuit filed against a customer for damages due to lost profits from rejected contracts and for unpaid receivables. The case is in final appeal, and legal counsel advises that it is probable Dinoco will prevail and be awarded $100 million.

402   CHAPTER 8   Current Liabilities

Calculate and analyze
ratios (LO6)

P8–9A Selected financial data regarding current assets and current liabilities for
The Home Depot and **Lowe's**, two close competitors in the building supply industry,
are as follows:

($ in millions)	The Home Depot	Lowe's
Current assets:		
Cash and cash equivalents	$ 519	$ 245
Current investments	6	416
Net receivables	972	166
Inventory	10,673	8,209
Other current assets	1,192	215
Total current assets	$13,362	$9,251
Current liabilities:		
Accounts payable	$ 8,221	$4,543
Short-term debt	1,767	1,021
Other current liabilities	1,165	2,458
Total current liabilities	$11,153	$8,022

Required:

1. Calculate the current ratio for The Home Depot and Lowe's. Which company has
   the better ratio? Compare your calculations with those for **United Airlines** and
   Southwest Airlines reported in the chapter text. Which industry maintains a higher
   current ratio?
2. Calculate the acid-test (quick) ratio for The Home Depot and Lowe's. Which
   company has the better ratio? Compare your calculations with those for United
   Airlines and Southwest Airlines reported in the chapter text. Which industry
   maintains a higher acid-test ratio?
3. How would the purchase of additional inventory on credit affect the current ratio?
   How would it affect the acid-test ratio?

PROBLEMS: SET B

Review current liability
terms and concepts (LO1)

P8–1B Listed below are several terms and phrases associated with current liabilities.
Pair each item from List A (by letter) with the item from List B that is most
appropriately associated with it.

List A	List B
_____ 1. Interest expense is recorded in the period interest is incurred rather than in the period interest is paid.	a. The riskiness of a business's obligations.
_____ 2. Payment is reasonably possible and can be reasonably estimated.	b. Current portion of long-term debt.
_____ 3. Cash, current investments, and accounts receivable all divided by current liabilities.	c. Recording a contingent liability.
_____ 4. Payment is probable and can be reasonably estimated.	d. Disclosure of a contingent liability.
_____ 5. Gift certificates.	e. Interest expense.
_____ 6. Long-term debt maturing within one year.	f. FICA.
_____ 7. Social Security and Medicare.	g. Commercial paper.
_____ 8. Unsecured notes sold in minimum denominations of $25,000 with maturities up to 270 days.	h. Acid-test ratio.
	i. Accrual accounting.
	j. Unearned revenues.
_____ 9. Classifying liabilities as either current or long-term helps investors and creditors assess this.	
_____ 10. Incurred on notes payable.	

P8–2B Eskimo Joe's, designer of the world's second best-selling T-shirt (just behind Hard Rock Cafe), borrows $20 million cash on November 1, 2012. Eskimo Joe's signs a six-month, 9% promissory note to Stillwater National Bank under a prearranged short-term line of credit. Interest on the note is payable at maturity. Each firm has a December 31 year-end.

Record notes payable and notes receivable **(LO2)**

Required:

1. Prepare the journal entries on November 1, 2012, to record (a) the notes payable for Eskimo Joe's and (b) the notes receivable for Stillwater National Bank.
2. Record the adjustment on December 31, 2012, for (a) Eskimo Joe's and (b) Stillwater National Bank.
3. Prepare the journal entries on April 30, 2013, to record payment of (a) the notes payable for Eskimo Joe's and (b) the notes receivable for Stillwater National Bank.

P8–3B Kashi Sales, L.L.C., produces healthy, whole-grain foods such as breakfast cereals, frozen dinners, and granola bars. Assume payroll for the month of January was $400,000 and the following withholdings, fringe benefits, and payroll taxes apply:

Record payroll **(LO3)**

Federal and state income tax withheld	$125,000
Health insurance premiums (Blue Cross) paid by employer	12,000
Contribution to retirement plan (Fidelity) paid by employer	50,000
FICA tax rate (Social Security and Medicare)	7.65%
Federal and state unemployment tax rate	6.20%

Assume that Kashi has paid none of the withholdings or payroll taxes by the end of January (record them as payables).

Required:

1. Record the employee salary expense, withholdings, and salaries payable.
2. Record the employer-provided fringe benefits.
3. Record the employer payroll taxes.

P8–4B Emily Turnbull, president of Aerobic Equipment Corporation, is concerned about her employees' well-being. The company offers its employees free medical, dental, and life insurance coverage. It also matches employee contributions to a voluntary retirement plan up to 5% of their salaries. Assume that no employee's cumulative wages exceed the relevant wage bases. Payroll information for the biweekly payroll period ending January 24 is listed below.

Record payroll **(LO3)**

Wages and salaries	$2,000,000
Employee contribution to voluntary retirement plan	100,000
Medical insurance premiums	40,000
Dental insurance premiums	14,000
Life insurance premiums	7,000
Federal and state income tax withheld	430,000
FICA tax rate	7.65%
Federal and state unemployment tax rate	6.20%

Required:

1. Record the employee salary expense, withholdings, and salaries payable.
2. Record the employer-provided fringe benefits.
3. Record the employer payroll taxes.

P8–5B Named in honor of the late Dr. F. C. "Phog" Allen, the Kansas Jayhawks' head coach for 39 years, Allen Fieldhouse is labeled by many as one of the best places in America to watch a college basketball game. Allen Fieldhouse has a seating capacity of 16,300. Assume the basketball arena sells out all 15 home games before the season begins, and the athletic department collects $12,225,000 in ticket sales.

Record unearned revenues **(LO4)**

Required:

1. What is the average price per season ticket and average price per individual game ticket sold?
2. Record the advance collection of $12,225,000 in ticket sales.
3. Record the revenue earned after the first home game is completed.

Record unearned revenues and sales taxes (LO4)

P8–6B Logan's Roadhouse opened a new restaurant in November. During its first two months of operation, the restaurant sold gift cards in various amounts totaling $1,800. The cards are redeemable for meals within one year of the purchase date. Gift cards totaling $689 were presented for redemption during the first two months of operation prior to year-end on December 31. The sales tax rate on restaurant sales is 6%, assessed at the time meals (not gift cards) are purchased. Logan's will remit sales taxes in January.

Required:

1. Record (in summary form) the $1,800 in gift cards sold (keeping in mind that, in actuality, each sale of a gift card or a meal would be recorded individually).
2. Record the $689 in gift cards redeemed, including the 6% sales tax assessed.
3. Determine the balance in the Unearned Revenue account (remaining liability for gift cards) to be reported on the December 31 balance sheet.

Record contingencies (LO5)

P8–7B Compact Electronics is a leading manufacturer of digital camera equipment. Assume the following transactions occur during the year ended December 31, 2012.

Required:

Record any amounts as a result of each of these contingencies.

1. Sales were $28 million (all credit) for 2012. Although no customer accounts have been shown to be uncollectible, the company estimates that 2% of credit sales will eventually prove uncollectible.
2. Compact Electronics is the plaintiff in a $4 million lawsuit filed against a supplier. The suit is in final appeal, and attorneys advise it is virtually certain that Compact Electronics will win and be awarded $2.5 million.
3. In November 2012, Compact Electronics became aware of a design flaw in one of its digital camera models. A product recall appears probable and would likely cost the company $500,000.
4. Compact Electronics is the defendant in a patent infringement lawsuit brought by a competitor. It appears reasonably likely Compact Electronics will lose the case, and potential losses are estimated to be in the range of $1.5 to $2.5 million.

Record contingencies (LO5)

P8–8B Authors Academic Publishing faces three potential contingency situations, described below. Authors' fiscal year ends December 31, 2012.

Required:

Determine the appropriate means of reporting each situation for the year ended December 31, 2012, and record any necessary entries. Explain your reasoning.

1. In August 2012, a worker was injured in an accident, partially as a result of his own negligence. The worker has sued the company for $1 million. Legal counsel believes it is reasonably possible that the outcome of the suit will be unfavorable, and that the settlement would cost the company from $250,000 to $500,000.
2. A suit for breach of contract seeking damages of $2,000,000 was filed by an author on October 4, 2012. Legal counsel believes an unfavorable outcome is probable. A reasonable estimate of the award to the plaintiff is between $1 million and $1.5 million. No amount within this range is a better estimate of potential damages than any other amount.
3. Authors is the plaintiff in a pending court case. Its lawyers believe it is probable that Authors will be awarded damages of $2 million.

Calculate and analyze ratios (LO6)

P8–9B Selected financial data regarding current assets and current liabilities for American Airlines and Delta Airlines are provided as follows:

($ in millions)	American	Delta
Current assets:		
Cash and cash equivalents	$1,225	$ 4,684
Current investments	3,104	1,351
Net receivables	811	1,844
Inventory	525	388
Other current assets	270	637
Total current assets	$5,935	$ 8,904
Current liabilities:		
Accounts payable	$6,702	$ 6,991
Short-term debt	2,672	2,407
Other current liabilities		1,604
Total current liabilities	$9,374	$11,002

Required:

1. Calculate the current ratio for American Airlines and Delta Airlines. Compare your calculations with those for **United Airlines** and **Southwest Airlines** reported in the chapter text. Which of the four airlines has the best current ratio?
2. Calculate the acid-test (quick) ratio for American Airlines and Delta Airlines. Compare your calculations with those for United Airlines and Southwest Airlines reported in the chapter text. Which of the four airlines has the best acid-test ratio?
3. How would the cash purchase of additional inventory affect the current ratio? How would it affect the acid-test ratio?

For additional problems, visit **www.mhhe.com/succeed** *for Problems: Set C.*

ADDITIONAL PERSPECTIVES

Great Adventures

(This is a continuation of the Great Adventures problem from earlier chapters.)

AP8–1 Great Adventures is a defendant in litigation involving a biking accident during one of its adventure races. The front tire on one of the bikes came off during the race, resulting in serious injury to the rider. However, Great Adventures can document that each bike was carefully inspected prior to the race. It may have been that the rider loosened the wheel during the race and then forgot to tighten the quick-release mechanism.

Continuing Problem

Required:

For each of the following scenarios, determine the appropriate way to report the situation. Explain your reasoning and record any necessary entry.

1. The likelihood of a payment occurring is probable, and the estimated amount is $120,000.
2. The likelihood of a payment occurring is probable, and the amount is estimated to be in the range of $100,000 to $150,000.
3. The likelihood of a payment occurring is reasonably possible, and the estimated amount is $120,000.
4. The likelihood of a payment occurring is remote, while the estimated potential amount is $120,000.

American Eagle Outfitters, Inc.

Financial Analysis

AP8–2 Financial information for **American Eagle** is presented in Appendix A at the end of the book.

Required:

1. Calculate the current ratio for the past two years. Did the current ratio improve or weaken in the more recent year?
2. Calculate the acid-test (quick) ratio for the past two years. Did the acid-test ratio improve or weaken in the more recent year?
3. If American Eagle used $100 million in current investments to pay $100 million in accounts payable, how would its current ratio and acid-test ratio change? Show your calculations.

Financial Analysis

The Buckle, Inc.

AP8–3 Financial information for **The Buckle** is presented in Appendix B at the end of the book.

Required:

1. Calculate the current ratio for the past two years. Did the current ratio improve or weaken in the more recent year?
2. Calculate the acid-test (quick) ratio for the past two years. Did the acid-test ratio improve or weaken in the more recent year?
3. If The Buckle purchased $50 million of inventory by debiting Inventory and crediting Accounts Payable, how would its current ratio and acid-test ratio change? Show your calculations.

Comparative Analysis

American Eagle Outfitters, Inc., vs. The Buckle, Inc.

AP8–4 Financial information for **American Eagle** is presented in Appendix A at the end of the book, and financial information for **The Buckle** is presented in Appendix B at the end of the book.

Required:

1. Calculate the current ratio for both companies for the year ended January 30, 2010. Which company has the better ratio? Compare your calculations with those for **United Airlines** and **Southwest Airlines** reported in the chapter text. Which industry maintains a higher current ratio?
2. Calculate the acid-test (quick) ratio for both companies for the year ended January 30, 2010. Which company has the better ratio? Compare your calculations with those for United Airlines and Southwest Airlines reported in the chapter text. Which industry maintains a higher acid-test ratio?
3. How would the purchase of additional inventory with accounts payable affect the current ratio for these two companies? Why is the answer for American Eagle and The Buckle opposite that for United Airlines?

Ethics

AP8–5 Eugene Wright is CFO of Caribbean Cruise Lines. The company designs and manufactures luxury boats. It's near year-end, and Eugene is feeling kind of queasy. The economy is in a recession, and demand for luxury boats is way down. Eugene did some preliminary liquidity analysis and noted the company's current ratio is slightly below the 1.2 minimum stated in its debt covenant with First Federal Bank. Eugene realizes that if the company reports a current ratio below 1.2 at year-end, the company runs the risk that First Federal will call its $10 million loan. He just cannot let that happen.

Caribbean Cruise Lines has current assets of $12 million and current liabilities of $10.1 million. Eugene decides to delay the delivery of $1 million in inventory purchased on account from the originally scheduled date of December 26 to a new arrival date of January 3. This maneuver will decrease inventory and accounts payable by $1 million at December year-end. Eugene believes the company can somehow get by without the added inventory, as manufacturing slows down some during the holiday season.

Required:

1. How will the delay in the delivery of $1 million in inventory purchased on account affect the company's current ratio on December 31? Provide supporting calculations of the current ratio before and after this proposed delivery delay.
2. Is this practice ethical? Provide arguments both for and against.

Internet Research

AP8–6 A very helpful site to learn about individual publicly traded companies is *finance.yahoo.com*. Go to this website and look up a well-known publicly traded company. Once you find the company page, perform the following tasks.

Required:

1. Click on "Basic Chart." How has the stock price changed over the past year?
2. Click on "Profile." In what industry does the company operate?
3. Click on "Key Statistics." What is the current ratio for the company?
4. Click on "SEC Filings." When was the most recent 10-K, also called the annual report, submitted?
5. Click on "Competitors." Who are the company's primary competitors?

Written Communication

AP8–7 Western Manufacturing is involved with several potential contingent liabilities. Your assignment is to draft the appropriate accounting treatment for each situation described below. Western's fiscal year-end is December 31, 2012, and the financial statements will be issued in early February 2013.

   a. During 2012, Western experienced labor disputes at three of its plants. Management hopes an agreement will soon be reached. However, negotiations between the company and the unions have not produced an acceptable settlement, and employee strikes are currently under way. It is virtually certain that material costs will be incurred, but the amount of possible costs cannot be reasonably estimated.
   b. Western warrants most products it sells against defects in materials and workmanship for a period of a year. Based on its experience with previous product introductions, warranty costs are expected to approximate 2% of sales. A new product introduced in 2012 had sales of $2 million, and actual warranty expenditures incurred so far on the product are $25,000. The only entry made so far relating to warranties on this new product was to debit Warranty Expense $25,000 and credit Cash $25,000.
   c. Western is involved in a suit filed in January 2013 by Crump Holdings seeking $88 million, as an adjustment to the purchase price in connection with the company's sale of its textile business in 2012. The suit alleges that Western misstated the assets and liabilities used to calculate the purchase price for the textile division. Legal counsel advises that it is reasonably possible that Western could lose up to $88 million.

Required:

In a memo, describe the appropriate means of reporting each situation and explain your reasoning.

408   CHAPTER 8   Current Liabilities

Earnings Management

AP8–8 Quattro Technologies, a hydraulic manufacturer in the aeronautics industry, has reported steadily increasing earnings over the past few years. The company reported net income of $120 million in 2010 and $140 million in 2011. The stock is receiving increasing analyst attention because many investors expect the steady earnings growth to continue well into the future.

One of the factors increasing sales is the superior warranty Quattro offers. Based on experience, warranty expense in 2012 should be around $40 million. However, in a recent executive meeting it was suggested that the CFO report a larger, more conservative, estimate of warranty expense. Income before warranty expense in 2012 is $210 million. By recording a warranty expense of $50 million this year, Quattro could maintain its steady earnings growth and be in a better position to maintain earnings growth again next year.

Required:

1. Can Quattro use warranty expense to manage its earnings? How?
2. Assume income before warranty expense is $210 million in 2012 and 2013, and total warranty expense over the two years is $80 million. What is the impact of the executive meeting suggestion on income in 2012? In 2013?
3. Is the executive meeting suggestion ethical? What would you do if you were the CFO?

Answers to the Self-Study Questions

1. c   2. a   3. c   4. b   5. b   6. d   7. a   8. a   9. c   10. b

CHAPTER

9

Long-Term Liabilities

AFTER STUDYING THIS CHAPTER, YOU SHOULD BE ABLE TO:

- **LO1** Explain financing alternatives.
- **LO2** Identify the characteristics of bonds.
- **LO3** Determine the price of a bond issue.
- **LO4** Account for the issuance of bonds.
- **LO5** Record the retirement of bonds.
- **LO6** Identify other major long-term liabilities.

Analysis

- **LO7** Make financial decisions using long-term liability ratios.

SIX FLAGS: THE UPS AND DOWNS OF BORROWING

Can you name the largest chain of amusement parks in the world? Would you guess **Disney**? **Six Flags** actually is larger, with over 20 amusement and water parks across North America. The first Six Flags amusement park, *Six Flags Over Texas*, was built in 1961 in Arlington, between Dallas and Fort Worth. The park is named for the six different flags that have flown over the state of Texas during its history—the flags of Spain, France, Mexico, the Republic of Texas, the United States, and the Confederate States of America.

What is the top-rated amusement park in the world? Six Flags? Disney? Guess again. Cedar Point, in Sandusky, Ohio, is known as the roller-coaster capital of the world and was rated the *Best Amusement Park in the World* for eleven consecutive years (*www.amusementtoday.com*). The park boasts an unheard-of 17 roller coasters! With a lineup that includes three of the top 10 steel roller coasters, Cedar Point is a coaster lover's dream come true. Its parent firm, **Cedar Fair Entertainment Company**, currently owns and operates 12 amusement parks in North America.

Comparing the financial information for Six Flags and Cedar Fair is revealing. Both companies are listed on the New York Stock Exchange, Six Flags under the ticker symbol SIX and Cedar Fair under the ticker symbol FUN. Both carry a very high level of long-term debt. However, the profitability of the two companies is quite different. From 2006–2008, Six Flags reported an average net loss each year of $238 million, and in 2009 Six Flags entered into bankruptcy proceedings. During this same time, Cedar Fair reported an average annual net income of about $30 million.

As you will learn in this chapter, assuming more debt can be either good or bad. If a company earns a rate of return higher than the interest rate on its debt, borrowing additional funds can increase overall profitability. On the other hand, if a company earns a rate of return lower than the interest rate on its debt, borrowing additional funds will further reduce profitability and may even result in bankruptcy proceedings.

PART A

OVERVIEW OF LONG-TERM DEBT

In the previous chapter, we discussed current liabilities. In this chapter we focus on long-term liabilities, primarily bonds. Parts A, B, and C deal with various aspects of bonds. Part D discusses other long-term liabilities such as installment notes and leases. We conclude the chapter by looking at how debt affects the riskiness and profitability of **Coca-Cola** and **Pepsi**.

Suppose you are the chief financial officer (CFO) for RC Enterprises, a company that designs, manufactures, and installs steel roller coasters. The executives at your company have an idea for a new ride that could revolutionize the amusement park industry. A ride like this could spur a huge increase in sales volume and create the opportunity to expand the idea to amusement parks around the world. But growth requires funding. What are RC Enterprises's choices? To answer that question, let's consider the financing alternatives available.

Financing Alternatives

■ **LO1**
Explain financing alternatives.

Some of the financing needed to fund a company's growth can come from the profits generated by operations. Frequently, though, companies must find additional external financing to meet their needs for cash. Let's look back at the basic accounting equation:

$$\underbrace{\textbf{Assets}}_{\text{(resources)}} \quad = \quad \underbrace{\textbf{Liabilities} \quad + \quad \textbf{Stockholders' Equity}}_{\text{(claims to resources)}}$$

The right side of the accounting equation reveals the two sources of external financing available to RC Enterprises: Debt financing refers to borrowing money (liabilities). Equity financing refers to obtaining additional investment from stockholders (stockholders' equity).

Companies in the auto industry, like **Ford**, typically lean toward liabilities for their financing. Companies in the computer industry, like **Microsoft**, use stockholders' equity to a greater extent to finance their asset growth. The mixture of liabilities and stockholders' equity a business uses is called its capital structure.

Decision Point	Question ❓	Accounting information 📄	Analysis 🔍
	How do you determine a company's capital structure?	Balance sheet	An equity capital structure would have fewer liabilities than stockholders' equity. A debt capital structure would have a higher portion of liabilities relative to stockholders' equity.

Why would a company choose to borrow money rather than issue additional stock in the company? One of the primary reasons relates to taxes. **Interest expense incurred when borrowing money is tax-deductible, whereas dividends paid to stockholders are *not* tax-deductible.** Interest expense incurred on debt reduces taxable income; paying dividends to stockholders does not reduce taxable income because dividends are not an expense. Therefore, debt can be a less costly source of external financing.

KEY POINT

Companies obtain external funds through debt financing (liabilities) and equity financing (stockholders' equity). One advantage of debt financing is that interest on borrowed funds is tax-deductible.

Companies have three primary sources of long-term debt financing: bonds, notes, and leases. Medium- and large-sized corporations often choose to borrow cash by issuing bonds. In fact, **bonds are the most common form of corporate debt.** A company also can borrow cash from a bank or other financial institution through notes payable. A third source of debt financing that continues to grow in popularity is leasing. We discuss each of these sources of long-term debt financing in this chapter.

What Are Bonds?

A bond is a formal debt instrument that obligates the borrower to repay a stated amount, referred to as the *principal* or *face amount,* at a specified maturity date. In return for the use of the money borrowed, the borrower also agrees to pay *interest* over the life of the bond. Sound familiar? It should. That's the way we described notes payable in the preceding chapter. Bonds are very similar to notes. Bonds, though, usually are issued to many lenders, while notes most often are issued to a single lender such as a bank. Traditionally, interest on bonds is paid twice a year (semiannually) on designated interest dates, beginning six months after the original bond issue date.

Perhaps your local school board issued bonds to build a new football stadium for the high school, or maybe your hometown issued bonds to build a new library. To build the stadium or library, a city needs external financing, so it borrows money from people in the community. Bonds provide a way to borrow the money needed from many community members, each willing to lend a small amount. In return, those investing in the bonds receive interest over the life of the bonds, say 20 years, and repayment of the principal amount at the end of the bonds' life.

For most large corporations, bonds are sold, or *underwritten,* by investment houses. The three largest bond underwriters are **JPMorgan**, **Citibank**, and **Bank of America**. The issuing company—the borrower—pays a fee for these underwriting services. Other costs include legal, accounting, registration, and printing fees. To keep costs down, the issuing company may choose to sell the debt securities directly to a single investor, such as a large investment fund or an insurance company. This is referred to as a private placement. Issue costs for private placements are lower because these bonds are not subject to the costly and lengthy process of registering with the SEC that is required of all public offerings.

Why do some companies issue bonds rather than borrow money directly from a bank? A company that borrows by issuing bonds is effectively bypassing the bank and borrowing directly from the investing public—usually at a lower interest rate than it would in a bank loan. However, issuing bonds entails significant bond issue costs that can exceed 5% of the amount borrowed. For smaller loans, the additional bond issuance costs exceed the savings from a lower interest rate, making it more economical to borrow from a bank. For loans of $20 million or more, the interest rate savings often exceed the additional bond issuance costs, making a bond issue more attractive.

A bond issue, in effect, breaks down a large debt into manageable parts—usually $1,000 units. This avoids the necessity of finding a single investor who is both willing and able to loan a large amount of money at a reasonable interest rate. So rather than signing a $50 million note to borrow cash, a company may find it more practicable to sell $1,000 bonds to as many as 50,000 separate investors.

CAREER CORNER

Bond Characteristics

A **bond indenture** is a contract between a firm issuing bonds to borrow money (the issuer) and the corporations or individuals who purchase the bonds as investments (the investors). Because it would not be practical for the corporation to enter into a direct agreement with each of the many bondholders, the bond indenture is held by a trustee, usually a commercial bank or other financial institution, appointed by the issuing firm to represent the rights of the bondholders. If the firm fails to live up to the terms of the bond indenture, the trustee may bring legal action against the company on behalf of the bondholders.

For any particular bond, the bond may be secured or unsecured, term or serial, callable, or convertible. We'll discuss each of these characteristics below.

SECURED AND UNSECURED BONDS

■ **LO2**
Identify the characteristics of bonds.

When you buy a house and finance your purchase with a bank loan, you sign a mortgage agreement assigning your house as collateral. If later you are unable to make the payments, the bank is entitled to take your house. **Secured bonds** are similar. They are supported by specific assets the issuer has pledged as collateral. For instance, mortgage bonds are backed by specific real estate assets. If the borrower defaults on the payments, the lender is entitled to the real estate pledged as collateral.

However, **most bonds are unsecured. Unsecured bonds**, also referred to as *debentures*, are not backed by a specific asset. These bonds are secured only by the "full faith and credit" of the borrower.

TERM AND SERIAL BONDS

Term bonds require payment of the full principal amount of the bond at a single maturity date (the end of the loan term). Most bonds have this characteristic. Borrowers often plan ahead for the repayment by setting aside funds throughout the term to maturity. For example, let's say a city borrows $20 million to build a new sports park by issuing 7% term bonds due in 10 years. To ensure that sufficient funds are available to pay the $20 million 10 years later, the borrower sets aside money in a "sinking fund." A **sinking fund** is a designated fund to which an organization makes payments each year over the life of its outstanding debt. The city might put $2 million each year for 10 years into a sinking fund, so that $20 million is available to pay the bonds when they become due.

Serial bonds require payments in installments over a series of years. Rather than issuing $20 million in bonds that will be due at the *end* of the 10th year, the city may issue $20 million worth of 7% serial bonds, of which $2 million is due *each year* for the next 10 years. This makes it easier for the city to meet its bond obligations as they become due. Since **most bonds are term bonds,** we focus on term bonds in this chapter.

CALLABLE BONDS

Suppose your company issued bonds a few years ago that pay 10% interest. Now market interest rates have declined to 6%, but you're obligated to pay 10%

interest for the remaining time to maturity. How can you avoid this unfortunate situation?

Most corporate bonds are callable, or redeemable. This feature allows the borrower to repay the bonds before their scheduled maturity date at a specified call price. The *call price* is stated in the bond contract and usually exceeds the bond's face amount.

A call feature helps protect the borrower against future decreases in interest rates. If interest rates decline, the borrower can buy back the high-interest-rate bonds at a fixed price and issue new bonds at the new, lower interest rate. Just think about any loans that you may currently have, maybe a car loan or credit card balance. If interest rates drop, wouldn't it be nice to pay off your debt and reestablish it at the lower interest rate? Many home loans, in fact, provide the option to pay the loan early and refinance at a lower rate.

CONVERTIBLE BONDS

While a bond could be both callable and convertible, **a call feature is more common than a conversion feature.** Another important distinction is that callable bonds are designed to benefit the borrower, whereas convertible bonds benefit both the borrower and the lender. Convertible bonds allow the lender (the investor) to convert each bond into a specified number of shares of common stock. For example, let's say a $1,000 convertible bond can be converted into 20 shares of common stock. In this case, convertible bondholders benefit if the market price of the common stock goes above $50 per share (= $1,000 ÷ 20 shares), assuming the current market price of the bond is $1,000. If the company's stock price goes to $60 per share, the convertible bondholder can trade the $1,000 bond for 20 shares of stock worth $60 per share (or $1,200). Prior to conversion, the bondholder still receives interest on the convertible bond. The borrower also benefits. Convertible bonds sell at a higher price and require a lower interest rate than bonds without a conversion feature.

INTERNATIONAL FINANCIAL REPORTING STANDARDS (IFRS)

Using IFRS, we would divide the issue price of convertible debt into its liability (bonds) and equity (conversion option) elements. Under U.S. GAAP, the entire issue price is recorded as a liability.

For more discussion, see Appendix E.

Illustration 9–1 summarizes bond characteristics.

Bond Characteristic	Definition	
Secured	Bonds are backed by collateral.	**ILLUSTRATION 9–1**
Unsecured	Bonds are not backed by collateral.	Summary of Bond
Term	Bond issue matures on a single date.	Characteristics
Serial	Bond issue matures in installments.	
Callable	Borrower can pay off bonds early.	
Convertible	Lender can convert bonds to common stock.	

KEY POINT

The distinguishing characteristics of bonds include whether they are backed by collateral (secured or unsecured), become due at a single specified date or over a series of years (term or serial), can be redeemed prior to maturity (callable), or can be converted into common stock (convertible).

Corporations normally issue bonds in the millions of dollars. However, to simplify the illustrations in this chapter, we drop three digits and illustrate the issuance of bonds in thousands rather than in millions. We begin with the following example and build upon it as we progress through the chapter.

Assume that on January 1, 2012, RC Enterprises decides to raise money for development of its new roller coaster by issuing $100,000 of bonds paying a stated interest rate of 7%. The bonds are due in 10 years, with interest payable semiannually on June 30 and December 31 each year. **In practice, most corporate bonds pay interest semiannually (every six months) rather than paying interest monthly, quarterly, or annually.** Thus, investors in RC Enterprises's bonds will receive (1) the *face amount* of $100,000 at the end of 10 years and (2) *interest payments* of $3,500 (= $100,000 × 7% × 1/2 year) every six months for 10 years. That's a total of 20 interest payments of $3,500 each (= $70,000). Illustration 9–2 provides a timeline of the cash flows related to the bond issue.

ILLUSTRATION 9–2

Timeline of a
Bond Issue

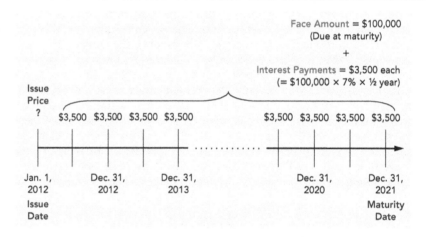

Over the 10-year period, bondholders will receive a total of $170,000, which is the face amount of $100,000 due at maturity plus semiannual interest payments totaling $70,000. How much are investors willing to pay the company today (January 1, 2012) for the right to receive $170,000 over the next 10 years? Certainly less than $170,000, because the cash flows are in the future. In the next section we see how to determine that price.

PART B

PRICING A BOND

We can calculate the issue price of a bond as the present value of the face amount *plus* the present value of the periodic interest payments. To calculate the issue price of RC Enterprises's $100,000 bonds, we need to determine the face amount of the bonds, the interest payment each period, the market interest rate per period, and the number of periods to maturity.

■ **LO3**
Determine the price
of a bond issue.

Bonds Issued at Face Amount

For RC, the face amount equals $100,000. The interest payment every six months is $3,500 (= $100,000 × 7% × 1/2 year). The market interest rate represents the true interest rate used by investors to value RC's bond issue. The market rate can be equal to, less than, or greater than the stated 7% interest rate paid to investors. As we will see later, the market rate is determined for each bond issue by the forces of supply and demand. The stated interest rate is the rate quoted in the bond contract used to calculate the cash payments for interest.

Common Terms The
market rate is also
known as the *effective
interest rate* or *yield rate*.

Let's first assume the market interest rate is 7%, the same as the stated interest rate. (Later we will calculate the bond issue price when the market interest rate is less than or greater than the stated interest rate.) The number of periods to maturity is the number of years to maturity multiplied by the number of interest payments per year. Since RC's bonds pay interest semiannually (twice per year) for 10 years, there are 20 periods to maturity.

One way to determine the issue price of bonds is to use your financial calculator. Illustration 9–3 shows the calculator inputs used to obtain an issue price at the face amount of $100,000.

CALCULATOR INPUT

Bond Characteristics	Key	Amount
1. Face amount	FV	$100,000
2. Interest payment each period	PMT	$3,500 = $100,000 × 7% × 1/2 year
3. Market interest rate each period	I	3.5% = 7% ÷ 2 semiannual periods
4. Periods to maturity	N	20 = 10 years × 2 periods each year

CALCULATOR OUTPUT

Issue price	PV	$100,000

ILLUSTRATION 9–3

Pricing Bonds Issued at Face Amount Using a Financial Calculator

An alternative to using a financial calculator is to calculate the price of bonds in Excel. Illustration 9–4 demonstrates the inputs and the formula used to calculate the issue price.

	C7		f_x	=-PV(C4, C5, C3, C2, 0)		
	A	B	C	D	E	F
1						
2	Face amount		$100,000.00			
3	Interest payment		$3,500.00			
4	Market interest rate		3.5%			
5	Number of periods		20			
6						
7	Issue price		$100,000.00			
8						
9						

Sheet1 Sheet2 Sheet3

Ready   100%

ILLUSTRATION 9–4

Pricing Bonds Issued at Face Amount Using Excel

A third alternative is to calculate the price of the bonds using present value tables. In Illustration 9–5 we calculate the price of the bonds using the present value tables provided at the back of the textbook.

Present value of face amount	= $100,000 × 0.50257*	= $ 50,257
Present value of interest payments	= $3,500[1] × 14.21240**	= 49,743
Issue price of the bonds		$100,000

ILLUSTRATION 9–5

Pricing Bonds Issued at Face Amount Using Present Value Tables

[1]$100,000 × 7% × 1/2 year = $3,500
*Table 2, i = 3.5%, n = 20
**Table 4, i = 3.5%, n = 20

We use Table 2, the present value of $1, to calculate the present value of the face amount since it's just one amount ($100,000) due at maturity. We use Table 4, the present value of an ordinary annuity of $1, to calculate the present value of the interest payments since they are a series of equal amounts ($3,500 each) paid every semiannual interest period.

Using any of these three alternatives, the issue price of the bonds is equal to $100,000. All three methods have their advantages. A financial calculator and Excel are simple to use and provide greater flexibility regarding the choice of different interest rates and time periods. On the other hand, present value tables provide a better conceptual understanding of how bond prices are determined.

We assumed a market rate of 7%, which is exactly equal to the 7% stated rate of interest on the bond contract. The market rate is the interest rate investors determine for each bond issue through the forces of supply and demand. Market rates change continuously. Announcements by the Federal Reserve regarding its intentions to increase the federal funds rate (the interest rate the Federal Reserve charges to banks), political unrest, an increase in the price of oil, and fears of growing inflation, to name a few, can cause an increase in market interest rates.

Another important point to remember is that the market rate is not the same for all companies issuing bonds. Market rates vary based on the default risk of the company issuing the bonds. Default risk refers to the possibility that a company will be unable to pay the bond's face amount or interest payments as they become due. As a company's default risk increases, investors demand a higher market interest rate on their bond investments. For example, would you pay the same for a $1,000 bond paying 7% interest issued by Six Flags as you would for a $1,000 bond paying 7% interest issued by Cedar Fair? Probably not. As we discussed earlier, Six Flags lost money in each of the past three years. This means there is a greater chance of default by Six Flags. By paying less for Six Flags' $1,000, 7% bond, investors are effectively increasing their market rate of return. **The higher the market interest rate, the lower the bond issue price will be.**

Bonds Issued at a Discount

Now let's assume that RC Enterprises issues the same $100,000 of 7% bonds when other bonds of similar risk and maturity are paying 8%. RC's bonds are less attractive to investors, because investors can purchase bonds of similar risk that are paying the higher 8% rate. Because of this, to make the bonds more attractive, RC will have to issue its 7% bonds *below* its $100,000 face amount. Bonds issued *below* face amount are said to be issued at a discount.

In this instance, the bonds will be issued for less than the $100,000 face amount. How much less? Let's calculate the bond issue price using I = 4% (= 8% ÷ 2) rather than the 3.5% used in the previous example. In Illustration 9–6 we recalculate the issue price of the bonds, assuming the market rate of interest is now 8% per year (4% every semiannual period).

ILLUSTRATION 9–6

Pricing Bonds Issued at a Discount Using a Financial Calculator

CALCULATOR INPUT

Bond Characteristics	Key	Amount
1. Face amount	FV	$100,000
2. Interest payment each period	PMT	$3,500 = $100,000 × 7% × 1/2 year
3. Market interest rate each period	I	4% = 8% ÷ 2 semiannual periods
4. Periods to maturity	N	20 = 10 years × 2 periods each year

CALCULATOR OUTPUT

Issue price	PV	$93,205

Illustration 9–7 demonstrates how to use Excel to determine the issue price.

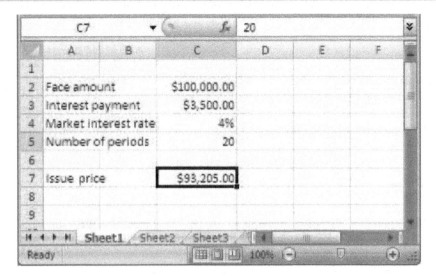

ILLUSTRATION 9–7

Pricing Bonds Issued at a Discount Using Excel

In Illustration 9–8 we calculate the price of the bonds using the present value tables provided at the back of the textbook, assuming the market rate of interest is 8% per year, or 4% every semiannual period.

Present value of principal	= $100,000 × 0.45639*	=	$45,639
Present value of interest payments	= $3,500[1] × 13.59033**	=	47,566
Issue price of the bonds			$93,205

[1]$100,000 × 7% × 1/2 year = $3,500
*Table 2, $i = 4\%$, $n = 20$
**Table 4, $i = 4\%$, $n = 20$

ILLUSTRATION 9–8

Pricing Bonds Issued at a Discount Using Present Value Tables

In practice, investors might refer to the bonds as being "issued at 93.2." This means the bonds were issued at approximately 93.2% of the $100,000 face value, or $93,200.

We see that in this instance the bond issue price is below the face amount of $100,000. The issuing company receives only $93,205 from investors, but will pay back $100,000 when the bonds mature in 10 years. Why? Because the bonds pay only 7% interest when the market rate for bonds of similar risk and maturity is 8%. By issuing the bonds for only $93,205, the issuer is effectively raising the interest earned by investors from the stated rate of 7% to the market rate of 8%. In other words, an investor paying $93,205 for the 7% bonds will earn the same rate of return on the investment (8%) as if he paid $100,000 for 8% bonds.

 COMMON MISTAKE

The interest rate we use to calculate the bond issue price is always the *market* rate, never the stated rate. Some students get confused and incorrectly use the stated rate to calculate present value. Use the stated rate to calculate the interest payment each period, but use the market rate to calculate the present value of the cash flows.

Bonds Issued at a Premium

Now let's assume that RC Enterprises issues $100,000 of 7% bonds when other bonds of similar risk and maturity are paying only 6%. Investors will pay *more* than $100,000 for these 7% bonds since they look relatively attractive compared with bonds paying only 6%. These bonds will sell at a premium. A **premium** occurs when the issue price of a bond is *above* its face amount. In this case, RC's bonds will sell for more than $100,000. How much more? In Illustration 9–9 we recalculate the issue price using a market rate of 6% (3% semiannually).

ILLUSTRATION 9–9

Pricing Bonds Issued at a Premium Using a Financial Calculator

CALCULATOR INPUT

Bond Characteristics	Key	Amount
1. Face amount	FV	$100,000
2. Interest payment each period	PMT	$3,500 = $100,000 × 7% × 1/2 year
3. Market interest rate each period	I	3% = 6% ÷ 2 semiannual periods
4. Periods to maturity	N	20 = 10 years × 2 periods each year

CALCULATOR OUTPUT

Issue price	PV	$107,439

Illustration 9–10 demonstrates how to use Excel to determine the issue price.

ILLUSTRATION 9–10

Pricing Bonds Issued at a Premium Using Excel

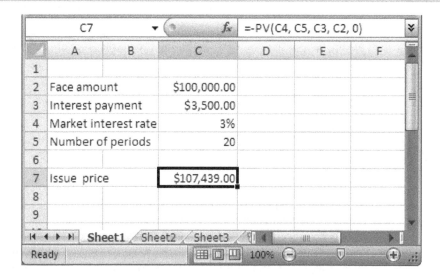

Illustration 9–11 calculates the price of the bonds using the present value tables provided at the back of the textbook, again assuming the market rate of interest is 6% (3% semiannually).

ILLUSTRATION 9–11

Pricing Bonds Issued at a Premium Using Present Value Tables

Present value of principal	= $100,000 × 0.55368*	=	$ 55,368
Present value of interest payments	= $3,500[1] × 14.87747**	=	52,071
Issue price of the bonds			$107,439

[1]$100,000 × 7% × 1/2 year = $3,500
*Table 2, i = 3%, n = 20
**Table 4, i = 3%, n = 20

In practice, investors might refer to these bonds as being "issued at 107.4." This means the bonds were issued at approximately 107.4% of the $100,000 face value, or $107,400.

Here, we see that the bond issue price is above the face amount of $100,000. RC Enterprises receives $107,439 from investors, but will need to pay back only $100,000 when the bonds mature in 10 years. Why? Because the bonds pay 7% interest when the market rate for bonds of similar risk is only 6%. By issuing the bonds for $107,439, the company is effectively lowering the interest earned by investors from the stated rate of 7% to the market rate of 6%.

Illustration 9–12 shows the relation between the stated interest rate, the market interest rate, and the bond issue price.

Stated Interest Rate		Market Interest Rate	Bonds Issued at
7%	<	8%	Discount
7%	=	7%	Face amount
7%	>	6%	Premium

ILLUSTRATION 9–12

Stated Rate, Market Rate, and the Bond Issue Price

If the bonds' stated interest rate is less than the market interest rate, then the bonds will issue below face amount (discount). If the bonds' stated interest rate equals the market interest rate, then the bonds will issue at face amount. Finally, if the bonds' stated interest rate is more than the market interest rate, the bonds will issue above face amount (premium).

Which is most common in practice—bonds issued at face amount, a discount, or a premium? Most bonds initially are issued at a slight discount. Because there is a delay between when the company determines the characteristics of the bonds and when the bonds actually are issued, the company must estimate the market rate of interest. Bond issuers usually adopt a stated interest rate that is close to, but just under, the expected market interest rate. However, in future periods, the bonds may trade at either a discount or a premium depending on changes in market interest rates.

 KEY POINT

The price of a bond is equal to the present value of the face amount (principal) payable at maturity, plus the present value of the periodic interest payments. Bonds can be issued at face amount, below face amount (at a discount), or above face amount (at a premium).

Assume that on January 1, 2012, Wally World issues $200,000 of 9% bonds, due in 10 years, with interest payable semiannually on June 30 and December 31 each year.

Let's Review

Required:

1. If the market rate is 9%, will the bonds issue at face amount, a discount, or a premium? Calculate the issue price.

2. If the market rate is 10%, will the bonds issue at face amount, a discount, or a premium? Calculate the issue price.

3. If the market rate is 8%, will the bonds issue at face amount, a discount, or a premium? Calculate the issue price.

Solution:

1. If the market rate is 9%, the bonds will issue at face amount.

CALCULATOR INPUT

Bond Characteristics	Key	Amount
1. Face amount	FV	$200,000
2. Interest payment each period	PMT	$9,000 = $200,000 × 9% × 1/2 year
3. Market interest rate each period	I	4.5% = 9% ÷ 2 semiannual periods
4. Periods to maturity	N	20 = 10 years × 2 periods each year

CALCULATOR OUTPUT

Issue price	PV	$200,000

C7			f_x	=-PV(C4, C5, C3, C2, 0)		
	A	B	C	D	E	F
1						
2	Face amount		$200,000.00			
3	Interest payment		$9,000.00			
4	Market interest rate		4.5%			
5	Number of periods		20			
6						
7	Issue price		$200,000.00			
8						
9						

Sheet1   Sheet2   Sheet3

Ready   100%

PRESENT VALUE TABLES

Present value of principal	= $200,000 × 0.41464* =	$ 82,928
Present value of interest payments	= $9,000[1] × 13.00794** =	117,072
Issue price of the bonds		$200,000

[1]$200,000 × 9% × 1/2 year = $9,000
*Table 2, i = 4.5%, n = 20
**Table 4, i = 4.5%, n = 20

2. If the market rate is 10%, the bonds will issue at a discount. The only change we make in the calculation is that now I = 5% rather than 4.5%.

CALCULATOR INPUT

Bond Characteristics	Key	Amount
1. Face amount	FV	$200,000
2. Interest payment each period	PMT	$9,000 = $200,000 × 9% × 1/2 year
3. Market interest rate each period	I	5% = 10% ÷ 2 semiannual periods
4. Periods to maturity	N	20 = 10 years × 2 periods each year

CALCULATOR OUTPUT

Issue price	PV	$187,538

PRESENT VALUE TABLES

Present value of principal	= $200,000 × 0.37689*	=	$ 75,378
Present value of interest payments	= $9,000[1] × 12.46221**	=	112,160
Issue price of the bonds			$187,538

[1]$200,000 × 9% × 1/2 year = $9,000
*Table 2, i = 5%, n = 20
**Table 4, i = 5%, n = 20

3. If the market rate is 8%, the bonds will issue at a premium. The only change we make in the calculation is that now I = 4%.

CALCULATOR INPUT

Bond Characteristics	Key	Amount
1. Face amount	FV	$200,000
2. Interest payment each period	PMT	$9,000 = $200,000 × 9% × 1/2 year
3. Market interest rate each period	I	4% = 8% ÷ 2 semiannual periods
4. Periods to maturity	N	20 = 10 years × 2 periods each year

CALCULATOR OUTPUT

Issue price	PV	$213,590

PRESENT VALUE TABLES

Present value of principal	= $200,000 × 0.45639* =	$ 91,278
Present value of interest payments	= $9,000[1] × 13.59033** =	122,312
Issue price of the bonds		$213,590

Suggested Homework:
BE9-3, BE9-4;
E9-3, E9-4;
P9-1A&B

[1]$200,000 × 9% × 1/2 year = $9,000
*Table 2, i = 4%, n = 20
**Table 4, i = 4%, n = 20

PART C

RECORDING BONDS PAYABLE

Now that we have seen how companies price bonds, let's look at how they record the bond issue and the related interest.

Accounting for a Bond Issue

■ **LO4**
Account for the issuance of bonds.

To see how to record the issuance of bonds, let's return to our initial example. On January 1, 2012, RC Enterprises issues $100,000 of 7% bonds, due in 10 years, with interest payable semiannually on June 30 and December 31 each year.

RECORDING BONDS ISSUED AT FACE VALUE

The bonds issue for exactly $100,000, assuming a 7% market interest rate. RC Enterprises records the bond issue as:

A = L + SE
+100,000
    +100,000

January 1, 2012	Debit	Credit
Cash	100,000	
Bonds Payable		100,000
(Issue bonds at face amount)		

RC Enterprises reports bonds payable in the long-term liabilities section of the balance sheet. Nine years from now, when the bonds are within one year of maturity, the firm will reclassify the bonds as current liabilities.

On June 30, 2012, RC Enterprises records the first semiannual interest payment:

A = L + SE
    −3,500 Exp↑
−3,500

June 30, 2012	Debit	Credit
Interest Expense	3,500	
Cash		3,500
(Pay semiannual interest)		
($3,500 = $100,000 × 7% × 1/2)		

The firm will record another semiannual interest payment on December 31, 2012. In fact, it will record semiannual interest payments at the end of every six-month period for the next 10 years.

RECORDING BONDS ISSUED AT A DISCOUNT

In the preceding example we assumed the stated interest rate (7%) and the market interest rate (7%) were the same. How will the entries differ if the stated interest rate is less than the market rate of, say, 8%? The bonds will issue at only $93,205. This is less than $100,000 because the bonds are paying only 7%, while investors can purchase bonds of similar risk paying 8%. When bonds issue at less than face value, we say they issue at a discount. RC Enterprises records the bond issue at a discount as:

January 1, 2012	Debit	Credit	A	=	L	+	SE
Cash	93,205		+93,205				
Bonds Payable		93,205			+93,205		
(Issue bonds at a discount)							

We initially record the Bonds Payable account at $93,205.[1] The balance in the Bonds Payable account is the carrying value. The carrying value will increase from the amount originally borrowed ($93,205) to the amount due at maturity ($100,000) over the 10-year life of the bonds.

 INTERNATIONAL FINANCIAL REPORTING STANDARDS (IFRS)

Including the discount or premium as part of the carrying value of bonds payable (called the *net method*) is the preferred method of reporting under IFRS. This is also how companies in the United States report bonds payable on the balance sheet. An alternative approach (referred to as the *gross method*), in which bonds payable is recorded at face value and the discount or premium is recorded in a separate account, is covered in more advanced accounting courses.

For more discussion, see Appendix E.

We calculate each period's interest expense as the carrying value (the amount actually owed during that period) times the market rate (4% semiannually or 8% annually, in our example).[2] For the first interest payment, interest expense is:

$$
\begin{array}{ccccc}
\textbf{Interest} & = & \textbf{Carrying value} & \times & \textbf{Market interest} \\
\textbf{expense} & & \textbf{of bond} & & \textbf{rate per period} \\
\$3,728 & = & \$93,205 & \times & 8\% \times 1/2
\end{array}
$$

However, the bond agreement specifies that cash paid for interest is equal to the face amount times the stated rate (3.5% semiannually or 7% annually, in our example):

$$
\begin{array}{ccccc}
\textbf{Cash paid} & = & \textbf{Face amount} & \times & \textbf{Stated interest} \\
\textbf{for interest} & & \textbf{of bond} & & \textbf{rate per period} \\
\$3,500 & = & \$100,000 & \times & 7\% \times 1/2
\end{array}
$$

Notice that when the bond sells at a discount, interest expense ($3,728) is *more* than the cash paid for interest ($3,500). (The opposite is true when the bond sells at a premium: Interest expense is less than the cash paid for interest.) On June 30, 2012, RC Enterprises records interest expense, an increase in the carrying value of bonds payable, and the cash paid for interest as follows:

June 30, 2012	Debit	Credit	A	=	L	+	SE
Interest Expense (= $93,205 × 8% × 1/2)................................	3,728						−3,728 Exp↑
Bonds Payable (difference)......................................		228			+228		
Cash (= $100,000 × 7% × 1/2).................................		3,500	−3,500				
(Pay semiannual interest)							

---

[1]Recording bonds payable, net of the discount or plus the premium, is how companies report bonds payable on the balance sheet. Companies also record the flip side, investment in bonds, net of the discount or plus the premium. Using the net method to record both bonds payable and the investment in bonds is (1) consistent with the actual reporting used by companies in practice and (2) easier to understand than recording the discount or premium separately.

[2]We cover the effective interest method, as this is the generally accepted method under both U.S. GAAP and IFRS. The straight-line amortization method, which is allowed only if it does not materially differ from the effective interest method, is discussed as an alternative approach in more advanced accounting courses.

COMMON MISTAKE

Students sometimes incorrectly record interest expense using the stated rate rather than the market rate. Remember that interest expense is the carrying value times the market rate, while the cash paid for interest is the face amount times the stated rate.

Because the carrying value of debt issued at a discount increases over time, interest expense also will increase each semiannual interest period. We record interest for the next semiannual interest period on December 31, 2012, as:

A = L + SE		Debit	Credit
−3,737 Exp	**December 31, 2012**		
+237	Interest Expense (= [$93,205 + $228] × 8% × 1/2).................	3,737	
−3,500	Bonds Payable (difference)....................................		237
	Cash (= $100,000 × 7% × 1/2)..............................		3,500
	(Pay semiannual interest)		

An amortization schedule provides a convenient summary of the cash interest payments, interest expense, and changes in carrying value for each semiannual interest period. Illustration 9–13 provides an amortization schedule for the bonds issued at a discount. Note that the amounts for the June 30, 2012, and the December 31, 2012, semiannual interest payments shown above can be taken directly from the amortization schedule.

ILLUSTRATION 9–13

Amortization Schedule for Bonds Issued at a Discount

	(1)	(2) Cash Paid for Interest	(3) Interest Expense	(4) Increase in Carrying Value	(5) Carrying Value
	Date	Face Amount × Stated Rate	Carrying Value × Market Rate	(3)−(2)	Prior Carrying Value + (4)
	1/1/12				$ 93,205
	6/30/12	$3,500	$3,728	$228	93,433
	12/31/12	3,500	3,737	237	93,670
	*	*	*	*	*
	*	*	*	*	99,057
	6/30/21	3,500	3,962	462	99,519
	12/31/21	3,500	3,981	481	100,000

The amortization schedule shows interest calculations every six months because interest is paid semiannually. The entire amortization schedule would be 20 rows long. To save space, we show only the amortization for the first and last years. The eight years in the middle are represented by asterisks. Cash paid is $3,500 (= $100,000 × 7% × 1/2) every six months. Interest expense is the carrying value times the market rate. Interest expense for the six months ended June 30, 2012, is $3,728 (= $93,205 × 4%). The difference between interest expense and the cash paid increases the carrying value of the bonds. At the maturity date, the carrying value will equal the face amount of $100,000.

Decision Maker's Perspective   Carrying Value and Market Value

Is the carrying value of bonds payable reported on the balance sheet really what the bonds are worth? Yes, but only on the date issued and on the final maturity date. Between these two dates, the carrying value of bonds payable reported on the balance sheet can vary considerably from the true underlying market value of the liability.

The reason is that the market interest rate is constantly changing. The market value of bonds moves in the opposite direction of interest rates: When market interest rates go up, the market value of bonds goes down. However, the carrying value of bonds is not adjusted for changes in market interest rates after the issue date.

Refer back to the amortization schedule for the bonds issued at a discount by RC Enterprises. The carrying value of $93,205 on the date of issue equals the market value of the bonds. However, the carrying value one year later on December 31, 2012 ($93,670), will equal market value *only* if the market rate of interest continues to be 8%. If market interest rates go up during the year, the value of bonds payable will fall. Similarly, if market rates go down during the year, the value of bonds payable will increase.

Current generally accepted accounting principles allow the option to report some or all of a company's financial assets and liabilities at fair value. If a company chooses to report a financial liability such as bonds payable at fair value, then it reports changes in fair value as gains and losses in the income statement. •

RECORDING BONDS ISSUED AT A PREMIUM

Now assume RC Enterprises issues $100,000 of 7% bonds when other bonds of similar risk are paying only 6%. The bonds will issue at $107,439. Investors will pay more than $100,000 for these 7% bonds because bonds of similar risk are paying only 6% interest. When bonds issue at more than face value, we say they issue at a premium. RC Enterprises records the bond issue at a premium as:

January 1, 2012	Debit	Credit	A	=	L	+	SE
Cash	107,439		+107,439				
Bonds Payable		107,439			+107,439		
(Issue bonds at a premium)							

Initially, we record the Bonds Payable account at $107,439. However, RC Enterprises will need to pay back only $100,000 when the bonds mature in 10 years. Therefore, the carrying value will decrease from $107,439 (issue price) to $100,000 (face amount) over the 10-year life of the bonds. We still calculate interest expense as the carrying value times the market rate (3% semiannually). On June 30, 2012, RC Enterprises records interest, assuming the bonds were issued at a premium, as follows:

June 30, 2012	Debit	Credit	A	=	L	+	SE
Interest Expense (= $107,439 × 6% × 1/2)...............................	3,223						−3,223 Exp↑
Bonds Payable (difference)..	277				−277		
Cash (= $100,000 × 7% × 1/2)...		3,500	−3,500				
(Pay semiannual interest)							

When bonds are issued at a premium, the carrying value of the debt decreases over time. That's why we *debit* Bonds Payable, because Bonds Payable is decreasing over time. Since the carrying value of the debt decreases over time, interest expense will also decrease each semiannual interest period. RC Enterprises records interest for the next semiannual interest period on December 31, 2012, as:

December 31, 2012	Debit	Credit	A	=	L	+	SE
Interest Expense (= [$107,439 − $277] × 6% × 1/2)................	3,215						−3,215 Exp↑
Bonds Payable (difference)..	285				−285		
Cash (= $100,000 × 7% × 1/2)...		3,500	−3,500				
(Pay semiannual interest)							

The amortization schedule in Illustration 9–14 summarizes the recording of interest expense for the bonds issued at a premium.

ILLUSTRATION 9–14

Amortization Schedule for Bonds Issued at a Premium

(1) Date	(2) Cash Paid for Interest Face Amount × Stated Rate	(3) Interest Expense Carrying Value × Market Rate	(4) Decrease in Carrying Value (2) − (3)	(5) Carrying Value Prior Carrying Value − (4)
1/1/12				$107,439
6/30/12	$3,500	$3,223	$277	107,162
12/31/12	3,500	3,215	285	106,877
*	*	*	*	*
*	*	*	*	100,956
6/30/21	3,500	3,029	471	100,485
12/31/21	3,500	3,015	485	100,000

Just as in the discount example, the amounts for the June 30, 2012, and the December 31, 2012, semiannual interest payments can be obtained directly from the amortization schedule. Now, however, with a bond premium, the difference between cash paid and interest expense *decreases* the carrying value each period from $107,439 at bond issue down to $100,000 (the face amount) at bond maturity.

Illustration 9–15 shows how carrying value changes as a bond approaches its maturity date.

ILLUSTRATION 9–15

Changes in Carrying Value over Time

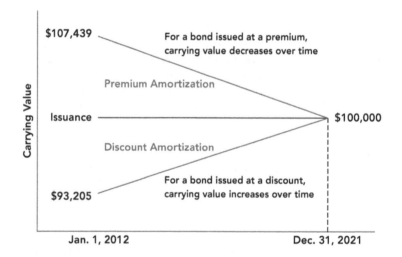

KEY POINT

When bonds issue at face amount, the carrying value and the corresponding interest expense *remain constant* over time. When bonds issue at a discount (below face amount), the carrying value and the corresponding interest expense *increase* over time. When bonds issue at a premium (above face amount), the carrying value and the corresponding interest expense *decrease* over time.

Assume that on January 1, 2012, Wally World issues $200,000 of 9% bonds, due in 10 years, with interest payable semiannually on June 30 and December 31 each year.

Let's Review

Required:

1. If the market rate is 9%, the bonds will issue at $200,000. Record the bond issue on January 1, 2012, and the first two semiannual interest payments on June 30, 2012, and December 31, 2012.

2. If the market rate is 10%, the bonds will issue at $187,538. Record the bond issue on January 1, 2012, and the first two semiannual interest payments on June 30, 2012, and December 31, 2012.

3. If the market rate is 8%, the bonds will issue at $213,590. Record the bond issue on January 1, 2012, and the first two semiannual interest payments on June 30, 2012, and December 31, 2012.

Solution:

1. Record the bonds issued at face amount and the first two semiannual interest payments:

January 1, 2012	Debit	Credit
Cash	200,000	
Bonds Payable		200,000
(*Issue bonds at face amount*)		
June 30, 2012		
Interest Expense	9,000	
Cash (= $200,000 \times 9\% \times 1/2$)		9,000
(*Pay semiannual interest*)		
December 31, 2012		
Interest Expense	9,000	
Cash (= $200,000 \times 9\% \times 1/2$)		9,000
(*Pay semiannual interest*)		

2. Record the bonds issued at a discount and the first two semiannual interest payments:

January 1, 2012	Debit	Credit
Cash	187,538	
Bonds Payable		187,538
(*Issue bonds at a discount*)		
June 30, 2012		
Interest Expense (= $187,538 \times 10\% \times 1/2$)	9,377	
Bonds Payable (difference)		377
Cash (= $200,000 \times 9\% \times 1/2$)................................		9,000
(*Pay semiannual interest*)		
December 31, 2012		
Interest Expense (= [$187,538 + $377] $\times 10\% \times 1/2$)	9,396	
Bonds Payable (difference)		396
Cash (= $200,000 \times 9\% \times 1/2$)................................		9,000
(*Pay semiannual interest*)		

3. Record the bonds issued at a premium and the first two semiannual interest payments:

January 1, 2012	Debit	Credit
Cash	213,590	
Bonds Payable		213,590
(Issue bonds at a premium)		
June 30, 2012		
Interest Expense (= $213,590 × 8% × 1/2)	8,544	
Bonds Payable (difference)	456	
Cash (= $200,000 × 9% × 1/2)...		9,000
(Pay semiannual interest)		
December 31, 2012		
Interest Expense (= [$213,590 − $456] × 8% × 1/2)	8,525	
Bonds Payable (difference)	475	
Cash (= $200,000 × 9% × 1/2)...		9,000
(Pay semiannual interest)		

Suggested Homework:
BE9-6, BE9-7;
E9-6, E9-7;
P9-2A&B, P9-4A&B

Accounting for Bond Retirements

■ **LO5**
Record the retirement of bonds.

When the issuing corporation buys back its bonds from the investors, we say the company has **retired** those bonds. The corporation can wait until the bonds mature to retire them, or frequently (for reasons we describe below), the issuer will choose to buy the bonds back from the bondholders early.

BOND RETIREMENTS AT MATURITY

Regardless of whether bonds are issued at face amount, a discount, or a premium, **their carrying value at maturity will equal their face amount.** RC Enterprises records the retirement of its bonds at maturity (December 31, 2021) as:

A	=	L	+	SE
		−100,000		
−100,000				

December 31, 2021	Debit	Credit
Bonds Payable	100,000	
Cash		100,000
(Retire bonds at maturity)		

BOND RETIREMENTS BEFORE MATURITY

Earlier we noted that a call feature accompanies most bonds, allowing the issuer to buy back bonds at a fixed price. Even when bonds are not callable in this way, the issuing company can retire bonds early by purchasing them on the open market. Regardless of the method, when the issuer retires debt of any type before its scheduled maturity date, the transaction is an early extinguishment of debt.

Let's return to our example of RC Enterprises issuing $100,000 of 7% bonds maturing in 10 years when other bonds of similar risk are paying 8%. The bonds were issued on January 1, 2012, below face amount (at a discount) at $93,205. Let's assume that market interest rates drop from 8% to 6% during 2012 and RC Enterprises decides to repurchase the bonds one year after issuance on December 31,

2012, when the carrying value of the bonds is now $93,670 (see the amortization table in Illustration 9–13).

When interest rates go down, bond prices go up. If the market rate drops to 6%, it will now cost $106,877 to retire the bonds on December 31, 2012.[3] The bonds have a carrying value on December 31, 2012, of only $93,670, but it will cost the issuing company $106,877 to retire them. RC Enterprises will record a loss for the difference. RC Enterprises records the retirement as:

December 31, 2012	Debit	Credit	A	=	L	+	SE
Bonds Payable (account balance)	**93,670**				−93,670		
Loss (difference)	**13,207**						−13,207 Exp↑
Cash (amount paid)		**106,877**	−106,877				
(*Retire bonds before maturity*)							

Losses (and gains) on the early extinguishment of debt are reported as nonoperating items (similar to losses and gains on the sale of long-term assets) in the income statement. Losses have the effect of reducing net income, while gains increase net income.

Why Buy Back Debt Early?

In the example above, RC Enterprises recorded a loss of $13,207 due to a decrease in market interest rates of 2%. One way a company can protect itself from decreases in interest rates is to include a call feature allowing the company to repurchase bonds at a fixed price (such as 2% over face amount, which in our example would be $102,000). When interest rates decrease, companies with a call provision are more likely to repurchase higher-cost debt and then reissue debt at new, lower interest rates. This type of buyback and reissue lowers future interest expense.

Another reason to repay debt early is to improve the company's debt ratios (discussed later in the chapter). Six Flags sold seven amusement parks for just over $300 million and used the proceeds to reduce its overall debt.

Early extinguishment of debt can also be timed to manage reported earnings. Since bonds payable are reported at carrying values and not market values, firms can time their repurchase of bonds to help meet earnings expectations. For instance, when interest rates go up, bond prices go down. In this case, RC Enterprises will record a gain rather than a loss on early extinguishment. ●

Decision Maker's Perspective

KEY POINT

No gain or loss is recorded on bonds retired at maturity. For bonds retired before maturity, we record a gain or loss on early extinguishment equal to the difference between the price paid to repurchase the bonds and the bonds' carrying value.

---

[3]The repurchase price of $106,877 is based on the following financial calculator inputs: future value, $100,000; interest payment each period, $3,500; market interest rate each period, 3% (6% ÷ 2 semiannual periods); and periods to maturity, 18 (9 years left × 2 periods each year).

ETHICAL DILEMMA

On January 1, 2012, West-Tex Oil issued $50 million of 8% bonds maturing in 10 years. The market interest rate on the issue date was 9%, which resulted in the bonds being issued at a discount. In December 2013, Tex Winters, the company CFO, notes that in the two years since the bonds were issued, interest rates have fallen almost 3%. Tex suggests that West-Tex might consider repurchasing the 8% bonds and reissuing new bonds at the lower current interest rates.

Another executive, Will Bright, asks, "Won't the repurchase result in a large loss to our financial statements?" Tex agrees, indicating that West-Tex is likely to just meet earnings targets for 2013. It would probably not meet them with an added loss on bond repurchase in the millions. However, 2014 looks to be a record-breaking year. They decide that maybe they should wait until 2014 to repurchase the bonds.

How could the repurchase of debt cause a loss to be reported in net income? Explain how the repurchase of debt might be timed to manage reported earnings. Is it ethical to time the repurchase of bonds to help meet earnings targets?

PART D

OTHER LONG-TERM LIABILITIES

■ LO6
Identify other major long-term liabilities.

Companies report many long-term liabilities other than bonds payable. In this section, we briefly discuss two of them: installment notes and leases. (Deferred taxes, a third long-term liability, discussed in Chapter 8, are classified as either current or long-term.) The emphasis in this discussion is on the big picture, saving the details for more advanced accounting courses.

Installment Notes

You may have purchased a car, or maybe even a house. If so, unless you paid cash, you signed a note promising to pay the purchase price over, say, four years for the car or 30 years for the house. Car and house loans usually call for payment in monthly installments rather than by a single amount at maturity. Companies, too, often borrow using installment notes. **Each installment payment includes both an amount that represents interest and an amount that represents a reduction of the outstanding loan balance.** The periodic reduction of the balance is enough that at maturity the note is completely paid.

To illustrate, assume that RC Enterprises obtains a $25,000, 6%, four-year loan for a new truck on January 1, 2012. Payments of $587.13 are required at the end of each month for 48 months.[4] Illustration 9–16 (next page) provides an amortization schedule for the loan.

Notice that the carrying value begins at $25,000 and decreases each month to a final carrying value of $0 at the end of the four-year loan. Also, notice that interest

---

[4]The monthly payment of $587.13 is based on the following financial calculator inputs: future value, $0; present value, $25,000; market interest rate, 0.5% (6% ÷ 12 periods each year); periods to maturity, 48 (4 years × 12 periods each year)—and solving for the monthly payment (PMT).

(1) Date	(2) Cash Paid for Interest	(3) Interest Expense	(4) Decrease in Carrying Value	(5) Carrying Value	
		Carrying Value × Market Rate	(2)−(3)	Prior Carrying Value − (4)	
1/1/12				$25,000.00	
1/31/12	$587.13	$125.00	$462.13	24,537.87	
2/28/12	587.13	122.69	464.44	24,073.43	
*	*	*	*	*	
*	*	*	*	*	
11/30/15	587.13	5.83	581.30	584.21	
12/31/15	587.13	2.92	584.21	0	

ILLUSTRATION 9–16

Amortization Schedule for an Installment Note

expense decreases with each monthly payment. In each of the following months, the amount that goes to interest expense becomes less and the amount that goes to decreasing the carrying value (referred to as the principal) becomes more. Why is this? Interest expense decreases over time because the carrying value decreases over time, and interest is a constant percentage of carrying value.

We record the note and the first two monthly installment payments as follows:

January 1, 2012	Debit	Credit	A	=	L	+	SE
Cash	25,000		+25,000				
Notes Payable		25,000			+25,000		
(*Issue a note payable*)							
January 31, 2012			A	=	L	+	SE
Interest Expense (= $25,000 × 6% × 1/12)	125.00						−125.00 Exp↑
Notes Payable (difference)	462.13				−462.13		
Cash (monthly payment)		587.13	−587.13				
(*Pay monthly installment on note*)							
February 28, 2012			A	=	L	+	SE
Interest Expense (= $24,537.87 × 6% × 1/12)	122.69						−122.69 Exp↑
Notes Payable (difference)	464.44				−464.44		
Cash (monthly payment)		587.13	−587.13				
(*Pay monthly installment on note*)							

 KEY POINT

Most notes payable require periodic installment payments. Each installment payment includes an amount that represents interest expense and an amount that represents a reduction of the outstanding loan balance.

Leases

If you have ever leased a car or an apartment, you are familiar with leasing. A lease is a contractual arrangement by which the *lessor* (owner) provides the *lessee* (user) the right to use an asset for a specified period of time. For accounting purposes, we have two basic types of leases: operating leases and capital leases.

Operating leases are like rentals. If you lease a car for a week, you really have no intention of owning the car. Short-term car rentals and most apartment leases are operating leases. The lessor owns the asset, and the lessee simply uses the asset temporarily. Over the lease term, the lessee records rent expense and the lessor records rent revenue.

However, not all leases are simply rentals. Capital leases occur when the lessee essentially buys an asset and borrows the money through a lease to pay for the asset. For example, let's say RC Enterprises leases rather than buys a truck, signing a four-year lease at 6% interest that automatically transfers ownership of the car to RC Enterprises at the end of the lease term. The dealership (the lessor) calculates the lease payments to cover the purchase price of the truck and 6% interest. In substance, RC Enterprises (the lessee) bought the car and borrowed the money at 6% interest to pay for it, even though RC signed a so-called lease agreement. RC would record the lease just as if it had bought the car and borrowed the money from the dealer—except "notes payable" would be labeled "lease payable." In turn, the dealership records the sale like other sales on credit.[5]

Decision Maker's Perspective

Why Do Some Companies Lease Rather Than Buy?

Leasing continues to grow in popularity. Approximately one-third of all debt financing in the United States is through leasing. Why do so many companies choose to lease rather than buy?

1. ***Leasing improves cash flows through up to 100% financing.*** In a purchase, most lenders require a down payment up to 20%. In contrast, leasing may allow you to finance up to the entire purchase price, freeing cash for other uses.

2. ***Leasing improves the balance sheet by reducing long-term debt.*** As long as the lessee can structure the lease as an operating lease, the lessee reports only rent expense, avoiding the reporting of long-term debt in a purchase with debt financing.

3. ***Leasing can lower income taxes.*** Many companies today find that purchasing equipment causes them to be faced with an extra income tax burden under the alternative minimum tax (AMT) calculations. Leasing is one way to help avoid these additional taxes. ●

 KEY POINT

An operating lease is recorded just like a rental. In a capital lease, the lessee essentially "buys" the asset and borrows the money to pay for it.

Decision Point

Question ?	Accounting information 🗎	Analysis 🔍
Does the company have significant obligations related to operating leases?	Disclosure of lease commitments in the notes to the financial statements	Operating lease commitments are not reported as liabilities on the balance sheet, but are disclosed in the notes to the financial statements. They need to be considered when calculating important debt ratios such as the debt to equity ratio.

---

[5]Lease accounting can be complex. Therefore, the details regarding the accounting for capital leases are covered in more advanced accounting classes.

DEBT ANALYSIS
Coca-Cola vs. PepsiCo

Business decisions include risk. Failure to properly consider risk in those decisions is one of the most costly, yet most common, mistakes investors and creditors make. Long-term debt is one of the first places decision makers should look when trying to get a handle on risk. As stated in the feature story at the beginning of the chapter, **Six Flags** entered into bankruptcy proceedings in 2009 due to difficulties in repaying its long-term debt. Illustration 9–17 describes steps taken by Six Flags to reduce its long-term debt.

ANALYSIS

■ **LO7**
Make financial decisions using long-term liability ratios.

> **SIX FLAGS, INC.**
> **Notes to the Financial Statements (excerpt)**
>
> Six Flags, Inc., has entered into an agreement to sell three of its water parks and four of its theme parks to PARC 7F-Operations Corporation (PARC) of Jacksonville, Florida, for $312 million, consisting of $275 million in cash and a note receivable for $37 million.
>   The disposition of these seven parks is a key component of the Company's overall strategy to reduce debt and enhance operational and financial flexibility. Company management stated that its intent was to reduce debt by several hundred million dollars over the next several years.

ILLUSTRATION 9–17
Six Flags's Disclosure of Long-Term Debt

Here, we look at two ratios frequently used to measure financial risk related to long-term liabilities: (1) debt to equity and (2) times interest earned.

DEBT TO EQUITY RATIO

To measure a company's risk, we often calculate the debt to equity ratio:

$$\text{Debt to equity ratio} = \frac{\text{Total liabilities}}{\text{Stockholders' equity}}$$

Debt requires payment on specific dates. Failure to repay debt or the interest associated with the debt on a timely basis may result in default and perhaps even bankruptcy. Other things being equal, the higher the debt to equity ratio, the higher the risk of bankruptcy. When a company assumes more debt, risk increases.

Debt also can be an advantage. It can enhance the return to stockholders. If a company earns a return in excess of the cost of borrowing the funds, shareholders are provided with a total return greater than what could have been earned with equity funds alone. Unfortunately, borrowing is not always favorable. Sometimes the cost of borrowing the funds exceeds the returns they generate. This illustrates the risk–reward trade-off faced by shareholders.

Have you ever ordered a Pepsi and then found out the place serves only Coke products? Amusement parks often have exclusive contracts for soft drinks. The official soft drink of **Six Flags** is Coca-Cola, while **Cedar Point** serves only Pepsi products. Illustration 9–18 provides selected financial data for **Coca-Cola** and **PepsiCo**.

ILLUSTRATION 9–18

Financial Information for Coca-Cola and PepsiCo

Selected Balance Sheet Data December 31, 2008 and 2007 ($ in millions)				
	Coca-Cola		PepsiCo	
	2008	2007	2008	2007
Total assets	$40,519	$43,269	$35,994	$34,628
Total liabilities	$20,047	$21,525	$23,888	$17,394
Stockholders' equity	20,472	21,744	12,106	17,234
Total liabilities and equity	$40,519	$43,269	$35,994	$34,628

Income Statements For the year ended December 31, 2008 ($ in millions)		
	Coca-Cola	PepsiCo
Net sales	$31,944	$43,251
Cost of goods sold	11,374	20,351
Gross profit	20,570	22,900
Operating expenses	12,693	15,550
Interest expense	438	329
Tax expense	1,632	1,879
Net income	$ 5,807	$ 5,142

Illustration 9–19 compares the 2008 debt to equity ratio for Coca-Cola and PepsiCo.

ILLUSTRATION 9–19

Debt to Equity Ratio for Coca-Cola and PepsiCo

($ in millions)	Total Liabilities	÷	Stockholders' Equity	=	Debt to Equity Ratio
Coca-Cola	$20,047	÷	$20,472	=	0.98
PepsiCo	$23,888	÷	$12,106	=	1.97

The debt to equity ratio is higher for PepsiCo. Debt to equity is a measure of financial leverage. Thus, PepsiCo has higher leverage than Coca-Cola. Leverage enables a company to earn a higher return using debt than without debt, in the same way a person can lift more weight with a lever than without it.

Decision Point

Question	Accounting information	Analysis
Which company has higher leverage?	Debt to equity ratio	Debt to equity is a measure of financial leverage. Companies with more debt will have a higher debt to equity ratio and higher leverage.

PepsiCo is assuming more debt, and therefore its investors are assuming more risk. Remember, this added debt could be good or bad depending on whether the company earns a return in excess of the cost of borrowed funds. Let's explore this further by revisiting the return on assets introduced in Chapter 7. Recall that return on assets measures the amount of income generated for each dollar invested in assets. In Illustration 9–20 we calculate the return on assets for Coca-Cola and PepsiCo.

$$\text{Return on assets} = \frac{\text{Net income}}{\text{Average total assets}}$$

($ in millions)	Net Income	÷	Average Total Assets	=	Return on Assets
Coca-Cola	$5,807	÷	$41,894*	=	13.9%
PepsiCo	$5,142	÷	$35,311**	=	14.6%

*($40,519 + $43,269) ÷ 2
**($35,994 + $34,628) ÷ 2

ILLUSTRATION 9–20

Return on Assets for Coca-Cola and PepsiCo

The return on assets indicates a company's overall profitability, ignoring specific sources of financing. PepsiCo's profitability slightly exceeds Coca-Cola's. Note that both Coca-Cola and PepsiCo have a strong return on assets.

What happens when we compare the companies' return on equity, which indicates their ability to generate earnings from the resources that *owners* provide? Illustration 9–21 shows the calculation for return on equity.

$$\text{Return on equity} = \frac{\text{Net income}}{\text{Average stockholders' equity}}$$

($ in millions)	Net Income	÷	Average Stockholders' Equity	=	Return on Equity
Coca-Cola	$5,807	÷	$21,108*	=	27.5%
PepsiCo	$5,142	÷	$14,670**	=	35.1%

*($20,472 + $21,744) ÷ 2
**($12,106 + $17,234) ÷ 2

ILLUSTRATION 9–21

Return on Equity for Coca-Cola and PepsiCo

The difference between the return on assets and return on equity measures is due to the difference in leverage: PepsiCo's higher leverage results in a 7.6% higher return on equity compared to only a 0.7% higher return on assets. PepsiCo increased its return on equity 2.4 times (35.1% ÷ 14.6%) the return on assets. Coca-Cola increased its return on equity only 2.0 times (27.5% ÷ 13.9%) the return on assets. So, as long as both companies have strong returns in excess of the rate charged on borrowed funds, the greater leverage of PepsiCo will result in a higher return to investors. However, if returns should fall below the rate charged on borrowed funds, PepsiCo's greater leverage will result in lower overall returns to PepsiCo than to Coca-Cola. That's where the risk comes in.

Decision Point	Question ?	Accounting information 📄	Analysis 🔍
	How does leverage affect a company's return on equity?	Debt to equity ratio; return on equity ratio	Leverage increases risk. In good times, higher leverage results in higher return on equity. In down times, higher leverage results in lower return on equity.

TIMES INTEREST EARNED RATIO

Lenders require interest payments in return for the use of their money. Failure to pay interest when it is due may invoke penalties, possibly leading to bankruptcy. A ratio often used to measure this risk is the times interest earned ratio. This ratio compares interest expense with income available to pay those charges.

At first glance, you might think we can calculate this simply by dividing net income by interest expense. But remember, interest is one of the expenses subtracted in determining net income. So to measure the amount available to pay interest, we need to add interest back to net income. Similarly, because interest is deductible for income tax purposes, we need to add back tax expense as well.

To illustrate the need to add back interest expense and tax expense, assume a company has the following income statement:

Income before interest and taxes	$100,000
Interest expense	(20,000)
Income before taxes	80,000
Income tax expense (40%)	(32,000)
Net income	$ 48,000

What's the maximum amount of interest the company *could have incurred* and still break even? Is it $48,000? No, it's $100,000:

Income before interest and taxes	$100,000
Interest expense	(100,000)
Income before taxes	0
Income tax expense (40%)	(0)
Net income	$ 0

Notice that the $100,000 is equal to net income plus income tax expense plus interest expense.

We compute the times interest earned ratio as:

$$\text{Times interest earned ratio} = \frac{\text{Net income} + \text{Interest expense} + \text{Tax expense}}{\text{Interest expense}}$$

Illustration 9–22 compares the times interest earned ratios for Coca-Cola and PepsiCo to see which company is better able to meet interest payments.

ILLUSTRATION 9–22

Times Interest Earned Ratio for Coca-Cola and PepsiCo

($ in millions)	Net Income + Interest Expense + Tax Expense	÷	Interest Expense	=	Times Interest Earned Ratio
Coca-Cola	$7,877	÷	$438	=	18.0
PepsiCo	$7,350	÷	$329	=	22.3

PepsiCo has a higher times interest earned ratio than Coca-Cola. However, both companies exhibit strong earnings in relation to their interest expense, and both companies appear well able to meet interest payments as they become due.

KEY POINT

The debt to equity ratio is a measure of financial leverage. Taking on more debt (higher leverage) can be good or bad depending on whether the company earns a return in excess of the cost of borrowed funds. The times interest earned ratio measures a company's ability to meet interest payments as they become due.

Decision Point

Question	Accounting information	Analysis
Can a company meet its interest obligations?	Times interest earned ratio	A high times interest earned ratio indicates the ability of a company to meet its interest obligations.

KEY POINTS BY LEARNING OBJECTIVE

LO1 Explain financing alternatives.

Companies obtain external funds through debt financing (liabilities) and equity financing (stockholders' equity). One advantage of debt financing is that interest on borrowed funds is tax-deductible.

LO2 Identify the characteristics of bonds.

The distinguishing characteristics of bonds include whether they are backed by collateral (secured or unsecured), become due at a single specified date or over a series of years (term or serial), can be redeemed prior to maturity (callable), or can be converted into common stock (convertible).

LO3 Determine the price of a bond issue.

The price of a bond is equal to the present value of the face amount (principal) payable at maturity, plus the present value of the periodic interest payments. Bonds can be issued at face amount, below face amount (at a discount), or above face amount (at a premium).

LO4 Account for the issuance of bonds.

When bonds issue at face amount, the carrying value and the corresponding interest expense *remain constant* over time. When bonds issue at a discount (below face amount), the carrying value and the corresponding interest expense *increase* over time. When bonds issue at a premium (above face amount), the carrying value and the corresponding interest expense *decrease* over time.

LO5 Record the retirement of bonds.

No gain or loss is recorded on bonds retired at maturity. For bonds retired before maturity, we record a gain or loss on early extinguishment equal to the difference between the price paid to repurchase the bonds and the bonds' carrying value.

LO6 Identify other major long-term liabilities.

Most notes payable require periodic installment payments. Each installment payment includes an amount that represents interest expense and an amount that represents a reduction of the outstanding loan balance.

An operating lease is recorded just like a rental. In a capital lease, the lessee essentially "buys" the asset and borrows the money to pay for it.

Analysis

LO7 Make financial decisions using long-term liability ratios.

The debt to equity ratio is a measure of financial leverage. Assuming more debt (higher leverage) can be good or bad depending on whether the company earns a return in excess of the cost of borrowed funds. The times interest earned ratio measures a company's ability to meet interest payments as they become due.

440   CHAPTER 9   Long-Term Liabilities

Amortization schedule: Provides a summary of the cash interest payments, interest expense, and changes in carrying value for debt instruments. **p. 426**

Bond: A formal debt instrument that obligates the borrower to repay a stated amount, referred to as the principal or face amount, at a specified maturity date. **p. 413**

Bond indenture: A contract between a firm issuing bonds and the corporations or individuals who purchase the bonds. **p. 414**

Callable: A bond feature that allows the borrower to repay the bonds before their scheduled maturity date at a specified call price. **p. 415**

Capital lease: Contract in which the lessee essentially buys an asset and borrows the money through a lease to pay for the asset. **p. 434**

Capital structure: The mixture of liabilities and stockholders' equity in a business. **p. 412**

Carrying value: The balance in the bonds payable account, which equals the face value of bonds payable minus the discount or the face value plus the premium. **p. 425**

Convertible: A bond feature that allows the lender (or investor) to convert each bond into a specified number of shares of common stock. **p. 415**

Debt financing: Obtaining additional funding from lenders. **p. 412**

Debt to equity ratio: Total liabilities divided by total stockholders' equity; measures a company's risk. **p. 435**

Default risk: The risk that a company will be unable to pay the bond's face amount or interest payments as it becomes due. **p. 418**

Discount: A bond's issue price is below the face amount. **p. 418**

Early extinguishment of debt: The issuer retires debt before its scheduled maturity date. **p. 430**

Equity financing: Obtaining additional funding from stockholders. **p. 412**

Installment payment: Includes both an amount that represents interest and an amount that represents a reduction of the outstanding balance. **p. 432**

Lease: A contractual arrangement by which the lessor (owner) provides the lessee (user) the right to use an asset for a specified period of time. **p. 433**

Market interest rate: Represents the true interest rate used by investors to value a bond. **p. 416**

Operating lease: Contract in which the lessor owns the asset and the lessee simply uses the asset temporarily. **p. 433**

Premium: A bond's issue price is above the face amount. **p. 420**

Private placement: Sale of debt securities directly to a single investor. **p. 413**

Return on assets: Net income divided by average total assets; measures the income generated per dollar of assets. **p. 437**

Return on equity: Net income divided by average stockholders' equity; measures the income generated per dollar of equity. **p. 437**

Secured bonds: Bonds that are supported by specific assets pledged as collateral. **p. 414**

Serial bonds: Bonds that require payment of the principal amount of the bond over a series of maturity dates. **p. 414**

Sinking fund: An investment fund used to set aside money to be used to pay debts as they come due. **p. 414**

Stated interest rate: The rate quoted in the bond contract used to calculate the cash payments for interest. **p. 416**

Term bonds: Bonds that require payment of the full principal amount of the bond at a single maturity date. **p. 414**

Times interest earned ratio: Ratio that compares interest expense with income available to pay those charges. **p. 438**

Unsecured bonds: Bonds that are *not* supported by specific assets pledged as collateral. **p. 414**

■ **LO1**

1. Which of the following is *not* a primary source of corporate debt financing?
   a. Bonds.
   b. Notes.
   c. Leases.
   d. Receivables.

■ **LO2**

2. Serial bonds are:
   a. Bonds backed by collateral.
   b. Bonds that mature in installments.

c. Bonds the issuer can repurchase at a fixed price.

d. Bonds issued below the face amount.

3. Convertible bonds: ■ LO2
   a. Provide potential benefits only to the issuer.
   b. Provide potential benefits only to the investor.
   c. Provide potential benefits to both the issuer and the investor.
   d. Provide no potential benefits.

4. The price of a bond is equal to: ■ LO3
   a. The present value of the face amount plus the present value of the stated
      interest payments.
   b. The future value of the face amount plus the future value of the stated interest
      payments.
   c. The present value of the face amount only.
   d. The present value of the interest only.

5. Which of the following is true for bonds issued at a discount?   ■ LO4
   a. The stated interest rate is greater than the market interest rate.
   b. The market interest rate is greater than the stated interest rate.
   c. The stated interest rate and the market interest rate are equal.
   d. The stated interest rate and the market interest rate are unrelated.

6. Interest expense on bonds payable is calculated as: ■ LO4
   a. Face amount times the stated interest rate.
   b. Carrying value times the market interest rate.
   c. Face amount times the market interest rate.
   d. Carrying value times the stated interest rate.

7. When bonds are issued at a discount, what happens to the carrying value and ■ LO4
   interest expense over the life of the bonds?
   a. Carrying value and interest expense increase.
   b. Carrying value and interest expense decrease.
   c. Carrying value decreases and interest expense increases.
   d. Carrying value increases and interest expense decreases.

8. Lincoln County retires a $50 million bond issue when the carrying value of the ■ LO5
   bonds is $48 million, but the market value of the bonds is $54 million. Lincoln
   County will record the retirement as:
   a. A debit of $6 million to Loss due to early extinguishment.
   b. A credit of $6 million to Gain due to early extinguishment.
   c. No gain or loss on retirement.
   d. A debit to Cash for $54 million.

9. Which of the following leases is essentially the purchase of an asset with debt ■ LO6
   financing?
   a. An operating lease.
   b. A capital lease.
   c. Both an operating lease and a capital lease.
   d. Neither an operating lease nor a capital lease.

10. Which of the following ratios measures financial leverage?   ■ LO7
    a. The return on assets ratio.
    b. The return on equity ratio.
    c. The times interest earned ratio.
    d. The debt to equity ratio.

Check out
www.mhhe.com/succeed
for more multiple-choice
questions.

Note: For answers, see the last page of the chapter.

REVIEW QUESTIONS

■ **LO1**   1. What is capital structure? How do the capital structures of **Ford** and **Microsoft** differ?

■ **LO1**   2. Why would a company choose to borrow money rather than issue additional stock?

■ **LO1**   3. What are bond issue costs? What is an underwriter?

■ **LO1**   4. Why do some companies issue bonds rather than borrow money directly from a bank?

■ **LO2**   5. Contrast the following types of bonds:
         a. Secured and unsecured.
         b. Term and serial.
         c. Callable and convertible.

■ **LO2**   6. What are convertible bonds? How do they benefit both the investor and the issuer?

■ **LO3**   7. How do we calculate the issue price of bonds? Is it equal to the present value of the principal? Explain.

■ **LO3**   8. Explain the difference in each of these terms used for bonds:
         a. Face amount and carrying value.
         b. Stated interest rate and market interest rate.

■ **LO3**   9. If bonds issue at a *discount*, is the stated interest rate less than, equal to, or more than the market interest rate? Explain.

■ **LO3**   10. If bonds issue at a *premium*, is the stated interest rate less than, equal to, or more than the market interest rate? Explain.

■ **LO3**   11. Extreme Motion issues $500,000 of 6% bonds due in 20 years with interest payable semiannually on June 30 and December 31. What is the amount of the cash payment for interest every six months? How many interest payments will there be?

■ **LO3**   12. Extreme Motion issues $500,000 of 6% bonds due in 20 years with interest payable semiannually on June 30 and December 31. Calculate the issue price of the bonds assuming a market interest rate of:
         a. 5%
         b. 6%
         c. 7%

■ **LO4**   13. If bonds issue at a *discount*, what happens to the carrying value of bonds payable and the amount recorded for interest expense over time?

■ **LO4**   14. If bonds issue at a *premium*, what happens to the carrying value of bonds payable and the amount recorded for interest expense over time?

■ **LO4**   15. Explain how each of the columns in an amortization schedule is calculated, assuming the bonds are issued at a discount. How is the amortization schedule different if bonds are issued at a premium?

■ **LO5**   16. Why would a company choose to buy back bonds before their maturity date?

■ **LO5**   17. If bonds with a carrying value of $280,000 are retired early at a cost of $330,000, is a gain or loss recorded by the issuer retiring the bonds? How does the issuer record the retirement?

■ **LO6**   18. How do interest expense and the carrying value of the note change over time for an installment note with fixed monthly loan payments?

■ **LO6**   19. Explain the difference between an operating lease and a capital lease.

■ **LO7**   20. What are the potential risks and rewards of carrying additional debt?

BRIEF EXERCISES

BE9–1 Water Emporium issues $20 million of 4% convertible bonds that mature in 10 years. Each $1,000 bond is convertible into 20 shares of common stock. The current market price of Water Emporium stock is $40 per share.
1. Explain why Water Emporium might choose to issue convertible bonds.
2. Explain why investors might choose Water Emporium's convertible bonds.

Explain the conversion feature of bonds (LO2)

BE9–2 Ultimate Butter Popcorn issues 6%, 20-year bonds with a face amount of $50,000. The market interest rate for bonds of similar risk and maturity is 6%. Interest is paid semiannually. At what price will the bonds issue?

Calculate the issue price of bonds (LO3)

BE9–3 Ultimate Butter Popcorn issues 6%, 10-year bonds with a face amount of $50,000. The market interest rate for bonds of similar risk and maturity is 7%. Interest is paid semiannually. At what price will the bonds issue?

Calculate the issue price of bonds (LO3)

BE9–4 Ultimate Butter Popcorn issues 6%, 15-year bonds with a face amount of $50,000. The market interest rate for bonds of similar risk and maturity is 5%. Interest is paid semiannually. At what price will the bonds issue?

Calculate the issue price of bonds (LO3)

BE9–5 Pretzelmania, Inc., issues 6%, 10-year bonds with a face amount of $60,000 for $60,000 on January 1, 2012. The market interest rate for bonds of similar risk and maturity is 6%. Interest is paid semiannually on June 30 and December 31.
1. Record the bond issue.
2. Record the first interest payment on June 30, 2012.

Record bond issue and related semiannual interest (LO4)

BE9–6 Pretzelmania, Inc., issues 6%, 10-year bonds with a face amount of $60,000 for $55,736 on January 1, 2012. The market interest rate for bonds of similar risk and maturity is 7%. Interest is paid semiannually on June 30 and December 31.
1. Record the bond issue.
2. Record the first interest payment on June 30, 2012.

Record bond issue and related semiannual interest (LO4)

BE9–7 Pretzelmania, Inc., issues 6%, 10-year bonds with a face amount of $60,000 for $64,676 on January 1, 2012. The market interest rate for bonds of similar risk and maturity is 5%. Interest is paid semiannually on June 30 and December 31.
1. Record the bond issue.
2. Record the first interest payment on June 30, 2012.

Record bond issue and related semiannual interest (LO4)

BE9–8 Pretzelmania, Inc., issues 6%, 10-year bonds with a face amount of $60,000 for $60,000 on January 1, 2012. The market interest rate for bonds of similar risk and maturity is 6%. Interest is paid *annually* on December 31.
1. Record the bond issue.
2. Record the first interest payment on December 31, 2012.

Record bond issue and related annual interest (LO4)

BE9–9 Pretzelmania, Inc., issues 6%, 10-year bonds with a face amount of $60,000 for $55,786 on January 1, 2012. The market interest rate for bonds of similar risk and maturity is 7%. Interest is paid *annually* on December 31.
1. Record the bond issue.
2. Record the first interest payment on December 31, 2012. (*Hint:* Interest expense is 7% times the carrying value of $55,786.)

Record bond issue and related annual interest (LO4)

BE9–10 Pretzelmania, Inc., issues 6%, 10-year bonds with a face amount of $60,000 for $64,633 on January 1, 2012. The market interest rate for bonds of similar risk and maturity is 5%. Interest is paid *annually* on December 31.
1. Record the bond issue.
2. Record the first interest payment on December 31, 2012. (*Hint:* Interest expense is 5% times the carrying value of $64,633.)

Record bond issue and related annual interest (LO4)

BE9–11 On January 1, 2012, Lizzy's Lemonade issues 7%, 15-year bonds with a face amount of $90,000 for $82,219, priced to yield 8%. Interest is paid semiannually. What amount of interest expense will be recorded on June 30, 2012, the first interest payment date?

Calculate interest expense (LO4)

Calculate interest expense (LO4)

BE9–12 On January 1, 2012, Lyle's Limeade issues 3%, 20-year bonds with a face amount of $80,000 for $69,034, priced to yield 4%. Interest is paid semiannually. What amount of interest expense will be recorded in the December 31, 2012, annual income statement?

Interpret a bond amortization schedule (LO4)

BE9–13 Presented below is a partial amortization schedule for Discount Pizza.

(1) Period	(2) Cash Paid for Interest	(3) Interest Expense	(4) Increase in Carrying Value	(5) Carrying Value
Issue date				$55,736
1	$1,800	$1,951	$151	55,887
2	1,800	1,956	156	56,043

1. Record the bond issue.
2. Record the first interest payment.
3. Explain why interest expense increases each period.

Interpret a bond amortization schedule (LO4)

BE9–14 Presented below is a partial amortization schedule for Premium Pizza.

(1) Period	(2) Cash Paid for Interest	(3) Interest Expense	(4) Decrease in Carrying Value	(5) Carrying Value
Issue date				$64,677
1	$1,800	$1,617	$183	64,494
2	1,800	1,612	188	64,306

1. Record the bond issue.
2. Record the first interest payment.
3. Explain why interest expense decreases each period.

Record early retirement of bonds issued at a discount (LO5)

BE9–15 Discount Pizza retires its 6% bonds for $58,000 before their scheduled maturity. At the time, the bonds have a carrying value of $56,043. Record the early retirement of the bonds.

Record early retirement of bonds issued at a premium (LO5)

BE9–16 Premium Pizza retires its 6% bonds for $62,000 before their scheduled maturity. At the time, the bonds have a carrying value of $64,306. Record the early retirement of the bonds.

Record installment notes (LO6)

BE9–17 On January 1, 2012, Corvallis Carnivals borrows $20,000 to purchase a delivery truck by agreeing to a 7%, four-year loan with the bank. Payments of $478.92 are due at the end of each month, with the first installment due on January 31, 2012. Record the issuance of the note payable and the first monthly payment.

Calculate ratios (LO7)

BE9–18 CEC Entertainment, which owns the Chuck E. Cheese pizza chain, has the following selected data ($ in millions):

CEC ENTERTAINMENT Selected Balance Sheet Data	2008	2007
Total assets	$747	$738
Total liabilities	618	520
Total stockholders' equity	129	218

CEC ENTERTAINMENT Selected Income Statement Data	
Sales revenue	$815
Interest expense	17
Tax expense	34
Net income	56

Based on these amounts, calculate the following ratios for 2008:
1. Debt to equity ratio.
2. Return on assets ratio.
3. Return on equity ratio.
4. Times interest earned ratio.
Why is the return on equity higher than the return on assets?

EXERCISES

E9–1 Penny Arcades, Inc., is trying to decide between the following two alternatives to finance its new $25 million gaming center:

a. Issue $25 million of 6% bonds at face amount.

b. Issue 1 million shares of common stock for $25 per share.

Compare financing alternatives (**LO1**)

	Issue Bonds	Issue Stock
Operating income	$10,000,000	$10,000,000
Interest expense (bonds only)		
Income before tax		
Income tax expense (30%)		
Net income	$	$
Number of shares	3,000,000	4,000,000
Earnings per share (Net income/# of shares)	$	$

Required:

1. Assuming bonds or shares of stock are issued at the beginning of the year, complete the income statement for each alternative.

2. Which alternative results in the highest earnings per share?

E9–2 Listed below are terms and definitions associated with bonds.

Match bond terms with their definitions (**LO2**)

Terms

_____ 1. Bond indenture.

_____ 2. Secured bond.

_____ 3. Unsecured bond.

_____ 4. Term bond.

_____ 5. Serial bond.

_____ 6. Callable bond.

_____ 7. Convertible bond.

_____ 8. Bond issue costs.

Definitions

a. Allows the issuer to pay off the bonds early at a fixed price.

b. Matures in installments.

c. Secured only by the "full faith and credit" of the issuing corporation.

d. Allows the investor to transfer each bond into shares of common stock.

e. A contract between the issuer and the investor.

f. Matures on a single date.

g. Supported by specific assets pledged as collateral by the issuer.

h. Includes underwriting, legal, accounting, registration, and printing fees.

Required:

Match (by letter) the bond terms with their definitions. Each letter is used only once.

E9–3 On January 1, 2012, Frontier World issues $40 million of 8% bonds, due in 15 years, with interest payable semiannually on June 30 and December 31 each year. The proceeds will be used to build a new ride that combines a roller coaster, a water ride, a dark tunnel, and the great smell of outdoor barbeque, all in one ride.

Calculate the issue price of bonds (**LO3**)

Required:

1. If the market rate is 7%, will the bonds issue at face amount, a discount, or a premium? Calculate the issue price.

2. If the market rate is 8%, will the bonds issue at face amount, a discount, or a premium? Calculate the issue price.

3. If the market rate is 9%, will the bonds issue at face amount, a discount, or a premium? Calculate the issue price.

Calculate the issue price of bonds (LO3)

E9–4 On January 1, 2012, Water World issues $25 million of 6% bonds, due in 20 years, with interest payable semiannually on June 30 and December 31 each year. Water World intends to use the funds to build the world's largest water avalanche and the "tornado"— a giant outdoor vortex in which riders spin in progressively smaller and faster circles until they drop through a small tunnel at the bottom.

Required:
1. If the market rate is 5%, will the bonds issue at face amount, a discount, or a premium? Calculate the issue price.
2. If the market rate is 6%, will the bonds issue at face amount, a discount, or a premium? Calculate the issue price.
3. If the market rate is 7%, will the bonds issue at face amount, a discount, or a premium? Calculate the issue price.

Record bonds issued at face amount (LO4)

E9–5 On January 1, 2012, Splash City issues $400,000 of 8% bonds, due in 15 years, with interest payable semiannually on June 30 and December 31 each year.

Required:
Assuming the market interest rate on the issue date is 8%, the bonds will issue at $400,000. Record the bond issue on January 1, 2012, and the first two semiannual interest payments on June 30, 2012, and December 31, 2012.

Record bonds issued at a discount (LO4)

E9–6 On January 1, 2012, Splash City issues $400,000 of 8% bonds, due in 15 years, with interest payable semiannually on June 30 and December 31 each year.

Required:
Assuming the market interest rate on the issue date is 9%, the bonds will issue at $367,422.
1. Complete the first three rows of an amortization table.
2. Record the bond issue on January 1, 2012, and the first two semiannual interest payments on June 30, 2012, and December 31, 2012.

Record bonds issued at a premium (LO4)

E9–7 On January 1, 2012, Splash City issues $400,000 of 8% bonds, due in 15 years, with interest payable semiannually on June 30 and December 31 each year.

Required:
Assuming the market interest rate on the issue date is 7%, the bonds will issue at $436,784.
1. Complete the first three rows of an amortization table.
2. Record the bond issue on January 1, 2012, and the first two semiannual interest payments on June 30, 2012, and December 31, 2012.

Record bonds issued at face amount (LO4)

E9–8 On January 1, 2012, White Water issues $500,000 of 6% bonds, due in 20 years, with interest payable semiannually on June 30 and December 31 each year.

Required:
Assuming the market interest rate on the issue date is 6%, the bonds will issue at $500,000. Record the bond issue on January 1, 2012, and the first two semiannual interest payments on June 30, 2012, and December 31, 2012.

Record bonds issued at a discount (LO4)

E9–9 On January 1, 2012, White Water issues $500,000 of 6% bonds, due in 20 years, with interest payable semiannually on June 30 and December 31 each year.

Required:
Assuming the market interest rate on the issue date is 7%, the bonds will issue at $446,612.
1. Complete the first three rows of an amortization table.
2. Record the bond issue on January 1, 2012, and the first two semiannual interest payments on June 30, 2012, and December 31, 2012.

E9–10 On January 1, 2012, White Water issues $500,000 of 6% bonds, due in 20 years, with interest payable semiannually on June 30 and December 31 each year.

Record bonds issued at a premium (LO4)

Required:

Assuming the market interest rate on the issue date is 5%, the bonds will issue at $562,757.

1. Complete the first three rows of an amortization table.
2. Record the bond issue on January 1, 2012, and the first two semiannual interest payments on June 30, 2012, and December 31, 2012.

E9–11 On January 1, 2012, White Water issues $500,000 of 6% bonds, due in 20 years, with interest payable annually on December 31 each year.

Record bonds issued at face amount with interest payable annually (LO4)

Required:

Assuming the market interest rate on the issue date is 6%, the bonds will issue at $500,000. Record the bond issue on January 1, 2012, and the first two interest payments on December 31, 2012, and December 31, 2013.

E9–12 On January 1, 2012, White Water issues $500,000 of 6% bonds, due in 20 years, with interest payable annually on December 31 each year.

Record bonds issued at a discount with interest payable annually (LO4)

Required:

Assuming the market interest rate on the issue date is 7%, the bonds will issue at $447,030.

1. Complete the first three rows of an amortization table. (*Hint:* Use Illustration 9–13, except the dates for the first three rows will be 1/1/12, 12/31/12, and 12/31/13 since interest is payable *annually* rather than semiannually. Interest expense for the period ended December 31, 2012, is calculated as the carrying value of $447,030 times the market rate of 7%.)
2. Record the bond issue on January 1, 2012, and the first two interest payments on December 31, 2012, and December 31, 2013.

E9–13 On January 1, 2012, White Water issues $500,000 of 6% bonds, due in 20 years, with interest payable annually on December 31 each year.

Record bonds issued at a premium with interest payable annually (LO4)

Required:

Assuming the market interest rate on the issue date is 5%, the bonds will issue at $562,311.

1. Complete the first three rows of an amortization table. (*Hint:* Use Illustration 9–14, except the dates for the first three rows will be 1/1/12, 12/31/12, and 12/31/13 since interest is payable *annually* rather than semiannually. Interest expense for the period ended December 31, 2012, is calculated as the carrying value of $562,311 times the market rate of 5%.)
2. Record the bond issue on January 1, 2012, and the first two interest payments on December 31, 2012, and December 31, 2013.

E9–14 On January 1, 2012, Splash City issues $400,000 of 8% bonds, due in 15 years, with interest payable semiannually on June 30 and December 31 each year. The market interest rate on the issue date is 9% and the bonds issued at $367,422.

Record the retirement of bonds (LO5)

Required:

1. Using an amortization schedule, show that the bonds have a carrying value of $369,706 on December 31, 2013.
2. If the market interest rate drops to 7% on December 31, 2013, it will cost $433,781 to retire the bonds. Record the retirement of the bonds on December 31, 2013.

E9–15 On January 1, 2012, White Water issues $500,000 of 6% bonds, due in 20 years, with interest payable semiannually on June 30 and December 31 each year. The market interest rate on the issue date is 5% and the bonds issued at $562,757.

Record the retirement of bonds (LO5)

Required:

1. Using an amortization schedule, show that the bonds have a carrying value of $556,810 on December 31, 2014.
2. If the market interest rate increases to 7% on December 31, 2014, it will cost $450,748 to retire the bonds. Record the retirement of the bonds on December 31, 2014.

Record installment
notes (LO6)

E9–16 On January 1, 2012, Tropical Paradise borrows $40,000 by agreeing to a 6%, five-year note with the bank. The funds will be used to purchase a new BMW convertible for use in promoting resort properties to potential customers. Loan payments of $773.31 are due at the end of each month with the first installment due on January 31, 2012.

Required:
Record the issuance of the installment note payable and the first two monthly payments.

Calculate and analyze
ratios (LO7)

E9–17 Two leading online travel companies are Expedia and Priceline. Selected financial data for these two close competitors are as follows:

($ in thousands)	Expedia	Priceline
Total assets	$5,937,156	$1,834,224
Total liabilities	3,254,475	476,610
Total stockholders' equity	2,682,681	1,357,614
Sales revenue	$2,955,426	$2,338,212
Interest expense	84,233	24,084
Tax expense	154,400	47,168
Net income	299,526	489,472

Required:
1. Calculate the debt to equity ratio for Expedia and Priceline. Which company has the higher ratio? Compare your calculations with those for Coca-Cola and PepsiCo reported in the chapter. Which industry maintains a higher debt to equity ratio?
2. Calculate the times interest earned ratio for Expedia and Priceline. Which company is better able to meet interest payments as they become due? Compare your calculations with those for Coca-Cola and PepsiCo reported in the chapter. Which industry has a better times interest earned ratio?

For additional exercises, visit www.mhhe.com/succeed for Exercises: Set B.

PROBLEMS: SET A

Calculate the issue
price of a bond and
prepare amortization
schedules (LO3, 4)

P9–1A Coney Island Entertainment issues $1,000,000 of 6% bonds, due in 15 years, with interest payable semiannually on June 30 and December 31 each year.

Required:
Calculate the issue price of a bond and complete the first three rows of an amortization schedule when:
1. The market interest rate is 6% and the bonds issue at face amount.
2. The market interest rate is 7% and the bonds issue at a discount.
3. The market interest rate is 5% and the bonds issue at a premium.

Record bond issue and
related interest (LO4)

P9–2A On January 1, 2012, Twister Enterprises, a manufacturer of a variety of transportable spin rides, issues $500,000 of 7% bonds, due in 20 years, with interest payable semiannually on June 30 and December 31 each year.

Required:
1. If the market interest rate is 7%, the bonds will issue at $500,000. Record the bond issue on January 1, 2012, and the first two semiannual interest payments on June 30, 2012, and December 31, 2012.
2. If the market interest rate is 8%, the bonds will issue at $450,518. Record the bond issue on January 1, 2012, and the first two semiannual interest payments on June 30, 2012, and December 31, 2012.

3. If the market interest rate is 6%, the bonds will issue at $557,787. Record the bond issue on January 1, 2012, and the first two semiannual interest payments on June 30, 2012, and December 31, 2012.

P9–3A On January 1, 2012, Vacation Destinations issues bonds that pay interest semiannually on June 30 and December 31. Portions of the bond amortization schedule appear below:

Understand a bond amortization schedule (LO4)

(1) Date	(2) Cash Paid for Interest	(3) Interest Expense	(4) Increase in Carrying Value	(5) Carrying Value
1/1/2012				$28,048,810
6/30/2012	$1,200,000	$1,262,196	$ 62,196	28,111,006
12/31/2012	1,200,000	1,264,995	64,995	28,176,001
*	*	*	*	*
*	*	*	*	29,719,099
6/30/2021	1,200,000	1,337,360	137,360	29,856,459
12/31/2021	1,200,000	1,343,541	143,541	30,000,000

Required:
1. Were the bonds issued at face amount, a discount, or a premium?
2. What is the original issue price of the bonds?
3. What is the face amount of the bonds?
4. What is the term to maturity in years?
5. What is the stated annual interest rate?
6. What is the market annual interest rate?
7. What is the total cash interest paid over the term to maturity?

P9–4A On January 1, 2012, Universe of Fun issues $800,000, 9% bonds that mature in 10 years. The market interest rate for bonds of similar risk and maturity is 10%, and the bonds issue for $750,151. Interest is paid semiannually on June 30 and December 31.

Prepare a bond amortization schedule and record transactions for the bond issuer (LO4)

Required:
1. Complete the first three rows of an amortization schedule.
2. Record the issuance of the bonds on January 1, 2012.
3. Record the interest payments on June 30, 2012, and December 31, 2012.

P9–5A On January 1, 2012, Gundy Enterprises purchases an office for $250,000, paying $50,000 down and borrowing the remaining $200,000, signing an 8%, 30-year mortgage. Installment payments of $1,467.53 are due at the end of each month, with the first payment due on January 31, 2012.

Record and analyze installment notes (LO6)

Required:
1. Record issuance of the mortgage installment note on January 1, 2012.
2. Complete the first three rows of an amortization schedule similar to Illustration 9–16.
3. Record the first monthly mortgage payment on January 31, 2012. How much of the first payment goes to interest expense and how much goes to reducing the carrying value of the loan?
4. Total payments over the 30 years are $528,311 ($1,467.53 × 360 monthly payments). How much of this is interest expense and how much is actual payment of the loan?

P9–6A Thrillville has $40 million in bonds payable. One of the contractual agreements in the bond indenture is that the debt to equity ratio cannot exceed 2.0. Thrillville's total assets are $80 million, and its liabilities other than the bonds payable are $10 million. The company is considering some additional financing through leasing.

Explore the impact of leases on the debt to equity ratio (LO6, 7)

450   CHAPTER 9   Long-Term Liabilities

Required:

1. Calculate total stockholders' equity using the balance sheet equation.
2. What is the debt to equity ratio?
3. Explain the difference between an operating lease and a capital lease.
4. The company enters a lease agreement requiring lease payments with a present value of $15 million. Will this lease agreement affect the debt to equity ratio differently if the lease is recorded as an operating lease versus a capital lease?
5. Will entering into the lease cause the debt to equity ratio to be in violation of the contractual agreement in the bond indenture? Show your calculations (a) assuming an operating lease and (b) assuming a capital lease.

Calculate and analyze ratios (LO7)

P9–7A Two leading hotel chains in the United States are **Starwood Hotels and Resorts** (owners of Sheraton, Westin, etc.) and **Marriott**. Selected financial data for these two close competitors are as follows:

($ in millions)	Starwood		Marriott	
	2008	**2007**	**2008**	**2007**
Total assets	$9,703	$9,622	$ 8,903	$8,942
Total liabilities	8,082	7,546	7,523	7,513
Total stockholders' equity	1,621	2,076	1,380	1,429
Sales revenue	$5,907		$12,879	
Interest expense	210		163	
Tax expense	76		350	
Net income	329		362	

Required:

1. Calculate the debt to equity ratio for Starwood and Marriott for the most recent year. Which company has the higher ratio? Compare your calculations with those for **Coca-Cola** and **PepsiCo** reported in the chapter. Which industry maintains a higher debt to equity ratio?
2. Calculate the return on assets and the return on equity for Starwood and Marriott. Which company has the better profitability ratios? How do they compare with those for Coca-Cola and PepsiCo reported in the chapter?
3. Calculate the times interest earned ratio for Starwood and Marriott. Which company is better able to meet interest payments as they become due? Compare your calculations with those for Coca-Cola and PepsiCo reported in the chapter. Which industry has a better times interest earned ratio?

PROBLEMS: SET B

Calculate the issue price of a bond and prepare amortization schedules (LO3, 4)

P9–1B Christmas Anytime issues $750,000 of 7% bonds, due in 10 years, with interest payable semiannually on June 30 and December 31 each year.

Required:

Calculate the issue price of a bond and complete the first three rows of an amortization schedule when:

1. The market interest rate is 7% and the bonds issue at face amount.
2. The market interest rate is 8% and the bonds issue at a discount.
3. The market interest rate is 6% and the bonds issue at a premium.

Record bond issue and related interest (LO4)

P9–2B Viking Voyager specializes in the design and production of replica Viking boats. On January 1, 2012, the company issues $2,000,000 of 8% bonds, due in 10 years, with interest payable semiannually on June 30 and December 31 each year.

Required:
1. If the market interest rate is 8%, the bonds will issue at $2,000,000. Record the bond issue on January 1, 2012, and the first two semiannual interest payments on June 30, 2012, and December 31, 2012.
2. If the market interest rate is 9%, the bonds will issue at $1,869,921. Record the bond issue on January 1, 2012, and the first two semiannual interest payments on June 30, 2012, and December 31, 2012.
3. If the market interest rate is 7%, the bonds will issue at $2,142,124. Record the bond issue on January 1, 2012, and the first two semiannual interest payments on June 30, 2012, and December 31, 2012.

P9–3B Temptation Vacations issues bonds on January 1, 2012, that pay interest semiannually on June 30 and December 31. Portions of the bond amortization schedule appear below:

Understand a bond amortization schedule (LO4)

(1) Date	(2) Cash Paid for Interest	(3) Interest Expense	(4) Decrease in Carrying Value	(5) Carrying Value
1/1/2012				$55,338,768
6/30/2012	$2,000,000	$1,936,857	$ 63,143	55,275,625
12/31/2012	2,000,000	1,934,647	65,353	55,210,272
*	*	*	*	*
*	*	*	*	50,474,924
6/30/2031	2,000,000	1,766,622	233,378	50,241,546
12/31/2031	2,000,000	1,758,454	241,546	50,000,000

Required:
1. Were the bonds issued at face amount, a discount, or a premium?
2. What is the original issue price of the bonds?
3. What is the face amount of the bonds?
4. What is the term to maturity in years?
5. What is the stated annual interest rate?
6. What is the market annual interest rate?
7. What is the total cash interest paid over the term to maturity?

P9–4B Super Splash issues $900,000, 8% bonds on January 1, 2012, that mature in 20 years. The market interest rate for bonds of similar risk and maturity is 7%, and the bonds issue for $996,098. Interest is paid semiannually on June 30 and December 31.

Prepare a bond amortization schedule and record transactions for the bond issuer (LO4)

Required:
1. Complete the first three rows of an amortization schedule.
2. Record the issuance of the bonds on January 1, 2012.
3. Record the interest payments on June 30, 2012, and December 31, 2012.

P9–5B On January 1, 2012, Stoops Entertainment purchases a building for $500,000, paying $100,000 down and borrowing the remaining $400,000, signing a 7%, 15-year mortgage. Installment payments of $3,595.31 are due at the end of each month, with the first payment due on January 31, 2012.

Record and analyze installment notes (LO6)

Required:
1. Record issuance of the mortgage installment note on January 1, 2012.
2. Complete the first three rows of an amortization schedule similar to Illustration 9–16.
3. Record the first monthly mortgage payment on January 31, 2012. How much of the first payment goes to interest expense and how much goes to reducing the carrying value of the loan?
4. Total payments over the 15 years are $647,156 ($3,595.31 × 180 monthly payments). How much of this is interest expense and how much is actual payment of the loan?

Explore the impact of leases on the debt to equity ratio (LO6, 7)

P9–6B Chunky Cheese Pizza has $60 million in bonds payable. The bond indenture states that the debt to equity ratio cannot exceed 3.0. Chunky's total assets are $200 million, and its liabilities other than the bonds payable are $90 million. The company is considering some additional financing through leasing.

Required:

1. Calculate total stockholders' equity using the balance sheet equation.
2. What is the debt to equity ratio?
3. Explain the difference between an operating and a capital lease.
4. The company enters a lease agreement requiring lease payments with a present value of $5 million. Will this lease agreement affect the debt to equity ratio differently if the lease is recorded as an operating lease versus a capital lease?
5. Will entering into the lease cause the debt to equity ratio to be in violation of the contractual agreement in the bond indenture? Show your calculations (a) assuming an operating lease and (b) assuming a capital lease.

Calculate and analyze ratios (LO7)

P9–7B Two of the world's leading cruise lines are **Royal Caribbean Cruises** and **Carnival Corporation**. Selected financial data for these two close competitors are as follows:

($ in millions)	Royal Caribbean		Carnival	
	2008	**2007**	**2008**	**2007**
Total assets	$16,463	$14,982	$33,400	$34,181
Total liabilities	9,660	8,225	14,302	14,218
Total stockholders' equity	6,803	6,757	19,098	19,963
Sales revenue	$ 6,533		$14,646	
Interest expense	327		414	
Tax expense	–		47	
Net income	574		2,330	

Required:

1. Calculate the debt to equity ratio for Royal Caribbean and Carnival for the most recent year. Which company has the higher ratio? Compare your calculations with those for **Coca-Cola** and **PepsiCo** reported in the chapter.
2. Calculate the return on assets and the return on equity for Royal Caribbean and Carnival. Which company has the better profitability ratios? How do they compare with those for Coca-Cola and PepsiCo reported in the chapter?
3. Calculate the times interest earned ratio for Royal Caribbean and Carnival. Which company is better able to meet interest payments as they become due? Compare your calculations with those for Coca-Cola and PepsiCo reported in the chapter. Which industry has a better times interest earned ratio?

*For additional problems, visit **www.mhhe.com/succeed** for Problems: Set C.*

ADDITIONAL PERSPECTIVES

Continuing Problem

Great Adventures

(This is a continuation of the Great Adventures problem from earlier chapters.)

AP9–1 Tony's favorite memories of his childhood were the times he spent with his dad at camp. Tony was daydreaming of those days a bit as he and Suzie jogged along a nature trail and came across a wonderful piece of property for sale. He turned to Suzie and said, "I've always wanted to start a camp where families could get away and spend some quality time together. If we just had the money, I know this would be the perfect place." They called several banks and on January 1, 2014, Great Adventures obtained a $500,000, 6%, 10-year installment loan from Summit Bank. Monthly payments of $5,551 are required at the end of each month over the life of the 10-year loan. Each monthly payment of $5,551 includes both interest expense and principal payments (i.e., reduction of the loan amount.)

Late that night Tony exclaimed, "$500,000 for our new camp, this has to be the best news ever." Suzie snuggled close and said, "There's something else I need to tell you, Tony, I'm expecting!" They decided right then, if it was a boy, they would name him Venture.

Required:

1. Complete the first three rows of an amortization table.
2. Record the note payable on January 1, 2014, and the first two payments on January 31, 2014, and February 28, 2014.

American Eagle Outfitters, Inc.

Financial Analysis

AP9–2 Financial information for **American Eagle** is presented in Appendix A at the end of the book.

Required:

1. Calculate the debt to equity ratio for the past two years. Did the ratio improve or weaken in the more recent year?
2. Calculate the return on equity. Would investors obtain a higher return on equity if American Eagle borrowed more money?
3. *Review the balance sheet and note 8 to the financial statements.* Based on this information, how would you rate the bankruptcy risk of American Eagle?

The Buckle, Inc.

Financial Analysis

AP9–3 Financial information for **The Buckle** is presented in Appendix B at the end of the book.

Required:

1. Calculate the debt to equity ratio for the past two years. Did the ratio improve or weaken in the more recent year?
2. Calculate the return on equity. Would investors obtain a higher return on equity if The Buckle borrowed more money?
3. *Review the balance sheet and note E to the financial statements.* Based on this information, how would you rate the bankruptcy risk of The Buckle?

American Eagle Outfitters, Inc., vs. The Buckle, Inc.

Comparative Analysis

AP9–4 Financial information for **American Eagle** is presented in Appendix A at the end of the book, and financial information for **The Buckle** is presented in Appendix B at the end of the book.

Required:

1. Calculate the debt to equity ratio for American Eagle and The Buckle for the most recent year. Which company has the better ratio? Compare your calculations with those for **Coca-Cola** and **PepsiCo** reported earlier in the chapter. Which industry maintains a higher debt to equity ratio?
2. Calculate the return on assets and the return on equity for American Eagle and The Buckle for the most recent year. Which company has the better profitability ratios?

Ethics

AP9–5 The Tony Hawk Skate Park was built in early 2010. The construction was financed by $10 million of 5% bonds issued at face value, due in 10 years, with interest payable on June 30 and December 31 each year. The park did well initially, reporting net income in both 2010 and 2011. However, the discussion at the executive board meeting in late 2012 focused on falling skate-park revenues and increasing maintenance expenses. While several ideas were proposed, Jim Trost, the VP of finance, had an intriguing short-term solution. Jim stated, "Interest rates have steadily climbed the past three years. At the current market interest rate of 9%, we could repurchase our bonds for just under $8 million, recording a gain of over $2 million on the repurchase. We could then reissue new bonds at the current 9% rate."

Required:

1. Calculate the actual repurchase price on December 31, 2012, assuming the 10-year, 5% bonds paying interest semiannually were initially issued at a face value of $10 million three years earlier on January 1, 2010. (*Hint:* The periods to maturity (n) will now be 14, calculated as 7 years remaining times 2 periods each year.)
2. Record the bond retirement on December 31, 2012.
3. Is it ethical to time the repurchase of bonds in 2012 in order to include a $2 million gain on repurchase in a bad year? What if the transaction is fully disclosed?
4. From a business standpoint, is the retirement of 5% bonds and the reissue of 9% bonds a good idea? Explain why or why not.

Internet Research

AP9–6 Standard & Poor's is a global leader in credit ratings and credit risk analysis. Go to its website at *standardandpoors.com*. Select "U.S." Click on "Products and Services."

Required:

1. Begin on the homepage. Click on "About S&P" listed at the top right of the page. About how much debt is covered by Standard & Poor's credit ratings?
2. Go back to the homepage. Click on "Ratings." Click on "Learn About Corporate Ratings." Click on "Corporates: News & Commentary" at the bottom of the page. Briefly summarize an item in the news today.
3. Go back to the homepage. Click on "Indices." Click on "S&P 500." When did the S&P 500 begin?
4. Go back to the homepage. Click on "Products and Services." Briefly summarize one of the products listed.

Written Communication

AP9–7 Western Entertainment is considering issuing bonds to finance its business expansion. The company contacts you, a business consultant charging $200 an hour, to answer the following questions.
1. What are the advantages of issuing bonds over borrowing funds from a bank?
2. What are the advantages of issuing bonds over issuing common stock?
3. How is a bond price determined?

Required:

Write a memo providing answers worthy of your billing rate.

Earnings Management

AP9–8 Adrenaline Entertainment is struggling financially and its CFO, David Plesko, is starting to feel the heat. Back on January 1, 2010, Adrenaline Entertainment issued $100 million of 6% bonds, due in 15 years, with interest payable semiannually on June 30 and December 31 each year. The market interest rate on the date of issue was 5%.

It is now the end of 2014, and David has a plan to increase reported net income in 2014. The market interest rate has risen to 9% by the end of 2014. David wants to retire the $100 million, 6% bonds and reissue new 9% bonds instead.

Required:
1. Show that the bonds originally were issued on January 1, 2010, for $110,465,146.
2. Calculate the carrying value of the bonds five years later on December 31, 2014. (*Hint:* Use a market rate of 2.5% (5% ÷ 2), and the number of periods is now 20 semiannual periods.)
3. Calculate the market value of the bonds five years later on December 31, 2014. (*Hint:* The market rate is now 4.5% (9% ÷ 2) rather than 2.5% (5% ÷ 2), and the number of periods is now 20 semiannual periods.)
4. Record the early retirement of the bonds on December 31, 2014. Does the transaction increase net income? By how much (ignoring any tax effect)?
5. Is David Plesko's plan ethical? Do you think investors would agree with David Plesko that the retirement of the 6% bonds and the reissue of 9% bonds is a good idea? Explain why or why not.

Answers to the Self-Study Questions
1. d   2. b   3. c   4. a   5. b   6. b   7. a   8. a   9. b   10. d

CHAPTER

10

Stockholders' Equity

DECKERS OUTDOOR: **FROM DOWN UNDER TO TOP TEN**

David Letterman has made the "Top Ten" list famous. His top ten things you *don't* want to hear from your accountant include, "Listen, I'm not good with math," "The good news is you're getting a huge refund—the bad news is you'll have to hide in Costa Rica for a while," "Do you have any dedemptions or exuptions or whatever?," and "Relax, everything here will be fine—I used to work for Enron."

Wouldn't it be nice to know the top ten best stock investments for the future? Although we can't predict the future, we can learn from the past. The ten best stock investments and their investment return over the past decade from 2000 through 2009 were:

Company	Main Product or Service	Return, 2000–2009
Green Mountain Coffee	Coffee	7,434%
Hansen Natural	Beverages	6,455%
Terra Nitrogen	Fertilizers	6,156%
Bally	Slot machines	5,965%
Southwestern Energy	Natural gas	5,411%
Clean Harbors	Hazardous waste disposal	5,464%
Amedisys	Home health care	4,452%
Quality Systems	Accounting and other financial software	3,592%
Deckers Outdoor	Footwear	3,549%
XTO Energy	Oil and natural gas	3,533%

Green Mountain Coffee was the top investment over the past decade. You may be more familiar with Starbucks, but Green Mountain was the better investment. If you had invested $1,000 in the company in 2000, your investment would have grown to over $74,000 by the end of 2009. The second-place finisher, **Hansen Natural**, provides a variety of all-natural beverages such as soda, energy drinks like the Monster brand, juice, and tea. A $1,000 investment in Hansen Natural would have grown to over $64,000 ten years later. Another company you might be familiar with is **Deckers Outdoor**. The company designs and manufactures trendy footwear like Teva sandals and UGG sheepskin boots, available in most shopping malls.

What do these great stock investments have in common? They all were very profitable in relation to the initial investment made by stockholders. In this chapter you will learn how to compare earnings in relation to equity—both the stockholders' equity recorded in the company balance sheet and the market value of equity as determined by the price per share times the number of shares.

Feature Story

Recall from the accounting equation that assets equal liabilities plus stockholders' equity.

$$\underbrace{\text{Assets}}_{\text{(resources)}} \quad = \quad \underbrace{\text{Liabilities} \quad + \quad \text{Stockholders' Equity}}_{\text{(claims to resources)}}$$

Common Terms
Stockholders' equity sometimes is referred to as *shareholders' equity.*

In Chapters 4–7 we focused on assets and in Chapters 8–9 on liabilities. Here, in Chapter 10, we focus on the third component of the accounting equation—stockholders' equity. Because assets represent resources of the company and liabilities are creditors' claims to those resources, equity represents the owners' residual claim to those resources. Stated another way, equity is equal to what we own (assets) minus what we owe (liabilities). We use the term *stockholders'* equity (as opposed to *owners'* equity) because our focus throughout the book is on corporations.

Stockholders' equity consists of three primary classifications: paid-in capital, retained earnings, and treasury stock. Paid-in capital is the amount stockholders have invested in the company. Retained earnings is the amount of earnings the corporation has kept or retained—that is, the earnings not paid out in dividends. Treasury stock is the corporation's own stock that it has reacquired. Illustration 10–1 shows those components in the stockholders' equity section of the balance sheet for American Eagle.

ILLUSTRATION 10–1

Stockholders' Equity Section for American Eagle

AMERICAN EAGLE Balance Sheet January 31, 2009	
(Dollars and number of shares in thousands)	
Total assets	$1,963,676
Total liabilities	$ 554,645
Stockholders' equity:	
Preferred stock, $0.01 par value	–0–
Common stock, $0.01 par value	2,485
Additional paid-in capital	513,574
Total paid-in capital	516,059
Retained earnings	1,679,772
Treasury stock, 43,248 (thousand) shares	(786,800)
Total stockholders' equity	$1,409,031
Total liabilities and stockholders' equity	$1,963,676

At this point, simply note that total stockholders' equity for American Eagle consists of total paid-in capital, retained earnings, and treasury stock. It is increased by paid-in capital and retained earnings and reduced by treasury stock. We'll fill in the details as we progress through the chapter.

In Part A of the chapter, we discuss transactions involving paid-in capital. A better description might be "invested capital" since it's the amount stockholders invest when they purchase a company's stock. In Part B, we examine transactions involving retained earnings. A better description might be "earned capital," since it's the amount the company has *earned* for the stockholders. In Part C, we look at the reporting of stockholders' equity.

INVESTED CAPITAL

Invested capital is the amount of money paid into a company by its owners. The owners of a corporation are its stockholders. Recall from Chapter 1 that a company can be formed as a sole proprietorship, a partnership, or a corporation. A sole proprietorship is a business owned by one person, whereas a partnership is a business owned by two or more persons. A **corporation** is an entity that is legally separate from its owners and even pays its own income taxes. Most corporations are owned by many stockholders, although some corporations are owned entirely by one individual.

While sole proprietorships are the most common form of business, corporations dominate in terms of total sales, assets, earnings, and employees. That's why we focus on corporations in this book. To better understand the composition of invested capital, it is helpful to know more about the corporate form of ownership.

Corporations

Corporations are formed in accordance with the laws of individual states. For instance, **American Eagle** is based in Pennsylvania but incorporated in the state of Delaware. Many corporations choose to incorporate in Delaware due to the favorable incorporation laws found there. State incorporation laws share many similarities, thanks to the widespread adoption of the Model Business Corporation Act. This act serves as a guide to states in the development of their corporate statutes.

The state incorporation laws, in turn, guide corporations as they write their articles of incorporation (sometimes called the *corporate charter*). The articles of incorporation describe (a) the nature of the firm's business activities, (b) the shares of stock to be issued, and (c) the initial board of directors. The board of directors establishes corporate policies and appoints officers who manage the corporation. Illustration 10–2 presents an organization chart tracing the line of authority for a typical corporation.

PART A

■ **LO1**
Identify the advantages and disadvantages of the corporate form of ownership.

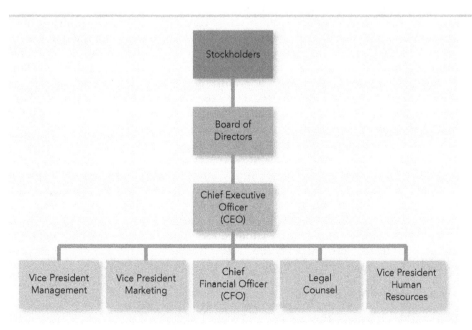

ILLUSTRATION 10–2
Organization Chart

Ultimately, a corporation's stockholders control the company. They are the owners of the corporation. By voting their shares, stockholders determine the makeup of the board of directors—which in turn appoints the management to run the company.

STAGES OF EQUITY FINANCING

Most corporations that end up selling stock to the general public don't begin that way. Instead, there's usually a progression of equity financing stages leading to a public offering, as summarized in Illustration 10–3.

ILLUSTRATION 10–3
Stages of Equity
Financing

Stages of Equity Financing

The progression leading to a public offering might include some or all of these steps:

(1) Investment by the founders of the business.
(2) Investment by friends and family of the founders.
(3) Outside investment by "angel" investors and venture capital firms.
(4) Initial public offering (IPO).

Most corporations first raise money by selling stock to the founders of the business and to their friends and family. As the equity financing needs of the corporation grow, companies prepare a business plan and seek outside investment from "angel" investors and venture capital firms. Angel investors are wealthy individuals in the business community willing to risk investment funds on a promising business venture. Individual angel investors may invest from a few thousand dollars to over a million dollars in the corporation. Venture capital firms provide additional financing, often in the millions, for a percentage ownership in the company. Many venture capital firms look to invest in promising companies to which they can add value through business contacts, financial expertise, or marketing channels. Most corporations do not consider issuing stock to the general public ("going public") until their equity financing needs exceed $20 million.

The first time a corporation issues stock to the public is called an initial public offering (IPO). Future stock issues by the company are called *seasoned equity offerings (SEOs)*. Like the issuance of bonds in Chapter 9, the public issuance of stock is a major event requiring the assistance of an investment banking firm (underwriter), lawyers, and public accountants. Major investment bankers, such as Citigroup, Morgan Stanley, and Goldman Sachs, can charge up to 6 percent of the issue proceeds for their services. That's $6 million for a $100 million stock offering. Legal and accounting fees also are not cheap, often running over $200 an hour for services performed in preparation for a public stock offering.

PUBLIC OR PRIVATE

Corporations may be either public or private. The stock of a publicly held corporation trades on the New York Stock Exchange (NYSE) or National Association of Securities Dealers Automated Quotations (NASDAQ), or by over-the-counter (OTC) trading. Many of the largest companies in the world such as Walmart, Exxon-Mobil, and General Electric are traded on the NYSE. The NASDAQ is home to many of the largest high-tech companies, including Microsoft, Intel, and Cisco. Over-the-counter trading takes place outside one of the major stock exchanges. Because these trades are not on any major stock exchange and there is less research done on them in the financial market, they are considered to be more risky. All publicly held corporations are regulated by the Securities and Exchange Commission (SEC), resulting in significant additional reporting and filing requirements.

A privately held corporation does not allow investment by the general public and normally has fewer stockholders than a public corporation. Three of the largest private corporations in the United States are Cargill (agricultural commodities), Koch Industries (oil and gas), and Chrysler (cars). Corporations whose stock is privately held do not need to file financial statements with the SEC.

Frequently, companies begin as smaller, privately held corporations. Then, as success broadens opportunities for expansion, the corporation goes public. For example, Google was a private corporation until it decided to take the company public in order to raise large amounts of outside investment funds. The result was the largest technology IPO ever.

STOCKHOLDER RIGHTS

Whether public or private, stockholders are the owners of the corporation and have certain rights: the right to vote on certain matters (including electing the board of directors), the right to receive dividends, the right to share in the distribution of assets if the company is liquidated, and (sometimes) the right to maintain their percentage share of ownership (the *preemptive right*). Illustration 10–4 further explains these stockholder rights.

ILLUSTRATION 10–4

Stockholder Rights

(1) **Right to Vote—** Stockholders *vote* on matters that come before the stockholders, including the election of corporate directors.

(2) **Right to Receive Dividends—** Stockholders share in profits when the company declares *dividends*. The percentage of shares a stockholder owns determines his or her share of the dividends distributed.

(3) **Right to Share in the Distribution of Assets—** Stockholders share in *the distribution of assets* if the company is liquidated. The percentage of shares a stockholder owns determines his or her share of the assets, which are distributed after creditors and preferred stockholders are paid.

(4) **Preemptive Right—** The *preemptive right* allows a stockholder to maintain his or her percentage share of ownership when new shares are issued. Each stockholder can buy a percentage of any new shares issued equal to the percentage of shares he or she owns. However, most corporations have dropped this right due to difficulties it causes when corporations issue new shares.

ADVANTAGES OF A CORPORATION

A corporation offers three primary advantages over sole proprietorships and partnerships. These are: (1) limited liability, (2) ability to raise capital, and (3) lack of mutual agency.

Limited liability. Limited liability guarantees that stockholders in a corporation can lose no more than the amount they invested in the company, even in the event of bankruptcy. In contrast, owners in a sole proprietorship or a partnership can be held personally liable for debts the company has incurred, above and beyond the investment they have made.

Ability to raise capital. A corporation is better suited to raising capital than is a sole proprietorship or a partnership. Because corporations sell ownership interest in the form of shares of stock, ownership rights are easily transferred. An investor can sell his or her ownership interest (shares of stock) at any time and without affecting the structure of the corporation or its operations. As a result, attracting outside investment is easier for a corporation than for a sole proprietorship or a partnership.

Lack of mutual agency. Another favorable aspect of investing in a corporation is the *lack of mutual agency*. Mutual agency means that individual partners in a partnership each have the power to bind the business to a contract. Therefore, an investor in a partnership must be very careful to investigate the character and business savvy of his or her fellow partners. In contrast, stockholders' participation in the affairs of a corporation is limited to voting at stockholders' meetings (unless the stockholder also is a manager). For example, owning shares of Microsoft stock doesn't allow you to transact business or enter into a contract in Microsoft's name. Consequently, a stockholder needn't exercise the same degree of care that partners must in selecting co-owners.

DISADVANTAGES OF A CORPORATION

A corporation has two primary disadvantages relative to sole proprietorships and partnerships. These are (1) additional taxes and (2) more paperwork.

Additional taxes. Owners of sole proprietorships and partnerships are taxed once, when they include their share of earnings in their personal income tax returns. However, corporations have double taxation: As a legal entity separate from its owners, a corporation pays income taxes on its earnings. Then, when it distributes the earnings to stockholders in dividends, the stockholders—the company's owners—pay taxes a second time on the corporate dividends they receive. In other words, corporate income is taxed once on earnings at the corporate level and again on dividends at the individual level.

More paperwork. To protect the rights of those who buy a corporation's stock or who lend money to a corporation, the federal and state governments impose extensive reporting requirements on the company. The additional paperwork is intended to ensure adequate disclosure of the information investors and creditors need.

Illustration 10–5 summarizes the primary advantages and disadvantages of a corporation compared to a sole proprietorship or partnership.

ILLUSTRATION 10–5

Advantages and
Disadvantages of a
Corporation

Advantages

(1) **Limited liability**
A stockholder can lose no more
than the amount invested.

(2) **Ability to raise capital**
Attracting outside investment is
easier for a corporation.

(3) **Lack of mutual agency**
Stockholders cannot legally bind
the corporation to a contract.

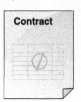

Disadvantages

(1) **Additional taxes**
Corporate earnings are taxed
twice—at the corporate level
and individual stockholder level.

(2) **More paperwork**
Federal and state governments
impose additional reporting
requirements.

Limited Liability *and* Beneficial Tax Treatment

Wouldn't it be nice to get the best of both worlds—enjoy the limited liability of a corporation and the tax benefits of a sole proprietorship or partnership? An S corporation allows a company to enjoy limited liability as a corporation, but tax treatment as a partnership. Because of these benefits, many companies that qualify choose to incorporate as S corporations. One of the major restrictions is that the corporation cannot have more than 100 stockholders, so S corporations appeal more to smaller, less widely held businesses.

Two additional business forms have evolved in response to liability issues and tax treatment—*limited liability companies* (LLCs) and *limited liability partnerships* (LLPs). Most accounting firms in the United States adopt one of these two business forms because they offer limited liability and avoid double taxation, but with no limits on the number of owners as in an S corporation. ●

**Decision Maker's
Perspective**

 KEY POINT

The primary advantages of the corporate form of business are limited liability, ability to raise capital, and lack of mutual agency. The primary disadvantages are additional taxes and more paperwork.

Common Stock

■ LO2
Record the issuance
of common stock.

If a corporation has only one kind of stock, it usually is labeled as common stock. We can think of the common stockholders as the "true owners" of the business. The number of shares of common stock in a corporation are described as being authorized, issued, or outstanding.

AUTHORIZED, ISSUED, AND OUTSTANDING STOCK

Authorized stock is the total number of shares available to sell, stated in the company's articles of incorporation. The authorization of stock is not recorded in the accounting records. However, the corporation is required to disclose the number of shares authorized. Issued stock is the number of shares that have been sold to investors. A company usually does not issue all its authorized stock. Outstanding stock is the number of shares held *by investors*. Issued and outstanding are the same amounts as long as the corporation has not repurchased any of its own shares. Repurchased shares, called *treasury stock*, are included as part of shares issued, but excluded from shares outstanding. We discuss treasury stock in more detail later in the chapter. Illustration 10–6 summarizes the differences between authorized, issued, and outstanding shares.

ILLUSTRATION 10–6
Authorized, Issued, and Outstanding Stock

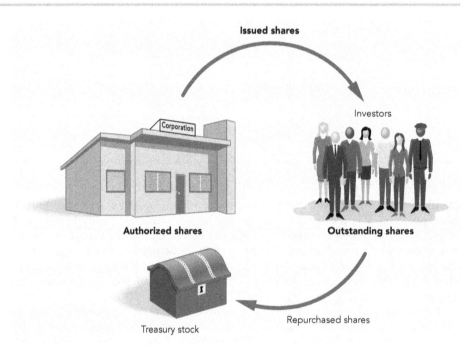

Type of Stock	Definition
Authorized	Shares available to sell (issued and unissued)
Issued	Shares actually sold (includes treasury stock)
Outstanding	Shares held by investors (excludes treasury stock)

Authorized − Unissued = Issued
Issued − Treasury Stock = Outstanding

Decision Point

Question		Accounting information		Analysis	
How many of a company's shares are authorized, issued, and outstanding?		Balance sheet		The number of authorized, issued, and outstanding shares is normally reported in the stockholders' equity section of the balance sheet. If the number of issued and outstanding shares differs, look for a separate line in the equity section called *treasury stock*.	

PAR VALUE

Par value is the legal capital per share of stock that's assigned when the corporation is first established. Par value originally indicated the real value of a company's shares of stock. During the late 19th and early 20th centuries, many cases of selling shares for *less* than par value (known as *watered shares*) triggered a number of lawsuits. To escape potential litigation, companies began issuing shares with very low par values—often pennies. Today, **par value has no relationship to the market value of the common stock.** For instance, American Eagle's common stock has a par value of $0.01 per share but a market value over $15 per share.

Laws in some states permit corporations to issue no-par stock. No-par value stock is common stock that has not been assigned a par value. Most new corporations, and even some established corporations such as Nike or Procter & Gamble, issue no-par value common stock. In some cases, a corporation assigns a stated value to the shares. Stated value is treated and recorded in the same manner as par value shares.

 COMMON MISTAKE

Some students confuse par value with market value. Par value is the legal capital per share that is set when the corporation is first established and actually is unrelated to "value." The market value per share is equal to the current share price. In most cases, the market value per share will far exceed the par value.

ACCOUNTING FOR COMMON STOCK ISSUES

When a company receives cash from issuing common stock, it debits Cash. If it issues no-par value stock, the corporation credits the equity account entitled Common Stock. For example, let's assume Canadian Falcon, a specialty retailer of casual apparel and accessories, issues 1,000 shares of no-par value common stock at $30 per share. We record this transaction as:

	Debit	Credit
Cash (= 1,000 shares × $30)	30,000	
Common Stock		30,000
(Issue no-par value common stock)		

A   =   L   +   SE
+30,000
               +30,000

If the company issues par value stock rather than no-par value stock, we record the transaction slightly differently. In that case, we credit two equity accounts. We credit the Common Stock account for the number of shares issued times the par value per share (as before), *and* we credit Additional Paid-in Capital for the portion of the cash proceeds above par value.

For example, assume that Canadian Falcon issues 1,000 shares of $0.01 par value common stock at $30 per share. The company credits the Common Stock account for par value. One thousand shares issued times $0.01 per share is $10. The company credits Additional Paid-in Capital for the portion of the cash proceeds above par value.

Common Terms
Additional paid-in capital is simply the amount paid for stock over par value. It is also called *paid-in capital in excess of par.*

A	=	L	+	SE

+30,000

             +10
        +29,990

	Debit	Credit
Cash (= 1,000 shares × $30)	**30,000**	
Common Stock (= 1,000 shares × $0.01)		**10**
Additional Paid-in Capital (difference)......................................		**29,990**
(*Issue common stock above par*)		

What if the common stock had a *stated value* of $0.01, rather than a *par value* of $0.01? We would record the same entry as in the par value example. For accounting purposes, **stated value is treated in the same manner as par value.**

Occasionally, a company will issue shares of stock in exchange for noncash goods or services. For example, what if 1,000 shares of common stock were issued to an attorney in payment for $30,000 in legal services? We would record the transaction in the same way as above, except we debit Legal Fees Expense, rather than Cash, for $30,000. The noncash exchange of stock, in this case for legal services, must be recorded at the fair value of the goods or services received.

 KEY POINT

If no-par value stock is issued, the corporation debits Cash and credits Common Stock. If par value or stated value stock is issued, the corporation debits Cash and credits two equity accounts—Common Stock at the par value or stated value per share and Additional Paid-in Capital for the portion above par or stated value.

Preferred Stock

■ **LO3**
Contrast preferred stock with common stock and bonds payable.

About 20% of the largest U.S. companies have preferred stock outstanding.

In order to attract wider investment, some corporations issue preferred stock in addition to common stock. American Eagle has been authorized to issue 5 million shares of preferred stock, but the company has yet to issue any of these shares. Preferred stock is "preferred" over common stock in two ways:

1. Preferred stockholders usually have first rights to a specified amount of dividends (a stated dollar amount per share or a percentage of par value per share). If the board of directors declares dividends, preferred shareholders will receive the designated dividend before common shareholders receive any.

2. Preferred stockholders receive preference over common stockholders in the distribution of assets in the event the corporation is dissolved.

However, unlike common stock, most preferred stock does not have voting rights, leaving control of the company to common stockholders.

COMPARISON OF FINANCING ALTERNATIVES

Preferred stock actually has a mixture of attributes somewhere between common stock (equity) and a bond (liability). Investors in common stock are the owners of the corporation because they have voting rights. Investors in bonds are creditors who have loaned money to the corporation. Preferred stockholders have characteristics of both. Illustration 10–7 provides a comparison of common stock, preferred stock, and bonds along several dimensions. Note that preferred stock falls in the middle between common stock and bonds for each of these factors.

Factor	Common Stock	Preferred Stock	Bonds
Voting rights	Yes	Usually no	No
Risk to the investor	Highest	Middle	Lowest
Expected return to the investor	Highest	Middle	Lowest
Risk of contract violations	Lowest	Middle	Highest
Preference for payments	Lowest	Middle	Highest
Tax deductibility of payments	No	Usually no	Yes

ILLUSTRATION 10–7
Comparison of Financing Alternatives

FEATURES OF PREFERRED STOCK

Preferred stock is especially interesting due to the flexibility allowed in its contractual provisions. For instance, preferred stock might be convertible, redeemable, and/or cumulative:

Convertible   Shares can be exchanged for common stock.

Redeemable   Shares can be returned to the corporation at a fixed price.

Cumulative   Shares receive priority for future dividends, if dividends are not paid in a given year.

Preferred stock may be convertible, which allows the stockholder to exchange shares of preferred stock for common stock at a specified conversion ratio. Xerox Corporation at one time had outstanding 6.4 million shares of convertible preferred stock.

Occasionally, preferred stock is redeemable at the option of either stockholders or the corporation. A redemption privilege might allow preferred stockholders the option, under specified conditions, to return their shares for a predetermined redemption price. Similarly, shares may be redeemable at the option of the issuing corporation.

INTERNATIONAL FINANCIAL REPORTING STANDARDS (IFRS)

Under U.S. accounting rules, we usually record preferred stock in the stockholders' equity section of the balance sheet just above common stock. However, sometimes preferred stock shares features with debt. Redeemable preferred stock with a fixed redemption date (called *mandatorily redeemable*) is reported, like bonds payable, in the liability section of the balance sheet.[1] However, under IFRS, most preferred stock is reported as debt, with the dividends reported in the income statement as interest expense. Under U.S. GAAP, that's the case only for "mandatorily redeemable" preferred stock.

For more discussion, see Appendix E.

Preferred stock usually is cumulative: If the specified dividend is not paid in a given year, unpaid dividends (called dividends in arrears) accumulate, and the firm must pay them in a later year before paying any dividends on common stock. For instance, assume that a company issues 1,000 shares of 8%, $30 par value cumulative

---

[1]FASB ASC Topic 480: Distinguishing Liabilities from Equity.

preferred stock and 1,000 shares of $1 par value common stock. The company owes a dividend on the preferred stock of $2,400 each year (= 1,000 shares × 8% × $30 par value). If the dividend is not paid in 2010 or 2011, dividends in arrears for the two years will total $4,800. Now, let's say the company declares a dividend of $10,000 in 2012. Before it can pay dividends to common stockholders, it must pay the $4,800 in unpaid dividends for 2010 and 2011, and then the current dividend on preferred stock of $2,400 in 2012. After paying the preferred stock dividends, the company can pay the remaining balance of $2,800 (= $10,000 − $4,800 − $2,400) in dividends on common stock. However, if the preferred stock is noncumulative, any dividends in arrears are lost. The dividend of $10,000 in 2012 will be split, with $2,400 paid to preferred stockholders for the current year and the remaining $7,600 paid to common stockholders.

Because dividends are not an actual liability until they are declared by the board of directors, dividends in arrears are not reported as a liability in the balance sheet. However, information regarding any dividends in arrears is disclosed in the notes to the financial statements.

ACCOUNTING FOR PREFERRED STOCK ISSUES

We record the issuance of preferred stock similar to the way we did for the issue of common stock. Assume that Canadian Falcon issues 1,000 shares of $30 par value preferred stock for $40 per share. We record the transaction as:

A = L + SE		Debit	Credit
+40,000	**Cash** (= 1,000 shares × $40)	**40,000**	
+30,000	**Preferred Stock** (= 1,000 shares × $30)....................................		**30,000**
+10,000	**Additional Paid-in Capital** (difference).....................................		**10,000**
	(*Issue preferred stock above par*)		

Illustration 10–8 displays the stockholders' equity section of the balance sheet for Canadian Falcon following the issuance of both common and preferred stock. We discuss the retained earnings balance later in the chapter.

ILLUSTRATION 10–8

Stockholders' Equity Section

CANADIAN FALCON **Balance Sheet (partial)** **December 31, 2012**	
Stockholders' equity:	
Preferred stock, $30 par value; 100,000 shares authorized; 1,000 shares issued and outstanding	$ 30,000
Common stock, $0.01 par value; 1 million shares authorized; 1,000 shares issued and outstanding	10
Additional paid-in capital	39,990
Total paid-in capital	70,000
Retained earnings	30,000
Total stockholders' equity	$100,000

KEY POINT

Preferred stock has features of both common stock and bonds and is usually included in stockholders' equity. However, some preferred stock (mandatorily redeemable) is so similar to bonds that we include it with bonds payable in the liability section of the balance sheet.

Treasury Stock

■ **LO4**
Account for treasury stock.

We just examined the issuance of common and preferred stock. Next, we look at what happens when companies reacquire shares they have previously issued. Most medium- and large-size companies buy back some of their own shares. Many have formal share repurchase plans. **Treasury stock** is the name given to a corporation's own stock that it has reacquired.

Just as issuing shares increases stockholders' equity, buying those shares back decreases stockholders' equity. Buying back shares is quite different from buying the shares of another corporation. For example, when Gap buys its own stock, it decreases stockholders' equity and records the repurchase as treasury stock. On the other hand, if Gap purchases shares of The Limited, it records this transaction as an investment (an asset) and not as treasury stock (a reduction of stockholders' equity). We discuss equity investments in Appendix D.

Share buybacks are more common than ever. Over two-thirds of all publicly traded companies report treasury stock in their balance sheets. What would motivate a company to buy back its own stock?

Why Corporations Repurchase Their Stock

Decision Maker's Perspective

Companies buy back their own stock for various reasons:

1. **To boost underpriced stock.** When company management feels the market price of its stock is too low, it may attempt to support the price by decreasing the supply of stock in the marketplace. A Johnson & Johnson announcement that it planned to buy up to $5 billion of its outstanding shares triggered a public buying spree that pushed the stock price up by more than 3%.
2. **To distribute surplus cash without paying dividends.** While dividends usually are a good thing, investors do pay personal income tax on them. Another way for a firm to distribute surplus cash to shareholders without giving them taxable *dividend* income is to use the excess cash to repurchase its own stock.
3. **To boost earnings per share.** Earnings per share is calculated as earnings divided by the number of shares outstanding. Stock repurchases reduce the number of shares outstanding, thereby increasing earnings per share. However, with less cash in the company, it's more difficult for companies to maintain the same level of earnings following a share repurchase.
4. **To satisfy employee stock ownership plans.** Perhaps the primary motivation for stock repurchases is to acquire shares used in employee stock award and stock option compensation programs. Microsoft, for example, reported that its board of directors had approved a program to repurchase shares of its common stock to offset the increase in shares from stock option and stock purchase plans. ●

American Eagle reported its treasury stock transactions in the notes to its financial statements as shown in Illustration 10–9.

ILLUSTRATION 10–9

Disclosure of Treasury Stock Transactions by American Eagle

AMERICAN EAGLE OUTFITTERS, INC.
Notes to the Financial Statements (excerpt)

The Company's Board authorized an additional 60.0 million shares of its common stock to be repurchased under the Company's share repurchase program. Subsequent to this authorization, the Company repurchased 18.7 million shares of its common stock. The shares were repurchased for approximately $438.3 million, at a weighted average share price of $23.38. As of March 25, 2010, the Company had 30.0 million shares remaining authorized for repurchase.

ACCOUNTING FOR TREASURY STOCK

Treasury stock is the repurchase of a company's own issued stock. As noted above, buying back stock decreases stockholders' equity. Rather than reducing the stock accounts directly, though, we record treasury stock as a "negative" or "contra" account. Recall that liability and stockholders' equity accounts normally have credit balances. So, treasury stock is included in the stockholders' equity section of the balance sheet with an opposite, or debit, balance. When a corporation repurchases its own stock, it increases (debits) Treasury Stock, while it decreases (credits) Cash.

 COMMON MISTAKE

Sometimes students confuse the purchase of treasury stock with investments in another company. An equity investment is the purchase of stock *in another corporation*, and we record it as an increase in assets. Treasury stock is the repurchase of a *corporation's own stock*, and we record it as a reduction in stockholders' equity. It is not an asset; a company cannot invest in itself.

We record treasury stock at the *cost* of the shares reacquired. For example, let's assume that Canadian Falcon repurchases 100 shares of its own $0.01 par value common stock at $30 per share. We record this transaction as:

A	=	L	+	SE		Debit	Credit
				−3,000	Treasury Stock (= 100 shares × $30)...	3,000	
−3,000					Cash		3,000
					(Repurchase treasury stock)		

Notice that the stock's par value has no effect on the entry to record treasury stock. We record treasury stock at its cost, which is $30 per share in this example. The debit to Treasury Stock reduces stockholders' equity. Illustration 10–10 displays the stockholders' equity section of the balance sheet following the repurchase of treasury stock.

ILLUSTRATION 10–10

Stockholders' Equity after Purchase of Treasury Stock

CANADIAN FALCON Balance Sheet (partial)	
Stockholders' equity:	
Preferred stock, $30 par value; 100,000 shares authorized; 1,000 shares issued and outstanding	$30,000
Common stock, $0.01 par value; 1 million shares authorized; 1,000 shares issued and 900 shares outstanding	10
Additional paid-in capital	39,990
Total paid-in capital	70,000
Retained earnings	30,000
Treasury stock, 100 shares	(3,000)
Total stockholders' equity	$97,000

Treasury stock is reported as a contra equity, or negative amount, since treasury stock reduces total stockholders' equity.

Now let's assume that Canadian Falcon later reissues the 100 shares of treasury stock for $35. Recall that these shares originally were purchased for $30 per share, so the $35 reissue price represents a $5 per share increase in additional paid-in capital. It's *not* recorded as a $5 per share gain in the income statement, as we would for the sale of an investment in another company, since the company is reissuing its own stock. We record this transaction as:

	Debit	Credit	A	=	L	+	SE
Cash (= 100 shares × $35)	3,500		+3,500				
Treasury Stock (= 100 shares × $30)		3,000					+3,000
Additional Paid-in Capital² (= 100 shares × $5)		500					+500
(Reissue treasury stock above cost)							

We debit Cash at $35 per share to record the inflow of cash from reissuing treasury stock. We recorded the 100 shares of treasury stock in the accounting records at a cost of $30 per share at the time of purchase. Now, when we reissue the treasury shares, we must reduce the Treasury Stock account at the same $30 per share. We record the $500 difference (= 100 shares × $5 per share) as Additional Paid-in Capital. Illustration 10–11 presents the stockholders' equity section of the balance sheet immediately after the sale of treasury stock.

ILLUSTRATION 10–11

Stockholders' Equity after Sale of Treasury Stock

CANADIAN FALCON Balance Sheet (partial)	
Stockholders' equity:	
Preferred stock, $30 par value; 100,000 shares authorized; 1,000 shares issued and outstanding	$ 30,000
Common stock, $0.01 par value; 1 million shares authorized; 1,000 shares issued and outstanding	10
Additional paid-in capital	40,490
Total paid-in capital	70,500
Retained earnings	30,000
Treasury stock	0
Total stockholders' equity	$100,500

What if the stock price goes down, and we reissue the treasury stock for less than we paid to buy back the shares? Let's assume Canadian Falcon later reissues the 100 shares of treasury stock for only $25 rather than $35. It records this transaction as:

	Debit	Credit	A	=	L	+	SE
Cash (= 100 × $25)	2,500		+2,500				
Additional Paid-in Capital³ (= 100 × $5)	500						−500
Treasury Stock (= 100 × $30).................................		3,000					+3,000
(Reissue treasury stock below cost)							

By repurchasing 100 shares of its own stock for $30 per share and reselling them for only $25 per share, Canadian Falcon experienced a decrease in additional

---

²Some companies credit "Additional Paid-in Capital from Treasury Stock Transactions" as a separate account from "Additional Paid-in Capital from Common Stock Transactions." We combine all additional paid-in capital entries into one "Additional Paid-in Capital" account, similar to how most companies report additional paid-in capital on the balance sheet.

³Companies debit Retained Earnings rather than Additional Paid-in Capital if there is not a sufficient prior credit balance in Additional Paid-in Capital from treasury stock transactions. The details are covered in more advanced financial accounting courses.

472   CHAPTER 10   Stockholders' Equity

paid-in capital. This is reflected in the entry as a debit to the Additional Paid-in Capital account. It's not recorded as a $5 per share loss in the income statement, as we would for the sale of an investment in another company, since the company is reissuing its own stock.

 KEY POINT

We include treasury stock in the stockholders' equity section of the balance sheet as a reduction in stockholders' equity. When we reissue treasury stock, we report the difference between its cost and the cash received as an increase or decrease in additional paid-in capital.

PART B

■ **LO5**
Describe retained earnings and record cash dividends.

EARNED CAPITAL

In Part A of the chapter, we discussed transactions involving "invested capital," because when investors buy a corporation's stock, they are investing in the company. Here, in Part B, we examine transactions involving retained earnings. Similarly, we might refer to this source of stockholders' equity as "earned capital," because it represents the net assets of the company that have been *earned* for the stockholders rather than *invested* by the stockholders.

Retained Earnings and Dividends

As noted at the beginning of the chapter, retained earnings represent the earnings retained in the corporation—earnings not paid out as dividends to stockholders. In other words, the amount of retained earnings equals all net income, less all dividends, since the company began.

In a company's early years, the amount of retained earnings tends to be small, and total paid-in capital—money invested into the corporation—tends to be large. As the years go by, the earnings retained in the business continue to grow and, for many profitable companies, can exceed the total amount originally invested in the corporation. Unfortunately, for some companies, expenses sometimes are more than revenues, so a net loss rather than net income is recorded. Just as net income increases retained earnings, a net loss *decreases* retained earnings.

Retained Earnings has a normal credit balance, consistent with other stockholders' equity accounts. However, if losses exceed income since the company began, Retained Earnings will have a debit balance. A debit balance in Retained Earnings is called an accumulated deficit. We subtract an accumulated deficit from total paid-in capital in the balance sheet to arrive at total stockholders' equity. Many companies in the start-up phase or when experiencing financial difficulties report an accumulated deficit. For instance, Amazon.com had an accumulated deficit of $730 million at the end of 2008 due to net losses reported in earlier years.

 COMMON MISTAKE

Some students think, incorrectly, that retained earnings represents a *cash* balance set aside by the company. In fact, the size of retained earnings has no relationship to the balance in the Cash account. American Eagle reported $1.3 billion in retained earnings, but only $60 million in cash.

Dividends are distributions by a corporation to its stockholders. Investors pay careful attention to cash dividends. A change in the quarterly or annual cash dividend paid by a company can provide useful information about its future prospects.

For instance, an increase in dividends often is perceived as good news. Companies tend to increase dividends when the company is doing well and future prospects look bright.

Many investors choose to automatically reinvest their dividends. Automatic dividend reinvestment works similar to compound interest in a savings account. The investor does not receive dividends directly as cash; instead, his or her dividends are directly reinvested into more shares of the company. This allows the investment to grow at a faster rate.

Why Don't Some Companies Pay Dividends?

Decision Maker's Perspective

Some companies are unprofitable and, therefore, unable to pay cash dividends. However, many profitable companies *choose* not to pay cash dividends. Companies with large expansion plans, called *growth companies,* prefer to reinvest earnings in the growth of the company rather than distribute earnings back to investors in the form of cash dividends. **Starbucks** is a nice example. As companies mature and their growth opportunities diminish, they tend to pay out more dividends. **Microsoft** and **Walmart** did not pay dividends in their early growth years, but began paying them in more recent years. ●

Why do investors buy stock in companies like **Starbucks** if they do not receive dividends? Investors make money through dividends, but they also make money when a company's share price increases. **American Eagle** has experienced tremendous increases in share price, but it has paid relatively small dividends. For instance, investors holding American Eagle stock in 2009 enjoyed a total return of 73%. This return includes a share price increase of about 71% and dividends of about 2%. Thus, the gains to American Eagle investors have come almost entirely from share price increases rather than dividend payments. Illustration 10–12 presents the disclosure of American Eagle's dividend policy.

ILLUSTRATION 10–12
American Eagle's Dividend Policy

AMERICAN EAGLE OUTFITTERS, INC.
Notes to the Financial Statements (excerpt)

Subsequent to the fourth quarter, our Board declared a quarterly cash dividend of $0.075 per share, payable on April 13, to stockholders of record at the close of business on March 30. The payment of future dividends is at the discretion of our Board and is based on future earnings, cash flow, financial condition, capital requirements, changes in U.S. taxation and other relevant factors. It is anticipated that any future dividends paid will be declared on a quarterly basis.

Note that it is the board of directors that declares the cash dividend to be paid. The day this occurs is known as the declaration date. The declaration of a cash dividend creates a binding legal obligation for the company declaring the dividend. On that date, we (a) increase Dividends, a temporary account that is closed into Retained Earnings at the end of each period, and (b) increase the liability account, Dividends Payable. The board of directors also indicates a specific date on which the company will determine the registered owners of stock and therefore who will receive the dividend. This date is called the record date. Investors who own stock on the date of record are entitled to receive the dividend. The date of the actual cash distribution is the payment date.

To illustrate the payment of a cash dividend, assume that on March 15 Canadian Falcon declares a $0.25 per share dividend on its 2,000 outstanding shares—1,000 shares of common stock and 1,000 shares of preferred stock. We record the declaration of cash dividends as:

A   =   L   +   SE

−500

+500

March 15 (declaration date)	Debit	Credit
Dividends (= 2,000 shares × $0.25)	**500**	
Dividends Payable		**500**
(Declare cash dividends)		

The Dividends account is a *temporary* stockholders' equity account that is closed into Retained Earnings at the end of each period, as discussed in Chapter 3.

Let's continue our example and assume that the dividend declared by Canadian Falcon is paid on April 15 to stockholders of record at the close of business on March 31. We make no entry on March 31, the date of record. We record the payment of cash dividends on April 15 as:

A   =   L   +   SE

−500

−500

April 15 (payment date)	Debit	Credit
Dividends Payable (= 2,000 shares × $0.25)	**500**	
Cash		**500**
(Pay cash dividends)		

As we will show in Part C later in the chapter, the amount of cash dividends the company declares and pays will be reported in the statement of stockholders' equity.

 KEY POINT

The declaration of cash dividends decreases Retained Earnings and increases Dividends Payable. The payment of cash dividends decreases Dividends Payable and decreases Cash. The net effect, then, is a reduction in both retained earnings and cash.

Decision Point

Question ?	Accounting information	Analysis
How much did the company pay in cash dividends?	Statement of stockholders' equity	The statement of stockholders' equity provides a summary of the activity in each equity account during the period. Any dividends declared and paid during the year will be reported in this statement.

Let's Review

Slacks 5th Avenue has two classes of stock authorized: $100 par preferred and $1 par common. As of the beginning of 2012, 1,000 shares of common stock and no preferred shares have been issued. The following transactions affect stockholders' equity during 2012:

January	15	Issue 2,000 additional shares of common stock for $20 per share.
February	1	Issue 100 shares of preferred stock for $110 per share.
June	1	Declare a cash dividend of $5 per share on preferred stock and $1 per share on common stock to all stockholders of record on June 15.
June	30	Pay the cash dividend declared on June 1.
October	1	Repurchase 200 shares of treasury stock for $25 per share.
November	1	Reissue 100 shares of the treasury stock purchased on October 1 for $28 per share.

Slacks 5th Avenue has the following beginning balances in its stockholders' equity accounts on January 1, 2012: Preferred Stock, $0: Common Stock, $1,000; Paid-in Capital, $14,000; and Retained Earnings, $5,000.

Required:

1. Record each transaction.
2. Indicate whether each transaction increases (+), decreases (−), or has no effect (NE), on total assets, total liabilities, and total stockholders' equity.

Solution:

1. Entries to record each transaction:

	Debit	Credit
January 15, 2012		
Cash (= 2,000 × $20)	40,000	
Common Stock (= 2,000 × $1)		2,000
Additional Paid-in Capital (difference)...............................		38,000
(*Issue common stock above par*)		
February 1, 2012		
Cash (= 100 × $110)	11,000	
Preferred Stock (= 100 × $100)..		10,000
Additional Paid-in Capital (difference)		1,000
(*Issue preferred stock above par*)		
June 1, 2012		
Dividends*	3,500	
Dividends Payable		3,500
(*Declare cash dividends*)		
*=(100 preferred shares × $5) + (3,000 common shares × $1)		
June 30, 2012		
Dividends Payable	3,500	
Cash		3,500
(*Pay cash dividends*)		
October 1, 2012		
Treasury Stock (= 200 shares × $25)	5,000	
Cash		5,000
(*Repurchase treasury stock*)		
November 1, 2012		
Cash (= 100 shares × $28)	2,800	
Treasury Stock (= 100 shares × $25)		2,500
Additional Paid-in Capital (= 100 × $3)		300
(*Reissue treasury stock above cost*)		

2. Effects of transactions on the components of the accounting equation:

Transaction	Total Assets	Total Liabilities	Total Stockholders' Equity
Issue common stock	+	NE	+
Issue preferred stock	+	NE	+
Declare cash dividends	NE	+	−
Pay cash dividends	−	−	NE
Purchase treasury stock	−	NE	−
Reissue treasury stock	+	NE	+

Suggested Homework:
BE10-3, BE10-4;
E10-5, E10-6;
P10-2A&B

Stock Dividends and Stock Splits

■ LO6
Explain the effect of stock dividends and stock splits.

Sometimes corporations distribute to shareholders additional shares of the companies' own stock rather than cash. These are known as stock dividends or stock splits depending on the size of the stock distribution. Suppose you own 100 shares of stock. Assuming a 10% stock dividend, you'll get 10 additional shares. If it's a 20% stock dividend, you'll get 20 more shares. A 100% stock dividend, equivalent to a 2-for-1 stock split, means 100 more shares.

Large stock dividends (25% or higher) and stock splits are declared primarily due to the effect they have on stock prices. Let's say that before the 100% stock dividend, your shares are trading at $40 a share, so your 100 shares are worth $4,000. After the 100% stock dividend, you will have twice as many shares. It sounds good, but let's look closer. Since the company as a whole still has the same value, each share of stock is now worth one-half what it was worth before the stock dividend. Your 200 shares still have a value of $4,000, the same as your 100 shares before the stock dividend. However, now each share is worth half as much—$20 rather than $40 per share.

Think of the company as a pizza. A 100% stock dividend is like changing an 8-slice pizza into 16 slices by cutting each slice in half. You are no better off with 16 half-slices than with the original 8 slices. Whether it's cut in 8 large slices or 16 smaller slices, it's still the same-sized pizza. Whether a company is represented by 1 million shares worth $40 each or 2 million shares worth $20 each, it's the same $40 million company. **Total assets, total liabilities, and total stockholders' equity do not change as a result of a stock dividend.**

 COMMON MISTAKE

Unfortunately, people often misuse the term *stock dividends* to refer to cash dividends on stock. Stock dividends, though, as you've learned, are distributions of additional shares of stock to shareholders, unlike cash dividends, which are distributions of cash to shareholders.

STOCK DIVIDENDS

Accounting standards distinguish between stock splits, large stock dividends, and small stock dividends (less than 25%). We look first at the accounting for stock splits and large stock dividends because they are more common in practice.

Stock splits/Large stock dividends.   When a company declares a stock split, we do not record a transaction. After a 2-for-1 stock split, the Common Stock account balance (total par value) represents twice as many shares. For instance, assume Canadian Falcon declares a 2-for-1 stock split on its 1,000 shares of $0.01 par value common stock. The balance in the Common Stock account is 1,000 shares times $0.01 par value per share, which equals $10. With no journal entry, the balance remains $10 despite the number of shares doubling. As a result, the par value *per share* is reduced by one-half to $0.005 (2,000 shares times $0.005 par per share still equals $10).

As you might expect, having the par value per share change in this way is cumbersome and expensive. All records, printed or electronic, that refer to the previous amount must be changed to reflect the new amount. Fortunately there is an alternative: To avoid the inconvenience and added cost, a company can choose to account for the large stock distribution as a stock *dividend* rather than a stock *split*. We account for a large stock dividend by recording an increase in the Common

Stock account in the amount of the par value of the additional shares distributed, as presented below:

	Debit	Credit	A	=	L	+	SE
Stock Dividends (= 1,000 shares × $0.01)	10						−10
Common Stock		10					+10
(Declare 100% [large] stock dividend)							

So, to avoid changing the par value per share, most companies report a 100% stock distribution as a *stock split to be recorded as a stock dividend*.

Similar to cash dividends, the Stock Dividends account is a temporary stockholders' equity account that is closed into Retained Earnings. Because an increase to stock dividends reduces retained earnings, we decrease one equity account, Retained Earnings, and increase another equity account, Common Stock. Note that the above entry does not change total assets, total liabilities, or total stockholders' equity. Illustration 10–13 presents the stockholders' equity section of the balance sheet for Canadian Falcon before and after the 2-for-1 stock split accounted for as a 100% stock dividend.

CANADIAN FALCON Balance Sheet (partial)		
	Before 100% Stock Dividend	After 100% Stock Dividend
Stockholders' equity:		
Preferred stock, $30 par value	$ 30,000	$ 30,000
Common stock, $0.01 par value	10	20
Additional paid-in capital	40,490	40,490
Total paid-in capital	70,500	70,510
Retained earnings	29,500	29,490
Total stockholders' equity	$100,000	$100,000
Common shares outstanding	1,000	2,000
Par value per share	$0.01	$0.01
Share price	$30	$15

ILLUSTRATION 10–13

Stockholders' Equity before and after a 2-for-1 Stock Split Accounted for as a 100% Stock Dividend

Notice that total stockholders' equity remains at $100,000 before and after the stock distribution. Common stock increased by $10, while retained earnings decreased by $10.

Why Declare a Stock Split?

Why would a company declare a 2-for-1 stock split when the stockholders are not really receiving anything of substance? The primary reason is to lower the trading price of the stock to a more acceptable trading range, making it attractive to a larger number of potential investors. Many companies like their stock to trade under $100 per share—$20 to $40 per share is common. For instance, after a company declares a 2-for-1 stock split with a per share market price of $80, it then has twice the number of shares outstanding, each with an approximate market value reduced to a more marketable trading range of $40.

Decision Maker's Perspective

However, there are exceptions to the normal trading range. Google's stock trades in the several-hundred-dollars-per-share range. Berkshire Hathaway's "A" shares trade at over $100,000 per share, making it accessible only to wealthier investors. Berkshire Hathaway is founded by billionaire investor Warren Buffett. While still an outspoken critic of stock dividends and stock splits, even Warren Buffett is giving in a little. In January 2010, Berkshire Hathaway's "B" shares, designed for general public investment, were split 50 to 1. The shares had a value of about $3,500 before the split and a value in a more acceptable trading range of about $70 ($3,500 ÷ 50) after the stock split. ●

Small stock dividends. Let's also look briefly at small stock dividends. Recall that we record large stock dividends at the *par value* per share. We record small stock dividends at the *market value,* rather than the par value, per share. Assume, for example, the market value of Canadian Falcon common stock is $30 per share when Canadian Falcon declares a 10% dividend on its 1,000 shares outstanding of $0.01 par value common stock. After the 10% stock dividend, Canadian Falcon will have 1,100 shares outstanding. The company records this small stock dividend as:

			A = L + SE

June 30, 2012	Debit	Credit	
Stock Dividends (= 1,000 × 10% × $30)	3,000		−3,000
Common Stock (= 1,000 × 10% × $0.01)...............................		1	+1
Additional Paid-in Capital (difference)......................................		2,999	+2,999
(*Pay 10% [small] stock dividend*)			

So, small stock dividends are recorded at the market value per new share, while large stock dividends are recorded at the par value per share. Why the inconsistency? Some believe that a small stock dividend will have little impact on the market price of shares currently outstanding, arguing for the recording of small stock dividends at market value. However, this reasoning is contrary to research evidence, which finds the market price adjusts for both large and small stock dividends.[4] A 10% stock dividend will result in 10% more shares, but each share will be worth 10% less, so the investor is no better off. Note that the above entry still does not change total assets, total liabilities, or total stockholders' equity. The debit to Stock Dividends simply decreases one equity account, Retained Earnings, while the credits increase two other equity accounts, Common Stock and Additional Paid-in Capital.

American Eagle is a prime candidate for stock splits since its share price has risen dramatically in prior years. Illustration 10–14 presents the disclosure of American Eagle's 3-for-2 stock split.

ILLUSTRATION 10–14
American Eagle's Stock Split

AMERICAN EAGLE OUTFITTERS, INC.
Notes to the Financial Statements

On November 13, the Company's Board approved a 3-for-2 stock split. This stock split was distributed on December 18, to stockholders of record on November 24. All share amounts and per share data presented herein have been restated to reflect this stock split.

---

[4]Taylor W. Foster and Don Vickrey. 1978. "The Information Content of Stock Dividend Announcements." *Accounting Review 53*, no. 2 (April), pp. 360–70; and J. David Spiceland and Alan J. Winters. 1986. "The Market Reaction to Stock Distributions: The Effect of Market Anticipation and Cash Returns." *Accounting and Business Research 16*, no. 63 (Summer), pp. 211–25.

ETHICAL DILEMMA

Intercontinental Clothing Distributors has paid cash dividends every year since the company was founded in 1990. The dividends have steadily increased from $0.05 per share to the latest dividend declaration of $1.00 per share. The board of directors is eager to continue this trend despite the fact that earnings fell significantly during the recent quarter as a result of worsening economic conditions and increased competition. The chair of the board proposes a solution. She suggests a 5% stock dividend in lieu of a cash dividend, to be accompanied by the following press announcement: "In place of our regular $1.00 per share cash dividend, Intercontinental will distribute a 5% stock dividend on its common shares, currently trading at $20 per share. Changing the form of the dividend will permit the company to direct available cash resources to the modernization of facilities in order to better compete in the 21st century."

Is a 5% stock dividend equivalent to a $1.00 per share cash dividend when shares are trading at $20 per share? Is the chair's suggestion ethical?

KEY POINT

Declaring stock dividends and stock splits is like cutting a pizza into more slices. Everyone has more shares, but each share is worth proportionately less than before.

REPORTING STOCKHOLDERS' EQUITY

PART C

We now can apply what we've learned so far in the chapter to analyze the stockholders' equity of an actual company—American Eagle. In this section, we show the financial statement presentation of stockholders' equity in the balance sheet and differentiate it from the statement of stockholders' equity.

Stockholders' Equity in the Balance Sheet

Illustration 10–15 (next page) presents the stockholders' equity section of the balance sheet for American Eagle, introduced briefly at the beginning of the chapter. Preferred stock is listed before common stock in the balance sheet. American Eagle has 5 million shares of preferred stock authorized but has not yet issued any preferred shares. Can you determine how many shares of common stock the company has issued? Common stock is reported at its par value of $0.01 per share. If we take the Common Stock account balance of $2,485,000 ($2,485 in thousands) and divide it by $0.01 per share, we find that the company has issued just under 250 million shares (248,500,000). The number of shares outstanding is equal to the number of shares issued (248,500,000) minus the number of shares bought back (the 43,248,000 treasury shares), or 205,252,000 shares.

Notice that the Additional Paid-in Capital account balance is much larger than the Common Stock account balance. This is to be expected. Remember, American Eagle has a par value of only $0.01 per share, so most of the money invested in the company was credited to Additional Paid-in Capital rather than Common Stock.

■ **LO7**
Prepare and analyze the stockholders' equity section of a balance sheet and the statement of stockholders' equity.

ILLUSTRATION 10–15

Stockholders' Equity
Section of American
Eagle's Balance Sheet

AMERICAN EAGLE Balance Sheet (partial) January 31, 2009	
(Dollars and number of shares in thousands)	
Total assets	$ 1,963,676
Total liabilities	$ 554,645
Stockholders' equity:	
Preferred stock, $0.01 par value	–0–
Common stock, $0.01 par value	2,485
Additional paid-in capital	513,574
Total paid-in capital	516,059
Retained earnings	1,679,772
Treasury stock, 43,248 (thousand) shares	(786,800)
Total stockholders' equity	$1,409,031
Total liabilities and stockholders' equity	$ 1,963,676

Now look at retained earnings. When a company is started, most of the equity is in the paid-in capital section because that's the amount invested by stockholders. But then, if a company is profitable, like American Eagle, and pays little in dividends, the retained earnings section of equity grows and often exceeds the amount invested by stockholders. For American Eagle, the amount of retained earnings is so large that it actually exceeds total stockholders' equity. How can this happen? American Eagle has been very profitable over the years, building retained earnings. It has used a portion of the company's earnings to buy back treasury shares, which decreases stockholders' equity. American Eagle has applied this strategy to such an extent that the balance in treasury stock (representing the cost of shares repurchased by the company) now exceeds total paid-in capital (representing the total cost of shares originally issued).

American Eagle has been very active in acquiring treasury shares. Has it benefited from the treasury stock repurchases? Dividing the treasury stock balance of $786,800 by the 43,248 shares repurchased, we can estimate an average purchase cost of $18.19 per share. That average repurchase price is nearly double the current trading price of $9 per share at January 31, 2009. Thus, at this point in time, it looks like American Eagle has not benefited from the treasury stock repurchase. However, if stock prices should again rise above $18.19 per share, the company could sell the treasury shares for more than the average purchase price.

Statement of Stockholders' Equity

The stockholders' equity section of the balance sheet, like the one we just examined for American Eagle, shows the balance in each equity account *at a point in time*. In contrast, the statement of stockholders' equity summarizes the *changes* in the balance in each stockholders' equity account *over a period of time*.

To contrast the stockholders' equity section of the balance sheet and the statement of stockholders' equity, let's compare both statements for our continuing example company—Canadian Falcon. Illustration 10–16 (next page) shows the stockholders' equity section reported in Canadian Falcon's balance sheet.

Compare that snapshot of stockholders' equity at the end of 2012 with Illustration 10–17 (next page) showing the statement of stockholders' equity for Canadian Falcon.

CANADIAN FALCON
Balance Sheet (partial)
December 31, 2012

Stockholders' equity:

Preferred stock, $30 par value; 100,000 shares authorized; 1,000 shares issued and outstanding	$ 30,000
Common stock, $0.01 par value; 1 million shares authorized; 2,000 shares issued and outstanding	20
Additional paid-in capital	40,490
Total paid-in capital	70,510
Retained earnings	29,490
Treasury stock	–0–
Total stockholders' equity	$100,000

ILLUSTRATION 10–16

Stockholders' Equity Section—Canadian Falcon

CANADIAN FALCON
Statement of Stockholders' Equity
For the year ended December 31, 2012

	Preferred Stock	Common Stock	Additional Paid-in Capital	Retained Earnings	Treasury Stock	Total Stockholders' Equity
Balance, January 1	$ –0–	$–0–	$ –0–	$ –0–	$ –0–	$ –0–
Issued common stock		10	29,990			30,000
Issued preferred stock	30,000		10,000			40,000
Repurchase of treasury stock					(3,000)	(3,000)
Sale of treasury stock			500		3,000	3,500
Cash dividends				(500)		(500)
100% stock dividend		10		(10)		–0–
Net income				30,000		30,000
Balance, December 31	$30,000	$20	$40,490	$29,490	$ –0–	$100,000

ILLUSTRATION 10–17

Statement of Stockholders' Equity—Canadian Falcon

Each of the beginning balances in Illustration 10–17 is zero because this is the first year of operations. (The beginning balances for the following year, January 1, 2013, are the same as the ending balance this year, December 31, 2012.)

The statement of stockholders' equity reports how each equity account changed during the year. For instance, the Common Stock account increased because Canadian Falcon issued common stock and declared a 100% stock dividend. The Additional Paid-in Capital account increased from the issuance of common stock, the issuance of preferred stock, and the sale of treasury stock for more than its original cost. Retained Earnings increased due to net income and decreased due to both cash and stock dividends. The repurchase of treasury stock is shown as a reduction because treasury stock reduces total stockholders' equity. The ending balance in Treasury Stock is zero, since all the treasury stock purchased was resold by the end of the year.

KEY POINT

The stockholders' equity section of the balance sheet presents the balance of each equity account *at a point in time*. The statement of stockholders' equity shows the change in each equity account balance *over time*.

Let's Review

This exercise is a continuation of the Let's Review exercise presented earlier. Recall that Slacks 5th Avenue has two classes of stock authorized: $100 par preferred and $1 par value common. As of the beginning of 2012, 1,000 shares of common stock have been issued and no shares of preferred stock have been issued. The following transactions affect stockholders' equity during 2012:

January	15	Issue 2,000 additional shares of common stock for $20 per share.
February	1	Issue 100 shares of preferred stock for $110 per share.
June	1	Declare a cash dividend of $5 per share on preferred stock and $1 per share on common stock to all stockholders of record on June 15.
June	30	Pay the cash dividend declared on June 1.
October	1	Repurchase 200 shares of common treasury stock for $25 per share.
November	1	Reissue 100 shares of treasury stock purchased on October 1 for $28 per share.

Slacks 5th Avenue has the following beginning balances in its stockholders' equity accounts on January 1, 2012: Preferred Stock, $0; Common Stock, $1,000; Paid-in Capital, $14,000; and Retained Earnings, $5,000. Net income for the year ended December 31, 2012, is $4,000.

Required:

Taking into consideration all of the transactions during 2012, prepare the following for Slacks 5th Avenue:

1. The stockholders' equity section as of December 31, 2012.

2. The statement of stockholders' equity for the year ended December 31, 2012.

Solution:

1. Stockholders' equity section:

SLACKS 5TH AVENUE Balance Sheet (partial) December 31, 2012	
Stockholders' equity:	
Preferred stock, $100 par value	$10,000
Common stock, $1 par value	3,000
Additional paid-in capital	53,300
Total paid-in capital	66,300
Retained earnings	5,500
Treasury stock	(2,500)
Total stockholders' equity	$69,300

2. Statement of stockholders' equity:

SLACKS 5TH AVENUE
Statement of Stockholders' Equity
For the year ended December 31, 2012

	Preferred Stock	Common Stock	Additional Paid-in Capital	Retained Earnings	Treasury Stock	Total Stockholders' Equity
Balance, January 1	$ –0–	$1,000	$14,000	$5,000	$ –0–	$20,000
Issued common stock		2,000	38,000			40,000
Issued preferred stock	10,000		1,000			11,000
Cash dividends				(3,500)		(3,500)
Repurchase of treasury stock					(5,000)	(5,000)
Sale of treasury stock			300		2,500	2,800
Net income				4,000		4,000
Balance, December 31	$10,000	$3,000	$53,300	$5,500	$(2,500)	$69,300

Suggested Homework:
BE10-13, BE10-14;
E10-10, E10-11;
P10-5A&B

EQUITY ANALYSIS

Deckers Outdoor vs. Timberland

ANALYSIS

Earnings are the key to a company's long-run survival. However, we need to evaluate earnings in comparison to the size of the investment. For instance, earnings of $500,000 may be quite large for a small business, but would be a rather disappointing outcome for a major corporation like American Eagle. A useful summary measure of earnings that considers the relative size of the business is the return on equity.

■ **LO8**
Evaluate company performance using information on stockholders' equity.

RETURN ON EQUITY

The return on equity (ROE) measures the ability of company management to generate earnings from the resources that owners provide. We compute the ratio by dividing net income by average stockholders' equity.

$$\text{Return on equity} = \frac{\text{Net income}}{\text{Average stockholders' equity}}$$

Deckers Outdoor was listed at the beginning of the chapter as one of the top ten investments of the past decade. The company is probably best known for its footwear products such as Teva sandals and UGG sheepskin boots. We can compare its profitability with a close competitor in the footwear industry, Timberland. Illustration 10–18 (next page) provides selected financial data for Deckers Outdoor and Timberland.

ILLUSTRATION 10–18

Financial Information for Deckers Outdoor and Timberland

Selected Balance Sheet Data December 31, 2009 and 2008 ($ in thousands)				
	Deckers Outdoor		**Timberland**	
	2009	**2008**	**2009**	**2008**
Total assets	$599,043	$483,721	$859,907	$849,399
Total liabilities	$107,685	$ 99,469	$264,290	$272,861
Stockholders' equity	491,358	384,252	595,617	576,538
Total liabilities and equity	$599,043	$483,721	$859,907	$849,399
Stock price, ending	$101.72		$17.83	
Shares outstanding (in thousands)	12,868		85,660	

Selected Income Statement Data For the year ended December 31, 2009 ($ in thousands)		
	Deckers Outdoor	**Timberland**
Net sales	$813,177	$1,285,876
Net income	$116,786	$56,644

The return on equity for both companies is calculated in Illustration 10–19.

ILLUSTRATION 10–19

Return on Equity for Deckers Outdoor and Timberland

($ in thousands)	Net Income	÷	Average Stockholders' Equity	=	Return on Equity
Deckers Outdoor	$116,786	÷	($384,252 + $491,358)/2	=	26.7%
Timberland	$56,644	÷	($576,538 + $595,617)/2	=	9.7%

As might be expected for a top-10 investment, Deckers Outdoor has a significantly higher return on equity of 26.7% compared to a respectable 9.7% for Timberland. A return on equity of 26.7% suggests that for every $1 of investors' resources, the company has earned almost $0.27 for its investors. Similarly, a return on equity of 9.7% suggests that for every $1 of investors' resources, the company has earned almost $0.10 for its investors. Although the return on equity is useful when comparing the effectiveness of management in employing resources provided by owners, analysts must be careful not to view it in isolation or without considering how the ratio is derived.

RETURN ON THE MARKET VALUE OF EQUITY

To supplement the return on equity ratio, analysts often relate earnings to the market value of equity, which is calculated as the ending stock price times the number of shares outstanding. The return on the market value of equity is computed as net income divided by the market value of equity, as shown in Illustration 10–20 (next page).

Once again, Deckers Outdoor has a higher return than Timberland. Notice that the return on the market value of equity for both companies is much lower than their return on equity. The reason is that the average stockholders' equity for Deckers Outdoor and Timberland is much lower than the market value of equity. For

($ in thousands)	Net Income	÷	Market Value of Equity (Ending stock price × Number of shares)	=	Return on the Market Value of Equity
Deckers Outdoor	$116,786	÷	($101.72 × 12,868)	=	8.9%
Timberland	$56,644	÷	($17.83 × 85,660)	=	3.7%

ILLUSTRATION 10–20

Return on the Market Value of Equity for Deckers Outdoor and Timberland

some companies, the return on equity is a meaningful measure of earnings performance. For others, the return on the market value of equity is a better measure, especially when the recorded balance in stockholders' equity and the market value of equity differ greatly.

Why Doesn't Stockholders' Equity Equal the Market Value of Equity?

Decision Maker's Perspective

The *market* value of equity is the price investors are willing to pay for a company's stock. The market value of equity equals the stock price times the number of shares outstanding. On the other hand, the *book* value of equity equals total stockholders' equity reported in the balance sheet. Market value and book value generally are not the same, and often are vastly different. For example, Deckers Outdoor reported total stockholders' equity of $491 million in 2009, yet its market value at this same time was over $1.3 billion. Why?

Keep in mind that stockholders' equity is equal to assets minus liabilities. An asset's book value usually equals its market value *on the date it's purchased*. However, the two aren't necessarily the same after that. For instance, an asset such as a building might increase in value over time, but it continues to be reported in the balance sheet at historical cost minus accumulated depreciation. Consider another example: **Deckers Outdoor** creates brand awareness and increases market value through advertising, but under accounting rules, it expenses all its advertising costs as it incurs them. This causes the true market value of assets and stockholders' equity to be greater than the amount recorded for assets and stockholders' equity in the accounting records. ●

Decision Point

Question	Accounting information	Analysis
What is a company's return on investment?	Return on equity and return on market value of equity	A high return on equity or market value of equity in relation to industry competitors indicates a strong return on investment. Note the return on market value of equity will normally be lower than the return on equity.

EARNINGS PER SHARE

Earnings per share (EPS) measures the net income earned per share of common stock. We calculate earnings per share as net income minus dividends on preferred stock divided by the average shares of common stock outstanding during the period:

$$\text{Earnings per share} = \frac{\text{Net income} - \text{Dividends on preferred stock}}{\text{Average shares of common stock outstanding}}$$

The upper half of the fraction measures the income available to common stockholders. We subtract any dividends paid to preferred stockholders from net income to arrive at the income available to the true owners of the company—the common stockholders. If a company does not issue preferred stock, the top half of the fraction is simply net income. We then divide income available to common stockholders by the average shares outstanding during the period to calculate earnings per share.

Earnings per share is useful in comparing earnings performance for the same company over time. It is *not* useful for comparing earnings performance of one company with another because of wide differences in the number of shares outstanding among companies. For instance, assume two companies, Alpha and Beta, both report net income of $1 million and are valued by the market at $20 million. Quite comparable, right? But, if Alpha has one million shares outstanding and Beta has two million shares outstanding, their earnings per share amounts will not be comparable. Alpha will have a share price of $20 (= $20 million ÷ 1 million shares) and an EPS of $1.00 (= $1 million in earnings ÷ 1 million shares). Beta, on the other hand, will have a share price of $10 (= $20 million ÷ 2 million shares) and an EPS of $0.50 (= $1 million in earnings ÷ 2 million shares). Is the earnings performance for Alpha better than that for Beta? Of course not. They both earned $1 million. Alpha's earnings per share is higher simply because it has half as many shares outstanding. (Same pizza, fewer slices.)

If Alpha declared a 2-for-1 stock split, its earnings per share would match Beta's exactly. The key point is that earnings per share is useful in comparing either Alpha's earnings over time, or Beta's earnings over time, but it is not useful in comparing the companies *with each other*.

Investors use earnings per share extensively in evaluating the earnings performance of a company over time. Investors are looking for companies with the potential to increase earnings per share. Analysts also forecast earnings on a per share basis. If reported earnings per share fall short of analysts' forecasts, this is considered negative news, usually resulting in a decline in a company's stock price.

PRICE-EARNINGS RATIO

Another measure analysts use extensively is the price-earnings ratio (PE ratio). It indicates how the stock is trading in relationship to current earnings. We calculate the PE ratio as the stock price divided by earnings per share, so that both stock price and earnings are expressed on a per share basis:

$$\text{Price-earnings ratio} = \frac{\textbf{Stock price}}{\textbf{Earnings per share}}$$

Price-earnings ratios are commonly in the range of 15 to 20. A high PE ratio indicates that the market has high hopes for a company's stock and has bid up the price. Growth stocks are stocks whose future earnings investors expect to be higher. Their stock prices are high in relation to current earnings because investors expect future earnings to be higher. On the other hand, value stocks are stocks that are priced low in relation to current earnings. The low price in relation to earnings may be justified due to poor future prospects, or it might suggest an underpriced "sleeper" stock. Illustration 10–21 calculates the price-earnings ratio for Deckers Outdoor and Timberland.

ILLUSTRATION 10–21

Price-Earnings Ratios for Deckers Outdoor and Timberland

($ in thousands)	Stock Price	÷	Earnings per Share	=	Price-Earnings Ratio
Deckers Outdoor	$101.72	÷	$116,786/12,868	=	11.2
Timberland	$ 17.83	÷	$ 56,644/85,660	=	27.0

The price-earnings ratio for Deckers Outdoor and Timberland is 11.2 and 27.0, respectively. A low price-earnings ratio indicates to investors that a stock is priced low in relation to its current earnings. Deckers Outdoor has a much lower stock price in relation to its current earnings, making it a potentially more attractive investment.

 KEY POINT

The return on equity measures the ability to generate earnings from the owners' investment. It is calculated as net income divided by average stockholders' equity. The return on the market value of equity is another useful measure, especially when the recorded balance in stockholders' equity and the market value of equity differ substantially. Earnings per share measures the net income earned per share of common stock. The price-earnings ratio indicates how the stock is trading in relationship to current earnings.

Decision Point

Question	Accounting information	Analysis
Do investors expect future earnings to grow?	Price-earnings ratio (PE ratio)	A high PE ratio indicates investors expect future earnings to be higher. A low PE ratio indicates investors' lack of confidence in future earnings growth.

 KEY POINTS BY LEARNING OBJECTIVE

LO1 Identify the advantages and disadvantages of the corporate form of ownership.

The primary advantages of the corporate form of business are limited liability, ability to raise capital, and lack of mutual agency. The primary disadvantages are additional taxes and more paperwork.

LO2 Record the issuance of common stock.

If no-par value stock is issued, the corporation debits Cash and credits Common Stock. If par value or stated value stock is issued, the corporation debits Cash and credits two equity accounts—Common Stock at the par value or stated value per share and Additional Paid-in Capital for the portion above par or stated value.

LO3 Contrast preferred stock with common stock and bonds payable.

Preferred stock has features of both common stock and bonds and is usually included in stockholders' equity. However, mandatorily redeemable preferred stock is so similar to bonds that we include it with bonds payable in the liability section of the balance sheet.

LO4 Account for treasury stock.

We include treasury stock in the stockholders' equity section of the balance sheet as a reduction

in stockholders' equity. When we reissue treasury stock, we report the difference between its cost and the cash received as an increase or decrease in Additional Paid-in Capital.

LO5 Describe retained earnings and record cash dividends.

The declaration of cash dividends decreases Retained Earnings and increases Dividends Payable. The payment of dividends decreases Dividends Payable and decreases Cash. The net effect, then, is a reduction in both retained earnings and cash.

LO6 Explain the effect of stock dividends and stock splits.

Declaring stock dividends and stock splits is like cutting a pizza into more slices. Everyone has more shares, but each share is worth proportionately less than before.

LO7 Prepare and analyze the stockholders' equity section of a balance sheet and the statement of stockholders' equity.

The stockholders' equity section of the balance sheet presents the balance of each equity account *at a point in time*. The statement of stockholders' equity shows the change in each equity account balance *over time*.

Analysis

LO8 Evaluate company performance using information on stockholders' equity.

The return on equity measures the ability to generate earnings from the owners' investment. It is calculated as net income divided by average stockholders' equity. The return on the market value of equity is another useful measure, especially when the recorded balance in stockholders' equity and the market value of equity differ substantially. Earnings per share measures the net income earned per share of common stock. The price-earnings ratio indicates how the stock is trading in relationship to current earnings.

GLOSSARY

Accumulated deficit: A debit balance in Retained Earnings. **p. 472**

Additional paid-in capital: The portion of the cash proceeds above par value. **p. 458**

Angel investors: Wealthy individuals in the business community willing to risk investment funds on a promising business venture. **p. 460**

Articles of incorporation: Describes the nature of the firm's business activities, the shares to be issued, and the composition of the initial board of directors. **p. 459**

Authorized stock: The total number of shares available to sell, stated in the company's articles of incorporation. **p. 464**

Convertible: Shares can be exchanged for common stock. **p. 467**

Cumulative: Shares receive priority for future dividends, if dividends are not paid in a given year. **p. 467**

Declaration date: The day on which the board of directors declares the cash dividend to be paid. **p. 473**

Dividends: Distributions by a corporation to its stockholders. **p. 472**

Dividends in arrears: Unpaid dividends on cumulative preferred stock. **p. 467**

Double taxation: A corporation pays income taxes on its earnings, and when dividends are distributed to stockholders, the stockholders pay taxes a second time on the corporate dividends they receive. **p. 462**

Earnings per share: Measures the net income earned per share of common stock. **p. 485**

Growth stocks: Stocks that tend to have higher price-earnings ratios and are expected to have higher future earnings. **p. 486**

Initial public offering: The first time a corporation issues stock to the public. **p. 460**

Issued stock: The number of shares sold to investors; includes treasury shares. **p. 464**

Limited liability: Stockholders in a corporation can lose no more than the amount they invested in the company. **p. 462**

Model Business Corporation Act: Serves as a guide to states in the development of their corporate statutes. **p. 459**

Mutual agency: Individual partners each have power to bind the partnership to a contract. **p. 462**

No-par value stock: Common stock that has not been assigned a par value. **p. 465**

Organization chart: Traces the line of authority for a typical corporation. **p. 459**

Outstanding stock: The number of shares held by investors; excludes treasury shares. **p. 464**

Paid-in capital: The amount stockholders have invested in the company. **p. 458**

Par value: The legal capital assigned per share of stock. **p. 465**

Payment date: The date of the actual cash distribution of dividends. **p. 473**

Preferred stock: Stock with preference over common stock in the payment of dividends and the distribution of assets. **p. 466**

Price-earnings ratio: The stock price divided by earnings per share so that both stock price and earnings are expressed on a per share basis. **p. 486**

Privately held corporation: Does not allow investment by the general public and normally has fewer stockholders. **p. 461**

Publicly held corporation: Allows investment by the general public and is regulated by the Securities and Exchange Commission. **p. 460**

Record date: A specific date on which the company will determine the registered owners of stock and, therefore, who will receive the dividend. **p. 473**

Redeemable: Shares can be returned to the corporation at a fixed price. **p. 467**

Retained earnings: Represents all net income, less all dividends, since the company began. **pp. 458, 472**

Return on equity: Net income divided by average stockholders' equity; measures the income generated per dollar of equity. **p. 483**

Return on the market value of equity: Net income divided by the market value of equity. **p. 484**

S corporation: Allows a company to enjoy limited liability as a corporation, but tax treatment as a partnership. **p. 463**

Stated value: The legal capital assigned per share to no-par stock. **p. 465**

Statement of stockholders' equity: Summarizes the changes in the balance in each stockholders' equity account over a period of time. **p. 480**

Stock dividends: Additional shares of a company's own stock given to stockholders. **p. 476**

Stock split: A large stock dividend that includes a reduction in the par or stated value per share. **p. 476**

Treasury stock: A corporation's own stock that it has reacquired. **p. 458**

Value stocks: Stocks that tend to have lower price-earnings ratios and are priced low in relation to current earnings. **p. 486**

Venture capital firms: Provide additional financing, often in the millions, for a percentage ownership in the company. **p. 460**

SELF-STUDY QUESTIONS

1. Which of the following is a publicly traded company?   ■ LO1
   a. American Eagle.
   b. Cargill.
   c. Ernst & Young.
   d. Koch Industries.

2. The disadvantages of owning a corporation include: ■ LO1
   a. Lack of mutual agency.
   b. Additional taxes.
   c. Limited liability.
   d. Ability to raise capital.

3. The correct order from the smallest number of shares to the largest number   ■ LO2
   of shares is:
   a. Authorized, issued, and outstanding.
   b. Outstanding, issued, and authorized.
   c. Issued, outstanding, and authorized.
   d. Issued, authorized, and outstanding.

4. Preferred stock: ■ LO3
   a. Is always recorded as a liability.
   b. Is always recorded as part of stockholders' equity.
   c. Can have features of both liabilities and stockholders' equity.
   d. Is not included in either liabilities or stockholders' equity.

5. Treasury stock: ■ LO4
   a. Has a normal credit balance.
   b. Decreases stockholders' equity.
   c. Is recorded as an investment.
   d. Increases stockholders' equity.

6. Retained earnings: ■ LO5
   a. Has a normal debit balance.
   b. Decreases stockholders' equity.
   c. Is equal to the balance in cash.
   d. Increases stockholders' equity.

7. We record cash dividends on the:
   a. Declaration date, record date, and payment date.
   b. Record date and payment date.
   c. Declaration date and payment date.
   d. Declaration date and record date.

8. Both cash dividends and stock dividends: ■ LO6
   a. Reduce total assets.
   b. Reduce total liabilities.
   c. Reduce total stockholders' equity.
   d. Reduce retained earnings.

490   CHAPTER 10   Stockholders' Equity

■ LO7   9. How does the stockholders' equity section in the balance sheet differ from the statement of stockholders' equity?
             a. The stockholders' equity section shows balances at a point in time, whereas the statement of stockholders' equity shows activity over a period of time.
             b. The stockholders' equity section shows activity over a period of time, whereas the statement of stockholders' equity is at a point in time.
             c. There are no differences between them.
             d. The stockholders' equity section is more detailed than the statement of stockholders' equity.

■ LO8   10. The PE ratio:
             a. Tends to be lower for growth stocks.
             b. Tends to be higher for value stocks.
             c. Indicates how a stock is trading in relation to current earnings.
             d. Typically is less than 1.

Check out
www.mhhe.com/succeed
for more multiple-choice
questions.

Note: For answers, see the last page of the chapter.

REVIEW QUESTIONS

■ LO1   1. Corporations typically do not first raise capital by issuing stock to the general public. What are the common stages of equity financing leading to an initial public offering (IPO)?

■ LO1   2. What is the difference between a public and a private corporation? Provide an example of each.

■ LO1   3. What are the four basic ownership rights of common stockholders?

■ LO1   4. Which form of business organization is most common? Which form of business organization is larger in terms of total sales, total assets, earnings, and number of employees?

■ LO1   5. Describe the primary advantages and disadvantages of a corporation.

■ LO1   6. Explain how an LLC or an S corporation represents the "best of both worlds" in terms of business ownership.

■ LO2   7. Explain the difference between authorized, issued, and outstanding shares.

■ LO2   8. The articles of incorporation allow for the issuance of 1 million shares of common stock. During its first year, California Clothing issued 100,000 shares and reacquired 10,000 shares it held as treasury stock. At the end of the first year, how many shares are authorized, issued, and outstanding?

■ LO2   9. What is par value? How is it related to market value? How is it used in recording the issuance of stock?

■ LO3   10. What are the three potential features of preferred stock? Indicate whether each feature makes the preferred stock appear more like stockholders' equity or more like long-term liabilities.

■ LO3   11. Explain why preferred stock often is said to be a mixture of attributes somewhere between common stock and bonds.

■ LO4   12. What would motivate a company to buy back its own stock?

■ LO4   13. How is the accounting for a repurchase of a company's own stock (treasury stock) different from the purchase of stock in another corporation?

■ LO5   14. Explain why some companies choose not to pay cash dividends. Why do investors purchase stock in companies that do not pay cash dividends?

15. Describe the declaration date, record date, and payment date for a cash dividend.   ■ **LO5**

16. How does a 100% stock dividend or a 2-for-1 stock split affect total assets, total liabilities, and total stockholders' equity?   ■ **LO6**

17. Contrast the effects of a cash dividend and a stock dividend on total assets, total liabilities, and total stockholders' equity.   ■ **LO6**

18. What happens to the par value, the share's trading price, and the number of shares outstanding in a 2-for-1 stock split?   ■ **LO6**

19. Indicate the correct order in which to report the following accounts in the stockholders' equity section of the balance sheet: Additional Paid-in Capital, Common Stock, Preferred Stock, Treasury Stock, and Retained Earnings.   ■ **LO7**

20. How is the stockholders' equity section of the balance sheet different from the statement of stockholders' equity?   ■ **LO7**

21. Why doesn't total stockholders' equity equal the market value of the firm?   ■ **LO8**

22. Which tends to be larger, the return on equity or the return on the market value of equity? Explain why.   ■ **LO8**

23. What does "PE" stand for in the PE ratio, and how do investors use this ratio?   ■ **LO8**

BRIEF EXERCISES

BE10–1 Waldo is planning to start a clothing store helping big and tall men blend in with the crowd. Explain to Waldo the advantages and disadvantages of a corporation in comparison to a sole proprietorship or partnership.

Cite advantages and disadvantages of a corporation **(LO1)**

BE10–2 Renaldo heard that an S corporation combines the benefits of a corporation with the benefits of a partnership. Explain to Renaldo the specific benefits of an S corporation and any drawbacks to organizing as an S corporation.

Understand an S corporation **(LO1)**

BE10–3 Western Wear Clothing issues 2,000 shares of its $0.01 par value common stock to provide funds for further expansion. Assuming the issue price is $12 per share, record the issuance of common stock.

Record issuance of common stock **(LO2)**

BE10–4 Gothic Architecture is a new chain of clothing stores specializing in the color black. Gothic issues 1,000 shares of its $1 par value common stock at $20 per share. Record the issuance of the stock. How would the entry differ if Gothic issued no-par value stock?

Record issuance of common stock **(LO2)**

BE10–5 Equinox Outdoor Wear issues 1,000 shares of its $0.01 par value preferred stock for cash at $22 per share. Record the issuance of the preferred shares.

Record issuance of preferred stock **(LO3)**

BE10–6 Match each of the following preferred stock features with its description.

Recognize preferred stock features **(LO3)**

Preferred Stock Features	Description
_____ 1. Convertible	a. Shares receive dividend priority, if a dividend is not paid.
_____ 2. Redeemable	b. Shares can be sold at a predetermined price.
_____ 3. Cumulative	c. Shares can be exchanged for common stock.

BE10–7 Rachel's Designs has 1,000 shares of 6%, $50 par value cumulative preferred stock issued at the beginning of 2010. All remaining shares are common stock. Due to cash flow difficulties, the company was not able to pay dividends in 2010 or 2011. The company plans to pay total dividends of $10,000 in 2012. How much of the $10,000 dividend will be paid to preferred stockholders and how much will be paid to common stockholders?

Determine the amount of preferred stock dividends **(LO3)**

492   CHAPTER 10   Stockholders' Equity

Record purchase of
treasury stock (LO4)

BE10–8 California Surf Clothing Company issues 1,000 shares of $1 par value common stock at $25 per share. Later in the year, the company decides to repurchase 100 shares at a cost of $28 per share. Record the purchase of treasury stock.

Record sale of treasury
stock (LO4)

BE10–9 Refer to the situation described in BE10–8. Record the transaction if California Surf reissues the 100 shares of treasury stock at $30 per share. How would it be different if the shares reissue at $26 per share rather than at $30 per share?

Record cash
dividends (LO5)

BE10–10 Divine Apparel has 3,000 shares of common stock outstanding. On October 1, the company declares a $0.50 per share dividend to stockholders of record on October 15. The dividend is paid on October 31. Record all transactions on the appropriate dates for cash dividends.

Record stock
dividends (LO6)

BE10–11 On June 30, the board of directors of Sandals, Inc., declares a 100% stock dividend on its 20,000, $1 par, common shares. The market price of Sandals common stock is $25 on June 30. Record the stock dividend.

Analyze a stock
split (LO6)

BE10–12 Refer to the situation described in BE10–11, but assume a 2-for-1 stock split instead of the 100% stock dividend. Explain why Sandals did not record a 2-for-1 stock split. What are the number of shares, par value per share, and market price per share immediately after the 2-for-1 stock split?

Indicate effects on total
stockholders' equity (LO7)

BE10–13 Indicate whether each of the following transactions increases (+), decreases (−), or has no effect (NE) on total assets, total liabilities, and total stockholders' equity. The first transaction is completed as an example.

Transaction	Total Assets	Total Liabilities	Total Stockholders' Equity
Issue common stock	+	NE	+
Issue preferred stock			
Purchase treasury stock			
Sale of treasury stock			

Prepare the stockholders'
equity section (LO7)

BE10–14 Silk Station has the following accounts at December 31: Common Stock, $1 par value, 1,000,000 shares; Paid-in Capital, $17 million; Retained Earnings, $10 million; and Treasury Stock, 50,000 shares, $1.1 million. Prepare the stockholders' equity section of the balance sheet.

Calculate the return on
equity (LO8)

BE10–15 The financial statements of **Limited Brands, Inc.,** include the following selected data ($ in millions): sales, $9,043; net income, $220; beginning stockholders' equity, $2,219; and ending stockholders' equity, $1,874. Calculate the return on equity.

EXERCISES

Match terms with their
definitions (LO1)

E10–1 Match (by letter) the following terms with their definitions. Each letter is used only once.

Terms

_____ 1. Publicly held corporation.
_____ 2. Model Business Corporation Act.
_____ 3. Articles of incorporation.
_____ 4. Limited liability.
_____ 5. Mutual agency.
_____ 6. Double taxation.
_____ 7. S corporation.
_____ 8. Limited liability company.

Definitions

a. Shareholders can lose no more than the amount they invest in the company.

b. Corporate earnings are taxed twice—at the corporate level and individual shareholder level.

c. Like an S corporation, but there are no limitations on the number of owners as in an S corporation.

d. Designed to serve as a guide to states in the development of their corporate statutes.

e. Allows for legal treatment as a corporation, but tax treatment as a partnership.

f. Has stock traded on a stock exchange such as the New York Stock Exchange (NYSE).

g. Individual partners in a partnership have the power to bind the business to a contract.

h. Describes (a) the nature of the firm's business activities, (b) the shares to be issued, and (c) the composition of the initial board of directors.

E10–2 Your friend, Jonathon Fain, is an engineering major with an entrepreneurial spirit. He wants to start his own corporation and needs your accounting expertise. He has no idea what the following terms mean: (1) authorized stock, (2) issued stock, (3) outstanding stock, (4) preferred stock, and (5) treasury stock.

Explain the meaning of terms used in stockholders' equity (LO2, 3, 4)

Required:
Write a note to Jonathon carefully explaining what each term means and how they are different from each other.

E10–3 Clothing Frontiers began operations on January 1, 2012, and engages in the following transactions during the year related to stockholders' equity.

Record the issuance of common stock (LO2)

January 1   Issues 600 shares of common stock for $40 per share.

April   1   Issues 100 additional shares of common stock for $44 per share.

Required:
1. Record the transactions, assuming Clothing Frontiers has no-par common stock.
2. Record the transactions, assuming Clothing Frontiers has $1 par value common stock.
3. Record the transactions, assuming Clothing Frontiers' common stock has a $1 stated value, rather than a $1 par value.

E10–4 Nathan's Athletic Apparel has 1,000 shares of 7%, $100 par value preferred stock the company issued at the beginning of 2011. All remaining shares are common stock. The company was not able to pay dividends in 2011, but plans to pay dividends of $15,000 in 2012.

Determine the amount of preferred stock dividends (LO3)

Required:
1. Assuming the preferred stock is cumulative, how much of the $15,000 dividend will be paid to preferred stockholders and how much will be paid to common stockholders in 2012?
2. Assuming the preferred stock is noncumulative, how much of the $15,000 dividend will be paid to preferred stockholders and how much will be paid to common stockholders in 2012?

E10–5 Italian Stallion has the following transactions during the year related to stockholders' equity.

Record common stock, preferred stock, and dividend transactions (LO2, 3, 5)

February 1   Issues 5,000 shares of no-par common stock for $15 per share.

May   15   Issues 500 shares of $10 par value preferred stock for $12 per share.

October   1   Declares a cash dividend of $0.75 per share to all stockholders of record (both common and preferred) on October 15.

October 15   Date of record.

October 31   Pays the cash dividend declared on October 1.

Required:
Record each of these transactions.

Record issuance of stock and treasury stock transactions (LO2, 3, 4)

E10–6 Finishing Touches has two classes of stock authorized: 8%, $10 par preferred, and $1 par value common. The following transactions affect stockholders' equity during 2012, its first year of operations:

January	2	Issues 100,000 shares of common stock for $25 per share.
February	6	Issues 2,000 shares of 8% preferred stock for $12 per share.
September	10	Repurchases 10,000 shares of its own common stock for $30 per share.
December	15	Reissues 5,000 shares of treasury stock at $35 per share.

Required:
Record each of these transactions.

Prepare the stockholders' equity section (LO7)

E10–7 Refer to the information in E10–6. In its first year of operations, Finishing Touches has income of $150,000 and pays dividends at the end of the year of $95,000 ($1 per share) on all common shares outstanding and $1,600 on all preferred shares outstanding.

Required:
Prepare the stockholders' equity section of the balance sheet for Finishing Touches as of December 31, 2012.

Record cash dividends (LO5)

E10–8 On March 15, American Eagle declares a quarterly cash dividend of $0.075 per share payable on April 13 to all stockholders of record on March 30.

Required:
Record American Eagle's declaration and payment of cash dividends for its 220 million shares.

Record common stock, treasury stock, and cash dividends (LO2, 4, 5)

E10–9 Power Drive Corporation designs and produces a line of golf equipment and golf apparel. Power Drive has 100,000 shares of common stock outstanding as of the beginning of 2012. Power Drive has the following transactions affecting stockholders' equity in 2012.

March	1	Issues 55,000 additional shares of $1 par value common stock for $52 per share.
May	10	Repurchases 5,000 shares of treasury stock for $55 per share.
June	1	Declares a cash dividend of $1.50 per share to all stockholders of record on June 15. (*Hint:* Dividends are not paid on treasury stock.)
July	1	Pays the cash dividend declared on June 1.
October	21	Reissues 2,500 shares of treasury stock purchased on May 10 for $60 per share.

Required:
Record each of these transactions.

Prepare the stockholders' equity section (LO7)

E10–10 Refer to the information in E10–9. Power Drive Corporation has the following beginning balances in its stockholders' equity accounts on January 1, 2012: Common Stock, $100,000; Paid-in Capital, $4,500,000; and Retained Earnings, $2,000,000. Net income for the year ended December 31, 2012, is $600,000.

Required:
Taking into consideration all of the transactions recorded in E10–9, prepare the stockholders' equity section of the balance sheet for Power Drive Corporation as of December 31, 2012.

Prepare a statement of stockholders' equity (LO7)

E10–11 Refer to the information in E10–9. Power Drive Corporation has the following beginning balances in its stockholders' equity accounts on January 1, 2012: Common

Stock, $100,000; Paid-in Capital, $4,500,000; and Retained Earnings, $2,000,000. Net income for the year ended December 31, 2012, is $600,000.

Required:

Taking into consideration all the transactions recorded in E10–9, prepare the statement of stockholders' equity for Power Drive Corporation for the year ended December 31, 2012, using the format provided.

POWER DRIVE CORPORATION
Statement of Stockholders' Equity
For the year ended December 31, 2012

	Common Stock	Additional Paid-in Capital	Retained Earnings	Treasury Stock	Total Stockholders' Equity
Balance, January 1	$100,000	$4,500,000	$2,000,000	$ -0-	$6,600,000
Issued common stock					
Repurchased treasury stock					
Cash dividends					
Sold treasury stock					
Net income					
Balance, December 31					

E10–12 Indicate whether each of the following transactions increases (+), decreases (−), or has no effect (NE) on total assets, total liabilities, and total stockholders' equity. The first transaction is completed as an example.

Indicate effects on total stockholders' equity (LO7)

Transaction	Total Assets	Total Liabilities	Total Stockholders' Equity
Issue common stock	+	NE	+
Issue preferred stock			
Repurchase treasury stock			
Sale of treasury stock			
Declare cash dividend			
Pay cash dividend			
100% stock dividend			
2-for-1 stock split			

E10–13 United Apparel has the following balances in its stockholders' equity accounts on December 31, 2012: Treasury Stock, $750,000; Common Stock, $500,000; Preferred Stock, $2,600,000; Retained Earnings, $1,700,000; and Additional Paid-in Capital, $7,800,000.

Prepare the stockholders' equity section (LO7)

Required:

Prepare the stockholders' equity section of the balance sheet for United Apparel as of December 31, 2012.

E10–14 The financial statements of **Limited Brands, Inc.**, include the following selected data (in millions):

Calculate and analyze ratios (LO8)

($ in millions)	2009	2008
Sales	$9,043	$10,134
Net income	$220	$718
Stockholders' equity	$1,874	$2,219
Shares outstanding (in millions)	321	–
Stock price	$7.92	–

Required:

1. Calculate the return on equity in 2009. Compare it with the amount calculated for **Deckers Outdoor** and **Timberland** in the chapter.
2. Calculate the return on the market value of equity in 2009. Compare it with the amount calculated for Deckers Outdoor and Timberland in the chapter.
3. Calculate earnings per share in 2009. Why is it not reasonable to compare it with the earnings per share for Deckers Outdoor and Timberland?
4. Calculate the price-earnings ratio in 2009. Compare it with the amount calculated for Deckers Outdoor and Timberland in the chapter.

Calculate and analyze ratios (LO8)

E10–15 Financial information for Forever 18 includes the following selected data (in millions):

($ in millions)	2012	2011
Net income	$210	$180
Dividends on preferred stock	$25	$20
Shares outstanding (in millions)	240	220
Stock price	$11.52	$10.47

Required:

1. Calculate earnings per share in 2011 and 2012. Did earnings per share increase in 2012?
2. Calculate the price-earnings ratio in 2011 and 2012. In which year is the stock priced lower in relation to reported earnings?

For additional exercises, visit www.mhhe.com/succeed for Exercises: Set B.

PROBLEMS: SET A

Connect
|ACCOUNTING

Match terms with their definitions (LO1)

P10–1A Match (by letter) the following terms with their definitions. Each letter is used only once.

Terms

_____ 1. Cumulative.
_____ 2. Retained earnings.
_____ 3. Outstanding stock.
_____ 4. Limited liability.
_____ 5. Treasury stock.
_____ 6. Issued stock.
_____ 7. Angel investors.
_____ 8. Paid-in capital.
_____ 9. Authorized stock.
_____ 10. Redeemable.

Definitions

a. The amount invested by stockholders.
b. Shares available to sell.
c. Shares can be returned to the corporation at a predetermined price.
d. The earnings not paid out in dividends.
e. Shares actually sold.
f. Shares receive priority for future dividends, if dividends are not paid in a given year.
g. Shares held by investors.
h. Shareholders can lose no more than the amount they invested in the company.
i. Wealthy individuals in the business community willing to risk investment funds on a promising business venture.
j. The corporation's own stock that it reacquired.

P10–2A Donnie Hilfiger has two classes of stock authorized: $1 par preferred and $0.01 par value common. As of the beginning of 2012, 200 shares of preferred stock and 3,000 shares of common stock have been issued. The following transactions affect stockholders' equity during 2012:

Record equity transactions and indicate the effect on the balance sheet equation (LO2, 3, 4, 5)

March	1	Issues 1,000 shares of common stock for $32 per share.
May	15	Repurchases 600 shares of treasury stock for $25 per share.
July	10	Reissues 100 shares of treasury stock purchased on May 15 for $30 per share.
October	15	Issues 100 shares of preferred stock for $35 per share.
December	1	Declares a cash dividend on both common and preferred stock of $0.75 per share to all stockholders of record on December 15. (*Hint:* Dividends are not paid on treasury stock.)
December	31	Pays the cash dividends declared on December 1.

Donnie Hilfiger has the following beginning balances in its stockholders' equity accounts on January 1, 2012: Preferred Stock, $200; Common Stock, $30; Additional Paid-in Capital, $66,000; and Retained Earnings, $25,500. Net income for the year ended December 31, 2012, is $9,800.

Required:
1. Record each of these transactions.
2. Indicate whether each of these transactions would increase (+), decrease (−), or have no effect (NE) on total assets, total liabilities, and total stockholders' equity by completing the following chart.

Transaction	Total Assets	Total Liabilities	Total Stockholders' Equity
Issue common stock			
Repurchase treasury stock			
Reissue treasury stock			
Issue preferred stock			
Declare cash dividends			
Pay cash dividends			

P10–3A Sammy's Sportshops has been very profitable in recent years and has seen its stock price steadily increase to over $100 per share. The CFO thinks the company should consider either a 100% stock dividend or a 2-for-1 stock split.

Indicate effect of stock dividends and stock splits (LO6)

Required:
1. Complete the following chart comparing the effects of a 100% stock dividend versus a 2-for-1 stock split on the stockholders' equity accounts, shares outstanding, par value, and share price.

	Before	After 100% Stock Dividend	After 2-for-1 Stock Split
Common stock, $1 par value	$ 1,000		
Additional paid-in capital	49,000		
Total paid-in capital	50,000		
Retained earnings	22,850		
Total stockholders' equity	$72,850		
Shares outstanding	1,000		
Par value per share	$1		
Share price	$110		

2. What is the primary reason companies declare a large stock dividend or a stock split?

Analyze the stockholders' equity section (LO7)

P10–4A The stockholders' equity section of Velcro World is presented here.

VELCRO WORLD	
Balance Sheet (partial)	
($ in thousands)	
Stockholders' equity:	
Preferred stock, $1 par value	$ 5,000
Common stock, $1 par value	20,000
Additional paid-in capital	575,000
Total paid-in capital	600,000
Retained earnings	278,000
Treasury stock, 10,000 common shares	(220,000)
Total stockholders' equity	$658,000

Required:

Based on the stockholders' equity section of Velcro World, answer the following questions. Remember that all amounts are presented in thousands.

1. How many shares of preferred stock have been issued?
2. How many shares of common stock have been issued?
3. If the common shares were issued at $20 per share, at what price per share were the preferred shares issued?
4. If retained earnings at the beginning of the period was $240 million and $20 million was paid in dividends during the year, what was the net income for the year?
5. What was the average cost per share of the treasury stock acquired?

Understand stockholders' equity and the statement of stockholders' equity (LO7)

P10–5A Refer to the information provided in P10–2A.

Required:

Taking into consideration all the transactions during 2012, respond to the following for Donnie Hilfiger:

1. Prepare the stockholders' equity section of the balance sheet as of December 31, 2012.
2. Prepare the statement of stockholders' equity for the year ended December 31, 2012.
3. Explain how *Requirements* 1 and 2 are similar and how they are different.

Record equity transactions and prepare the stockholders' equity section (LO2, 3, 4, 5, 7)

QB

P10–6A Major League Apparel has two classes of stock authorized: 5%, $10 par preferred, and $1 par value common. The following transactions affect stockholders' equity during 2012, its first year of operations:

January	2	Issue 100,000 shares of common stock for $60 per share.
February	14	Issue 50,000 shares of preferred stock for $11 per share.
May	8	Repurchase 10,000 shares of its own common stock for $50 per share.
May	31	Reissue 5,000 shares of treasury stock for $55 per share.
December	1	Declare a cash dividend on its common stock of $0.50 per share and a $25,000 (5% of par value) cash dividend on its preferred stock payable to all stockholders of record on December 15. The dividend is payable on December 30. (*Hint:* Dividends are not paid on treasury stock.)
December	30	Pay the cash dividends declared on December 1.

Required:

1. Record each of these transactions.
2. Prepare the stockholders' equity section of the balance sheet as of December 31, 2012. Net income for the year was $480,000.

Calculate and analyze ratios (LO8)

P10–7A **Abercrombie & Fitch** is a close competitor of **Deckers Outdoor** and **Timberland** in the apparel industry. Selected financial data for Abercrombie is provided as follows:

($ in millions)	2009	2008
Sales	$3,540	$3,750
Net income	272	476
Total assets	$2,848	$2,568
Total liabilities	$1,003	$ 949
Stockholders' equity	1,845	1,619
Total liabilities and stockholders' equity	$2,848	$2,568
Shares outstanding (in millions)	103	–
Stock price	$29	–

Required:

1. Calculate the return on equity for Abercrombie in 2009. How does it compare with the return on equity for Deckers Outdoor and Timberland reported in the chapter?
2. Calculate the return on the market value of equity for Abercrombie in 2009. How does it compare with the return on the market value of equity for Deckers Outdoor and Timberland reported in the chapter?
3. Why is the return on the market value of equity for Abercrombie, Deckers Outdoor, and Timberland so much lower than the return on equity?
4. Calculate the price-earnings ratio for Abercrombie in 2009. How does it compare with the price-earnings ratio for Deckers Outdoor and Timberland reported in the chapter? Which is trading at a lower price per dollar of earnings?

PROBLEMS: SET B

P10–1B Match (by letter) the following terms with their definitions. Each letter is used only once.

Match terms with their definitions **(LO1 to 8)**

Terms

_____ 1. PE ratio.
_____ 2. Stockholders' equity section of the balance sheet.
_____ 3. Accumulated deficit.
_____ 4. Growth stocks.
_____ 5. 100% stock dividend.
_____ 6. Statement of stockholders' equity.
_____ 7. Treasury stock.
_____ 8. Value stocks.
_____ 9. Return on equity.
_____ 10. Retained earnings.

Definitions

a. A debit balance in Retained Earnings.
b. Priced high in relation to current earnings as investors expect future earnings to be higher.
c. Effectively the same as a 2-for-1 stock split.
d. The earnings not paid out in dividends.
e. The stock price divided by earnings per share.
f. Summarizes the *changes* in the balance in each stockholders' equity account *over a period of time.*
g. Priced low in relation to current earnings.
h. Measures the ability of company management to generate earnings from the resources that owners provide.
i. Shows the balance in each equity account *at a point in time.*
j. The corporation's own stock that it reacquired.

500   CHAPTER 10   Stockholders' Equity

Record equity transactions
and indicate the effect
on the balance sheet
equation (LO2, 3, 4, 5)

P10–2B Nautical has two classes of stock authorized: $10 par preferred, and $1 par value common. As of the beginning of 2012, 100 shares of preferred stock and 2,000 shares of common stock have been issued. The following transactions affect stockholders' equity during 2012:

March	1	Issue 2,000 additional shares of common stock for $15 per share.
April	1	Issue 200 additional shares of preferred stock for $30 per share.
June	1	Declare a cash dividend on both common and preferred stock of $0.50 per share to all stockholders of record on June 15.
June	30	Pay the cash dividends declared on June 1.
August	1	Repurchase 200 shares of common treasury stock for $12 per share.
October	1	Reissue 100 shares of treasury stock purchased on August 1 for $14 per share.

Nautical has the following beginning balances in its stockholders' equity accounts on January 1, 2012: Preferred Stock, $1,000; Common Stock, $2,000; Paid-in Capital, $18,500; and Retained Earnings, $10,500. Net income for the year ended December 31, 2012, is $7,150.

Required:
1. Record each of these transactions.
2. Indicate whether each of these transactions would increase (+), decrease (−), or have no effect (NE) on total assets, total liabilities, and total stockholders' equity by completing the following chart.

Transaction	Total Assets	Total Liabilities	Total Stockholders' Equity
Issue common stock			
Issue preferred stock			
Declare cash dividends			
Pay cash dividends			
Repurchase treasury stock			
Reissue treasury stock			

Indicate effect of stock
dividends and stock
splits (LO6)

P10–3B The Athletic Village has done very well the past year, and its stock price is now trading at $82 per share. Management is considering either a 100% stock dividend or a 2-for-1 stock split.

Required:
Complete the following chart comparing the effects of a 100% stock dividend versus a 2-for-1 stock split on the stockholders' equity accounts, shares outstanding, par value, and share price.

	Before	After 100% Stock Dividend	After 2-for-1 Stock Split
Common stock, $0.01 par value	$ 10		
Additional paid-in capital	24,990		
Total paid-in capital	25,000		
Retained earnings	15,000		
Total stockholders' equity	$40,000		
Shares outstanding	1,000		
Par value per share	$0.01		
Share price	$82		

P10–4B The stockholders' equity section of The Seventies Shop is presented here.

```
┌─────────────────────────────────────────┐
│            THE SEVENTIES SHOP             │
│          Balance Sheet (partial)          │
├─────────────────────────────────────────┤
│ ($ in thousands)                          │
│ Stockholders' equity:                     │
│ Preferred stock, $50 par value   $   –0–  │
│ Common stock, $5 par value          15,000│
│ Additional paid-in capital          45,000│
│   Total paid-in capital             60,000│
│ Retained earnings                   48,000│
│ Treasury stock                      (2,700)│
│     Total stockholders' equity    $105,300│
└─────────────────────────────────────────┘
```

Required:

Based on the stockholders' equity section of The Seventies Shop, answer the following questions. Remember that all amounts are presented in thousands.

1. How many shares of preferred stock have been issued?
2. How many shares of common stock have been issued?
3. Total paid-in capital is $60 million. At what price per share were the common shares issued?
4. If retained earnings at the beginning of the period was $40 million and net income during the year was $10,850,000, how much was paid in dividends for the year?
5. If the treasury stock was reacquired at $18 per share, how many shares were reacquired?
6. How much was the dividend per share? (*Hint:* Dividends are not paid on treasury stock.)

P10–5B Refer to the information provided in P10–2B.

Understand stockholders' equity and the statement of stockholders' equity (LO7)

Required:

Taking into consideration all the transactions during 2012, respond to the following for Nautical:

1. Prepare the stockholders' equity section of the balance sheet as of December 31, 2012.
2. Prepare the statement of stockholders' equity for the year ended December 31, 2012.
3. Explain how *Requirements* 1 and 2 are similar and how they are different.

P10–6B National League Gear has two classes of stock authorized: 6%, $20 par preferred, and $5 par value common. The following transactions affect stockholders' equity during 2012, National League's first year of operations:

Record equity transactions and prepare the stockholders' equity section (LO2, 3, 4, 5, 7)

February	2	Issue 1 million shares of common stock for $25 per share.
February	4	Issue 500,000 shares of preferred stock for $22 per share.
June	15	Repurchase 100,000 shares of its own common stock for $20 per share.
August	15	Reissue 75,000 shares of treasury stock for $35 per share.
November	1	Declare a cash dividend on its common stock of $1 per share and a $600,000 (6% of par value) cash dividend on its preferred stock payable to all stockholders on record on November 15. (*Hint:* Dividends are not paid on treasury stock.)
November	30	Pay the dividends declared on November 1.

Required:

1. Record each of these transactions.
2. Prepare the stockholders' equity section of the balance sheet as of December 31, 2012. Net income for the year was $4,800,000.

P10–7B Gap is a close competitor of **Deckers Outdoor** and **Timberland** in the teenage apparel industry. Gap also owns the **Old Navy** and **Banana Republic** clothing chains. Gap reported higher earnings than Deckers Outdoor and Timberland in 2009.

Calculate and analyze ratios (LO8)

502   CHAPTER 10   Stockholders' Equity

Does that mean Gap is more profitable? Maybe, but we need to control for the differences in company size in order to accurately compare the profitability of the companies. Selected financial data for Gap is provided as follows:

($ in millions)	2009	2008
Sales	$14,526	$15,763
Net income	967	833
Total assets	$ 7,564	$ 7,838
Total liabilities	$ 3,177	$ 3,564
Stockholders' equity	4,387	4,274
Total liabilities and stockholders' equity	$ 7,564	$ 7,838
Shares outstanding (in millions)	694	–
Stock price	$16	–

Required:

1. Calculate the return on equity for Gap in 2009. How does it compare with the return on equity for Deckers Outdoor and Timberland reported in the chapter?
2. Calculate the return on the market value of equity for Gap in 2009. How does it compare with the return on the market value of equity for Deckers Outdoor and Timberland reported in the chapter?
3. Why is the return on the market value of equity for Gap so much lower than the return on equity?
4. Calculate the price-earnings ratio for Gap in 2009. How does it compare with the price-earnings ratio for Deckers Outdoor and Timberland reported in the chapter? Which is trading at a lower price per dollar of earnings?

*For additional problems, visit **www.mhhe.com/succeed** for Problems: Set C.*

ADDITIONAL PERSPECTIVES

Great Adventures

(This is a continuation of the Great Adventures problem from earlier chapters.)

Continuing Problem

AP10–1 Tony and Suzie purchased land costing $500,000 for a new camp in January 2014. Now they need money to build the cabins, dining facility, a ropes course, and an outdoor swimming pool. Tony and Suzie first checked with Summit Bank to see if they could borrow another million dollars, but unfortunately the bank turned them down as too risky. Undeterred, they promoted their idea to close friends they had made through the outdoor clinics and TEAM events. They decided to go ahead and sell shares of stock in the company to raise the additional funds for the camp. Great Adventures has two classes of stock authorized: 8%, $10 par preferred, and $1 par value common.

When the company began on July 1, 2012, Tony and Suzie each purchased 10,000 shares of $1 par value common stock at $1 per share. The following transactions affect stockholders' equity during 2014, its third year of operations:

Jul.	2	Issue an additional 100,000 shares of common stock for $12 per share.
Sep.	10	Repurchase 10,000 shares of its own common stock (i.e., treasury stock) for $15 per share.
Nov.	15	Reissue 5,000 shares of treasury stock at $16 per share.
Dec.	1	Declare a cash dividend on its common stock of $115,000 ($1 per share) to all stockholders of record on December 15. The dividend is payable on December 31.

Required:
1. Record each of these transactions.
2. Great Adventures has net income of $150,000 in 2014. Retained earnings at the beginning of 2014 was $140,000. Prepare the stockholders' equity section of the balance sheet for Great Adventures as of December 31, 2014.

American Eagle Outfitters, Inc.

Financial Analysis

AP10–2 Financial information for the year ended January 31, 2009, is presented in the text of the chapter. Financial information for **American Eagle** for the year ended January 31, 2010, is presented in Appendix A at the end of the book. Using the financial information presented in Appendix A, answer the following.

Required:
1. What is the par value per share for the common stock?
2. How many common shares were issued at the end of the most recent year?
3. Did the company have any treasury stock? How many shares?
4. How much did the company pay in cash dividends in the most recent year?

The Buckle, Inc.

Financial Analysis

AP10–3 Financial information for **The Buckle** is presented in Appendix B at the end of the book.

Required:
1. What is the par value per share for the common stock?
2. How many common shares were issued at the end of the most recent year?
3. Did the company have any treasury stock? How many shares?
4. How much did the company pay in cash dividends in the most recent year?
5. Has the company ever issued a stock dividend or stock split? If so, describe.

American Eagle Outfitters, Inc., vs. The Buckle, Inc.

Comparative Analysis

AP10–4 Financial information for **American Eagle** is presented in Appendix A at the end of the book, and financial information for **The Buckle** is presented in Appendix B at the end of the book. The stock prices as of January 30, 2010, for American Eagle and The Buckle were $15.89 and $30.34, respectively.

Required:
1. Calculate the return on equity for American Eagle and The Buckle in 2010. Which company has a higher return on equity?
2. Calculate the return on the market value of equity for American Eagle and The Buckle in 2010. Which company has a higher return on the market value of equity?
3. Why is the return on the market value of equity for American Eagle and The Buckle so much lower than the return on equity?
4. Calculate the price-earnings ratio for American Eagle and The Buckle. Which is trading at a lower price per dollar of earnings?

Ethics

AP10–5 Put yourself in the shoes of a company president: The extremely successful launch of a new product has resulted in an additional $5 million in unexpected operating cash flows. You can think of several ways to use the extra $5 million.

One alternative is to pay out a special dividend to the shareholders. As president, you are accountable to the board of directors, which is elected by the shareholders. Rather than pay a dividend, you could repurchase shares of the company's own stock. The stock seems currently to be underpriced, and by purchasing treasury shares you are distributing surplus cash to shareholders without giving them taxable dividend income.

You could also pay a special year-end bonus to your employees. With 500 employees, that would average $10,000 per employee, quite a nice holiday bonus. After all, it was the employees' hard work and dedication that earned the money in the first place.

Or you could use the money to reinvest in the company. By reinvesting the money, it might be easier to continue the upward earnings trend in the future.

Finally, you could approach the board of directors for a compensation adjustment of your own. It's been a great year, and you are the president of the company. Shouldn't you at least share in the success?

Required:
Determine how you would allocate the additional $5 million. Are there other areas in which to spend the money not mentioned in the above case? Is it ethical for the president to be directly compensated based on the company's performance each year?

Internet Research

AP10–6 EDGAR, the Electronic Data Gathering, Analysis, and Retrieval system, is a giant database of documents the U.S. Securities and Exchange Commission (SEC) requires that companies submit. All publicly traded domestic companies use EDGAR to make the majority of their filings. (Filings by foreign companies are not required to be filed on EDGAR, but many of these companies do so voluntarily.) Form 10-K, which includes the annual report, is an important document required to be filed on EDGAR. The SEC makes this information available, free to the public, on the Internet.

Required:
1. Access EDGAR on the Internet. The web address is *www.sec.gov*.
2. Search for a public company with which you are familiar. Access its most recent 10-K filing, and search or scroll to find the statement of stockholders' equity.
3. Determine from the statement the transactions that affected common stock during the past year.
4. Determine from the statement the transactions that affected retained earnings during the past year.
5. Explain how the totals on the statement of stockholders' equity agree with the amounts reported in the stockholders' equity section in the balance sheet.

Written Communication

AP10–7 Preferred stock has characteristics of both liabilities and stockholders' equity. Convertible bonds are another example of a financing arrangement that blurs the line between liabilities and stockholders' equity. Items like these have led some to conclude that the present distinction between liabilities and equity should be eliminated. Under this approach, liabilities and equity would be combined into one category that includes both creditor and owner claims to resources.

Required:
1. Define liabilities and stockholders' equity.
2. Provide arguments in support of maintaining the distinction between liabilities and stockholders' equity in the balance sheet.
3. Provide arguments in support of eliminating the distinction between liabilities and stockholders' equity in the balance sheet.
4. Which do you recommend? Why?

Earnings Management

AP10–8 Renegade Clothing is struggling to meet analysts' forecasts. It's early December 2012, and the year-end projections are in. Listed below are the projections for the year ended 2012 and the comparable actual amounts for 2011.

	Projected 2012	Actual 2011
Sales	$14,000,000	$16,023,000
Net income	878,000	1,113,000
Total assets	$ 6,500,000	$ 6,821,000
Total liabilities	$ 2,500,000	$ 2,396,000
Stockholders' equity	4,000,000	4,425,000
Total liabilities and stockholders' equity	$ 6,500,000	$ 6,821,000
Shares outstanding	950,000	950,000

Analysts forecast earnings per share for 2012 to be $0.95 per share. It looks like earnings per share will fall short of expectations in 2012.

Ronald Outlaw, the director of marketing, has a creative idea to improve earnings per share and the return on equity for 2012. He proposes the company borrow additional funds and use the proceeds to repurchase some of its own stock—treasury shares. Is this a good idea?

Required:
1. Calculate the projected earnings per share and return on equity for 2012 before any repurchase of stock.

Now assume Renegade Clothing purchases 100,000 shares of its own stock at $10 per share. The projections for 2012 will change as follows:

	2012	2011
Sales	$14,000,000	$16,023,000
Net income	878,000	1,113,000
Total assets	$ 6,500,000	$ 6,821,000
Total liabilities	$ 3,500,000	$ 2,396,000
Stockholders' equity	3,000,000	4,425,000
Total liabilities and stockholders' equity	$ 6,500,000	$ 6,821,000
Shares outstanding	850,000	950,000

2. Calculate the new projected earnings per share and return on equity for 2012, assuming the company goes through with the treasury stock repurchase.
   (*Hint:* In computing earnings per share, average shares outstanding is now 900,000 = (850,000 + 950,000) ÷ 2.)
3. Explain how the repurchase of treasury stock near year-end improves earnings per share and the return on equity ratio.

Answers to the Self Study Questions
1. a 2. b 3. b 4. c 5. b 6. d 7. c 8. d 9. a 10. c

CHAPTER

11

Statement of Cash Flows

AFTER STUDYING THIS CHAPTER, YOU SHOULD BE ABLE TO:

- **LO1** Classify cash transactions as operating, investing, or financing activities.
- **LO2** Prepare the operating activities section of the statement of cash flows using the indirect method.
- **LO3** Prepare the investing activities section and the financing activities section of the statement of cash flows.

Analysis

- **LO4** Perform financial analysis using the statement of cash flows.

Appendix

- **LO5** Prepare the operating activities section of the statement of cash flows using the direct method.

APPLE, INC.: **CASH FLOWS AT THE CORE**

Net income represents all revenues less expenses of a company during a reporting period. Operating cash flows represent the cash inflows less cash outflows related to the very same revenue and expense activities. Although you might expect these two amounts to be similar, fairly large differences sometimes exist. For instance, here are the 2009 net income and operating cash flows for three well-known companies in the electronics industry ($ in millions):

Feature
Story

Company Name	Net Income	Operating Cash Flows
Apple	$ 5,704	$10,159
Hewlett-Packard	7,660	13,379
Microsoft	14,569	19,037

All three companies report higher operating cash flows than net income. For **Apple** and **Hewlett-Packard**, operating cash flow is almost twice net income. One reason may be that certain items, like depreciation expense, decrease net income but have no effect on operating cash flows. Both net income and operating cash flows are important indicators in explaining stock prices. Which is more important to investors—net income or operating cash flows? The financial press discusses net income more than cash flows, but many finance courses emphasize that "cash is king."

However, in comparing net income with operating cash flows, research consistently finds that net income, not cash, is king. Net income works better than operating cash flow in forecasting not only future net income, but also future cash flow.[1] The research also finds that stock returns (the change in stock price plus dividends) are more closely related to net income than to operating cash flow.[2] Net income helps smooth out the unevenness or lumpiness in year-to-year operating cash flow, producing a better estimate of ongoing company profitability.

While net income may win in a direct competition with operating cash flow, it's important to remember that both net income and operating cash flow provide important information. An investor or creditor who analyzes both net income and operating cash flow will do better than one who focuses solely on net income. For instance, a company with increasing earnings but decreasing operating cash flow is probably not as good an investment as a company with increasing earnings and increasing operating cash flow. Net income and operating cash flows are each so valuable that we might think of them both as financial royalty.

---

[1]M. Barth, C. Cram, and K. Nelson. 2001. "Accruals and the Prediction of Future Cash Flows." *The Accounting Review* 76 (January), pp. 27–58; and C. Finger. 1994. "The Ability of Earnings to Predict Future Earnings and Cash Flow." *Journal of Accounting Research* 32 (Autumn), pp. 210–23.
[2]P. Dechow. 1994. "Accounting Earnings and Cash Flow as Measures of Firm Performance: The Role of Accounting Accruals." *Journal of Accounting and Economics* (July), pp. 3–42.

PART A	# FORMATTING THE STATEMENT OF CASH FLOWS

A **statement of cash flows** provides a summary of cash inflows and cash outflows during the reporting period. Illustration 11–1 presents the statement of cash flows for E-Games, Inc.

ILLUSTRATION 11–1

Statement of Cash Flows

E-GAMES, INC. Statement of Cash Flows For the year ended December 31, 2012		
Cash Flows from Operating Activities		
Net income	$42,000	
Adjustments for noncash effects:		
Depreciation expense	9,000	
Loss on sale of land	4,000	
Changes in current assets and current liabilities:		
Increase in accounts receivable	(7,000)	
Decrease in inventory	10,000	
Increase in prepaid rent	(2,000)	
Decrease in accounts payable	(5,000)	
Increase in interest payable	1,000	
Decrease in income tax payable	(2,000)	
Net cash flows from operating activities		$50,000
Cash Flows from Investing Activities		
Purchase of investment	(35,000)	
Sale of land	6,000	
Net cash flows from investing activities		(29,000)
Cash Flows from Financing Activities		
Issuance of common stock	5,000	
Payment of cash dividends	(12,000)	
Net cash flows from financing activities		(7,000)
Net increase (decrease) in cash		14,000
Cash at the beginning of the period		48,000
Cash at the end of the period		$62,000
Note: Noncash Activities		
Purchased equipment by issuing a note payable		$20,000

We will use this statement as an example throughout the chapter. Don't be concerned about the details just yet. That's what the rest of the chapter is all about.

Classification of Transactions

■ LO1

Classify cash transactions as operating, investing, or financing activities.

The three primary categories of cash flows are (1) cash flows from operating activities, (2) cash flows from investing activities, and (3) cash flows from financing activities. Classifying each cash flow by source (operating, investing, or financing activities) is more informative than simply listing the various cash flows.

REPORTING CASH FLOW ACTIVITIES

Operating activities include cash receipts and cash payments for transactions relating to revenue and expense activities. These are essentially the very same activities reported on the income statement. In other words, cash flows from operating activities include the elements of net income, but reported on a cash basis. Common examples of operating activities include the collection of cash from customers or the payment of cash for inventory purchases, salaries, and rent.

Investing activities include cash transactions involving the purchase and sale of long-term assets and current investments. Companies periodically invest cash to replace or expand productive facilities such as buildings, land, and equipment. They might also invest in other assets, such as stocks or bonds of other firms, with the expectation of a return on those investments. Eventually, many of these assets are sold. Investment in and sale of long-term assets and investments are common examples of investing activities.

Financing activities are both inflows and outflows of cash resulting from the external financing of a business. A major portion of financing for many companies comes from external sources, specifically stockholders and lenders. Common financing activities are borrowing and repaying debt, issuing and repurchasing stock, and paying dividends.

 INTERNATIONAL FINANCIAL REPORTING STANDARDS (IFRS)

In a joint project on financial reporting presentation with the FASB, the IASB recently proposed extending the operating, investing, and financing classifications used in the statement of cash flows to the income statement and the balance sheet. If the proposal goes through, all the major financial statements will be organized along the lines of operating, investing, and financing activities.

For more discussion, see Appendix E.

Illustration 11–2 lists common cash receipts and cash payments for operating, investing, and financing activities. **Review this illustration carefully** (you may even want to bookmark it); it will come in handy in solving many of the questions, exercises, problems, and cases at the end of the chapter.

Cash Flows from Operating Activities	
Cash Inflows	**Cash Outflows**
Sale of goods or services	Purchase of inventory
Receipt of interest and dividends	For operating expenses
	For interest
	For income taxes
Cash Flows from Investing Activities	
Cash Inflows	**Cash Outflows**
Sale of investments	Purchase of investments
Sale of property, plant, and equipment or intangibles	Purchase of property, plant, and equipment or intangibles
Collection of notes receivable	Lending with notes receivable
Cash Flows from Financing Activities	
Cash Inflows	**Cash Outflows**
Issuance of bonds or notes payable	Repayment of bonds or notes payable
Issuance of stock	Reacquisition of stock (treasury stock)
	Payment of dividends

ILLUSTRATION 11–2

Operating, Investing, and Financing Activities

Let's look at a few of the cash flows. For example, we report interest and dividends received from investments with operating activities rather than investing activities. Similarly, we report interest paid on bonds or notes payable with operating activities rather than financing activities. Why are these classified as operating activities? They are included in operating activities because each is a cash flow from an activity reported in the income statement—interest revenue, dividend revenue, and interest expense. As we discussed earlier, operating activities are those we report on the income statement.

On the other hand, we record dividends paid as a financing activity. Recall that dividends are not an expense and, therefore, paying dividends has no effect on net income. The payment of dividends simply reduces assets (cash) and stockholders' equity (retained earnings).

COMMON MISTAKE

Students sometimes misclassify dividends in preparing the statement of cash flows. Dividends *received* are included in operating activities. Dividends *paid* are included in financing activities.

As we saw in Chapter 3, we prepare the income statement, the statement of stockholders' equity, and the balance sheet directly from the adjusted trial balance. Unfortunately, though, the accounts listed on the adjusted trial balance do not directly provide the cash inflows and cash outflows we report on the statement of cash flows. We need to rely on other sources to determine the amounts necessary to prepare the statement of cash flows. Illustration 11–3 outlines the three primary sources.

ILLUSTRATION 11–3

Information Sources for Preparing the Statement of Cash Flows

Information Sources	Explanation
1. Income statement	The income statement provides important information in determining cash flows from operating activities.
2. Balance sheet	We look at the change in asset, liability, and stockholders' equity accounts from the end of the last period to the end of this period to find cash flows from operating, investing, and financing activities.
3. Detailed accounting records	Sometimes we need additional information from the accounting records to determine specific cash inflows or cash outflows for the period.

KEY POINT

Operating activities relate to income statement items. Investing activities primarily involve changes in long-term assets. Financing activities primarily involve changes in long-term liabilities and stockholders' equity.

Illustration 11–4 summarizes the relationship of the income statement and balance sheet to the operating, investing, and financing sections in the statement of cash flows.

ILLUSTRATION 11–4

Relationship of the Income Statement and Balance Sheet to the Statement of Cash Flows

REPORTING NONCASH ACTIVITIES

Suppose a company borrows $200,000 cash from a bank, issuing a long-term note payable for that amount. The firm reports this transaction in a statement of cash flows as a *financing activity*. Now suppose the company uses that cash to purchase new equipment. It reports this second transaction as an *investing activity*. But what if, instead of two separate transactions, the company acquired $200,000 of new equipment by issuing a $200,000 long-term note payable in a *single transaction*? Since this transaction does not affect cash, it is excluded from the statement of cash flows.

However, undertaking a significant investing activity and a significant financing activity as two parts of a single transaction does not lessen the value of reporting these activities. For that reason, transactions that do not increase or decrease cash, but that result in significant investing and financing activities, are reported as noncash activities either directly after the cash flow statement or in a note to the financial statements. Examples of significant noncash investing and financing activities include:

1. Purchase of long-term assets by issuing debt.
2. Purchase of long-term assets by issuing stock.
3. Conversion of bonds payable into common stock.
4. Exchange of long-term assets.

Having a better overall picture of total investing and financing activities is important for investors and creditors. Thus, they should consider both the investing and financing activities reported in the statement of cash flows and the noncash investing and financing activities reported in the notes to the financial statements.

Decision Point

Question ?	Accounting information 📄	Analysis 🔍
Did the company have any significant noncash investing and financing activities?	Reported either directly after the cash flow statement or in a note to the financial statements	The disclosure of noncash investing and financing activities can be combined with information reported on the statement of cash flows to provide a better overall picture of total investing and financing activities.

Let's Review

Indicate whether each of the following items is classified as an operating activity, investing activity, financing activity, or a significant noncash activity.
1. Dividends received from an investment.
2. Dividends paid to shareholders.
3. Property, plant, and equipment purchased for cash.
4. Property, plant, and equipment purchased by issuing stock.
5. Notes receivable accepted for lending cash.
6. Notes payable issued for borrowing cash.

Solution:

1. Operating.
2. Financing.
3. Investing.
4. Noncash.
5. Investing.
6. Financing.

Suggested Homework:
BE11-1, BE11-2;
E11-3, E11-4;
P11-1A&B

OPERATING ACTIVITIES—INDIRECT AND DIRECT METHODS

We have two ways to determine and report cash flows from operating activities in a statement of cash flows—the indirect method and the direct method. The methods differ only in the presentation format for operating activities. **The total net cash flows from operating activities are identical under both methods.** Also, the two methods affect only the operating section. We report investing, financing, and noncash activities identically under both methods.

Using the indirect method, we begin with net income and then list adjustments to net income, in order to arrive at operating cash flows. The indirect method is more popular because it is generally easier and less costly to prepare. In fact, nearly all major companies in the United States (about 99%) prepare the statement of cash flows using the indirect method.[3] For this reason, we emphasize the indirect method.

Using the direct method, we adjust the items on the income statement to directly show the cash inflows and outflows from operations such as cash received from customers and cash paid for inventory, salaries, rent, interest, and taxes. If a company decides to use the direct method to report operating activities, it must also report the indirect method either along with the statement of cash flows or in a separate note to the financial statements.

We discuss the indirect method in the next section. We present the direct method using the same example in an appendix to this chapter.

KEY POINT

Companies choose between the indirect method and the direct method in reporting operating activities in the statement of cash flows. The indirect method is less costly to prepare and is used in practice by the majority of companies. The direct method more logically presents the cash inflows and outflows from operations. The investing and financing sections of the statement of cash flows are identical under both methods.

PART B   PREPARING THE STATEMENT OF CASH FLOWS

In this section, we first look at the steps involved in preparing the statement of cash flows, and its basic format. Then we work through these steps in preparing the operating, investing, and financing activities sections of the statement of cash flows.

Steps in Preparing the Statement of Cash Flows

Illustration 11–5 summarizes the four basic steps in preparing the statement of cash flows.

ILLUSTRATION 11–5

Steps in Preparing the Statement of Cash Flows

Step 1. Calculate net cash flows from *operating activities*, using information from the income statement and changes in current assets (other than cash) and current liabilities from the balance sheet.

Step 2. Determine the net cash flows from *investing activities*, by analyzing changes in long-term asset accounts from the balance sheet.

Step 3. Determine the net cash flows from *financing activities*, by analyzing changes in long-term liabilities and stockholders' equity accounts from the balance sheet.

Step 4. Combine the operating, investing, and financing activities, and make sure the total change from these three activities agrees with the net increase (decrease) in cash shown at the bottom of the statement of cash flows.

---

[3] *Accounting Trends and Techniques—2009.* 2009. (New York: American Institute of Certified Public Accountants).

Illustration 11–6 provides the income statement, balance sheet, and additional information for E-Games, Inc. We will use this information to prepare the statement of cash flows following the four basic steps.

E-GAMES, INC.
Income Statement
For the year ended December 31, 2012

Revenues		$1,012,000
Expenses:		
Cost of goods sold	$650,000	
Operating expenses (salaries, rent, utilities)	286,000	
Depreciation expense	9,000	
Loss on sale of land	4,000	
Interest expense	5,000	
Income tax expense	16,000	
Total expenses		970,000
Net income		$ 42,000

ILLUSTRATION 11–6

Income Statement, Balance Sheet, and Additional Information for E-Games, Inc.

E-GAMES, INC.
Balance Sheet
December 31, 2012 and 2011

	2012	2011	Increase (I) or Decrease (D)
Assets			
Current assets:			
Cash	$ 62,000	$ 48,000	$14,000 (I)
Accounts receivable	27,000	20,000	7,000 (I)
Inventory	35,000	45,000	10,000 (D)
Prepaid rent	4,000	2,000	2,000 (I)
Long-term assets:			
Investments	35,000	0	35,000 (I)
Land	70,000	80,000	10,000 (D)
Equipment	90,000	70,000	20,000 (I)
Accumulated depreciation	(23,000)	(14,000)	9,000 (I)
Total assets	$300,000	$251,000	
Liabilities and Stockholders' Equity			
Current liabilities:			
Accounts payable	$ 22,000	$ 27,000	$ 5,000 (D)
Interest payable	2,000	1,000	1,000 (I)
Income tax payable	5,000	7,000	2,000 (D)
Long-term liabilities:			
Notes payable	95,000	75,000	20,000 (I)
Stockholders' equity:			
Common stock	105,000	100,000	5,000 (I)
Retained earnings	71,000	41,000	30,000 (I)
Total liabilities and stockholders' equity	$300,000	$251,000	

(continued)

ILLUSTRATION 11-6
(*concluded*)

Additional Information for 2012:
1. Purchased stock in Intendo Corporation for $35,000.
2. Sold land originally costing $10,000 for $6,000, resulting in a $4,000 loss on sale of land.
3. Purchased $20,000 in equipment by issuing a $20,000 note payable due in three years. No cash was exchanged in the transaction.
4. Issued common stock for $5,000 cash.
5. Declared and paid a cash dividend of $12,000.

Basic Format

In preparing the statement of cash flows, it's helpful to first set up the basic format. As Illustration 11–7 shows, the last three lines of the statement of cash flows include amounts for the net increase (decrease) in cash, cash at the beginning of the period, and cash at the end of the period obtained from the E-Games balance sheet. Cash at the beginning of the period is $48,000 (the balance for cash in the 2011 balance sheet column), and cash at the end of the period is $62,000 (the balance for cash in the 2012 balance sheet column). The $14,000 change in the cash balance will be our "check figure," which means the cash inflows and cash outflows we identify must net to this amount. After all, the purpose of the statement of cash flows is to explain *why* cash increased by $14,000.

ILLUSTRATION 11-7

Basic Format for the Statement of Cash Flows

E-GAMES, INC. Statement of Cash Flows For the year ended December 31, 2012	
Cash Flows from Operating Activities	$_____
Cash Flows from Investing Activities	_____
Cash Flows from Financing Activities	_____
Net increase (decrease) in cash	14,000
Cash at the beginning of the period	48,000
Cash at the end of the period	$62,000
Note: Noncash Activities	
List of noncash transactions	_____

Operating Activities—Indirect Method

■ **LO2**
Prepare the operating activities section of the statement of cash flows using the indirect method.

As we learned in Illustration 11–5, the first step in preparing the statement of cash flows is to calculate net cash flows from *operating activities* using information from the income statement and changes in current assets (other than cash) and current liabilities from the balance sheet.

The key to understanding the operating activities section of the statement of cash flows is to understand that both net income and cash flows from operating activities represent the same operating activities: The income statement reports net income on an *accrual basis*. That is, we report revenues when we earn them, regardless of when cash is received, and expenses when we incur them, regardless of when cash is paid. On the other hand, the statement of cash flows reports the very same activities on a *cash basis*—revenues when we receive cash, and expenses when we pay cash.

Net income includes both cash and noncash components. *Our task, when preparing a statement of cash flows, is to convert net income from an accrual basis to a cash basis.* In other words, we remove noncash components from net income so that what's left is cash flows only. We can classify the noncash components as:

(a)   revenues and expenses that don't affect cash at all (adjustments for non-cash components of net income), and

(b)   revenues and expenses that do affect cash, but not by the amount reported as the revenue or expense (adjustments for changes in current assets and current liabilities).

We look at each of those two adjustments for noncash components in the sections that follow.

Question		Accounting information		Analysis		**Decision Point**
Is a company's net income supported by strong operating cash flows?		Operating activities section of the statement of cash flows using the indirect method		The operating activities section using the indirect method reconciles net income to operating cash flows. Net income is considered to be of higher quality when backed by strong operating cash flows.		

ADJUSTMENTS FOR NONCASH COMPONENTS OF NET INCOME

Using the indirect method, we first adjust net income for revenues and expenses that don't affect cash at all. Here are two common examples.

Depreciation expense.   Depreciation expense reduces net income. Remember, though, depreciation expense does not correspond to a cash outflow in the current period. Recording depreciation expense results in increases to the Depreciation Expense and Accumulated Depreciation accounts. In recording depreciation, we're simply allocating the cost of an asset over the periods the asset is used. But since we deducted this noncash expense in the determination of net income, we need to add it back in order to eliminate it. Amortization of intangible assets is treated the same way as depreciation of tangible assets. We add back both depreciation expense and amortization expense to net income in arriving at cash flows from operating activities.

E-Games, Inc., reports net income of $42,000 and depreciation expense of $9,000 in its income statement. Since depreciation expense reduces net income by $9,000, E-Games will add the $9,000 back to net income as a step in arriving at net cash flows from operations. Illustration 11–8 shows how E-Games reports depreciation expense in the statement of cash flows under the indirect method.

E-GAMES, INC.
Statement of Cash Flows (partial)

Cash Flows from Operating Activities	
Net income	$42,000
Adjustments for noncash effects:	
Depreciation expense	9,000

ILLUSTRATION 11–8

Adjustment for Depreciation Expense

Loss on sale of land.   Gains on the sale of long-term assets increase net income, while losses on the sale of those assets decrease net income. E-Games, Inc., reports a $4,000 loss on sale of land in its income statement. To see how to treat the loss, let's re-create how E-Games recorded the sale of land. We see from additional-information item (2) that E-Games sold land originally costing $10,000 for only $6,000, resulting in a $4,000 loss.

A = L + SE		Debit	Credit
+6,000	Cash	6,000	
−4,000 Exp↑	Loss	4,000	
−10,000	Land		10,000
	(Record loss on sale of land)		

The cash effect of this transaction is a cash increase of $6,000. The sale of land, though, is an investing activity, so this cash inflow is reported in the investing section of the statement of cash flows. Note that the loss is simply the difference between cash received in the sale of land (reported as an investing activity) and the cost of the land. It is not a cash inflow or cash outflow. And yet, we subtracted the $4,000 loss on the income statement in the determination of net income, so we need to add it back in order to eliminate this noncash component of net income. Illustration 11–9 shows how E-Games adds back the loss on sale of land to net income in arriving at net cash flows from operating activities.

ILLUSTRATION 11–9

Adjustment for Loss on Sale of Land

E-GAMES, INC.		
Statement of Cash Flows (partial)		
Cash Flows from Operating Activities		
Net income		$42,000
Adjustments for noncash effects:		
Depreciation expense		9,000
Loss on sale of land		4,000

What if E-Games, Inc., had a gain of $4,000, rather than a loss, on the sale of land? Since we would have added the $4,000 gain in the determination of net income, we would need to subtract it from net income to eliminate it.

 COMMON MISTAKE

Students sometimes are unsure whether to add or subtract a loss on the sale of assets. Just remember that a loss is like an expense—both reduce net income. Treat a loss on the sale of assets like depreciation expense and add it back to net income. A gain on the sale of long-term assets is the opposite of an expense, so we subtract it from net income to arrive at net cash flows from operating activities.

ADJUSTMENTS FOR CHANGES IN CURRENT ASSETS AND CURRENT LIABILITIES

For components of net income that increase or decrease cash, but *by an amount different from that reported on the income statement,* we adjust net income for changes in the balances of related balance sheet accounts to convert the effects of those items to a cash basis. For example, E-Games reports sales revenue of $1,012,000 in its income statement. This does not mean, however, that E-Games collected $1,012,000 cash from its customers during the reporting period. Since accounts receivable increased during the year, some of the sales revenue the company earned must not yet have been collected. We need, then, to make an adjustment to net income for the change in accounts receivable to convert the sales revenue number to a cash basis. To similarly convert other income statement components from accrual basis to cash basis, we adjust net income for changes in all current assets (other than cash) and current liabilities. Let's look at the changes in current assets and current liabilities for E-Games to see how this works.

Increase in accounts receivable.   E-Games' accounts receivable increased $7,000 during the year (from $20,000 in 2011 to $27,000 in 2012). This tells us that the company must not have collected all of its $1,012,000 sales revenue in cash. Why? Because customers owe the company $7,000 more than before. Let's confirm this by recording the selling and collection activities during the year:

	Debit	Credit	A	=	L	+	SE
Cash (to balance)	1,005,000		+1,005,000				
Accounts Receivable (= $27,000 − $20,000)	7,000		+7,000				
Revenues (from income statement)		1,012,000					+1,012,000 Rev↑
(Record increase in accounts receivable)							

We record an increase in Revenues with a credit and an increase in Accounts Receivable with a debit. Cash received from customers of $1,005,000 is the number we need for the debits and credits to equal.

The $7,000 increase in accounts receivable represents $7,000 of credit sales that E-Games reported as part of net income but that did not result in operating cash inflows. Therefore, to adjust net income to operating cash flows, we need to eliminate $7,000 from net income, as shown in Illustration 11–10.

E-GAMES, INC. Statement of Cash Flows (partial)	
Cash Flows from Operating Activities	
Net income	$42,000
Adjustments for noncash effects:	
Depreciation expense	9,000
Loss on sale of land	4,000
Changes in current assets and current liabilities:	
Increase in accounts receivable	(7,000)

ILLUSTRATION 11–10
Adjustment for Change in Accounts Receivable

A decrease in accounts receivable would have the opposite effect. We would *add* a decrease in accounts receivable to net income to arrive at net cash flows from operating activities. A decrease in accounts receivable indicates that we collected more cash from customers than we recorded as credit sales.

Decrease in inventory.   E-Games' inventory balance decreased by $10,000 during the year. This tells us that the company purchased $10,000 less inventory than is reflected in cost of goods sold in the income statement. In other words, $10,000 of E-Games' cost of goods sold was a result of reducing its inventory, rather than a purchase of new inventory and a corresponding cash outflow. Therefore, we need to eliminate the noncash portion of cost of goods sold from net income as part of our conversion of net income to operating cash flows. To eliminate the effect of this $10,000 expense, we add the $10,000 decrease in inventory to net income. Illustration 11–11 shows this adjustment.

ILLUSTRATION 11–11

Adjustment for Change
in Inventory

E-GAMES, INC. Statement of Cash Flows (partial)	
Cash Flows from Operating Activities	
Net income	$42,000
Adjustments for noncash effects:	
Depreciation expense	9,000
Loss on sale of land	4,000
Changes in current assets and current liabilities:	
Increase in accounts receivable	(7,000)
Decrease in inventory	10,000

Increase in prepaid rent.   E-Games' prepaid rent increased $2,000 during the year. The company paid $2,000 cash for an asset (prepaid rent) for which there is no corresponding expense (rent expense). In other words, the cash outflow for prepaid rent caused cash to decrease by $2,000, but net income remained unaffected. To adjust for this, we subtract the $2,000 increase in prepaid rent from net income to reflect the $2,000 cash outflow not reflected in net income. Illustration 11–12 shows this adjustment.

ILLUSTRATION 11–12

Adjustment for Change
in Prepaid Rent

E-GAMES, INC. Statement of Cash Flows (partial)	
Cash Flows from Operating Activities	
Net income	$42,000
Adjustments for noncash effects:	
Depreciation expense	9,000
Loss on sale of land	4,000
Changes in current assets and current liabilities:	
Increase in accounts receivable	(7,000)
Decrease in inventory	10,000
Increase in prepaid rent	(2,000)

Decrease in accounts payable.   E-Games' accounts payable decreased $5,000 during the year. Reducing the amount owed to suppliers means the company paid $5,000 more cash than the cost of goods purchased. The decrease in accounts payable indicates that the company paid $5,000 cash to reduce its liability (accounts payable) but reported no corresponding expense (cost of goods sold) during the period. In other words, total cash outflows to reduce accounts payable were $5,000 greater than total related expenses. To adjust for the greater cash outflows, we subtract the $5,000 decrease in accounts payable from net income, as shown in Illustration 11–13.

ILLUSTRATION 11–13

Adjustment for Change
in Accounts Payable

E-GAMES, INC. Statement of Cash Flows (partial)	
Cash Flows from Operating Activities	
Net income	$42,000
Adjustments for noncash effects:	
Depreciation expense	9,000
Loss on sale of land	4,000
Changes in current assets and current liabilities:	
Increase in accounts receivable	(7,000)
Decrease in inventory	10,000
Increase in prepaid rent	(2,000)
Decrease in accounts payable	(5,000)

Increase in interest payable. E-Games' interest payable increased $1,000 during the year. That means the company owes $1,000 more than previously, so it must have paid $1,000 less cash than the interest expense included in net income. As shown in Illustration 11–14, the company adds the increase in interest payable to net income to adjust for the fact that cash outflows are less than interest expense, increasing overall cash flows.

Decrease in income tax payable. E-Games' income tax payable decreased $2,000 during the year. A change in income tax payable indicates a difference between income tax expense and income taxes paid. A $2,000 decrease in income tax payable indicates E-Games paid $2,000 more to reduce its tax liability (income tax payable) than it recorded as an expense (income tax expense) in net income. To adjust for the fact that cash outflow is greater than tax expense, we subtract $2,000 from net income to calculate operating cash flows. Illustration 11–15 shows this adjustment and calculates total net cash flows from operating activities of $50,000.

CAREER CORNER

Are you good at analyzing information? If so, you might consider a career as a financial analyst. A career in this field involves understanding the operations of companies, assessing the reasonableness of their stock price, and predicting their future performance. Investment analysts rely heavily on financial statements as a source of information in predicting stock price movements. Since financial statements, including the cash flow statement covered in this chapter, are accounting-based, it is no surprise that a strong background in accounting is necessary for a career as a financial analyst. A background in accounting is useful, not only in preparing accounting information, but analyzing and interpreting that information as well.

E-GAMES, INC. Statement of Cash Flows (partial)	
Cash Flows from Operating Activities	
Net income	$42,000
Adjustments for noncash effects:	
Depreciation expense	9,000
Loss on sale of land	4,000
Changes in current assets and current liabilities:	
Increase in accounts receivable	(7,000)
Decrease in inventory	10,000
Increase in prepaid rent	(2,000)
Decrease in accounts payable	(5,000)
Increase in interest payable	1,000

ILLUSTRATION 11–14

Adjustment for Change in Interest Payable

E-GAMES, INC. Statement of Cash Flows (partial)	
Cash Flows from Operating Activities	
Net income	$42,000
Adjustments for noncash effects:	
Depreciation expense	9,000
Loss on sale of land	4,000
Changes in current assets and current liabilities:	
Increase in accounts receivable	(7,000)
Decrease in inventory	10,000
Increase in prepaid rent	(2,000)
Decrease in accounts payable	(5,000)
Increase in interest payable	1,000
Decrease in income tax payable	(2,000)
Net cash flows from operating activities	$50,000

ILLUSTRATION 11–15

Adjustment for Change in Income Tax Payable

Illustration 11–16 provides a summary of the adjustments we make to convert net income to net cash flows from operating activities.

ILLUSTRATION 11–16

Summary of Adjustments to Net Income

Cash Flows from Operating Activities

Net income

Adjustments for noncash effects:

For noncash components of income:
+ Depreciation expense
+ Amortization expense
+ Loss on sale of assets
− Gain on sale of assets

For changes in current assets and current liabilities:
− Increase in a current asset
+ Decrease in a current asset
+ Increase in a current liability
− Decrease in a current liability

= Net cash flows from operating activities

This illustration is a helpful reference when completing the homework exercises at the end of the chapter. Remember that for noncash components of income, we add back expenses and losses and subtract gains. For changes in current liabilities, we add an increase in a current liability and subtract a decrease. We do just the opposite for changes in current assets.

 KEY POINT

Using the indirect method, we start with net income and adjust this number for (a) revenue and expense items that do not represent cash and (b) changes in current assets and current liabilities.

Investing and Financing Activities

■ LO3

Prepare the investing activities section and the financing activities section of the statement of cash flows.

As noted earlier, we prepare the investing and financing activities in the statement of cash flows the same whether we use the indirect or the direct method. Here, we take a detailed look at how investing and financing activities are determined in our E-Games, Inc., example.

INVESTING ACTIVITIES

As we learned in Illustration 11–5, the second step in preparing the statement of cash flows is to determine the net cash flows from *investing* activities by analyzing changes in long-term asset accounts from the balance sheet. The long-term assets section of the balance sheet is the place to look for investing activities.[4] Looking at that section of E-Games' balance sheet, we determine the following cash flows from investing activities.

---

[4]Although not used as an example in this chapter, it's also possible to have investing activities related to changes in current investments or current notes receivable.

Increase in investments. E-Games' investments in stock increased $35,000 during the year (from $0 in 2011 to $35,000 in 2012). In the absence of contrary evidence, it's logical to assume the increase is due to the purchase of investments during the year. Additional-information item (1) in Illustration 11–6 confirms this assumption. As Illustration 11–17 (see below) shows, we report the purchase of Intendo Corporation stock as a cash outflow of $35,000 from investing activities.

Decrease in land. The Land account decreased $10,000 during the year, indicating that E-Games sold land costing $10,000. Additional-information item (2) in Illustration 11–6 indicates that we originally recorded the land at a cost of $10,000 but sold it for only $6,000 (resulting in a loss on the sale of land of $4,000, as recorded in the operating activities section). We report $6,000 as a cash inflow from investing activities—the actual amount of cash proceeds received from the sale. (See Illustration 11–17, below.)

 COMMON MISTAKE

Some students mistakenly record a cash inflow from investing activities equal to the change in the asset account, $10,000 in this case. Remember, though, that the statement of cash flows reports the *actual* cash received or paid, which is not always the same as the change in the balance sheet accounts.

Increase in equipment. E-Games' Equipment account increased by $20,000 during the year. If E-Games purchased the equipment with cash, we would record a cash outflow from investing activities of $20,000. However, additional-information item (3) in Illustration 11–6 indicates that the firm paid for the equipment by issuing a $20,000 note payable. No cash was exchanged in the transaction. The increase in equipment therefore represents a noncash activity, which is disclosed in the cash flow footnote. Illustration 11–17 provides a summary of the cash flows from investing activities and disclosure of the noncash activity.

ILLUSTRATION 11–17

Cash Flows from Investing Activities

E-GAMES, INC. Statement of Cash Flows (partial)	
Cash Flows from Investing Activities	
Purchase of investment	$(35,000)
Sale of land	6,000
Net cash flows from investing activities	$ (29,000)
Note: Noncash Activities	
Purchased equipment by issuing a note payable	$ 20,000

FINANCING ACTIVITIES

The third step in preparing the statement of cash flows is to determine the net cash flows from *financing* activities. We can find a firm's financing activities by examining changes in long-term liabilities and stockholders' equity accounts from the balance sheet.[5] Referring back to E-Games' balance sheet, we find the following cash flows from financing activities.

---

[5]Although not used as an example in this chapter, it is also possible for financing activities to be indicated by changes in current liability accounts, such as current notes payable.

Increase in notes payable. E-Games has only one long-term liability. The company reports an increase in notes payable of $20,000. As we saw earlier, this was in payment for equipment and represents a noncash activity disclosed in a note to the cash flow statement.

Increase in common stock. Common stock increased by $5,000 during the year. Item (4) of the additional information in Illustration 11–6 confirms that this was the result of issuing $5,000 of common stock. As Illustration 11–18 (see below) shows, the $5,000 inflow of cash is reported as a financing activity.

Increase in retained earnings. E-Games' Retained Earnings balance increased by $30,000 during the year. Recall from earlier chapters that the balance of Retained Earnings increases with net income and decreases with dividends:

Retained Earnings

		41,000	Beginning balance
Dividends	?	42,000	Net income
(*decreases* RE)			(*increases* RE)
		71,000	Ending balance

Since net income is $42,000 and retained earnings increased by only $30,000, the company must have declared dividends of $12,000 during the year:

Retained earnings, beginning balance	$41,000
+ Net income	42,000
− Dividends	(12,000)
Retained earnings, ending balance	$71,000

Additional-information item (5) in Illustration 11–6 confirms that E-Games declared and paid dividends of $12,000 during the year. As shown in Illustration 11–18, we report the payment of cash dividends as a cash outflow from financing activities.

ILLUSTRATION 11–18

Cash Flows from
Financing Activities

E-GAMES, INC.
Statement of Cash Flows (partial)

Cash Flows from Financing Activities		
Issuance of common stock	$ 5,000	
Payment of cash dividends	(12,000)	
Net cash flows from financing activities		(7,000)

Only the dividends actually paid in cash during the year are reported in the statement of cash flows. If the company declares dividends in 2012 but does not pay them until 2013, it will report the dividends paid as a cash outflow in 2013, not in 2012.

KEY POINT

Most investing activities can be explained by changes in long-term asset accounts. Most financing activities can be explained by changes in long-term liability and stockholders' equity accounts.

The fourth and final step in preparing the statement of cash flows (see Illustration 11–5) is to combine the operating, investing, and financing activities and make sure the total of these three activities *agrees* with the net increase (decrease) in cash. Illustration 11–19 shows the complete statement of cash flows for E-Games, with all three sections—operating, investing, and financing—included along with the note for noncash activities.

E-GAMES, INC. Statement of Cash Flows—Indirect Method For the year ended December 31, 2012		
Cash Flows from Operating Activities		
Net income	$42,000	
Adjustments for noncash effects:		
Depreciation expense	9,000	
Loss on sale of land	4,000	
Changes in current assets and current liabilities:		
Increase in accounts receivable	(7,000)	
Decrease in inventory	10,000	
Increase in prepaid rent	(2,000)	
Decrease in accounts payable	(5,000)	
Increase in interest payable	1,000	
Decrease in income tax payable	(2,000)	
Net cash flows from operating activities		$50,000
Cash Flows from Investing Activities		
Purchase of investment	(35,000)	
Sale of land	6,000	
Net cash flows from investing activities		(29,000)
Cash Flows from Financing Activities		
Issuance of common stock	5,000	
Payment of cash dividends	(12,000)	
Net cash flows from financing activities		(7,000)
Net increase (decrease) in cash		14,000
Cash at the beginning of the period		48,000
Cash at the end of the period		$62,000
Note: Noncash Activities		
Purchased equipment by issuing a note payable		$20,000

ILLUSTRATION 11–19

Complete Statement of Cash Flows for E-Games, Inc.

This is the moment of truth. The sum of the net cash flows from operating, investing, and financing activities should equal the net increase (decrease) in cash for the period. In Illustration 11–19, we see that the total of the cash flows from operating (+$50,000), investing (−$29,000), and financing (−$7,000) activities equals the net increase in cash of $14,000 for the year. This amount was the increase in cash from the balance sheet in Illustration 11–6.

Let's Review

Provided below are the income statement, balance sheet, and additional information for E-Phones, Inc.

E-PHONES, INC.
Income Statement
For the year ended December 31, 2012

Revenues		$2,200,000
Gain on sale of investment		5,000
Expenses:		
Cost of goods sold	$1,100,000	
Operating expenses	450,000	
Depreciation expense	25,000	
Income tax expense	217,000	
Total expenses		1,792,000
Net income		$ 413,000

E-PHONES, INC.
Balance Sheet
December 31, 2012 and 2011

	2012	2011	Increase (I) or Decrease (D)
Assets			
Current assets:			
Cash	$ 32,000	$ 48,000	$ 16,000 (D)
Accounts receivable	32,000	40,000	8,000 (D)
Inventory	100,000	70,000	30,000 (I)
Long-term assets:			
Investments	0	50,000	50,000 (D)
Land	280,000	180,000	100,000 (I)
Equipment	200,000	140,000	60,000 (I)
Accumulated depreciation	(53,000)	(28,000)	25,000 (I)
Total assets	$591,000	$500,000	
Liabilities and Stockholders' Equity			
Current liabilities:			
Accounts payable	$ 52,000	$ 62,000	$ 10,000 (D)
Income tax payable	55,000	12,000	43,000 (I)
Long-term liabilities:			
Bonds payable	0	200,000	200,000 (D)
Stockholders' equity:			
Common stock	200,000	100,000	100,000 (I)
Retained earnings	284,000	126,000	158,000 (I)
Total liabilities and stockholders' equity	$591,000	$500,000	

Additional Information for 2012:
1. Sold an investment in stock costing $50,000 for $55,000, resulting in a $5,000 gain on sale of investment.
2. Purchased $100,000 in land, issuing $100,000 of common stock as payment. No cash was exchanged in the transaction.
3. Purchased equipment for $60,000 cash.
4. Retired the $200,000 balance in bonds payable at the beginning of the year.
5. Declared and paid a cash dividend of $255,000.

Required:

Prepare the statement of cash flows using the *indirect method*. Disclose any non-cash transactions in an accompanying note.

Solution:

E-PHONES, INC. Statement of Cash Flows—Indirect Method For the year ended December 31, 2012		
Cash Flows from Operating Activities		
Net income	$413,000	
Adjustments for noncash effects:		
Depreciation expense	25,000	
Gain on sale of investment	(5,000)	
Changes in current assets and current liabilities:		
Decrease in accounts receivable	8,000	
Increase in inventory	(30,000)	
Decrease in accounts payable	(10,000)	
Increase in income tax payable	43,000	
Net cash flows from operating activities		$444,000
Cash Flows from Investing Activities		
Sale of investment	55,000	
Purchase of equipment	(60,000)	
Net cash flows from investing activities		(5,000)
Cash Flows from Financing Activities		
Retirement of bonds payable	(200,000)	
Payment of cash dividends	(255,000)	
Net cash flows from financing activities		(455,000)
Net increase (decrease) in cash		(16,000)
Cash at the beginning of the period		48,000
Cash at the end of the period		$ 32,000
Note: Noncash Activities		
Purchased land by issuing common stock		$100,000

Suggested Homework:
BE11-4, BE11-5;
E11-7, E11-8;
P11-2A&B; P11-4A&B

CASH FLOW ANALYSIS
Apple vs. Dell

ANALYSIS

Throughout this text, we have emphasized the analysis of financial statements from a decision maker's perspective. Often that analysis includes the development and comparison of financial ratios. Each of the ratios discussed in Chapters 5 through 10 is based on income statement and balance sheet amounts.

■ **LO4**
Perform financial analysis using the statement of cash flows.

Cash Flow Ratios

Decision Maker's Perspective

Analysts often supplement their investigation of income statement and balance sheet amounts with cash flow ratios. Some cash flow ratios are derived by substituting net cash flows from operating activities in place of net income—not to replace those ratios but to complement them. Substituting cash flow from operations in place of net income offers additional insight in the evaluation of a company's profitability and financial strength.[6] Positive cash flow from operations is important to a company's survival in the long run. ●

Now we reexamine the financial ratios introduced in Chapter 7—return on assets, profit margin, and asset turnover—substituting net cash flows from operating activities, also called **operating cash flows**, in place of net income. Illustration 11–20 provides selected financial data for Apple and Dell.

ILLUSTRATION 11–20

Selected Financial Data for Apple and Dell

($ in millions)	2009	2008
Apple		
Net sales	$36,537	$32,479
Net income	5,704	4,834
Operating cash flows	10,159	9,596
Total assets	53,851	39,572
Dell		
Net sales	$61,101	$61,133
Net income	2,478	2,947
Operating cash flows	1,894	3,949
Total assets	26,500	27,561

RETURN ON ASSETS

Return on assets, introduced in Chapter 7, is calculated as net income divided by average total assets. Illustration 11–21 presents return on assets for Apple and Dell.

ILLUSTRATION 11–21

Return on Assets for Apple and Dell

($ in millions)	Net Income	÷	Average Total Assets	=	Return on Assets
Apple	$5,704	÷	($53,851 + $39,572)/2	=	12.2%
Dell	$2,478	÷	($26,500 + $27,561)/2	=	9.2%

Both Apple and Dell report strong return on assets, with Apple's return on assets of 12.2% being higher than Dell's at 9.2%. Thus, Apple generated more income for each dollar invested in assets.

CASH RETURN ON ASSETS

We can gain additional insights by examining a similar measure called the cash return on assets. We calculate it as:

Cash return on assets = Operating cash flows ÷ Average total assets

Illustration 11–22 presents the cash return on assets for Apple and Dell.

ILLUSTRATION 11–22

Cash Return on Assets for Apple and Dell

($ in millions)	Operating Cash Flows	÷	Average Total Assets	=	Cash Return on Assets
Apple	$10,159	÷	($53,851 + $39,572)/2	=	21.7%
Dell	$1,894	÷	($26,500 + $27,561)/2	=	7.0%

---

[6]Proposals for informative sets of cash flow ratios are offered by Charles A. Carslaw and John R. Mills. 1991. "Developing Ratios for Effective Cash Flow Statement Analysis." *Journal of Accountancy* 172 (November), pp. 63–70; Don E. Giacomino and David E. Mielke. 1993. "Cash Flows: Another Approach to Ratio Analysis." *Journal of Accountancy* 174 (March), pp. 55–58; and John Mills and Jeanne H. Yamamura. 1998. "The Power of Cash Flow Ratios." *Journal of Accountancy* 186 (October), pp. 53–61.

Apple's cash return on assets of 21.7% is much higher than Dell's cash return on assets of only 7.0%. Note that operating cash flows exceed net income for Apple, while operating cash flows are less than net income for Dell. This causes a greater difference in *cash* return on assets for Apple and Dell, in comparison to the spread between the two companies for return on assets presented in Illustration 11–21. Apple's net income is supported by even higher operating cash flows, while Dell's is not.

COMPONENTS OF CASH RETURN ON ASSETS

Let's explore the cash return on assets further by separating the ratio into two separate parts, as shown in Illustration 11–23.

Cash return on assets	=	Cash flow to sales	×	Asset turnover
$\dfrac{\text{Operating cash flows}}{\text{Average total assets}}$	=	$\dfrac{\text{Operating cash flows}}{\text{Net sales}}$	×	$\dfrac{\text{Net sales}}{\text{Average total assets}}$

ILLUSTRATION 11–23

Components of Cash Return on Assets

Cash return on assets can be separated into cash flow to sales and asset turnover. Cash flow to sales measures the operating cash flows generated for each dollar of sales. (It is the cash flow equivalent to profit margin, introduced in Chapter 7.) Asset turnover, also covered in Chapter 7, measures the sales revenue generated per dollar of assets. Cash flow to sales and asset turnover represent two primary strategies that companies have for increasing their cash return on assets. One strategy, used by Apple, is to sell highly innovative products that yield very high cash inflows from customers in relationship to the cash outflows to produce their products. Another strategy, which Dell uses, is to pursue high asset turnover by selling at lower prices than the competition. In Illustrations 11–24 and 11–25, we calculate cash flow to sales and asset turnover for both companies. We then can see whether our expectations regarding Apple and Dell are supported.

($ in millions)	Operating Cash Flows	÷	Net Sales	=	Cash Flow to Sales
Apple	$10,159	÷	$36,537	=	27.8%
Dell	$1,894	÷	$61,101	=	3.1%

ILLUSTRATION 11–24

Cash Flow to Sales for Apple and Dell

($ in millions)	Net Sales	÷	Average Total Assets	=	Asset Turnover
Apple	$36,537	÷	($53,851 + $39,572)/2	=	0.8 times
Dell	$61,101	÷	($26,500 + $27,561)/2	=	2.3 times

ILLUSTRATION 11–25

Asset Turnover for Apple and Dell

The cash flow ratios support our expectations regarding the different business strategies of Apple and Dell. Apple, with its innovative products such as the iPod, iPad, and the iPhone, generates higher cash flow from each dollar of sales than Dell, as Illustration 11–24 shows. However, Dell, with its innovative marketing, distribution, and discount pricing strategies, generates nearly three times the asset turnover of Apple, as Illustration 11–25 shows. To maximize cash flow from operations, a company strives to increase *both* cash flow per dollar of sales (cash flow to sales) and sales per dollar of assets invested (asset turnover).

KEY POINT

Cash return on assets indicates the amount of operating cash flow generated for each dollar invested in assets. We can separate cash return on assets into two components—cash flow to sales and asset turnover—to examine two important business strategies.

Decision Point

Question	Accounting information	Analysis
Are the company's cash flows based more on selling at higher prices or on increasing sales volume?	Cash flow to sales and asset turnover ratios	Companies with high cash flow to sales ratios obtain high cash inflows from sales to customers in relation to the cash outflows to produce the products. Companies with high asset turnover ratios may not make as much on each sale, but they make money through higher sales volume.

ETHICAL DILEMMA

Ebenezer is CEO of a successful small business. One day he stops by to see Tim Cratchit, the new branch manager at First National Bank. Ebenezer would like to double the size of his loan with the bank from $500,000 to $1 million. Ebenezer explains, "Business is booming, sales and earnings are up each of the past three years, and we could certainly use the funds for further business expansion." Tim Cratchit has a big heart, and Ebenezer has been a close friend of the family. He thinks to himself this loan decision will be easy, but he asks Ebenezer to e-mail the past three years' financial statements as required by bank policy.

In looking over the financial statements sent by Ebenezer, Tim becomes concerned. Sales and earnings have increased just as Ebenezer said. However, receivables, inventory, and accounts payable have grown at a much faster rate than sales. Furthermore, he notices a steady decrease in operating cash flows over the past three years, with negative operating cash flows in each of the past two years.

Who are the stakeholders, and what is the ethical dilemma? Do you think Tim should go ahead and approve the loan?

APPENDIX

OPERATING ACTIVITIES—DIRECT METHOD

■ **LO5**
Prepare the operating section of the statement of cash flows using the direct method.

The presentation of cash flows from operating activities in the chapter is referred to as the indirect method. By this method, we determine the cash effect of each operating activity or income statement item indirectly, starting with reported net income and working backward to convert to a cash basis.

An alternative is the **direct method,** by which we report the cash inflows and cash outflows directly on the statement of cash flows. For instance, we report *cash received from customers* as the cash effect of sales activities, and *cash paid to suppliers* as the cash effect of cost of goods sold. Income statement items that have *no* cash effect—such as depreciation expense or gains and losses on the sale of assets— are simply not reported under the direct method.

Here, we repeat the example for E-Games, Inc., this time presenting cash flows from operating activities using the direct method. For convenience, the income statement, balance sheet, and additional information for E-Games, Inc., are repeated in Illustration 11–26.

ILLUSTRATION 11–26

Income Statement, Balance Sheet, and Additional Information for E-Games, Inc.

E-GAMES, INC.
Income Statement
For the year ended December 31, 2012

Revenues		$1,012,000
Expenses:		
Cost of goods sold	$650,000	
Operating expenses (salaries, rent, utilities)	286,000	
Depreciation expense	9,000	
Loss on sale of land	4,000	
Interest expense	5,000	
Income tax expense	16,000	
Total expenses		970,000
Net income		$ 42,000

E-GAMES, INC.
Balance Sheet
December 31, 2012 and 2011

	2012	2011	Increase (I) or Decrease (D)
Assets			
Current assets:			
Cash	$ 62,000	$ 48,000	$14,000 (I)
Accounts receivable	27,000	20,000	7,000 (I)
Inventory	35,000	45,000	10,000 (D)
Prepaid rent	4,000	2,000	2,000 (I)
Long-term assets:			
Investments	35,000	0	35,000 (I)
Land	70,000	80,000	10,000 (D)
Equipment	90,000	70,000	20,000 (I)
Accumulated depreciation	(23,000)	(14,000)	9,000 (I)
Total assets	$300,000	$251,000	
Liabilities and Stockholders' Equity			
Current liabilities:			
Accounts payable	$ 22,000	$ 27,000	$ 5,000 (D)
Interest payable	2,000	1,000	1,000 (I)
Income tax payable	5,000	7,000	2,000 (D)
Long-term liabilities:			
Notes payable	95,000	75,000	20,000 (I)
Stockholders' equity:			
Common stock	105,000	100,000	5,000 (I)
Retained earnings	71,000	41,000	30,000 (I)
Total liabilities and stockholders' equity	$300,000	$251,000	

(continued)

ILLUSTRATION 11–26 (concluded)	**Additional Information for 2012:** 1. Purchased stock in Intendo Corporation for $35,000. 2. Land costing $10,000 was sold for only $6,000, resulting in a $4,000 loss on sale of land. 3. Purchased $20,000 in equipment by issuing a $20,000 note payable due in three years. No cash was exchanged in the transaction. 4. Issued common stock for $5,000 cash. 5. The company declared and paid a cash dividend of $12,000.

Remember from Illustration 11–5 that the first step in preparing the statement of cash flows is to calculate net cash flows from *operating* activities using information from the income statement and changes in current assets and current liabilities from the balance sheet.

The income statement reports revenues earned during the year, *regardless of when cash is received,* and the expenses incurred in generating those revenues, *regardless of when cash is paid.* This is the *accrual concept* of accounting that we've discussed throughout the book. Cash flows from operating activities, on the other hand, are both inflows and outflows of cash that result from activities reported in the income statement. In other words, it's the elements of net income, but **reported on a cash basis.** Using the direct method, we examine each account in the income statement and convert it from an accrual amount to a cash amount. We directly report the cash inflows and cash outflows from operations as shown in Illustration 11–27.

ILLUSTRATION 11–27
Operating Activities Using the Direct Method
	Cash Flows from Operating Activities
	Cash inflows:
	    Cash received from customers
	    Cash received from interest
	    Cash received from dividends
	Cash outflows:
	    Cash paid to suppliers
	    Cash paid for operating expenses
	    Cash paid for interest
	    Cash paid for income taxes
	
	= Net cash flows from operating activities

The best way to apply the direct method is to convert each revenue and expense item to its cash-basis amount. We do this by considering how each income statement account is affected by related changes in current asset and current liability accounts.

Cash received from customers. E-Games reports revenues of $1,012,000 as the first item in its income statement. Did E-Games receive $1,012,000 in cash from those revenues? We can answer this by looking at the change in accounts receivable. If accounts receivable increases, this indicates that revenues exceed cash receipts from customers. That's why customers owe more than they did before. If accounts receivable decreases, the opposite will be true. Recall that accounts receivable increased $7,000. Therefore, we deduct the $7,000 increase in accounts receivable from revenues to obtain cash received from customers of $1,005,000, as shown in Illustration 11–28.

Revenues	$ 1,012,000	**ILLUSTRATION 11–28**
− Increase in accounts receivable	(7,000)	Cash Received from
Cash received from customers	**$1,005,000**	Customers

Let's consider this again from a couple of different perspectives. Accounts receivable increases when customers buy on credit and decreases when we receive cash from customers. We can compare sales and the change in accounts receivable during the year to determine the amount of cash we received from customers. In T–account format the relationship looks like this:

Accounts Receivable

Beginning balance	20,000			
Credit sales	1,012,000	?	Cash received	
(*increases A/R*)			(*decreases A/R*)	
Ending balance	27,000			

We see from this analysis that *cash received from customers* must have been $1,005,000. Still another way to view the situation is to think about how E-Games recorded these selling and collection activities during the year:

	Debit	Credit	A	=	L	+	SE
Cash (to balance)	**1,005,000**		+1,005,000				
Accounts Receivable (= $27,000 − $20,000)	**7,000**		+7,000				
Revenues (from income statement)		**1,012,000**					+1,012,000 Rev↑
(*Receive cash from customers*)							

We record an increase in Revenues with a credit and an increase in Accounts Receivable with a debit. Cash received from customers must be $1,005,000 for debits to equal credits.

Cash paid to suppliers.   Moving down the income statement, we see that E-Games reports cost of goods sold of $650,000. Did E-Games pay cash of $650,000 to suppliers of those goods during the year? To answer this, we look to the two current balance sheet accounts affected by merchandise purchases—Inventory and Accounts Payable.

First, compare cost of goods sold with the change in inventory to determine the cost of goods purchased (not necessarily cash paid) during the year. Inventory decreased by $10,000. We can visualize the relationship in T-account format:

Inventory

Beginning balance	45,000			
Cost of goods purchased	?	650,000	Cost of goods sold	
(*increases inventory*)			(*decreases inventory*)	
Ending balance	35,000			

The number needed to explain the change is $640,000. That's the cost of goods *purchased* during the year. It's not necessarily true, though, that E-Games paid $640,000 cash to suppliers of these goods. We need to look at the change in accounts payable to determine the cash paid to suppliers:

Accounts Payable

		27,000	Beginning balance
Cash paid to suppliers	?	640,000	Cost of goods purchased
(*decreases A/P*)			(*increases A/P*)
		22,000	Ending balance

We now see that cash paid to suppliers is $645,000. We can confirm this by looking at how E-Games recorded inventory purchases and sales during the year:

A = L + SE		Debit	Credit
−650,000 Exp↑	Cost of Goods Sold (from income statement)	650,000	
−5,000	Accounts Payable (= $27,000 − $22,000)	5,000	
−10,000	Inventory (= $45,000 − $35,000)		10,000
−645,000	Cash (to balance)		645,000
	(Pay cash for inventory)		

We record an increase in Cost of Goods Sold with a debit, a decrease in Inventory with a credit, and a decrease in Accounts Payable with a debit. Cash paid to suppliers is the "plug" figure we need for debits to equal credits in the journal entry.

Alternatively, we can analyze the situation this way: Inventory decreased $10,000 for the year, so E-Games needed to purchase only $640,000 of goods in order to sell $650,000 of goods; $10,000 came from existing inventory. Because accounts payable decreased by $5,000, cash paid to suppliers must have been $5,000 more than purchases, so we add the decrease in accounts payable to purchases of $640,000 to arrive at cash paid to suppliers of $645,000, as shown in Illustration 11–29.

ILLUSTRATION 11–29

Cash Paid to Suppliers

Cost of goods sold	$ 650,000
− Decrease in inventory	(10,000)
= Purchases	640,000
+ Decrease in accounts payable	5,000
= Cash paid to suppliers	$645,000

Cash paid for operating expenses.   Operating expenses of $286,000 appear next in the income statement. We examine the changes in current assets and current liabilities for any accounts related to operating expenses. Rent expense is included in operating expenses, so we must consider the change in prepaid rent. Increasing prepaid rent takes additional cash. Prepaid rent increased by $2,000, so we need to add this change to operating expenses to determine the cash paid for operating expenses, as shown in Illustration 11–30.

ILLUSTRATION 11–30

Cash Paid for
Operating Expenses

Operating expenses	$ 286,000
+ Increase in prepaid rent	2,000
= Cash paid for operating expenses	$288,000

We see no current assets or current liabilities associated with other operating expenses such as salaries expense or utilities expense, so we make no adjustments to these expenses. Therefore, the amounts we report for these expenses in the income statement must equal the amount of cash we paid for these items.

Let's check our calculation by recording the payment for operating expenses during the year:

	Debit	Credit	A = L + SE
Operating Expenses (from the income statement).....................	**286,000**		−286,000 Exp↑
Prepaid Rent (= $4,000 − $2,000)...	**2,000**		+2,000
Cash (to balance)...		**288,000**	−288,000
(*Pay operating expenses*)			

Depreciation expense and loss on sale of land. The next expense listed in the income statement is depreciation expense of $9,000. Depreciation expense has no effect on cash flows. It is merely an allocation in the current period of a prior cash expenditure (to acquire the depreciable asset). Therefore, unlike the other expenses to this point, depreciation is *not* reported on the statement of cash flows under the direct method.

Similar to depreciation expense, the loss on sale of land is *not* reported because it, too, has no effect on *operating* cash flows. Additional-information item (2) in Illustration 11–26 indicates that land we originally purchased at a cost of $10,000 was sold for $6,000, resulting in a loss on the sale of land of $4,000. E-Games records the sale as:

	Debit	Credit	A = L + SE
Cash (selling price)	**6,000**		+6,000
Loss (difference)	**4,000**		−4,000 Exp↑
Land (cost)		**10,000**	−10,000
(*Receive cash from sale of land*)			

As we discussed previously, we report the $6,000 cash inflow as an investing activity, because both investing in land and later selling it are considered investing activities. The original cost of the land, and thus the loss, has no effect on operating cash flows.

Cash paid for interest. E-Games next reports interest expense of $5,000 in the income statement. The related current asset or current liability in the balance sheet is interest payable. If interest payable increases, interest expense exceeds cash paid for interest. Interest payable increases $1,000. As shown in Illustration 11–31, we deduct the increase in interest payable from interest expense to arrive at cash paid for interest.

Interest expense	$ 5,000
− Increase in interest payable	(1,000)
= Cash paid for interest	$4,000

ILLUSTRATION 11–31

Cash Paid for Interest

We can check our calculation by recording the payment for interest during the year:

	Debit	Credit	A = L + SE
Interest Expense (from income statement).................................	**5,000**		−5,000 Exp↑
Interest Payable (= $2,000 − $1,000)......................................		**1,000**	+1,000
Cash (to balance)...		**4,000**	−4,000
(*Pay interest*)			

Cash paid for income taxes. The final item reported in the income statement is income tax expense of $16,000. The related current asset or current liability in the balance sheet is income tax payable. Income tax payable decreased $2,000. This means that E-Games paid $2,000 more than the income tax expense recorded. As shown in Illustration 11–32, we add the decrease in income tax payable to income tax expense to calculate cash paid for income taxes.

ILLUSTRATION 11–32	Income tax expense $\qquad$ $ 16,000
Cash Paid for Income Taxes	+ Decrease in income tax payable $\qquad$ 2,000
	= Cash paid for income taxes $\qquad$ $18,000

Recording the payment of taxes during the year confirms this:

A = L + SE		Debit	Credit
−16,000 Exp	Income Tax Expense (from income statement)...........................	16,000	
−2,000	Income Tax Payable (= $7,000 − $5,000)...................................	2,000	
−18,000	Cash (to balance)...		18,000
	(Pay income taxes)		

Illustration 11–33 shows the completed operating activities section using the direct method.

ILLUSTRATION 11–33	
Operating Activities Using the Direct Method	

E-GAMES, INC. Statement of Cash Flows (partial)—Direct Method	
Cash Flows from Operating Activities	
Cash received from customers	$1,005,000
Cash paid to suppliers	(645,000)
Cash paid for operating expenses	(288,000)
Cash paid for interest	(4,000)
Cash paid for income taxes	(18,000)
Net cash flows from operating activities	$50,000

Note that the net cash flows from operating activities is $50,000—**the same amount we calculated earlier in Illustration 11–15 using the indirect method.** This will always be the case. The indirect method begins with net income, whereas the direct method considers each of the individual accounts that make up net income. Both methods take into consideration the *same changes* in current asset and current liability accounts.

KEY POINT

The indirect method and direct method differ only in the presentation of operating activities. In the indirect method, we start with net income and make adjustments to arrive at net cash flows from operating activities. In the direct method, we convert each individual line item in the income statement to its cash basis and directly list the cash inflows and cash outflows from operating activities. The net cash flows from operating activities are *the same under both methods.*

The income statement, balance sheet, and additional information from the accounting records of E-Phones, Inc., are provided below.

Let's Review

E-PHONES, INC.
Income Statement
For the year ended December 31, 2012

Revenues		$2,200,000
Gain on sale of investment		5,000
Expenses:		
Cost of goods sold	$1,100,000	
Operating expenses	450,000	
Depreciation expense	25,000	
Income tax expense	217,000	
Total expenses		1,792,000
Net income		$ 413,000

E-PHONES, INC.
Balance Sheet
December 31, 2012 and 2011

	2012	2011	Increase (I) or Decrease (D)
Assets			
Current assets:			
Cash	$ 32,000	$ 48,000	$ 16,000 (D)
Accounts receivable	32,000	40,000	8,000 (D)
Inventory	100,000	70,000	30,000 (I)
Long-term assets:			
Investments	0	50,000	50,000 (D)
Land	280,000	180,000	100,000 (I)
Equipment	200,000	140,000	60,000 (I)
Accumulated depreciation	(53,000)	(28,000)	25,000 (I)
Total assets	$591,000	$500,000	
Liabilities and Stockholders' Equity			
Current liabilities:			
Accounts payable	$ 52,000	$ 62,000	$ 10,000 (D)
Income tax payable	55,000	12,000	43,000 (I)
Long-term liabilities:			
Bonds payable	0	200,000	200,000 (D)
Stockholders' equity:			
Common stock	200,000	100,000	100,000 (I)
Retained earnings	284,000	126,000	158,000 (I)
Total liabilities and stockholders' equity	$591,000	$500,000	

Additional Information for 2012:
1. Sold an investment in stock costing $50,000 for $55,000, resulting in a $5,000 gain on sale of investment.
2. Purchased $100,000 in land issuing $100,000 of common stock as payment. No cash was exchanged in the transaction.
3. Purchased equipment for $60,000 cash.
4. Retired the $200,000 balance in bonds payable at the beginning of the year.
5. Declared and paid a cash dividend of $255,000.

536   CHAPTER 11   Statement of Cash Flows

Required:

Prepare the statement of cash flows using the *direct method* for reporting operating activities. Disclose any noncash transactions in a note to the statement of cash flows.

Solution:

E-PHONES, INC.
Statement of Cash Flows—Direct Method
For the year ended December 31, 2012

Cash Flows from Operating Activities		
Cash received from customers	$2,208,000	
Cash paid to suppliers	(1,140,000)	
Cash paid for operating expenses	(450,000)	
Cash paid for income taxes	(174,000)	
Net cash flows from operating activities		$444,000
Cash Flows from Investing Activities		
Sale of investment	55,000	
Purchase of equipment	(60,000)	
Net cash flows from investing activities		(5,000)
Cash Flows from Financing Activities		
Retire bonds payable	(200,000)	
Payment of cash dividends	(255,000)	
Net cash flows from financing activities		(455,000)
Net increase (decrease) in cash		(16,000)
Cash at the beginning of the period		48,000
Cash at the end of the period		$ 32,000
Note: Noncash Activities		
Purchased land by issuing common stock		$100,000

Here are the supporting calculations for cash flows from operating activities under the direct method:

Revenues	$ 2,200,000
+ Decrease in accounts receivable	8,000
= Cash received from customers	$2,208,000
Cost of goods sold	$ 1,100,000
+ Increase in inventory	30,000
= Purchases	1,130,000
+ Decrease in accounts payable	10,000
= Cash paid to suppliers	$1,140,000
Cash paid for operating expenses	$ 450,000
Income tax expense	$ 217,000
− Increase in income tax payable	(43,000)
= Cash paid for income taxes	$ 174,000

Suggested Homework:
BE11-12, BE11-13;
E11-13, E11-14;
P11-6A&B; P11-7A&B

KEY POINTS BY LEARNING OBJECTIVE

LO1 Classify cash transactions as operating, investing, or financing activities.

Operating activities relate to income statement items. Investing activities primarily involve changes in long-term assets. Financing activities primarily involve changes in long-term liabilities and stockholders' equity.

Companies choose between the indirect method and direct method in reporting operating activities in the statement of cash flows. The indirect method is less costly to prepare, and most companies use it. The direct method more logically presents the cash inflows and outflows from operations. The investing and financing sections of the statement of cash flows are identical under both methods.

LO2 Prepare the operating activities section of the statement of cash flows using the indirect method.

Using the indirect method, we start with net income and adjust this number for (a) revenue and expense items that do not represent cash and (b) changes in current assets and current liabilities.

LO3 Prepare the investing activities section and the financing activities section of the statement of cash flows.

Most investing activities can be explained by changes in long-term asset accounts. Most

financing activities can be explained by changes in long-term liability and stockholders' equity accounts.

Analysis

LO4 Perform financial analysis using the statement of cash flows.

Cash return on assets indicates the amount of operating cash flow generated for each dollar invested in assets. We can separate cash return on assets to two components—cash flow to sales and asset turnover—to examine two important business strategies.

Appendix

LO5 Prepare the operating activities section of the statement of cash flows using the direct method.

The indirect method and direct method differ only in the presentation of operating activities. In the indirect method, we start with net income and make adjustments to arrive at net cash flows from operating activities. In the direct method, we convert each individual line item in the income statement to its cash basis and directly list the cash inflows and cash outflows from operating activities. The net cash flows from operating activities are *the same* under both methods.

GLOSSARY

Asset turnover: Sales revenue divided by average total assets; measures the sales revenue generated per dollar of assets. **p. 527**

Cash flow to sales: Net cash flows from operating activities divided by sales revenue; measures the operating cash flow generated per dollar of sales. **p. 527**

Cash return on assets: Net cash flows from operating activities divided by average total assets; measures the operating cash flow generated per dollar of assets. **p. 526**

Direct method: Adjusts the items on the income statement to directly show the cash inflows and outflows from operations, such as cash received from customers and cash paid for inventory, salaries, rent, interest, and taxes. **p. 512**

Financing activities: Includes cash transactions resulting from the external financing of a business. **p. 509**

Indirect method: Begins with net income and then lists adjustments to net income in order to arrive at operating cash flows. **p. 512**

Investing activities: Includes cash transactions involving the purchase and sale of long-term assets and current investments. **p. 508**

Noncash activities: Significant investing and financing activities that do not affect cash. **p. 511**

Operating activities: Includes cash receipts and cash payments for transactions relating to revenue and expense activities. **p. 508**

Statement of cash flows: A summary of cash inflows and cash outflows during the reporting period sorted by operating, investing, and financing activities. **p. 508**

SELF-STUDY QUESTIONS

■ LO1   1. The purchase of a long-term asset is classified in the statement of cash flows as a(n):
a. Operating activity.
b. Investing activity.
c. Financing activity.
d. Noncash activity.

■ LO1   2. The issuance of common stock is classified in the statement of cash flows as a(n):
a. Operating activity.
b. Investing activity.
c. Financing activity.
d. Noncash activity.

■ LO1   3. The payment of bonds payable is classified in the statement of cash flows as a(n):
a. Operating activity.
b. Investing activity.
c. Financing activity.
d. Noncash activity.

■ LO1   4. Which of the following is an example of a noncash activity?
a. Sale of land for more than its cost.
b. Purchase of land by issuing common stock.
c. Sale of land for less than its cost.
d. Purchase of land using cash proceeds from issuance of common stock.

■ LO2   5. We can identify operating activities from income statement information and changes in:
a. Current asset and current liability accounts.
b. Long-term asset accounts.
c. Long-term liability accounts.
d. Stockholders' equity accounts.

■ LO2   6. The indirect and direct methods:
a. Are used by companies about equally in actual practice.
b. Affect the presentations of operating, investing, and financing activities.
c. Arrive at different amounts for net cash flows from operating activities.
d. Are two allowable methods to present operating activities in the statement of cash flows.

■ LO3   7. Which of the following is an example of a cash inflow from an investing activity?
a. Receipt of cash from the issuance of common stock.
b. Receipt of cash from the sale of equipment.
c. Receipt of cash from the issuance of a note payable.
d. Receipt of cash from the sale of inventory.

■ LO3   8. Which of the following is an example of a cash outflow from a financing activity?
a. Payment of interest.
b. Purchase of an intangible asset.
c. Payment of cash dividends.
d. Purchase of land.

■ LO4   9. We can separate cash return on assets into:
a. Cash flow to sales and return on assets.
b. Profit margin and asset turnover.
c. Cash flow to sales and profit margin.
d. Cash flow to sales and asset turnover.

10. Which of the following items do we report in the statement of cash flows using the direct method?
    ■ LO5
    a. Depreciation expense.
    b. Gain on sale of an asset.
    c. Cash paid to suppliers.
    d. Loss on sale of an asset.

Note: For answers, see the last page of the chapter.

Check out
www.mhhe.com/succeed
for more multiple-choice
questions.

REVIEW QUESTIONS

1. Identify and briefly describe the three categories of cash flows reported in the statement of cash flows.
    ■ LO1

2. Changes in current assets and current liabilities are used in determining net cash flows from operating activities. Changes in which balance sheet accounts are used in determining net cash flows from investing activities? Changes in which balance sheet accounts are used in determining net cash flows from financing activities?
    ■ LO1

3. Explain what we mean by noncash activities and provide an example.
    ■ LO1

4. Why is it necessary to use an income statement, balance sheet, and additional information to prepare a statement of cash flows?
    ■ LO1

5. Describe the basic format used in preparing a statement of cash flows, including the heading, the three major categories, and what is included in the last three lines of the statement.
    ■ LO1

6. Briefly describe the four steps outlined in the text for preparing a statement of cash flows.
    ■ LO1

7. Distinguish between the indirect method and the direct method for reporting net cash flows from operating activities. Which method is more common in practice? Which method provides a more logical presentation of cash flows?
    ■ LO1

8. Describe the most common adjustments we use to convert net income to net cash flows from operations under the indirect method.
    ■ LO2

9. The executives at Peach, Inc., are confused. The company reports a net loss of $200,000, and yet its net cash flow from operating activities increased $300,000 during the same period. Is this possible? Explain.
    ■ LO2

10. Explain how we report depreciation expense in the statement of cash flows using the indirect method. Why do we report it this way?
    ■ LO2

11. Describe how we report a gain or loss on the sale of an asset in the statement of cash flows using the indirect method. Why do we report it this way?
    ■ LO2

12. Indicate whether we add or subtract each of the following items from net income in preparing the statement of cash flows using the indirect method: (a) an increase in current assets, (b) a decrease in current assets, (c) an increase in current liabilities, and (d) a decrease in current liabilities.
    ■ LO2

13. How does an increase in accounts receivable affect net income in relation to operating cash flows? Why? How does a decrease in accounts receivable affect net income in relation to operating cash flows? Why?
    ■ LO2

14. Bell Corporation purchases land by issuing its own common stock. How do we report this transaction, if at all?
    ■ LO3

540   CHAPTER 11   Statement of Cash Flows

■ LO2, 3   15. A $10,000 investment on the books of a company is sold for $9,000. Under the indirect method, how does this transaction affect operating, investing, and financing activities?

■ LO3   16. Provide three examples of financing activities reported in the statement of cash flows.

■ LO4   17. Explain the difference between the calculation of return on assets and cash return on assets. How can cash-based ratios supplement the analysis of ratios based on income statement and balance sheet information?

■ LO4   18. Describe the two primary strategies firms use to increase cash return on assets. Which strategy does Apple use, and which does Dell use?

■ LO5   19. What are the primary cash inflows and cash outflows under the direct method for determining net cash flows from operating activities?

■ LO5   20. Why do we exclude depreciation expense and the gain or loss on sale of an asset from the operating activities section of the statement of cash flows under the direct method?

BRIEF EXERCISES

Determine proper classification (LO1)
BE11–1 Classify each of the following items as an operating, investing, or financing activity.
1. Dividends paid.
2. Repayment of notes payable.
3. Payment for inventory.
4. Purchase of equipment.
5. Interest paid.

Determine proper classification (LO1)
BE11–2 The following selected transactions occur during the first year of operations. Determine how each should be reported in the statement of cash flows.
1. Issued one million shares of common stock at $20 per share.
2. Paid $75,000 to suppliers for inventory.
3. Paid a dividend of $1 per share to common stockholders.
4. Loaned $50,000 to an employee and accepted a note receivable.

Understand the basic format for the statement of cash flows (LO2)
BE11–3 Place the following items in the correct order as they would appear in the statement of cash flows.
1. Financing activities.
2. Net increase (decrease) in cash.
3. Operating activities.
4. Beginning cash balance.
5. Ending cash balance.
6. Investing activities.

Calculate operating activities—indirect method (LO2)
BE11–4 Laser World reports net income of $550,000. Depreciation expense is $40,000, accounts receivable increases $10,000, and accounts payable decreases $20,000. Calculate net cash flows from operating activities using the indirect method.

Calculate operating activities—indirect method (LO2)
BE11–5 Macrosoft Company reports net income of $65,000. The accounting records reveal depreciation expense of $80,000 as well as increases in prepaid rent, accounts payable, and income tax payable of $60,000, $12,000, and $18,000, respectively. Prepare the operating activities section of Macrosoft's statement of cash flows using the indirect method.

Calculate operating activities—indirect method (LO2)
BE11–6 Hi-Tech, Inc., reports net income of $60 million. Included in that number are depreciation expense of $5 million and a loss on the sale of equipment of $1 million. Records reveal increases in accounts receivable, accounts payable, and inventory of

$2 million, $3 million, and $4 million, respectively. What are Hi-Tech's net cash flows from operating activities?

BE11–7 Engineering Wonders reports net income of $60 million. Included in that number is building depreciation expense of $5 million and a gain on the sale of land of $1 million. Records reveal decreases in accounts receivable, accounts payable, and inventory of $2 million, $3 million, and $4 million, respectively. What are Engineering Wonders' net cash flows from operating activities?

Calculate operating activities—indirect method (LO2)

BE11–8 Creative Sound Systems sold investments, land, and its own common stock for $30 million, $15 million, and $40 million, respectively. Creative Sound Systems also purchased treasury stock, equipment, and a patent for $21 million, $25 million, and $12 million, respectively. What amount should the company report as net cash flows from investing activities?

Calculate net cash flows from investing activities (LO3)

BE11–9 Refer to the situation described in BE11–8. What amount should Creative Sound Systems report as net cash flows from financing activities?

Calculate net cash flows from financing activities (LO3)

BE11–10 The balance sheet of Cranium Gaming reports total assets of $400,000 and $700,000 at the beginning and end of the year, respectively. Sales revenues are $1.1 million, net income is $65,000, and operating cash flows are $55,000. Calculate the cash return on assets, cash flow to sales, and asset turnover for Cranium Gaming.

Calculate the cash return on assets (LO4)

BE11–11 The balance sheet of Innovative Products reports total assets of $520,000 and $720,000 at the beginning and end of the year, respectively. The cash return on assets for the year is 20%. Calculate Innovative Products' net cash flows from operating activities (operating cash flows) for the year.

Calculate the net cash flows from operating activities (LO4)

BE11–12 Video Shack's accounts receivable decreases during the year by $8 million. What is the amount of cash received from customers during the reporting period if its sales are $63 million?

Determine cash received from customers (LO5)

BE11–13 Electronic Superstore's inventory increases during the year by $4 million, and its accounts payable to suppliers increases by $6 million during the same period. What is the amount of cash paid to suppliers of merchandise during the reporting period if its cost of goods sold is $35 million?

Determine cash paid to suppliers (LO5)

BE11–14 Wireless Solutions reports operating expenses of $885,000. Operating expenses include both rent expense and salaries expense. Prepaid rent increases during the year by $20,000 and salaries payable increases by $15,000. What is the cash paid for operating expenses during the year?

Determine cash paid for operating expenses (LO5)

BE11–15 Computer World reports income tax expense of $240,000. Income taxes payable at the beginning and end of the year are $55,000 and $65,000, respectively. What is the cash paid for income taxes during the year?

Determine cash paid for income taxes (LO5)

EXERCISES

E11–1 Match (by letter) the following items with the description or example that best fits. Each letter is used only once.

Match terms with their definitions (LO1, 2, 3, 4, 5)

Terms

_____ 1. Operating activities.
_____ 2. Investing activities.
_____ 3. Financing activities.
_____ 4. Noncash activities.
_____ 5. Indirect method.
_____ 6. Direct method.
_____ 7. Depreciation expense.
_____ 8. Cash return on assets.

542   CHAPTER 11   Statement of Cash Flows

Descriptions

a. Begins with net income and then lists adjustments to net income in order to arrive at operating cash flows.
b. Item included in net income, but excluded from net operating cash flows.
c. Net cash flows from operating activities divided by average total assets.
d. Cash transactions involving lenders and investors.
e. Cash transactions involving net income.
f. Cash transactions for the purchase and sale of long-term assets.
g. Purchase of long-term assets by issuing stock.
h. Shows the cash inflows and outflows from operations such as cash received from customers and cash paid for inventory, salaries, rent, interest, and taxes.

Determine proper classification (LO1)

E11–2 Discount Computers is in its second year of business providing computer repair services in the local community and reselling used computers on the Internet. The company is owned by 10 investors, each investing $100,000. Justin Lake was hired as president and CEO, with one stipulation: He would receive no salary unless the company achieved annual operating cash flows exceeding $200,000. If the $200,000 was achieved, Justin would receive a $100,000 bonus, and each of the 10 investors would receive a dividend of $10,000.

At the end of the year, Justin had Nicole Roberts, one of the business interns from the local college, calculate a preliminary statement of cash flows. Operating cash flows were $185,000. Justin carefully looked over the calculations that night and then met with Nicole in the morning. Justin starts out: "Nicole, you did an excellent job in preparing the statement of cash flows. The only change I could find is that we need to move the $25,000 increase in notes payable to the bank from financing activities to operating activities. We borrowed that money three months ago and plan to pay it back within a year. After you finish the changes, round up the rest of the interns. Lunch is on me."

Required:
Do you agree with the change recommended by Justin Lake? Is there anything unethical about his actions? What should Nicole do in this situation?

Determine proper classification (LO1)

E11–3 Analysis of an income statement, balance sheet, and additional information from the accounting records of Gadgets, Inc., reveals the following items.

1. Purchase of a patent.
2. Depreciation expense.
3. Decrease in accounts receivable.
4. Issuance of a note payable.
5. Increase in inventory.
6. Collection of notes receivable.
7. Purchase of equipment.
8. Exchange of long-term assets.
9. Decrease in accounts payable.
10. Payment of dividends.

Required:
Indicate in which section of the statement of cash flows each of these items would be reported: operating activities (indirect method), investing activities, financing activities, or a separate noncash activities note.

Determine proper classification (LO1)

E11–4 Wi-Fi, Inc., has the following selected transactions during the year.

1. Issues $20 million in bonds.
2. Purchases equipment for $80,000.
3. Pays a $20,000 account payable.
4. Collects a $15,000 account receivable.
5. Exchanges land for a new patent. Both are valued at $300,000.
6. Declares and pays a cash dividend of $100,000.
7. Loans $50,000 to a customer, accepting a note receivable.
8. Pays $75,000 to suppliers for inventory.

Required:

Indicate in which section of the statement of cash flows each of these items would be reported: operating activities (indirect method), investing activities, financing activities, or a separate noncash activities note.

E11–5 Ernie's Electronics had the following transactions with Bert's Bargain House:

1. Ernie sold Bert land, originally purchased for $180,000, at a sales price of $195,000, resulting in a gain on sale of land of $15,000.
2. Ernie borrowed $100,000 from Bert, signing a three-year note payable.
3. Ernie purchased $1 million in common stock in Bert's Bargain House through a private placement.
4. Ernie received a dividend of $40,000 from the common stock investment in Bert's Bargain House.

Determine proper classification **(LO1)**

Flip Side of E11–6

Required:

Analyze each of the four transactions from the perspective of Ernie's Electronics. Indicate in which section of the statement of cash flows each of these items would be reported for Ernie's Electronics: operating activities (indirect method), investing activities, financing activities, or a separate noncash activities note.

E11–6 Refer to the transactions between Ernie's Electronics and Bert's Bargain House recorded in E11–5.

Determine proper classification **(LO1)**

Flip Side of E11–5

Required:

Analyze each of the four transactions from the perspective of Bert's Bargain House. Indicate in which section of the statement of cash flows each of these items would be reported for Bert's Bargain House: operating activities (indirect method), investing activities, financing activities, or a separate noncash activities note.

E11–7 Technology Solutions' format for the statement of cash flows was corrupted by a computer virus, as follows:

Prepare the basic format for the statement of cash flows **(LO2, 3)**

TECHNOLOGY SOLUTIONS
Statement of Cash Flows
For the year ended December 31, 2012

Cash at the beginning of the period	$$$
Cash at the end of the period	$$$
Net increase (decrease) in cash	$$$
Cash Flows from Financing Activities	
List of cash inflows and outflows from financing activities	
Net cash flows from financing activities	$$$
Noncash Activities	
List of noncash transactions	$$$
Cash Flows from Investing Activities	
List of cash inflows and outflows from investing activities	
Net cash flows from investing activities	$$$
Cash Flows from Operating Activities	
List of items adjusting net income to operating cash flows	
Adjustments	
Net income	
Net cash flows from operating activities	$$$

Required:

Prepare a correct format for Technology Solutions to use in preparing the statement of cash flows.

544   CHAPTER 11   Statement of Cash Flows

Calculate operating
activities—indirect
method (LO2)

E11–8 Hardware Suppliers reports net income of $155,000. Included in net income is a gain on the sale of land of $15,000. A comparison of this year's and last year's balance sheets reveals an increase in accounts receivable of $25,000, an increase in inventory of $15,000, and a decrease in accounts payable of $45,000.

Required:
Prepare the operating activities section of the statement of cash flows using the indirect method. Do you see a pattern in Hardware Suppliers' adjustments to net income to arrive at operating cash flows? What might this imply?

Calculate operating
activities—indirect
method (LO2)

E11–9 Software Distributors reports net income of $55,000. Included in that number is depreciation expense of $10,000 and a loss on the sale of land of $5,000. A comparison of this year's and last year's balance sheets reveals a decrease in accounts receivable of $25,000, a decrease in inventory of $15,000, and an increase in accounts payable of $45,000.

Required:
Prepare the operating activities section of the statement of cash flows using the indirect method. Do you see a pattern in Software Distributors' adjustments to net income to arrive at operating cash flows? What might this imply?

Prepare a statement
of cash flows—indirect
method (LO2, 3)

E11–10 The balance sheet for Plasma Screens Corporation along with additional information is provided below:

PLASMA SCREENS CORPORATION
Balance Sheet
December 31, 2012 and 2011

	2012	2011
Assets		
Current assets:		
Cash	$ 112,000	$ 120,000
Accounts receivable	78,000	92,000
Inventory	95,000	80,000
Prepaid rent	4,000	2,000
Long-term assets:		
Land	480,000	480,000
Equipment	790,000	670,000
Accumulated depreciation	(428,000)	(268,000)
Total assets	$1,131,000	$1,176,000
Liabilities and Stockholders' Equity		
Current liabilities:		
Accounts payable	$ 99,000	$ 85,000
Interest payable	6,000	12,000
Income tax payable	8,000	5,000
Long-term liabilities:		
Notes payable	100,000	200,000
Stockholders' equity:		
Common stock	700,000	700,000
Retained earnings	218,000	174,000
Total liabilities and stockholders' equity	$1,131,000	$1,176,000

Additional Information for 2012:
1. Net income is $69,000.
2. The company purchases $120,000 in equipment.
3. Depreciation expense is $160,000.
4. The company repays $100,000 in notes payable.
5. The company declares and pays a cash dividend of $25,000.

Required:

Prepare the statement of cash flows using the indirect method.

E11–11 Portions of the financial statements for Peach Computer are provided below.

Calculate operating activities—indirect method **(LO2)**

PEACH COMPUTER
Income Statement
For the year ended December 31, 2012

Revenues		$1,800,000
Expenses:		
Cost of goods sold	$1,050,000	
Operating expenses	560,000	
Depreciation expense	50,000	
Income tax expense	40,000	
Total expenses		1,700,000
Net income		$ 100,000

PEACH COMPUTER
Selected Balance Sheet Data
December 31

	2012	2011	Increase (I) or Decrease (D)
Cash	$102,000	$85,000	$17,000 (I)
Accounts receivable	45,000	49,000	4,000 (D)
Inventory	75,000	55,000	20,000 (I)
Prepaid rent	3,000	5,000	2,000 (D)
Accounts payable	45,000	37,000	8,000 (I)
Income tax payable	5,000	10,000	5,000 (D)

Required:

Prepare the operating activities section of the statement of cash flows for Peach Computer using the *indirect* method.

E11–12 Google has the following selected data ($ in millions):

Calculate financial ratios **(LO4)**

	2009	2008
Net sales	$23,651	$21,796
Net income	6,520	4,227
Operating cash flows	9,316	7,853
Total assets	40,497	31,768

Required:

1. Calculate the return on assets. Compare it with the amounts calculated for **Apple** and **Dell** in Illustration 11–21.
2. Calculate the cash return on assets. Compare it with the amounts calculated for Apple and Dell in Illustration 11–22.
3. Calculate the cash flow to sales ratio and the asset turnover ratio. Compare the ratios with those calculated for Apple and Dell in Illustrations 11–24 and 11–25. Is Google's business strategy closer to Apple's or to Dell's?

E11–13 Refer to the information provided for Peach Computer in E11–11.

Calculate operating activities—direct method **(LO5)**

Required:

Prepare the operating activities section of the statement of cash flows for Peach Computer using the *direct* method.

Calculate operating activities—direct method (LO5)

E11–14 Mega Screens, Inc., reports sales revenue of $2,700,000, cost of goods sold of $1,500,000, and income tax expense of $140,000 for the year ended December 31, 2012. Selected balance sheet accounts are as follows:

MEGA SCREENS, INC. Selected Balance Sheet Data December 31			
	2012	**2011**	**Increase (I) or Decrease (D)**
Cash	$145,000	$185,000	$40,000 (D)
Accounts receivable	275,000	225,000	50,000 (I)
Inventory	120,000	155,000	35,000 (D)
Accounts payable	115,000	127,000	12,000 (D)
Income tax payable	20,000	15,000	5,000 (I)

Required:
Calculate cash received from customers, cash paid to suppliers, and cash paid for income taxes.

Calculate operating activities—direct method (LO5)

E11–15 The income statement for **Hewlett-Packard** reports revenues of $91,658 million and cost of goods sold of $69,178 million. An examination of balance sheet amounts indicates accounts receivable increased $1,723 million, inventory increased $873 million, and accounts payable to suppliers decreased $1,957 million.

Required:
Using the direct method, calculate (1) cash received from customers and (2) cash paid to suppliers.

*For additional exercises, visit **www.mhhe.com/succeed** for Exercises: Set B.*

PROBLEMS: SET A

Determine proper classification (LO1)

P11–1A Listed below are several transactions. For each transaction, indicate by letter whether the cash effect of each transaction is reported in a statement of cash flows as an operating (O), investing (I), financing (F), or noncash (NC) activity. Also, indicate whether the transaction is a cash inflow (CI) or cash outflow (CO), or has no effect on cash (NE). The first answer is provided as an example.

Transaction	Type of Activity	Cash Inflow or Outflow
1. *Payment of employee salaries.*	O	CO
2. Sale of land for cash.		
3. Purchase of rent in advance.		
4. Collection of an account receivable.		
5. Issuance of common stock.		
6. Purchase of inventory.		
7. Collection of notes receivable.		
8. Payment of income taxes.		
9. Sale of equipment for a note receivable.		
10. Issuance of bonds.		
11. Loan to another firm.		
12. Payment of a long-term note payable.		
13. Purchase of treasury stock.		
14. Payment of an account payable.		
15. Sale of equipment for cash.		

P11–2A Seth Erkenbeck, a recent college graduate, has just completed the basic format to be used in preparing the statement of cash flows (indirect method) for ATM Software Developers. All amounts are in thousands (000s).

Basic format for the statement of cash flows (LO2, 3)

ATM SOFTWARE DEVELOPERS Statement of Cash Flows For the year ended December 31, 2012	
Cash Flows from Operating Activities	
Net income	$
Adjustments for noncash effects:	
Net cash flows from operating activities	_____
Cash Flows from Investing Activities	
Net cash flows from investing activities	_____
Cash Flows from Financing Activities	
Net cash flows from financing activities	_____
Net increase (decrease) in cash	$2,565
Cash at the beginning of the period	7,410
Cash at the end of the period	$9,975

Listed below in random order are line items to be included in the statement of cash flows.

Cash received from the sale of land	$ 8,550
Issuance of common stock	12,825
Depreciation expense	5,415
Increase in accounts receivable	3,990
Decrease in accounts payable	1,710
Issuance of long-term notes payable	16,245
Purchase of equipment	39,615
Decrease in inventory	1,425
Decrease in prepaid rent	855
Payment of dividends	6,270
Net income	11,400
Purchase of treasury stock	2,565

Required:

Prepare the statement of cash flows for ATM Software Developers using the *indirect* method.

P11–3A Portions of the financial statements for Alliance Technologies are provided below.

Calculate operating activities—indirect method (LO2)

ALLIANCE TECHNOLOGIES Income Statement For the year ended December 31, 2012		
Revenues		$305,000
Expenses:		
Cost of goods sold	$185,000	
Operating expenses	60,000	
Depreciation expense	16,000	
Income tax expense	22,000	
Total expenses		283,000
Net income		$ 22,000

ALLIANCE TECHNOLOGIES
Selected Balance Sheet Data
December 31, 2012, compared to December 31, 2011

Decrease in accounts receivable	$ 6,000
Increase in inventory	13,000
Decrease in prepaid rent	9,000
Increase in operating expenses payable	5,000
Decrease in accounts payable	8,000
Increase in income tax payable	20,000

Required:

Prepare the operating activities section of the statement of cash flows for Alliance Technologies using the *indirect* method.

Prepare a statement of cash flows—indirect method (LO2, 3)

P11–4A The income statement, balance sheet, and additional information for Video Phones, Inc., are provided.

VIDEO PHONES, INC.
Income Statement
For the year ended December 31, 2012

Revenues		$3,036,000
Expenses:		
Cost of goods sold	$1,950,000	
Operating expenses	858,000	
Depreciation expense	27,000	
Loss on sale of land	8,000	
Interest expense	15,000	
Income tax expense	48,000	
Total expenses		2,906,000
Net income		$ 130,000

VIDEO PHONES, INC.
Balance Sheet
December 31

	2012	2011
Assets		
Current assets:		
Cash	$186,000	$144,000
Accounts receivable	81,000	60,000
Inventory	105,000	135,000
Prepaid rent	12,000	6,000
Long-term assets:		
Investments	105,000	0
Land	210,000	240,000
Equipment	270,000	210,000
Accumulated depreciation	(69,000)	(42,000)
Total assets	$900,000	$753,000
Liabilities and Stockholders' Equity		
Current liabilities:		
Accounts payable	$ 66,000	$ 81,000
Interest payable	6,000	10,000
Income tax payable	15,000	14,000
Long-term liabilities:		
Notes payable	285,000	225,000
Stockholders' equity:		
Common stock	300,000	300,000
Retained earnings	228,000	123,000
Total liabilities and stockholders' equity	$900,000	$753,000

Additional Information for 2012:

1. Purchase investment in bonds for $105,000.
2. Sell land costing $30,000 for only $22,000, resulting in an $8,000 loss on sale of land.
3. Purchase $60,000 in equipment by borrowing $60,000 with a note payable due in three years. No cash is exchanged in the transaction.
4. Declare and pay a cash dividend of $25,000.

Required:

Prepare the statement of cash flows using the *indirect* method. Disclose any noncash transactions in an accompanying note.

P11–5A Google and **Yahoo** are competitors in the Internet search engine business. Selected financial data for Google and Yahoo are as follows:

Calculate and analyze ratios (LO4)

($ in millions)	2009	2008
Google		
Net sales	$23,651	$21,796
Net income	6,520	4,227
Operating cash flows	9,316	7,853
Total assets	40,497	31,768
Yahoo		
Net sales	$ 6,460	$ 7,209
Net income	598	424
Operating cash flows	1,310	1,880
Total assets	14,936	13,690

Required:

1. Calculate the return on assets for both companies. Compare the ratios with those calculated for **Apple** and **Dell** in Illustration 11–21.
2. Calculate the cash return on assets for both companies. Compare the ratios with those calculated for Apple and Dell in Illustration 11–22.
3. Calculate the cash flow to sales ratio and the asset turnover ratio for both companies. Compare the ratios with those calculated for Apple and Dell in Illustrations 11–24 and 11–25. Are Google's and Yahoo's business strategies closer to Apple's or to Dell's?

P11–6A Refer to the information provided in P11–3A for Alliance Technologies.

Calculate operating activities—direct method (LO5)

Required:

Prepare the operating activities section of the statement of cash flows for Alliance Technologies using the *direct* method.

P11–7A Data for Video Phones, Inc., is provided in P11–4A.

Calculate operating activities—direct method (LO5)

Required:

Prepare the statement of cash flows for Video Phones, Inc., using the *direct* method. Disclose any noncash transactions in an accompanying note.

P11–8A Cash flows from operating activities for both the indirect and direct methods are presented for Reverse Logic. All amounts are in thousands (000s).

Prepare an income statement using operating cash flow information—indirect and direct methods (LO2, 5)

Cash Flows from Operating Activities (Indirect method)	
Net income	$164
Adjustments for noncash effects:	
Depreciation expense	52
Changes in current assets and current liabilities:	
Increase in accounts receivable	(28)
Decrease in inventory	40
Increase in prepaid rent	(4)
Decrease in accounts payable	(16)
Decrease in income tax payable	(8)
Net cash flows from operating activities	$200

(continued)

550   CHAPTER 11   Statement of Cash Flows

(concluded)   **Cash Flows from Operating Activities (Direct method)**

Cash received from customers	$ 4,020
Cash paid to suppliers	(2,580)
Cash paid for operating expenses	(1,152)
Cash paid for income taxes	(88)
Net cash flows from operating activities	$200

Required:

Complete the following income statement for Reverse Logic. Assume all accounts payable are to suppliers.

REVERSE LOGIC
Income Statement
For the year ended December 31, 2012

Revenues		$?
Expenses:		
Cost of goods sold	$?	
Operating expenses	?	
Depreciation expense	52	
Income tax expense	?	
Total expenses		?
Net income		$164

[Hint: Use the following calculations and work backwards from bottom (in red) to top for each item.]

   Revenues
± Change in accounts receivable   _____
= Cash received from customers   =========

   Cost of goods sold
± Change in inventory   _____
= Purchases
± Change in accounts payable   _____
= Cash paid to suppliers   =========

   Operating expenses
± Change in prepaid rent   _____
= Cash paid for operating expenses   =========

   Income tax expense
± Change in income tax payable   _____
= Cash paid for income taxes   =========

PROBLEMS: SET B

Determine proper classification **(LO1)**

P11–1B Listed below are several transactions. For each transaction, indicate by letter whether the cash effect of each transaction is reported in a statement of cash flows as an operating (O), investing (I), financing (F), or noncash (NC) activity. Also, indicate whether the transaction is a cash inflow (CI) or cash outflow (CO), or has no effect on cash (NE). The first answer is provided as an example.

Transaction	Type of Activity	Cash Inflow or Outflow
1. *Issuance of common stock.*	*F*	*CI*
2. Sale of land for cash.		
3. Purchase of treasury stock.		
4. Collection of an account receivable.		
5. Issuance of a note payable.		
6. Purchase of inventory.		
7. Repayment of a note payable.		
8. Payment of employee salaries.		
9. Sale of equipment for a note receivable.		
10. Issuance of bonds.		
11. Investment in bonds.		
12. Payment of interest on bonds payable.		
13. Payment of a cash dividend.		
14. Purchase of a building.		
15. Collection of a note receivable.		

P11–2B Natalie Daniels has completed the basic format to be used in preparing the statement of cash flows (indirect method) for CPU Hardware Designers. All amounts are in thousands (000s).

Basic format for the statement of cash flows **(LO2, 3)**

CPU HARDWARE DESIGNERS
Statement of Cash Flows
For the year ended December 31, 2012

Cash Flows from Operating Activities
Net income
Adjustments for noncash effects:

Net cash flows from operating activities _____

Cash Flows from Investing Activities

Net cash flows from investing activities _____

Cash Flows from Financing Activities

Net cash flows from financing activities _____

Net increase (decrease) in cash	$(50,000)
Cash at the beginning of the period	80,000
Cash at the end of the period	$ 30,000

Below, in random order, are line items to be included in the statement of cash flows.

Cash received from the sale of land	$ 3,000
Issuance of common stock	250,000
Depreciation expense	20,000
Increase in accounts receivable	60,000
Increase in accounts payable	10,000
Loss on sale of land	7,000
Purchase of equipment	220,000
Increase in inventory	30,000
Increase in prepaid rent	10,000
Payment of dividends	40,000
Net income	70,000
Repayment of notes payable	50,000

Required:
Prepare the statement of cash flows for CPU Hardware Designers using the *indirect* method.

Calculate operating activities—indirect method **(LO2)**

P11–3B Portions of the financial statements for Software Associates are provided below.

SOFTWARE ASSOCIATES		
Income Statement		
For the year ended December 31, 2012		
Revenues		$610,000
Expenses:		
Cost of goods sold	$370,000	
Operating expenses	120,000	
Depreciation expense	32,000	
Income tax expense	44,000	
Total expenses		566,000
Net income		$ 44,000

SOFTWARE ASSOCIATES	
Selected Balance Sheet Data	
December 31, 2012, compared to December 31, 2011	
Decrease in accounts receivable	$ 9,000
Decrease in inventory	12,000
Increase in prepaid rent	2,000
Decrease in operating expenses payable	3,000
Increase in accounts payable	6,000
Increase in income tax payable	7,000

Required:
Prepare the operating activities section of the statement of cash flows for Software Associates using the *indirect* method.

Prepare a statement of cash flows—indirect method **(LO2, 3)**

P11–4B The income statement, balance sheet, and additional information for Virtual Gaming Systems are provided.

VIRTUAL GAMING SYSTEMS		
Income Statement		
For the year ended December 31, 2012		
Revenues		$2,500,000
Gain on sale of land		2,000
Total revenues		2,502,000
Expenses:		
Cost of goods sold	$1,600,000	
Operating expenses	605,000	
Depreciation expense	23,000	
Interest expense	24,000	
Income tax expense	70,000	
Total expenses		2,322,000
Net income		$ 180,000

VIRTUAL GAMING SYSTEMS
Balance Sheet
December 31

	2012	2011
Assets		
Current assets:		
Cash	$199,000	$144,000
Accounts receivable	75,000	90,000
Inventory	145,000	135,000
Prepaid rent	4,000	6,000
Long-term assets:		
Investments	185,000	100,000
Land	210,000	260,000
Equipment	230,000	210,000
Accumulated depreciation	(128,000)	(105,000)
Total assets	$920,000	$840,000
Liabilities and Stockholders' Equity		
Current liabilities:		
Accounts payable	$ 30,000	$ 88,000
Interest payable	4,000	3,000
Income tax payable	21,000	24,000
Long-term liabilities:		
Notes payable	245,000	225,000
Stockholders' equity:		
Common stock	350,000	300,000
Retained earnings	270,000	200,000
Total liabilities and stockholders' equity	$920,000	$840,000

Additional Information for 2012:

1. Purchase additional investment in stocks for $85,000.
2. Sell land costing $50,000 for $52,000, resulting in a $2,000 gain on sale of land.
3. Purchase $20,000 in equipment by borrowing $20,000 with a note payable due in three years. No cash is exchanged in the transaction.
4. Declare and pay a cash dividend of $110,000.
5. Issue common stock for $50,000.

Required:

Prepare the statement of cash flows using the *indirect* method. Disclose any noncash transactions in an accompanying note.

P11–5B **Hewlett-Packard** and **IBM** are close competitors in the sale of computer products and technology consulting. Selected financial data for Hewlett-Packard and IBM are as follows:

Calculate and analyze ratios **(LO4)**

($ in millions)	2009	2008
Hewlett-Packard		
Net sales	$114,552	$118,364
Net income	7,660	8,329
Operating cash flows	13,379	14,591
Total assets	114,799	113,331
IBM		
Net sales	$ 95,758	$103,630
Net income	13,425	12,334
Operating cash flows	20,773	18,812
Total assets	109,022	109,524

Required:
1. Calculate the return on assets for both companies. Compare the ratios with those calculated for **Apple** and **Dell** in Illustration 11–21.
2. Calculate the cash return on assets for both companies. Compare the ratios with those calculated for Apple and Dell in Illustration 11–22.
3. Calculate the cash flow to sales ratio and the asset turnover ratio for both companies. Which company has the better ratios, Hewlett-Packard or IBM? Are Hewlett-Packard's and IBM's business strategies closer to Apple's or to Dell's?

Calculate operating activities—direct method **(LO5)**

P11–6B Refer to the information provided in P11–3B for Software Associates.

Required:
Prepare the operating activities section of the statement of cash flows for Software Associates using the *direct* method.

Calculate operating activities—direct method **(LO5)**

P11–7B Data for Virtual Gaming Systems is provided in P11–4B.

Required:
Prepare the statement of cash flows for Virtual Gaming Systems using the *direct* method. Disclose any noncash transactions in an accompanying note.

Prepare an income statement using operating cash flow information—indirect and direct methods **(LO2, 5)**

P11–8B Cash flows from operating activities for both the indirect and direct methods are presented for Electronic Transformations.

Cash Flows from Operating Activities (Indirect method)		
Net income	$35,000	
Adjustments for noncash effects:		
Depreciation expense	8,000	
Changes in current assets and current liabilities:		
Increase in accounts receivable	(12,000)	
Increase in accounts payable	7,000	
Increase in income tax payable	5,000	
Net cash flows from operating activities		$43,000

Cash Flows from Operating Activities (Direct method)		
Cash received from customers	$78,000	
Cash paid for operating expenses	(25,000)	
Cash paid for income taxes	(10,000)	
Net cash flows from operating activities		$43,000

Required:
Complete the following income statement for Electronic Transformations. Assume all accounts payable are to suppliers.

ELECTRONIC TRANSFORMATIONS		
Income Statement		
For the year ended December 31, 2012		
Revenues		$?
Expenses:		
Operating expenses	$?	
Depreciation expense	8,000	
Income tax expense	?	
Total expenses		?
Net income		$35,000

[*Hint:* Use the calculations on the next page and work backwards from bottom (in red) to top for each item.]

Revenues
± Change in accounts receivable
= Cash received from customers _____

Operating expenses
± Change in accounts payable
= Cash paid for operating expenses _____

Income tax expense
± Change in income tax payable
= Cash paid for income taxes _____

For additional problems, visit **www.mhhe.com/succeed** for Problems: Set C.

ADDITIONAL PERSPECTIVES

Great Adventures

(This is a continuation of the Great Adventures problem from earlier chapters.)

AP11–1 The income statement, balance sheet, and additional information for Great Adventures, Inc., are provided below.

Continuing Problem

GREAT ADVENTURES, INC. Income Statement For the year ended December 31, 2014		
Revenues:		
Service revenue (clinic, racing, TEAM)	$543,000	
Sales revenue (MU watches)	118,000	
Total revenues		$661,000
Expenses:		
Cost of goods sold (watches)	70,000	
Operating expenses	304,276	
Depreciation expense	50,000	
Interest expense	29,724	
Income tax expense	57,000	
Total expenses		511,000
Net income		$150,000

GREAT ADVENTURES, INC. Balance Sheet December 31, 2014 and 2013			
	2014	**2013**	**Increase (I) or Decrease (D)**
Assets			
Current assets:			
Cash	$ 322,362	$138,000	$ 184,362 (I)
Accounts receivable	45,000	35,000	10,000 (I)
Inventory	17,000	14,000	3,000 (I)
Other current assets	13,000	11,000	2,000 (I)

(continued)

(concluded)

GREAT ADVENTURES, INC. Balance Sheet December 31, 2014 and 2013			
	2014	**2013**	**Increase (I) or Decrease (D)**
Long-term assets:			
Land	$ 500,000	$ 0	$ 500,000 (I)
Buildings	1,000,000	0	1,000,000 (I)
Equipment	65,000	65,000	
Accumulated depreciation	(75,250)	(25,250)	50,000 (I)
Total assets	$1,887,112	$237,750	
Liabilities and Stockholders' Equity			
Current liabilities:			
Accounts payable	$ 12,000	$ 9,000	$ 3,000 (I)
Interest payable	750	750	
Income tax payable	57,000	38,000	19,000 (I)
Long-term liabilities:			
Notes payable	492,362	30,000	462,362 (I)
Stockholders' equity:			
Common stock	120,000	20,000	100,000 (I)
Paid-in capital	1,105,000	0	1,105,000 (I)
Retained earnings	175,000	140,000	35,000 (I)
Treasury stock	(75,000)	0	(75,000) (I)
Total liabilities and stockholders' equity	$1,887,112	$237,750	

Additional Information for 2014:

1. Borrowed $500,000 in January 2014. Made 12 monthly payments during the year, reducing the balance of the loan by $37,638.
2. Issued common stock for $1.2 million.
3. Purchased 10,000 shares of treasury stock for $15 per share.
4. Reissued 5,000 shares of treasury stock at $16 per share.
5. Declared and paid a cash dividend of $115,000.

Required:

Prepare the statement of cash flows for the year ended December 31, 2014, using the *indirect* method.

Financial Analysis

American Eagle Outfitters, Inc.

AP11–2 Financial information for **American Eagle** is presented in Appendix A at the end of the book.

Required:

1. What was the amount of increase or decrease in cash and cash equivalents for the most recent year?
2. What was net cash from operating activities for the most recent year? Is net cash from operating activities increasing each year? What is the largest reconciling item between net income and net operating cash flows during the most recent year?
3. What was net cash from investing activities for the most recent year? Is it positive or negative? What is the largest investing activity during the most recent year?

4. What was net cash from financing activities for the most recent year? Is negative financing activities a good sign or a bad sign? What is the largest financing activity during the most recent year?

The Buckle, Inc.

AP11–3 Financial information for The Buckle is presented in Appendix B at the end of the book.

Financial Analysis

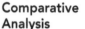

Required:

1. What was the amount of increase or decrease in cash and cash equivalents for the most recent year?
2. What was net cash from operating activities for the most recent year? Is net cash from operating activities increasing each year? What is the largest reconciling item between net income and net operating cash flows during the most recent year?
3. What was net cash from investing activities for the most recent year? Is it positive or negative? What is the largest investing activity during the most recent year?
4. What was net cash from financing activities for the most recent year? Is negative financing activities a good sign or a bad sign? What is the largest financing activity during the most recent year?

American Eagle Outfitters, Inc., vs. The Buckle, Inc.

AP11–4 Financial information for American Eagle is presented in Appendix A at the end of the book, and financial information for The Buckle is presented in Appendix B at the end of the book.

Comparative Analysis

Required:

1. Calculate American Eagle's cash return on assets, cash flow to sales, and asset turnover ratio.
2. Calculate The Buckle's cash return on assets, cash flow to sales, and asset turnover ratio.
3. Which company is doing better based on cash return on assets? Which company has the higher cash flow to sales? Which company has the higher asset turnover?

Ethics

AP11–5 Aggressive Corporation approaches Matt Taylor, a loan officer for Oklahoma State Bank, seeking to increase the company's borrowings with the bank from $100,000 to $150,000. Matt has an uneasy feeling as he examines the loan application from Aggressive Corporation, which just completed its first year of operations. The application included the following financial statements.

AGGRESSIVE CORPORATION		
Income Statement		
For the year ended December 31, 2012		
Revenues		$200,000
Expenses:		
Cost of goods sold	$110,000	
Operating expenses	50,000	
Depreciation expense	10,000	
Total expenses		170,000
Net income		$ 30,000

AGGRESSIVE CORPORATION Balance Sheet December 31		
	2012	**2011**
Assets		
Current assets:		
Cash	$ 10,000	$0
Accounts receivable	60,000	0
Inventory	40,000	0
Long-term assets:		
Equipment	100,000	0
Accumulated depreciation	(10,000)	0
Total assets	$200,000	$0
Liabilities and Stockholders' Equity		
Current liabilities:		
Accounts payable	$ 20,000	$0
Interest payable	10,000	0
Long-term liabilities:		
Note payable	100,000	0
Stockholders' equity:		
Common stock	40,000	0
Retained earnings	30,000	0
Total liabilities and stockholders' equity	$200,000	$0

The income statement submitted with the application shows net income of $30,000 in the first year of operations. Referring to the balance sheet, this net income represents a more-than-acceptable 15% rate of return on assets of $200,000.

Matt's concern stems from his recollection that the $100,000 note payable reported on the balance sheet is a three-year loan from his bank, approved earlier this year. He recalls another promising new company that, just recently, defaulted on its loan due to its inability to generate sufficient cash flows to meet its loan obligations.

Seeing Matt's hesitation, Larry Bling, the CEO of Aggressive Corporation, closes the door to the conference room and shares with Matt that he owns several other businesses. He says he will be looking for a new CFO in another year to run Aggressive Corporation along with his other businesses and Matt is just the kind of guy he is looking for. Larry mentions that as CFO, Matt would receive a significant salary. Matt is flattered and says he will look over the loan application and get back to Larry concerning the $50,000 loan increase by the end of the week.

Required:

1. Prepare a statement of cash flows for Aggressive Corporation.
2. Explain how Aggressive Corporation can have positive net income but negative operating cash flows. How does the finding of negative operating cash flows affect your confidence in the reliability of the net income amount?
3. Why do you think Larry mentioned the potential employment position? Should the potential employment position with Aggressive Corporation have any influence on the loan decision?

Internet Research

AP11–6 EDGAR, the Electronic Data Gathering, Analysis, and Retrieval system, is a giant database of documents required to be submitted to the U.S. Securities and Exchange Commission (SEC). All publicly traded domestic companies use EDGAR to make the majority of their filings. (Filings by foreign companies are not required to be filed on EDGAR, but many of these companies do so voluntarily.) Form 10-K, which

includes the annual report, is an important document required to be filed on EDGAR. The SEC makes this information available, free to the public, on the Internet.

Required:
1. Access EDGAR on the Internet. The web address is *www.sec.gov*.
2. Search for a public company with which you are familiar. Access its most recent 10-K filing. Search or scroll to find the statement of cash flows.
3. Is the direct or indirect method used to report operating activities? What is the largest adjustment to net income in reconciling net income and cash flows from operations in the most recent year?
4. What has been the most significant investing activity for the company in the most recent three years?
5. What has been the most significant financing activity for the company in the most recent three years?

Written Communication

AP11–7 "Why can't we pay our shareholders a dividend?" shouts your new boss at Polar Opposites. "This income statement you prepared for me says we earned $5 million in our first year!" You recently prepared the financial statements below.

POLAR OPPOSITES Income Statement For the year ended December 31, 2012	
	($ in millions)
Sales revenue	$65
Cost of goods sold	(35)
Depreciation expense	(4)
Operating expenses	(21)
Net income	$ 5

POLAR OPPOSITES Balance Sheet December 31, 2012	
	($ in millions)
Cash	$ 1
Accounts receivable (net)	16
Merchandise inventory	14
Machinery (net)	44
Total	$75
Accounts payable	$ 7
Accrued expenses payable	9
Notes payable	29
Common stock	25
Retained earnings	5
Total	$75

Although net income was $5 million, cash flow from operating activities was a negative $5 million. This just didn't make any sense to your boss.

Required:
Prepare a memo explaining how net income could be positive and operating cash flows negative. Include in your report a determination of operating cash flows of negative $5 million using the *indirect* method.

Earnings Management

AP11–8 Bryan Eubank began his accounting career as an auditor for a Big 4 CPA firm. He focused on clients in the high-technology sector, becoming an expert on topics such as inventory write-downs, stock options, and business acquisitions. Impressed with his technical skills and experience, General Electronics, a large consumer electronics chain, hired Bryan as the company controller responsible for all of the accounting functions within the corporation. Bryan was excited about his new position—for about a week, until he took the first careful look at General Electronics' financial statements.

The cause of Bryan's change in attitude is the set of financial statements he's been staring at for the past few hours. For some time prior to his recruitment, he had been aware that his new employer had experienced a long trend of moderate profitability. The reports on his desk confirm the slight but steady improvements in net income in recent years. The disturbing trend Bryan is now noticing, though, is a decline in cash flows from operations. Bryan has sketched out the following comparison ($ in millions):

	2012	2011	2010	2009
Operating income	$1,400	$1,320	$1,275	$1,270
Net income	385	350	345	295
Cash flows from operations	16	110	120	155

Profits? Yes. Increasing profits? Yes. So what is the cause of his distress? The trend in cash flows from operations, which is going in the opposite direction of net income. Upon closer review, Bryan noticed a couple events that, unfortunately, seem related:
a. The company's credit policy has been loosened, credit terms relaxed, and payment periods lengthened. This has resulted in a large increase in accounts receivable.
b. Several of the company's salary arrangements, including that of the CEO and CFO, are based on reported net income.

Required:
1. What is likely causing the increase in accounts receivable? How does an increase in accounts receivable affect net income differently than operating cash flows?
2. Explain why salary arrangements for officers, such as the CEO and CFO, might increase the risk of earnings management.
3. Why is the trend in cash flows from operations, combined with the additional events, such a concern for Bryan?
4. What course of action, if any, should Bryan take?

Answers to the Self-Study Questions
1. b   2. c   3. c   4. b   5. a   6. d   7. b   8. c   9. d   10. c

Subject Index

Note: Page numbers followed by *n* indicate material in footnotes.